INTERNATIONAL LAW AND THE PROLIFERATION OF WEAPONS OF MASS DESTRUCTION

International Law and the Proliferation of Weapons of Mass Destruction

DANIEL H. JOYNER

OXFORD

UNIVERSITY PRESS

OXFORD

UNIVERSITY PRESS

Great Clarendon Street, Oxford OX2 6DP

Oxford University Press is a department of the University of Oxford.
It furthers the University's objective of excellence in research, scholarship,
and education by publishing worldwide in

Oxford New York

Auckland Cape Town Dar es Salaam Hong Kong Karachi
Kuala Lumpur Madrid Melbourne Mexico City Nairobi
New Delhi Shanghai Taipei Toronto

With offices in

Argentina Austria Brazil Chile Czech Republic France Greece
Guatemala Hungary Italy Japan Poland Portugal Singapore
South Korea Switzerland Thailand Turkey Ukraine Vietnam

Oxford is a registered trade mark of Oxford University Press
in the UK and in certain other countries

Published in the United States
by Oxford University Press Inc., New York

British Library Cataloguing in Publication Data

Data available

Library of Congress Cataloging in Publication Data

Data available

Typeset by Newgen Imaging Systems (P) Ltd., Chennai, India
Printed in Great Britain
on acid-free paper by
CPI Antony Rowe, Chippenham, Wiltshire

ISBN 978–0–19–920490–8

1 3 5 7 9 10 8 6 4 2

To My Father, Ronald W. Joyner and
My Mother, Elizabeth H. Joyner

Table of Contents

Acknowledgments

This book is the product of six years of work on the topic of international law and WMD proliferation. During that time I have been professionally located in several institutions, and have benefited from many collegial relationships. I would like to express my appreciation to Gary Bertsch, under whose guidance I was first introduced to this area at the University of Georgia. I am also indebted to Lee Bridges, who gave me my first faculty job and a chance to pursue my research at the University of Warwick. Also at Warwick, I would like to thank Jan Aart Scholte, Director of the Centre for the Study of Globalisation and Regionalisation, for his generous support of my work. I would also like to thank Rosemary Foot, under whose supervision I worked at Oxford University. Finally, I would like to thank Ken Randall for my current academic home at the University of Alabama, and for his generous support of my research. Substantively, this book has greatly benefited from review of chapters and discussion of ideas with many colleagues, to whom I am particularly grateful. These include Scott Jones, Mike Beck, Seema Gahlaut, Nathan Busch, Matt Happold, Rob Cryer, Julian Robinson, Petros Mavroidis, Tom Schoenbaum, Vaughan Lowe, Malcolm Shaw, Andrew Williams, Sir Adam Roberts, Andrew Hurrell, Istvan Pogany, Nico Krisch, Elizabeth Wilmshurst, Lady Hazel Fox, Gillian Triggs, Dan Bodansky, Kenneth Rosen and Mark Drumbl. I cannot refrain from particularly thanking Michael Byers, who first taught me international law, and who has been a friend and mentor ever since; as well as Michael Lionberger, lifelong friend and whetstone. Not leastly, I would like to thank my wife, Yvette, for standing by me for twelve years, and in many impermanent homes. *Amor in aeternum.*

Table of Cases

Introduction

On March 17, 2003, U.S. President George W. Bush declared to an anxious world:

Intelligence gathered by this and other governments leaves no doubt that the Iraq regime continues to possess and conceal some of the most lethal weapons ever devised...the danger is clear: using chemical, biological, or one day nuclear weapons, obtained with the help of Iraq, the terrorists could fulfill their stated ambition and kill thousands or hundreds of thousands of innocent people in our country or any other.[1]

Two days later on March 19, a coalition of states led by the United States began what has been aptly described as "the world's first nonproliferation war."[2]

While the 2003 Iraq intervention was the first large scale military conflict to be waged primarily for the purpose of removing a perceived threat from weapons of mass destruction, the fear of war involving these, the most destructive weapons in human history, had been for decades the defining independent variable influencing international politics.

For the 56 years following the first detonation of atomic bombs over Japan in August of 1945, this fear of mutually assured reciprocal use of thermonuclear weapons on a massive scale between the two Cold War superpowers, was arguably the single greatest contributor to peace and world order.[3] However, the world paid a heavy price for this security, living constantly with the knowledge that it stood every moment upon the precipice of its own existence.

For foreign policy officials, advancements in weapons technologies after World War II, some of which were entirely unprecedented and some of which were simply innovations increasing the effectiveness of older destructive technologies, fundamentally altered strategic calculations regarding uses of force both aggressive and defensive, and understandings of the power projection capabilities of states and non-state actors.

Through the succeeding decades, the acquisition by an increasing number of states of nuclear, chemical, and biological weapons, whose destructive capacities compressed the amount of time and effort required to kill massive numbers of people by relatively indiscriminate means, was disconcerting particularly to the most powerful members of the international community.[4] This concern was due

---

[1] "Address to the Nation on War with Iraq," remarks in Cross Hall, Washington, March 17, 2003. Available at <http://www.whitehouse.gov/news/releases/2003/03/20030317-7.html>.

[2] J. Cirincione et al., Deadly Arsenals, Nuclear, Biological and Chemical Threats (Carnegie Endowment, 2nd edn, 2005) 333.

[3] S.D. Sagan and K.N. Waltz, The Spread of Nuclear Weapons (2nd edn, 2003).

[4] See generally R. Forsberg et al., Nonproliferation Primer: Preventing the Spread of Nuclear, Chemical and Biological Weapons (1995).

not only to the distant possibilities of the use of such weapons against them in aggressive fashion, but also as it became clear that the latent potential utility of these weapons itself had fundamentally altered the strategic calculus employed in the former days of the exclusive availability of what came to be known as "conventional" weapons.

Under this previous calculus, the ability of an international actor to wield and to project power could be derived through a fairly simple calculus of the physical and territorial resources of that actor. Now however, it became possible for smaller states and even some non-state actors to change this security dynamic through possession and threat of use of these more destructive weapons technologies, which eventually came to be grouped together through customary usage under the new categorical nomenclature of "weapons of mass destruction" (WMD).[5] Through these means, international actors with relatively small resource bases could gain useful leveraging and deterrent capabilities against a larger state or group of states, wholly disproportionate to their conventional military capabilities.

I. Non-proliferation Law

Due particularly to these fears of the spread to other states and non-state actors of WMD technologies, a phenomenon known as "horizontal proliferation," while on one level there was almost unbridled development of WMD programs and production and operational fielding of the most lethal WMD systems ever seen by the superpowers during the long decades of the Cold War, there were concurrently during these years at another level significant efforts, in many cases led by the superpowers, to at a minimum limit the proliferation of WMD outside of a very select group of states.[6]

---

[5] See the discussion in Chapter 2 below on the term "weapons of mass destruction" and its variants. It was in fact only after the break-up of the Soviet Union and the ending of the Cold War in the early 1990s that the term "weapons of mass destruction" and its acronym "WMD" came into their own as descriptors of the triumvirate of non-conventional weapons—nuclear, chemical, and biological—particularly in public discourse and by senior government officials. Among specialists, the acronyms "NBC" and particularly "CBRN" have come to be used more commonly in describing this class of non-conventional weapons, in the case of the latter in order to include sub-critical radiological weapons ("dirty bombs").

[6] See J. Goldblat, Arms Control: The New Guide to Negotiations and Agreements (2002); B. Kellman, *Bridling the International Trade of Catastrophic Weaponry*, 43 American University Law Review 755 (1994); C. Blacker and J. Duffy, International Arms Control (1984); J. Dahlitz, Nuclear Arms Control with Effective International Agreements (1983); J. Dhanapala, Regional Approaches to Disarmament: Security and Stability (1993); Keating et al. (eds), Nuclear Nonproliferation and the Nonproliferation Treaty (1990); J. Goldblat, Nonproliferation: The Why and the Wherefore (1985); J.P. Robinson, The Rise of CB Weapons (1971).

The first example of this effort at the multilateral level is to be found in the nuclear weapons area, with the conclusion in 1968 of the Nuclear Nonproliferation Treaty (NPT), which forms the cornerstone of the modern nuclear non-proliferation regime.[7] Following the conclusion of the NPT, there were efforts to conclude similar multilateral non-proliferation agreements in the areas of biological and chemical weapons. These efforts led to the conclusion in 1972 of the Biological Weapons Convention (BWC).[8] A multilateral non-proliferation treaty on the subject of chemical weapons, however, would have to wait until the conclusion of the Chemical Weapons Convention (CWC) in 1993.[9] Each of these treaties sought to address the problem of horizontal proliferation of WMD through provisions, variously adapted within each of the treaties, proscribing possession, development, and transfer of both single-use WMD-related materials (i.e. those items and technologies primarily suited for use in WMD development programs) as well as dual-use WMD-related materials (i.e. items and technologies which have both civilian and military applications).

In addition to addressing the problem of horizontal proliferation of their subject technologies through their proscriptive provisions, these three treaties also addressed, with some significant variation in method, the problem of "vertical proliferation," or the development and possession of WMD technologies within each of the states which acceded to their membership. Each of the treaties has as its ultimate stated objective the complete disarmament by all member states of their subject weapons technologies.

These multilateral non-proliferation treaties, building upon and supported by other treaties as well as rules of customary international law, form the foundation of the modern regulation of WMD proliferation in international law. Parts I and II of this book will review and analyze these foundational treaties, as well as the normative regimes of both hard and soft law character which have been instituted to supplement them, including monitoring and verification regimes and multilateral export control regimes. It will further review and analyze other

---

[7] Treaty on the Nonproliferation of Nuclear Weapons, opened for signature July 1, 1968, 21 U.S.T. 483, T.I.A.S. No. 6839, 729 U.N.T.S. 161. On the NPT see J. Goldblat, ARMS CONTROL: THE NEW GUIDE TO NEGOTIATIONS AND AGREEMENTS (2nd edn, 2002) chs 4–6; THE NUCLEAR NONPROLIFERATION REGIME: ASSESSMENT AND PROSPECTS (1997); TWENTY YEARS OF THE NONPROLIFERATION TREATY: IMPLEMENTATION AND PROSPECTS (1990); J. Simpson and D. Howlett (eds), THE FUTURE OF THE NONPROLIFERATION TREATY (1995).

[8] Convention on the Prohibition of the Development, Production and Stockpiling of Bacteriological (Biological) and Toxin Weapons and on Their Destruction, opened for signature April 10, 1972, 26 U.S.T. 583, T.I.A.S. No. 8062, 1015 U.N.T.S. 163.

[9] Convention on the Prohibition of the Development, Production and Stockpiling and Use of Chemical Weapons and on Their Destruction, opened for signature, Paris, January 13, 1993, entered into force April 29, 1997, 32 INTERNATIONAL LEGAL MATERIALS 800. See generally T. Bernauer, THE PROJECTED CHEMICAL WEAPONS CONVENTION: A GUIDE TO THE NEGOTIATIONS IN THE CONFERENCE ON DISARMAMENT (1990); M. Lumsden, INCENDIARY WEAPONS (1975); A. Westing (ed.), HERBICIDES IN WAR THE LONG-TERM ECOLOGICAL AND HUMAN CONSEQUENCES (1984).

sources of international law, including particularly provisions of the World Trade Organization's General Agreement on Tariffs and Trade, and the United Nations Charter, as additional sources of international law which relate in material ways to the regulation of the subject of WMD proliferation.

This volume will employ the term "non-proliferation law" as an umbrella categorization of sources of international law, including but not limited to the above-mentioned sources of law, which regulate the proliferation of WMD. To be clear, the sources of international law reviewed herein in depth do not represent the totality of rules of international law which relate in material ways to the regulation of WMD proliferation. The sources to be reviewed have been selected by the author as comprising the most important, or in some cases most controversial, sources of law within the umbrella category of non-proliferation law, and can be viewed as representing the broad contours of this area of law for purposes of considering its strengths and its limitations.

The study of sources of international law relating materially to the regulation of WMD proliferation, which much of this volume represents, should not be confused with a study of all sources of international law materially relating to WMD. The first two Parts of this book will thus be concerned with a review and analysis of sources of international law which, in their own way, seek to regulate the proliferation of WMD. The "regulation" embodied in the provisions of these sources of international law has as a general rule been structured so as to have as its primary regulating purpose the proscription, or at least limitation of the horizontal and vertical proliferation of WMD.

This book does not attempt to include within its scope a comprehensive review of other sources of international law which relate materially to WMD, but which do not primarily seek to regulate WMD proliferation as thus defined. Other such sources of international law exist in relative abundance in substantive areas of international law including, inter alia, international environmental law, international criminal law, the law of the sea, and space law. Sources of international humanitarian law which regulate the use of WMD in armed conflict are also not given comprehensive coverage within the scope of this volume, although some provisions of international humanitarian law on this subject will be addressed as they are presented incidentally within the context of review and analysis particularly of the cornerstone multilateral non-proliferation treaties.

Another distinction which must be made clear is that between non-proliferation law, as that category of legal sources has been defined herein, on the one hand, and arms control law on the other. This distinction is essentially one of scope. In terms of its breadth of coverage, arms control law is a broader jurisprudential framework than is non-proliferation law, importantly conceptually including the international legal regulation of development, possession, and proliferation of WMD, which comprises non-proliferation law as this volume utilizes that term, but also including the legal regulation of conventional weapons technologies.[10] Non-proliferation law is thus a lesser included concept within the larger substantive area of arms control law.

II. The Modern Threat of WMD

The base assertion that proliferation of WMD is a threat to international peace and security, requiring the expenditure of resources by the international community in establishing and maintaining the edifice of non-proliferation law to be reviewed herein, deserves some small attention itself before moving on.[11] While it may seem a subject hardly worthy of debate to the average person on the street, arguments over the effects of weapons proliferation upon international peace and security, and on the character of those effects as either positive or negative, have subsisted among members of the academy for years.[12]

This debate has been renewed somewhat famously of late in the context of the spread of nuclear weapons technologies, between Kenneth Waltz and Scott Sagan.[13] Drawing on Cold War observations of a relative state of lasting peace between the nuclear superpowers, Waltz argues that the slow spread of nuclear weapons horizontally (i.e. to other states) is actually preferable from an international security perspective than is either no proliferation at all or very quick proliferation. He argues that international security is advantaged by having additional members of the nuclear club, because states with nuclear weapons are less likely to be attacked by other states due to the additional cost of such an action to the attacker posed by the potential nuclear response of the target. Thus Waltz argues that the wider presence of such a nuclear deterrent among states will decrease the likelihood of international military conflict generally, presenting a more stable international order.[14]

Sagan responds that Waltz has adopted as a backdrop to his arguments an unrealistically simple view of states as rational, unitary actors that will without

---

[10] See H. Schutz, "Arms Control," ENCYCLOPAEDIA OF PUBLIC INTERNATIONAL LAW I, at 259–267; H. Bull, THE CONTROL OF THE ARMS RACE: DISARMAMENT AND ARMS CONTROL IN THE MISSILE AGE (2nd edn, 1965); J. Goldblat, ARMS CONTROL (2nd edn, 2002); Z. Yihdego, THE ARMS TRADE AND INTERNATIONAL LAW (2007); G. Den Dekker, THE LAW OF ARMS CONTROL (2001).

[11] See D.H. Joyner, "International Legal Responses to WMD Proliferation" in C. Hughes and R. Devetak (eds), THE GLOBALIZATION OF POLITICAL VIOLENCE (2007).

[12] For a summary of this debate since the 1940s, see P.R. Lavoy, *The Strategic Consequences of Nuclear Proliferation*, SECURITY STUDIES 4, no. 4 (Summer 1995). See also F.H. Hinsley, POWER AND THE PURSUIT OF PEACE (1963); P.N. Rosecrance, ACTION AND REACTION IN WORLD POLITICS (1963); P. Gallois, THE BALANCE OF TERROR: STRATEGY FOR THE NUCLEAR AGE (1961). See also the WMD Commission final report: *Weapons of Terror: Freeing the World of Nuclear, Biological and Chemical Arms*, released June 1, 2006. Available at <http://www.wmdcommission.org/files/Weapons_of_Terror.pdf>.

[13] See their co-edited volume of their own papers on the subject: S.D. Sagan and K.N. Waltz, THE SPREAD OF NUCLEAR WEAPONS (2nd edn, 2003).

[14] Ibid. at ch. 1.

exception respond in this predictable manner to the presence of such a deterrent in a potential target state. He argues that government behavior is better understood through organizational theory, which views the rationality of state actors in making decisions as being bounded, or limited, in significant ways by factors inherent in the structure of their organizations. Understanding state action in this light, Sagan argues, produces a much more sceptical view of whether states will in fact act consistently in this objectively rational manner with regard to decisions to use their nuclear capabilities.[15]

This debate has been contributed to in a new book by Nathan Busch, who adopts a more empirical methodology to question Waltz's implicit assumptions of the rational and unitary nature of states in the real world.[16] Through a detailed empirical study of the command and control systems of five nuclear states, Busch questions the actual capability of governments both to control the actions of government officials and technical personnel all the way down the chains of command to operational control over the weapons themselves, as well as to provide adequate physical protection for nuclear materials in their possession and to guard against theft or diversion.[17]

III. The Khan Network

Recent revelations of a long-standing clandestine nuclear materials smuggling ring headed by the father of Pakistan's gas centrifuge program, Dr. Abdul Qadeer Khan seem to bear out these concerns in a high-profile and sensational manner.[18] Emerging from the illicit procurement network developed by Dr. Khan and his associates in the 1970s to supply the infant Pakistani gas centrifuge program, the channels of this network eventually began to be used as a conduit for the flow of single and dual-use nuclear goods out of Pakistan, and under the radar screens of both national and multilateral export control and non-proliferation frameworks. The Khan network orchestrated the diversion of nuclear materials and centrifuge and other related technologies, including nuclear bomb designs (received by

---

[15] Ibid. at ch. 2.

[16] N.E. Busch, No End in Sight: The Continuing Menace of nuclear proliferation (2004).

[17] See also L. Goldstein, Preventive Attack and Weapons of Mass Destruction: A Comparative Historical Analysis (2006).

[18] See G. Corera, Shopping for Bombs (2006); W. Langewiesche, The Atomic Bazaar (2007); G. Milholin and K. Motz, "Nuikes 'R' Us", *The New York Times*, March 4, 2004, A31; D. Henninger, "Terror's Truth: Saddam Will Shop Till He Drops", *Wall Street Journal*, March 14, 2003; F. Stockman, "U.S. Prods U.N. for a Nuclear Export Rule Measure Sought to Halt the Spread of Weapons Data," *The Boston Globe*, April 4, 2004, A4; D. Albright and C. Hinderstein, "Uncovering the Nuclear Black Market: Working Toward Closing Gaps in the International Proliferation Regime," Institute for Science and International Security, July 2, 2004; D.H. Joyner, "International Legal Responses to WMD Proliferation" in C. Hughes and R. Devetak (eds), The Globalization of Political Violence (2007).

Pakistan from China in the early 1980s), from the control of national laboratories in Pakistan. It has become clear that through this network, in operation possibly for decades, single and dual-use nuclear materials were channelled to Libya, North Korea, and Iran largely if not exclusively on a private, profiteering basis.

However, perhaps even more troubling than the original diversion of these technologies from public to private hands, is the shadowy world of brokers and illicit transshipment points which the narrative of the Khan network reveals were used to keep this long standing network running so successfully for so long. These transactions were not structured as direct transfers of items and technologies from the hands of Pakistani scientists to officials of other countries. The manufacturing of items from sub-components and raw materials smuggled out of Pakistan, and the actual transport of items all along the supply and production chain, was accomplished through the regular processes, and through the standard vehicles of private international commerce—through the instrumentality of various manufacturers, brokers, and transit companies in Europe, South Africa, Malaysia, and Turkey, with many of the items at some point passing through the customs black hole of Dubai in the United Arab Emirates. The network operated through both active and intentional deception, as well as through unwitting and ignorant participation in some cases, on the part of manufacturers and transit companies on many continents.

As two authors have recently commented "the workshops that contracted to make components for the network typically imported the necessary items, such as metals, equipment, or sub-components. After they made the item, they would then send it—either assembled or as a finished centrifuge component—to Dubai under a false end-user certificate. Then it would be repackaged and sent off to Libya."[19] Mohamed El Baradei, Director General of the IAEA, has similarly noted of the Khan network: "Nuclear components designed in one country could be manufactured in another, shipped through a third (which may have appeared to be a legitimate user), assembled in a fourth, and designated for eventual turn-key use in a fifth."[20]

This network and its success provides one illustration of how globalized international business processes, in which the flow of goods between and through states has become increasingly difficult to monitor much less control, are making the task of limiting the proliferation of weapons-sensitive technologies harder than ever before. Particularly when such a regulation-light international business transactions environment in the developed world is combined with the reality, in parts of the developing world, of states with little or no effective national controls over transshipment and re-export of imported goods, the enormity

---

[19] D. Albright and C. Hinderstein, "Uncovering the Nuclear Black Market: Working Toward Closing Gaps in the International Proliferation Regime," Institute for Science and International Security, July 2, 2004.

[20] Ibid.

and intractability of the task confronting international non-proliferation efforts becomes readily apparent.[21]

There are simply more states now that have the capacity to produce weapons and related dual-use technologies, and to put them on the international WMD black market than there were when Waltz originally put forward his proliferation-optimistic arguments in the early 1980s. Arguably, this fact itself is a result of the forces of globalization increasing access horizontally among states to foreign investment capital and oversees markets. Furthermore, alliances among states and allegiances of interest, which if antithetical were at least fairly clear in the Cold War era, have fractured and have been replaced with *ad hoc* coalitions of states, much less sure of their like-mindedness in matters of strategic calculus and definitions of threat.[22]

These facts can be argued to frustrate Waltz's hope of a slow and managed horizontal proliferation of WMD technologies, resulting in a much less predictable pattern of proliferation and the possibility of a build-up of such weapons in regions of the world in which the arguably stabilizing geopolitics of bipolar superpower conflict are no longer a force of restraint upon the ambitions of regional powers.

Global production chains, through which weapons-related high technology is produced in its final form from composite parts, potentially from a number of different countries of origin, make the task of monitoring and regulating where those final products end up a much more difficult task than in the Cold War era, when research relating to, and actual production of high-end weapons-related technologies was funded almost exclusively by, and therefore much more tightly controlled by, a relatively small number of state governments.[23] In the post-Cold War environment, states began to find that they were much better off loosening their hold over domestic production of such technologies, and allowing them to be developed primarily, but not exclusively, for state consumption, by private companies where quality was higher and costs lower. This "off the shelf" environment of weapons technology development and production by companies whose own corporate structures are increasingly international, however, makes keeping track, particularly of dual-use items, increasingly difficult for states.[24]

---

[21] S. Jones, The Evolution of the Ukrainian Export Control System: State Building and International Cooperation (2002); M. Beck et al., To Supply or To Deny: Comparing Nonproliferation Export Controls in Five Key Countries (2003); D.H. Joyner, "International Legal Responses to WMD Proliferation" in C. Hughes and R. Devetak (eds), The Globalization of political Violence (2007).

[22] See D.H. Joyner, *Restructuring the Multilateral Export Control Regime System*, Journal of Conflict and Security Law, Vol. 9 Issue 2 (2004).

[23] Ibid.; W.W. Keller and J.E. Nolan, *The Arms Trade: Business as Usual?* 109 Foreign Policy 113 (Winter 1997/1998).

[24] See *Strengthening Multilateral Export Controls: A Nonproliferation Priority* (Center for International Trade and Security report, September 2002); W.A. Reinsch, *Export Controls in the Age of Globalization*, The Monitor: Nonproliferation Demilitarization and Arms

Also counter to Waltz's worldview is the modern reality of the state-like violent capabilities of some non-state actors, including sophisticated international terrorist organizations. These actors, possessed of organizational structures and often motivated by ideologies which make them immune to classical forces of deterrence and containment, do not fit neatly into the optimistic proliferation framework Waltz describes.[25] Globalized markets in general and increased access thereby to information technology specifically, have facilitated the capacity of such groups to form and maintain networks capable of coordinating devastating uses of destructive force such as the September 11, 2001 attacks in the United States. These developments, along with the lessons of the A.Q. Khan network, have given rise to the quite reasonable fear that through the regular processes of international commerce, weapons of mass destruction could be obtained by such non-state actors, either through the purposive assistance of sympathetic states, or through theft and diversion from state control, or, which is increasingly more likely, simply through acquisition from the private sector.

IV. Counterproliferation

Non-proliferation law, or the "non-proliferation treaties and regimes system," as the web of hard and soft international law normative frameworks regulating the proliferation of WMD has come to be known in proliferation studies circles, is as discussed above, purposed in combating the threat to international peace and security caused by horizontal and vertical WMD proliferation.[26] However, as will be discussed in Part III of this book, this non-proliferation normative system

---

CONTROL 5 (Summer 1999); *Defense Industry Consolidation: Competitive Effects of Mergers and Acquisitions* (Testimony, March 4, 1998 GAO/T-NSIAD-98-112).

[25] See D. Smith, DETERRING AMERICA: ROGUE STATES AND THE PROLIFERATION OF WEAPONS OF MASS DESTRUCTION (2006).

[26] See D.S. Gualtieri, "The System of Nonproliferation Export Controls," in D. Shelton (ed.) COMMITMENT AND COMPLIANCE: THE ROLE OF NON-BINDING NORMS IN THE INTERNATIONAL LEGAL SYSTEM (2000); R. Forsberg et al., NONPROLIFERATION PRIMER: PREVENTING THE SPREAD OF NUCLEAR, CHEMICAL AND BIOLOGICAL WEAPONS (1995); B. Kellman, *Bridling the International Trade of Catastrophic Weaponry*, 43 AMERICAN UNIVERSITY LAW REVIEW 755 (1994); P. Van Ham, MANAGING NONPROLIFERATION REGIMES IN THE 1990's: POWER, POLITICS AND POLICIES (1993); T. Bernauer, THE CHEMISTRY OF REGIME FORMATION: EXPLAINING INTERNATIONAL COOPERATION FOR A COMPREHENSIVE BAN ON CHEMICAL WEAPONS (1993); M. Lipson, *The Reincarnation of COCOM: Explaining Post-Cold War Export Controls*, THE NONPROLIFERATION REVIEW (Winter 1999); G.K. Bertsch and S. Gillot, ARMS ON THE MARKET: REDUCING THE RISK OF PROLIFERATION IN THE FORMER SOVIET UNION (1998); R. Cupitt and S. Gillot, *COCOM is Dead, Long Live COCOM: Persistence and Change in Multilateral Security Institutions*, 27 BRITISH JOURNAL OF POLITICAL SCIENCE 361 (1997); E.H. Noehrenberg, MULTILATERAL EXPORT CONTROLS AND INTERNATIONAL REGIME THEORY: THE EFFECTIVENESS OF COCOM (1995). Regimes are defined by Stephen Krasner as the "principles, norms, rules and decision-making structures" that influence the behavior of states in various issue areas. See S.D. Krasner, *Structural Causes and Regime Consequences: Regimes as Intervening Variables*, in Krasner (ed.), INTERNATIONAL REGIMES 2 (1983).

has long been known to be inherently limited in its ability to effectively regulate WMD proliferation due to fundamental aspects of its normative character.

Among these limitations of the treaties and regimes system is the problem of its non-universality, meaning that not all actors of WMD proliferation concern are members of the non-proliferation normative system.[27] A further limitation is to be found in the non-state actor problem, arising from the fact that all of the international legal obligations imposed by the non-proliferation treaties and regimes frameworks are addressed to states, and that therefore there is no international legal regulation directly applicable to the actions of non-state actors in this area.[28]

As will be explained more fully in Chapter 6 below, concern among states flowing both from the realities of WMD proliferation, and from these inherent limitations of the treaties and regimes system, has been aggravated in recent years by two phenomena in particular. The first is the phenomenon of secondary proliferation, or proliferation by and to states not members of the treaties and regimes system, and thus not subject to its normative prescriptions.[29] The second is the aforementioned rise to prominence and capability of well-funded and sophisticated international terrorist organizations.

Since the attacks of September 11, 2001 there have been a number of voices in the international community, and particularly from states which feel especially threatened by and vulnerable to WMD attacks staged by ideology-driven non-state actors, who have called for a refocusing of attention, and a lesser reliance on the traditional treaties and regimes approach to stemming the proliferation of WMD. These commentators point to the previously described limitations of the non-proliferation treaties and regimes system, and argue that, either as a supplement to or a replacement of this system of diplomatic relations and normative multilateral frameworks, states should increase their emphasis on and employment of proactive and forceful efforts of counterproliferation, including the use of both pre-emptive and preventive strategies for dealing with potential threats of WMD proliferation and use.[30]

---

[27] See S. Gahlaut and V. Zaborsky, *Do Regimes Have the Members They Need?*, Center for International Trade and Security Working Paper (Athens; Center for International Trade and Security, February 2003); R.T. Cupitt and I. Khripunov, *New Strategies for the Nuclear Suppliers Group (NSG)*, 16 COMPARATIVE STRATEGY 305 (1997); G.K. Bertsch and S. Gillot (eds), ARMS ON THE MARKET: REDUCING THE RISK OF PROLIFERATION IN THE FORMER SOVIET UNION (1998).

[28] M. Asada, *WMD Terrorism and Security Council Resolution 1540: Conditions for Legitimacy in International Legislation*, IILJ Working Paper 2007/9, available at <http://www.iilj.org/publications/2007-9Asada.asp>; J. du Preez, *The 2005 NPT Review Conference: Can it Meet the Nuclear Challenge?*, ARMS CONTROL TODAY (April 2005).

[29] See C. Braun and C. Chyba, *Proliferation Rings: New Challenges to the Nuclear Nonproliferation Regime*, 29 INTERNATIONAL SECURITY, No. 2, 5–49 (Fall 2004).

[30] J.D. Ellis, *The Best Defense: Counterproliferation and U.S. National Security*, THE WASHINGTON QUARTERLY 26:2 (Spring 2003); J.D. Ellis and G.D. Kiefer, COMBATTING PROLIFERATION: STRATEGIC INTELLIGENCE AND NATIONAL POLICY (2003); H. Muller and M. Reiss, *Counterproliferation : Putting New Wine in Old Bottles*, THE WASHINGTON QUARTERLY

The chapters of Part III of this book will therefore examine this shift within some states' policies toward a greater emphasis upon such counterproliferation strategies as a means of combating WMD proliferation, and a lesser emphasis and reliance upon the non-proliferation treaties and regimes system. The analysis in these chapters will focus on the relational dynamics between this shift in the policy of some powerful states on the one hand, and rules of international law, including particularly provisions of the law of the sea and international use of force law, on the other.

The analysis in Part III will conclude that there exists a significant gap between the provisions of existing international law on the one hand, and the perceptions of a significant number of important states of the realities of the international political issue area that law is meant to regulate—here the proliferation of WMD and state responses thereto—on the other. While this gap is principally located within the context of international use of force law, it is in fact a composite result of the limitations of non-proliferation law, the realities of WMD proliferation, and the limited possibilities for normative construction in international use of force law. This identified gap is therefore a systemic gap in the sources of international law meaningfully related to the regulation of WMD proliferation and of state responses thereto; a normative lagging that the best efforts of the international community have so far proven unable to rectify. Chapter 9 will then proceed to identify one path, entailing a fundamental re-construction of the normative character of sources of international law governing uses of force, which could be taken by the international community in order address this gap in the formal sources of international law.

V. Summation

In summary, then, in Parts I and II this volume seeks to provide a review and analysis of existing sources of international law regulating the proliferation of WMD. In Part III it will proceed from that analysis to additionally consider international legal questions posed by the shift in some states' policies away from a reliance upon the non-proliferation treaties and regimes normative system for combating the proliferation of WMD, and toward an increased emphasis upon counterproliferation strategies for this purpose. These latter international legal questions arise primarily within the context of international use of force law. Thus, particular consideration will be given in Chapter 9 to the future of international use of force law in the age of WMD proliferation. However, in the end, all of the

18:2 (Spring 1996); T.G. Mahnken, *A Critical Appraisal of the Defense Counterproliferation Initiative*, NATIONAL SECURITY STUDIES QUARTERLY 5:3 (Summer 1999); G. Andreani, *The Disarray of U.S. Nonproliferation Policy*, SURVIVAL 41:4 (Winter 1999); B. Roberts, *Proliferation and Nonproliferation in the 1990s: Looking for the Right Lessons*, NONPROLIFERATION REVIEW 6:4 (Fall 1999).

international legal issues to be discussed in this volume should be viewed within the broader systemic context of sources of international law meaningfully related to the regulation of WMD proliferation and of state responses thereto.

VI. Nature of the Work

A word, finally, on the nature of this book and its intended audience. This book is principally a legal text, i.e. a text which seeks to identify and analyze sources of international law regulating WMD proliferation and state responses thereto. In its analysis of legal issues it seeks to consider the political and theoretical context in which the law exists.

Notwithstanding its principal character as a legal text, this book has from the beginning been intended to address an interdisciplinary and interprofessional audience, i.e. an audience not exclusively comprised of international lawyers. This intended audience additionally includes both scholars and students in other academic disciplines (e.g. political science, proliferation studies). It also includes practitioners in government agencies, and in inter-governmental and non-governmental organizations. It is hoped that the legal analysis and proposals for change included herein will be of use across this interdisciplinary and interprofessional spectrum.

In order to make this text accessible and useful to such a wide audience, care has been taken to thoroughly explain the sources of international legal obligation, and the principles which guide interpretation of those obligations. Specialists in international law may find some of this basic explanation superfluous. However, its inclusion is intended in order to allow for the use of the book as a reference work both by international lawyers and by non-legal specialists.

PART I

NON-PROLIFERATION LAW

1

The Nuclear Non-proliferation Regime

I know not with what weapons World War III will be fought, but World War IV will be fought with sticks and stones.

Albert Einstein

During the period of East–West superpower rivalry that has come to be known as the Cold War, whilst on one level there was almost unbridled development of nuclear weapons programs and vertical proliferation of nuclear weapons within the superpowers, there were concurrently at another level significant efforts involving those actors as well as other members of the international community to limit the horizontal proliferation of nuclear weapons outside of a very select group.[1]

The idea for a treaty specifically to limit the wider and deeper dissemination of nuclear weapons, as distinct from ongoing efforts to achieve general and complete disarmament (GCD) of nuclear weapons, had its origin in proposals made by Ireland to the United Nations General Assembly during its 13th session in 1958.

These proposals took two forms. The first was a draft resolution offered to the General Assembly, which sought to

establish an ad hoc committee to study the dangers inherent in the further dissemination of nuclear weapons and recommend to the General Assembly at its fourteenth session appropriate measures for averting these dangers.[2]

The second preambular paragraph of this draft resolution recognized that

the danger now exists that an increase in the number of States possessing nuclear weapons may occur, aggravating international tension and the difficulty of maintaining

---

[1] See J. Goldblat, Arms Control: The New Guide to Negotiations and Agreements (2002); J. Cirincione, Bomb Scare: The History and Future of Nuclear Weapons (2007); B. Kellman, *Bridling the International Trade of Catastrophic Weaponry*, 43 American University Law Review 755 (1994); C. Blacker and J. Duffy, International Arms Control (1984); J. Dahlitz, Nuclear Arms Control with Effective International Agreements (1983); J. Dhanapala, Regional Approaches to Disarmament: Security and Stability (1993); N. Keatinge et al. (eds), Nuclear Nonproliferation and the Nonproliferation Treaty (1990); J. Goldblat, Nonproliferation: The Why and the Wherefore (1985).

[2] GAOR, 13th Sess., Anns., a.i. 64, 70 and 72, Doc A/C.1/L.206, 17 October 1958.

world peace, and thus rendering more difficult the attainment of a general disarmament agreement...[3]

The second form of the Irish proposals was a set of proposed additions to a seventeen-power draft resolution on the suspension of nuclear weapons tests. Pursuant to these proposed amendments, the draft would provide that states

shall not supply other states with nuclear weapons while these negotiations are taking place and during the period of any suspension of tests that may result therefrom.[4]

It further called upon "all states which are not now producing nuclear weapons to refrain from undertaking their manufacture" during the same term.

Mr. Frank Aiken, Minister for External Affairs for Ireland, argued that there were two especial reasons why the proliferation of nuclear weapons needed urgently to be checked:

The first was the slowness with which negotiations toward general disarmament were proceeding. The second was that failure to halt the spread of nuclear weapons during the long period of negotiations on general disarmament was likely to make those negotiations abortive.[5]

With regard to the proposed amendments to the seventeen-power draft reso-lution, Mr. Aiken argued:

It was essential that the "nuclear powers" should undertake not to transfer nuclear weapons to other states, if manufacture of those weapons by the "non-nuclear powers" was to be avoided. Indeed, until the "nuclear powers" formally undertook to refrain from doing so, the "non-nuclear powers" might fear a possible transfer to an enemy or rival, and strive to offset that risk by trying to manufacture their own nuclear weapons.[6]

As Mohamed Shaker has explained:

The danger was conceived by Mr. Aiken as increasing not only in proportion to the number of states possessing nuclear weapons but in geometric progression. While nuclear weapons were in the hands of a few highly developed states which had much to lose and little to gain by a nuclear war, and therefore felt a sense of deep responsibility regarding their use, the smaller states would have much less to lose and a temptation to exploit the enormous temporary advantage deriving from the possession of these weapons. Also by falling into the hands of revolutionary groups and organizations—and as history has shown, local wars and revolutions almost always involved great-power rivalry—the use of nuclear weapons by a small state or a revolutionary group could easily set off a world-wide nuclear war.[7]

---

[3] Ibid.
[4] Ibid. at Doc. A/3974 and Add. 1 and 2, 3 and 4 November 1958, para. 22.
[5] Ibid. at 970th mtg, 31 October 1958, para. 49.
[6] Ibid. at para. 52.
[7] M. Shaker, THE NUCLEAR NONPROLIFERATION TREATY: ORIGIN AND IMPLEMENTATION 1959–1979, Vol. 1 (1980) 5.

While a good deal of support existed as to the substance of the Irish proposals, there was concern that the establishment of a new committee to review the issue of nuclear proliferation would largely duplicate the work already underway in the U.N. Disarmament Commission, which was to be enlarged in the same General Assembly session to include all U.N. members. With regard to the proposed amendments to the seventeen-power draft resolution, it was eventually decided by the Irish representative that the question of the proliferation of nuclear weapons should, in order to garner the maximum level of support, be kept separate from the question of nuclear testing. Thus, timing and other circumstances surrounding the Irish proposals in 1958 were perceived as non-ideal, and the Irish delegation withdrew them.[8]

However, efforts by the Irish delegation to the General Assembly on the issue of nuclear non-proliferation, and particularly on the subject of an international convention on nuclear non-proliferation, continued over the next three years. These efforts eventually resulted in the unanimous passage by the General Assembly on December 4, 1961 of a resolution on the "prevention of wider dissemination of nuclear weapons."[9] Because of the efforts of the Irish delegation leading up to the passage of this resolution, it has become commonly referred to in non-proliferation circles as the "Irish Resolution." The resolution:

1. Calls upon all states, and in particular upon the states at present possessing nuclear weapons, to use their best endeavours to secure the conclusion of an international agreement containing provisions under which the nuclear states would undertake to refrain from relinquishing control of nuclear weapons and from transmitting the information necessary for their manufacture to states not possessing such weapons, and provisions under which states not possessing nuclear weapons would undertake not to manufacture or otherwise acquire control of such weapons;
2. Urges all states to cooperate to those ends.

The Irish Resolution of 1961 was remarkable in laying out for the first time in a broad multilateral statement some of the basic principles of a treaty on nuclear weapons non-proliferation; principles which would eventually underpin the provisions of Articles I and II of the NPT. It was further remarkable in placing upon nuclear weapons possessing states the primary onus of responsibility for the negotiation and conclusion of such a treaty.[10]

For their part, the superpowers voiced early support for the principles contained in the Irish Resolution. The United States had that same year put forward proposals to the General Assembly entitled "Declaration on Disarmament: The

---

[8] Ibid. at 9–10.   [9] General Assembly Resolution 1665.
[10] M. Shaker, THE NUCLEAR NONPROLIFERATION TREATY: ORIGIN AND IMPLEMENTATION 1959–1979, Vol. 1, 25 (1980).

United States Programme for General and Complete Disarmament in a Peaceful World," which included the provision:

States owning nuclear weapons shall not relinquish control of such weapons to any nation not owning them and shall not transmit to any such nation the information or material necessary for their manufacture. States not owning nuclear weapons shall not manufacture such weapons, attempt to obtain control of such weapons belonging to other states, or seek or receive information or materials necessary for their manufacture.[11]

Proposals forwarded to the General Assembly by the Soviet Union the same year under the heading "Memorandum of the Government of the Union of Soviet Socialist Republics on Measures to Ease International Tension, Strengthen Confidence among States and Contribute to General and Complete Disarmament" included, under the sub-heading "[m]easures to prevent the further spread of nuclear weapons" the following paragraph:

The Soviet Government considers that there is at present a possibility of concluding an agreement by which the nuclear powers would undertake not to give nuclear weapons to other countries, and those states which do not possess nuclear weapons would undertake not to make them or obtain them from the nuclear powers.[12]

Even with the general support of the superpowers, it was not until 1965 that the General Assembly next agreed upon a significant resolution progressing the agenda of achieving a treaty on nuclear weapons proliferation. In Resolution 2028 the General Assembly, acting under its powers pursuant to Article 11(1) of the U.N. Charter which will be discussed at length in Chapter 4 below, agreed upon five "main principles" which were to underpin a treaty on the non-proliferation of nuclear weapons. The negotiation of the treaty was entrusted by the General Assembly in Resolution 2028 to the auspices of the Conference of the Eighteen-Nation Committee on Disarmament (ENDC), a Geneva-based multilateral negotiation forum established in 1961 with close institutional ties to the United Nations. The five principles agreed in Resolution 2028 were:

(a) The treaty should be void of any loop-holes which might permit nuclear or non-nuclear Powers to proliferate, directly or indirectly, nuclear weapons in any form;
(b) The treaty should embody an acceptable balance of mutual responsibilities and obligations of the nuclear and non-nuclear Powers;
(c) The treaty should be a step towards the achievement of general and complete disarmament and, more particularly, nuclear disarmament;
(d) There should be acceptable and workable provisions to ensure the effectiveness of the treaty; and

---

[11] GAOR, 16th Sess., Anns. (Vol. I), a.i. 19, Doc. A/4891, 25 September 1961 (Stage I, para. C, subpara (e)).
[12] Ibid. at para. 22.

(e) Nothing in the treaty should adversely affect the right of any group of States to conclude regional treaties in order to ensure the total absence of nuclear weapons in their respective territories.

The principles in Resolution 2028 were the product of the Irish proposals of 1958, as well as the Irish Resolution of 1961 and four subsequent years of discussions of nuclear non-proliferation particularly in the ENDC and in the U.N. Disarmament Commission. During these discussions, both the United States and the Soviet Union presented draft treaties to U.N. organs, giving further support to the continuing momentum for the establishment of a multilateral convention.[13]

The five principles of Resolution 2028 became important guiding considerations in the negotiations which followed between 1965 and 1968 on a treaty text for the NPT, and their meaning and correct interpretation were the subject of much debate. The ENDC became the focal point for negotiations, and forum for convergence of resolutions passed by the General Assembly and the Disarmament Commission.

Members of the ENDC took wide soundings from other nations not formally members of the group, and included those inputs in the formulation of treaty drafts. Issues such as the sharing of control between nuclear powers and non-nuclear powers—an ability desired by the U.S. and its European allies but disapproved of by the Soviet Union—and the safeguards and inspection regime to be included in Article III of the NPT, were the subject of protracted negotiation between the superpowers and among the wider membership of the ENDC.

On March 11, 1968, the United States and the Soviet Union submitted to the ENDC a joint draft treaty. This text was made the subject of several revisions over the course of the succeeding two months, but was finalized in a draft of May 31 and submitted to the General Assembly. The draft was adopted as Resolution 2373 by the General Assembly on June 12, 1968 by a vote of 95 to 4 with 21 abstentions, included among which were France and three members of the ENDC.

On the same day, the United States, the United Kingdom, and the Soviet Union fulfilled a commitment made during the course of negotiations on a treaty text, by submitting to the Security Council a draft resolution giving security assurances to non-nuclear weapon states. The draft was accepted by the Council and passed as Resolution 255. In its resolution the Council:

1. *Recognizes* that aggression with nuclear weapons or the threat of such aggression against a non-nuclear-weapon State would create a situation in which the Security Council, and above all its nuclear-weapon state permanent members, would have to act immediately in accordance with their obligations under the United Nations Charter; and

---

[13] The U.S. draft treaty was presented to the ENDC on August 17, 1965, and the Soviet draft treaty was presented to the General Assembly on September 24, 1965.

2. *Welcomes* the intention expressed by certain States that they will provide or support immediate assistance, in accordance with the Charter, to any non-nuclear-weapon State Party to the Treaty on the Nonproliferation of Nuclear Weapons that is a victim of an act or an object of a threat of aggression in which nuclear weapons are used; ...

The NPT was opened for signature on July 1, 1968 at Washington, London, and Moscow.[14] It was signed that first day by the three depository governments and by more than 50 other states. The treaty entered into force on March 5, 1970, when, according to Article IX, the three depository governments and 40 other states had deposited their instruments of ratification. In 2007, the membership of the NPT stands at 187 states, and the treaty continues to serve as the cornerstone legal instrument of the nuclear non-proliferation system.[15]

I. The Grand Bargain of the NPT

From the original Irish proposals in 1958, an international agreement purposed in stopping nuclear weapons proliferation had been conceptualized as one consisting of two distinct sets of obligations; one set for states already in possession of nuclear weapons, and a different set for states not in possession of nuclear weapons.

States possessing nuclear weapons were to take upon themselves the obligation not to proliferate those weapons or technologies which could lead to the development of those weapons, to states that did not possess nuclear weapons. They further accepted an obligation to eventually disarm themselves of nuclear weapons, in keeping with concurrent efforts toward general and complete nuclear disarmament.[16]

---

[14] Treaty on the Nonproliferation of Nuclear Weapons, opened for signature July 1, 1968, 21 U.S.T. 483, T.I.A.S. No. 6839, 729 U.N.T.S. 161.

[15] On the NPT generally see M. Willrich, NONPROLIFERATION TREATY: FRAMEWORK FOR NUCLEAR ARMS CONTROL (1969); M. Shaker, THE NUCLEAR NONPROLIFERATION TREATY: ORIGIN AND IMPLEMENTATION 1959–1979 (1980); M. Fry, N. Keatingue, and J. Rotblat (eds), NUCLEAR NONPROLIFERATION AND THE NONPROLIFERATION TREATY (1990); I. Bellamy, C. Blacker, and J. Gallacher, THE NUCLEAR NONPROLIFERATION TREATY (1985); C. Moxley, NUCLEAR WEAPONS AND INTERNATIONAL LAW IN THE POST-COLD WAR WORLD (2000); H. Athanasopulos, NUCLEAR DISARMAMENT IN INTERNATIONAL LAW (2000); L. Jensen, RETURN FROM THE NUCLEAR BRINK: NATIONAL INTEREST AND THE NUCLEAR NONPROLIFERATION TREATY (1974); J. Rhinelander and A. Scheinman (eds), AT THE NUCLEAR CROSSROADS: CHOICES ABOUT NUCLEAR WEAPONS AND EXTENSION OF THE NONPROLIFERATION TREATY (1995); S. Schrafsetter, AVOIDING ARMAGEDDON: EUROPE, THE UNITED STATES AND THE STRUGGLE FOR NUCLEAR NONPROLIFERATION, 1945–1970 (2004); D. Thomson, A GUIDE TO THE NUCLEAR ARMS CONTROL TREATIES (2001); J. Dhanapala, MULTILATERAL DIPLOMACY AND THE NPT: AN INSIDER'S ACCOUNT (2005); J. Goldblat (ed.), NUCLEAR DISARMAMENT: OBSTACLES TO BANISHING THE BOMB (2000).

[16] See, e.g., General Assembly Resolutions 1378, 1660, 1664, 1665, 1722.

For their part, states not possessing nuclear weapons were to take upon themselves an obligation neither to acquire such weapons from nuclear weapon states, nor to manufacture such weapons indigenously. In exchange for their commitment to forgo what would otherwise be their right, equal to that of the nuclear weapon states, to obtain nuclear weapons technologies, non-nuclear weapon states demanded that the treaty provide not only a recognition of their right to use nuclear technologies for purposes of civilian power generation, but also a further reciprocal obligation on the part of nuclear weapon states to provide positive assistance to non-nuclear weapon states in the development of their civilian nuclear power programs.[17]

This *quid pro quo* relationship of differential and reciprocal obligations between nuclear weapon states and non-nuclear weapon states, which the NPT came to codify, has become known as the "grand bargain" of the NPT, and is the fulfillment of the guiding principle of balanced mutuality enunciated in U.N. General Assembly Resolution 2028(b).[18]

The fact that the NPT is the codification of a *quid pro quo* relationship between two classes of states parties, each class having differing rights and obligations accorded them under the treaty, serves to differentiate the NPT from most other large multilateral treaties, e.g. the 1948 Genocide Convention, and the 1982 Law of the Sea Convention. These other broadly subscribed multilateral treaties are referred to in legal terminology as *traité-loi*, or lawmaking treaties, and have as their chief characteristic under this classification a set of rules which are applied universally across the full spectrum of states parties. Generally speaking, lawmaking treaties do not set up a *quid pro quo* relationship between states parties or groups thereof, and there is no consideration given between states in exchange for the undertaking of obligations.[19] Thus, lawmaking treaties are comparable to a degree with legislation under domestic law, binding each member equally to their rules without consideration.[20]

The NPT, because of the fundamental *quid pro quo* nature of the obligations contained in it, and the classification of states parties into two groups with distinct sets of rights and obligations, should rather be classified as a *traite-contrat*, or contract treaty; a treaty format more commonly used in private international law to define business transactions.[21]

---

[17] See J. Cirincione, Bomb Scare (2007) 30–31.

[18] See C. Chyba, "Second-Tier Suppliers and Their Threat to the Nuclear Nonproliferation Regime," in J. Pilat (ed.), Atoms for Peace: A Future After Fifty Years? (2007) 120–122.

[19] See generally, however, H. Caminos and M. Molitor, *Progressive Development of International Law and the Package Deal*, 79 American Journal of International Law 871 (1985).

[20] See P. Malanczuk, Akehurst's Modern Introduction to International Law (7th edn, 1997) 37–38; H. Thirlway, "The Sources of International Law," in M. Evans (ed.), International Law (2nd edn, 2006) 119–120; R. Bernhardt, "Treaties," in Encyclopedia of Public International Law, Vol. IV, 928–929; I. Brownlie, Principles of Public International Law (6th edn, 2003) 12 ("Law-making treaties create *general* norms for the future conduct of the parties in terms of legal propositions, and the obligations are basically the same for all parties.")

[21] Ibid.

It should be clear that this classification as a contract treaty, and not a law-making treaty, does not in any way affect the binding nature of the commitments entered into by the states parties of the NPT under international law.[22] Nor does it result in different rules of interpretation being applied to the treaty. The interpretation of the NPT is subject, as are all treaties, to the rules of treaty interpretation contained in the 1969 Vienna Convention on the Law of Treaties (VCLT), and in parallel custom.[23]

However, this difference in classification of the NPT can have an impact upon the actual interpretation and application of the NPT's terms. While the same VCLT rules on interpretation, contained in Articles 31 and 32 of the VCLT, apply to treaties under both the contract and lawmaking classifications, as Rudolph Bernhardt has explained, those rules may properly be applied to produce differing results depending upon a treaty's classification.[24] Article 31(1) of the VCLT provides:

1. A treaty shall be interpreted in good faith in accordance with the ordinary meaning to be given to the terms of the treaty in their context and in the light of its object and purpose.

The object and purpose of a contract treaty, with its *sine qua non* of a *quid pro quo* reciprocal commitment between the parties, is quite different from the object and purpose of a lawmaking treaty, which is to bind all states parties to the same rules without any particular consideration passing between the parties for their individual commitments. Thus, in terms of application of the object and purpose rule of VCLT Article 31(1), whereas in the case of a lawmaking treaty one party's breach of a universal rule will not necessarily have any particular bearing upon the continuing obligatory nature of that rule or other rules of the treaty upon the other treaty parties, because of the *quid pro quo* nature of the object and purpose of a contract treaty, a breach by one party can strike at the heart of the treaty's object and purpose, and therefore render the reciprocal obligation of another party null and void.[25]

In the case of a large, multilateral treaty like the NPT, with two categories of states parties each with multiple members, the breach by one state of its obligations will likely not be sufficient to render null and void the obligations under the

---

[22] H. Thirlway, "The Sources of International Law," in M. Evans (ed.), INTERNATIONAL LAW (2nd edn, 2006) 119–120.

[23] The ICJ has firmly established that Articles 31 and 32 of the VCLT reflect customary law. See, e.g., the *India/Malaysia* case, ICJ Reports 2002, para. 37; the *Libya/Chad* case, ICJ Reports 1994, paras 6, 21–22. See also I. Brownlie, PRINCIPLES OF PUBLIC INTERNATIONAL LAW (6th edn, 2003) 602–207; M. Shaw, INTERNATIONAL LAW, Pg. 839 (5th edn, 2003).

[24] R. Bernhardt, *Treaties*, in ENCYCLOPEDIA OF PUBLIC INTERNATIONAL LAW, Vol. IV (2000) 928–929; "Interpretation in International Law," in ENCYCLOPEDIA OF PUBLIC INTERNATIONAL LAW, Vol. II (1995) 1421–1422.

[25] See the discussion on 66–67 below regarding the operation of VCLT Article 60(2) on termination or suspension.

treaty of the entirety of the other category of states. However, if, under the NPT scenario, an entire category of states parties (e.g. the NWS) are found to be in breach of their fundamental obligations under the treaty, then the fact of the *quid pro quo* object and purpose of the treaty will likely serve to render the obligations of the other category of states (the NNWS) null and void. Thus, the NPT's distinction as a contract treaty, while not meaningful in altering the binding force of its terms or changing the rules regarding its interpretation, is meaningful in the application of its provisions to the behavior of its parties, and to the effect of that behavior upon the obligations of other states parties.

II. Article I

Article I of the NPT establishes the obligations of nuclear weapon states parties, which are defined in Article IX as states which had "manufactured and exploded a nuclear weapon or other nuclear explosive device prior to January 1, 1967." The original NWS states parties to the NPT were the United States, the United Kingdom, and the Soviet Union. The remaining two states which had met the Article IX criteria for exploding a nuclear device, China and France, did not join the NPT as NWS parties until March 9, 1992 and August 3, 1992 respectively.

Article I obligates NWS firstly "not to transfer to any recipient whatsoever nuclear weapons or other nuclear explosive devices or control over such weapons or explosive devices directly, or indirectly." The wording of this provision had been the subject of long and careful negotiation. The final language of this provision, termed inclusively in order to create a comprehensive ban upon transfers of nuclear weapons outside of the group of nuclear weapon states, to any recipient whether state or non-state actor, closely mirrors that of the 1954 U.S. Atomic Energy Act. This language, however, notably prohibits only the transfer of complete nuclear weapons, and not of components, related materials, and design information. This wording was desired by the United States specifically to allow for the continuation of U.S.–U.K. cooperative nuclear weapons development programs.[26]

---

[26] J. Simpson, "The Nuclear Nonproliferation Treaty," in N. Busch and D.H. Joyner, COMBATING WEAPONS OF MASS DESTRUCTION: THE FUTURE OF INTERNATIONAL NONPROLIFERATION POLICY (2009). On June 26, 2008, the Federation of American Scientists reported that the United States had secretly, and unexpectedly, removed all of its nuclear weapons from the United Kingdom, ending a 54-year presence of U.S. nuclear weapons in the country. The 110 B-61 gravity bombs had been stationed at the Royal Air Force base at Lakenheath. It was not immediately clear why the transfer was made, or why it was kept clandestine. The weapons had been rendered largely obsolete due to technological advances, and their presence in the U.K. had come to be seen as largely symbolic. See J. Borger, "U.S. Removes its Nuclear Arms from Britain," *The Guardian*, June 26, 2008.

Still, the terms "nuclear weapons" and "other nuclear explosive devices" are not defined in the NPT text.[27] Article 5 of the Treaty of Tlatelolco, which had been signed in February of 1967 by Latin American and Caribbean states, defines nuclear weapons as

any device which is capable of releasing nuclear energy in an uncontrolled manner and which has a group of characteristics that are appropriate for use for warlike purposes. An instrument that may be used for the transport or propulsion of the device is not included in this definition if it is separable from the device and not an indivisible part thereof.

This language was largely derived from the 1954 U.S. Atomic Energy Act, which defines "atomic weapon" as

any device utilizing atomic energy, exclusive of the means for transporting or propelling the device (where such means is a separable and divisible part of the device) the principal purpose of which is for use as, or development of, a weapon, a weapon prototype, or a weapon test device.[28]

Notably, however, while the Atomic Energy Act definition requires a "principal purpose" test for the characterization of a device as a nuclear weapon, the Treaty of Tlatelolco definition provides for an objective test, focusing on the physical characteristics of the device itself.[29]

The only guidance offered on definition by the text of NPT Article I itself is the presence of the separate terms "nuclear weapons" and "other nuclear explosive devices." This seems to indicate a distinction between, on the one hand nuclear explosive devices which, by virtue of their physical characteristics or their intended use, are to be classified as weapons; and on the other hand nuclear explosive devices which are by the same measures to be classified as non-weapons. Devices in the latter category would include those used for peaceful research, and for other civilian uses such as civil engineering.[30] The prohibitive terms of NPT Article I cover nuclear explosive devices of both weapon and non-weapon varieties. However, it is not clear from the NPT text, as it is clear from both the Treaty of Tlatelolco definition and the U.S. Atomic Energy Act definition, whether the means of transport or propulsion of nuclear explosive devices are also covered by the terms of Article I.[31]

---

[27] For an excellent review of the history and science of nuclear weapons, see J. Cirincione, BOMB SCARE (2007).

[28] Atomic Energy Act of 1954, Section 11(d).

[29] See M. Willrich, NONPROLIFERATION TREATY: FRAMEWORK FOR NUCLEAR ARMS CONTROL (1969) 68.

[30] M. Shaker, THE NUCLEAR NONPROLIFERATION TREATY: ORIGIN AND IMPLEMENTATION 1959–1979, Vol. 1 (1980) 204. See NPT Article V.

[31] The position of the United States has long been that means of transport or propulsion are not covered by Article I. See M. Shaker, THE NUCLEAR NONPROLIFERATION TREATY: ORIGIN AND IMPLEMENTATION 1959–1979, Vol. 1 (1980) 202.

The second clause in Article I obligates NWS not to "in any way assist, encourage, or induce any non-nuclear weapon state to manufacture or otherwise acquire nuclear weapons or other nuclear explosive devices..." This more broad formulation of the prohibition on sharing of nuclear technologies, components, and designs was made specifically applicable to NWS sharing with NNWS, thus leaving untouched the sharing of nuclear weapons technologies between NWS parties, yet at the same time providing a mandate for the regulation of international transfers of nuclear technologies from NWS to NNWS through export controls in national legal systems.[32]

III. Article II

Under Article II, all NNWS parties to the NPT undertake

not to receive the transfer from any transferor whatsoever of nuclear weapons or other nuclear explosive devices or of control over such weapons or explosive devices directly, or indirectly; not to manufacture or otherwise acquire nuclear weapons or other nuclear explosive devices; and not to seek or receive any assistance in the manufacture of nuclear weapons or other nuclear explosive devices.

One issue which has produced controversy from the earliest days of negotiation of the NPT, and which involves the obligations of both NWS under NPT Article I and NNWS under NPT Article II, is the issue of nuclear sharing agreements between the U.S. and its NNWS NATO allies.[33] Such nuclear sharing arrangements date to the Cold War era, and six such arrangements with NNWS NATO states are still in place today, with approximately 200 U.S. B-61 gravity bombs stationed in these countries.[34] Nuclear sharing between the U.S. and NNWS NATO countries takes the form of U.S. nuclear weapons being physically located within the territory of a NATO state, generally at domestic military installations, and all components and items necessary for delivery of such

---

[32] See J. Simpson, "The Nuclear Nonproliferation Treaty," in N. Busch and D.H. Joyner, COMBATING WEAPONS OF MASS DESTRUCTION: THE FUTURE OF INTERNATIONAL NONPROLIFERATION POLICY (2009).

[33] See generally M. Willrich, NONPROLIFERATION TREATY: FRAMEWORK FOR NUCLEAR ARMS CONTROL (1969) Chapter IV; M. Shaker, THE NUCLEAR NONPROLIFERATION TREATY: ORIGIN AND IMPLEMENTATION 1959–1979, Vol. 1 (1980) 191–245; J. Simpson and J. Nielsen, *The NPT and Nuclear Sharing,* <http://www.mcis.soton.ac.uk>; K. Koster, *An Uneasy Alliance: NATO Nuclear Doctrine & the NPT,* DISARMAMENT DIPLOMACY, Issue No. 49, August 2000; A. Makhijani and N. Deller, *NATO and Nuclear Disarmament: An Analysis of the Obligations of the NATO Allies of the United States under the Nuclear Nonproliferation Treaty and the Comprehensive Test Ban Treaty,* Institute for Energy & Environmental Research Report, October 2003, available at <http://www.ieer.org/reports/nato/fullrpt.pdf>; O. Nassauer, *NATO's Nuclear Posture Review, Should Europe End Nuclear Sharing?,* BITS Policy Note 02.1, April 2002. Available at <http://www.bits.de/public/policynote/pn02-1.htm>.

[34] See K. Koster, *An Uneasy Alliance: NATO Nuclear Doctrine & the NPT,* DISARMAMENT DIPLOMACY, Issue No. 49, August 2000.

weapons (e.g. trained bomber squadrons and appropriately fitted aircraft) being maintained by the host state's military. Both physical possession and operational control over the nuclear weapons themselves remain with the U.S. in times of peace. The launch codes are held exclusively by the U.S. military, and can only be used upon authorization of the U.S. President. However, NATO strategic policy has long provided that in time of general war, the U.S. president could authorize the activation of the weapons and the delegation of physical control over the weapons to the armed forces of NNWS NATO states, under the overall command of the NATO Supreme Allied Commander Europe. In practice, this means that the weapons would be armed and that the host state military would have physical control over their use—i.e. the weapons would be transported in and dropped by aircraft commanded and operated by the host state military, subject to the NATO chain of command.[35]

Such nuclear sharing arrangements between the U.S. and its NNWS NATO allies have long been a source of concern as to their compliance with Articles I and II of the NPT. The U.S. has maintained that they are in compliance with NPT rules, as under these arrangements control over the nuclear weapons themselves (as distinct from control over their means of delivery) is never surrendered to NNWS allies until a general state of war has commenced, and that in such a case of general war the NPT would no longer be a controlling legal framework.[36]

Critics quite correctly dispute this legal analysis, and argue that no principle of either humanitarian law or the law governing international uses of force serves *ipso facto* to render existing provisions of treaty law inoperable in a time of general war as among belligerents. On the contrary, the survival of basic rules of positive international law, and in particular those relevant to the prosecution of armed conflict, in times of armed conflict is a principle which has been consistently upheld since the Nuremburg war crimes trials.[37] The Third Draft Report of Professor Ian Brownlie, the Special Rapporteur of the International Law Commission's work on the subject of the effect of armed

---

[35] Ibid.

[36] See Message from the President of the United States, Transmitting Treaty on the Nonproliferation of Nuclear Weapons to U.S. Senate, 90th Congress, 2nd Session, Ex. H, 6, July 1, 1968, reprinted in M. Willrich, NONPROLIFERATION TREATY: FRAMEWORK FOR NUCLEAR ARMS CONTROL (1969) 75. See also a reprinting of a letter by Secretary of State Dean Rusk stating this reasoning in M. Shaker, THE NUCLEAR NONPROLIFERATION TREATY: ORIGIN AND IMPLEMENTATION 1959–1979, Vol. 1 (1980) 234.

[37] L. Green, THE CONTEMPORARY LAW OF ARMED CONFLICT (2nd edn, 2000) 55; D. Schindler and J. Toman, THE LAWS OF ARMED CONFLICTS (1988) 373–594; *Nicaragua* case (*Military and Paramilitary Activities in and Against Nicaragua*), ICJ Reports 1986, 14; *Oil Platforms* case (*Oil Platforms (Iran v. U.S.)*, Merits, Judgment of November 6, 2003, text available at 42; INTERNATIONAL LEGAL MATERIALS (2003), 1334); *Legal Consequences of the Construction of a Wall in the Occupied Palestinian Territory*, ICJ Reports 2004; *Armed Activities on the Territory of the Congo* (*Democratic Republic of the Congo v. Uganda*), ICJ Reports 2005.

conflict on treaties, supports this latter view.[38] The Report's Draft Article 3 states:

The outbreak of an armed conflict does not necessarily terminate or suspend the operation of treaties as:

(a) Between the parties to the armed conflict;
(b) Between one or more parties to the armed conflict and a third State.

Draft Article 4 continues:

1. The susceptibility to termination or suspension of treaties in case of an armed conflict is determined in accordance with the intention of the parties at the time the treaty was concluded.
2. The intention of the parties to a treaty relating to its susceptibility to termination or suspension shall be determined in accordance:
   (a) With the provisions of articles 31 and 32 of the Vienna Convention on the Law of Treaties; and
   (b) The nature and extent of the armed conflict in question.

Applying the principles of VCLT Article 31, the object and purpose of the NPT is to prohibit the further spread of nuclear weapons, and thus limit the extent and severity of any nuclear exchange between belligerents.[39] Thus, the object and purpose of this treaty would not appear to justify a decision on the part of any state to suspend its implementation during time of war for the purpose of increasing the potential for and scope of nuclear exchange, which is the essential effect of such nuclear sharing agreements.[40] Under this analysis, any transfer of physical and/or operational control over nuclear weapons from the United States to an NPT NNWS, whether NATO member or not, whether in peacetime or in time of war, would be a breach of both NPT Article I on the part of the United States, and NPT Article II on the part of the NNWS concerned.

Critics further argue that such nuclear sharing arrangements are a violation of the spirit of the NPT, in that they result in the de facto continuing proliferation of nuclear weapons to NNWS which would otherwise not have nuclear weapons on their territory, with the attendant increased risk of their use in wars involving those countries. They argue that such programs constitute long standing and open policies of planned breach of NPT rules and thus do continuing violence to the fundamental principle of NPT Articles I and II, which is to prohibit the proliferation of nuclear weapons to the control of NNWS under any circumstances.

---

[38] See U.N. Doc A/CN.4/578 (2007). See also M.J. Matheson, *The Fifty-Seventh Session of the International Law Commission*, 100 AMERICAN JOURNAL OF INTERNATIONAL LAW 416, 422–424 (2006).

[39] The parties to the NPT state in the preamble their belief "that the proliferation of nuclear weapons would seriously enhance the danger of nuclear war."

[40] I. Detter, THE LAW OF WAR (2nd edn, 2000) 346–349.

Another issue relevant particularly to the meaning of the second clause of Article II is the interpretation of the obligation accepted by NNWS therein not to "manufacture" nuclear weapons or other nuclear explosive devices. Most of the emphasis on nuclear weapons non-proliferation in the NPT's provisions has as its operative object the regulation of fissile materials. Thus, in Article III(1) the purpose of "preventing diversion of nuclear energy from peaceful uses to nuclear weapons or other nuclear explosive devices," is to be accomplished by a system of IAEA administered safeguards which are to be applied on "all source or special fissionable material in all peaceful nuclear activities within the territory of such State, under its jurisdiction, or carried out under its control anywhere." As will be more fully discussed below, the IAEA draws its monitoring and verification mandate from NPT Article III and the independent safeguards agreements which it concludes with NPT NNWS. Its mandate is thus essentially limited to detecting diversions of declared nuclear material from use for civilian purposes to use for military purposes.

However, the manufacture of a nuclear weapon involves not only the acquisition or production of a sufficient amount of the correct type of fissile material, it further requires the acquisition or construction of a mechanical device capable of properly manipulating that fissile material and channeling its energy into an explosive weapon. There has been considerable controversy regarding the scope of the Article II prohibition on manufacture, particularly as it applies to the manufacture of a nuclear warhead. There is no universally agreed interpretation of this term. However, the most often cited definition comes from testimony which William C. Foster, the head of the U.S. delegation to the NPT negotiations, gave before the U.S. Senate Foreign Relations Committee in 1968:

Facts indicating that the purpose of a particular activity was the acquisition of a nuclear explosive device would tend to show non-compliance. (Thus, the construction of an experimental prototype nuclear explosive device would be covered by the term "manufacture" as would be the production of components which would only have relevance to a nuclear explosive device.) Again, while the placing of a particular activity under safeguards would not, in and of itself, settle the question of whether that activity was in compliance with the treaty, it would of course be helpful in allaying any suspicion of non-compliance.[41]

This set of purposive criteria, commonly known as the Foster criteria, is useful in providing a guide for interpretation of the term "manufacture" in NPT Article II. It would seem to argue that any activity the purpose of which could reasonably

---

[41] Senate Committee on Foreign Relations, *Remarks Submitted by William C. Foster*, 89th Cong., 2d sess., July 10, 1968. See also G. Bunn and R.M. Timerbaev, *Nuclear Verification under the NPT*, Program for Promoting Nuclear Nonproliferation (PPNN) Study No. 5 (University of Southampton, England: Mountbatten Centre for International Studies, 1994) 4–5. Jozef Goldblat has stated that the Foster criteria represent the "unchallenged U.S. interpretation, given in the course of the negotiation of the treaty." THE NEW GUIDE TO NEGOTIATIONS AND AGREEMENTS (2nd edn, 2002) 102.

be none other than to contribute to the construction of a nuclear explosive device would run afoul of the prohibition on manufacture in NPT Article II. However, exactly how far back along the process of component construction, and particularly design, this prohibition extends, is less clear. Arguments have been made by NNWS that the prohibition on manufacture does not extend to research into and development of design information regarding nuclear explosive devices, so long as actual production of the device does not begin.[42]

The question of which of the two primary elements comprised within the Article II term "manufacture"—i.e. the fissile material element or the explosive device element—if detected, is most important in determining whether an NNWS is engaging in a prohibited nuclear weapon manufacturing program, was raised in the context of the December 2007 U.S. National Intelligence Estimate concerning Iran's nuclear activities.[43] As the New York Times explained:

For years, Washington had based its assessment that Iran was pursuing nuclear weapons largely on its steady work to enrich uranium, which could be used for bombs but which Iran says it wants to fuel power reactors. Forcing Iran to give up enrichment became the goal. The December estimate, by contrast, focused on weapons design. Based on fresh intelligence that Iran's bomb design program was suspended in 2003, it said Iran was not pursuing nuclear weapons, even though uranium enrichment continued.[44]

This shift in emphasis to detection of warhead design and production was hotly contested within U.S. intelligence circles.[45] Some observers have speculated that this rather sudden shift is attributable to the intelligence debacle of the 2003 Iraq intervention, in which U.S. intelligence agencies were subjected to harsh criticism regarding their interpretation of information concerning Iraq's WMD programs.[46] Under this reasoning, the shift to an emphasis on detecting NNWS possession of nuclear warhead designs and production efforts, and away from a focus on detecting diversions of fissile materials, essentially represents a shift toward a more objectively verifiable detection goal.[47] Due to the profoundly dual use nature of fissile materials and the processes of their refinement and extraction, the relatively more single use nature of activities and technologies involved in design and production of nuclear warhead components represents an attractive

---

[42] See "Arms Control Implications of Peaceful Nuclear Explosions," working paper submitted to Geneva disarmament conference by Japan, CCD/454, July 7, 1975 (Arms Control and Disarmament Agency [ACDA] Documents on Disarmament, 1975); L. Weiss, "The Nuclear Nonproliferation Treaty: Strengths and Gaps," in H. Sokolski (ed.), FIGHTING PROLIFERATION: NEW CONCERNS FOR THE NINETIES (1996).

[43] <http://www.dni.gov/press_releases/20071203_release.pdf>.

[44] W.J. Broad and D.E. Sanger, "Meeting on Arms Data Reignites Iran Debate," *The New York Times* (online) (March 3, 2008).

[45] Ibid.

[46] See ibid., quoting P. Pillar: "Intel officers are human too. What we might be seeing here is the price to be paid for the vilification of the community on the Iraq issue."

[47] See J. Acton and C. Newman, *IAEA Verification of Military Research and Development*, VERTIC Research Reports, Number 5, July 2006, 13–14.

subject for detection efforts, as a detection of the latter would be far less susceptible to demurrer on the basis of argued civilian purpose.

However, it should be reiterated that the IAEA does not have a mandate, and is generally ill-equipped to engage in detection efforts aimed at uncovering warhead design and production programs. Thus, a shift in emphasis away from detection of fissile materials diversion, and toward warhead design, production, or acquisition, may also represent an intent to, or at the least will have the effect of, marginalizing the IAEA's role in monitoring and verification of nuclear obligations. It may represent a desired shift in emphasis to the detection efforts of national intelligence services, and away from those of the IAEA, which has been seen particularly by some U.S. officials as less than effective in uncovering illicit, clandestine activities.[48]

IV. Article III.1

In order to verify compliance and aid in the implementation of the obligations undertaken by NWS and NNWS in Articles I and II, Article III of the NPT provides for two separate mechanisms aimed at preventing the proliferation of nuclear weapons technologies from NWS to NNWS, as well as among NNWS, or by indigenous manufacture within NNWS. These two mechanisms are safeguards, as described in Article III.1, and export controls, as provided in Article III.2.

Under Article III.4, NNWS are required to accept the imposition of safeguards administered by the International Atomic Energy Agency (IAEA) to verify compliance with the provisions of the NPT, and specifically to detect diversions of nuclear materials from peaceful uses, such as civilian power generation, to the production of nuclear weapons or other nuclear explosive devices.[49] Each NNWS agrees under Article III.4 to conclude an independent bilateral safeguards agreement with the IAEA. Under the terms of these safeguards agreements, all nuclear materials in peaceful uses at civilian facilities within the jurisdiction of the NNWS must be declared to the IAEA, whose inspectors are to be given regular access to the facilities for purposes of monitoring and inspections.

The IAEA itself pre-dates the conclusion of the NPT by eleven years, having been established in 1957 as an outgrowth of the "Atoms for Peace" plan, first envisaged by U.S. President Dwight Eisenhower in a speech to the U.N. General

---

[48] See W. Pinkus and D. Milbank, "Bush Clings to Dubious Allegations about Iraq," *Washington Post*, March 18, 2003.
[49] See generally M. Willrich, NONPROLIFERATION TREATY: FRAMEWORK FOR NUCLEAR ARMS CONTROL (1969) ch. V. The operative obligation of Article III with regard to safeguards is the obligation in Article III.4 to conclude an independent agreement with the IAEA. Paragraphs 1 through 3 of Article III describe aspects of the character and attributes of the safeguards which are to be the subject of that agreement.

Assembly on December 8, 1953.[50] As part of this plan, states possessing nuclear materials and related technology were to contribute to an international pool of resources, which was to be under the supervision of an international organization tasked with supplying the materials to states not possessing such technologies for peaceful purposes. The aim of the plan was to control and supervise the use of nuclear technologies through a collective international organization, in order to ensure the exclusively peaceful use of such technologies. The IAEA was originally conceived and designed to fulfill this role of international conduit for the regulated dispersal of nuclear materials for peaceful purposes.[51]

The fact of this original design can be viewed in the construction of the IAEA Statute. Article III of the Statute, which lists the functions of the Agency, includes seven paragraphs, six of which have to do with this originally intended role under the Atoms for Peace concept. The first such paragraph mandates the Agency:

1. To encourage and assist research on, and development and practical application of, atomic energy for peaceful uses throughout the world; and, if requested to do so, to act as an intermediary for the purposes of securing the performance of services or the supplying of materials, equipment, or facilities by one member of the Agency for another; and to perform any operation or service useful in research on, or development or practical application of, atomic energy for peaceful purposes...[52]

It is only in Article III(A)(5), the last paragraph in the functions section to be negotiated by the Statute's framers, where the Agency is given the role for which it has become best known—the administration of safeguards on nuclear fuel cycle activities within NNWS treaty parties. As stated in the paragraph, this role is:

5. To establish and administer safeguards designed to ensure that special fissionable and other materials, services, equipment, facilities, and information made available by the Agency or at its request or under its supervision or control are not used in such a way as to further any military purpose; and to apply safeguards, at the request of the parties, to any bilateral or multilateral arrangement, or at the request of a State, to any of that State's activities in the field of atomic energy...

The IAEA's role in administering safeguards arrangements began modestly, as in the early 1960s the limited number of inter-state transfers of nuclear materials

---

[50] See generally D. Fischer, The International Atomic Energy Agency: The First Forty Years and Reflections (1997).

[51] Eisenhower's original "Atoms for Peace" concept shared elements with the Baruch plan, which had been considered by the United Nations in 1946; in particular the establishment of an international uranium repository to which all able countries would contribute. The IAEA, which was originally conceived to act as this repository, was then to share out fissile materials on an equitable, supervised, and monitored basis. By the time the IAEA Statute was drafted, however, this role as a uranium repository had been scrapped primarily due to the reluctance of both superpowers to cooperate with the concept. Thus, the IAEA was given a somewhat more modest role of intermediary for programs of nuclear energy technology exchange and development assistance. See generally J. Pilat (ed.), Atoms for Peace: A Future after Fifty Years? (2007).

[52] Article III(A)(1).

and technologies which did occur were monitored, and the subsequent handling of the materials by the receiving state was supervised, by the supplying states themselves. However, as such transfers increased in number and frequency, supplier states became more eager to shift the burden of continuing monitoring of receiving states' uses of such materials and technology, and safeguarding of the exclusively peaceful purposes to which such technologies would be applied, to the IAEA.[53]

In response to this increased demand for the Agency's services in administering safeguards arrangements between states, and after long discussions with experts and among the IAEA's Board of Governors, the Agency adopted its first "Safeguards Document," clarifying the principles and procedures which were to guide the Agency in its fulfillment of its vaguely worded Article III(A)(5) role under its Statute.

This safeguards system, eventually defined in document INFCIRC/66, was designed to allow the IAEA to supervise the handling and uses of nuclear materials transferred to non-nuclear weapon states, and to ensure that such materials would not be diverted to military uses. The INFCIRC/66 system was originally designed not to cover the entirety of nuclear fuel cycle activity within a state, as later systems would, but rather to be applied to specific lots of nuclear materials, or specific facilities or installations. This specificity in application fitted the INFCIRC/66 system for the Agency's purposes during the 1960s, but after the signing of the NPT in 1968, and the new primary role for the IAEA under the NPT framework, it became clear that a new safeguards system would have to be devised to provide for more comprehensive safeguards on all nuclear-related sites within NNWS parties.[54]

In 1972, two years after the coming into force of the NPT, this new IAEA safeguards system was brought online and defined in document INFCIRC/153, entitled "The Structure and Content of Agreements Between the Agency and States Required in Connection With the Treaty on the Nonproliferation of Nuclear Weapons." INFCIRC/153 sets out the principles which should be included in a safeguards agreement between the IAEA and NNWS. The basic system established by INFCIRC/153 is one in which states have an obligation to keep detailed records "on all source or special fissionable material in all peaceful nuclear activities," and to provide the IAEA with design information on facilities in which such materials are kept, as well as access to such facilities for IAEA inspectors.[55]

The IAEA's role is essentially one of verification of the details on the location and handling of nuclear materials provided to the Agency through national reporting. In order to fulfill this role, the IAEA is to engage in routine inspections

---

[53] B. Sanders, *IAEA Safeguards and the NPT*, The 2005 NPT Review Conference, DISARMAMENT FORUM, Volume 4 (2004). Available at <http://www.unidir.org/pdf/articles/pdf-art2189.pdf>.
[54] Ibid.   [55] Ibid.

of declared facilities, including sampling of the environment within and outside of such facilities. However, the INFCIRC/153 system was constructed to impose the minimum burden necessary upon NNWS, and to be applied in a manner designed "to avoid hampering" technological development, "to avoid undue interference" in civilian nuclear energy, and "to reduce to a minimum the possible inconvenience and disturbance to the State." Thus, as one result, IAEA inspectors are not granted rights of access to all parts of safeguarded facilities, but only to agreed "strategic points" within facilities.[56]

INFCIRC/153 does provide, in Article 77, for the IAEA to be granted authority in safeguards agreements to conduct "special inspections" in addition to these routine inspections, through which the Agency might "obtain access in agreement with the State to information or locations in addition to the access specified in paragraph 76 above for *ad hoc* and routine inspections." However, the idea of special inspections was met with considerable opposition from NNWS, and the system which evolved in practice over the next two decades created an environment in which IAEA inspectors did not feel able to make such requests, and in fact did not make them. Thus, the IAEA's role remained one of verification of national reports through routine inspections of declared facilities.

Despite its shortcomings in practice, due to the comprehensive character of the INFCIRC/153 system, covering all sites involved in nuclear fuel cycle activity within a state, this safeguards system came to be referred to as the "Full Scope Safeguards System" (FSSG).[57]

In the aftermath of the 1991 Iraq war, IAEA inspectors returning to Iraq discovered that the Hussein regime had pursued a nuclear weapons program to an advanced stage, involving activities in facilities located all over the country. This program, according to IAEA Deputy Director of Inspections David Kay, had progressed to being within 12 to 18 months of acquiring sufficient fissile material to construct a nuclear explosive device.[58]

This revelation of a large scale clandestine nuclear weapons program in a state which had signed an INFCIRC/153 agreement with the IAEA, and which was under active Agency safeguards, was troubling. Even more disturbing was the fact that one of the undeclared nuclear installations, the Tuwaitha Nuclear Research Center, was virtually next door to a declared, safeguarded research reactor. Iraq's ability to conceal such an advanced program literally under the noses of IAEA inspectors shook international confidence in the INFCIRC/153 safeguards system.[59]

---

[56] Ibid.

[57] See F. Schmidt, *NPT Export Controls and the Zangger Committee*, NONPROLIFERATION REVIEW, CNS, Vol. 7 No. 3, (Fall–Winter 2000).

[58] U.S. Senate, Committee on Foreign Relations, *Nuclear Proliferation: Learning from the Iraq Experience*, Hearing before the Committee on Foreign Relations, 102 Cong., 1st Sess., October 17, 1991, 20.

[59] T. Hirsch, *The IAEA Additional Protocol: What it is and Why it Matters*, THE NONPROLIFERATION REVIEW (Fall–Winter 2004).

Again, that system relies almost entirely upon the declarations of facilities and materials made by states, and the IAEA's role under that system is to review those declarations and accounts to verify that the numbers add up, and that all fissile material is accounted for. However, under the INFCIRC/153 system the IAEA had almost no facility for determining the completeness of such reports, or of detecting undeclared nuclear activities.

Speaking at the 46th Session of the General Assembly in 1991, IAEA Director General Hans Blix called for the construction of an IAEA safeguards system with "more teeth." Soon afterward, a committee of IAEA member states began negotiation on a protocol to strengthen and supplement the INFCIRC/153 system. This process led to the adoption by the IAEA Board of Governors in 1997 of the Model Additional Protocol (INFCIRC/540).

The Additional Protocol has been characterized as "an effort to transform IAEA inspectors from accountants to detectives."[60] It attempts to do this by supplementing the INFCIRC/153 safeguards system in two primary areas. First, the Additional Protocol requires states to produce a more expanded declaration regarding nuclear fuel cycle activity being carried out within its territory than that required by the INFCIRC/153 system. This expanded declaration is to include details on nuclear materials and the facilities involved in producing, processing, and utilizing them, as required under INFCIRC/153, but in addition must also include information on all nuclear fuel cycle-related research and development activities that do not themselves involve nuclear materials, but which may be used in the production of nuclear materials, including activities being carried out in privately owned facilities. This expansion of information required from the states significantly widens the Agency's understanding of the full range of nuclear-related activities being carried on within a state. This more complete understanding allows the IAEA to better assess the purpose and direction of nuclear programs within NNWS.[61]

Second, the Additional Protocol provides for the IAEA to have "complementary access" to that it enjoys under the INFCIRC/153 system. INFCIRC/540 gives the IAEA the right of access "on a selective basis in order to assure the absence of undeclared nuclear material" to "any place" on the site of a declared facility, and not only to agreed strategic points, as under the INFCIRC/153 system. It further provides for IAEA access to all sites on which information has been provided by the state regarding research and development activities on nuclear fuel cycle-related technologies, in order "to resolve a question relating to the correctness and completeness of the information provided."[62]

Additionally, INFCIRC/540 provides for IAEA access to "any location specified by the Agency" in order to carry out "location-specific environmental monitoring." This provision enables IAEA inspectors to nominate undeclared

---

[60] Ibid. at 143.   [61] Ibid. at 143–144.   [62] Ibid.

locations at which they would like to take soil, water, and air samples in order to detect the presence of fissile materials, and thus potentially produce evidence of undeclared nuclear activities.[63]

The notice requirements for the carrying out of inspections under the Additional Protocol are significantly shortened from their length under the INFCIRC/153 system, and are typically set at 24 hours, down from the normal one-week notice period under INFCIRC/153. The Additional Protocol further requires the state to grant multi-entry visas to inspectors. Under the INFCIRC/153 system, this was not a requirement, and the necessity in many states of inspectors obtaining entry visas, often a month-long process, served to give the state even earlier warning of impending inspections.

These supplements to the information gathering ability of the IAEA, as well as its ability to conduct inspections in a more efficient and effective manner, are significant improvements to the Agency's ability to verify not only the correctness, but also the completeness of state declarations. They allow for increased confidence in the determinations of the IAEA that no undeclared nuclear-related activity is being carried out in a safeguarded territory.

The INFCIRC/540 Additional Protocol is voluntary for NPT member states, in that conclusion of an INFCIRC/540 agreement is not a part of the fundamental NNWS safeguards obligation under Article III.4 of the NPT. NPT NNWS may, if they choose, maintain only the standard INFCIRC/153 agreement with the IAEA. However, since its adoption in 1997, INFCIRC/540 agreements have been signed and have come into force in 78 IAEA member states.

Compliance with IAEA safeguards agreements is verified by IAEA inspectors under these inspection systems and reports regarding compliance are submitted to the IAEA Board of Governors. If that body determines that there has been a breach of a safeguards agreement, it will, pursuant to Article XII of the IAEA Statute, typically ask the state in question to clarify or provide further information regarding the status of its programs or facilities. The Board will, if necessary, provide direction to the state to take corrective action in order to bring itself back into compliance with its safeguards commitments.

If a breach continues, or, pursuant to Article 19 of INFCIRC/153, if the IAEA is "not able to verify that there has been no diversion of nuclear material required to be safeguarded under the Agreement to nuclear weapons or other nuclear explosive devices," and the state is resistant to the directions of the Board of Governors, the IAEA Board can in accordance with Article XII(C) of its Statute refer the matter to the United Nations Security Council for that body's

---

[63] The two fissile materials most appropriate for nuclear weapons are uranium and plutonium. These materials exist in several alternative forms (isotopes) that differ only in their atomic weight, which is indicated in common usage by a number appearing after their name. The two isotopes most capable of sustaining the fast-neutron chain reaction necessary for a nuclear weapon are uranium 235 and plutonium 239.

deliberation and action, and for its potential authorization of measures to remedy the breach, including at the extreme the use of the Security Council's powers under Chapter VII of the U.N. Charter.

Despite the advantages of increased information provision and complementary inspector access provided for under the Additional Protocol, the IAEA safeguards system even as supplemented by the Additional Protocol is still dependant upon the cooperation of the state in which safeguards are applied for its success. Even under the Additional Protocol, there are ample reservations of authority for states to allow them to severely restrict the activities of IAEA inspectors, while remaining in full compliance with the Additional Protocol.[64] Thus, while the IAEA safeguards system overall is esteemed as an effective tool for verifying NNWS compliance with NPT Article II obligations, its limitations as a system imposed upon sovereign entities, by an international organization system with limited compulsory powers and abilities, are apparent.

Furthermore, despite its attempts to be seen as an independent "nuclear watchdog" and objective verifier of NPT commitments, the IAEA has not escaped criticisms of politicization, and of being unduly influenced by powerful Western states wishing to use the organization as a tool to accomplish political agendas.[65] Such criticism has been made in the context of the recent institutional escalation of tensions surrounding the 2002 revelations of undeclared nuclear fuel cycle sites in Iran, in breach of its IAEA safeguards agreement. While the details of the Iranian case will be more fully explored below, observers have noted the fact-similarity of the case with another case in which revelations were made concerning undeclared nuclear experimentation.

On August 17, 2004, South Korea's Ministry of Science and Technology (MOST) reported to the IAEA that South Korea had, during three experiments in January and February 2000, used a process known as atomic vapor laser isotope separation to produce approximately 0.2 grams of uranium of an average enrichment of 10% presence of U-235. The peak level of enrichment achieved during the experiments was 77% presence of U-235, a level sufficient for weapons-usable fissile material, and close to the 85% threshold of weapons-grade fissile material. The experiments had been carried out at the Laboratory for Quantum Optics at the Korea Atomic Energy Research Institute (KAERI). MOST further informed the IAEA that KAERI scientists had, during April to May of 1982, separated about a milligram of plutonium from approximately 2.5 kilograms of spent fuel discharged from a research reactor.[66]

---

[64] T. Hirsch, *The IAEA Additional Protocol: What it is and Why it Matters*, THE NON-PROLIFERATION REVIEW (Fall–Winter 2004) 143–144.

[65] See J. Joseph, "IAEA Set Unwise Precedent on S. Korea," Defensenews.com, January 3, 2005. Available at <http://www.defensenews.com/story.php?F=580844&C=commentary>.

[66] See D. Pinkston, "South Korea's Nuclear Experiments," Center for Nonproliferation Studies, November 9, 2004. Available at <http://cns.miis.edu/pubs/week/041109.htm>.

Both the uranium enrichment experiments and the plutonium separation experiments had to that point been undeclared to the IAEA, and were thus in breach of South Korea's INFCIRC/153 agreement with the IAEA which had been in place since 1975. The uranium enrichment experiments, having achieved a weapons-usable level of enrichment, were also arguably in breach of South Korea's fundamental obligations under Article II of the NPT. The fact that the experiments had remained undisclosed for so many years (for over two decades in the case of the 1982 plutonium experiments), in addition to the well known facts of South Korea's efforts, later abandoned, to pursue a nuclear weapons program in the 1970s, and in particular the fact that the 2000 experiments had succeeded in enriching uranium to weapons-usable level, made the admissions from South Korean officials a shocking revelation to the IAEA.[67]

The reason South Korean officials finally disclosed the experiments to the IAEA in August 2004, is almost certainly because South Korea had ratified an Additional Protocol (INFCIRC/540) agreement with the IAEA in February of 2004, and knew that the results of the experiments would be detected by the environmental sampling IAEA inspectors were sure to undertake pursuant to that agreement. South Korean officials had in fact denied IAEA inspectors entry in 2002 and 2003 into sites associated with the laser enrichment program that was used in the 2000 uranium experiments. Even in their admission, the South Korean Government's initial statements regarding the experiments contained a number of inconsistencies which fueled suspicion regarding South Korea's commitment to its NPT obligations, as well as its control over national nuclear laboratories.[68]

In spite of South Korean pressure, including threats to undermine his candidacy for a third term as Director General of the IAEA, Mohammed ElBaradei reported the admissions to the IAEA Board of Governors on September 15, 2004.[69] The Board of Governors completed their deliberations and issued a brief set of conclusions on the implementation of safeguards in South Korea on November 26. In its conclusions the Board

shared the Director General's view that given the nature of the nuclear activities described in his report, the failure of the Republic of Korea to report these activities in accordance with its safeguards agreements is of serious concern. At the same time, the Board noted that the quantities of nuclear material involved have not been significant, and that to date there is no indication that the undeclared experiments have continued.[70]

The Board ended its conclusions by encouraging South Korea to continue its "active cooperation" with the Agency, and by requesting the Director General to report on the situation as appropriate.

---

[67] Ibid.   [68] Ibid.   [69] IAEA Document GOV/2004/84.
[70] Available at <http://www.iaea.org/NewsCenter/News/2004/south_korea.html>.

These conclusions by the Board of Governors, not even amounting to a denunciation of South Korea's breaches of its safeguards agreement, let alone referral of the case to the U.N. Security Council, were in stark contrast to its resolution adopted exactly one year previously on Iran after that country's admission to having conducted uranium enrichment and plutonium extraction experiments at undeclared sites.

In its November 26, 2003 resolution, the Board "strongly deplore[d]" Iran's "past failures and breaches of its obligation to comply with the provisions of its Safeguards Agreement," and noted with concern Iran's "past...pattern of concealment resulting in breaches of safeguard obligations..." The Board further recognized that Iran had a particular onus of cooperation and transparency in order to "provide and maintain the assurances required by Member States" and "restore confidence."[71] Such an increased standard of responsibility to restore the confidence of the IAEA was noticeably absent in the Board's November, 2004 conclusions regarding South Korea.

Iran's perceived failure to meet this enhanced standard, uniquely imposed upon it by the IAEA Board of Governors, led to the Board's February 4, 2006 referral of the Iranian case to the U.N. Security Council, notwithstanding the fact that no evidence of a nuclear weapons program in Iran had been found by IAEA inspectors, and Iran had no history of nuclear weapons program development. This again was quite inexplicable when compared to the Board's kid-glove treatment of South Korea, which had been found to have enriched uranium to weapons-usable levels, and which had pursued a nuclear weapons program in the past.

To many observers, the reasons for this inconsistency in treatment between the Iranian and South Korean safeguards cases cannot be explained by differences in the facts of the cases themselves, the material points of which are quite strikingly similar, or by differences in the subsequent level of cooperation with the IAEA by the states concerned. The difference in the standards applied in the two cases by the IAEA Board, and the resulting institutional escalation in the Iranian case, seem more persuasively explained by the character of the two states themselves and their broader relationships with members of the IAEA Board of Governors, and in particular the United States.

The fact that South Korea is an important U.S. ally in Northeast Asia (particularly in the context of ongoing tensions with North Korea over its nuclear weapons program), compared with the long and torrid history of U.S.–Iranian relations, seems to many to be the missing independent variable, which when added to these two fact-similar cases of safeguards agreement violation produces what many see as prejudicial and politically-driven treatment of Iran by the IAEA. This perceived use of the IAEA as a vehicle for the pursuit of U.S. foreign policy serves to undermine the credibility of the organization as an independent

---

[71] IAEA Document GOV/2003/81.

body, and in measure serves to reduce the confidence of NNWS, particularly those not on good terms with the U.S., in the IAEA as an objective verifier of NPT commitments.[72]

V. Article III.2

Article III.2 provides the international legal basis for all nuclear export controls. It specifies that all parties to the treaty will not transfer nuclear (fissionable) materials, as well as "any equipment or material especially designed or prepared for the processing, use or production of special fissionable material" to non-nuclear weapon states for peaceful purposes unless such material is subject to the IAEA safeguards specified in Article III.1.[73]

This provision, providing only the most vague of standards both on the subjects of criteria for applying national export controls, and on the question of exactly what materials should be the subject of national export controls, created an urgent need for clarification of the NPT's meaning in this regard. This was particularly the case as the regulation of trade in nuclear-related technologies between states formed the most practical continuing concern for states in possession of such technologies, and the issue area in which the implementation of NPT rules was to be most impactful upon the national laws and policies of the NWS and other supplier states of nuclear-related technologies.

Due to this need, in March 1971, shortly after the NPT's entry into force, a group of such supplier states gathered for the purpose of clarifying the technical implications of NPT export controls, as well as to establish a continuing forum for interpretation of Article III.2's broad export control provisions. This meeting was the nucleus of a group which came to be known as the Zangger Committee, after its first Chairman, Professor Claude Zangger.

The Zangger Committee continued to meet periodically and eventually established both a set of Understandings adopted by all Committee members, and a Trigger List composed of items the export of which should "trigger" the requirement of safeguards. The Committee's declared purpose has from the beginning not been to establish additional obligations binding upon it members.[74] This fact is evident by the nature of acceptance of the Understandings by each member, which is accomplished through simple exchange of notes and

---

[72] See J. Joseph, "IAEA Set Unwise Precedent on S. Korea," Defensenews.com, January 3, 2005. Available at <http://www.defensenews.com/story.php?F=580844&C=commentary>.

[73] See generally D.H. Joyner, *The Nuclear Suppliers Group: History and Functioning*, INTERNATIONAL TRADE LAW & REGULATION 11(2), 33–42 (2005); idem, *The Nuclear Suppliers Group: Present Challenges and Future Prospects*, INTERNATIONAL TRADE LAW & REGULATION 11(3), 84–96 (2005).

[74] See F. Schmidt, *The Zangger Committee: Its History and Future Role*, Vol. 2 No. 3, NONPROLIFERATION REVIEW, CNS (Fall 1994) 38.

a unilateral declaration that the Understandings will be made effective through national export legislation.[75] Rather, the Committee's understood role is to provide a forum for harmonization of export control policies and the setting of mutually understood minimum standards for compliance with the export control provisions of NPT Article III.2.[76]

The Zangger Committee's Understandings were published in September 1974 as IAEA document INFCIRC/209, and are divided into two separate memoranda addressing export controls on a category of items described in Article III.2. Memorandum A covers source and special fissionable material, and Memorandum B covers equipment and material specifically designed or prepared for the processing, use, or production of special fissionable material. The memoranda provide that nuclear suppliers should, in the context of a transfer of subject items to a non-nuclear weapon state not party to the NPT:

a) obtain assurances from the recipient state that the exported materials will not be used in a nuclear explosion;
b) subject such items, and materials on the Trigger List produced through their use, to IAEA safeguards; and
c) ensure that items on the Trigger List are not re-exported to a third party recipient state unless that recipient state meets the criteria laid out in a) and b).

The Trigger List, which clarifies and provides detail regarding the equipment listed in the memoranda is updated regularly in accordance with technological innovations. The Zangger Committee's Trigger List and memoranda together comprised the first major agreement among supplier states regarding nuclear export controls.

---

[75] It has been argued that there is a substantive difference between the joint declaration mode of accession to membership which has been employed in the NSG, and the exchange of notes between members which is the *modus operandi* in the Zangger Committee. The contention being that this exchange of notes creates a more binding foundational understanding among Zangger Committee members. However, an analysis of the notes exchanged as part of this process makes clear that the notes are not intended by their issuers to constitute an understanding of a treaty relationship, which is the only type of agreement enforceable in international law. This understanding of the issuing states governs the issue of creation of legal relationship in this context as per Articles 11 and 13 of the 1969 Vienna Convention on the Law of Treaties. Thus it is correct to maintain that both the Zangger Committee and the NSG are examples of inter-governmental agreements which are not legally binding as a matter of international law.

[76] See F. Schmidt, *NPT Export Controls and the Zangger Committee*, NONPROLIFERATION REVIEW, CNS, Vol. 7 No. 3 (Fall–Winter 2000) 137. ("The Committee does not decide 'ex cathedra' what the export control requirements of the NPT should be. Instead, its members—NPT parties who are major suppliers confronted regularly with the question of how to interpret Art. III.2 obligations—meet to negotiate what minimum requirements should be applied. They seek to harmonize their understandings, aiming at the widest possible membership, to try to prevent commercial transactions from weakening nonproliferation objectives.")

The explosion of a nuclear device by India in May 1974, in addition to increased activity among other NNWS to create a full nuclear fuel cycle, led to heightened concern among supplier states regarding nuclear proliferation. In 1975 a new group of supplier states met in London with the purpose of supplementing the Zangger Committee's work in the field of nuclear export controls. Over successive meetings, this group became known unofficially as the "London Club," and officially as the Nuclear Suppliers Group (NSG). The NSG's chief distinction from the Zangger Committee was initially to be found in the character of its membership. The Zangger Committee had from its inception been comprised exclusively of NPT member states. The NSG by contrast was consciously envisioned to include non-parties to the NPT and, importantly, France, a major supplier state not yet a party to the NPT and therefore also not a member of the Zangger Committee. The establishment of the NSG thus expanded the number of important voices and interests in deliberations regarding nuclear export control standards.[77]

In 1976 NSG member states produced a document entitled "Guidelines on Nuclear Transfers," which was accepted by all 15 members in 1977 and published in February 1978 as IAEA document INFCIRC/254. The NSG guidelines incorporated the Zangger Committee Trigger List and largely mirrored the Zangger Committee's Understandings, with the notable addition of going beyond the context of the NPT to cover nuclear transfers to any non-nuclear weapon state. The NSG guidelines further tightened export control standards in a number of areas including in the transfer of nuclear facilities and technology supporting them.

Following the adoption of the guidelines in 1977, the NSG did not meet again officially for 13 years, although during this time the NSG Guidelines were implemented by member states through national measures and 12 more states from both the West and the East formally accepted the Guidelines. From 1978 to 1990 no changes were made to NSG documents, including updates to the NSG Trigger List, although during the same period the Zangger Committee continued to function and regularly updated its Trigger List.[78] Tadeusz Strulak, Chairman of the 1992 meeting of the NSG, has noted of this period of relative inactivity:

In my opinion, the major cause of the group's inactivity was the unwillingness of some NSG suppliers to move beyond the conditions for nuclear exports established in 1977. The motive behind this unwillingness was commercial interest. An example to support this view is the case of full-scope safeguards. Discussion on the extent of the safeguards that recipients should be required to agree to as a condition of nuclear supplies dates back to the early NSG period before the acceptance of the guidelines. There was no agreement on this point then, and later attempts in the mid-1980's by some countries to begin a

---

[77] See T. Strulak, *The Nuclear Suppliers Group,* THE NONPROLIFERATION REVIEW, Vol. 1, No. 1 (Fall 1993).
[78] Ibid.

discussion on making full-scope safeguards a condition of export failed as well. Some suppliers unilaterally adopted the requirement of full-scope safeguards.[79]

However, interest in the NSG as a separate institution underwent a revival and the NSG entered a period of renewed activity beginning with the ending of the Cold War, a revival which was greatly enhanced through the experience of the 1990–91 Gulf War. With the collapse of the Soviet Union, a period of political reformation began in Central and Eastern Europe, one result of which was a renewal in many former Soviet states of non-proliferation commitments, which generally strengthened the hand of the NSG as well as the other multilateral non-proliferation regimes. Even more importantly, however, the confrontation between East and West, which had dominated both the formal and informal agendas of most international institutions, including the multilateral export control regimes, during the Cold War was replaced by a new list of regional proliferation concerns. Cooperation regarding these disparate problems was seen by many to be better facilitated, in the nuclear export control context, through the more inclusive frameworks of the Nuclear Suppliers Group.[80]

A. Dual-Use Gap

However, if the ending of the Cold War allowed greater attention to be focused on regional issues, the Gulf War and the lessons learned particularly by Western supplier states from it, brought home in compelling fashion the necessity of greater attention to harmonization and tightening of multilateral nuclear export controls in general. This was particularly perceived as it became clear that items and technologies directly involved in the processes of weapons manufacture were not the only or even the most important problem for export control systems to deal with. As the war progressed, and particularly in its aftermath, it became clear that one of the greatest facilitators of the formidable yet clandestine Iraqi nuclear weapons program was the importation, through various methods ranging from open purchase to covert indirect acquisition, of items from Western companies which were not directly nuclear-related but which were rather dual-use in nature, i.e. items which had legitimate civilian uses but which could also be adapted for use in weapons programs.[81]

The Trigger Lists and foundational principles both of the Zangger Committee and the NSG had up to that point been concentrated on nuclear materials and those items and technologies "especially designed" for their production, as

---

[79] Ibid. at 3.

[80] T. Perry, *The Origins and Implementation of the 1992 Nuclear Suppliers Group (NSG) Agreement*, Doctoral Dissertation, University of Michigan (2003).

[81] J. Holmes and G. Bertsch, *Tighten Export Controls*, DEFENSE NEWS, May 5, 2003. D. Albright and M. Hibbs, *Iraq and the Bomb, Were They Even Close?*, THE BULLETIN OF ATOMIC SCIENTISTS 16–28 (April, 1992); D.A. Kay, *Denial and Deception of WMD Proliferators*, THE WASHINGTON QUARTERLY 18:1, 90 (November 1994).

specified in Article III.2 of the NPT. Now, however, it was realized that a sizeable "dual-use gap" existed as between the normative foundations of the multilateral nuclear export control regimes and the realities of the modern security environment. The recognition of this dual-use gap, and a commonly perceived imperative to narrow it, contributed significantly to the revival of the NSG.[82]

At the NSG plenary meeting in the Hague in March, 1991, the members agreed to bring the NSG control list up-to-date by broadening it to include the items which had been added to the Zangger Committee's control list since the last NSG meeting in 1977. The group also decided on the implementation of a revised process of review and consultation (which had been used infrequently up to that point) and also of information exchange. However, the most noteworthy achievement of the Hague meeting was the decision to create a supplementary regime within the NSG framework to control exports of nuclear-related dual-use materials and technology. This arrangement was formally adopted by the 27 NSG members at the 1992 plenary meeting in Warsaw, and both the resulting guidelines and Trigger List were published by the IAEA in July 2002 as INFCIRC/254/REV 1.Part 2.

The NSG arrangement for dual-use nuclear export controls, now referred to as NSG Part 2, consists of a set of guidelines for transfers of nuclear dual-use items and a list of approximately 65 items including equipment and technology. The "Basic Principle" of the guidelines states that suppliers should not authorize transfers of equipment, materials, software, or related technology identified on the list if 1) they are to be used by a non-nuclear weapon state in a nuclear explosive activity or an unsafeguarded nuclear fuel cycle; 2) there is in general an unacceptable risk of diversion to such an activity; or 3) the transfers are contrary to the objective of averting the proliferation of nuclear weapons.

Other important provisions in the guidelines specify criteria for assessing the risk level specified in the Basic Principle, and conditions for transfers and re-transfers (i.e., end-use statements or assurances of non-use for explosive or unsafeguarded nuclear fuel cycle activity). Also adopted at Warsaw was a Memorandum of Understanding, clarifying a number of important matters regarding implementation of the Part 2 guidelines.[83]

In addition to the creation of a new dual-use regime and its related documentation, the Warsaw plenary saw significant steps being taken to strengthen and update the original NSG regime for controlling nuclear transfers (NSG Part 1). Since the signing of the NPT there had been debate regarding the requirement of full scope safeguards for transfers of nuclear materials and related items. The text of NPT Article III.4 requires NNWS parties to undertake a commitment to accept IAEA safeguards on all peaceful nuclear activities. However, this

---

[82] See C.E. Thorne (ed.), A GUIDE TO NUCLEAR EXPORT CONTROLS (5th edn, 2002).

[83] See T. Strulak, *The Nuclear Suppliers Group,* THE NONPROLIFERATION REVIEW, Vol. 1, No. 1 (Fall 1993).

safeguards requirement which NPT parties take upon themselves was not made applicable under the terms of the treaty to non-NPT members receiving exports of nuclear-related items from NPT parties. Some argued afterwards that the intent of the NPT was to require the same safeguards commitment of non-party recipients, but this interpretation was not widely accepted and state practice in the years following the signing of the NPT indicated that this was not the conclusion of most NPT parties.

However, at the Warsaw meeting in April 1992 NSG members accepted a declaration requiring suppliers not to transfer Trigger List items to non-nuclear weapon states (NPT member or not) unless the recipient state has concluded a bilateral agreement with the IAEA implementing full scope safeguards on all nuclear facilities within the recipient state. This declaration, published as IAEA INFCIRC/405, was an important step toward universalization of nuclear non-proliferation principles and represented a significant tightening of the nuclear export control regime.

Other important institutional modifications to the NSG which occurred during the decade of the 1990s include the extension in 1995 of the "no-undercutting" rule to both NSG Parts 1 and 2. Paragraph 4(b) of the 1992 dual-use regime Memorandum of Understanding states that member governments

should not authorize a transfer of equipment, materials, software, or related technology identified in the Annex which is essentially identical to a transfer which was not authorized by another Subscribing Government where this decision was notified pursuant to subparagraph (a), without consulting the Subscribing Government which provided the notice.

The observance of this rule on undercutting transfers is vital to the maintenance of an effective procedure for information sharing in the area of denial notifications. This principle and the other implementing principles of the MOU for "leveling the playing field" among members became available for acceptance by all NSG members in 1997.

It is worth noting that there has been some discussion within legal circles, and particularly among legal experts in Non-Aligned Movement (NAM) countries regarding the nature of the NSG dual-use regime and its character as being a step removed from the legitimizing provisions of Article III.2 of the NPT in its attempts to regulate trade in dual-use technologies.[84] It will be remembered that Article III.2 of the NPT addresses export controls on both nuclear materials and "equipment or material especially designed or prepared for the processing, use or production of special fissionable material." There is no mention within the text of

---

[84] On the NAM, see <http://www.nam.gov.za/background/background.htm>; J. Simpson and T. Ogilvie-White (eds), NPT Briefing Book, Vol. i: The Evolution of the Nuclear Nonproliferation Regime (2003); T. Ogilvie-White, *International Responses to Iranian Nuclear Defiance: The Non-Aligned Movement and the Issue of Non-Compliance*, 18 European Journal of International Law 453 (2007).

dual-use items, primary uses for which in many cases are only indirectly related to nuclear materials and which, by the same token, are capable of non-nuclear peaceful civilian use.

Trade in such dual-use items is of particular interest to developing states at the early stages of energy production capacities. Many such states have voiced concern that the NSG's regulation in this area is overly restrictive, and on a more fundamental level that the NSG itself is outside of the legal regime for multilateral regulation of nuclear materials, with the NPT as its cornerstone. They have protested the characterization of NSG standards and policies as being authoritatively or normatively incumbent upon non-NSG members, whether NPT parties or not. They have further protested criticisms from NSG members regarding non-compliance of the policies of non-NSG members with NSG norms.[85] They have argued that the NSG is essentially a supplier-state cartel whose policies unduly target states legitimately attempting to develop civilian power generation facilities.[86]

B. Legal Implications

The question of the international legal import of the guidelines of both the Zangger Committee and, perhaps more importantly, the NSG is indeed an interesting one. Both groups are clearly not treaty-based, nor do the guidelines of either group per se establish rules of law binding upon states, whether group members or not. At first glance, one is tempted to think of both groups, and particularly of the larger membership NSG, as comprising a subset of states parties to the NPT "whose interests are specially affected"[87] by the issue of the international supply of nuclear-related items and technologies, i.e. because they are groups composed of the states, relatively few in number, which are in possession of such technologies. This is in contrast to other NPT member states which do not possess such technologies in significant amounts, and are therefore not able to engage in state practice and *opinio juris* in this issue area. This distinction has been argued to be significant in according special influence to a subgrouping of states, even a minority of states, in their ability to create customary international law binding upon all states. A classic example of this is the special influence of the state practice and *opinio juris* of coastal states, as contrasted with

---

[85] One basis for such characterizations is provided in the NSG Part 2 Guidelines, paragraph 9, which states "In the interest of international peace and security, the adherence of all states to the Guidelines would be welcome."

[86] See, e.g., NAM Summit Declaration, Cartagena, Colombia, 18–20 October 1995. Available at <http://www.nam.gov.za/xisummit/index.html>. In this Declaration, NAM members "noted with concern the growing restraint placed on access to material, equipment and technology for peaceful uses of nuclear energy by the developed countries through imposition of ad-hoc export control regimes."

[87] *North Sea Continental Shelf,* Judgment, ICJ Reports 1969, 3, para. 74.

landlocked states, in the creation of customary law in the issue area of the law of the sea.[88]

However, while the membership of these groups would seem to fit nicely into this specially interested category, and the activities of the groups in passing guidelines and harmonizing their actions in pursuance therewith would seem to reflect a common and consistent state practice in this issue area, the customary law analysis of the Zangger Committee and the NSG fails on the point of *opinio juris*. From all of the foundational documents of the two groups it is clear that their members do not view the groups' guidelines as comprising legally binding statements of rules. Rather, they view them simply as commonly agreed norms or principles which give meaning and specificity to the obligation of NPT Article III.2, and which should be adhered to by NSG members, in accordance with each state's national laws. This absence of *opinio juris* with regard to the agreed pronouncements of the Zangger Committee and the NSG is fatal to a determination of the existence of customary law in the guidelines of the groups.

However, the absence of a customary law foundation to the guidelines of the Zangger Committee and the NSG does not mean that the statements agreed by these groups, and the actions taken pursuant thereto by their members, are devoid of legal effect. Article 31(3) of the 1969 Vienna Convention on the Law of Treaties (VCLT), which is itself a rule of customary law,[89] provides that in interpretation of the terms of a treaty, reference should be had to

(a) any subsequent agreement between the parties regarding the interpretation of the treaty or the application of its provisions;
(b) any subsequent practice in the application of the treaty which establishes the agreement of the parties regarding its interpretation...

The issue is first raised whether subsequent agreement between a subset of the parties to a treaty, and action taken in pursuance thereof, will fit within the meaning of these provisions on treaty interpretation.[90] It is interesting to note in this regard that Article 31(2), which addresses the subject of the context of the treaty, includes as documents which may serve to comprise the context for purposes of interpretation

(a) any agreement relating to the treaty which was made between all the parties in connection with the conclusion of the treaty;

---

[88] See H. Thirlway, "The Sources of International Law," in M. Evans (ed.), INTERNATIONAL LAW (2nd edn, 2006) 123; M. Shaw, INTERNATIONAL LAW (5th edn, 2003) 75–76.

[89] See *Maritime Delimitation and Territorial Questions* case (*Qatar v. Bahrain*), ICJ Reports 1995, 6, para 18.

[90] Note that a subsequent agreement pursuant to VCLT Article 31(3)(a) need not be of the same formal character as the treaty it interprets. See R. Gardiner, TREATY INTERPRETATION (2008) 220. ("The judgment of the ICJ in the *Botswana/Namibia* case...was cited by the Arbitral Tribunal in *Methanex v. USA*, in conjunction with other materials, as showing that Article 31(3)(a) does not envisage that a subsequent agreement need be concluded with the same formal requirements as a treaty for such an agreement to play a role in treaty interpretation.")

(b) any instrument which was made by one or more parties in connection with the conclusion of the treaty and accepted by the other parties as an instrument related to the treaty...

In thus specifically differentiating in Article 31(2)(a) and Article 31(2)(b) between agreements made between all parties to a treaty, and those made between a subset of parties to a treaty, the drafters of the 1969 VCLT showed themselves to be conscious of this distinction, and capable of making this distinction clear when desired. The fact that the subsequent Article 31(3) does not so distinguish, but rather simply uses the phrases "agreement between the parties" and "agreement of the parties" thus introduces some ambiguity into the question of the proper interpretation of these provisions. It would seem that an interpretation of these phrases as meaning that such agreements are to include all parties to the treaty concerned, as well as the alternate meaning that such agreements need only include a subset of the parties to the treaty concerned, are equally persuasive.

However, some light can be shed on this question of interpretation by applying the VCLT's own rules of interpretation to its provisions. As the plain meaning of the terms of Article 31(3) does not render a clear interpretation, the interpreter may proceed to examine the terms of the treaty, taking into account the provisions of the selfsame Article 31(3), which in paragraph (c) includes a consideration of "any relevant rules of international law applicable in the relations between the parties." Under this paragraph, in order to aid in the interpretation of the phrases "agreement of the parties" and "agreement between the parties" found in Article 31(3), the interpreter should look for rules of international law on the subject of the meaning of the concept of agreement among states, particularly in the context of the interpretation and application of rules of international law.

In this context, an argument can be made that such a "relevant rule of international law" exists in the rule referenced above regarding the disproportionate influence which can be attached to the understandings and actions of states "whose interests are specially affected" by an issue area in the creation of customary law in that issue area. Notwithstanding its origin in the area of customary law formation, this relevant rule can be applied through the operation of VCLT Article 31(3)(c) to the treaty interpretation question of the meaning of the phrases "agreement of the parties" and "agreement between the parties" found in VCLT Article 31(3)(a) & (b). When so applied, this relevant rule would seem to argue for the result that the proper interpretation of these phrases includes within their meaning cases in which the subsequent agreement between treaty parties, and subsequent practice of treaty parties, is carried out as among a subset of states parties to the treaty concerned, as long as that subset is comprised of states "whose interests are specially affected" by the issue area in which they have expressed agreed interpretations of meaning and have taken actions pursuant thereto.

It is clear that the guidelines of both the Zangger Committee and the NSG were created by their members in order to establish agreed interpretations as among themselves regarding the meaning of the terms of Article III.2 of the NPT, as well as to flesh out and add substance to the interpretation of their own obligations as suppliers of nuclear-related items and technologies under Article III.2.[91] It is further clear that the members of these groups represent, if not perfectly then approximately, the subset of NPT parties able to engage in practice in this issue area because they, unlike the rest of the NPT membership, possess nuclear-related items and technologies in significant quantities (i.e. they are supplier states). It can thus be argued that the guidelines of the Zangger Committee and the NSG, and the actions of members of these groups in pursuance of those agreed interpretations of Article III.2 of the NPT, are the "subsequent agreement[s] ... regarding the interpretation of the treaty or the application of its provisions" and "subsequent practice in the application of the treaty" of a subset of states "whose interests are specially affected" by this issue area.[92]

Thus, according to the interpretation of Article 31(3)(a) and (b) of the VCLT detailed above, the guidelines of the Zangger Committee and the NSG, and the actions of member states of those groups taken in pursuance thereof, are indicia of meaning to be taken into account when interpreting Article III.2 of the NPT, at least as regards the actions of members of those groups, and possibly also as regards the actions of group non-members. This does not mean that these indicia of meaning should be taken as conclusive of meaning in interpreting Article III.2. However it may be the case that, since the guidelines of the Zangger Committee and the NSG, and actions taken by members of these groups in pursuance thereof, are predominantly unopposed by states not members of the two groups, the supplementary weight of general state acquiescence may be added to the weight of influence of these agreements and actions by supplier states in interpretation of Article III.2.[93]

---

[91] See IAEA Document INFCIRC/539 at para. 4, 10. It is significant that in these guidelines, the member states of the Zangger Committee and the NSG seek particularly to control and regulate their own actions, through clarification of their obligations under the NPT. In the *South West Africa* case (ICJ Reports 1950, 135) the ICJ found such subsequent agreed statements by treaty parties to be particularly meaningful: "Interpretations placed upon legal instruments by the parties to them, though not conclusive as to their meaning, have considerable probative value when they contain recognition by a party of its own obligations under an instrument."

[92] In addition to their legal weight per se, the NSG Part 1 Trigger List has been incorporated by reference into Security Council resolutions sanctioning both Iran (Resolution 1737) and North Korea (Resolution 1718). For this purpose, the NSG Part 1 Trigger List has been adopted as a United Nations document (S/2006/814).

[93] See D.J. Harris, CASES AND MATERIALS ON INTERNATIONAL LAW (6ᵗʰ edn, 2004) 837. ("Presumably, however, acquiescence is relevant so that the practice of one party of which the other parties have or can be deemed to have knowledge can, through lack of protest, establish the common interpretation of the parties.")

C. The U.S.–India "Global Partnership"

A recent case of controversy regarding the obligations of NPT parties under Article III.2 is the case of the "global partnership" between the United States and India, which was announced on July 18, 2005 and signed into law in the U.S. on December 18, 2006. Under this partnership, the United States has undertaken to supply India with civilian nuclear materials and technology, including importantly nuclear fuel for India's Tarapur nuclear reactor, and potentially including the supply of new design nuclear reactors. For its part, India has under the terms of the global partnership, agreed to separate its civilian and military nuclear facilities and programs, declare its civilian facilities to the IAEA and voluntarily place those civilian facilities under IAEA safeguards. It has further agreed to conclude an Additional Protocol agreement with the IAEA, continue its unilateral moratorium on nuclear testing, and participate in international non-proliferation efforts including negotiations on the establishment of a Fissile Material Cut Off Treaty (FMCT).[94]

This decision by the United States to supply civilian nuclear materials and technology to a state which is not a member of the NPT, and which is in possession of nuclear weapons, marked a reversal of 30 years of U.S. law and policy, and efforts on the international plane to limit transfers of nuclear technologies to only those non-nuclear weapon states which had committed to an exclusively civilian nuclear program, and which had accepted the imposition of full-scope safeguards, meaning safeguards on all nuclear facilities within the state, by the IAEA.[95]

In terms of U.S. law, the 1978 Nuclear Nonproliferation Act, passed in response to India's 1974 explosion of a nuclear device, imposed upon U.S. exporters of civilian nuclear technologies the obligation not to transfer such technologies to states that have not both committed to having an exclusively peaceful nuclear program, and accepted full-scope safeguards as administered by the IAEA. On the international plane, the United States was a founding member of the NSG which, as discussed above, in 1992 agreed by consensus that supplies of nuclear technologies should only be made to states which had accepted full-scope safeguards.

It was this commitment by all NSG members which was the basis of harsh criticism by the United States of Russia's 2001 transfer of low-enriched uranium to the Terapur reactor in India. At a special meeting in December 2000, upon

---

[94] See S.Squassoni, "U.S. Nuclear Cooperation with India: Issues for Congress," Congressional Research Service Report for Congress (RL33016), January 12, 2006; G. Perkovich, *Faulty Promises: The U.S.–India Nuclear Deal*, POLICY OUTLOOK (CNS, September 2005); S. Gahlaut, "Misfiring at the India Nuclear Deal," Foreign Policy Web Exclusive (February 2006). Available at <http://www.foreignpolicy.com/story/cms.php?story_id=3404>.

[95] Interview with Lawrence Scheinman, "New U.S.–India Agreement Undercuts U.S. Allegiance to Nonproliferation of Nuclear Weapons," Council on Foreign Relations website (November 3, 2005). Available at <http://www.cfr.org/publication/9149/scheinman.html>.

news of the proposed transfer, 32 of 34 NSG members declared that the shipment would be inconsistent with Russia's commitments under the NSG guidelines. On February 16, 2001, the U.S. State Department issued the following condemnation of the Russian shipments:

> We deeply regret that the Russian Federation has shipped nuclear fuel to the Terapur power reactors in India in violation of Russia's nonproliferation commitments. As a member of the 39-nation Nuclear Suppliers Group, Russia is committed not to engage in nuclear cooperation with any country that does not have comprehensive International Atomic Energy Agency safeguards on all its nuclear facilities...At a December 2000 meeting of the Nuclear Suppliers Group, the overwhelming majority of the members expressed their strong concerns about Russia's planned shipment of nuclear fuel to India, which they regarded as inconsistent with Russia's commitments. We join other nuclear suppliers in calling on Russia to cancel this supply arrangement and live up to its non-proliferation commitments. Russia's disregard of its Nuclear Supplier Group commitments, together with its sensitive nuclear assistance to Iran, raises serious questions about Russia's support for the goal of preventing nuclear proliferation.[96]

To explain its about face on this issue of nuclear transfer policy, previously deemed a fundamental part of international non-proliferation strategy, the U.S. administration has noted its "desire to transform relations with India" as being "founded upon a strategic vision that transcends even today's most pressing security concerns."[97] The U.S. has argued that, due to India's record of non-proliferation efforts particularly since its acquisition of nuclear weapons technologies in 1974, and due to its status as the world's largest democracy and a U.S. ally in a volatile region of the world, an exception should be made both to U.S. law as well as to international non-proliferation law and policy in India's case.[98] Many observers have seen in these explanations a subtext of support for Indian development in the energy sector, as well as in other economic sectors, in order to better enable India to play a role of regional counterweight to the escalating economic and military power of China.

The U.S. has, as of March 2008, successfully amended the 1978 Nuclear Nonproliferation Act to create an exception for transfers of civilian nuclear technologies to India. India has negotiated a safeguards agreement with the IAEA under the terms of the U.S. supply deal, and a little over a month ago the Nuclear Suppliers Groop agreed by consensus to allow trade in nuclear materials and technologies with India as an exception to its normal standards. The way has thus been formally cleared for transfers of nuclear materials and technology to commence under the partnership agreement.

---

[96] P.T. Reeker, U.S. Department of State, Office of the Spokesman, February 16, 2001.

[97] Statement of Under-Secretary of State for Political Affairs, R. Nicholas Burns, September 8, 2005, House Committee on International Relations, Hearing on "The U.S. and India: An Emerging Entente?"

[98] See S. Squassoni, "U.S. Nuclear Cooperation with India: Issues for Congress," Congressional Research Service Report for Congress (RL33016), January 12, 2006.

In terms of the NPT Article III.2 obligations of the United States, the U.S. has argued that civilian nuclear cooperation with India, including transfers to India of nuclear fuel and enrichment technologies, is not in violation of its Article III.2 obligation not to "provide source or fissionable material . . . or equipment or material especially designed or prepared for the processing, use or production of special fissionable material, to any non-nuclear weapons state . . . ," firstly because India is not a non-nuclear weapon state party to the NPT. The question of whether the term "non-nuclear weapon State" as used in Article III.2 of the NPT refers only to non-nuclear weapon states parties to the treaty, as specified in other NPT provisions, or whether the term in this Article refers more broadly to any state not in possession of nuclear weapons, whether NPT party or not, is one which is debated by international lawyers.[99] However, in the case of India, this distinction is largely moot as India is in possession of nuclear weapons and thus could not be included in any definition of a non-nuclear weapon state. Thus, the U.S. argues that transfers to India are not subject to this provision of the NPT.

However, critics argue that, even if not a violation of the letter of the NPT's provisions, the U.S.–India nuclear supply deal is undermining of the spirit of the NPT and of the grand bargain among NPT parties which the treaty represents.[100] They argue that in concluding this deal to provide civilian nuclear technology to India, the United States, a Nuclear Weapon State under the NPT, is giving concessions to a state which has never undertaken the limiting obligations of the NPT, and which has in fact developed and is in possession of nuclear weapons. To NPT NNWS which have undertaken the obligations of the NPT and not pursued nuclear weapons programs as a result, and which have submitted all nuclear sites within their territory to full-scope IAEA safeguards, this deal appears to give to India, in exchange for only the most basic of non-proliferation commitments, the reward which NPT NNWS were required to undertake and maintain these much more stringent obligations to obtain.[101] Many NPT NNWS see this granting of nuclear technology concessions to India by an NPT NWS as a positive reward for India's decision to remain outside the NPT framework, and develop and maintain a nuclear weapons arsenal, which is the precise opposite to the incentive structure which the NPT sought to codify into international law.

This positive discrimination in favor of India, and its undermining effects upon the spirit of the NPT grand bargain, are most saliently seen in the

---

[99] See the letter from 10 NPT experts addressed to members of the U.S. Congress concerning NPT Article I in the context of the U.S.–India Global Partnership, sent under the auspices of the Nonproliferation Policy Education Center, June 20, 2006, available at <http://www.npec-web.org/Essays/20060620-LetterOnArticleOne.pdf>.

[100] See Interview with Lawrence Scheinman, "New U.S.–India Agreement Undercuts U.S. Allegiance to Nonproliferation of Nuclear Weapons, Council on Foreign Relations Website (November 3, 2005). Available at <http://www.cfr.org/publication/9149/scheinman.html>.

[101] Ibid.

contrasting cases of Brazil, the Ukraine, and South Africa.[102] Each of these states had active nuclear weapons development programs and chose to give up their pursuit of nuclear weapons in order to take advantage of the NPT grand bargain, and the promise of positive assistance in the development of their civilian nuclear energy programs offered by NWS under the NPT framework.[103] For India, which has not undertaken the reciprocal obligations of the NPT grand bargain, and which under the global partnership deal would still be allowed to maintain its nuclear weapons program untouched by the limited IAEA safeguards system to be administered only at civilian nuclear facilities nominated by the Indian Government, now to be given the same concessions from a NWS that these other states obtained only through complete renunciation of their nuclear weapons programs and submission to full-scope IAEA safeguards, the double standard this deal represents and the resulting evisceration of the fundamental tenets of the agreement they struck with NWS in their acceptance of the NPT is clear.

The U.S.–India nuclear supply deal does appear to significantly weaken the NPT system by causing all NNWS, and particularly states like Iran which are the subject of what they see as prejudicial applications of nuclear non-proliferation law, to question anew their commitment to Article II of the NPT in light of the breakdown in the incentive structure of the NPT system of reciprocal, *quid pro quo* obligations which this deal represents.[104]

D. Missiles

It is worth noting before moving on the existence of another multilateral export control regime supplementary to the NSG; the Missile Technology Control Regime (MTCR).[105] While missile technologies are relevant to the delivery of chemical and biological weapons as well as nuclear weapons, concern regarding the proliferation of missiles is most compelling with regard to the possible incorporation of nuclear weapons technologies and missile technologies by states

---

[102] Ibid.

[103] See J. Cirincione et al., DEADLY ARSENALS: NUCLEAR BIOLOGICAL AND CHEMICAL THREATS (2nd edn, 2005), chs 18, 20, and 21.

[104] C. Chyba, "Second-Tier Suppliers and Their Threat to the Nuclear Nonproliferation Regime," in J. Pilat (ed.), ATOMS FOR PEACE: A FUTURE AFTER FIFTY YEARS? (2007) 121. On October 5, 2008, the deputy head of Iran's Atomic Energy Organization, Mohammad Saeedi, was quoted by the official IRNA news agency as saying of the U.S.–India deal that "cooperation in the area of transfer of nuclear technology to the NPT non-members will endanger the treaty." "The method used by several nuclear states to transfer the technology to non-members of the NPT will create new crises for the international community": "Iran Refuses to Halt Enrichment for Fuel Guarantees," Global Security Newswire, October 6, 2008.

[105] See S. Jones, "Emptying the Haunted Air: The Current and Future Missile Control Regime," in D.H. Joyner (ed.), NONPROLIFERATION EXPORT CONTROLS: ORIGINS, CHALLENGES AND PROPOSALS FOR STRENGTHENING (Ashgate, 2006).

and non-state actors of concern, and the production thereby of nuclear weapons which can be delivered over long distances and remotely detonated.

Notwithstanding the importance of this technology issue area and its close relationship with WMD technologies which have been the subject of regulation under international law, there is currently no multilateral treaty regulating either possession, development, or trade in missile technologies. This area of technology has always bedeviled and resisted efforts of formal multilateral normative regulation due largely to the fact that missile technologies are by far the most dual-use in character among all WMD-related technologies.[106] Missile components have many legitimate civilian uses quite apart from their military uses, many of which are themselves widely considered to be legitimate. These include, most importantly, use in peaceful space exploration and development. To add to the difficulty, there is virtually no means available to distinguish between a civilian space missile program and a military missile program up until the very late stages of its development. Thus normative progression in this area has been effectively stalled over difficulties in addressing the specific technologies involved by means of formally binding instruments, due to the inability of such an instrument to effectively distinguish between legitimate materials and technologies and those which should be subject to regulation in this rapidly changing technological landscape.[107]

However, the MTCR was founded as a non-binding political arrangement in 1987 for the purpose of controlling the proliferation of rocket and unmanned air vehicle systems capable of delivering WMD, and their associated materials and technology. Its membership currently stands at 34 countries, which use the MTCR as a forum for coordination of export control measures specifically related to the two categories of missile-related items contained in the MTCR Annex. Its intended goal as a concept was to restrict exports of these sensitive items, and therefore inhibit their proliferation outside the boundaries of MTCR membership.[108]

At the 15th plenary meeting of MTCR member states in October 2000, a draft International Code of Conduct (ICoC) generating demand-side norms was circulated and discussed, and by April 2002, 80 countries had purportedly agreed

---

[106] See B. Jasani (ed.), PEACEFUL AND NON-PEACEFUL USES OF OUTER SPACE: PROBLEMS OF DEFINITION FOR THE PREVENTION OF AN ARMS RACE (1991); A. Karp, BALLISTIC MISSILE PROLIFERATION: THE POLITICS AND TECHNICS (1996); Stutzle et al. (ed.), THE ABM TREATY: TO DEFEND OR NOT TO DEFEND? (1987); D.A. Ozga, *A Chronology of the Missile Technology Control Regime*, THE NONPROLIFERATION REVIEW, 1:2 (1994); W. Bowen, *U.S. Policy on Ballistic Missile Proliferation: The MTCR's First Decade (1987–1997)*, THE NONPROLIFERATION REVIEW 5:1 (1997); *Missile Proliferation and Defenses: Problems and Prospects*, CNS Occasional Paper No. 7 (2001) available at <http://cns.miis.edu/pubs/opapers/op7/op7.pdf>.

[107] See V. Zaborsky, *The New Code of Conduct: A Solution or a Problem?* WORLD AFFAIRS, Winter 2003; M. Smith, *Rules for the Road? The International Code of Conduct Against Ballistic Missile Proliferation*, DISARMAMENT DIPLOMACY No. 63 (2002).

[108] J. Goldblat, ARMS CONTROL: THE NEW GUIDE TO NEGOTIATIONS AND AGREEMENTS (2nd edn, 2002).

on a draft of the ICoC at a meeting in Paris. The draft ICoC was to contain a recitation of agreed-upon principles, commitments, incentives for compliance, and confidence building measures. And while the commitments were carefully worded so as to avoid the attachment of legal obligation to their terms, they did include commitments by states parties to ratify a number of international treaties on space exploration, to undertake measures to prevent the proliferation of WMD-capable missiles, to reduce national holdings of the same, to exercise vigilance in the consideration of assistance to space launch vehicle programs in other countries (a notorious front for military-use missile and WMD delivery system programs), and not to support ballistic missile programs in countries which "might be developing or acquiring weapons of mass destruction in a way incompatible with the norms established by the disarmament and nonproliferation treaties."

The resulting Hague Code of Conduct Against Ballistic Missile Proliferation was finally agreed on November 25, 2002 as a non-binding arrangement among its original 93 (now 124) declarants, and as a supplement to the supply-side controls of the MTCR.[109] However, it remains the case that there are no serious prospects for formalization of this regime into a binding legal framework within the foreseeable future.[110] Nevertheless, as the current author has argued elsewhere, the potential effectiveness of soft law, non-binding multilateral export control regimes such as the MTCR should not be underestimated.[111] As Scott Jones has observed specifically on the subject of the MTCR:

In the absence of a missile nonproliferation treaty, the MTCR has been a useful tool in countering the proliferation of missile components, technologies, and materials by establishing international norms against missile technology sales. The existence of the MTCR and U.S. sanctions based partly on them has provided a basis for U.S. diplomatic-political efforts to constrain questionable exports from countries such as China and Russia. It has positively impacted export control practices of several European nations and others, likely preventing the "best teams" from transferring systems and technologies. Although difficult to measure, the growth in the relative sophistication of the missile threat to the United States and its friends and allies from rogue or irresponsible nations has probably been slowed. As a consequence of the MTCR, proliferators have been forced to indigenize their missile programmes—increasing the difficulties of their programmes and the unreliability of their missiles. Indeed, the greatest source of expanding missile capabilities, especially in relative sophistication and range, has been from countries not party to

---

[109] Text available at <http://projects.sipri.se/expcon/hcocfinal.htm>. See A. Karp, *Going Ballistic? Reversing Missile Proliferation*, ARMS CONTROL TODAY (June 2005); A. Karp, 'The Spread of Ballistic Missile Missiles and the Transformation of Global Security', THE NONPROLIFERATION REVIEW (Spring–Summer 2000).

[110] See D. Mistry, CONTAINING MISSILE PROLIFERATION (2003).

[111] See D.H. Joyner, *Restructuring the Multilateral Export Control Regime System*, 9 JOURNAL OF CONFLICT & SECURITY LAW 181 (2004).

the MTCR, such as North Korea, which, to date, has been limited to providing systems based on Scud technology (the so-called "Scud barrier").[112]

VI. Article IV

1. Nothing in this Treaty shall be interpreted as affecting the inalienable right of all the Parties to the Treaty to develop research, production and use of nuclear energy for peaceful purposes without discrimination and in conformity with articles I and II of this Treaty.
2. All the Parties to the Treaty undertake to facilitate, and have the right to participate in, the fullest possible exchange of equipment, materials and scientific and technological information for the peaceful uses of nuclear energy. Parties to the Treaty in a position to do so shall also cooperate in contributing alone or together with other States or international organizations to the further development of the applications of nuclear energy for peaceful purposes, especially in the territories of non-nuclear-weapon States Party to the Treaty, with due consideration for the needs of the developing areas of the world.

The two paragraphs of Article IV should be read along with the two preambular paragraphs on the topic of peaceful application of nuclear technologies, which serve to flesh out the terms of Article IV:[113]

Affirming the principle that the benefits of peaceful applications of nuclear technology, including any technological by-products which may be derived by nuclear-weapon States from the development of nuclear explosive devices, should be available for peaceful purposes to all Parties of the Treaty, whether nuclear-weapon or non-nuclear-weapons States,

Convinced that, in furtherance of this principle, all Parties to the Treaty are entitled to participate in the fullest possible exchange of scientific information for, and to contribute alone or in cooperation with other States to, the further development of the applications of atomic energy for peaceful purposes...

The most fundamental tension within the NPT framework is contained in the coexistence of the interest of all states parties in the non-proliferation of nuclear weapons on the one hand, and the interest of all states to pursue peaceful uses of nuclear technologies, including particularly the generation of nuclear energy, on the other. The interest in nuclear weapons non-proliferation is clearly laid out in Articles I and II of the NPT, and implemented through the paragraphs of

---

[112] S. Jones, "Emptying the Haunted Air: The Current and Future Missile Control Regime", in D.H. Joyner (ed.), Nonproliferation Export Controls: Origins, Challenges and Proposals for Strengthening (Ashgate, 2006).

[113] See generally M. Willrich, Nonproliferation Treaty: Framework for Nuclear Arms Control (1969) ch. VI.

Article III. The concurrent interest of states parties, and in particular NNWS, in peaceful uses of nuclear technologies, and a framework for the coexistence of these two interests, is the subject of Article IV.

Article IV was desired by NNWS, first in order to obtain an acknowledgment of their residual entitlement to possess and use nuclear technologies and materials for peaceful purposes, notwithstanding the obligations not to pursue nuclear weapons which they were to undertake in Article II. It was further desired in order to secure a reciprocal concession from NWS and from technologically advanced NNWS, in the form of a positive obligation to assist particularly developing NNWS in their development of peaceful nuclear energy programs, in exchange for the commitments of NNWS in Article II. These dual aims of the NNWS are mirrored in the two-paragraph structure of Article IV.

It is important to note that the principles of Article IV were not included in the original drafts of the NPT produced by the United States and the Soviet Union. Article IV was only added to the agreed drafts in August of 1967 at the insistence of NNWS, who gathered around a proposal made by Mexico in March of 1967. Article IV clearly has its origins in the desires of NNWS parties to the NPT, and was only included in the final draft by concession of the NWS parties.[114]

The article begins in Paragraph 1 by identifying this residual entitlement as an "inalienable right." This is strong language intended to convey deep legal meaning, analogous to the recognition in Article 51 of the U.N. Charter of an "inherent right" of self-defense.[115] This phrasing is intent upon characterizing the right guaranteed by this provision not simply as a right created by the present positive conventional instrument, but rather as a pre-existing right independent of the treaty, and only recognized by its terms. Whether the treaty drafters intended the understanding of this pre-existence to be based upon customary law existing prior to the convention, or whether the inalienability of the right was seen to be rooted in a more naturalistic sense within the bundle of rights inuring to a state by virtue of its sovereignty (i.e. as an attribute of statehood), the right is by this characterization proclaimed to possess a firmer foundation than that conferred upon it simply through its definition in the present treaty instrument.[116]

This inalienable right to develop research, production, and use of nuclear energy for peaceful purposes is recognized to exist in all parties to the treaty

---

[114] M. Shaker, THE NUCLEAR NONPROLIFERATION TREATY: ORIGIN AND IMPLEMENTATION 1959–1979, Vol. 1 (1980) 276–277; J. Cirincione, BOMB SCARE (2007) 30–31; C. Chyba, "Second-Tier Suppliers and Their Threat to the Nuclear Nonproliferation Regime," in J. Pilat (ed.), ATOMS FOR PEACE: A FUTURE AFTER FIFTY YEARS? (2007) 120–122.

[115] On the recognition of the customary right of self-defense in U.N. Charter Article 51, see D. Bowett, SELF-DEFENCE IN INTERNATIONAL LAW (1958) 185. ("It is . . . fallacious to assume that members have only those rights which the Charter accords to them; on the contrary they have those rights which general international law accords to them except in so far as they have surrendered them under the Charter . . . [T]he view of Committee I at San Francisco was that this prohibition [Article 2(4)] left the right of self-defense unimpaired.")

[116] See S. Hall, *The Persistent Spectre: Natural Law, International Order and the Limits of Legal Positivism*, 12 EUROPEAN JOURNAL OF INTERNATIONAL LAW 269 (2001).

without discrimination. The discrimination referred to here is the divide between nuclear weapon states and non-nuclear weapon states, which is so meaningful in the context of other articles of the treaty. This provision serves to clarify that this distinction is not meaningful in the context of the right to develop peaceful applications of nuclear technologies.[117]

Paragraph 1 also provides that the research, production, and use of nuclear energy for peaceful purposes, which is the inalienable right of all states parties, must be carried out in conformity with Articles I and II of the treaty.[118] Upon the first reading of this paragraph, the recognition of an inalienable right in the first part of the paragraph, and the limitation of that inalienable right by reference to two other Articles of the present conventional instrument, seems to be self-contradictory.

Some have argued that this stipulation that the activities included within the inalienable right to pursue peaceful application of nuclear technologies be carried out "in conformity with" Articles I and II should be taken to mean that the inalienable right recognized herein is in fact only a subsidiary right, and that the terms of Articles I and II take precedence over this right, and leave only a limited entitlement, and one which is made subject to the discretion of supplier states in their interpretation and application of Articles I and II.[119]

However, this interpretation does no justice to the peculiarity of the term "inalienable right" and its deep legal meaning, just as the subsequent conventional terms of Article 51 of the U.N. Charter do not serve to make subsidiary the previously existing inalienable right of states to self-defense, but rather quite the reverse are interpreted as including and being informed in their interpretation by the substance of that prior law.[120] Thus in the case of U.N. Charter Article 51, the principle of anticipatory self-defense is widely accepted to be a continuingly viable legal right, although the basis for that right is to be found in pre-Charter

---

[117] M. Shaker, THE NUCLEAR NONPROLIFERATION TREATY: ORIGIN AND IMPLEMENTATION 1959–1979, Vol. 1 (1980) 294–295.

[118] The Final Document of the 2000 NPT Review Conference expands this relationship to include Article III in addition to Articles I and II.

[119] See L. Scheinman, "Article IV of the NPT: Background, Problems, Some Prospects" (Paper commissioned by the Weapons of Mass Destruction Commission, available at <http://www.wmdcommission.org/files/No5.pdf>).

[120] See *Nicaragua v. United States*, ICJ Reports 1986, 14, para. 176. ("Article 51 of the Charter is only meaningful on the basis that there is a 'natural' or 'inherent' right of self-defence, and it is hard to see how this can be other than of a customary nature...Moreover the Charter, having itself recognized the existence of this right, does not go on to regulate directly all aspects of its content. For example, it does not contain any specific rule whereby self-defence would warrant only measures which are proportional to the armed attack and necessary to respond to it, a rule well-established in customary international law. Moreover, a definition of the 'armed attack' which, if found to exist, authorizes the exercise of the 'inherent right' of self-defence, is not provided in the Charter, and is not part of treaty law. It cannot therefore be held that Article 51 is a provision which 'subsumes and supervenes' customary international law. It rather demonstrates that in the field in question...customary international law continues to exist alongside treaty law.") See discussion of the inherent right of self-defense in Chapter 7 below.

customary law, which is in fact at seeming odds with the plain meaning of the subsequent terms of Article 51.[121]

In the context of NPT Article IV, Articles I and II should be understood not to take precedence over the inalienable right first recognized in the Article, but rather to carve out a limited conventional exception to that inalienable right in the case of the existence of clear evidence that a NNWS party to the treaty is using the assistance in peaceful nuclear applications to which it is entitled, in order to contribute to the development of a nuclear weapons program. In such a case, the force of Articles I and II serves to justify the cessation of such assistance, and further penalties and sanctions as provided for in the treaty. Other interpretations which seek to emasculate the inalienable right by making its enjoyment more broadly subject to the principles of Articles I and II, diminish one of the chief reciprocal obligations and resulting benefits which NNWS demanded under the NPT framework in exchange for their Article II commitment, and do violence to the incentive structure established under the grand bargain. The natural result of such an interpretation by supplier states is to cause NNWS to quite reasonably question whether the benefit of their understood bargain in acceding to the NPT is being secured through the implementation of the treaty's provisions by supplier states.[122]

Article IV proceeds in paragraph 2 to provide an obligation undertaken by all NPT members to "facilitate... the fullest possible exchange of equipment, materials and scientific and technological information for the peaceful uses of nuclear energy." Paragraph 2 further provides that all NPT parties "in a position to do so" are obligated to "cooperate in contributing... to the further development of the applications of nuclear energy for peaceful purposes, especially in the territories of non-nuclear-weapon States Party to the Treaty, with due consideration for the needs of the developing areas of the world."

It is firstly important to discuss the nature of the terms of paragraph 2, and to clarify that the term "undertake" as used in paragraph 2 does create legal obligations for all NPT members as provided in the paragraph. Some commentators have argued to the contrary, and have based their analysis upon the negotiating history of Article IV, and specifically upon the rejection by other states in 1967 of a Mexican proposal of language for Article IV which identified the obligation undertaken therein as a "duty."[123] Carefully read, however, the objections by NWS and other technologically advanced NNWS to the Mexican draft were only with regard to the scope of the obligation, and not

---

[121]   See a fuller discussion of Article 51 in Chapter 7 below.

[122]   C. Chyba, "Second-Tier Suppliers and Their Threat to the Nuclear Nonproliferation Regime," in J. Pilat (ed.), ATOMS FOR PEACE: A FUTURE AFTER FIFTY YEARS? (2007) 120–122.

[123]   See L. Scheinman, "Article IV of the NPT: Background, Problems, Some Prospects" (paper commissioned by the Weapons of Mass Destruction Commission, available at <http://www.wmdcommission.org/files/No5.pdf>). For background on the Mexican proposal see M. Shaker, THE NUCLEAR NONPROLIFERATION TREATY: ORIGIN AND IMPLEMENTATION 1959–1979, Vol. 1 (1980) 328–329.

to the nature of the commitment undertaken in the article as a legally binding obligation.

Furthermore, even if the obligatory nature of the term "undertake" were to come into question by reference to certain statements and documents included in the preparatory work of the NPT, it must be remembered that as a matter of treaty interpretation, this negotiating history is in fact immaterial to the interpretation of the terms of Article IV. This language of commitment appears within the context of an unambiguously legally binding treaty, and thus is presumed, as a lesser part of the greater whole, to be binding by nature of that inclusion, absent clear distinguishing language manifesting altered intent. Within this obligatory context, the ordinary meaning of the term "undertake" is most consonant with the concept of the undertaking of a legally binding obligation.[124] Thus, according to the rules on treaty interpretation contained in Articles 31 and 32 of the 1969 Vienna Convention on the Law of Treaties, this plain meaning of the terms of Article IV leaves no need, or justification, for resort to the *travaux préparatoires* of the treaty to determine the meaning of the terms.

As to the scope of these obligations, the paragraph 2 obligations should be given a broad interpretation, as within the context of the NPT they comprise some of the chief reciprocal obligations (the others having been included in Article VI, to be discussed below), especially falling upon NWS and particularly demanded by NNWS in exchange for their obligations under Article II. The clear intent of NNWS in including this right was to provide for a balancing of obligations between groups of states parties to the treaty, and to meet the development needs of NNWS. This latter objective was "imperative," in the words of the Belgian representative to the First Committee of the U.N. General Assembly

if we want to avoid introducing into the civilian area the distinction accepted in the military area, which would be unacceptable and would inevitably lead to the calling into question of the treaty.[125]

---

[124] See U.S. Supreme Court Justice Stephen Breyer's consideration of the term "undertake" within the context of its occurrence in Article 94 of the U.N. Charter, in his dissent in the recently decided *Medellin* case (*Medellin v. Texas*, 552 U.S. ___, 17–18): "I recognize, as the majority emphasizes, that the U.N. Charter uses the words 'undertakes to comply,' rather than, say, 'shall comply' or 'must comply.' But what is inadequate about the word 'undertak[e]'? A leading contemporary dictionary defined it in terms of 'lay[ing] oneself under obligation...to perform or to execute.'" Webster's New International Dictionary 2770 (2nd edn, 1939). And that definition is just what the equally authoritative Spanish version of the provision (familiar to Mexico) says directly: The words "*compromete a cumplir*" indicate a present obligation to execute, without any tentativeness of the sort the majority finds in the English word "undertakes." See Carta de las Naciones Unidas, Articulo 94, 59 Stat. 1175 (1945); Spanish and English Legal and Commercial Dictionary 44 (1945) (defining "*comprometer*" as "become liable"); ibid. at 59 (defining "*cumplir*" as "to perform, discharge, carry out, execute"); see also Art. 111, 59 Stat. 1054 (Spanish-language version equally valid); *Percheman*, 7 Pet., at 88–89 (looking to Spanish version of a treaty to clear up ambiguity in English version). Compare *Todok v. Union State Bank of Harvard*, 281 U. S. 449, 453 (1930) (treating a treaty provision as self-executing even though it *expressly* stated what the majority says the word "undertakes" *implicitly* provides: that "'[t]he United States...shall be at liberty to make respecting this matter, such laws as they think proper')".

[125] A/c.1/PV. 1571 (prov.), 20 May 1968, 49–50.

The obligations in paragraph 2 include not only direct transfers of nuclear fuel and facilities for nuclear energy production, including reactors, but also technical and design information to allow for the indigenous production of nuclear fuel and facilities in NNWS.[126]

Notwithstanding the terms of Article IV, paragraph 2, and the overall importance of the article in the context of the NPT, some NWS particularly have taken a very narrow view of their obligations under the provision. For example, the U.S. Atomic Energy Commission in 1969 in Senate hearings on the NPT, stated:

> We do not, however, interpret Article IV as meaning that the U.S. will be compelled to embark on any costly new programs or as obliging the U.S. to meet all requests and demands. Neither do we construe Article IV as overriding the provisions of the U.S. Atomic Energy Act, nor will it remove the discretion we have in determining the nature of our cooperative relationships with other countries, on a case by case basis.[127]

This restrictive reading of the paragraph 2 obligations of assistance, and claim to a wide residual discretion in supplier states to determine with which NNWS peaceful nuclear sharing should take place, if accepted, would set up a fundamental inconsistency within the treaty framework. It would serve to make the Article IV obligations, which are particularly incumbent upon NWS and other technologically advanced states, conditional upon the national discretion of individual treaty parties, whereas the reciprocal obligations of NNWS in Article II are absolute and independently verified by the IAEA. Under this interpretation, the grand bargain of the NPT becomes severely one-sided and subject to the subjective determinations of individual powerful states. This interpretation further weakens the incentive of NNWS to maintain their Article II obligations.[128]

Some have argued that a more expansive interpretation of this right would mean unjustifiably giving up to NNWS, and particularly developing NNWS, something that other nations had to work hard to achieve, thus resulting in an undue windfall for developing states.[129] However, in exchange for this obligation on the part particularly of NWS, it must be remembered that consideration is passing between the parties under the NPT, because of the reciprocal, *quid pro quo* framework of the treaty. It must be remembered that in Article II, NNWS are giving up a legal right which they would otherwise have, and that that renunciation of right by NNWS is of value to NWS and other supplier NNWS. Thus, the benefit of the NPT bargain to NWS should not be forgotten, and consideration should be given to ensuring that NNWS feel that they, in return for

---

[126] M. Shaker, THE NUCLEAR NONPROLIFERATION TREATY: ORIGIN AND IMPLEMENTATION 1959–1979, Vol. 1 (1980) 330.

[127] Hearings on NPT, 1969, 498.

[128] C. Chyba, "Second-Tier Suppliers and Their Threat to the Nuclear Nonproliferation Regime," in J. Pilat (ed.), ATOMS FOR PEACE: A FUTURE AFTER FIFTY YEARS? (2007) 120–122.

[129] Comments of the U.K. Representative to the ENDC, ENDC/PV. 337, 10 October 1967, para. 42.

this consideration, are receiving enough of a benefit from their bargain to justify continued support of, and participation in, the NPT regime.

This understanding of the nature and scope of the terms of Article IV is important in informing the understanding of supplier states, particularly including NWS, regarding the correct posture to take toward the fundamental tension mentioned above between the concurrent and at times competing interests of NPT members in nuclear weapons non-proliferation and the peaceful use of nuclear materials and technologies.

In the present author's view, the implementation both of the inalienable right of NNWS as well as the obligation of all NPT parties contained in Article IV, must be based upon rules of law and objectively and consistently established principle. Thus, in order to fulfill their obligations under Article IV, and in consideration of the balance of both fundamental interests identified above, the approach of supplier states to the issue of assistance to NNWS in the area of peaceful nuclear uses should be firstly to require that the receiving state be a NNWS party to the NPT (per the considerations explained above through the case of the recent U.S–India partnership). Second, the recipient state should be subject to full-scope safeguards as administered by the IAEA.

If a state meets these criteria, and if no positive and objectively demonstrable evidence has been produced by IAEA inspectors either of incompleteness of the state's declaration of its nuclear activities to the IAEA, or of the actual diversion of nuclear materials to non-peaceful use, then transfers of items and technologies for peaceful use to the state should continue per the request of that state.[130] This should be the understood meaning of the right to peaceful use held by NNWS, and the obligation of all NPT parties to assist developing states in their peaceful nuclear programs contained in Article IV. It should further be accepted as the correct interpretation of the relationship between Article IV and Articles I and II. Such a treaty-rule-based approach, supplemented by the most broadly agreed terms of supply contained in the NSG guidelines, should serve to remove much of the subjectivity and potential politicization from the issue of the compatibility of the two fundamental interests.

In line with this interpretation and approach to the reconciliation of fundamental interests, it is argued herein that NNWS should insist in their negotiations with the IAEA in the context of the conclusion and maintenance of safeguards agreements, upon the non-inclusion in such agreements of the right of the IAEA Board of Governors, as recommended in paragraph 19 of INFCIRC/153, to refer

---

[130] Subject, of course, to any other applicable laws and normal conditions of business, including payment, licensing, etc. This standard further assumes that the NNWS in question has not been clearly demonstrated to have breached its Article II obligations on transfer, acquisition, manufacture, and assistance. Such a determination does present evidentiary problems, as the IAEA is not mandated to monitor or verify these Article II obligations per se. Thus, demonstration of breach would need to be accomplished through other means, preferably through enunciation by a multilateral body, and ideally the U.N. Security Council.

states to the U.N. Security Council for enforcement action upon the simple finding that Agency inspectors are "not able to verify that there has been no diversion of nuclear material required to be safeguarded under the Agreement to nuclear weapons or other nuclear explosive devices." This finding, which constitutes a finding of an inability of Agency inspectors to prove a negative, i.e. the practically near impossible determination that a state has not done something, provides too low a standard for institutional escalation by referral to the Security Council, and one which is too easily susceptible to manipulation for political ends by the Board of Governors. It is a standard which is inconsistent with the respect which should be given by the IAEA to states' inalienable right to engage in peaceful uses of nuclear technologies under Article IV, and finds no justification elsewhere in the NPT.

Further following from this understanding of the contours of the obligation of NPT parties to assist NNWS, and particularly developing countries, in development of peaceful nuclear programs, is the observation that this obligation should inform both the making and implementation of NSG guidelines on transfers from supplier states, as well as national export control laws which the NSG seeks to harmonize. In this regard, it is important to remember that in any case in which the clear interpretation of the terms of the NPT is found to be inconsistent with the guidelines of the NSG, the treaty rule must prevail and the conflicting NSG guideline will not serve to absolve a state from liability for violation of the treaty rule. Thus, even though great emphasis is placed upon the Basic Principle within the NSG guidelines as a catch-all norm justifying withholding of transfers of sensitive items and technologies when there is concern regarding the risk of diversion to military use by an end user, this principle cannot be held to trump the rights of developing NNWS under Article IV of the NPT, as properly interpreted.

VII. Iran

In the context of Article IV, the recent case of Iran's nuclear program, and Western suspicions regarding its scope and related intentions, resulting in institutional escalation of the situation from the IAEA to the Security Council, are illustrative.[131]

In late 2002, the world learned from Iranian opposition groups in exile that Iran had concealed from the IAEA for 18 years the existence of facilities at Natanz and Arak engaged in experiments involving uranium enrichment and

---

[131] See generally C. Ferguson and R. Takeyh, *Making the Right Call: How the World Can Limit Iran's Nuclear Program*, ARMS CONTROL TODAY (March 2006); S. Squassoni, "The Iranian Nuclear Program," in N. Busch and D.H. Joyner (eds), COMBATING WEAPONS OF MASS DESTRUCTION: THE FUTURE OF INTERNATIONAL NONPROLIFERATION POLICY (2009); M. Fitzpatrick, *Lessons Learned from Iran's Pursuit of Nuclear Weapons*, THE NONPROLIFERATION REVIEW, Vol. 13, No. 3 (2006).

plutonium separation. Upon a report by IAEA inspectors detailing their findings of the undeclared activities, the IAEA Board of Governors reached the conclusion in a Resolution passed November 26, 2003 that, due to this concealment and to other reporting omissions, Iran had "in a number of instances" failed to meet its obligations under its INFCIRC/153 safeguards agreement.[132] As noted previously, in its resolution the Board further recognized that Iran had a particular onus of cooperation and transparency in order to "provide and maintain the assurances required by Member States" and "restore confidence." Iran subsequently agreed upon a temporary suspension of its uranium enrichment activities and in December 2003 signed the IAEA Additional Protocol.

Despite these concessions, Iran has continuously maintained that all of its work with fissile materials and related technologies, including work at these undeclared sites, has been aimed at furthering its capacity to produce nuclear energy. They have thus argued, notwithstanding their failure to comply with reporting requirements under their safeguards agreement, that they have always been in compliance with their substantive obligations under the NPT. In this argument, they have relied specifically upon the inalienable right of all states to engage in peaceful uses of nuclear technologies recognized in Article IV, paragraph 1.

However, suspicions have become widespread particularly among Western states, that Iran does indeed have nuclear weapons ambitions, and that particularly the uranium enrichment work which Iran has carried out is intended not solely for use in peaceful energy production, but for the creation of nuclear weapons. Notwithstanding these suspicions, IAEA inspectors have to date found no conclusive evidence to support allegations of a clandestine nuclear weapons program in Iran.

Despite this lack of evidence of a weapons program, the IAEA Board of Governors took the decision on February 4, 2006 to refer Iran's case to the U.N. Security Council. This referral, without a supporting report by IAEA inspectors providing evidence that Iran was in breach of its substantive NPT obligations, or that it was in continuing breach of its safeguards agreement, led some to criticize the Board's decision as premature. However, notwithstanding these concerns, on July 31, 2006 the Security Council passed Resolution 1696 in which, acting under Article 40 of Chapter VII of the U.N. Charter, it demanded that Iran suspend all uranium enrichment-related and reprocessing activities, and requested a report from the IAEA Director General by August 31 to confirm this suspension.

Iran's failure to abide by the terms of this resolution, insisting that its activities are firmly within its rights under Article IV, has led to the issuance of further Security Council resolutions under Chapter VII, and an increasing atmosphere of tension between Iran and, particularly, Western powers whom it alleges are the

---

[132] IAEA Document GOV/2003/81.

prime movers behind the institutional escalation and application of international pressure.

In consideration of the legal merits of Iran's claim of justification of its activities by reference to Article IV of the NPT, it is important first to note that uranium enrichment, when declared, is not an NPT violation per se. Certainly when uranium is enriched to a U-235 presence of less than 20%, and can thus still be classified as Low-Enriched Uranium (LEU), that enrichment activity is one that is fully includable within the Article IV inalienable right to engage in peaceful uses of nuclear technologies. This understanding was clear at the time of the drafting of the NPT. As the Director of the U.S. Arms Control and Disarmament Agency told the Senate Foreign Relations Committee in 1968:

> It may be useful to point out, for illustrative purposes, several activities which the United States would not consider per se to be violations of the prohibitions in Article II. Neither uranium enrichment nor the stockpiling of fissionable material in connection with a peaceful program would violate Article II so long as these activities were safeguarded under Article III. Also clearly permitted would be the development, under safeguards, of plutonium fueled power reactors, including research on the properties of metallic plutonium, nor would Article II interfere with the development or use of fast breeder reactors under safeguards.[133]

Japan and a number of other NNWS parties to the NPT have carried out enrichment of uranium for the purpose of nuclear power generation for many years without complaint from the IAEA Board of Governors. Japan has in fact separated and stockpiled at least 43.1 tons of plutonium, as well as having a robust and productive gas centrifuge program for uranium enrichment at its facility in Rokkasho, Aomori prefecture, thus illustrating that even the overproduction and stockpiling of fissile materials is deemed permissible by the IAEA[134] It is only when this enrichment activity by an NNWS is undeclared to the IAEA that a violation of an IAEA safeguards agreement results. Even this, however, is not a violation of the NPT per se. Only if enrichment proceeds to the production of Highly-Enriched Uranium (HEU), at approximately 20% presence of U-235, does it produce a weapons-usable material. Undeclared enrichment of weapons-usable HEU would create a prima facie case of breach of Article II of the NPT, and such activity would not be justifiable by reference to Article IV.

In this context, it is instructive to note again the treatment received by South Korea, as explained above, when it was found to have engaged in undeclared

[133] Extension of Remarks By Mr. Foster in Response To Question Regarding Nuclear Explosive Devices, Hearings Before the Committee on Foreign Relations, U.S. Senate, Ninetieth Congress, Second Session, Executive H, Treaty on the Nonproliferation of Nuclear Weapons, July 10, 11, 12, 17, 1968, p. 39.

[134] See report from Kyodo news agency, available at <http://www.redorbit.com/news/science/231519/japans_separated_plutonium_stockpile_increases_to_43_tons/index.html>. Uranium enrichment through centrifuge cascade is also carried out, for example, at the Almelo facility in the Netherlands, and at the Gronau facility in Germany.

uranium enrichment and to have proceeded to the production of weapons-usable HEU. This case again demonstrates that even this prima facie case, clearly made out against South Korea, does not guarantee reprimand by the IAEA Board of Governors, or the imposition of remedial sanctions. As stated above, the most persuasive reason for the difference in the severity of treatment received by Iran from the IAEA and the Security Council, in response to its activities which did not present a prima facie case of breach of Article IV and were in fact squarely within that right as illustrated by the Board's history of condoning other cases of uranium enrichment by NNWS, does not have to do with an application of NPT rules, but rather the judgment of the IAEA Board of Governors that the Iran case is somehow different.

While the Board of Governors has the right to make such a determination, under Article XII(C) of its Statute, the fact that in this case this determination is unsupported by (and in fact inconsistent with) previous precedent, and cannot be explained objectively by clear differences in facts between cases, nor by any positive evidence presented by IAEA inspectors that Iran has embarked upon a nuclear weapons program, provides a dubious foundation for institutional escalation. Indeed, as noted above the more persuasive location of causation for this decision lies in the undue influence of the political and ideological dispositions of some powerful IAEA Board members.[135]

In the present author's view, as a matter of law Iran was quite correct in its interpretation of the coverage of its uranium enrichment activities by Article IV of the NPT until July 31, 2006. The basis of its case was not altered by previous IAEA urgings that Iran cease uranium enrichment, as the IAEA's only legal competence is in the administration of safeguards agreements, and the continuation of uranium enrichment in declared sites, under IAEA safeguards, poses no challenge to the provisions of Iran's safeguards agreement. The legal landscape did change, however, on July 31, 2006 with the passage of Security Council Resolution 1696, under which the Council exercised its authority under Chapter VII of the U.N. Charter to order Iran to cease uranium enrichment.

Regardless of the prudence or other merit of this demand by the Council, in passing this resolution the Council did change the legal underpinnings of Iran's case for justifying its enrichment activities by reference to NPT Article IV.[136] This issue can be approached legally under a number of different theories. The first theory focuses on the provisions of the U.N. Charter, of which Iran is a member, which in Article 103 specifies that "[i]n the event of a conflict between the obligations of the Members of the United Nations under the present Charter and their obligations under any other international agreement, their obligations

---

[135] T. Ogilvie-White, *International Responses to Iranian Nuclear Defiance: The Non-Aligned Movement and the Issue of Non-Compliance*, 18 EUROPEAN JOURNAL OF INTERNATIONAL LAW 453 (2007).

[136] See the discussion of the limits of the Security Council's Chapter VII authority in Chapter 4 below.

under the present Charter shall prevail." The obligations of the Charter are thus declared superior to all other treaty rights and obligations by its own terms. One of the substantive obligations United Nations members undertake in the Charter is spelled out in Article 25, which states that "[t]he Members of the United Nations agree to accept and carry out the decisions of the Security Council in accordance with the present Charter."

Thus, under this analysis, with the passage of Resolution 1696, the Council invoked Iran's obligation as a U.N. member to abide by the Council's decisions under Article 25, which is an obligation superior to all other treaty obligations pursuant to Article 103, inclusive of the rights and duties contained in the NPT. Iran thus became legally obligated to comply with Resolution 1696, as well as with all other resolutions passed by the Security Council under its Chapter VII authority, and unable to rely upon its right to peaceful use of nuclear technologies in NPT Article IV to justify actions in disharmony with such Council decisions.

On this line of reasoning, there has been some question as to whether Article 103 serves to make the Charter pre-eminent over not only obligations in other treaties, but also over rights defined in other treaties. It is possible to consider that the distinction between obligations and rights as defined in treaties is largely a semantic one, at least in terms of the juridical nature of the two concepts and their equal susceptibility to being trumped by the terms of the Charter. The Security Council itself has previously leaned toward the interpretation that rights in treaties are includable, along with obligations in treaties, among those legal principles which are made secondary in priority to the Charter by virtue of Article 103. In Security Council Resolution 670, the Council invokes "the provisions of Article 103 of the Charter" and "decides that all States, notwithstanding the existence of any rights or obligations conferred or imposed by any international agreement...shall deny..." The failure of the Charter drafters to explicitly include the term "rights" in Article 103 could under this reasoning be explainable not as a recognition of a category of legal principles (i.e. rights) not subject to the higher priority of the terms of the Charter, but rather by this notion of the juridical sameness of the concept of obligations and rights in the context of treaty terms, and thus of their equal susceptibility to being trumped by the terms of the Charter, including decisions of the Security Council by operation of Article 25.[137]

However, perhaps a more persuasive theory for the superiority of Chapter VII resolutions over the rights of NPT Article IV is simply to be found in the reasoning that, as noted above, the rights defined in Article IV are not creations alone of the treaty terms of the NPT, but are rather rights recognized by the terms of the treaty but existing independently as within the bundle of rights inherent in the attributes of a state. Under this reasoning, while the Article IV rights are important features of the sovereign character of all NPT parties, they

---

[137] See B. Simma et al. (eds), THE CHARTER OF THE UNITED NATIONS: A COMMENTARY (2nd edn, 2002) Vol. II, 1295–1296.

are nonetheless categorizeable along with all other general state rights which are, by a state's consent to the terms of Article 25 of the Charter, made surmountable by and subject to the authority of the Security Council acting under Chapter VII. Any other understanding of the relationship between the generally inherent rights of states and Article 25 of the Charter would render the Security Council unable to authorize any remedial force under Articles 41 and 42 as a consequence of its determinations under Article 39 of threats to international peace and security.

The outcome of the institutional escalation to the Security Council of the question of Iran's nuclear programs remains to be seen. The December 3, 2007 release of a National Intelligence Estimate (NIE) by the U.S. intelligence community has provided a considerable setback to international efforts, led by the U.S, to pressure Iran regarding its nuclear program. Reversing a key high-confidence judgment contained in a 2005 NIE, the 2007 NIE contains a high-confidence judgment that, "in Fall 2003, Tehran halted its nuclear weapons program."[138] This acknowledgment that Iran is not currently pursuing a nuclear weapons program represents yet another instance of the significant escalation of international tensions on an issue of WMD proliferation, based in the end upon incorrect intelligence.[139] This revelation will likely make extremely difficult any significantly enhanced sanctions by the Security Council against Iran.

However, as the analysis above demonstrates, unless they are formally withdrawn or suspended, Iran is still formally under legal obligation to comply with Security Council decisions demanding that it cease uranium enrichment, notwithstanding its reliance to the contrary upon its NPT Article IV rights. The contradiction inherent in the recognition of Iran's non-pursuit of a weapons program on the one hand, and this continuing formal obligation upon Iran to suspend its concededly peaceful uranium enrichment program, at present in early 2008, seems rather glaring, and it is unclear what resolution to this impasse will be found. Whatever the outcome of this situation, because of the inconsistency of the IAEA's Board of Governors' decision in this case with its previous decisions, and due to the persuasive contention that the prejudicial application of standards to Iran has been the result of politicization in the workings of the IAEA as well as the Security Council, it can even at present be concluded that the decision of the IAEA to refer Iran to the Council, and the Council's decision to impose sanctions, represent a low point for the rule of law in the non-proliferation issue area, and are compelling evidence of the nature of both the IAEA and the Security Council first and foremost as political organs, and not as independent adjudicatory bodies which can be entrusted to objectively apply non-proliferation law.

138 <http://www.dni.gov/press_releases/20071203_release.pdf>.
139 See Chapter 7 below.

VIII. Article VI

As reviewed above, the inclusion of Article IV was a concession sought by NNWS parties to the NPT in part to ensure that the discriminatory situation regarding the rights and obligations of NPT parties in military uses of nuclear technologies, codified in Articles I and II, would not carry over into the ability of NNWS to engage in peaceful uses of nuclear technologies, and in particular for the production of nuclear energy.

In a similar vein, the inclusion of Article VI was the other chief concession sought by NNWS in order to ensure that the discriminatory situation of rights and obligations as among NPT parties codified in Articles I and II with regard to nuclear weapons would not be a permanent one.[140] Article VI importantly links the imperative of stopping the further proliferation of nuclear weapons with the imperative of disarmament of existing nuclear weapons stockpiles.[141]

Article VI imposes upon all NPT parties an obligation, particularly incumbent upon NWS parties as they are the only parties with nuclear weapons, "to pursue negotiations in good faith on effective measures relating to cessation of the nuclear arms race at an early date and to nuclear disarmament, and on a Treaty on general and complete disarmament under strict and effective international control."

Article VI is the codification of a number of provisions in the Preamble of the NPT, in which the parties express their intent by:

Declaring their intention to achieve at the earliest possible date the cessation of the nuclear arms race and to undertake effective measures in the direction of nuclear disarmament,

Urging the cooperation of all States in the attainment of this objective,

Recalling the determination expressed by the Parties to the 1963 Treaty banning nuclear weapon tests in the atmosphere, in outer space and under water in its Preamble to seek to achieve the discontinuance of all test explosions of nuclear weapons for all time and to continue negotiations to this end, [and]

Desiring to further the easing of international tension and the strengthening of trust between States in order to facilitate the cessation of the manufacture of nuclear weapons, the liquidation of all their existing stockpiles, and the elimination from national arsenals

---

[140] See J. Cirincione, Bomb Scare (2007) 30–31; C. Chyba, "Second-Tier Suppliers and Their Threat to the Nuclear Nonproliferation Regime," in J. Pilat (ed.), Atoms for Peace: A Future After Fifty Years? (2007) 120–122; M. ElBaradei, "Towards a Safer World," *The Economist*, October 16, 2003. ("In the climate of the mid-to-late-1960's in which the NPT negotiations took place, this bargain was the best that could be achieved. But the asymmetry it endorsed was never intended to be permanent.")

[141] M. Shaker, The Nuclear Nonproliferation Treaty: Origin and Implementation 1959–1979, Vol. II (1980) 564. On the link between disarmament and nonproliferation, see generally J. Cirincione, Bomb Scare (2007) 32–33; M. ElBaradei, "Towards a Safer World," *The Economist*, October 16, 2003; M. Shaker, "Toward Universal Nonproliferation and Disarmament," in J. Pilat (ed.), Atoms for Peace: A Future after Fifty Years? (2007) 65–66; C. Chyba, "Second-Tier Suppliers and Their Threat to the Nuclear Nonproliferation Regime," in J. Pilat (ed.), Atoms for Peace: A Future After Fifty Years? (2007) 123.

of nuclear weapons and the means of their delivery pursuant to a Treaty on general and complete disarmament under strict and effective international control...

Similar to the negotiating history of Article IV, the first submission of identical treaty drafts by the U.S. and U.S.S.R. on August 24, 1967 contained only preambular references to disarmament, and no mention of disarmament in any treaty article. However, from September to November of 1967, a movement grew among important non-nuclear weapons possessing states desiring that the obligations they were to undertake in Articles I and II be equitably met by the nuclear weapon states through a treaty obligation to disarm.[142] Among the states placing such proposals on record were Mexico, India, Brazil, Sweden, Romania, Switzerland, Canada, the United Arab Republic, and Germany. The result of these efforts was the inclusion of Article VI for the first time in the identical treaty drafts of January 18, 1968. The language of the article underwent alteration until its inclusion in the final draft of the treaty, and was adopted by the NNWS parties with only partial satisfaction.

Contrary to a number of proposals made by NNWS, the final language of Article VI provided for an obligation "to pursue negotiations," which many NNWS felt was insubstantial and ultimately unenforceable, as it did not specify a particular object of the obligation, the achievement of which could be shown either to have occurred or not to have occurred. Furthermore, the treaty text gave no specific indication of a time frame for the accomplishment of any concrete result from the required negotiations. Neither did it give any indication of what would constitute "effective measures relating to cessation of the nuclear arms race at an early date and to nuclear disarmament" which were to be the subject of the negotiations. Thus, many NNWS felt that their victory in securing the inclusion of a provision on disarmament in the NPT had been significantly lessened by the vague and ambiguous terms finally consented to by the NWS, and particularly the superpowers.[143]

However, the terms of Article VI are not completely bereft of justiciable legal principles. The obligation is not, in fact, simply one of negotiation, but rather an obligation to negotiate "in good faith." These words invoke a fundamental

---

[142] M. Shaker, The Nuclear Nonproliferation Treaty: Origin and Implementation 1959–1979, Vol. II (1980) 564.

[143] See J. du Preez, *The 2005 NPT Review Conference: Can it Meet the Nuclear Challenge?*, Arms Control Today (April 2005). ("The weakness to enforce treaty obligations also relates to the flip side of the nonproliferation deal: nuclear disarmament. Many non-nuclear-weapon states believe that the nuclear-weapon states are no longer fully committed to their obligations under Article VI of the treaty to make good faith efforts toward disarmament. They are especially bothered that some nuclear-weapon states appear to have walked away from the 'unequivocal undertaking' given at the 2000 NPT Review Conference to eliminate their nuclear arsenals as part of '13 practical steps' toward nuclear disarmament. This highlights what many view as one of the fundamental weaknesses in the treaty: the absence of a time frame for disarmament. While the nuclear-weapon states have always refused to accept such a time frame, many non-nuclear-weapon states now rightfully argue that, if the nonproliferation objectives of the treaty are to be backed by stricter verification and enforcement measures, so should the treaty's disarmament objectives.")

principle of international law.[144] As Christine Chinkin and Rabinder Singh have explained:

The Treaty obligation is thus not to disarm as such, but a positive obligation to pursue in good faith negotiations towards these ends, and to bring them to a conclusion. Good faith is the legal requirement for the process of carrying out of an existing obligation. In the *Nuclear Tests cases* the ICJ described the principle of good faith as *"one of the basic principles governing the creation and performance of legal obligations"*... The obligation of good faith has been described as not being one *"which obviously requires actual damage. Instead its violation may be demonstrated by acts and failures to act which, taken together, render the fulfilment of specific treaty obligations remote or impossible."* In the context of an obligation to negotiate in good faith this would involve taking no action that would make a successful outcome impossible or unlikely.[145]

Furthermore, the legal scope and meaning of the terms of Article VI have been given more clarity and certainty through their subsequent interpretation, both by the International Court of Justice, as well as by NPT parties themselves. Although not central to the question put to the International Court of Justice (ICJ) in the context of its 1996 *Advisory Opinion on the Threat or Use of Nuclear Weapons*, toward the end of its opinion the ICJ took up the question of the scope of the disarmament obligation in Article VI of the NPT, and found that in fact the effect of the presence of the principle of good faith in the text of Article VI is to create a particular object of the obligation to negotiate. As the Court states:

In these circumstances the Court appreciates the full importance of the recognition in Article VI of the Treaty on the Nonproliferation of Nuclear Weapons of an obligation to negotiate in good faith a nuclear disarmament... The legal import of that obligation goes beyond that of a mere obligation of conduct; the obligation involved here is an obligation to achieve a precise result—nuclear disarmament in all its aspects—by adopting a particular course of conduct, namely, the pursuit of negotiations on the matter in good faith.[146]

Thus, the Court's interpretation of the effect of the principle of good faith adds significantly to understanding of the legal contours of Article VI, in clarifying that the obligation is in fact not simply an obligation to negotiate, but rather an obligation to succeed through such negotiations in producing the effect of

---

[144] *Advisory Opinion on the Threat or Use of Nuclear Weapons*, ICJ Reports 1996, 26, para. 102; M.N. Shaw, INTERNATIONAL LAW (5th edn, 2003) 97–98.

[145] UK Trident Replacement a "Material Breach" of the NPT, Joint Opinion by Rabinder Singh QC and Professor Christine Chinkin, December 19, 2005, para. 69, quoting *Nuclear Tests cases (Australia v. France; New Zealand v. France)* ICJ Reports 1974, 253; 457, para. 46; and G. Goodwin-Gill, "State Responsibility and the 'Good Faith' Obligation in International Law", in M. Fitzmaurice and D. Sarooshi (eds), ISSUES OF STATE RESPONSIBILITY BEFORE INTERNATIONAL JUDICIAL INSTITUTIONS (2004) 75, 84. Available at <http://www.acronym.org.uk/docs/0512/doc06.htm>.

[146] ICJ Reports 1996, 26, para. 99.

complete nuclear disarmament, through such facilitating procedural steps as the conclusion of a treaty on disarmament.

The legal meaning of the terms of Article VI has been further supplemented through the negotiations of NPT member states at NPT review conferences, which by the operation of Article VIII(3) may occur at five-year intervals, and through the adoption of resolutions at such review conferences by the consensus of the parties attending. The final documents which have resulted from some of these review conferences are highly significant in manifesting the agreed interpretation of the obligations of NPT parties, held by the members themselves. Furthermore, according to Article 31(3) of the 1969 Vienna Convention on the Law of Treaties, such consensus statements by NPT parties are clearly categorizeable as "subsequent agreement[s] between the parties regarding the interpretation of the treaty or the application of its provisions," and are thus statements which may be "taken into account, together with the context" of the treaty in authoritatively interpreting its terms. Thus while not binding per se as sources of law, the resolutions in review conference final documents are significant as sources of treaty interpretation.[147]

As the 2005 NPT review conference concluded without agreement being reached on a final document, the two most recent such documents are from the 1995 and 2000 review conferences. The 1995 review conference, which was the first to take place after the ending of the Cold War, was also the forum for consideration by NPT parties, pursuant to Article X(2), of the question of whether the NPT should be indefinitely extended, or extended only for a fixed period. The importance of Article VI to NNWS was reaffirmed in the negotiations during the 1995 conference, and the decision to indefinitely extend the NPT was made in conjunction with two other agreements among the parties, one of which was entitled "Principles and Objectives for Nuclear Nonproliferation and Disarmament." In this document, all NPT member states in attendance at the conference, including NWS, agreed by consensus the following text on Article VI:[148]

The achievement of the following measures is important in the full realization and effective implementation of Article VI, including the programme of action as reflected below:

a) The completion by the Conference on Disarmament of the negotiations on a universal and internationally and effectively verifiable Comprehensive Nuclear-Test-Ban Treaty

---

[147] See B. Carnahan, *Treaty Review Conferences*, 81 American Journal of International Law, 226, 229 (1987).

[148] The vehicle of the NPT Review Conference, sanctioned as it is by Article VIII(3) of the treaty, operates as a forum for generating consensus statements by NPT parties which, as discussed herein, are relevant to interpretation of the NPT pursuant to VCLT Article 31(3). All NPT states parties are invited to attend Review Conferences. In the case of a failure by one or more states to attend a Review Conference, any resulting consensus statement by attending states will not be diluted in its interpretive weight by the failure of states to attend the Conference. This failure represents a waiving of the right of participation on the part of the non-attending state(s), and an acquiescence in the consensus statements of those attending.

no later than 1996. Pending the entry into force of a Comprehensive Test-Ban Treaty, the nuclear-weapon states should exercise utmost restraint;

b) The immediate commencement and early conclusion of negotiations on a non-discriminatory and universally applicable convention banning the production of fissile material for nuclear weapons or other nuclear explosive devices...;

c) The determined pursuit by the nuclear-weapon states of systematic and progressive efforts to reduce nuclear weapons globally, with the ultimate goals of eliminating those weapons, and by all states of general and complete disarmament under strict and effective international control.

This agreement thus added meaning to the terms of Article VI, and particularly to the obligation to negotiate in good faith "effective measures relating to cessation of the nuclear arms race at an early date and to nuclear disarmament," by enumerating a "programme of action," including concrete steps such as the conclusion of a comprehensive test-ban treaty (CTBT), and a fissile materials cut-off treaty (FMCT), which in the words of the agreement are "important in the full realization and effective implementation of Article VI."

At the 2000 review conference, the principles and objectives on disarmament iterated in the 1995 final document were given further clarification by translation into 13 "practical steps for the systematic and progressive efforts to implement Article VI..." The 13 steps in the 2000 review conference final document include the urgent ratification of the CTBT, negotiations toward the establishment of an FMCT, the adoption of the principle of irreversibility in disarmament efforts, a reiteration by NWS of their undertaking to totally eliminate their nuclear weapons arsenals per the Article VI obligation, the furtherance of efforts to bring into force the stalled START II process, and the permanent disposition of all fissile material no longer needed for military programs. Step 9 is particularly detailed and useful in its specification of "steps...leading to nuclear disarmament in a way that promotes international stability, and based on the principle of undiminished security for all." The designated steps are as follows:

- Further efforts by the nuclear-weapon States to reduce their nuclear arsenals unilaterally;
- Increased transparency by the nuclear-weapon States with regard to the nuclear weapons capabilities and the implementation of agreements pursuant to article VI and as a voluntary confidence building measure to support further progress on nuclear disarmament;
- The further reduction of non-strategic nuclear weapons, based on unilateral initiatives and as an integral part of the nuclear arms reduction and disarmament process;
- Concrete agreed measures to further reduce the operational status of nuclear weapons systems;

- A diminishing role for nuclear weapons in security policies to minimize the risk that these weapons will ever be used and to facilitate the process of their total elimination;
- The engagement as soon as appropriate of all the nuclear-weapon States in the process leading to the total elimination of their nuclear weapons.

While hailed at the time as an important step forward as an agreed framework for progress in fulfillment of Article VI obligations, the 13 steps adopted by consensus at the 2000 review conference have not enjoyed universal support in subsequent years.[149] The United States under the changed leadership of the Bush administration, in particular, has made it clear that it no longer supports all of the 13 steps.[150] Areas of disagreement include the early entry into force of the CTBT, which has been signed by 177 states and ratified by 138, and which the United States signed in 1999, but was rejected by the U.S. Senate the same year, and has not been put forward again to the Senate by the Bush administration. Other steps not favored by the Bush administration include the conclusion of a multilateral and "effectively verifiable" FMCT, the implementation of the principle of irreversibility in disarmament efforts, and an unconditional "undertaking by nuclear weapons states to accomplish the total elimination of their nuclear arsenals leading to nuclear disarmament."[151]

The United States is quick to point out that it has implemented a unilateral moratorium on nuclear weapons tests since 1992 and that it has, particularly through its bilateral agreements with the Soviet Union/Russia, achieved a significant reduction in its nuclear weapons stockpiles. It notes that over the past 16 years, and through a number of agreements including the 1987

---

[149] See J. du Preez, *The 2005 NPT Review Conference: Can it Meet the Nuclear Challenge?*, ARMS CONTROL TODAY (April 2005). ("What should remain clear is that the 1995 package allowed all states-parties to support the indefinite extension while also providing several practical steps for achieving progress toward nuclear disarmament and nonproliferation. The 2000 Review Conference reaffirmed this program of action, including the 'unequivocal undertaking,' and agreed on a set of specific practical 'systematic and progressive' steps to implement Article VI. Although these undertakings are of a political binding nature, they certainly derive from and are linked to the legal commitments and undertakings provided for in the treaty. Most importantly, the treaty clearly would not have been indefinitely extended had it not been for the program of action on nuclear disarmament built into the package that allowed that decision to be taken. The trend by some nuclear-weapon states, such as the United States, to roll back or, in some cases, simply ignore many of these political commitments and undertakings point out yet another weakness in the way the treaty is being implemented. If the nuclear-weapon states are allowed to cherry-pick which commitments they consider applicable, then why are non-nuclear-weapon states refused the same privilege?")

[150] Statement by J. Sherwood McGinnis, Deputy U.S. Representative to the Conference on Disarmament, to the Second Session of the Preparatory Committee for the 2005 NPT Review Conference, May 1, 2003. Available at <http://www.us-mission.ch/press2003/0501NPTMcGinnis.htm>.

[151] See L. Scheinman, *Disarmament: Have the Five Nuclear Powers Done Enough?* ARMS CONTROL TODAY (January/February 2005).

Intermediate-Range Nuclear Forces Treaty, and the 1991 START I process, dismantled over 13,000 nuclear weapons. The Moscow Treaty on Strategic Offensive Reductions, which is the latest such bilateral agreement, obligates the United States to reduce its operational arsenal from approximately 6,000 strategic nuclear warheads to between 1,700 and 2,200 by December 31, 2012. Such steps, the U.S. claims, are evidence that the United States is uphold-ing its obligation under Article VI in good faith, and engaging in progressive steps toward the complete fulfillment of that obligation, within the context of changing security realities including the September 11, 2001 terror attacks on the United States and the resulting "war on terror."[152]

However, added to this list of accomplishments in reducing nuclear stockpiles must be added, in the negative column, the failure of the U.S. to ratify the CTBT and lack of participation in the development of a FMCT discussed above, as well as a number of other policy choices which would seem to put the U.S. at odds with the 13 steps agreed at the 2000 Review Conference, as well as with the provisions of Article VI itself.[153] Many of these choices are expressed in the Bush administration's classified Nuclear Posture Review (NPR) document, which was submitted to Congress on December 31, 2001.[154]

This document makes clear the U.S. policy of expanding the use of nuclear weapons beyond their primary role as a deterrent, to include their potential use against targets able to withstand non-nuclear attack, or in retaliation for the use of chemical or biological weapons. In pursuance of this policy, the NPR sug-gests the need for a new generation of low-yield, tactical nuclear weapons which would be more readily usable for these purposes.[155] These policies are squarely at odds with the undertaking in step 9 of the 13 steps in the 2000 Review Conference final document, to implement "a diminished role for nuclear weapons in security policies to minimize the risk that these weapons will ever be used..."

The NPR further makes clear the intention of the United States to maintain a large stockpile of nuclear weapons for such purposes for the foreseeable future, and makes no mention of any plans to fully disarm itself of nuclear weapons. On the contrary, it notes the steps being taken by the U.S. to restore and maintain

---

[152] Statement by J. Sherwood McGinnis, Deputy U.S. Representative to the Conference on Disarmament, to the Second Session of the Preparatory Committee for the 2005 NPT Review Conference, May 1, 2003. Available at <http://www.us-mission.ch/press2003/0501NPTMcGinnis. htm>.

[153] See J.du Preez, *The 2005 NPT Review Conference: Can it Meet the Nuclear Challenge?* ARMS CONTROL TODAY (April 2005).

[154] See generally, J. du Preez, *The Impact of the Nuclear Posture Review on the International Nuclear Nonproliferation Regime*, THE NONPROLIFERATION REVIEW, Vol. 9, No. 3 (2002).

[155] pp. 34–35. See excerpts at <http://www.globalsecurity.org/wmd/library/policy/dod/npr. htm>.

its capacity to produce fissile material for nuclear weapons. As it states regarding several different aspects of this capacity:

"*Uranium Operations*:...Plans are underway to expand the capacity and capability of the Y-12 Plant [nuclear weapons development complex at Oak Ridge, TN] to meet the planned workload for replacing warhead secondaries, and other uranium components"..."*Plutonium Operations*:...For the long term a new modern production facility will be needed to deal with the large scale replacement of components and new production"..."*Other Component and Material Production*:....Additionally, warhead refurbishment plans require modern facilities at Y-12's Special Materials Complex for manufacturing unique materials."[156]

These policies are clearly at odds with the requirement in step 6 of the 2000 Review Conference final document's 13 steps, of "an unequivocal undertaking by the nuclear-weapon States to accomplish the total elimination of their nuclear arsenals," as well as the step 9 requirement of "further efforts by the nuclear-weapon States to reduce their nuclear arsenals unilaterally."

The NPR further notes the continued emphasis placed in U.S. policy upon missile defense. Since the U.S. withdrew from the 1972 Anti-Ballistic Missile Treaty (ABM) in 2002, it has proceeded with an ambitious program of installation of missile defense technologies both within the U.S. and on the territory of other states through bilateral agreements. The aim of this program is to create a missile defense "shield" enabling the U.S. to destroy enemy missiles in flight.[157] This policy is clearly at odds with the undertaking in step 7 of the 2000 Review Conference final document's 13 steps, to preserve and strengthen the ABM "as a cornerstone of strategic stability and as a basis for further reductions of strategic offensive weapons..."

Finally, the NPR notes the need for "a revitalized nuclear weapons complex that will...be able, if directed, to design, develop, manufacture, and certify now, warheads in response to new national requirements; and maintain readiness to resume underground nuclear testing if required," thus placing in question even the unilateral moratorium on nuclear testing which the U.S. currently maintains.[158] This policy derogates significantly from the undertaking in step 2 of the 2000 Review Conference final document's 13 steps, to maintain a moratorium on nuclear-weapon-test explosions, as well as the agreement in step one on the "importance and urgency...without delay and without conditions...to achieve the early entry into force of the Comprehensive Nuclear-Test Ban Treaty."

It should further be noted that a number of nuclear weapons reduction treaties which the U.S. has signed have, pursuant to the policies outlined in the NPR stressing flexibility in meeting new security challenges, not mandated the actual

---

[156] Quotes from pp. 14 and 33. See excerpts at <http://www.globalsecurity.org/wmd/library/policy/dod/npr.htm>.

[157] Ibid. at 9, 11, and 13.   [158] Ibid., quote from p. 30.

destruction of nuclear warheads, but rather the removing of warheads from operational status and their subsequent storage, which preserves their functionality and makes their return to operational status relatively easily and quickly achieved.[159] This indeed is the case with the 2002 Moscow Treaty noted earlier. Such policies are at variance with the undertaking in step 5 of the 2000 Review Conference final document's 13 steps, to implement the principle of irreversibility in nuclear disarmament.

With regard to these agreements to which the U.S. is so eager to refer as evidence of progressive compliance with the terms of Article VI, the arguments of U.S. officials in this regard make the mistake of confusing arms control efforts, which have as their aim the exercise of restraint upon or achievement of alteration of either the quantity or character of armaments, with disarmament efforts, the *sine qua non* of which is the intention to reduce numbers of armaments to absolute zero. This latter intention is expressed in the preambular language of the NPT to include "the cessation of the manufacture of nuclear weapons, the liquidation of all their existing stockpiles, and the elimination from national arsenals of nuclear weapons and the means of their delivery."[160]

The agreements referenced by the United States have been and are arms control agreements. None have been disarmament agreements of either a bilateral, or as Article VI calls for, a multilateral character. This is because, while these agreements were intent upon and designed to achieve a reduction of nuclear weapons stockpiles, as the NPR bears out at least in the case of the U.S. these agreements were not intended to produce, nor were they designed to produce, disarmament of nuclear stockpiles, per the obligation of Article VI. Thus, none of these arms control agreements can genuinely be referred to as evidence of U.S. compliance with the terms of NPT Article VI.

Furthermore, with regard to the other policies of the U.S. reviewed herein, more fundamental than their disharmony with the 13 steps included in the 2000 review conference final document, is the fact that these policies are in a number of cases in clear disharmony with the textual obligations of the U.S. under Article VI of the NPT, as interpreted by the ICJ. It must be remembered that the principle of good faith is a justiciable principle of international law. As reviewed previously, it requires states under treaty obligation to fulfill that obligation, and not to consistently take actions which are retrograde to its fulfillment. As noted by Guy Goodwin-Gill above regarding the principle of good faith in the upholding of treaty obligations: "its violation may be demonstrated by acts and failures

---

[159] See R. Norris and H. Kristensen, *NRDC Nuclear Notebook*, BULLETIN OF ATOMIC SCIENTISTS, January/February 2005.

[160] As stated in an op-ed written by George Schultz, Henry Kissinger, Sam Nunn, and William Perry: "Progress must be facilitated by a clear statement of our ultimate goal. Indeed, this is the only way to build the kind of international trust and broad cooperation that will be required to effectively address today's threats. Without the vision of moving toward zero, we will not find the essential cooperation required to stop our downward spiral." "Toward a Nuclear-Free World," *Wall Street Journal*, January 15, 2008.

to act which, taken together, render the fulfillment of specific treaty obligations remote or impossible."[161]

It is submitted that, in the case of U.S. policy with regard to nuclear weapons, the cumulative effect of the policies described above, and particularly those regarding the continued maintenance of a nuclear stockpile, the increasingly significant role accorded to nuclear weapons in U.S. security policy, the maintenance of a capacity to produce weapons-grade fissile materials and other weapons technologies, and the construction of new generations of tactical nuclear weapons, taken together, meet this test precisely. These are consistent policies maintained by a NWS party to the NPT which create an environment of national policy in which the fulfillment of the specific treaty obligation in Article VI, as interpreted by the ICJ, to move toward disarmament in good faith, is made remote or impossible. It can thus be concluded that the United States is in breach of the principle of good faith codified in the terms of Article VI, and thus in breach of its obligations under that article.[162]

As for the other NWS parties to the NPT, their national policies on nuclear weapons have not been as blatantly disharmonious with the program and steps enumerated in the 1995 and 2000 review conference final documents.[163] Indeed, Russia, the United Kingdom, and France have ratified the CTBT (China has also signed the CTBT and begun the ratification process, but awaits U.S. ratification before it will ratify); France and the United Kingdom have taken significant steps to implement the principle of irreversibility in their disarmament efforts, as well as steps to reduce the operational status of their nuclear weapons systems; and Russia has cooperated extensively with the largely successful cooperative nonproliferation programs funded by U.S. Government agencies.[164] However, all

---

[161] "State Responsibility and the 'Good Faith' Obligation in International Law," in M. Fitzmaurice and D. Sarooshi (eds), Issues of State Responsibility before International Judicial Institutions (2004) 75, 84.

[162] See UK Trident Replacement a "Material Breach" of the NPT, Joint Opinion by Rabinder Singh QC and Professor Christine Chinkin, December 19, 2005. Available at <http://www.acronym.org.uk/docs/0512/doc06.htm>.

[163] Russia's National Security Concept document, released in January 2000, does worryingly imply an increased understanding of the right to use nuclear weapons in a tactical manner, in response to threats of less than proportional magnitude. However, as Nikolai Sokov has explained: "The text of the Concept, however, creates the clear impression that reliance on nuclear weapons is intended to be a temporary 'fix' until conventional forces are reformed and modernized. While provisions pertaining to the nuclear doctrine are limited to barely two paragraphs, the document concentrates primarily on conventional modernization. Arguably, when this task is implemented, reliance on nuclear weapons could be reduced." *Russia's New National Security Concept: The Nuclear Angle*, NTI.org, January 2000. Available at <http://www.nti.org/db/nisprofs/over/concept.htm>.

[164] See E. Turpen and B. Finlay, "U.S.–Russia Cooperative Nonproliferation," in N. Busch and D.H. Joyner, (eds), Combating Weapons of Mass Destruction: The Future of International Nonproliferation Policy (2009) 302. ("In the fifteen years since inception, the cooperative nonproliferation programs (CNP) at the U.S. Departments of Defense (DoD), Energy (DoE), and State have proven an unparalleled national security success. These efforts have achieved numerous quantifiable disarmament goals and myriad less tangible accomplishments in stemming the potential threats of the Cold War legacy. More than 6,800 former Soviet

NPT NWS are still in possession of stockpiles of nuclear weapons, and continue to maintain those weapons systems and the means of their delivery. None are currently undertaking serious efforts to completely disarm themselves of nuclear weapons, as the terms of Article VI as well as the 1995 and 2000 final documents require.[165]

For all NWS parties to the NPT, the stark fact remains that forty years have passed since the establishment of the treaty, and no NWS state party has yet to fulfill its obligation to move toward disarmament in good faith under Article VI, as interpreted by the ICJ and subsequent review conference resolutions. The principle of good faith in the fulfillment of treaty obligations simply cannot be stretched that far. It is not possible for NWS to maintain that they are in fact complying with their Article VI obligations in good faith, when none of them currently manifests any intention through their national security policies of disarming their nuclear weapons stockpiles in an irreversible manner in the foreseeable future. Thus, the NWS parties to the NPT are individually and collectively in breach of the principle of good faith, and of their obligation under Article VI.

It will be recalled that earlier in this chapter the observation was made that the NPT is in fact categorizeable as a contract treaty and not as a lawmaking treaty. It was noted that this distinction has no bearing upon the obligatory nature of the terms of the NPT per se, but that its interpretation and continuing validity as a treaty could be called into question, because of the *quid pro quo* nature of the object and purpose of such a treaty, in a case in which an entire category of states parties were found to be in breach of a fundamental treaty obligation.[166]

It is thus argued herein that because NWS parties to the NPT are collectively in breach of their obligation to move toward disarmament in good faith under Article VI, and thus in abrogation of a fundamental provision of the treaty specifically secured by NNWS parties as a reciprocal obligation in return for NNWS acceptance of Article II of the treaty, that under a strictly legal analysis the obligations of NNWS in Article II are likely currently null and void, or are at least

---

nuclear warheads have been deactivated. Over 600 intercontinental ballistic missiles that once pointed at the United States and 150 strategic bombers that once prowled the skies preparing to drop their nuclear ordnance have been destroyed. Russian and other former Soviet facilities storing approximately 267 metric tons of fissile material have received either comprehensive or rapid security upgrades, and as of June 2006, 276 metric tons of highly enriched uranium (HEU) from dismantled nuclear weapons has been blended down to non-weapons-usable low-enriched uranium (LEU). Innovative new partnerships developed to promote peaceful joint U.S.–Russian research at forty-nine former biological weapons facilities are ensuring the nonproliferation of potentially nefarious knowledge to terrorists and rogue regimes"); B. Gill, "China's Approach to Nonproliferation," in N. Busch and D.H. Joyner (eds), COMBATING WEAPONS OF MASS DESTRUCTION: THE FUTURE OF INTERNATIONAL NONPROLIFERATION POLICY (2009).

[165] See, e.g., ibid.; B. Tertrais, *The Last to Disarm? The Future of France's Nuclear Weapons*, THE NONPROLIFERATION REVIEW, Vol. 14, No. 2 (2007); N. Busch, NO END IN SIGHT: THE CONTINUING MENACE OF NUCLEAR PROLIFERATION (2004).

[166] See below at 10.

voidable at the option of NNWS pursuant to VCLT Article 60(2) on material breach.

It is further proposed herein that the question of whether in fact NWS parties to the NPT are in breach of their obligations under Article VI of the NPT is one which is ripe for referral by the U.N. General Assembly to the International Court of Justice for the Court's exercise of its advisory jurisdiction. As the role of independent verifier of the compliance of NWS with their obligations under the NPT cannot be exercised by the IAEA (that organization having no legal competence over them under the NPT), nor entrusted to the U.N. Security Council (each NWS having a permanent, veto wielding seat upon the Council), the exercise of the advisory jurisdiction of the ICJ would seem particularly apposite in this circumstance.

As will be discussed in Chapter 5 below, the question put to the ICJ by the General Assembly in 1995, and which resulted in the Court's adoption of its rather disappointing *Advisory Opinion on the Threat or Use of Nuclear Weapons* in 1996, has been criticized by some as having been ill considered and controversial as to its justiciability. It is argued herein that the question of whether in fact NWS parties to the NPT are in breach of their obligations under Article VI of the NPT, presents a much more clearly justiciable question for the Court, along the lines of the analysis of the legal principle of good faith and the other terms of Article VI presented herein.[167]

A persuasive, reasoned opinion by the ICJ reaching the conclusion that the NPT NWS are in breach of their Article VI obligations would provide an important normative locus around which compliance pressuring, both from within and without the NWS, could be focused.

IX. Analysis of the NPT Regime

When considering the past, present, and future of the NPT regime, it must be remembered that the NPT was not originally conceived to be the apex of international agreement on a legal framework to address the problems of the existence and proliferation of nuclear weapons in the world. As is clear from General Assembly Resolution 2028(c) and the Preamble of General Assembly Resolution 2373 quoted above, as well as from the *travaux préparatoires* of the NPT itself, the NPT was originally designed to comprise an intermediary framework the primary goals of which were to stop the horizontal proliferation of nuclear weapons outside of the five established nuclear weapon states of 1968, provide reciprocal

---

[167] In order to avoid the imperfections of form present in the 1995 question, the question referred should be as specific, concise, discrete, and concrete as possible. One suggested form for this question would be *"Are the Nuclear Weapons States parties to the 1968 Treaty on the Nonproliferation of Nuclear Weapons, through their acts or omissions, individually or collectively in breach of their obligations under Article VI of the same?"*

energy benefits to non-nuclear weapon states, and provide intermediate disarmament obligations for nuclear weapon states (i.e. the obligation to move toward disarmament in good faith). These goals of the NPT were clearly not meant to be ends in themselves, but were rather understood to be intermediate goals—a half-way house in a sense—the purpose of which was to facilitate the accomplishment of the larger goals being formulated through concurrent negotiations on general and complete disarmament, and particularly general and complete nuclear disarmament.[168]

However, while the NPT has been an effective instrument in the accomplishment of its proliferation aims to an extent, with a number of success stories (including the renunciation by South Africa, Argentina, and Brazil of their nuclear programs, and the surrender by Ukraine of its nuclear arsenal after the break-up of the Soviet Union) to its credit, its effectiveness in accomplishing particularly the intermediate aim of stopping horizontal proliferation of nuclear weapons has over the long term been proven to be limited by fundamental aspects of its normative structure, and by the discriminatory application of its terms, as has been reviewed in this chapter.

Furthermore, the effectiveness of the NPT regime has been significantly undermined externally by the related problems of non-universality (currently four states in possession of nuclear weapons—India, Pakistan, Israel, and North Korea—are not NPT members) and secondary proliferation, or proliferation by and to actors outside of the regime; problems which have become increasingly compelling in recent years and which will be discussed in depth in Chapter 6 below.

On a fundamental level, many of these limitations of the effectiveness of the NPT regime stem directly from the two-tiered structure of the NPT, and its division of states parties into two separate categories, each with its own unique set of rights and responsibilities.[169] This artificially imposed, and unprincipled separation of obligations has led directly to many cases of inter-state tension regarding the application of NPT terms. It has further made unnecessarily controversial and politicized both the work of the NSG on the export control front, through its often controversial guidelines and conditions on the supply of items and technologies between categories of states; as well as the work of the IAEA in its attempts to verify the non-diversion of supplied materials in one category of states, while at the same time leaving unscrutinized and being disproportionately influenced in its decisions by members of the other category.

On a normative development level as well, the contract treaty nature of the NPT has not given the elements of customary law creation clear universal

---

[168] See M. ElBaradei, "Towards a Safer World," *The Economist*, October 16, 2003. ("In the climate of the mid-to-late-1960's in which the NPT negotiations took place, this bargain was the best that could be achieved. But the asymmetry it endorsed was never intended to be permanent.")

[169] See J. du Preez, *The 2005 NPT Review Conference: Can it Meet the Nuclear Challenge?*, ARMS CONTROL TODAY (April 2005).

principles to attach to, in order to enable the creation of parallel custom, unlike in the cases of the Chemical Weapons Convention (CWC) and the Biological Weapons Convention (BWC), to be discussed in detail below. Such parallel customary law in the cases of these other multilateral non-proliferation treaties constitutes an important supplemental source of legal obligation through which even non-parties, and particularly secondary proliferators of WMD technologies, may be bound to the terms of the cornerstone international legal instruments.[170]

The NPT's maintenance of a two-category, differential obligations structure between its parties, and recognition of the rights of one category of parties to develop and possess weapons technologies, has in fact always been anomalous, and quite enigmatic, when compared to these other foundational non-proliferation agreements. The BWC and CWC are unquestionably lawmaking treaties, providing for a blanket prohibition upon development and possession, as well as proliferation, of their subject weapons technologies, binding upon all states parties. In these other WMD technology areas, this blanket prohibition on possession and proliferation is maintained even though both treaties take care to allow a broad latitude for legitimate civilian/scientific use of their subject materials.

To explain this rather exceptional aspect of the character of the NPT, it is of course necessary to consider the important differences between the weapons technologies under discussion, and the unique role of nuclear weapons—by far the most destructive of WMD technologies, as discussed previously—in international politics since the final days of World War II. Miguel Bosch has written concerning the peculiar legitimacy which nuclear weapons gained in the perception of the international community through their role in ending World War II; a legitimacy which would only be reinforced through the conclusion of the NPT and the failure to realize the conclusion of a multilateral treaty on general and complete nuclear weapons disarmament. As Bosch observes:

The ethical questions posed by the appearance of atomic weapons were discussed intensely in the middle of the 1940's, especially among the atomic scientists themselves. It is thus difficult to explain how seemingly rational human beings would end up justifying the acquisition, the use and continued development of these weapons of mass destruction. The Allies' efforts to build an atomic bomb were viewed in the context of the crusade against the Axis Powers. When it was used in 1945, the relationship to the "ultimate weapon" changed in the United States and elsewhere. Incredible as it seems, the bomb became acceptable to leaders of many states. The Cold War would only serve to obfuscate the moral argument. However, what would they have said had Nazi Germany and not

---

[170] See M. Shaw, INTERNATIONAL LAW (5th edn, 2003) 90–92. Those provisions of the NPT which are of general applicability to the treaty membership, including importantly Article VI, could conceivably be replicated in parallel customary law. However, in the case of Article VI, notwithstanding an ostensible abundance of state *opinio juris* on the issue of nuclear disarmament through U.N. General Assembly Resolutions, state practice in this area is decidedly more mixed. Indeed, as has been argued herein, the NWS parties to the NPT have openly flouted their obligations under Article VI for decades. Because of these problems with state practice particularly, Article VI of the NPT has almost certainly not passed into parallel customary law.

the United States acquired the bomb first? They would probably have referred to it as "an evil weapon in evil hands." In short, there was no moral or legal justification for acquiring and using atomic bombs then, and there is none today.[171]

Again, it must be remembered as noted above that the NPT, unlike the BWC or the CWC, was not intended to be the last word on the subject of the legitimacy of continued possession of its subject weapons technologies. From its inception, the establishment of the NPT was understood to be an intermediary framework, put in place primarily in order to keep proliferation of nuclear weapons at the status quo, provide reciprocal energy benefits to non-nuclear weapon states, and establish obligations for nuclear weapon states to move toward disarmament in good faith. These intermediate goals were specifically designed to facilitate the accomplishment of the larger goal of general and complete nuclear disarmament; negotiations regarding which were concurrently proceeding at the time of the adoption of the NPT, but fell into inactivity as Cold War tensions between the superpowers heightened in the 1970s and 1980s.

Full and irreversible nuclear disarmament, and a universal ban on possession, were the aims of those negotiations. And though they never resulted in a multilateral disarmament convention, it is herein argued that this understanding that efforts at the highest levels to accomplish this larger goal formed the context for the conclusion of the NPT, not as a final solution to the problem of nuclear weapons possession but as an intermediate step or halfway-house on the path to the achievement of this larger goal, is important both to understanding the problems the NPT system currently faces, as well as to understanding what future direction the nuclear non-proliferation system should take.

Instead of responding ad hoc to the problems under which the NPT system currently labors, by attempting to fix the intermediary vehicle, the fundamental structure of which is itself the cause of many of these problems, it is herein argued that efforts and resources should now be turned away from attempts to shore up the failing NPT regime, and placed instead with renewed vigor toward the larger and more potentially effective agenda of general and complete nuclear disarmament. It is time for the cornerstone nuclear weapons non-proliferation treaty to be structured in the same way as the cornerstone non-proliferation treaties in the chemical and biological weapons areas, with the establishment of a universal ban upon the development, possession, and proliferation of nuclear weapons.

This argument is of course not a new one, and important efforts toward this end have been made in the past.[172] Interestingly, however, calls for a renaissance

---

[171] "The Nonproliferation Treaty and its Future," in P. Sands and L. Boisson de Chazournes (eds), INTERNATIONAL LAW, THE INTERNATIONAL COURT OF JUSTICE AND NUCLEAR WEAPONS (1999) 375, 383.

[172] See a detailed review of these past efforts in J. Goldblat, ARMS CONTROL: THE NEW GUIDE TO NEGOTIATIONS AND AGREEMENTS (2nd edn, 2002), ch. 7.

of attention to concerted efforts leading to general and complete nuclear disarmament, often led in the past by civil society movements and by officials of non-nuclear weapon states, have recently been joined by a number of seasoned world leaders of nuclear weapon states, including Mikhail Gorbachev, Henry Kissinger, William Perry, Sam Nunn, and George Shultz, who have written in the *Wall Street Journal* urging the United States and other nuclear weapon states to make renewed efforts toward complete nuclear disarmament. As an op-ed written by Kissinger, Perry, Nunn, and Shultz argues:

Nuclear weapons today present tremendous dangers, but also an historic opportunity. U.S. leadership will be required to take the world to the next stage—to a solid consensus for reversing reliance on nuclear weapons globally as a vital contribution to preventing their proliferation into potentially dangerous hands, and ultimately ending them as a threat to the world.

Nuclear weapons were essential to maintaining international security during the Cold War because they were a means of deterrence. The end of the Cold War made the doctrine of mutual Soviet-American deterrence obsolete. Deterrence continues to be a relevant consideration for many states with regard to threats from other states. But reliance on nuclear weapons for this purpose is becoming increasingly hazardous and decreasingly effective.

North Korea's recent nuclear test and Iran's refusal to stop its program to enrich uranium—potentially to weapons grade—highlight the fact that the world is now on the precipice of a new and dangerous nuclear era. Most alarmingly, the likelihood that non-state terrorists will get their hands on nuclear weaponry is increasing. In today's war waged on world order by terrorists, nuclear weapons are the ultimate means of mass devastation. And non-state terrorist groups with nuclear weapons are conceptually outside the bounds of a deterrent strategy and present difficult new security challenges.[173]

To these political and strategic arguments regarding the threat and potential military usefulness of nuclear weapons, can be added principles of international law which argue for the decreasing marginal legitimate usability of nuclear weapons. As clarified by the ICJ in its 1996 Advisory Opinion to be discussed in detail in Chapter 5 below, existing principles of international humanitarian law and international environmental law particularly already so severely limit the possibilities for the legal use of nuclear weapons, that the only question regarding the legal use of nuclear weapons which remains is that of their use in the most extreme case of necessity for reasons of self-defense and state survival, and that only in response to a proportionate use of force.[174] And of course even use in these circumstances is controversial, as can be seen through the analysis provided in a number of

---

[173] "A World Free of Nuclear Weapons," January 8, 2007.

[174] *Legality of the Use by a State of Nuclear Weapons in Armed Conflict*, Advisory Opinion, ICJ Reports 1996, 26. For a detailed review of these authorities, see J. Goldblat, "Ban on Use: An Essential Condition for Disarmament," in J. Goldblat (ed.), NUCLEAR DISARMAMENT: OBSTACLES TO BANISHING THE BOMB (2000) 29.

dissenting opinions to the 1996 Advisory Opinion, and in particular the comprehensive opinion of Judge Christopher Weeramantry. It may in fact be the case, as some have argued, that the totality of treaty and customary law already forbids the use of nuclear weapons completely.[175]

Add to this accumulation of international law on the use of nuclear weapons the fact that, per their NPT Article VI obligations, NWS are already legally obligated eventually to disarm themselves of nuclear weapons, and one arrives at the conclusion that since the possession and use of nuclear weapons is already so severely restricted under international law, which thus renders minimal the advantage of continuing possession of nuclear weapons, the move to a complete ban on possession through the conclusion of a multilateral treaty on disarmament would not in fact effect a large change upon the already existing legal situation regarding nuclear weapons, and thus would not present high marginal costs to states in the form of requirements of actions they are not already under obligation to perform. What the conclusion of such a treaty would usefully accomplish, however, is the clarification of that negative legal status regarding the possession of nuclear weapons, and the commitment of all states to disarmament and non-possession on a real and effectively verifiable basis, and within a meaningful time frame and procedural framework.

Regarding the practical advantages of the conclusion of such an instrument, a multilateral disarmament treaty establishing a universal ban on the development, possession, and proliferation of nuclear weapons would aid in the enforcement of nuclear non-proliferation law by universalizing and making consistent the obligation to disarm and remain disarmed. As IAEA Director General Mohamed ElBaradei has explained:

The very existence of nuclear weapons gives rise to the pursuit of them. They are seen as a source of global influence, and are valued for their perceived deterrent effect. And as long as some countries possess them (or are protected by them in alliances) and others do not, this asymmetry breeds chronic global insecurity.[176]

With this asymmetry comes a lack of moral authority in nuclear weapons possessing states to argue on a principled basis for non-proliferation objectives in other states. Currently when any of the NPT NWS complain about NPT breaches by NNWS, and particularly in cases where concern is expressed by NWS regarding

---

[175] See the discussion of the Advisory Opinion in Chapter 5 below. See in particular the Dissenting Opinion by Judge Weeramantry; C. Moxley, NUCLEAR WEAPONS AND INTERNATIONAL LAW IN THE POST-COLD WAR WORLD (2000); J. Gardam, "Necessity and Proportionality in Jus ad Bellum & Jus in Bello," in P. Sands and L. Boisson de Chazournes (eds), INTERNATIONAL LAW, THE INTERNATIONAL COURT OF JUSTICE AND NUCLEAR WEAPONS (1999) 275, 288–289. ("It is almost impossible to apply the proportionality and unnecessary suffering equations to [nuclear] weapons and end up with a result that is not at odds with any view of what is humane. Scholars have tended to avoid the fundamental question of the relationship between IHL and nuclear weapons, no doubt for that very reason.")

[176] "Towards a Safer World," *The Economist*, October 16, 2003.

suspected nuclear weapons programs on the territory of NNWS, the fact that the states making the accusations are themselves engaging in the selfsame conduct for which they condemn other states, regardless of the legal niceties of the case against the target NNWS under the NPT's terms, makes the air rank with hypocrisy. This result serves only to undermine the credibility of enforcement efforts, and causes disunity among states in efforts to curb nuclear weapons proliferation.

A universal prohibition, and the observance by all states of the established rule, would allow for credible collective outrage to be expressed at identified breaches, and would result in a more united voice of the international community in condemning such breaches, and calling for their rectification. Particularly as such a universal norm matures into parallel customary law binding upon both treaty party and non-party states, this added legal reach would additionally help to justify more proactive and forceful efforts of counterproliferation (more on which concept in Chapter 6 below) against states and non-state actors breaching the rule. This aspect particularly should be appealing to powerful states interested in taking such a proactive approach to the subject of stopping weapons proliferation. Again, counterproliferation actions now undertaken by powerful nuclear weapons possessing states are roundly criticized as hypocritical. These states would find more support if they too were subject to the rules they attempt to enforce upon others.[177]

Concerning the related problems of the potential collective action problem among states, and the issue of verifiability of a complete ban, it is doubtless true that nuclear weapon states will, quite rationally, not give up their nuclear weapons stockpiles except through reciprocal, structured, verifiable processes in coordination with other nuclear weapon states. This is a course of diplomatic dealing which has been pursued bilaterally between the United States and the U.S.S.R./Russia through the START process particularly, and in this context has achieved some significant success in decreasing nuclear stockpiles, though these efforts have not, nor were they intended to, lead to the complete nuclear disarmament of the two states. There seems to be no clear reason, other than the lack of political will by the parties concerned, why such a process could not be organized among all nuclear weapon states, both members of the NPT as well as non-members, and prosecuted to the ultimate end of full nuclear disarmament.

With the stated aim of aiding in the facilitation of this process, the Kissinger et al. *Wall Street Journal* op-ed includes a series of recommended steps purposed

---

[177] On the link between disarmament and non-proliferation, see generally J. Cirincione, BOMB SCARE (2007) 32–33; M. Shaker, "Toward Universal Nonproliferation and Disarmament," in J. Pilat (ed.), ATOMS FOR PEACE: A FUTURE AFTER FIFTY YEARS? (2007) 65–66; C. Chyba, "Second-Tier Suppliers and Their Threat to the Nuclear Nonproliferation Regime," in J. Pilat (ed.), ATOMS FOR PEACE: A FUTURE AFTER FIFTY YEARS? (2007) 123.

in laying the political groundwork for a process of multilateral nuclear disarmament. These steps include:

1. Changing the Cold War posture of deployed nuclear weapons to increase warning time and thereby reduce the danger of an accidental or unauthorized use of a nuclear weapon.
2. Continuing to reduce substantially the size of nuclear forces in all states that possess them.
3. Eliminating short-range nuclear weapons designed to be forward-deployed.
4. Initiating a bipartisan process with the U.S. Senate . . . to achieve ratification of the Comprehensive Test Ban Treaty, taking advantage of recent technical advances, and working to secure ratification by other key states.
5. Providing the highest possible standards of security for all stocks of weapons, weapons-usable plutonium, and highly enriched uranium everywhere in the world.
6. Getting control of the uranium enrichment process, combined with the guarantee that uranium for nuclear power reactors could be obtained at a reasonable price, first from the Nuclear Suppliers Group and then from the International Atomic Energy Agency (IAEA) or other controlled international reserves. It will also be necessary to deal with proliferation issues presented by spent fuel from reactors producing electricity.
7. Halting the production of fissile material for weapons globally; phasing out the use of highly enriched uranium in civil commerce and removing weapons-usable uranium from research facilities around the world and rendering the materials safe.
8. Redoubling our efforts to resolve regional confrontations and conflicts that give rise to new nuclear powers.[178]

As Mikhail Gorbachev explains regarding the process of disarmament itself:

The key to success is reciprocity of obligations and actions. The members of the nuclear club should formally reiterate their commitment to reducing and ultimately eliminating nuclear weapons. As a token of their serious intent, they should without delay take two crucial steps: ratify the comprehensive test ban treaty and make changes in their military doctrines, removing nuclear weapons from the Cold War-era high alert status. At the same time, the states that have nuclear-power programs would pledge to terminate all elements of those programs that could have military use.[179]

As the ban would be applicable to all states, it is of course true that any system of verification of a ban once achieved would be subject to cheating. There is also, however, always the counterbalancing threat of re-armament of other states in the event one state is found to be cheating. It is of course not possible to de-invent nuclear weapons or erase the knowledge of how to create such weapons from

---

[178] "A World Free of Nuclear Weapons," January 8, 2007.
[179] "The Nuclear Threat," *Wall Street Journal*, January 31, 2007.

the human mind. Thus, while on the one hand this reality leads to the continuing possibility of cheating, it equally provides for a counterweight to this threat in the form of the residual deterrent possibility of re-armament of other states. Notwithstanding these possibilities of cheating and re-armament, the pull-back to a status quo in which nuclear weapons arsenals have in the first instance at least been destroyed, would bring the international community back further from the brink of nuclear weapons use, either international or accidental, and would thus contribute to a more stable international security reality.[180]

Ideally this process would be led by the nuclear weapon states, as urged by the *Wall Street Journal* op-eds quoted above. Hopefully NPT NWS particularly would see their interests, both short-term and long-term, being served by the de-nuclearization of international security issues, and would be willing to undertake the complex and resource consuming efforts necessary in order to negotiate such an agreed mutual disarmament among themselves and among other nuclear weapon possessing states. Having the NPT NWS particularly take this leading role would make such a universal initiative most likely to succeed, as the newer nuclear states (Israel, North Korea, Pakistan, and India) would be more likely to agree to the initiative if it were led—in deed as well as in word—by the old NWS.

However, even if not led by the NWS, it is clear from voting records of the General Assembly on resolutions (not infrequently passed by the General Assembly) concerning nuclear disarmament, that by far the majority of states in the world would support such an initiative, and would likely become treaty parties.[181] This popular acceptance of the treaty by a supermajority of states, even without the NPT NWS could be enough, in time, for the universal disarmament and prohibition norms of the treaty to achieve the parallel status of customary law, binding even non-parties. It could, in time, even form the basis for a rule of *jus cogens*, binding even persistent objectors.

If nuclear weapon possessing states will not lead the way in accomplishing this larger objective of general and complete nuclear disarmament, then it will require momentum in the U.N. General Assembly, particularly, to begin the process of producing a U.N. sponsored treaty incorporating universal disarmament and possession ban obligations. Once produced, civil society movements, particularly including those within nuclear weapon states, will pressure states to sign the treaty, and those that do not will be forced to make difficult arguments to justify

---

[180] See J. Rotblat, "Toward and Nuclear Weapon-Free World as a Prelude to a War-Free World," in J. Goldblat (ed.), Nuclear Disarmament: Obstacles to Banishing the Bomb (2000) 3. See also N. Busch, No End in Sight: The Continuing Menace of Nuclear Proliferation (2004) for a description of nuclear command and control systems and their shortcomings, making accidental launch an all too real possibility.

[181] See an account and analysis of these voting records in M. Bosch, "The Nonproliferation Treaty and its Future," in P. Sands and L. Boisson de Chazournes (eds), International Law, the International Court of Justice and Nuclear Weapons (1999) 375, 384–386.

their decision not to sign. Reluctant governments will have to be shamed into this path, and shown that not doing so will be politically costly, as has been done with significant effect in the environmental issue area.[182]

General and complete nuclear disarmament is a controversial idea, but it is not, as its critics maintain, a fundamentally unrealistic notion. The maintenance of arguments originating during the Cold War for the necessary continued possession of nuclear weapons, and the two-tiered structure of the NPT which, quite contrary to its originally intended purpose, has produced in the minds of some a legitimization of that continued possession by NPT NWS, have had the cumulative effect of pushing the idea of general and complete nuclear disarmament to the margins of political debate. However, it should be recalled that this is an idea that has been at the fore of international attention in the past, and the subject of serious negotiation at the highest political levels of states across the power spectrum. It is not a non-starter. The start was simply forgotten, and proposals to renew this effort in earnest have been invariably pushed aside by Cold War arguments of the necessity of nuclear weapons arsenals to preserve peace. However, as the Kissinger et al. and Gorbachev op-eds quoted above take pains to clarify, times have changed, and these Cold War justifications no longer ring true.

As Mikhail Gorbachev concludes in his *Wall Street Journal* op-ed:

Over the past 15 years, the goal of the elimination of nuclear weapons has been so much on the back burner that it will take a true political breakthrough and a major intellectual effort to achieve success in this endeavor. It will be a challenge to the current generation of leaders, a test of their maturity and ability to act that they must not fail. It is our duty to help them to meet this challenge.[183]

---

[182] Ibid.

[183] "The Nuclear Threat," January 31, 2007. See also the focus on reviving disarmament and outlawing nuclear weapons in the WMD Commission final report: *Weapons of Terror: Freeing the World of Nuclear, Biological and Chemical Arms*, released June 1, 2006. Available at <http://www.wmdcommission.org/files/Weapons_of_Terror.pdf>. ("Weapons of mass destruction cannot be uninvented. But they can be outlawed, as biological and chemical weapons have been, and their use made unthinkable. Compliance, verification and enforcement rules can, with the requisite will, be effectively applied. And with that will, even the eventual elimination of nuclear weapons is not beyond the world's reach." 17)

2

The Chemical and Biological Weapons Non-proliferation Regimes

Gas! Gas! Quick, boys!—An ecstasy of fumbling,
Fitting the clumsy helmets just in time;
But someone still was yelling out and stumbling,
And flound'ring like a man in fire or lime ...
Dim, through the misty panes and thick green light,
As under a green sea, I saw him drowning.
In all my dreams, before my helpless sight,
He plunges at me, guttering, choking, drowning.

Wilfred Owen

Beginning on September 18, 2001 (only one week following the terrorist attacks of September 11) and lasting for several weeks, the United States was gripped with fear as a number of letters (now believed to have totaled seven), sent to major media outlets and government offices, were found to contain anthrax spores. In the end, more than 22 people, including office workers at the intended target organizations, as well as intermediaries such as postal employees, developed anthrax infections, with 11 suffering the most life-threatening inhalation variety of infection. Five of those suffering inhalation anthrax died as a result.[1]

As had the 1995 sarin gas attack on the Tokyo subway, perpetrated by the apocalyptic religious group Aum Shinrikyo and resulting in the deaths of 12 people, the 2001 anthrax attacks in the United States refocused both public and official attention on the threat of the use of chemical compounds and biological agents and toxins as weapons, potentially inflicting large numbers of casualties upon a target population and causing terror and disruption on a massive scale.

However, the use of chemical and biological weapons (CBW) has not been a feature of the experience of recent decades alone. The use of noxious chemicals and biological pathogens and derivative toxins as weapons is a practice which has been employed literally for millenia.

The use of toxins derived from the venom and other secretions of animals as well as plants has been used to augment the effectiveness of projectile weapons,

---

[1] See L. Parker and S. Sternberg, "Findings of First Death Reported in Medical Journal," *USA Today*, November 9, 2001.

such as arrowheads, in many parts of the world since the Neolithic era. Poisonous or irritating smoke or gas, such as produced from burning oil, mustard, or sulfur, was used militarily at least from the fifth century B.C. in Greece during the Peloponnesian Wars and from the fourth century B.C. in China. The Byzantine Greeks from the seventh century A.D. made particularly effective use of an incendiary chemical substance, likely petroleum-based, which history has termed "Greek Fire," and which was used particularly injuriously against enemy naval forces, as it burned even on the surface of water.[2]

Poisonous plants and fungi were further used in the ancient world as biological weapons to poison the wells and food supplies of enemy cities under siege. The use of catapults to hurl excrement and the corpses of people who had died of disease over the walls of besieged cities continued throughout the Middle Ages. In one of the better documented cases of germ warfare, during the French and Indian war (1756–1763) British commander Lord Jeffrey Amherst is reported to have authorized the distribution of smallpox-infected blankets to enemy Native-Americans.[3]

The first large scale battlefield deployment of lethal chemical weapons occurred during the First World War, beginning with the Second Battle of Ypres on April 22, 1915, when the German army attacked French, Canadian, and Algerian forces with chlorine gas. Both the Central Powers and Allied Forces continued to use weaponized chemical agents such as phosgene and mustard throughout the remainder of World War I. It is estimated that approximately 124,000 metric tons of chemicals had been used by all sides by the war's end, resulting in over 90,000 deaths and over a million injuries.[4]

In World War II, although the German army possessed large quantities of chemical weapons, including the nerve agents tabun and sarin which had been invented in Germany during the course of the war, chemical weapons were not used extensively on the battlefield in Europe, due to fears of Allied retaliation. However, the insecticide Zyklon B, which contains hydrogen cyanide, was used in gaseous form at concentration camps including Auschwitz and Majdanek to kill several million people, the vast majority of whom were civilians.

During the decades of the Cold War, both the United States and the Soviet Union stockpiled both chemical and biological weapons. The United States officially ended its offensive biological weapons program in 1969. Russia's deactivation of its biological weapons program is ongoing. Most major military states,

---

[2] See generally A. Mayor, GREEK FIRE, POISON ARROWS AND SCORPION BOMBS: BIOLOGICAL AND CHEMICAL WARFARE IN THE ANCIENT WORLD (2003).

[3] M. Wheelis, "Biological Warfare Before 1914," in E. Geissler and J. Ellis van Courtland Moon (eds), BIOLOGICAL AND TOXIN WEAPONS: RESEARCH, DEVELOPMENT AND USE FROM THE MIDDLE AGES TO 1945, (1999) 8–34; E. Fenn, POX AMERICANA: THE GREAT SMALLPOX EPIDEMIC OF 1775–82 (2001) 88–91; J. Guillemin, BIOLOGICAL WEAPONS (2005) 3.

[4] See J. Cirincione et al., DEADLY ARSENALS, NUCLEAR, BIOLOGICAL AND CHEMICAL THREATS (Carnegie Endowment, 2nd edn, 2005) 63; Jonathan Tucker, WAR OF NERVES (2006).

including both the United States and Russia, have committed, under the 1997 Chemical Weapons Convention, to disarm themselves of their chemical weapons stockpiles.

While it is difficult to determine definitively how many states continue to possess chemical and biological weapons stockpiles and programs, as most such remaining programs are largely clandestine, it has been alleged that seven countries (China, Iran, Israel, Egypt, North Korea, Syria, and Russia) may be maintaining biological weapons programs, and that six countries (China, Iran, Israel, Egypt, North Korea, and Syria) may be maintaining undeclared/clandestine chemical weapons programs.[5]

I. CBW

Before entering into an analysis of the international legal regimes regulating the proliferation of CBW, a brief description of chemical and biological weapons is needed. It should be noted that this treatment will seek only to give a basic outline of the various classifications of chemicals and biological agents and toxins regulated by the major non-proliferation legal regimes. For more detailed technical consideration of these materials, and their nature and use, reference should be made to more specialized treatments.[6]

A. Biological Weapons

Biological weapons consist of pathogenic microorganisms or toxins manufactured from living organisms which, when intentionally delivered, have the capacity to cause illness or death among human, animal, or plant populations.[7] The destructive capability of a biological agent as a weapon may be determined by the contours of its character as within four categories: virulence, infectiousness, stability, and ease of production.[8] Biological agents themselves can be grouped into four classes: bacterial agents (e.g. anthrax), viral agents (e.g. smallpox), rickettsial agents (e.g. epidemic typhus), and toxins.

Bacterial agents, viral agents, and rickettsial agents are of varying virulence, stability and ease of production, but primarily derive their destructive capability

---

[5] See J. Cirincione et al., DEADLY ARSENALS, NUCLEAR, BIOLOGICAL AND CHEMICAL THREATS, (Carnegie Endowment, 2nd edn, 2005) 57.

[6] See, e.g., A. Kelle, K. Nixdorff, and M. Dando, CONTROLLING BIOCHEMICAL WEAPONS: ADAPTING MULTILATERAL ARMS CONTROL FOR THE 21st CENTURY (2006).

[7] See generally M. Wheelis, L Rózsa, and M. Dando (eds), DEADLY CULTURES: BIOLOGICAL WEAPONS SINCE 1945 (2006); B. Kellman, BIOVIOLENCE: PREVENTING BIOLOGICAL TERROR AND CRIME (2007); J. Guillemin, BIOLOGICAL WEAPONS (2005).

[8] J. Cirincione et al., DEADLY ARSENALS, NUCLEAR, BIOLOGICAL AND CHEMICAL THREATS (Carnegie Endowment, 2nd edn, 2005) 57.

from their infectious nature, both in terms of primary infection of the agent as well as through the contagious effect of secondary diseases which may follow primary infection. Thus, if properly introduced into a target population, these biological agents not only attack the first hosts with which they come into contact, but have the potential through various means of transmission to spread among the population, inflicting illness and death among potentially hundreds of thousands in densely populated urban areas.

Biological toxins differ from bacterial, viral, and rickettsial agents in that toxins are not themselves alive, but are rather non-living protein or non-protein molecules, and thus are not capable of infectious transmission between hosts. Toxins are poisons either derived from living organisms (e.g. bacteria, fungi, algae, and plants), or more recently, synthetically created. Examples of biological toxins include botulinum toxin and ricin. While in some ways less dangerous than living pathogens due to their inability to spread through infectious transmission, biological toxins are often extremely potent, having toxicity levels several orders of magnitude higher than the most lethal chemical poisons. Both biological pathogens and biological toxins are generally most effectively distributed in inhalable, aerosolized form, though they can also be used to poison food and beverages.[9]

B. Chemical Weapons

As defined in the Chemical Weapons Convention, a chemical weapon is "any chemical which through its chemical action on life processes can cause death, temporary incapacitation or permanent harm to humans or animals."[10] Chemical weapons agents are produced by the mixture in specific ratios of more fundamental chemical precursors. Both chemical weapons agents and their precursors have become the subject of legal regulation. Approximately 70 chemical substances have been stockpiled as chemical weapons, having been found to be highly toxic yet stable enough to be stored without deterioration, and able to withstand the forces of heat or conditions of atmospheric water vapor and oxygen encountered during dispersal.[11]

Chemical weapons can be categorized into four groups: blood gases (e.g. hydrogen cyanide), blistering agents (e.g. mustard gas, phosgene oxime and lewisite), choking agents (e.g. chlorine and phosgene), and nerve agents (e.g. tabun, sarin, and V nerve agent (VX)). Chemical weapons are generally disseminated in liquid form, either through liquid droplets or an aerosol, though some can be used in gaseous form.[12]

---

[9] Ibid.   [10] Article 2(2).

[11] See generally J.B. Tucker, War of Nerves: Chemical Warfare from World War I to Al-Qaeda (2006).

[12] See J. Cirincione et al., Deadly Arsenals, Nuclear, Biological and Chemical Threats (Carnegie Endowment, 2nd edn, 2005) 57.

II. CBW = WMD?

The idea of classifying chemical and biological weapons as weapons of mass destruction must also receive some consideration before proceeding. The term "weapons of mass destruction" is of controversial origin in the English language. However, its first use by governments in an official context appears to have been in the first ever resolution of the United Nations General Assembly, passed at its seventeenth plenary meeting on January 24, 1946. In its Resolution 1, entitled "Establishment of a Commission to Deal with the Problems Raised by the Discovery of Atomic Energy," the General Assembly created the Atomic Energy Commission (AEC), and gave the new organization a mandate to "proceed with utmost despatch and inquire into all phases of the problem" of the discovery of atomic energy, and to make specific proposals inter alia "for the elimination from national armaments of atomic weapons and of all other major weapons adaptable to mass destruction."[13]

The reason for the inclusion of this action, and creation of this new classification of weapons technologies and accompanying nomenclature, in the very first General Assembly resolution was of course the fact that the world had only months earlier found out about the development by the United States of nuclear fission weapons, and their use on the cities of Hiroshima and Nagasaki, Japan in August 1945. During the decades of the Cold War which followed, with the threat of mutually assured nuclear destruction looming over the world, the term "weapons of mass destruction" continued to be used, along with other terms including "strategic weapons," most commonly to refer particularly to nuclear fusion or thermonuclear weapons.

It was only after the break-up of the Soviet Union and the ending of the Cold War in the early 1990s that the term "weapons of mass destruction" and its acronym "WMD" came into their own as descriptors of the triumvirate of non-conventional weapons—nuclear, chemical, and biological—particularly in public discourse and by senior government officials. Among specialists, the acronyms "NBC" and particularly "CBRN" have come to be used more commonly in describing this class of non-conventional weapons, in the case of the latter in order to include sub-critical radiological weapons ("dirty bombs").[14]

During the first Gulf War in 1991, extensive reference was made by U.S. officials to Iraq's chemical and biological weapons stockpiles as "weapons of mass destruction." Even more widespread use was made of the term, with the inclusion within its meaning of chemical and biological weapons, by U.S. and U.K. officials in the context of the lead-up to the 2003 invasion of Iraq. The prolific use of

---

[13] Para. 5.
[14] See C. Ferguson, "WMD Terrorism," in N. Busch and D.H. Joyner (eds), Combating Weapons of Mass Destruction: The Future of International Nonproliferation Policy (2009).

the term "weapons of mass destruction" in vernacular during this time led to its acronym form being voted the Word of the Year by the American Dialect Society in 2002.[15]

However, there is a serious argument to be made that including chemical and biological weapons along with nuclear weapons within the term weapons of mass destruction is analytically invalid, or at least sub-optimally descriptive. As the U.N. General Assembly first recognized in its separate categorization of nuclear weapons as a weapon "adaptable to mass destruction," the incomparable physical destructive power of nuclear fission and fusion weapons demands such a separate classification from any other weapon conventionally used by the world's militaries. The effects of a high-yield nuclear weapon detonation, including the massive destructive force of the initial blast, thermal radiation, and electromagnetic pulse, followed by the short, medium, and long-term effects of residual nuclear radiation on an area extending up to hundreds of miles from the epicenter of the detonation, are simply unmatched in their effects upon physical structures and upon human, animal, and plant life within the affected area.[16]

Because of their massive destructive power, and adaptability both as a battlefield weapon, as well as a weapon potentially usable by terrorists and other non-state actors against civilian centers, the independent variable of nuclear weapons possession by states and non-state actors has a highly significant effect upon the interests and behavior of states, and thus plays a deciding role in international politics and the foreign policy of states. The political uses of nuclear weapons range from the explicit threat of aggressive use, to the latent threat of use for the sake of deterrence of aggressive use by a rival state or non-state actor, to possession for simple political leverage to obtain concessions from states or other actors interested in curbing further nuclear proliferation.[17]

Due to both the destructive potential of the direct use of nuclear weapons themselves, as well as their secondary but highly significant effects upon the dynamics of international politics, some have argued that nuclear weapons are deserving of an exclusive, apex categorization under the term weapons of mass destruction.[18]

Bolstering this argument, it has been noted that both the Biological Weapons Convention and the Chemical Weapons Convention, in their attempts to comprehensively ban the use of their subject technologies as weapons, include within their regulation both lethal CBW as well as a wide range of non-lethal CBW. Thus, it is argued, only by rather tortured expansion of the term "weapons of mass destruction" could the full gamut of materials covered under the

---

[15] <http://www.americandialect.org/index.php/amerdial/2002_words_of_the_y/>.
[16] See E. Koppe, THE USE OF NUCLEAR WEAPONS AND THE PROTECTION OF THE ENVIRONMENT DURING INTERNATIONAL ARMED CONFLICT (2006).
[17] See J. Bayliss and R. O'Neill (eds), ALTERNATIVE NUCLEAR FUTURES: THE ROLE OF NUCLEAR WEAPONS IN THE POST-COLD WAR WORLD (2000).
[18] R. Thakur, "Introduction" in R. Thakur (ed.), THE CHEMICAL WEAPONS CONVENTION: IMPLEMENTATION, CHALLENGES AND OPPORTUNITIES (2006) 3.

foundational CBW non-proliferation legal instruments be included within its meaning. Alternatively, however, including only lethal CBW within the WMD classification runs an unacceptable risk of implicitly legitimizing non-lethal CBW which, if less physically destructive than lethal CBW, are yet importantly de-legitimized and made illegal by operation of the BWC and CWC.[19] Developments in the field of non-lethal CBW, as will be discussed later on, pose one of the most difficult challenges for the future strengthening of the CBW non-proliferation regimes, and thus their implicit legitimization through such a discriminatory classification would be particularly unhelpful. More generally, such partial legitimization of CBW would run the further risk of confusing and possibly undercutting the longstanding and pervasive taboo regarding use of CBW which, as will be discussed, is the principle guarantor of the effectiveness of the CBW non-proliferation legal regimes.

Classifying CBW along with nuclear weapons as weapons of mass destruction can pose further problems, both in terms of international non-proliferation policy as well as the foreign policy of states. Lumping CBW in together with nuclear weapons under the umbrella of WMD can lead to treating all WMD technologies similarly in proliferation-related analysis and debate. This practice incorporates a false understanding that the non-proliferation challenges facing the international community with regard to these very different weapons technologies, with very different legal regimes, histories, and records of success, are in fact similar. As Julian Robinson has explained:

"Nonproliferation" is itself another technical term that is problematic in its application to CBW, for international law is now either approaching or, depending on one's view, has long since reached the point at which any possession of CBW is illegal. To posit nonproliferation of CBW as a policy objective is therefore to imply that this legal regime is failing. There is no evidence whatsoever for this. Nor, in contrast to nuclear weapons, does any state have licence to possess CBW, not even the permanent members of the UN Security Council...The chapter therefore warns that express pursuit of WMD nonproliferation may damage the existing CBW governance regime, which is aimed at suppressing CBW and has proved largely successful in so doing.[20]

With regard to the foreign policy of states, the rather un-nuanced grouping of CBW along with nuclear weapons within the concept of WMD again has a tendency to bundle technologies together which are in most material ways analytically dissimilar, with potentially disastrous effects. For example, a number of states, including the United States, cite as a justification for the maintenance of their nuclear weapons arsenals the threat of WMD attack, including by definition

---

[19] J. Robinson, "Chemical and Biological Weapons," in N. Busch and D.H. Joyner (eds), COMBATING WEAPONS OF MASS DESTRUCTION: THE FUTURE OF INTERNATIONAL NONPROLIFERATION POLICY (2009) 74.

[20] Ibid. at 74.

an attack exclusively utilizing CBW. As stated in the 2002 United States National Strategy to Combat Weapons of Mass Destruction:

The United States will continue to make clear that it reserves the right to respond with overwhelming force—including through resort to all of our options—to the use of WMD against the United States, our forces abroad, and friends and allies. In addition to our conventional and nuclear response and defense capabilities, our overall deterrent posture against WMD threats is reinforced by effective intelligence, surveillance, interdiction, and domestic law enforcement capabilities. Such combined capabilities enhance deterrence both by devaluing an adversary's WMD and missiles, and by posing the prospect of an overwhelming response to any use of such weapons.[21]

As the number of states and non-state actors possessing, suspected of possessing, or potentially possessing CBW, with or without additionally possessing nuclear weapons, significantly exceeds the number possessing nuclear weapons alone, the inclusion of CBW within the concept of WMD thus allows for an expansion in the number of threats which may be cited as justifications for continued possession of nuclear weapons. Most strikingly, the foregoing statement must be read to proclaim the right of retaliation with nuclear weapons in response to WMD attack, again inclusive of an exclusively CBW attack.[22] As held by the International Court of Justice in its 1996 *Nuclear Weapons Advisory Opinion*, the proportionality principle contained both in international use of force law and international humanitarian law would likely render all imaginable exercises of this proclaimed right in the context of an exclusively CBW attack violative of international law, as unlike the case of a massive nuclear weapons attack it is difficult to conceive of an exclusively CBW attack upon a state, the result or threatened result of which would produce "an extreme case of self-defense, in which the very survival of a state would be at stake."[23]

Due to these concerns, a persuasive case can be made that CBW are indeed better dissociated terminologically from nuclear weapons and classed in a subsidiary category to WMD. One candidate for the name of this new category might be "weapons of mass casualty," owing to the capacity of CBW, if effectively used, to cause massive loss of human life notwithstanding the inability of CBW themselves (i.e. unless supplemented or delivered by conventional explosive weapons such as artillery shells) to cause massive physical destruction.[24]

Perhaps even more appropriately, however, this new category might be termed "weapons of mass terror." CBW are notoriously difficult to deploy effectively in order to cause large numbers of casualties, though in theory they can be so deployed, and have been so deployed on rare occasions in practice. Reasons for

---

[21] Available at <http://www.whitehouse.gov/news/releases/2002/12/WMDStrategy.pdf>.

[22] See R. Thakur, "Introduction" in R. Thakur (ed.), THE CHEMICAL WEAPONS CONVENTION: IMPLEMENTATION, CHALLENGES AND OPPORTUNITIES (2006) 3.

[23] Para. 105(2)(E).

[24] "Biological Weapons in the Former Soviet Union: An Interview with Kenneth Alibek," conducted by J.B. Tucker, 6 THE NONPROLIFERATION REVIEW 91 (Spring–Summer 1999).

this include technical barriers to weaponization and environmental and other challenges to effective deployment. As Julian Robinson has explained:

> Published military doctrine shows that most of the military and other utilities for which user-services have valued possession of CBW have depended on aggressive properties other than mass killing. One may view the available target effects of CBW as lying along spectra that have highly localized, say, or low-casualty effects at one end and large-area or mass-casualty effects at the other. Where along a spectrum a given chemical or biological weapon would manifest its effects is determined by the characteristics of the toxic/infective agent being used (such as the contagiousness of any disease it can cause) and the manner of its use, and by the vulnerability of the threatened population, this reflecting such factors as the health status of the population and degree of preparedness for protecting itself against disseminated agent. It remains the case today that, in the design of CBW, increasingly severe technological constraint sets in as the mass-destruction end of the spectrum is approached: the greater and more assured the area-effectiveness sought for the weapon, the greater the practical difficulties of achieving it. This is why the notion of mass-destruction terrorism using CBW is less plausible than its portrayals have often suggested.[25]

However, even a relatively minor deployment, or credible threat of deployment, of CBW is likely to incite widespread fear within either a military or a civilian target population. In the civilian context, this fear could very possibly lead to disruption of transportation and other services and activities necessary to the normal functioning of commerce and society. The effects of this fear and disruption to life particularly in urban centers, and the knock-on effects thereof to economies, are indeed likely the most effective results of which the threat or use of CBW are reasonably capable.

To be clear before proceeding, the questions of categorization and nomenclature regarding chemical and biological weapons under discussion, while important for the reasons described, and possibly indirectly relevant to legal considerations in, e.g., the area of use of force law as described above, have no material bearing on the interpretation, validity, or scope of the sources of international law relevant to CBW to be reviewed in this chapter. The legal terminology used in the provisions of these treaty sources (i.e. the Geneva Protocol, the BWC, and the CWC), which in turn forms the normative locus around which the parallel custom supporting these conventional instruments has developed, is not affected by any uncertainties regarding these categorizations or the semantics of their titles.

III. Scope of the Chapter

Finally, a note on the scope of this chapter, in its inclusion of consideration of both the biological weapons proliferation regime and the chemical weapons

---

[25] J. Robinson, "Chemical and Biological Weapons," in N. Busch and D.H. Joyner (eds), COMBATING WEAPONS OF MASS DESTRUCTION: THE FUTURE OF INTERNATIONAL NONPROLIFERATION POLICY (2009) 76–77.

proliferation regime. While some treatments maintain an analytical separation between the two regimes, this treatment has chosen to consider these regimes together for a number of reasons.

The first reason for this joint analysis is the profound historical and documentary links between the regulation through international law of biological weapons and chemical weapons. Both legal regimes are direct outgrowths of the same program of work that began in the late 1960s, the CWC simply taking longer to achieve realization due to Cold War politics and tensions. Their legal foundations as well are directly linked to the same legal progenitor—the 1925 Geneva Protocol. The texts of the BWC and the CWC themselves are expressly linked. The BWC's Preamble is explicit in its recognition of the BWC as constituting only the first step in regulating the entire area of chemical and biological weapons, and mentions ongoing efforts to broaden regulation to cover chemical weapons as well. Article IX of the BWC in fact obligates states parties to continue in negotiations toward the conclusion of a treaty on chemical weapons prohibition. This article of the BWC is reciprocally expressly mentioned in the Preamble to the CWC, and the relation of the two treaties is specially addressed in Article XIII of the CWC.

The second reason for a joined up analysis of the BWC and the CWC regimes is that both areas of regulation enjoy a similar, peculiar normative and moral support for their prohibitive efforts. This support stems from a strong historical aversion in international society to the use of chemical and biological weapons, which has translated into a strong communal norm that such use is, in a word, taboo.[26] As the BWC itself states, such use would be "repugnant to the conscience of mankind." The origins of the particular opprobrium attached to the use of chemicals and biological agents in warfare are ancient, descending at least from the Romans, some of whom considered the use of poisons in battle disgraceful, though to be fair adherence to this taboo in the ancient world was spotty at best.[27] The taboo was strengthened in the early twentieth century by observations of the horrific effects of the full-scale battlefield use of these weapons in World War I, as best chronicled in the poem by Wilfred Owen which opened the chapter. This and other chronicles of the use of chemical weapons seared into the mind of future generations poignant images of the strange and horrific suffering caused thereby. As Julian Robinson, one of the foremost authorities on chemical and biological weapons, has explained:

First and foremost, CBW may resemble other categories of weapon in that they can attack life, killing their victims no less dead than can bullets or bayonets, but they may also be targeted to disrupt individual processes that contribute to life, which other weapons cannot do save by accident, not design. The nerve gases, for example, target nerve-signal

---

[26] J. Guillemin, Biological Weapons (2005) 1–20.

[27] See A. Mayor, Greek Fire, Poison Arrows and Scorpion Bombs: Biological and Chemical Warfare in the Ancient World (2003) 37.

transmission; the blood gases, cellular respiration. Advances in the life sciences and in those allied technologies that allow the analysis and construction of complex biologically active molecules could eventually make it possible to design a CBW agent that will interfere with any life process that can be understood in molecular terms, whether it be the process of development, inheritance, reproduction, locomotion, sensation, cognition or indeed any other process that keeps us functioning properly, according to expectations. The potential is there, inasmuch as it has not materialized already, for inducing many different forms of malfunction, maybe even ones that discriminate between ethnic groups of human beings. It is this potential for manipulating at will our very humanity, in pursuit of who-knows-what strategy of adversary subjugation, repression or coercion, that makes CBW especially menacing.[28]

As noted in Chapter 1 above, there is perhaps little in the way of objective criteria by which to justify the differential presence of this taboo in the area of chemical and biological weapons, and its relative absence in the area of nuclear weapons. The horrific devastation of Hiroshima and Nagasaki, and the nature of the effects of nuclear weapons as including massive instantaneous destruction and loss of life, as well as widespread non-lethal injuries such as burning; and even further the medium and long-term effects upon victims' health caused by exposure to radiation, not to mention the devastating effects of nuclear weapons upon a target environment, all amply and graphically chronicled in literature such as Ibuse Masuji's classic *Black Rain*, would seem fertile sod for the production of a similarly pervasive air of obloquy. As explained in Chapter 1 above, the difference in attachment of moral censure likely has to do with the role nuclear weapons played in bringing World War II to a close, and the positive associations to which the results of this use gave rise in Western consciousness, which successfully drew a curtain over and obscured the horrors of the use of nuclear weapons. This difference may, in frankness, also have significantly to do with the fact that the use in World War I of chemical weapons was as against Europeans, and the use in World War II of nuclear weapons was as against Asians, though this must remain speculation. What is more clear is that the absence of a similar taboo in the nuclear weapons area made more reasonable and objectively unassailable the retention of right in the NWS to possess nuclear weapons under the grand bargain of the NPT, and secured the absence of any moral condemnation of nuclear weapons or their use per se in the text of the NPT, similar to that contained in the BWC Preamble.

As will be discussed further below, this peculiar yet pervasive taboo regarding chemical and biological weapons is the single most significant reason for the successes achieved in implementation of the BWC and CWC.

The third reason for joint analysis of the BWC and CWC regimes is the decreasingly clear line separating biological weapons and chemical weapons. The

---

[28] J. Robinson, "Chemical and Biological Weapons," in N. Busch and D.H. Joyner (eds), COMBATING WEAPONS OF MASS DESTRUCTION: THE FUTURE OF INTERNATIONAL NONPROLIFERATION POLICY (2009) 75–76.

fields of chemistry and biology are converging, as evident in the recent rise to prominence of the field of molecular biology, and this convergence has blurred whatever clear distinctions were perceived to exist between biological and chemical weaponizable materials.[29] There has always been some overlap in the coverage of the BWC and CWC, as for example both treaties cover biological toxins, or poisonous chemicals which are produced by some living organisms. However the science of biological weapons and chemical weapons is increasingly merging and overlapping, e.g. as scientists are now able to synthetically produce compounds previously only obtainable from natural sources, giving rise to entirely new fields of research into biochemical weapons.[30] The development of materials which defy classic criteria for categorization as between the two legal regimes argues for a more holistic approach to the area of biological and chemical weapons regulation generally.

Fourth and finally, from an institutional/regime perspective, due to the coverage of the Australia Group control lists of both chemical and biological materials and dual-use technologies, there is parsimony to be found in addressing both regimes within the scope of one chapter.

IV. CBW Regimes

A. The 1925 Geneva Protocol

The Hague Regulations of 1899 and 1907 provided the first multilaterally agreed prohibition of "poison or poisoned weapons." However, the proscriptions upon chemically enhanced weapons in the Regulations did not serve to clearly prohibit many potential uses of chemical weapons, in particular chemical gas weapons, in warfare, leading to the widespread use of such weapons in World War I.

By the signing in 1925 of the Protocol for the Prohibition of the Use in War of Asphyxiating, Poisonous or other Gases, and of Bacteriological Methods of Warfare (Geneva Protocol), the major industrialized military states, with the significant exception of the United States, had come to the conclusion that the "use in war of asphyxiating, poisonous or other gases, and of all analogous liquids, materials or devices, has been justly condemned by the general opinion of the civilized world…" Through the Geneva Protocol, the High Contracting Parties (now totaling 132) accept (to the extent they had not already accepted through the

---

[29] Ibid. at 24.

[30] A. Kelle, K. Nixdorff, and M. Dando, CONTROLLING BIOCHEMICAL WEAPONS: ADAPTING MULTILATERAL ARMS CONTROL FOR THE 21ˢᵗ CENTURY (2006); M. Wheelis, *Biotechnology and Biochemical Weapons*, 9 THE NONPROLIFERATION REVIEW 48 (Spring 2002); Submission of the United States, BWC/CONF.III/4, Paragraph 5 (1991) ("the distinction between biology and chemistry is becoming blurred").

Hague Regulations) this prohibition on the use of chemical weapons in war, and agree to extend this prohibition as among themselves to the use of bacteriological, or biological, weapons in war.[31]

The Geneva Protocol is a short document, and is notoriously imprecise in its language, which forms one barrier to its effective implementation. In this regard, significant interpretive differences have arisen as to whether the Protocol covers herbicides and tear gas and other riot agents, i.e. toxic chemicals which are not lethal to humans. The interpretation largely turns on the meaning to be given to the rather vague phrase "or other gases," following the Protocol's prohibition of the use in war of asphyxiating and poisonous gases; an interpretive question complicated by the incongruity between terms used in the Protocol's two official languages at this point in the document.[32]

Another significant barrier to the effectiveness of the Protocol is posed by the character of obligations thereunder as existing only as among the High Contracting Parties themselves, and not as generalized obligations as toward any state. Finally, the number and character of the reservations appended by states to their signature of the Protocol has largely undermined its effectiveness, as with the numerous reservations stipulating that the application of the provisions will be based strictly upon reciprocity (thus the obligations become nullified in response to a prior attack using prohibited weapons). Though not a formal treaty reservation, a similar undermining effect was produced by the "understanding" adopted by the U.S. Senate upon its 1975 consent to ratification of the Protocol, exempting tear gas and herbicides (both of which having been used extensively by the U.S. in the Vietnam War).[33]

With regard to the problem of reservations conditioning compliance with the Protocol upon reciprocity, which in the words of one commentator "was to lend the Geneva Protocol the appearance of a 'no-first-use declaration' rather than a solemn renunciation by treaty of any use in war of chemical and biological weapons,"[34] it is material to note that many such reservations have over the succeeding decades been formally withdrawn by states. A number of these withdrawals occurred due to the conclusion in 1972 of the Biological Weapons Convention. The Irish Government, for example, in 1972 withdrew its reservation to the Geneva Protocol with the following explanatory statement:

Ireland considers that the Convention could be undermined if reservations made by the parties to the 1925 Geneva Protocol were allowed to stand, as the prohibition of possession

---

[31] See generally I. Detter, THE LAW OF WAR (2nd edn, 2000) 251–259.

[32] Ibid. at 256.

[33] 14 INTERNATIONAL LEGAL MATERIALS 1975, 49. See generally J.N. Moore, *Ratification of the Geneva Protocol on Gas and Bacteriological Warfare: A Legal and Political Analysis*, 3 VIRGINIA LAW REVIEW 419 (1972).

[34] N. Sims, "Legal Constraints on Biological Weapons," in M. Wheelis, L. Rosa, and M. Dando (eds), DEADLY CULTURES: BIOLOGICAL WEAPONS SINCE 1945 (2006) 330.

is incompatible with the right to retaliate. As the convention purports to strengthen the Geneva Protocol, there should be an absolute and universal prohibition of the use of the weapons in question.[35]

It is likely that the persuasive lesser included logic conveyed in this statement, now equally applicable in the context of the CWC and supplemented by that instrument's explicit prohibition on use of chemical weapons, together with the status of the 1925 Protocol, the BWC, and the CWC in customary international law (all three are with little doubt now supplemented and expanded in their obligational reach by parallel customary international law),[36] as well as state practice including withdrawals of reciprocity reservations, have together worked to produce a rule of customary international law forbidding even the retaliatory use of chemical and biological weapons.[37] This customary rule, in addition to the subsequent treaty provisions on possession and use themselves, almost certainly now trumps remaining reciprocity reservations to the 1925 Protocol per the interpretive cannon *lex posterior derogat priori*.[38]

Due in part to some of the above outlined concerns with the 1925 Protocol, momentum began to build particularly within the United Nations in the late 1960s toward the conclusion of a multilateral convention on the regulation of chemical and biological weapons.[39] Though the conclusion of such a treaty covering both chemical and biological weapons technologies was considered by inter alia the Eighteen Power Disarmament Conference (ENCD) and the Committee of the Conference on Disarmament (CCD), it became apparent that agreement on a multilateral prohibition on possession would be more easily achieved in the biological weapons area than in the chemical weapons area. Thus, the decision was made to separate the two branches of weapons technologies and focus first on the achievement of a treaty prohibiting biological weapons development, possession, and proliferation as a supplementary set of obligations to the 1925 Protocol's prohibition on use.

---

[35] World Armaments and Disarmament: SIPRI Yearbook 1976, 468, 474.

[36] J.-M. Henckaerts and L. Doswald-Beck, Customary International Humanitarian Law, Volume I: Rules (2005) 256–267. There is the rather anomalous fact that, while the use of chemical weapons and biological toxins is included under the definition of "war crimes" in Articles 8(2)(b)(xvii) & (xviii) of the Statute of the International Criminal Court, the use of biological agents themselves are arguably not included in Article 8(2)(b)(xvii)'s prohibition of use of "poison or poisoned weapons." This distinction can, however, be explained in the remaining distinction, notwithstanding significant overlap, as between customary international humanitarian law on the one hand, and customary international criminal law on the other. Thus, as the above cited ICRC study makes clear, the use of biological weapons, including biological agents, is prohibited under customary international humanitarian law, notwithstanding the arguable absence of international criminal liability attaching to such an action.

[37] Ibid.

[38] See A. Roberts and R. Guelff, Documents on the Laws of War (3rd edn, 2000) 160–167.

[39] See, e.g., General Assembly Resolutions 2262 (1970); 2827 (1971); 2933 (1972); 3077 (1973).

B. The Biological Weapons Convention

Article I

The Biological Weapons Convention (BWC)[40] was opened for signature in April 1972 and entered into force on March 26, 1975. In its Article I it states the undertaking of its states parties

> never in any circumstances to develop, produce, stockpile or otherwise acquire or retain: (1) Microbial or other biological agents, or toxins whatever their origin or method of production, of types and in quantities that have no justification for prophylactic, protective or other peaceful purposes...

Because of the profoundly dual-use nature of biological agents as well as some biological toxins, the conclusion was reached that possession of such materials could not be prohibited outright. The question thus became one of describing, in the necessarily vague language of a multilateral treaty, those biological materials which were to be classified as "biological weapons" subject to the prohibitions of the treaty. The purpose-related criteria included in Article I, often referred to as the general purpose criteria of the BWC, were an innovative attempt at concision in this regard. The terms "of types" and "in quantities" would seem best read disjunctively in this article, so as to produce two separate criteria, the satisfaction of either of which will suffice to render the substance in question prohibited under the treaty. Thus, some substances are of types for which no legitimate civilian purpose exists, and their possession in any amount is therefore prohibited. However, there are some substances which do have legitimate "prophylactic, protective or other peaceful purposes," and which may therefore be possessed by states parties in quantities necessary to the fulfilling of these purposes, but no more than these quantities.

While laying the foundation for defining which biological materials are subject to the convention's prohibitions, the general purpose criteria of Article I remain very difficult to implement as, among other reasons, they are not supplemented, as in the case of the CWC to be discussed below, by a listing of prohibited materials and equipment within the treaty text or other binding document.[41] BWC Review Conferences have similarly failed to conclude such a list of prohibited items in their final documents, although the final document of

---

[40] Formally the "Convention on the Prohibition of the Development, Production and Stockpiling of Bacteriological (Biological) and Toxin Weapons and on Their Destruction," opened for signature April 10, 1972, 26 U.S.T. 583, T.I.A.S. No. 8062, 1015 U.N.T.S. 163. See generally I. Detter, THE LAW OF WAR (2nd ed., 2000) 259–262; N. Sims, "Legal Constraints on Biological Weapons," in M. Wheelis, L. Rosa, and M. Dando (eds), DEADLY CULTURES: BIOLOGICAL WEAPONS SINCE 1945 (2006).

[41] See J. Beard, *The Shortcomings of Indeterminacy in Arms Control Regimes: The Case of the Biological Weapons Convention*, 101 AMERICAN JOURNAL OF INTERNATIONAL LAW 271(2007).

the Second Review Conference, held in 1986, did include the following statement ensuring the comprehensive character of the terms of Article I:

The Conference, conscious of apprehensions arising from relevant scientific and techno-logical developments, inter alia, in the fields of microbiology, genetic engineering and biotechnology, and the possibilities of their use for purposes inconsistent with the objectives and the provisions of the Convention, reaffirms that the undertaking given by the States Parties in Article I applies to all such developments. The Conference reaffirms that the Convention unequivocally applies to all natural or artificially created micro-bial or other biological agents or toxins whatever their origin or method of production. Consequently, toxins (both proteinaceous and non-proteinaceous) of a microbial, animal or vegetable nature and their synthetically produced analogues are covered.

This statement was supplemented by the final document of the Fourth Review Conference, held in 1996, which affirmed the extension of the BWC's terms to more recent developments in the fields of "microbiology, biotechnology, molecu-lar biology, genetic engineering" and further to "any applications resulting from genome studies."

The Australia Group, to be discussed below, does provide control lists of bio-logical dual-use technologies and biological agents and toxins which, per the analysis of VCLT Article 31(3) contained in Chapter 1, could along with other sources including Review Conference final documents be materially useful in interpretation of BWC Article I. However, as in the case of the NSG control list in the context of the NPT, the legal weight of this list for purposes of interpret-ation of Article I of the BWC is concededly limited by the limited-membership nature of the Australia Group and its non-incorporation into the BWC text.

The production of such a delineation of prohibited materials, their thresholds of use, and related equipment as a formal additional protocol to the BWC was one of the chief goals of the Ad Hoc Group of Governmental Experts to Identify and Examine Potential Verification Measures from a Scientific and Technical Standpoint (VEREX), a body of experts established at the Third BWC Review Conference in September 1991. As will be detailed below, the production of this report and the succeeding process purposed in producing an additional binding protocol for the BWC, culminated in a dramatic series of events in 2001, as a result of which the additional protocol was abandoned.

In a further effort of interpretive clarification of the reach of BWC Article I, the final documents of the Fourth and Sixth Review Conferences of the BWC have included consensus decisions of the treaty parties, interpreting BWC Article I as including an implied prohibition on the use of biological weapons in addition to its express prohibitions on development, production, stockpiling, acquisition, and reten-tion. As stated in the Final Document of the Fourth BWC Review Conference:

The Conference reaffirms that the use by the States Parties, in any way and under any circumstances, of microbial or other biological agents or toxins, that is not consistent with prophylactic, protective or other peaceful purposes, is effectively a violation of Article I of the convention.

This statement recognizing an extension of the meaning of the terms of Article I of the BWC to include use is an interesting use of the interpretive rights of treaty member states acting subsequent to the conclusion of the treaty. As discussed in the context of the NPT Review Conference final documents, the decisions of review conferences by the consensus of treaty parties do carry significant interpretive weight pursuant to Article 31(3) of the Vienna Convention on the Law of Treaties. While not determinative of correct interpretation, such statements do assist in providing the interpreter with valuable evidence of the understanding of the parties to the treaty as to its meaning, and should thus factor significantly into determinations of treaty interpretation.[42]

In the case of the extension of the terms of Article I to include a prohibition on use of biological weapons, as the membership overlap between the 1925 Geneva Protocol and the 1972 BWC is extensive, and as the significance of the former document is expressly noted in the Preamble of the BWC, it should not perhaps be surprising that the states parties of the BWC should see the obligation of non-use first established in the 1925 Protocol as running through and being both incorporated into and reinforced by the terms of the BWC. This incorporation of the prohibition into the BWC, and its continuing consistent and generalized implementation in state practice, add to the strength of the parallel customary law prohibition on the use of biological weapons binding upon all states, including non-parties of the Protocol or BWC.[43]

Article I(2)

In the context of Article I(2) of the BWC and the interpretation of the prohibition therein upon "weapons, equipment or means of delivery designed to use such agents or toxins for hostile purposes or in armed conflict," Nicholas Sims has usefully discussed a controversial case of interpretation of the term "designed." As Sims explains:

It was presumably on this reasoning that U.S. government lawyers were relying (those from the State Department reportedly dissenting) when they apparently advised that U.S. efforts to replicate key parts of a biological bomb designed in the former Soviet Union, in order to better understand the BW threat, would not be in breach of Article I. The absence of an intention "to use such agents or toxins for hostile purposes or in armed conflict" would on this argument (which depends crucially upon the interpretation of "designed" to mean the same as "intended") render the design of such a weapon compatible with U.S. obligations under the BWC. There remains the further objection that to advance such a permissive interpretation of the design criterion is undesirably

---

[42] See Chapter 1 at 59.

[43] See also generally B. Kellman's discussion of non-lethal biological agents in BIOVIOLENCE: PREVENTING BIOLOGICAL TERROR AND CRIME (2007) 197–205. As the most contentious legal debates regarding non-lethal weapons and their use against personnel are currently better located within the context of the provisions of the Chemical Weapons Convention, this treatment will review the issue of non-lethal CBW below within the framework of CWC Article 1.

subjective, allowing each state party to decide for itself whether its intention, in designing a biological bomb, is to hold it in readiness to use it for hostile purposes or in armed
conflict, or merely to acquire a better understanding of how others might use it in such
circumstances.[44]

For the reasons of unacceptable subjectivity of any other interpretation
correctly explained by Sims, the interpretation of the term "designed" in
Article I(2) should be understood to make reference to the objective character and primary latent usefulness of the "weapons, equipment or means of
delivery" themselves, and not to the intention of the state party who wishes to
develop or possess them.

Article II

In BWC Article II, states parties undertake "to destroy, or to divert to peaceful purposes, as soon as possible but not later than nine months after entry into
force of the Convention, all agents, toxins, weapons, equipment and means of
delivery specified in Article I of the Convention, which are in its possession or
under its jurisdiction or control." Thus, in contrast to the differential obligations
of the NPT, the obligation of non-possession of the BWC's prohibited materials
extends to all states parties, even to those whose possession at the time of signing
requires the action of destruction or diversion of such materials in order to attain
that state.

Article III

Article III requires states not to transfer "to any recipient whatsoever, directly
or indirectly," nor to assist, encourage, or support the manufacture or acquisition of the materials prohibited under Article I. Again, the relative simplicity of
the obligations of the BWC as compared to the NPT can be seen in the blanket prohibition on transfer "to any recipient whatsoever," in marked contrast to
the various exceptions on nuclear materials trade and transfer embedded within
Article I of the NPT particularly. In the final document of the Sixth BWC Review
Conference, BWC states parties adopted the following statement clarifying the
scope of this prohibition on transfer:

The Conference reaffirms that Article III is sufficiently comprehensive to cover
any recipient whatsoever at the international, national or sub-national levels. The
Conference calls for appropriate measures, including effective national export controls, by all States Parties to implement this Article, in order to ensure that direct
and indirect transfers relevant to the Convention, to any recipient whatsoever, are
authorized only when the intended use is for purposes not prohibited under the
Convention.

---

[44] N. Sims, "Legal Constraints on Biological Weapons," in M. Wheelis, L. Rózsa, and M.
Dando (eds), DEADLY CULTURES: BIOLOGICAL WEAPONS SINCE 1945 (2006) 352.

Article IV

In Article IV, states parties undertake to make any necessary modifications to their own national laws, regulations, and official processes, including to the procedures for enforcement of such laws, in order to fulfill their obligations undertaken in Articles I through III. BWC Review Conference final documents have urged states to view this requirement broadly, and to include the education of relevant private business entities and groups of professionals regarding the obligations of the BWC, and the encouragement of codes of conduct and self-regulatory mechanisms for such private entities.[45] The Final Document of the Second Review Conference of the BWC, held in 1986, specifically noted the importance in the context of the Article IV obligation of:

- legislative, administrative and other measures designed effectively to guarantee compliance with the provisions of the Convention within the territory under the jurisdiction or control of a State Party,
- legislation regarding the physical protection of laboratories and facilities to prevent unauthorised access to and removal of pathogenic or toxic material, and inclusion in textbooks and in medical, scientific and military educational programmes of information dealing with the prohibition of bacteriological (biological) and toxin weapons and the provisions of the Geneva Protocol.

Articles V & VI

Articles V and VI comprise the only system for verification and dispute resolution contained within the original BWC text. This system provides in the first instance for consultation and cooperation between states on questions regarding compliance with the provisions of the treaty. In implementation of this obligation of consultation and cooperation, the final documents of the Second and Third Review Conferences of the BWC established and refined a procedure and series of forms for the sharing of information between BWC members, and the voluntary undertaking of specified confidence building measures (CBM) by states parties. This process was to include annual reports by each member state on its information exchange and CBM activity to the United Nations Department for Disarmament Affairs (UNDA). This system remains in place and reports by a number of member states are submitted to the UNDA annually.

However, in the event that a state feels it has not achieved satisfaction through the consultative process of Article V, it may under Article VI(1) report an allegation of another party's breach of the BWC's provisions within the context of a complaint to the U.N. Security Council. The Security Council may then make

---

[45] See, e.g., the Sixth Review Conference Final Document. See generally T. Dunworth, R. Mathews, and T. McCormack, *National Implementation of the Biological Weapons Convention*, 11 JOURNAL OF CONFLICT & SECURITY LAW 93 (2006).

the matter the subject of investigation, and if it does so investigate, all BWC parties undertake in Article VI(2) to cooperate with the Council.

The weakness of the BWC's provisions with regard to verification were apparent from early on in the negotiation of the treaty.[46] Negotiations on the BWC got their start from a proposal put forward by the U.K. in 1968. However, as noted above, during this early period there was broad disagreement on the question of whether a single treaty covering both biological and chemical weapons should be pursued, or whether the two technologies should be addressed through separate instruments. By 1971, a superpower consensus had emerged in favor of a separated process of negotiations on chemical and biological weapons prohibition, and the view of the overall work program came to see a robust verification mechanism as necessary to the disarmament of chemical weapons stockpiles, while in the area of biological weapons verification measures were seen to be "dispensible."[47] The draft of the BWC which was put forward by the U.S. and Russia, and which was eventually signed in 1972, received only lukewarm support from a number of states due to its lack of verification and compliance provisions. In its decision not to sign the BWC in 1972, France particularly noted that verification "was a fundamental condition of our adherence," and that the lack of such mechanisms in the view of the French formed a barrier to their membership.[48] In describing its frustration with the treaty text, Sweden's pre-conference submission to the First BWC Review Conference in 1980 included the statement:

Verification of Articles I & II is not envisaged in the Convention. Therefore, violation can only be verified by chance or, possibly, by national means. The possibilities for clandestine violation on a smaller scale are substantial. Present trends of technological and scientific development within states—also states not party to the Convention—and organizations indicate that the potential for production of biological warfare agents is spreading globally.[49]

Succeeding Review Conferences attempted to address this dearth of meaningful verification procedures through consideration and in some cases adoption of a range of measures, from organized consultative groups to a variety of voluntary confidence building measures which could be undertaken by states through information exchange as discussed above. However there was palpable resistance to any proposals for serious reform of the BWC text itself, or to the imposition of significant new verification-related obligations through Review Conference

---

[46] See J. Beard, *The Shortcomings of Indeterminacy in Arms Control Regimes: The Case of the Biological Weapons Convention*, 101 AMERICAN JOURNAL OF INTERNATIONAL LAW 271(2007).

[47] See J. Littlewood, THE BIOLOGICAL WEAPONS CONVENTION: A FAILED REVOLUTION (2005) 16.

[48] ACDA, "Statement by the French Representative (Rapin) to the First Committee of the General Assembly: Biological and Chemical Weapons, November 26, 1973," *Documents on Disarmament 1973*, (U.S. Government Printing Office, 1973) 830.

[49] BWC 1RC, BWC/CONF.I/4 (20 February 1980), 24.

final documents. Jez Littlewood has very usefully described the dynamic of these negotiations as existing between states of a reformist orientation on the one hand, and states of a minimalist orientation on the other:[50]

In the BWC context, however, there was no corresponding political decision to introduce "suppleness" into the U.S. position on biological verification. For the U.S. the criterion remained effective verification and, as such, the BWC, according to the U.S., remained unverifiable... The U.S. preferred the status quo to the prospect of an improved BWC, whereas its Western Group allies accepted complete assurance via verification was unachievable. However, the latter believed that some verification mechanisms would provide them with greater confidence in the BWC. This debate split the Western Group.[51]

The VEREX group of experts met twice in 1992 and twice in 1993 and submitted a final report in September 1993 in which 21 different measures, including a listing of prohibited materials and related technologies, for strengthening the BWC's provisions in the area of verification and compliance monitoring were identified and evaluated. In September 1994 a Special Conference of States Parties was held to consider the VEREX report. One result of this conference was the establishment of an Ad Hoc Group, open to all states, and given a mandate to

consider appropriate measures, including possible verification measures, and draft proposals to strengthen the convention, to be included, as appropriate, in a legally binding instrument, to be submitted for the consideration of the States Parties. In this context, the Ad Hoc Group shall, inter alia consider:

- Definitions of terms and objective criteria, such as lists of bacteriological (biological) agents and toxins, their threshold quantities, as well as equipment and types of activities, where relevant for specific measures designed to strengthen the Convention;...
- A system of measures to promote compliance with the Convention, including, as appropriate, measures identified, examined and evaluated in the VEREX Report. Such measures should apply to all relevant facilities and activities, be reliable, cost effective, non-discriminatory and as non-intrusive as possible, consistent with the effective implementation of the system and should not lead to abuse...[52]

Furthermore, the proposals to be developed by the Ad Hoc Group were to "include, *inter alia*, potential verification measures, as well as agreed procedures and mechanisms for their efficient implementation and measures for the investigation of alleged use."[53]

Through its work in 24 sessions over the succeeding six years, the Ad Hoc Group produced a protocol instrument containing, in addition to a list of prohibited materials and their thresholds, a developed system of provisions for annual declarations by states of the existence on their territory of prohibited materials, procedures for technical assistance and cooperation among states

[50] See J. Littlewood, THE BIOLOGICAL WEAPONS CONVENTION: A FAILED REVOLUTION (2005) 10.
[51] Ibid. at 35.   [52] BWC/SPCONF/1.   [53] Ibid.

parties, and the carrying out of site inspections on the territory of states parties at the request of other states parties. It provided further for an organizational structure including a Conference of States Parties, Executive Council, and Technical Secretariat to administer this new verification and monitoring system. In all, the draft protocol provided for the BWC regime verification procedures and supporting organizational structures essentially equivalent to those found in the CWC and in its administrative body, the Organization for the Prohibition of Chemical Weapons; a reflection of the negotiations and drafting recently completed at the time in the chemical weapons area.

By the summer of 2001, work on the draft protocol had reached an advanced stage, and it appeared that, despite significant issues of disagreement among the states members of the Ad Hoc Group, resolution of these remaining issues was possible and that a final agreed draft of the protocol could be ready for presentation to a Special Conference of States Parties for adoption prior to the Fifth BWC Review Conference, scheduled for November. However, as Jez Littlewood has chronicled, in July of 2001 the United States, for some time a supporter of the reformist movement to produce a legally binding protocol to strengthen the verification provisions of the BWC, rather abruptly and conclusively rejected the proposed draft. It was both the abruptness and absoluteness of the U.S. rejection which seems to have bewildered many states which had, along with the U.S., spent many years developing the protocol. As Littlewood has written of the explanations given by the U.S. for its change in attitude toward the protocol:

None of the... issues were unsolvable; certainly they would have created new problems and prolonged the negotiations, but had the US turned to its allies in early July 2001 and stated that these issues required further consideration if the US was to accept the text, the Western Group would have almost certainly capitulated to the US demands. At this stage of the negotiations the US was in a position to present a *fait accompli* to its allies if it chose to go down that route. It did not do so, and the rejection of the composite text resulted in so much ire because of the lack of any effort whatsoever to address problems which could have been resolved. Again, it was not the text of the Protocol that was the problem *per se*; it was the politics in Washington and the change in political criteria under which the Protocol was judged that was used to reject the composite text...After tipping the balance of power in favour of the *reformists* in 1994, the US killed off a twenty-year *reformist* effort on July 25, 2001.[54]

With this sudden and conclusive shift of U.S. support away from the protocol, the momentum for the adoption of the protocol seemed to eviscerate overnight, and the work of the Ad Hoc Group effectively ground to a halt. As of early 2008 there has been no serious renaissance of attention by the Ad Hoc Group to the issue of the draft protocol, and no discernible progress toward its eventual adoption by BWC members. The "institutional deficit," the continuance of which was

---

[54] J. Littlewood, THE BIOLOGICAL WEAPONS CONVENTION: A FAILED REVOLUTION (2005) 214–215.

assured through the failure of the protocol negotiations, remains a most serious encumbrance upon the effectiveness of the BWC.[55]

Article X

Again reflecting the dual-use nature of many biological materials and related equipment and technologies, Article X(1) of the BWC codifies the residual right of BWC parties, in complement to the prohibitions agreed in Article I, to facilitate and participate in "the fullest possible exchange of equipment, materials and scientific and technological information for the use of bacteriological (biological) agents and toxins for peaceful purposes." And to further recognize the potential benefits to the international community derived from future peaceful innovations in the area of biology and biological chemistry, Article X(1) obligates able parties to "cooperate in contributing individually or together with other States or international organizations to the further development and application of scientific discoveries in the field of bacteriology (biology) for prevention of disease, or for other peaceful purposes."

Article X(2) is addressed to the impact of the BWC's provisions upon the economic development of states, and to the principle that the implementation of the provisions of the BWC should be designed to "avoid hampering the economic or technological development of States Parties... or international cooperation in the field of peaceful bacteriological (biological) activities..." In the final document of the First Review Conference of the BWC, held in 1980, the following text concerning Article X(2) was adopted by consensus:

The Conference notes that since the entry into force of the Convention, increasing importance has been attached by the International community to the principle that the disarmament process should help promote economic and social development, particularly in the developing countries. Accordingly, the Conference calls upon States Parties, especially developed countries, to increase, individually, or together with other States or international organizations, their scientific and technological co-operation, particularly with developing countries, in the peaceful uses of bacteriological (biological) agents and toxins. Such co-operation should include, *inter alia*, the transfer and exchange of

---

[55] See O. Kervers, *Strengthening Compliance with the Biological Weapons Convention: the Draft Protocol*, 8 JOURNAL OF CONFLICT AND SECURITY LAW 197 (2003); K.D. Ward, *The BWC Protocol: Mandate for Failure*, THE NONPROLIFERATION REVIEW, Volume 11:2 (Summer 2004); G.S. Pearson, *The Composite Protocol Text: An Evaluation of the Costs and Benefits to States Parties*, The BTWC Protocol Evaluation Paper No. 21 (University of Bradford, 2001); K.C. Bailey, *Why the United States Rejected the Protocol to the Biological and Toxin Weapons Convention*, National Institute for Public Policy, October 2002, <http://www.nipp.org/publications.php>. The Sixth Review Conference of the BWC decided in December 2006 to create and fund an Implementation Support Unit (ISU) within the Office for Disarmament Affairs (UNODA) of the United Nations Office at Geneva. The role of the ISU is "to support the work of States Parties during the 2007–2010 intersessional process; in the comprehensive implementation and universalization of the convention; and through the exchange of confidence-building measures." <http://www.unog.ch/80256EDD006B8954/(httpAssets)/53FC4512797DE8D0C125733A0034A554/$file/FLYER.pdf>.

information, training of personnel and transfer of materials and equipment on a more systematic and long-term basis.

Article X is of course a corollary to Article I as it establishes a category for treatment of materials which do not fall under the proscriptive provisions of the category established in Article I. The question of the difficulty in distinction between materials which is necessary to making this categorization, leads again to the question of definition of materials and delineation of thresholds which the VEREX group of experts and the Ad Hoc Group sought to address through their efforts. However, as explained above, no authoritative source for this effort of distinction has yet been produced.

C. The Chemical Weapons Convention

Following the horrific uses of chemical weapons by Iraq during its 1980–88 war with Iran, and particularly its use of chemical weapons to subdue the Iraqi Kurdish population in the north of the country in the late 1980s, momentum in the international community began to increase for the conclusion of a multilateral treaty banning the possession of chemical weapons outright. The movement for a treaty banning chemical weapons had begun at the same time as the movement for banning biological weapons in the late 1960s; however as explained above the politics of the Cold War prevented agreement in the area of chemical weapons until after the dissolution of the Soviet Union in 1991.

As with all multilateral treaties, the final draft of the Chemical Weapons Convention[56] which was opened for signature on January 13, 1993 was the result of years of sometimes difficult negotiations and significant compromise among its drafters. However, notwithstanding the difficulty in its production, the CWC text as it emerged in 1993, and came into force in 1997, can be viewed as one of the great accomplishments in the history of multilateral treaty-making, and a superior piece of legal draftsmanship. It is the product of a trend in multilateral treaty negotiation toward the production of texts not only incorporating substantive norms, but also creating by their terms supplementary organizational structures mandated to facilitate and monitor the implementation of those norms among treaty parties. Other treaty regimes of this type include the 1985 Vienna Convention for the Protection of the Ozone Layer and the 1994 World Trade Organization Agreement.

---

[56] Formally "The Convention on the Prohibition of the Development, Production, Stockpiling and use of Chemical Weapons and on their Destruction," opened for signature, January 13, 1993, Paris, entered into force April 29, 1997, 32 INTERNATIONAL LEGAL MATERIALS 800. See generally W. Krutzsch and R. Trapp, A COMMENTARY ON THE CHEMICAL WEAPONS CONVENTION (1994) 16–17; W. Krutzsch and R. Trapp, VERIFICATION PRACTICE UNDER THE CHEMICAL WEAPONS CONVENTION: A COMMENTARY (1999); R. Thakur (ed.), THE CHEMICAL WEAPONS CONVENTION: IMPLEMENTATION, CHALLENGES AND OPPORTUNITIES (2006); T. Bernauer, THE PROJECTED CHEMICAL WEAPONS CONVENTION: A GUIDE TO THE NEGOTIATIONS IN THE CONFERENCE ON DISARMAMENT (1990); I. Detter, THE LAW OF WAR (2nd edn, 2000) 263–266; E. Myjer (ed.), ISSUES OF ARMS CONTROL LAW AND THE CHEMICAL WEAPONS CONVENTION (2001).

The CWC establishes a highly developed regime of substantive prohibitions as well as positive duties in the area of chemical weapons proliferation, binding equally upon all treaty parties. These basic duties are refined in their scope by the inclusion of detailed, albeit non-exclusive, lists of covered materials in its Annex on Chemicals. These substantive duties are then supplemented by provisions in Article VIII of the convention which establish an international organization to aid in the verification of treaty commitments, and also by a comprehensive set of verification procedures and rules on implementation contained in the Convention's Annex on Implementation and Verification.

The developed, comprehensive, administratively robust international legal regime for regulating chemical weapons proliferation created by the CWC is in many ways a culmination of lessons learned through the experiences of the international community in the operation of the NPT/IAEA regime in the nuclear weapons area and the BWC regime in the biological weapons area. The seamless nature of the CWC text's inclusion of definitions of terms, lists of covered materials, as well as the administrative mechanism for verifying and facilitating compliance represent major improvements over both prior models.

Articles I and II

When interpreting the scope of the obligations of parties to the CWC, Articles I and II of the treaty must be read very much in concert with each other, as the definitions in Article II provide essential meaning to the basic recitations of obligation contained in Article I.

Thus, the obligations in Article I "never under any circumstances" to "develop, produce, otherwise acquire, stockpile or retain chemical weapons;" to "use chemical weapons;" to "transfer, directly or indirectly, chemical weapons to anyone;" to "engage in any military preparations to use chemical weapons;" or to "assist, encourage or induce, in any way, anyone to engage in any activity prohibited to a State Party under this Convention," are all contingent in their meaning upon the definitions given to the terms "chemical weapon," "toxic chemical," and "precursor" in Article II.

Within Article II(1), which defines the term "chemical weapon," we find the essential definition employing the purposive formula originating in Article I of the BWC.[57] Thus, chemical weapons are "[t]oxic chemicals and their precursors, except where intended for purposes not prohibited under this Convention, as long as the types and quantities are consistent with such purposes." Article II(2) then defines toxic chemicals as "[a]ny chemical which through its chemical action on life processes can cause death, temporary incapacitation or permanent harm to humans or animals. This includes all such chemicals, regardless of their origin or of their method of production, and regardless of whether they are produced in facilities, in munitions or elsewhere."

---

[57] G. Pearson, *The Importance of Implementation of the General Purpose Criterion of the Chemical Weapons Convention*, 55 KEMIJAU INDUSTRIJI 413 (2006).

Article II(9) further defines "Purposes not prohibited under this Convention" to include

(a) industrial, agricultural, research, medical, pharmaceutical or other peaceful purposes;
(b) protective purposes, namely those purposes directly related to protection against toxic chemicals and to protection against chemical weapons;
(c) military purposes not connected with the use of chemical weapons and not dependent on the use of the toxic properties of chemicals as a method of warfare;
(d) law enforcement including domestic riot control purposes.

As in the context of the BWC, this general purpose formula allows for comprehensive and inclusive application of the prohibitive terms of the convention, even to newly developed materials falling within the definitional ambit of "[t]oxic chemicals and their precursors," through the establishment of a presumption of prohibition. Thus, as Ralf Trapp has explained, under the terms of Article I *"Any* toxic or precursor chemical is regarded as a chemical weapon *unless* it has been developed, produced, stockpiled or used for purposes *not* prohibited, and only as long as types and quantities are consistent with such purposes."[58]

In the context of Article I(1), as defined in Article II, a number of important points bear mention. The first is with regard to the relationship between the materials listed in the Annex on Chemicals and the basic obligations of the general purpose criteria of Article I. As the parenthetical additions to Articles II(2) and II(3) make clear, the chemical agents listed in the Annex on Chemicals consist only of those toxic chemicals which have been "identified for the application of verification measures" contained within the Annex on Implementation and Verification. These chemical agents do not represent an exclusive list of agents subject to the terms of Article I and are not a substitute for the general purpose definitions of Article II. The agents listed in the schedules of the Annex on Chemicals thus comprise only a sub-grouping, or representative listing of materials subject to the terms of the CWC. As the Annex on Chemicals Section B states "Pursuant to Article II, subparagraph 1 (a), these Schedules do not constitute a definition of chemical weapons." This is an important distinction to bear in mind in preserving the comprehensive reach of the definitions of Article II particularly to newly developed materials.[59]

---

[58] R. Trapp, "The Chemical Weapons Convention—Multilateral Instrument with a Future," in R. Thakur, (ed.), The Chemical Weapons Convention: Implementation, Challenges and Opportunities (2006) 20.

[59] See Organization for the Prohibition of Chemical Weapons, Note by Director General, Report of the Scientific Advisory Board on Developments in Science and Technology, RC-1/DG.2/23 April 2003 ("The definition of CW contained in Article II, as well as the provisions of the Schedules of Chemicals, make it clear that the Schedules do not embrace the entire scope of the Convention. The Convention's prohibitions related to 'chemical weapons' apply to all toxic chemicals and their precursors, except when intended for purposes not prohibited by the Convention, as long as the

With regard to the scope of the obligations listed in Article I(1), a further element of the definition of "chemical weapon" in Article II(1) is instructive. Unlike other arms control and non-proliferation treaties, including the NPT, which define their subject "weapons" as the cumulative entirety of their component parts,[60] Article II(1) of the CWC defines a chemical weapon to mean the following "*together* or *separately*":

(a) Toxic chemicals and their precursors, except where intended for purposes not prohibited under this Convention, as long as the types and quantities are consistent with such purposes;

(b) Munitions and devices, specifically designed to cause death or other harm through the toxic properties of those toxic chemicals specified in subparagraph (a), which would be released as a result of the employment of such munitions and devices;

(c) Any equipment specifically designed for use directly in connection with the employment of munitions and devices specified in subparagraph (b).

Thus, the terms of the CWC apply their prohibitions not only to the totality of the component parts of a chemical weapon as traditionally conceived, but also equally to each of the component parts themselves. This means for example that artillery shells designed specifically to deliver binary chemical weapons, or non-toxic precursor chemicals manufactured in bulk for purposes of a chemical weapons program, are themselves considered chemical weapons even before they are incorporated into their intended end-product weapons. This expansive definition allows the prohibitions of the CWC to attach to a variety of materials, for example the dual-use low-toxicity precursor chemicals chlorine and phosgene, previously untouched by international law.[61]

Finally with regard to the Article I(1)(a) prohibition on transfers of chemical weapons, reference to the Annex on Implementation and Verification (AIV) provides an important delineation of obligations with regard to transfers of chemicals scheduled within the Annex on Chemicals. AIV Part VI(B) paragraph 3 provides that "A State Party may transfer Schedule 1 chemicals outside its territory only to

types and quantities are consistent with such purposes. Without that broad scope, chemical warfare agents of novel identity (including those which are as yet undisclosed or undiscovered) would remain outside the reach of the Convention.") See, e.g., R.D. Pinson, *Is Nanotechnology Prohibited by the Biological and Chemical Weapons Conventions?* 22 BERKELEY JOURNAL OF INTERNATIONAL LAW 279 (2004).

[60] One example is presented by the definition of nuclear weapons in the Treaty of Tlatelolco, Article 5: "For the purposes of this Treaty, a nuclear weapon is any device which is capable of releasing nuclear energy in an uncontrolled manner and which has a group of characteristics that are appropriate for use for warlike purposes. An instrument that may be used for the transport or propulsion of the device is not included in this definition if it is separable from the device and not an indivisible part thereof."

[61] R. Trapp, "The Chemical Weapons Convention—Multilateral Instrument with a Future," in R. Thakur (ed.), THE CHEMICAL WEAPONS CONVENTION: IMPLEMENTATION, CHALLENGES AND OPPORTUNITIES (2006) 20.

another State Party and only for research, medical, pharmaceutical or protective purposes…" Schedule 1 materials, which are those of the highest relative toxicity and/or risk to the object and purpose of the CWC, may therefore only be transferred between states parties to the CWC, and only for specific peaceful purposes.

Schedule 2 chemicals, those of the next highest relative toxicity and/or risk to the object and purpose of the CWC, were originally transferable by CWC member states either to other CWC member states or to states not members of the CWC, subject in the latter circumstance to the provision of an end-use certificate and to due diligence on the part of the exporting state. However, AIV Part VII(C) paragraph 31 provides: "Schedule 2 chemicals shall only be transferred to or received from States Parties. This obligation shall take effect three years after entry into force of this Convention." Thus, as of April 29, 2000, Schedule 2 chemicals cannot be exported to or imported from non-party states.

Pursuant to AIV Part VIII(C) paragraphs 26 and 27, Schedule 3 chemicals, those of lowest relative toxicity and/or risk to the object and purpose of the CWC within the schedules, as well as unfilled munitions and devices and equipment designed specifically to employ chemical weapons included in Schedule 3, may be transferred either to CWC states parties or to non-party states. However end-use certificates are currently required for exports of Schedule 3 chemicals and materials to non-party states.

Within the other subparagraphs of Article I additional fundamental obligations are to be found. In subparagraph 2, the parties undertake to destroy all chemical weapons possessed by them or located within territory under their jurisdiction or control. With regard to this latter category of location, Walter Krutzsch and Ralf Trapp have commented:

This compels states parties to use jurisdiction with regard to natural and legal persons on its territory, in other places under the jurisdiction outside the territory and on vessels flying its flag or on aircraft registered under the national law, to implement the destruction obligation. The same goes for places under the control of a state party, that means places over which the state party exercises factual power or authority, in particular occupied territories…In cases in which the legal status of a place is disputed, for instance in an occupied territory, the state party actually exercising the control is addressed by this provision.[62]

Pursuant to Article III(1)(a), states parties are to make a declaration of all chemical weapons which are to be destroyed under the Article I(2) obligation. Article IV(6) then specifies that the full destruction of subject materials shall be accomplished by each state party within 10 years of the coming into force of the convention for it, in accordance with the rate and sequence of destruction spelled out in the AIV. The AIV's basic obligation for the destruction of Schedule 1-based chemical weapons in terms of time period is not more that 10 years after entry into force of the convention. However AIV Part IV(C) allows states to apply to the OPCW on

---

[62] W. Krutzsch and R. Trapp, A COMMENTARY ON THE CHEMICAL WEAPONS CONVENTION (1994) 16–17.

the basis of "exceptional circumstances" for an extension of this deadline to no more than 15 years after entry into force. Thus, all CWC parties are obligated to destroy all Schedule 1-based chemical weapons at least by April 29, 2012.

The progress of the largest possessors of declared chemical weapons stockpiles in meeting their obligation of destruction of Schedule 1-based chemical weapons under CWC Article I(2) was summarized in April 2007 by the Arms Control Association using the following tabulated information:[63]

Table 2.1. Possessor States' Category I Destruction Implementation

	Declared Category 1 Stockpile	Revised Destruction Deadline	Agents	Remaining Stockpile	Projection
Albania	16 metric tons	4/29/2007	Mustard	Unknown	Generally estimated to miss deadline by several weeks.
India	1,055 metric tons	4/28/2009	Unknown	578 metric tons on 12/31/2005	Will meet deadline.
Libya	23.6 metric tons	12/31/2010	Lewisite, Mustard, Phosgene, Sarin, Tabun	23.6 metric tons	No projection.
Russia	40,000 metric tons	4/29/2012	Lewisite, Mustard, Phosgene, Sarin, Soman, VX	Russia projects 31,000 metric tons on 4/29/2007	Will not meet deadline; U.S. Government Accountability Office estimates 2007.
South Korea	605 metric tons	12/31/2008	Unknown	304 tons on 12/31/2005	Will probably meet deadline.
United States	27,771 metric tons	4/29/2012	Binary nerve agents, Lewisite, Mustard, Sarin, Soman, VX	16,317 tons on 3/11/2007	Will not meet deadline; U.S. Department of Defense estimates 2023.

[63] Original available at <http://www.armscontrol.org/factsheets/cwcglance.asp>. In presenting this information, the Arms Control Association notes: "these figures are inferences from the Organization for the Prohibition of Chemical Weapons December 2006 implementation report, *Report of the OCPW on the Implementation of the Convention of the Prohibition of the Development, Production, Stockpiling and Use of Chemical Weapons and on their Destruction in 2005.*" Because these figures must by necessity be based upon inferences (all but one of the six possessor states having withheld their declarations from public scrutiny), there are likely some errors of fact presented therein. The information has been reprinted here not to give an accurate accounting, which is an impossible task given the closed nature of sources, but rather to give the reader a general idea of the amounts and types of chemicals possessed by the largest possessor states, and schedules for destruction.

This obligation to destroy is extended in Article I(3) to all chemical weapons abandoned by states parties on the territory of another state party. This provision has particular relevance to Japan, and to that country's abandonment of approximately two million chemical weapon munitions on the territory of China during World War II. The Japanese Imperial Army had used chemical weapons during its conquest and occupation of China between 1937 and 1945. These chemical attacks resulted in approximately 10,000 fatalities and 80,000 injuries, according to Chinese sources. Most of these munitions contained a mustard gas–lewisite mixture and were abandoned primarily in the north-eastern provinces of Heilongjiang, Liaoning, and Jilin. Since the coming into force of the CWC, the Japanese and Chinese Governments have cooperated in fact-finding efforts and have agreed upon a protocol for destruction of these abandoned munitions, with Japan bearing the financial costs of the disposal.[64]

The subparagraph 3 obligation to destroy abandoned chemical weapons notably does not include chemical weapons abandoned on the territory of a non-state party, or abandoned on the high seas or other area not under the jurisdiction or control of a state party. Parts VII and XII of the 1982 Law of the Sea Convention, among other largely subscribed multilateral treaty provisions, include environmental protection obligations which effectively forbid the dumping of toxic chemicals at sea; however this does not address materials already abandoned at sea. Indeed, Article III(2) expressly states regarding the Article III obligations of declaration that:

[t]he provisions of this Article and the relevant provisions of Part IV of the Verification Annex shall not, at the discretion of a State Party, apply to chemical weapons buried on its territory before 1 January 1977 and which remain buried, or which had been dumped at sea before 1 January 1985.

Article I(1) and Non-Lethal Weapons

As Julian Robinson has described:

In the ability of CBW agents to target themselves on particular life processes, there is growing scope for users of weapons based on them to "tailor" the nature or severity of their effects to a strategic objective...That same tailoring can, however, provide weapons of an altogether more acceptable character, including ones having effects gentler than most other means of violence. Examples include the "tear gas" of police forces; the psychochemical weapons that, according to past US Army teaching, would cause the enemy to "linger in overpowering reverie"; and the entirely mythical knock-out agents of "war without death" that have figured in science fiction since the Nineteenth Century...A rather wide variety of commercial, political and military interests stand to benefit from exclusion of some or all of these non-WMD CBW from the governance regime. *Sub rosa* campaigning to that end has long been under way, most notably

---

[64] See "Abandoned Chemical Weapons in China," Monterrey Institute Center for Nonproliferation Studies, available at <http://www.nti.org/db/china/acwpos.htm>.

during the last months of the CWC negotiation in mid-1992, when the new protagonists of Non Lethal Warfare (NLW) came up against governmental officials charged with securing consensus on those parts of the CWC text that dealt with "riot control agents" (RCA). The issue turned then on whether RCA should or should not fall within the definition of "toxic chemicals", subject, thereby, to the general purpose criterion that would serve to regulate the duality of their application either in warfare (prohibited) or in law-enforcement (permitted). The USA favoured exclusion but, finding itself isolated in this position within the Western Group, secured a compromise in which the CWC expressly prohibited use of RCA "as a method of warfare" but remained silent on the toxic character of RCA, thus perpetuating a semblance of ambiguity on whether the toxicity criterion fundamental to the CWC did or did not capture RCA... The process that can be seen here is a surreptitious equation of toxicity with lethal toxicity, and in this attempt to loosen the CWC constraint on the weaponization of other forms of toxicity we have started to see a creeping legitimation of non-WMD CBW, which is a most serious challenge to the regime. A situation in which some types of toxic weapon are allowed but not others is certain to be unstable.[65]

The basic or presumptive rule of Article I(1) of the CWC is, as has been seen, that chemical weapons are prohibited (i.e. their possession, development, transfer, and use are prohibited). Through the definition of chemical weapon in Article II(1) this obligation is clarified as providing that toxic chemicals (among other things) are chemical weapons. Therefore the presumptive rule (in its lesser included form) restated is that toxic chemicals are prohibited by Article I(1). However, pursuant to Article II(1), if a toxic chemical is intended for purposes not prohibited by the convention (provided that types and quantities of the chemical are consistent with this purpose) then this purpose establishes an exception excluding the subject material from the application of the basic prohibitive rule regarding toxic chemicals.

Most, though not all, non-lethal chemicals used either for law enforcement or military purposes do fall under the definition of toxic chemicals provided in Article II(2), in that they at least cause temporary incapacitation in their targets (this being their *raison d'etre* in the context of either law enforcement or military use).

Thus, in order not to be prohibited as chemical weapons under the presumptive rule of Article I(1), toxic non-lethal chemicals (sometimes referred to categorically in this context as non-lethal weapons (NLW)) employed by militaries or law enforcement agencies must be intended for use for a purpose not prohibited under the CWC.[66] There are two provisions of Article II(9) which are most applicable in this context: subparagraphs (c) and (d).

---

[65] J. Robinson, "Chemical and Biological Weapons," in N. Busch and D.H. Joyner (eds), COMBATING WEAPONS OF MASS DESTRUCTION: THE FUTURE OF INTERNATIONAL NONPROLIFERATION POLICY (2009) 86–87.

[66] On the subject of toxic vs non-toxic chemicals and lethality, it is important to note that, in the end, the dose of the chemical in question can determine both its toxicity and its lethality.

Article II(9)(c)

Under Article II(9)(c), toxic non-lethal chemicals can be used for military purposes under two express conditions to be read conjunctively; each a separate condition precedent to the functioning of this exception from the Article I(1) presumptive prohibitive rule. Those military purposes for which toxic non-lethal chemicals are used must

1. not be connected with the use of chemical weapons; and
2. not be dependent on the use of the toxic properties of chemicals as a method of warfare.

In keeping with the basic definition of a chemical weapon, then, in order to satisfy condition precedent number one, toxic non-lethal chemicals used for military purposes must not accomplish their intended purpose through the operation upon a target of the toxicity of the material being utilized. Explosive chemicals, rocket fuels, incendiaries, and smoke devices which do not accomplish their intended purpose through the operation of toxicity would fall under this category.[67]

In order to satisfy condition precedent number two, the same use of toxic non-lethal chemicals for military purposes, in addition to not accomplishing its purpose through the use of the toxic properties of the material, must also not be a use of the material as a method of warfare.

The term "method of warfare" as a legal term of art first appears in the context of a multilateral treaty in Protocol I to the 1949 Geneva Conventions.[68] In its Article 35 the Protocol provides that "[i]n any armed conflict, the right of the parties to the conflict to choose methods or means of warfare is not unlimited." It is important to bear in mind, however, that the term "method of warfare" under consideration herein is the appearance of this term within the specific and independent context of the CWC, and thus while the meaning of the term in the context of its appearance in other treaties including Geneva Convention Protocol I is instructive to determining its meaning in the CWC context, it must be remembered that the treaty context is in the end different. Thus, in applying this term in the CWC context, one is not bound in interpretation to the parameters of the use of the same term in the Geneva Convention context, e.g. as to what sort of armed conflict can be applied the law of the Geneva Conventions, or on the principle of the exclusive application of the law of the Geneva Conventions as between parties to the Conventions.

See M. Wheelis, *Biotechnology and Biochemical Weapons*, 9 The Nonproliferation Review 48 (Spring 2002).

[67] W. Krutzsch and R. Trapp, A Commentary on the Chemical Weapons Convention (1994) 42.

[68] See generally E. Harper, *A Call for Definition of Method of Warfare in Relation to the Chemical Weapons Convention*, 48 Naval Law Review 132 (2001).

In applying the term "method of warfare" in the CWC context, therefore, distinction need not be made strictly along Geneva Convention lines between international armed conflict and non-international armed conflict.[69] Rather, the term must be interpreted using the interpretive method prescribed in the Vienna Convention on the Law of Treaties, Articles 31 and 32, which focuses on the ordinary meaning of treaty terms, in their context and in the light of the treaty's object and purpose.

Importantly for purposes of interpretation, this term in Article II(9)(c) of the CWC does not provide that toxic chemicals may be used for military purposes "in wartime." This rendering would emphasize the context of the conflict, and its legal status as "war" or "not war" as being determinative of the legality of the use of toxic chemicals including toxic non-lethal chemicals.

Rather, the provision provides that toxic chemicals including toxic non-lethal chemicals may not be used for military purposes as a "method of warfare." This rendering thus emphasizes the method, or the way in which the toxic chemical is used, and the importance of this inquiry in determining whether it is a prohibited method of warfare.[70]

A method of warfare can generally be defined as a means of violence, or procedure for applying a means of violence, used against enemy belligerents, including both regular armed forces and insurgents, in an armed conflict of either an international or non-international character.[71] This definition is in accord with modern definitions of war as encompassing both international armed conflict and some varieties of non-international armed conflict, as well as the trend in both international humanitarian law and international criminal law to extend the protections and obligations of international law to the prosecution of non-international armed conflicts.[72]

Thus, in determining whether a toxic chemical has been used for military purposes as a prohibited method of warfare, the most important question is not what is the character of the armed conflict in which the use takes place, but rather against whom is the chemical being used and in what context.

In applying this interpretation of the Article I(1) obligation in the particular context of toxic non-lethal chemicals including toxic riot control agents, it is clear that any use of toxic chemicals including toxic non-lethal chemicals against belligerents, including both regular armed forces and insurgents, in either an international or non-international armed conflict, is prohibited by the CWC, in

---

[69] See L.C. Green, THE CONTEMPORARY LAW OF ARMED CONFLICT (2nd edn, 2000) ch. 3.

[70] See Y. Sandoz et al. (eds), COMMENTARY ON THE ADDITIONAL PROTOCOLS OF 8 JUNE 1977 TO THE GENEVA CONVENTIONS OF 12 AUGUST 1949 (1987) 398, paras 1401 and 1402.

[71] W. Krutzsch and R. Trapp, A COMMENTARY ON THE CHEMICAL WEAPONS CONVENTION (1994) 18–19; J. Bond, THE RULES OF RIOT (1974) 51–58.

[72] M. Shaw, INTERNATIONAL LAW (5th edn, 2003) 1068–1072; I. Detter, THE LAW OF WAR (2nd edn, 2000) 17–26; A. Cassese, INTERNATIONAL CRIMINAL LAW (2003) 37–41.

addition to whatever other prohibitions may be in force flowing from the Geneva Conventions or other source of international law.

With regard to the scope of this obligation in the CWC context, unlike the 1949 Geneva Conventions, the CWC contains no limitation on the observance of its obligations with regard to conduct affecting non-parties to the CWC.[73] Thus, the obligations of Article I of the CWC are to be observed by CWC parties with regard to their conduct whether or not that conduct is pursued for the purpose of affecting CWC parties or non-parties. Again, there is no Geneva Convention-like limitation with regard to uses of toxic chemicals as against non-CWC members. The CWC's obligations are universal.

Having thus established this general obligation, some brief consideration will be given to the most controversial issues concerning the use of toxic non-lethal chemicals in situation of armed conflict. Such issues have included the use of such chemicals in peacekeeping operations, in occupied territories, and as against civilians in the context of insurgencies.

Again, using the interpretation of the Article I(1) obligation employed herein, the character of an armed conflict is not the most probative fact in determining whether the use of a toxic chemical for military purposes is a prohibited method of warfare. Thus, the fact of such a usage in the context of a peacekeeping operation or in occupied territories does not per se bear materially on this determination of legality.

As in the context of an international armed conflict, the use of a toxic chemical for military purposes in the context of a peacekeeping operation or in occupied territories will constitute a prohibited method of warfare if that use is against belligerents, including regular military forces or insurgents, in the prosecution of an armed conflict. The few military purposes justifying the use of toxic chemicals as against belligerents in an armed conflict include riot control in the context of prisoner of war camps or military prisons.[74]

As consideration turns to the subject of the use for military purposes of toxic chemicals, including toxic non-lethal chemicals such as riot control agents, as against civilians within the context of an occupation and/or insurgency, the question becomes one of the connection of civilian activity with the continuing armed conflict.[75] If a civilian group is actively supporting belligerents partici-pating in an armed conflict, then as a result of this connection, the use of toxic chemicals by opposing military forces against such civilians would be a method of warfare, and would thus be prohibited by Article I(1) of the CWC.

---

[73] See Common Article 2 of the Geneva Conventions.

[74] W. Krutzsch and R. Trapp, A COMMENTARY ON THE CHEMICAL WEAPONS CONVENTION (1994) 42.

[75] See by analogy the nexus test applied to ground international criminal liability for acts against civilians. See, e.g., the ICTY Appeals Chamber Judgment (June 12, 2002) in the *Kunarac* case, paras 58–59.

Article II(9)(d)

On the question of the use of toxic chemicals, including non-lethal chemicals such as riot control agents, against civilians by foreign military forces in an occupied territory where those civilians are not engaging in activity in connection with a continuing armed conflict, neither Article II(9)(c) nor Article II(9)(d) would appear to justify this purpose as one not prohibited by CWC Article I(1).

Article II(9)(d) provides that "law enforcement including domestic riot control" comprises an additional "purpose not prohibited," which can serve to exclude a use of toxic chemicals from the prohibitive terms of Article I(1). This provision effectively excludes most uses of toxic chemicals by government agents as against civilians within the domestic sovereign jurisdiction of the government, provided the use may be classified as law enforcement. Use of toxic chemicals, such as tear gas, for law enforcement often though not exclusively occurs in the riot control context.

Some have read Article II(9)(d) in a bifurcated manner, holding that the term "law enforcement" in the provision is broad in scope so as to include within its meaning both domestic law enforcement as well as law enforcement in territory not within the sovereign jurisdiction of a state, but rather only under its occupation jurisdiction, or jurisdiction otherwise conferred upon the state through, e.g., U.N. Security Council resolution. Under this reading, the terms "including domestic riot control" serve as a non-exclusive sub-delineation of activities included within the prior broadly exculpatory term "law enforcement."

A better reading, however, and one more in line with the *travaux préparatoires* of the CWC which clearly emphasizes domestic law enforcement, is that the entire provision refers only to domestic law enforcement, or law enforcement over territory within the sovereign jurisdiction of the acting state government. Under this reading, the inclusion of "domestic riot control" serves to delineate in an exclusionary manner that only domestic riot control, and not riot control in non-sovereign territory, is contemplated to be included within this exception from the general purpose criteria of Article I(1).

Thus, under this interpretation of Article II(9)(d), taken together with the previously determined interpretation of Article II(9)(c), it can be concluded that the use of toxic chemicals by a foreign military against civilians in an occupied territory is in all cases prohibited by Article I(1) of the CWC.[76]

---

[76] This conclusion is in disharmony with that advanced by I. Lombardo in "Chemical Non-Lethal Weapons—Why the Pentagon Wants them and Why Others Don't," Monterrey Institute of International Studies, Center for Nonproliferation Studies, June 8, 2007. Available at <http://cns.miis.edu/pubs/week/070608.htm>.

Application of the Scope of Article I(1)

The scope of the Article I(1) prohibition, as interpreted herein, will serve to find prohibited certain uses by the United States, for example, of toxic chemicals for military purposes in its continuing prosecution of armed conflicts in Iraq and Afghanistan. In Afghanistan, such a prohibited use of toxic chemicals occurred in the context of "cave clearing" activities against enemy belligerents, as described by James Fry:

At the beginning of the War in Afghanistan, some analysts encouraged the use of gases to force combatants out of the caves. Apparently the U.S. military had these same thoughts, as it made the use of CS tear gas a fundamental part of its cave-clearing techniques. When cave-clearing teams fear enemy attack in a cave, they use a burning type CS grenade (M7A2) and a Mity Mite Portable Blower to "flush the enemy from the tunnels." Once a cave is cleared, CS is placed throughout the cave and CS powder is blown into the cave's entrance by the Mity Mite in order to temporarily prevent re-entry by enemy forces until the cave complex can be completely demolished.[77]

As CWC Article I(1) prohibits inter alia development, possession, or military preparations to use prohibited toxic chemicals, the U.S. military's research regarding development and possession of chemicals and their precursors for the purpose of prohibited activities of this nature are also, independently, violations of the CWC's terms.[78]

Article I(5)

In light of the foregoing analysis and interpretation of Article I(1), Article I(5) seems a largely redundant addition to the terms of the treaty, as it simply re-identifies an obligation subsumed under the Article I(1) obligation. Article I(5) was clearly meant, as explained by Julian Robinson above, to introduce some ambiguity into the terms of the CWC on the question of the scope of Article I(1)'s prohibition of chemical weapons in the context of riot control agents.[79] However, as the analysis of the text as offered herein makes clear, the comprehensive scope of Article I(1) and its application to toxic non-lethal chemicals including many riot control agents stands independently of Article I(5) and there is no principle of treaty interpretation which demands any dimming of the clarity of this scope as a result of the addition of Article 1(5) to the treaty text, particularly when the *travaux préparatoires* of the convention, in which this somewhat subversive intent on the part of one state party is laid bare, is considered as provided in VCLT Article 32.

---

[77] *Contextualized Legal Reviews For The Methods And Means Of Warfare: Cave Combat And International Humanitarian Law*, 44 COLUMBIA JOURNAL OF TRANSNATIONAL LAW 453 (2006).

[78] See I. Lombardo "Chemical Non-Lethal Weapons—Why the Pentagon Wants them and Why Others Don't," Monterrey Institute of International Studies, Center for Nonproliferation Studies, June 8, 2007. Available at <http://cns.miis.edu/pubs/week/070608.htm>.

[79] See below 106–107.

To be clear, this should not be framed as an issue of *lex specialis*, or that of a more specific provision of a legal text being read out in favor of a more general provision in violation of this interpretive canon. Rather, it should be framed as an issue of redundancy in the provisions of the same legal text. In this case, Article I(5) should be seen as a redundant provision of lesser included scope which has obfuscatory rather than specifying intent. In such a case, the need for legal clarity should take precedence in interpretation over canons of interpretation favoring the attachment of meaning to every provision of a legal text.

This conclusion is further supported by the VCLT Article 31 rule of treaty interpretation, pursuant to which the meaning of a provision of a treaty is to be interpreted in its context within the treaty, and in light of the treaty's overall object and purpose. In the case of the CWC, the object and purpose of the treaty is clearly to establish a broad prohibition on the development, possession, transfer, and use of toxic chemicals for non-civilian, non-peaceful purposes. In context, as concluded above, the ordinary meaning of the terms of Article I(5) can be interpreted as redundant of the ordinary meaning of previous provisions. Taken together for purposes of interpretation, therefore, the object and purpose of the treaty, and the context of the provision within the treaty, both argue for primacy, independence, and universal application of the terms of Article I(1), and a reading of Article I(5) which does not in any way obscure or confuse the Article I(1) obligation, but rather simply reiterates a part of it.

If there is anything additionally meaningful contained in the obligation defined in Article 1(5), it is to be found in the clarification provided by definitional Article II(7) of the meaning of the term "riot control agent." This definition of riot control agent as "any chemical not listed in a Schedule, which can produce rapidly in humans sensory irritation or disabling physical effects which disappear within a short time following termination of exposure" would appear to extend the reach of the CWC's prohibitory terms to include non-toxic riot control agents, e.g. those which do not cause temporary incapacitation but only "sensory irritation," in addition to Article I(1)'s previously described regulation of toxic non-lethal chemicals, into which latter category fall most chemicals used for riot control purposes.

Thus, under this interpretation of Article I(5), even non-toxic chemicals which produce only sensory irritation may not be used as a method of warfare by CWC members, as that term has been interpreted herein.

Monitoring and Verification Mechanism

As previously noted, one of the chief successes of the CWC distinguishing it from both the NPT and the BWC was its inclusion within its text of a developed and universal scheme for monitoring and verification of its basic obligations contained in Article I.[80] This monitoring and verification mechanism, complete with *sui generis* supervisory administrative organs, is contained within Articles III through XI of the treaty, as supplemented by the Annex on Chemicals and the highly detailed AIV.

This mechanism may be summarized as follows. All CWC parties are to make a declaration of all chemical weapons and chemical weapons production facilities which it possesses, or which are on its territory. This declaration must be followed by a detailed plan for destruction of all such chemical weapons and chemical weapons production facilities. Each state shall proceed with its destruction of all chemical weapons and closing of all chemical weapons production facilities according to the guidelines and schedules specified in the convention.[81]

Each state shall further provide access to all such materials and facilities for the purpose of on-site inspection and verification by the Organization for the Prohibition of Chemical Weapons (OPCW), the umbrella organization for the various monitoring and verification organs and activities provided for within the CWC. Inspections by members of the OPCW Technical Secretariat proceed according to a schedule agreed between the organization and the subject member state, and detailed procedures for the conduct of inspections are laid out in the AIV. The OPCW states on its website that to date it has conducted over 3,000 such on-site inspections in 79 member states.[82] The OPCW further concludes standing arrangements with member states to continue monitoring sites through the use of video and other electronic detection equipment.

All states parties are to cooperate with other states parties in requests for information regarding chemical weapons and chemical weapons production facilities, particularly when such information is requested in order to clarify or resolve a matter which "may cause doubt about compliance with this Convention, or which gives rise to concerns about a related matter which may be considered ambiguous." Such requests for information may be made directly as between states parties, or alternatively through the intermediary offices of the OPCW.

If, however, a state party feels that it has not been satisfied through this process of interrogatory, it may request that the OPCW conduct a challenge inspection on "any facility or location in the territory or in any other place under the jurisdiction or control of any other State Party for the sole purpose of clarifying and resolving any questions concerning possible non-compliance

---

[80] See generally W. Krutzsch and R. Trapp, VERIFICATION PRACTICE UNDER THE CHEMICAL WEAPONS CONVENTION: A COMMENTARY (1999).

[81] See B. Kellman, *The Advent of International Chemical Regulation: The Chemical Weapons Convention Implementation Act*, 25 JOURNAL OF LEGISLATION 117 (1999).

[82] <http://www.opcw.org>.

with the provisions of this Convention."[83] The state against whom the challenge inspection has been requested is under a basic obligation to cooperate with the challenge inspection by members of the OPCW Technical Secretariat, unless the OPCW Executive Council (composed of 41 state party members based upon the principle of rotation) determines by a three-fourths vote that the inspection request is "frivolous, abusive, or clearly beyond the scope of [the] convention."[84]

On the basis of the report generated by the Technical Secretariat, the Executive Council may determine whether non-compliance with the CWC's terms has occurred and may instruct the offending state party on measures which it must take to remedy such non-compliance. If the measures directed by the Executive Council are not implemented by the offending state, the issue may be referred by the Council to the Conference of the States Parties (the Conference), the principal organ of the OPCW, comprised of a representative of all states parties. In its discretion, the Conference may restrict or suspend the rights of an offending state party under the convention, and may at the extreme in "cases of particular gravity," refer the matter to the U.N. Security Council.

The challenge inspection aspect of the CWC's monitoring and verification system has been rightly viewed as one if its most revolutionary accomplishments. The breadth of the presumptive right of states parties to request an inspection of any facility under the control of any other state party has the potential to be the ultimate guarantor of the effectiveness of the CWC regime. As Masahiko Asada has explained, this system can act as both a deterrent and confidence-building mechanism:

Although these two functions of deterrence and confidence-building can be found to varying degrees in any type of verification and are not necessarily unique to challenge inspections, the challenge inspection type of verification system could be expected to function far more effectively than others in both respects. This is because most other types of verification system, including the routine-type industry inspection system of the CWC, are based on the declarations made by the States Parties to the relevant treaty implementation bodies, and consequently are not expected to function effectively with regard to undeclared facilities, where proliferating countries may conduct clandestine illegal activities.[85]

Notwithstanding its potential, as of this writing there has not been a single instance of the use or request of the operation of the challenge inspection system. Possible reasons for the reluctance of states to use this procedure include

---

[83] Article IX(9).

[84] Article IX(17). See generally R. Greenlee, *The Fourth Amendment and Facilities Inspections under the Chemical Weapons Convention*, 65 UNIVERSITY OF CHICAGO LAW REVIEW 943 (1998).

[85] M. Asada, "The Challenge Inspection System of the Chemical Weapons Convention: Problems and Prospects," in R. Thakur (ed.), THE CHEMICAL WEAPONS CONVENTION: IMPLEMENTATION, CHALLENGES AND OPPORTUNITIES (2006) 77.

a lack of confidence in the ability of OPCW inspectors acting pursuant to their limited powers under the AIV to detect intentionally hidden non-compliance, generally political considerations averse to the use of compulsory verification procedures in such a sensitive issue area, and the fear of retaliatory challenge inspections and a spiraling, resource demanding, tit-for-tat acrimony between member states.[86]

Article XV

Among the other notable innovations of the CWC text is the bifurcated system for *ex post* alteration of the treaty text enshrined in Article XV. The need for this differential system arises from the presence in the CWC text both of substantive obligations as well as the Annexes which facilitate compliance with them. Thus, a formal amendment to the substantive obligations of the CWC may be made, pursuant to Article XV(2)–(3), through the rather traditional mechanism of proposal and consensual acceptance by all states parties. However there is also in Article XV(4)–(5) the novel addition of procedures for "change" to the provisions of the Annexes to the CWC, so long as the alterations proposed "are related only to matters of an administrative or technical nature." Detailed procedures for determining the propriety of a proposal for characterization as a "change" follow.

This bifurcated system of alteration to the treaty text is a creative response to the character of the CWC as containing both substantive obligations as well as a monitoring and verification mechanism within its text. This system allows for ongoing revision of the Annex on Chemicals and the procedures for verification laid out in the AIV as required by the dynamics of scientific advance and political change, with a realistic threshold for securing support for such change among states parties. At the same time it allows for maintenance of the consistency of the substantive provisions of the CWC and for the upholding of the consensual nature of the fundamentals of the treaty.

D. The Australia Group

The Australia Group (AG) was established upon the initiative of the Government of Australia in 1985, with an original membership of 15 countries plus the European Union as an observer. Its original purpose was to constitute a forum for coordination among its members on issues of chemical precursor and dual-use chemical equipment export controls, and for harmonization of national control lists and procedures on export authorization through the agreement of non-binding

---

[86] Ibid. at 88–90.

guidelines to be implemented according to national discretion.[87] The membership of the Australia group currently stands at 41 states.[88]

Like the Nuclear Suppliers Group, the AG is an informal association of states with no obligatory documentary foundation. Its guidelines and control lists are adopted by simple unilateral declaration of an adherent state. Also like the NSG, membership in the AG may only be gained by the unanimous consent of existing Group members. The AG has no standing organs or regular budget. The Australian embassy in Paris currently acts as the point of contact of the Group, and provides secretarial services for its annual meetings.

In 1990 the members of the AG agreed to expand the ambit of the Group's existing guidelines and lists on chemical agents and dual-use equipment, to additionally cover biological weapon agents and toxins, and related dual-use equipment. In 1992 control lists were established covering 18 bacteria, 4 rickettsiae, 25 viruses, and 14 toxins. A separate list covers dual-use equipment, such as fermenters, centrifuges, aerosol chambers, and some types of filter and freeze-drying equipment.[89] The next year the AG established a no-undercut policy within its guidelines similar to that established in 1992 by the Nuclear Suppliers Group.[90]

In 2002 the AG significantly expanded the scope of its guidelines, including for the first time a catch-all provision to be implemented in the domestic legal systems of adherents. Also included in the 2002 changes were additions to the guidelines on the subject of "intangible transfers of information and knowledge which could be used for chemical and biological weapons purposes."[91] The 2002 meeting further saw the addition of a number of biological toxins to its control lists, as part of the Group's continuing efforts to keep its six control lists current in reflection of scientific advance and the dynamics of potential use.

It should be noted that the analysis of the international legal import of the guidelines and statements of the AG, particularly in reference to interpretations

---

[87] See generally A. Kelle, "CBW Export Controls: Towards Regime Integration?" in D.H. Joyner (ed.), NONPROLIFERATION EXPORT CONTROLS: ORIGINS, CHALLENGES AND PROPOSALS FOR STRENGTHENING (2006) 102–103; J. Robinson, "The Australia Group: A Description and Assessment," in H.G. Brauch et al. (eds), CONTROLLING THE SPREAD AND DEVELOPMENT OF MILITARY TECHNOLOGY (1992); A. Smithson, *Separating Fact From Fiction: The Australia Group and the Chemical Weapons Convention*, Occasional Paper No. 34, The Henry L. Stimson Centre, Washington, DC (1997).

[88] <http://www.australiagroup.net>.

[89] A. Kelle, "CBW Export Controls: Towards Regime Integration?" in D.H. Joyner (ed.), NONPROLIFERATION EXPORT CONTROLS: ORIGINS, CHALLENGES AND PROPOSALS FOR STRENGTHENING (2006) 102–104.

[90] Ibid.

[91] Australia Group (2002), "Press Release: Australia Group Meeting," available at <http://www.australiagroup.net/en/releases/press_2002_06.htm>.

of the BWC and CWC, is essentially similar to that given in the context of the NSG and the Zangger Committee in Chapter 1.[92]

1. The AG and the BWC

With the failure of the negotiations in the BWC context regarding possible adoption of an additional protocol on verification, and in consideration of the continuing absence of an effective monitoring and verification mechanism in the BWC context, proponents of the AG contend that AG activities of coordination and harmonization of national control lists and export control policies are integral to its participant states' proper implementation of their obligations regarding transfer under BWC Article III, as well as their obligations of national implementation under BWC Article IV. As in the context of the NSG and its relationship with Article IV of the NPT, detractors of the AG argue that the Group is essentially a supplier-state cartel, whose policies unduly target states legitimately attempting to exercise their rights under Article X(1) of the BWC to participate in "the fullest possible exchange of equipment, materials and scientific and technological information for the use of bacteriological (biological) agents and toxins for peaceful purposes." They argue that the targeted controls of the AG are in disharmony with the Article X(2) obligation of states parties to implement the BWC "in a manner designed to avoid hampering the economic or technological development of states parties to the convention or international cooperation in the field of peaceful bacteriological (biological) activities..."[93]

While the countervailing obligations and rights identified in Article X of the BWC are similar to those contained in NPT Article IV, in the context of the BWC, the arguments of AG detractors lack the supportive strength of the presence in the NPT context of the *quid pro quo* relationship between NWS and NNWS, and the heightened obligation arising therefrom for NWS to assist NNWS in the development of peaceful uses of nuclear material in a non-discriminatory manner. This consideration, in addition to the absence of an effective monitoring and verification system supplementing the BWC regime, arguably serves to strengthen the arguments of AG proponents in the context of the BWC, and distinguish this context from that of the NPT/NSG.[94]

---

[92] See Chapter 1 below at 34–36.

[93] See generally <http://www.nam.gov.za/background/background.htm>; J. Simpson and T. Ogilvie-White (eds), NPT BRIEFING BOOK, VOL. I: THE EVOLUTION OF THE NUCLEAR NONPROLIFERATION REGIME (2003); T. Ogilvie-White, *International Responses to Iranian Nuclear Defiance: The Non-Aligned Movement and the Issue of Non-Compliance*, 18 EUROPEAN JOURNAL OF INTERNATIONAL LAW 453 (2007).

[94] See generally A. Kelle, "CBW Export Controls: Towards Regime Integration?" in D.H. Joyner (ed.), NONPROLIFERATION EXPORT CONTROLS: ORIGINS, CHALLENGES AND PROPOSALS FOR STRENGTHENING (2006).

2. *The AG and the CWC*

The relationship between the AG and the provisions of the CWC has, however, become a very contentious issue, with provisions of the CWC and aspects of its supportive procedural and institutional structure aligning persuasively behind the arguments of AG detractors.

In the CWC context, the obligations in Article I(1) with regard to transfers and Articles VI(2) and XI(2)(e) regarding national implementation, serve as the presumptive legal basis for CWC member states' continued participation in the AG.

However, these articles must be read in conjunction with Article XI(2)(c) which provides that CWC parties shall:

Not maintain among themselves any restrictions, including those in any international agreements, incompatible with the obligations undertaken under this Convention, which would restrict or impede trade and the development and promotion of scientific and technological knowledge in the field of chemistry for industrial, agricultural, research, medical, pharmaceutical or other peaceful purposes.

It is the clarity and specificity of this provision of the CWC which creates the most significant problem in reconciling the continued parallel existence of the AG's activities with regard to chemical precursors and related dual-use technologies. This is particularly true as the "obligations undertaken under this convention" referred to in Article XI(2)(c) clearly include the Article XI(1) obligation to implement the provisions of the CWC in a manner which "avoids hampering... international cooperation in the field of chemical activities for purposes not prohibited under this convention, including the international exchange of scientific and technical information and chemicals and equipment for the production, processing or use of chemicals for purposes not prohibited under this Convention." Further damning to arguments supporting CWC states parties' continued participation in the AG is the presence within the CWC regime of the developed monitoring and verification system embodied in the Annexes and in the role and activities of the OPCW, which would seem to create an unsupportable overlap of roles and redundancy of efforts.[95]

In realization of these problems, there have been arguments to move the work of the AG in the chemical weapons context under the auspices of the OPCW. During the Third Session of the Conference of States Parties of the OPCW in November 1998, member states Iran, Cuba, and Pakistan submitted a draft resolution to the Conference stating that the CWC "has not envisaged any export control restriction in chemical trade between States Parties for peaceful purposes," that "the OPCW should be seen as the sole responsible body to verify the compliance of the States Parties with their

---

[95] Ibid.

obligations undertaken under the Convention," and that CWC states parties "should abide by the provisions of the Convention and abolish existing export control regimes against states parties in order to render their national regulations...consistent with the obligations undertaken in accordance with the Article XI of the Convention."[96]

Perhaps not surprisingly, this resolution was not adopted by the Conference, in large part due to the opposition of powerful members of the AG including the United States, which strongly supports the continuing existence and role of the AG. Indeed, in the U.S. Senate Resolution consenting to the U.S. ratification of the CWC, the Senate declared

that the collapse of the informal forum of states known as the "Australia Group," either through changes in membership or lack of compliance with common export controls, or the substantial weakening of common Australia Group export controls and nonproliferation measures in force on the date of United States ratification of the Convention, would constitute a fundamental change in circumstances to United States ratification of the Convention.[97]

However, noting (with consternation) that Article 22 of the CWC disallowed the attachment of formal reservations to the U.S. ratification, the Senate proceeded to give its consent to ratification of the treaty in its entirety without being able to secure formal assurances as to the survival of the AG after the CWC came into force in 1997.

Arguments for the illegitimacy of the continuing activities of the AG in the field of chemical weapons are at their strongest as they identify areas in which the guidelines of the AG propose a more restrictive rule regarding transfers than does the CWC text itself, thus presenting a prima facie case of infringement of the Article X(I)(1) obligation not to hamper international cooperation and exchange. Such a case is presented in the AG's Chemical Weapons Precursors control list, and the observation that 24 of the 63 precursors on the AG list are nowhere listed in the schedules of the CWC.[98]

The arguments of AG detractors in the area of chemical weapons received considerable support from José Bustani, the Director General of the OPCW's Technical Secretariat, when in his opening statement to the Fifth Session of the Conference on State in 2000 parties he declared:

As more states join the CWC, and as their chemical producers support it, the arguments originally advanced for the maintenance of restrictions outside a credible reliable

---

[96] Islamic Republic of Iran, Cuba, and Pakistan (1998), "Draft Resolution Submitted by Islamic Republic of Iran, Cuba and Pakistan: Fostering of International Cooperation for Peaceful Purposes in the Field of Chemical Activities," C-III/NAT.4, November 19, 1998.

[97] Senate Resolution 75, 105th Congress, 1st Session, April 24, 1997.

[98] See A. Kelle, "CBW Export Controls: Towards Regime Integration?" in D.H. Joyner (ed.), Nonproliferation Export Controls: Origins, Challenges and Proposals for Strengthening (2006) 104.

international legal framework become increasingly redundant. Given this fact, the continuing existence of export controls by some States Parties against others is hard to understand and very difficult to justify.[99]

V. Overview of the CBW Legal Regime

In the end, the area of biological and chemical weapons regulation in international law can be seen to be both more and less complex than is the nuclear weapons regulatory regime described in Chapter 1.

It is fundamentally less complex because the starting point of both the BWC and CWC is a universal and comprehensive ban on possession, development, acquisition, and transfer of biological weapons and chemical weapons respectively, without any exceptions in the rights and obligations of parties. Both the BWC and the CWC are thus lawmaking treaties, as defined in Chapter 1. This aspect of the legal character of both the BWC and the CWC carries with it significant advantages both in establishing and maintaining a strong and uniform legal prohibitive norm. Unlike in the context of the NPT, no state party can claim special rights and, importantly, all states are subject to the same verification procedures.

The breadth of the bans codified in the BWC and the CWC adds to this comparative simplicity. For example, as reviewed above the prohibition on transfer in Article I of the CWC and Article III of the BWC is comprehensive as to transferees, meaning that transfer of the covered technologies is prohibited "to any recipient whatsoever," and member state assistance in developing covered weapons programs is clearly prohibited to any state assistee, whether party to the treaty or not. CWC Article I(1)(d) even expands this prohibition on assistance to cover such assistance to non-state actors as well as to states. In both cases, this is a much more comprehensive prohibition than that found in Article I of the NPT, particularly in its second clause, as reviewed previously.[100]

The breadth and universality of the obligations contained in the BWC and the CWC further aids in the development, maintenance, and strengthening of supplementary parallel customary law in both areas. This parallel custom, now undeniably established with regard to the fundamental substantive provisions of both the BWC and the CWC, serves to bind even non-parties, thus broadening the universal rules out past the immediate treaty membership in both areas.[101]

---

[99] Cited in D. Feakes, "Export Controls, Chemical Trade, and the CWC," in J. Tucker (ed.), The Chemical Weapons Convention: Implementation Challenges and Solutions, Monterey Institute of International Studies (2001) 47.

[100] See below p. 11–13.

[101] J.-M. Henckaerts and L. Doswald-Beck, Customary International Humanitarian Law, Volume I: Rules (2005) 256–267.

In terms of enforcement, the breadth and universality of the BWC and the CWC serve usefully to minimize the potential for hypocrisy in the application of obligations, lending moral authority to calls for compliance emanating from states who are themselves subject to the selfsame obligations, and whose conduct in implementing those obligations can itself be held up as exemplary.

All of these simplifying aspects and products of the legal character of the BWC and the CWC serve to minimize or obviate entirely many legal disputes that are occasioned in the NPT context by the two-tiered, non-universal structure of the NPT text.

The biological and chemical weapons regulatory environment can, however, be described as more complex than the nuclear weapons environment in that the subject materials themselves, inclusive of dual-use technologies, are themselves more complex and varied, and are even more dynamic in terms of development of new covered materials and technologies than is the case with the nuclear weapons regulatory environment.[102]

This complexity and dynamism of the underlying fields of biology and chemistry leads to problems for the legal regime, including problems in classification of new materials and technologies and problems of definition of legal terms, not present to the same degree in the nuclear context.[103]

In order to address this complexity and dynamism, both the BWC and the CWC employ versions of a general purpose test to define their scope. This purposive approach is of course aimed at providing a catch-all legal framework which can adjust without formal amendment to advances in the underlying disciplines and development of new materials and technologies. While this purposive approach does provide comprehensiveness, it can at the same time, and due to the same indefiniteness of its terms which gives rise to its scope, present challenges to its implementation in an objectively discernible, predictable, and consistent manner.[104] These implementation problems are exacerbated in the context of the international legal system due to the absence in many cases of the effectual interpretive aid of international courts and tribunals, as will be discussed in Chapter 5 below.

It could further be argued somewhat ironically that the universality and breadth of the prohibitive norm in both the BWC and the CWC, while conferring advantages on the regime as outlined previously, have also given rise to particular difficulties in implementation of these broad obligations. This difficulty can be most clearly seen in the BWC context, in which the universal prohibitive norm has arguably contributed to the stagnation of the legal

---

[102] See A. Kelle, K. Nixdorff, and M. Dando, CONTROLLING BIOCHEMICAL WEAPONS: ADAPTING MULTILATERAL ARMS CONTROL FOR THE 21ˢᵗ CENTURY (2006).

[103] Ibid.

[104] For a domestic analogy, see D.H. Joyner, *The Enhanced Proliferation Control Initiative: National Security Necessity or Unconstitutionally Vague?*, 32 GEORGIA JOURNAL OF INTERNATIONAL & COMPARATIVE LAW 107 (2004).

regime, and its inability to normatively develop and add further universally binding monitoring and verification obligations to increase its effectiveness. As Jez Littlewood has argued, regime minimalist states, including the U.S. and other powerful states, were the ultimate cause of the collapse of the additional protocol negotiations because they were unwilling to subject themselves to intrusive independent verification.[105] In the CWC context as well, though there is a challenge inspection procedure in place under Article IX whereby any state party may request verification of the compliance of any other party, thus far this compulsory verification system has not been triggered by any state party. As discussed above, this absence of challenge inspection requests, and particularly those targeted at powerful states, is likely explainable largely by fears of retaliation.

In both of these cases, it can be argued that the universality of the obligations of the regime has led to increased obstruction of the effective implementation of the regime particularly on the part of powerful states. In the NPT regime, it will be remembered, these same powerful states are given exceptional rights and immunities, and are arguably therefore more supportive of the strict implementation of the regime inclusive of intrusive verification procedures for those subject thereto, and are furthermore willing to place their considerable diplomatic weight behind the adoption of additional binding law purposed in increasing the effectiveness of the regime, with a case in point presented in the IAEA Additional Protocol.

The reluctance of powerful states particularly to agree to an intrusive and meaningful inspections process in the BWC context, and to properly support the existing process in the context of the CWC, can be argued to constitute the primary cause of the continuing problems experienced by both regimes in the area of implementation and verification.

VI. Conclusion

Viewed together, the biological and chemical weapons regulatory regimes, with the BWC and CWC as their cornerstones, have succeeded in establishing a comprehensive legal prohibition upon possession, development, proliferation, and use of biological and chemical weapons. This legal prohibition is supported by a pervasive and powerful ancient moral taboo particularly on the use of biological and chemical weapons. In the end, it is this reciprocally strengthening, symbiotic, and synergistic convergence of a universal legal ban and overwhelming moral taboo that gives the biological and chemical weapons regulatory regimes their strength and effectiveness, and has led to their enviable success in progressing

---

[105] J. Littlewood, THE BIOLOGICAL WEAPONS CONVENTION: A FAILED REVOLUTION (2005).

the agenda of biological and chemical weapons disarmament and non-use.[106] As Julian Robinson has summarized:

[M]odern customary and conventional international law has transformed an ancient taboo into an enforceable norm of international behaviour. Together these are the principal reasons why chemical and biological warfare are rare occurrences even in today's conflict-ridden world. Because of what CBW could become, they are treasure that must not be frittered away.[107]

---

[106] A. Kelle, *Assessing the Effectiveness of Security Regimes—the Chemical Weapons Control Regime's First Six years of Operation*, 41 INTERNATIONAL POLITICS 221 (2004); A. Kelle, *Strengthening the Effectiveness of the BTW Control Regime—Feasibility and Options*, 24 CONTEMPORARY SECURITY POLICY 95 (2003).

[107] J. Robinson, "Chemical and Biological Weapons," in N. Busch and D.H. Joyner (eds), COMBATING WEAPONS OF MASS DESTRUCTION: THE FUTURE OF INTERNATIONAL NON-PROLIFERATION POLICY (2009) 87.

3

The World Trade Organization and WMD Dual-Use Export Controls

Having considered the three substantive technology-specific WMD non-proliferation legal regimes and their supporting normative structures, this chapter will proceed to consider one further substantive area of international law which may be included under the umbrella category of non-proliferation law, in that it provides the rules and administrative structures concerned with cross-border transfers of a broad range of goods and services, inclusive of cross-border transfers (i.e. horizontal proliferation) of WMD related items and technologies.

The rules of international trade law most relevant to this consideration are to be found in the General Agreement on Tariffs and Trade (GATT) which, since 1995, has been housed within the administrative framework of the World Trade Organization (WTO). Of most direct relevance within the GATT are rules regarding the restriction of exports from the territory of WTO member states. Before considering the rules of the GATT, however, some consideration of the national measures they are addressed to regulating, and in particular national non-proliferation export control regulatory systems, is necessary.

I. Non-proliferation Export Controls

Many states have developed comprehensive domestic legal regulations whose focus is the control through licensing requirement of exports of both single-use and dual-use conventional and non-conventional (WMD) weapons technologies.[1]

---

[1] On the role that export controls can play in non-proliferation efforts as well as the limitations of export controls see M. Beck et al., TO SUPPLY OR TO DENY: COMPARING NONPROLIFERATION EXPORT CONTROLS IN FIVE KEY COUNTRIES (2003); K. Bailey, *Nonproliferation Export Controls: Problems and Alternatives*, in K. Bailey and R. Rudney (eds), PROLIFERATION AND EXPORT CONTROLS (1993); U.S. Congress, Office of Technology Assessment, *Export Controls and Nonproliferation Policy* (Washington, DC: GPO, May 1994), OTA-ISS-596; *Final Report of the Defense Science Board Task Force on Globalization and Security*, Office of the Under-Secretary of Defense for Acquisition and Technology (Washington, DC: DSB, December 1999); National Academy of Sciences, *Elements of a New Response: Multilateral Export Control Regimes, Finding Common Ground: U.S. Export Controls in a Changed Global Environment* (Washington, DC: National Academy Press, 1991); R.T. Cupitt, *Multilateral Nonproliferation Export Control*

Such export control regulatory regimes are an important element in international non-proliferation efforts. National export control regimes, as reviewed in Chapters 1 and 2, are coordinated and harmonized through the guidelines and control lists of the informal yet influential multilateral export control regimes (the Nuclear Suppliers Group, the Australia Group, and the Missile Technology Control Regime).[2]

One example of a developed national export control system can be found in the United States, as established under the authority of the Export Administration Act (EAA).[3] In 1979, the U.S. Congress passed the EAA to replace the provisions of the earlier 1949 Export Control Act. The stated aim of the EAA is to restrict the export of goods and technology which would make a significant contribution to the military capacities of nations posing a threat to the United States. Particularly, the EAA seeks to regulate dual-use items, i.e. those items with both legitimate civilian and potential military application. The regulation of such items is an especially sensitive area of any export control system due to the peaceful uses for which such goods and technologies may be, and usually are intended, and the tension between the dual goals of providing for national security on the one hand, and not excessively burdening the ordinary flow of such goods on the international market on the other. Thus the EAA seeks to strike a balance between the valid interests and concerns of both government and industry in keeping sufficiently open access to international demand for dual-use goods and technologies, and concerns over their diversion to uses which threaten U.S. national security.

The EAA's provisions delegate a degree of discretionary authority to the executive branch of government to craft regulations for the implementation of its goals and policies, and specifically for the implementation of a licensing system for goods of dual-use character. The resulting Export Administration Regulations (EAR) of the Department of Commerce establish a comprehensive regime for the licensing of dual-use goods to be administered by the Commerce Department's Bureau of Industry and Security (BIS). The basic structure of the EAR provisions governing dual-use items consists of a Commerce Control List (CCL) which provides detailed specifications for approximately 2,400 dual-use items including equipment, materials, software, and technology (including intangible goods such as digital data) the export of which is likely to require a license from BIS. Often, items on the CCL will require a license only if being exported to a particular

---

Arrangements in 2000: Achievements, Challenges and Reform, Center for Strategic and International Studies, Occasional Paper, September 2000.

  [2] See D.H. Joyner (ed.), Nonproliferation Export Controls: Origins, Challenges and Proposals for Strengthening (2006); idem, *Restructuring the Multilateral Export Control Regime System*, 9 Journal of Conflict & Security Law 181 (2004).

  [3] D.H. Joyner, *The Enhanced Proliferation Control Initiative: National Security Necessity or Unconstitutionally vague?* 32 Georgia Journal of International & Comparative Law 107 (2004).

country of concern, although some items, even if directed to a non-sensitive location, will yet require a license due to the significant risk of diversion to a destination of concern or because of the inherently sensitive nature of the item itself. The CCL is updated periodically to decontrol items broadly available in the market and to target restrictions on those critical technology items of particular proliferation concern.

Thus, when contemplating the export of a good or technology item, a U.S. individual or business must first classify the commodity to be exported by reference to the description of items on the CCL and thereby determine the commodity's Export Control Classification Number (ECCN). From there, the individual or entity must examine the country charts included in Section 738.1 of the EAR and find the country to which its item is destined. By comparing the item's ECCN to the list of ECCNs corresponding to the subject country, an exporter can determine whether or not a license must be first obtained from BIS before the item can in fact be exported. This process, while time consuming and complex, does provide a fairly systematic and predictable method for the classification of items and determination of the necessity of a license application.

However, due to concerns about the dynamic nature of the development of and demand for dual-use goods and technologies, the EAR supplements the CCL system with a set of regulations, contained in Sections 744.1–744.6 known as the Enhanced Proliferation Control Initiative (EPCI). The provisions of the EPCI, rather than being based on a set control list specifying sensitive items to be monitored by exporters, places its emphasis on exporters' knowledge of the activities and characteristics of end users, or final recipients, of their commodity and the uses to which their commodity will be put once in the hands of its destined recipient, including the potential for diversion of the export from its stated end uses to uses of WMD proliferation concern. Section 744.6 places obligations on U.S. exporters with regard to their knowledge of such facts and their efforts at acquiring such knowledge. In pertinent part, the regulations state:

(a)(1)(i) No U.S. person . . . may, without a license from BIS, export, re-export, or transfer to or in any country any item where the person knows that such items:

    (A) Will be used in the design, development, production, or use of nuclear explosive devices in or by a country listed in Country Group D:2 . . . ;

    (B) Will be used in the design, development, production, or use of missiles in or by a country listed in Country Group D:4 . . . ; or

    (C) Will be used in the design, development, production, stockpiling, or use of chemical or biological weapons in or by a country listed in Country Group D:3.

  (ii) No U.S. person shall, without a license from BIS, knowingly support an export, re-export, or transfer that does not have a license as required by this section. Support means any action, including financing, transportation, and freight forwarding, by which a person facilitates an export, re-export, or transfer without being the actual exporter or re-exporter.

The regulations continue in the same section to forbid any U.S. person from "perform[ing] any contract, service, or employment that the U.S. person knows will directly assist" in the development, production, or use of the aforementioned items in the specified nations of concern. They further define the term "know" and its derivations in the context of the regulation as "not only positive knowledge that [a] circumstance exists or is substantially certain to occur, but also an awareness of a high probability of its existence or future occurrence. Such awareness is inferred from evidence of the conscious disregard of facts known to a person and is also inferred from a person's willful avoidance of facts."[4]

The purpose of the EPCI provisions is to supplement the inherently limited quality of an enumerated list-based system of regulation with a more inclusive or "catch-all" normative framework that places positive obligations upon U.S. exporters to make themselves aware of the characteristics not only of their particular items and their potential for use in WMD programs, but of the particulars of the specific uses to which the item is to be put in its place of destination, along with the likelihood of its diversion by either primary or secondary parties and potential use in the manufacture of WMD.

II. GATT Rules on Export Restrictions

The General Agreement on Tariffs and Trade, which is the core substantive agreement administered under the WTO's institutional umbrella, is primarily purposed in channeling all national legal restrictions on trade in goods into the form of tariffs (i.e. taxes), and then both binding and lowering tariff rates across national economies. In theory, this process leads to efficiency of markets by facilitating the realization of comparative advantage among producers. It further creates transparency and a marketplace ruled by objective legal standards, as opposed to a system of preferential treatment for provincial interests. Underlying the most fundamental rules of the GATT is the principle of non-discrimination, both as between various foreign producers of like products (Articles I, XI, XIII, XX), as well as between foreign and domestic producers of like products (Article III).[5]

With its focus on tariffs, the rules of the GATT are most commonly applied to issues of importation of foreign produced goods. However, the cornerstone

---

[4] 15 CFR 772.1.

[5] See P. Mavroidis, Trade in Goods: The Gatt and Other Agreements Regulating Trade in Goods (2007); T. Cottier, P. Mavroidis, and P. Blatter (eds), Regulatory Barriers and the Principle of Non-discrimination in World Trade Law (2000); M. Matsushita, T. Schoenbaum, and P. Mavroidis, The World Trade Organization: Law, Practice and Policy (2003); J.H. Jackson, The World Trading System: Law and Policy of International Economic Relations (2nd edn, 1997); P. Van den Bossche, The Law and Policy of the World Trade Organization: Text, Cases and Materials (2005); M. Trebilcock and R. Howse, The Regulation of International Trade (3rd edn, 2005).

Most Favored Nation rule of Article I formally applies equally to exports as well as to imports. Additionally, Article XI of the GATT provides for a broad prohibition of both import and export restraints other than tariffs, inclusive of "import or export licenses."[6] The breadth of Article XI's coverage of all trade "measures" affecting imports or exports was clarified in the 1989 *Japan Trade in Semi-Conductors* GATT Panel Report.[7]

Article XI contains a number of fairly discrete exceptions to its broad prohibition, and these exceptions are of course supplemented by the general exceptions to GATT obligations found in Article XX. However, none of the exceptions either in Article XI or Article XX addresses export controls for national security or foreign policy purposes. Thus, on its face, Article XI can be viewed to clearly include within its prohibited scope national export control licensing requirements for national security or foreign policy purposes, inclusive of such regulatory regimes as the United States Export Administration Act system.

However, there is a further article of the GATT specifically addressed to excepting national regulatory provisions of defined types from the scope of the general obligations of the GATT, including Article XI, if those regulations are maintained out of a specific concern for national security. Article XXI provides as follows:

Nothing in this Agreement shall be construed

(a) to require any contracting party to furnish any information the disclosure of which it considers contrary to its essential security interests; or

(b) to prevent any contracting party from taking any action which it considers necessary for the protection of its essential security interests

    (i) relating to fissionable materials or the materials from which they are derived;

    (ii) relating to the traffic in arms, ammunition and implements of war and to such traffic in other goods and materials as is carried on directly or indirectly for the purpose of supplying a military establishment;

    (iii) taken in time of war or other emergency in international relations; or

(c) to prevent any contracting party from taking any action in pursuance of its obligations under the United Nations Charter for the maintenance of international peace and security.

With specific regard to national regulatory regimes controlling exports of WMD-related items and technologies through licensing requirements, the provisions of GATT Article XXI clearly legitimize some such regulations. However, there are significant unresolved questions as to the precise scope, character, and meaning of those provisions.[8]

---

[6] Art. XI. See *Japan—Trade in Semi-Conductors*, adopted May 4, 1988, GATT B.I.S.D. (35th Supp.) at 116 (1989). See P. Mavroidis, Trade in Goods: The Gatt and Other Agreements Regulating Trade in Goods (2007) noting that domestic quotas are not covered by Article XI.

[7] *Japan—Trade in Semi-Conductors*, adopted May 4, 1988, GATT B.I.S.D. (35th Supp., 1989).

[8] See M. Matsushita, T. Schoenbaum, and P. Mavroidis, The World Trade Organization: Law, Practice and Policy (2003) 226. ("There are many unanswered legal questions involving the compliance of export controls with GATT/WTO norms.")

Article XXI certainly works to legalize national export control licensing regulations covering both single-use nuclear materials under Article XXI(b)(i), and single-use biological and chemical materials under Article XXI(b)(ii). It also almost certainly works to legalize at least some national export control licensing requirements covering WMD dual-use items and technologies, also by virtue of Article XXI(b)(ii).

It is to this latter category of national export restrictions on WMD dual-use items and technologies that the most uncertainty attaches. This, again, is because WMD dual-use goods have civilian as well as military applications, and thus trade in dual-use goods comprises a not insignificant percentage of normal, legitimate international trade in goods.[9] While no authoritative study has measured the worldwide volume of trade in WMD dual-use goods, one can get an idea of the scope of this trade by examining the control lists of the various multilateral export control regimes, or developed national control lists such as the U.S. CCL, which contains approximately 2,400 items, covering a wide variety of high-tech goods ranging from machine tools, to microscopes, to computer processors, to piping/tubing made from particular metallic alloys, to an array of laboratory equipment such as weighing and measuring devices, autoclaves and compressors. A brief review of these lists is sufficient to convey an understanding that national export controls of WMD dual-use goods can and do restrict international trade in a variety of civilian-usable, highly commercially viable goods.

The question is thus raised, are all national regulations maintained by WTO member states restricting the export of WMD dual-use goods through licensing requirements indeed outside the prohibitive scope of GATT Articles I and XI?

On its face this premise would appear problematic. National export control regulation is an exercise of the national security policy of the state, and is thus fundamentally much more an art than a science, entailing political judgments at every turn and requiring the exercise of a very broad and largely unrestricted unilateral discretion on the part of national regulating bodies.[10]

Necessary judgments include the subject of which states or non-state actors, including private business entities, should be targeted by such controls. This judgment will be made based on many factors, but all of them subjective on the part of the regulating state. From a GATT perspective, such 'prohibited end user' judgments are by definition discriminatory applications of national export law

---

[9] On patterns of technology dissemination and the challenges presented thereby, see M. Moodie, *The Challenges of Chemical, Biological and Nuclear Weapons Enabling Technology*, in P. Gasprani Alves and K. Hoffman (eds), THE TRANSFER OF SENSITIVE TECHNOLOGY AND THE FUTURE OF THE CONTROL REGIMES (1997). See also W.W. Keller and J.E. Nolan, *Proliferation of Advanced Weaponry: Threat to Stability*, FOREIGN POLICY (Winter 1997–98); M. Hirsch, *The Great Technology Giveaway*, FOREIGN AFFAIRS, September/October 1998.

[10] See D.H. Joyner (ed.), NONPROLIFERATION EXPORT CONTROLS: ORIGINS, CHALLENGES AND PROPOSALS FOR STRENGTHENING (2006); K. Bailey and R. Rudney (eds), PROLIFERATION AND EXPORT CONTROLS (1993); G.K. Bertsch and W.C. Potter (eds), DANGEROUS WEAPONS, DESPERATE STATES (1999).

and policy. As such they necessarily do violence to the spirit, if not the letter, of fundamental non-discrimination principles enshrined in provisions throughout the GATT, and throughout other WTO agreements as well.

National export control regulation further entails judgments concerning the definition of 'dual-use goods,' and a delineation of which goods are to be the subject of regulation. This judgment on definition is problematic because there is no multilaterally agreed definition of WMD dual-use goods in any WMD-related technology area. The closest approximation to such a multilateral standard is to be found in the control lists of the multilateral export control regimes, but these regimes are of course non-binding, and are far from universal in membership. This unilateral discretion on the part of an exporting state to define the category of goods subject to national export control regulations produces unpredictability and non-transparency in the application of fundamental GATT rules such as Article XI.

On both the question of targets of dual-use goods export control regulation, and the question of goods subject to dual-use export control regulation, the breadth of the unilateral discretion which some have read Article XXI to allow to WTO member states arguably comes into direct conflict with the object and purpose of the GATT/WTO, which is to provide transparent, predictable, non-discriminatory, objectively determinable rules of law to order international trade in goods. Pursuant to extreme interpretations, the unilateral discretion granted to states to maintain national dual-use export control regulations provided by Article XXI creates a latent general escape clause, functioning to except states relying upon it from the core rules of the GATT whenever they subjectively determine it to be, under some definition also largely subjective in scope and meaning, in their 'essential security interest' to do so.[11] As John Jackson has written, while the GATT was intended to "reduce the danger and the damage of arbitrary exercise of economic power... The GATT security exception... can reopen the door to arbitrary abuse."[12]

Issues of national export control regulations have been especially controversial as they have become intertwined with larger economic and political tensions between the developed and the developing world. The perception long held by developing states members of the Non-Aligned Movement (NAM) that the national export control regulations of developed, Western states are targeted unfairly at denying high technology goods to developing states, while being grounded speciously in claims of national security interest, has become a mantraic rallying cry in debates of the U.N. General Assembly and in other *fora*.[13] Extreme interpretations of GATT Article XXI, granting broad unilateral

---

[11] See M. Hahn, *Vital Interests and the Law of GATT: An Analysis of GATT's Security Exception*, 12 Michigan Journal of International Law 558 (1991).

[12] J.H. Jackson, World Trade and the Law of GATT (1969) 752.

[13] On the NAM, see <http://www.nam.gov.za/background/background.htm>; J. Simpson and T. Ogilvie-White (eds), NPT Briefing Book, Vol. 1: The Evolution of the Nuclear

discretion to WTO members to exclude national export controls from the general
obligations of the GATT, add considerable fuel to these arguments.

III. The United States–Czechoslovakia Dispute of 1949

The first GATT dispute to formally deal with Article XXI concerned a dispute in
1949 between Czechoslovakia and the United States, regarding the application
by the United States of an export control licensing regime which had produced
denials of certain exports to Czechoslovakia.[14] Though there was some disagreement among the representatives of the two states regarding which items had
actually been denied export to Czechoslovakia, it was conceded by the United
States that exports of electrodes, x-ray tubes, tungsten wire, and mining drills
had in some cases been denied. Of these, the record of debate provides most
information regarding the denied mining drills.

The U.S. representative, John Evans, explained that during the processing of the
application for export of the drills, the "American press published an announcement of the discovery of an important uranium deposit in Czechoslovakia."
Evans then stated: "I am sure it is not necessary for me to refer again to the exception
in the General Agreement with respect to commodities relating to fissionable
materials."[15]

From his comments, it is clear that at least Mr. Evans believed that the GATT
Article XXI(b)(i) provision excepting from GATT obligations action which
a state considers necessary for the protection of its essential security interests
"relating to fissionable materials or the materials from which they are derived,"
was sufficient to justify export denial of mining drills which might be used to
drill for uranium ore.

In his response, Mr. Augenthaler of Czechoslovakia took this interpretation
to task:

One of the [] basic questions is the interpretation of the provisions of Article XXI as
to security exceptions. When this question was discussed at Havana many delegations
wished to have these security exceptions interpreted as narrowly as possible in order
to avoid misuses...How far a misinterpretation can go, I could demonstrate by the
example given by Mr. Evans concerning orders placed by Czechoslovakia in the U.S.

NONPROLIFERATION REGIME (2003); T. Ogilvie-White, *International Responses to Iranian Nuclear
Defiance: The Non-Aligned Movement and the Issue of Non-Compliance*, 18 EUROPEAN JOURNAL OF
INTERNATIONAL LAW 453 (2007).

   [14] Contracting Parties to the GATT, Third Session; GATT/CP.3/SR.22 (June 8, 1949); GATT/
CP.3/SR.20 (June 14, 1949); GATT/CP.3/33 (May 30, 1949)(Statement by the Head of the
Czechoslovak Delegation); GATT/CP.3/38 (June 2, 1949) (Reply by the Vice Chairman of the
U.S. Delegation); GATT/CP.3/39 (June 8, 1949) (Reply of the Head of the Czechoslovak
Delegation); see also J.H. Jackson, WORLD TRADE AND THE LAW OF GATT (1969) 749.
   [15] GATT/CP.3/38 (June 2, 1949) (Reply by the Vice Chairman of the U.S. Delegation).

for some mining drills...Mr. Evans invoked the proviso about fissionable materials which would mean that mining drills are probably considered fissionable material too. It seems that they became radioactive as a consequence of radiations from the U.S. factories.[16]

Implicit in Mr. Augenthaler's statement is the interpretation that, in order to be justified by reference to Article XXI(b)(i), a state action would have to relate in a direct fashion to "fissionable materials of the materials from which they are derived," and not in an indirect fashion as through application to dual-use items which might be used to procure such materials.

On this point, though not explicitly argued by either side in the 1949 dispute, while the expanding terms "directly or indirectly" are present as relating to the term "military establishment" in Article XXI(b)(ii), to be discussed below, they are not present to clearly expand the term "relating to" in the context of Article XXI(b)(i). This omission within the selfsame paragraph renders persuasive the presumption that a more direct link between a state action and fissionable or precursor material is required in order for the action to be included under the Article XXI(b)(i) exception, and that state actions more indirectly linked to fissionable or precursor material, as actions concerning dual-use items, are more properly suited for consideration under Article XXI(b)(ii).[17] If this directness of relation were not read in, it would be difficult to circumscribe the reach of the term "related to" in Article XXI(b)(i), as everything is in the end related to everything else at some degree of separation.[18] Thus in the export control context, the terms of Article XXI(b)(i) should be interpreted to be limited in their coverage to the denial of the export of actual fissionable material or precursor material, such as uranium ore itself.

Nevertheless, it is clear that the basis for the U.S. denial was the suspicion that the drills would be used for mining uranium ore, which could of course then be used for development of nuclear weapons. This fits the export license denial of these mining drills solidly within the category of a WMD dual-use export control license denial.

In the end, the *U.S.–Czechoslovakia* case unfortunately does not tell us much about the scope and meaning of the Article XXI(b)(ii) exception, as the only formal decision of the GATT Contracting Parties in the case was on the discrete question "whether the government of the United States had failed to carry out its obligations under the Agreement through its administration of the issues of export licenses," to which the response of the Contracting Parties was in the

---

[16] GATT/CP.3/39 (June 8, 1949) (Reply of the Head of the Czechoslovak Delegation).

[17] M. Hahn, *Vital Interests and the Law of GATT: An Analysis of GATT's Security Exception*, 12 MICHIGAN JOURNAL OF INTERNATIONAL LAW 558, 569 at fn. 56 (1991).

[18] The Appellate Body has followed this interpretive reasoning in its jurisprudence regarding GATT Article XX(g), and has in that context interpreted the term "relating to" to mean "primarily aimed at." See *United States—Standards for Reformulated and Conventional Gasoline*, WT/DS2/AB/R, adopted on May 20, 1996.

negative. As per GATT practice at the time, disputes were handled by diplomats, and not through the more formalistic, lawyerly procedures which would come to full maturity in the agreements of the WTO. Thus, the *U.S.–Czechoslovakia* case cannot be seen as a proper legal debate about the scope of Article XXI(b)(ii), but is rather confined to the particular facts of the case.

What can be divined from the statements of the various diplomats who participated in the debates is a subtle yet significant distinction in how the issue of the license denials was framed by the two sides. Czechoslovakia clearly framed it as an international legal issue, entailing the scope and meaning of Articles I, XI, XIII, and XXI of the GATT. Its argument was that the U.S. export control licensing regime was an inherently discriminatory barrier to trade, and as such fundamentally incompatible with U.S. obligations pursuant to the provisions of the GATT. It argued that the U.S. in its averment that the licensing regime fell within the Article XXI exception, was stretching beyond reasonable limits the interpretive scope of the security exception which, as previously noted, it felt should be interpreted extremely narrowly. It presented its complaint to the Contracting Parties by reference to the dispute settlement provision of the GATT, Article XXIII. In doing so, the Czechoslovakian delegation expressed its understanding that the issues in question were capable of objective determination as issues of treaty interpretation and application to state action.

The Czechoslovakian representative, Mr. Augenthaler, expressed his concerns regarding the effect of these alleged treaty breaches by the U.S. thus:

> Mr. Chairman, Fellow Delegates, we have signed the GATT confident that it would bring a certain sense of security and legality into international trade relations leading to an expanding exchange of goods and ensuring full employment. Instead we are faced with the greatest insecurity and with measures which are leading to an inevitable decrease in our trade with certain countries. How can our enterprises be expected to place their orders with the factories of those countries, in which, either through State intervention or the possibility of State intervention millions of our money remain, or may remain, frozen?...For all these reasons we expect your decision to be just and fair, and to renew the badly shaken confidence, because otherwise it would allow each country to do to other countries practically what it wishes...*As soon as you admit that a country may impose restrictions and special formalities on exports to some destinations and none to others, the Most-Favored-Nations-Treatment would cease to exist and we would be in the midst of wildest economic warfare instead of peaceful cooperation.*[19]

The focus of the U.S. representative's statements was on explaining why the U.S. export control licensing system should be seen to fit within the Article XXI exception to the general obligations of the GATT. To that extent at least in part his arguments met those of the Czechoslovakian representative. However, in those explanations there is little if any discussion of the scope and meaning of

---

[19] GATT/CP.3/33 (May 30, 1949) (Statement by the Head of the Czechoslovak Delegation), emphasis added.

the article, or a sustained argument explaining why the licensing program was justified by the terms of Article XXI; only the rather bald assertion that the export restriction in question fit "within our rights, if that restriction is based on the exceptions in the General Agreement on Tariffs and Trade."[20] In only minimally addressing the legal issues raised by the Czechoslovakian representative, Mr. Evans' statements on behalf of the U.S. give the clear impression that, in his opinion at least, the exceptions to the GATT, and particularly the security exception, were to be judged in their scope unilaterally by states claiming justification thereby, with little requirement to submit explanations concerning compliance to objective scrutiny or determination.[21]

The U.K. representative, Mr. Shackle, was even more explicit in this understanding of the unfettered discretion reserved to states to self-judge the harmony of their actions with the Article XXI security exception, as well as the supremacy of such judgments over any apparently limiting or contradictory GATT provisions.

His delegation did not seek to deny that export licensing control over those goods was discriminatory in its effects, since controls exercised for security reasons were by their nature discriminatory. No country could deny, or be expected to deny, itself the right to exercise such control where matters of national security were concerned... It was, he thought, a principle well recognized internationally, that it was for each country to judge for itself of its own security interests... Of course no one would deny that there was an extensive field of commodities which were capable both of war-like and peaceful uses, but where there was doubt his Government was obliged to reserve to itself fully the right to judge whether to give an export licence in any given case or not.... [S]ince the question clearly concerned Article XXI, the United States action would seem to be justified because every country must have the last resort on questions relating to its own security.[22]

Thus, in the end the *U.S.–Czechoslovakia* case illustrates two quite different perspectives in framing the issue of the U.S. license denials, but little in the way of helpful, authoritative answers as to the scope and meaning of principles of GATT law involved.[23]

---

[20] GATT/CP.3/38 (June 2, 1949) (Reply by the Vice Chairman of the U.S. Delegation).

[21] This position was made even more clear by the U.S. delegation during a 1986 dispute with Nicaragua, about which a GATT Panel Report was issued but never adopted (*United States—Trade Measures Affecting Nicaragua* (GATT Doc. L/6053, October 13, 1986)). The panel summarized one of the main headings of the U.S. argument thus: "The United States said that Article XXI applied to any action which the contracting party taking it considered necessary for the protection of its essential security interest. This provision, by its clear terms, left the validity of the security justification to the exclusive judgement of the contracting party taking the action. The United States could therefore not be found to act in violation of Article XXI." (Para. 4.6.)

[22] GATT/CP.3/SR.20 (June 14, 1949).

[23] See M. Hahn, *Vital Interests and the Law of GATT: An Analysis of GATT's Security Exception*, 12 MICHIGAN JOURNAL OF INTERNATIONAL LAW 558, 569–570 (1991).

Since 1949, there have been a limited number of other cases in which Article XXI has been invoked.[24] However, none has contributed significantly to our understanding of the scope and meaning of Article XXI(b)(ii). The *U.S–Czechoslovakia* dispute remains the most relevant GATT/WTO case to the issue of WMD dual-use export control licensing regulation.

IV. Textual Analysis of Article XXI(b)(ii)

Article XXI(b) is textually constructed to consist of two normative elements. The first is a subjective element, i.e. the subjective view of the state that an action is necessary to protect its essential security interest. This subjective element is arguably subject only to exercise in good faith, per VCLT Article 31.[25]

The second element is a delineation of three alternative objective circumstances, at least one of which must accompany the state's subjective determination in order for the state to avail itself of the exception.[26]

Thus, with regard to WMD dual-use export controls, Article XXI(b)(ii) should be interpreted to provide that, for export controls of goods not categorizeable as single-use military goods (i.e. the "other goods and materials" referred to in the provision) to be covered under the Article XXI exception, the goods subject to export control regulation must be items and technologies the export of which from the country concerned "is carried on directly or indirectly for the purpose of supplying a military establishment."

This provision emphasizes, similar to the general purpose criteria of both the BWC and CWC, the purpose to which the items will be put once exported to the target state, and provides that, in order for the exporting state to place export controls upon the items, justifiable by reference to Article XXI, the items must be exported "directly or indirectly for [this] purpose."

The term "purpose of supplying a military establishment" is debatable as to its scope and meaning, even with the additional qualifiers "directly or indirectly"

---

[24] See M. Hahn, *Vital Interests and the Law of GATT: An Analysis of GATT's Security Exception*, 12 Michigan Journal of International Law 558 (1991); P. Mavroidis, Trade in Goods: The Gatt and Other Agreements Regulating Trade in Goods (2007) 321; M. Matsushita, T. Schoenbaum, and P. Mavroidis, The World Trade Organization: Law, Practice and Policy (2003) 220–226.

[25] See D. Akande and S. Williams, *International Adjudication on National Security Issues: What Role for the WTO?* 43 Virginia Journal of International Law 365, 386–392 (2003). For the principle that WTO agreements should be interpreted in accordance with the VCLT, see *Reformulated Conventional Gasoline*, I WTO DSR at 14.

[26] See D. Akande and S. Williams, *International Adjudication on National Security Issues: What Role for the WTO?* 43 Virginia Journal of International Law 365, 399 (2003); M. Hahn, *Vital Interests and the Law of GATT: An Analysis of GATT's Security Exception*, 12 Michigan Journal of International Law 558, 584 (1991); M. Matsushita, T. Schoenbaum, and P. Mavroidis, The World Trade Organization: Law, Practice and Policy, (2003) 222.

being taken into account. John Jackson has noted that some have interpreted the purpose to which goods may be put by an end user so broadly as to extend to the maintenance of shoe production facilities, "because an army must have shoes!"[27] This example illustrates the sort of considerable tenuousness of relationship between the purpose to which exported goods will be put, and the supply of a military establishment, which some states would interpret the exception delineated in Article XXI(b)(ii) to cover. The potential for excessive breadth in interpretation of the connection embodied in this relationship, and the mischief which such an interpretation could create for the fundamental rules of the GATT, is readily apparent.

The potential for this mischief argues for a nexus test to be applied to the relationship between the purpose to which the goods will be put by the end user, and the supply of a military establishment. The precise contours of this nexus test would be subject to determination by the DSB, but might usefully require that the *primary purpose* of the use to which the goods will be put by the end user must be the supply of a military establishment. Such a test should rule purposes only tangentially, or minimally related to the supply of a military establishment, such as the export of materials purposed in maintaining shoe production facilities, as falling outside the scope of the Article XXI(b)(ii) head of the Article XXI(b) exception.

The requirement that the subject regulation restrict trade carried on for the purpose of supplying a military establishment, even without further content through interpretation, serves to limit the scope of the Article XXI(b)(ii) exception to cover only a sub-category of export controls currently maintained by many supplier countries. Export controls are applied to states and non-state actors for many reasons, some based more in political or economic consideration than security considerations. As one commentator has noted:

A stronger indication that the U.S. is not in compliance with GATT is the structure of the EAA. Most proliferation controls are categorized primarily as foreign policy controls, rather than national security controls. The statutory organization of the EAA places national security and foreign policy controls in different sections of the statute, rather than treating one as a subset of the other. National security controls are directed at restricting exports which would "make a significant contribution to the military potential...which would prove detrimental to the national security of the United States." Foreign policy controls, on the other hand, are intended to "further significantly the foreign policy of the United States." One of the major foreign policy aims they are intended to further is the suppression of international terrorism. While there is no statutory prohibition on imposing proliferation controls under the national security provisions of the EAA, the inclusion of missile technology and biological and chemical weapons in

---

[27] J.H. Jackson, THE WORLD TRADING SYSTEM: LAW AND POLICY OF INTERNATIONAL ECONOMIC RELATIONS (2nd edn, 1997) 230.

the foreign policy provisions of the EAA strongly indicates that Congress did not feel that these controls were of a national security nature.[28]

Even when based in national security concerns specifically, export controls can cast a wide net of reasons to deny a particular technology or material to a specific state or non-state actor. Strictly applying the criterion of a necessary purpose of directly or indirectly supplying a military establishment should serve to significantly limit the breadth of the controls which may be justifiable in reference to Article XXI(b)(ii).

The most obvious basis for restriction upon exports for reasons of national security concern which such an application would likely bring into question, relates to restrictions aimed at denying sensitive items and technologies to terrorist groups and related persons and entities. Particularly on the question of whether such non-state actors, which are the ultimate target of such controls, can be persuasively categorized as a "military establishment," there would seem to be cause for serious doubt. The term "military establishment" appears not to be a term of art taken from other legal sources by the drafters of the GATT. Thus there is little by way of material from concurrent or prior legal sources from which to draw analogous conclusions regarding interpretation. However, the term would seem to carry a meaning of some regularized, institutionally integrated military organization, and almost certainly contemplated as its paradigm of meaning the national armed forces of the states signing the GATT. The fitting of non-state terrorist organizations under this term would seem rather dubious without a purposefully excessive construction being imposed upon interpretation.[29]

The result of these interpretations of the text of Article XXI(b)(ii) is to add a measure of objectivity to its meaning, and some substantive restrictions upon state claims in reliance upon this exception. These restrictions upon the ability of states to claim exception for national export control regulations under Article XXI(b)(ii) do help in some measure to allay concerns regarding the breadth of the exception mentioned earlier. However, even with the measure of objectivity and restriction which can be imposed upon the Article XXI(b)(ii) exception through interpretation of provisions of its text, this provision does appear to persuasively include within its exceptional scope national export control licensing regulations on a wide range of exports of WMD dual-use goods, including discriminatory choices of target actors through the exercise of unilateral state discretion, and

---

[28] M. Gaugh, *GATT Article XXI and U.S. Export Controls: The Invalidity of Nonessential Nonproliferation Controls*, 8 NEW YORK INTERNATIONAL LAW REVIEW 51, 73 (1995).

[29] It might be argued that UNSC Resolution 1540's creation of an obligation for all U.N. members to establish within their domestic legal systems, "effective laws which prohibit any non-State actor to manufacture, acquire, possess, develop, transport, transfer or use nuclear, chemical or biological weapons and their means of delivery, in particular for terrorist purposes," works to trump this limitation of the scope of the GATT Article xxi(b)(ii) exception. However, as will be argued in Chapter 4 herein, Resolution 1540 should be understood to comprise an overreaching by the U.N. Security Council of its powers under the U.N. Charter, with the result that Resolution 1540 itself is null and void of legal effect.

unilateral state discretion on judgments regarding controlled technologies, which necessarily accompany such regulations.

V. Objective Interpretation of Article XXI(b)(ii)

Some have argued that objective interpretation of Article XXI, including the requirement of the existence of one of the three alternative circumstances stated in Article XXI(b)(ii), is unwarranted because Article XXI incorporates a reservation in matters of national security concern which is essentially self-judging on the part of states claiming it. This is in essence the position iterated by the U.S. and U.K. representatives in the context of the 1949 *U.S.–Czechoslovakia* case reviewed above.

However, nothing either in the text of the GATT or in its *travaux préparatoires* supports the idea that Article XXI issues are in any way exempt from the dispute settlement procedure of the GATT (Articles XXII and XXII), and now by extension the WTO Dispute Settlement Understanding (DSU). Thus, the provisions of Article XXI must be susceptible to independent review according to objectively determinable legal standards.[30] As Michael Hahn has argued:

Despite the strengthening of GATT's security exception during its development, it is worth noting that those deliberations did not affect the understanding that the security exception, susceptible to abuse, was to be subject to consultation, decision and control of legality under the future dispute settlement procedure. Moreover, such a procedure only makes sense if there is something worth submitting to legal assessment. This is not to underestimate the importance of political arguments in consultations under what is now Article XXII of the GATT. While such arguments are often very important, considerable lawyering is indispensable to the resolution of what is, after all, a legal as well as a political issue. This is even more the case in a regular dispute settlement procedure...which clearly involves the application of legal principles. The drafters of GATT must have therefore presumed that within such a procedure the objective prerequisites for the invocation of a security exception would be subject to review in principle. This perception was shared by the dominant economic power of the day (i.e. the United States) which was also the major protagonist behind the security exception. Furthermore, the U.S. analysis suggests the understanding that cases might arise in which invocation of the security exception was legally unjustified.[31]

More recently, Professors Matsushita, Schoenbaum and Mavroidis have noted:

Some authors have concluded that Article XXI is a self-judging provision, but this view seems untenable. The GATT rules are not designed to be self-judging, and unilateral action is specifically excluded in the Dispute Settlement Understanding. If any part of

---

[30] See M. Hahn, *Vital Interests and the Law of GATT: An Analysis of GATT's Security Exception*, 12 Michigan Journal of International Law 558, 567 (1991).

[31] Ibid. at 568–569.

Article XXI were intended to be self-judging, the parties to the GATT or WTO would have specified this. The vague and ambiguous wording of parts of Article XXI(b), including the "emergency" provision, may constitute a loophole in the GATT, but this does not mean that it is self-judging. In fact, the legislative history of the provision indicates the Article was not to be excluded from GATT dispute settlement procedures, so that it was not conceived of as a self-judging provision.[32]

In essence, this was the position iterated by the Czechoslovakian representative, Mr. Augenthaler, in the 1949 *U.S.–Czechoslovakia* case.[33] Within subsequent state practice and the jurisprudence of GATT/WTO dispute settlement panels, there is nothing to authoritatively contradict the conclusion that a states wishing to avail itself of the GATT Article XXI(b)(ii) exception in order to justify a program of national export control licensing of WMD dual-use goods must, in addition to a showing of good faith in its subjective determination that the action

---

[32] M. Matsushita, T. Schoenbaum, and P. Mavroidis, THE WORLD TRADE ORGANIZATION: LAW, PRACTICE AND POLICY (2nd edn, 2006) 597; See also D. Akande and S. Williams, *International Adjudication on National Security Issues: What Role for the WTO?* 43 VIRGINIA JOURNAL OF INTERNATIONAL LAW 365, 381–384 (2003).

[33] This position on justiciability and the susceptibility of Article XXI to objective interpretation is in essential accord with that of the Nicaraguan Government during its 1986 dispute with the United States over the latter's imposition of a two-way embargo upon Nicaragua. The GATT Panel summarized the response of the Nicaraguan representative to the U.S. invocation of Article XXI(b)(iii) in justification of the embargo, as well as U.S. assertions that its justification by reference to that article was essentially non-justiciable, as follows: "Nicaragua stated that the United States could not properly rely on Article XXI:(b)(iii) in this case. This provision could be invoked only if two conditions were met: first, the measure adopted had to be necessary for the protection of essential security interest and, second, the measure had to be taken in time of war or other emergency in international relations. Neither of these conditions were fulfilled in this present case. Obviously, a small developing country such as Nicaragua could not constitute a threat to the security of the United States. The embargo was therefore not necessary to protect any essential security interest of that country. Nor was there any 'emergency' in the sense of Article XXI. Nicaragua and the United States were not at war and maintained full diplomatic relations. If there was tension between the two countries, it was due entirely to actions by the United States in violation of international law. A country could not be allowed to base itself on the existence of an 'emergency' which it had itself created. In that respect, Article XXI was analogous to the right of self-defence in international law. This provision could be invoked only by a party subjected to direct aggression or armed attack and not by the aggressor or by parties indirectly at risk. Nicaragua added that it must be borne in mind that GATT did not exist in a vacuum but was an integral part of the wider structure of international law, and that the General Agreement must not be interpreted in a way inconsistent with international law. The International Court of Justice had found that the embargo was one element of a whole series of economic and military actions taken against Nicaragua in violation of international law and that it was not necessary for the protection of any essential security interest of the United States, and it had declared that the United States must make reparation for the damage caused. The Security Council (Resolution 562) and the General Assembly (Resolution 40/188) of the United Nations had also condemned the embargo for infringing the principles of free trade and had explicitly demanded its rescinding. Consequently, Nicaragua held that the United States could not base itself on Article XXI in the particular case, and that the trade measures under consideration constituted coercive measures applied for political reasons in contravention of paragraph 7(iii) of the Ministerial Declaration of November 1982, which obliged contracting parties to 'abstain from taking restrictive trade measures, for reasons of a non-economic character, not consistent with the General Agreement.'" (*United States—Trade Measures Affecting Nicaragua* (GATT Doc. L/6053, Para. 4.5, October 13, 1986).)

is necessary to protect its essential security interest, further establish objectively that the goods subject to export control regulation are goods the export of which "is carried on directly or indirectly for the purpose of supplying a military establishment." This latter objective element, like the good faith character of the subjective element, is reviewable by the WTO DSU process.[34]

VI. Other Provisions in Article XXI

In addition to Article XXI(b)(ii), other possible candidates among the provisions of Article XXI for the conferral of exceptional status upon national export control programs include Article XXI(b)(iii). It is of course important for states to be able to suspend their GATT obligations toward another WTO member in time of war or other emergency, and this exception should be read fairly liberally, though at the same time it must be recognized that Article XXI(b)(iii) comprises a legal exception to the fundamental legal obligations of the GATT, and thus that this provision, as all of the provisions of Article XXI, has objective content. As is the case with Article XXI(b)(ii), Article XXI(b)(iii) is not self-judging and is subject to independent review and assessment through the DSU process.[35] As Professors Matsushita, Shoenbaum, and Mavroidis have explained:

Despite its ambiguity, the phrase "emergency in international relations" has a certain objective content. The term "emergency" requires a certain degree of seriousness as

---

[34] In its unadopted report on the 1986 dispute between Nicaragua and the United States, the GATT Panel expressed its frustration with the limited nature of its mandate, in which it had been forbidden by the *special terms of reference* of the parties from examining or judging the validity of or motivation for the invocation of Article XXI(b)(iii) by the United States: "The above considerations and the conclusions to which the Panel had to arrive, given its limited terms of reference and taking into account the existing rules and procedures of the GATT, raise in the view of the Panel the following more general questions: If it were accepted that the interpretation of Article XXI was reserved entirely to the contracting party invoking it, how could the CONTRACTING PARTIES ensure that this general exception to all obligations under the General Agreement is not invoked excessively or for purposes other than those set out in this provision? If the CONTRACTING PARTIES give a panel the task of examining a case involving an Article XXI invocation without authorizing it to examine the justification of that invocation, do they limit the adversely affected contracting party's right to have its complaint investigated in accordance with Article XXIII:2? Are the powers of the CONTRACTING PARTIES under Article XXIII:2 sufficient to provide redress to contracting parties subjected to a two-way embargo? The Panel noted that in 1982 the CONTRACTING PARTIES took a 'Decision Concerning Article XXI of the General Agreement' which refers to the possibility of a formal interpretation of Article XXI and to a further consideration by the Council of this matter (BISD 29S/23-24). The Panel recommends that the CONTRACTING PARTIES, in any further consideration of this matter in accordance with that Decision, take into account the questions raised by the Panel above." (*United States—Trade Measures Affecting Nicaragua* (GATT Doc. L/6053, Para. 5.17–5.18, October 13, 1986)).

[35] M. Hahn, *Vital Interests and the Law of GATT: An Analysis of GATT's Security Exception*, 12 MICHIGAN JOURNAL OF INTERNATIONAL LAW 558, 567–569 (1991); D. Akande and S. Williams, *International Adjudication on National Security Issues: What Role for the WTO?* 43 VIRGINIA JOURNAL OF INTERNATIONAL LAW 365, 400 (2003).

distinguished from routine tensions or disagreements. The phrase certainly would apply to international situations that could pose a threat of future, armed conflict. But clearly "emergency" can refer to an economic, social, or political situation as well. The best reading of this phrase would seem to allow it to apply to almost any situation, but to confine it to those of a serious nature. This implies a case-by-case judgment by WTO dispute settlement panels.[36]

In terms of its application, Article XXI(b)(iii) seems far more apposite to the temporary application of targeted economic sanctions during a period of meaningful international crisis between WTO members than it does to states' continuing programs of WMD dual-use export control, even if rhetorically justified by reference to more constructed principles such as the "war on terror." As noted above, export controls can be applied to a state or non-state actor for many reasons, some more of a political or economic character than a security character.[37] Even when applied for genuine national security reasons, the relationship between export controlling states on the one hand and target states and private entities on the other, can usually be objectively characterized as relationships in a state of "war or other emergency" with only the most tenuous grasp upon persuasion. The application of Article XXI(b)(iii) to WMD dual-use export controls would thus in most cases be extremely difficult to uphold, and is generally unpersuasive.

As a final contender, Article XXI(c) is effective in exempting sanctions or export controls authorized by the U.N. Security Council under either Chapter VI or Chapter VII of the U.N. Charter. In addition to targeted, ad hoc requirements codified in U.N. Security Council resolutions, this article could be read to include the broad and continuing obligations upon states imposed by UNSC Resolution 1540, inclusive of obligations regarding the maintenance of effective national export control systems, which will be discussed in Chapter 4 below. However, as concluded in that analysis, Resolution 1540 should be understood to comprise an overreaching by the U.N. Security Council of its powers under the U.N. Charter, with the result that Resolution 1540 itself is null and void of legal effect. As will be discussed in Chapter 5's treatment of the powers of the International Court of Justice with regard to *ultra vires* acts of the Security Council, through the ICJ's powers of incidental review the Court could determine, if the issue were properly placed before it in a contentious case, pursuant to its broad jurisdiction *ratione materiae* as defined in Article 36(2) of its Statute, that GATT Articles I and XI are binding upon WTO members and are not restricted in their scope by Security Council Resolution 1540 through the operation of GATT Article XXI(c), because Resolution 1540 is *ultra vires* the Security Council's authority under the Charter. Such a case would, in fact, constitute

---

[36] M. Matsushita, T. Schoenbaum, and P. Mavroidis, THE WORLD TRADE ORGANIZATION: LAW, PRACTICE AND POLICY (2003) 223.

[37] See, e.g., G.Clyde Hufbauer et al., ECONOMIC SANCTIONS RECONSIDERED: HISTORICAL AND CURRENT POLICY (1990).

one of the most direct confrontations to the validity of Resolution 1540 possible under existing international law, and would arguably force the Court to exercise its powers of incidental review to declare Resolution 1540 void *ab initio*.

VII. Summary of Problem

So in summary, while some objective restrictions may be imposed upon the scope of the GATT Article XXI(b)(ii) exception with regard to WMD dual-use export controls through interpretation of provisions of its text, there is still a wide scope for persuasive justification of WMD dual-use national export controls by reference to Article XXI(b)(ii), including unilateral decisions by states concerning targets of controls as well as concerning designation of controlled items and technologies.

As noted previously, the precise scope of the Article XXI(b)(ii) exception as applied to WMD dual-use export controls has not yet been defined by the WTO DSB. This is simply because thus far the specific claim has not been made before the DSB, pursuant to Article XXIII of the GATT, that a WTO member's national export control regulations are in violation of GATT Articles I, XI, or XIII, and that as a result another WTO member's benefits under the GATT have been nullified or impaired. As noted previously, states tend to deal with issues in the area of trade and security not through the formalistic dispute settlement procedures of the WTO, but rather through more subtle and non-public avenues of diplomacy.

However, it is only a matter of time before such a claim is made and must be squarely faced by a WTO Panel. When this happens, it will present a serious problem for the WTO DSB, in which it will likely have to rule as a matter of law that the national export control regulation in dispute is justified by reference to the Article XXI(b)(ii) exception. However, this ruling will reignite old tensions between North and South, between developed states and developing states, and undercurrent controversies regarding the legality and legitimacy of national and multilateral export controls generally. Such a ruling by a WTO Panel could become a serious problem for the continuing perceived legitimacy of the WTO system in developing countries. It would be perceived as a ruling that developed states, who are the primary suppliers of high tech dual-use goods, can at their will violate the spirit of fundamental principles of the WTO in discriminatorily denying whatever technologies they see fit to developing states, and that WTO law countenances this apparent double standard.[38]

---

[38] J. Simpson and T. Ogilvie-White (eds), NPT Briefing Book, Vol. 1: The Evolution of the Nuclear Nonproliferation Regime (2003); T. Ogilvie-White, *International Responses to Iranian Nuclear Defiance: The Non-Aligned Movement and the Issue of Non-Compliance*, 18 European Journal of International Law 453 (2007).

VIII. Compromise Solution

In hopes of contributing to a compromise solution of sorts when this issue is eventually fully presented to the DSB, this chapter will proceed to make some observations concerning relevant WTO procedural jurisprudence on the subjects of burden of proof and remedies, and will forward proposals as to how this jurisprudence should be applied to such cases when they arise.

First, some background on WTO dispute resolution procedure in the context of the GATT is necessary.[39] There are two primary forms of complaint under GATT Article XXIII. They are violation complaints pursuant to Article XXIII(1)(a), and non-violation complaints pursuant to Article XXIII(1)(b). A violation complaint is brought to the DSB by a state which feels that the violation of a GATT rule by another state or states has nullified or impaired benefits accruing to it under the GATT. If a breach is found by a WTO Panel to have occurred, the DSB may "recommend" that the member concerned "bring the measure into conformity" with the GATT provision which has been violated.[40] The primary requirement is "withdrawal" of the offending state measure. The panel and the Appellate Body may "suggest ways in which the Member concerned could implement the recommendations."[41] Compliance with these recommendations will be required of the offending state within a reasonable period of time. If compliance is not forthcoming within a reasonable time, the offending state may offer compensation to the aggrieved state through the lifting of trade barriers to offset the amount of the injury due to non-compliance.[42] Compensation must be agreed between the winning and losing parties. If compensation cannot be agreed upon, the winning state may appeal to the DSB to authorize countermeasures, i.e. the "suspen[sion of] the application to the Member concerned of concessions or other obligations under the covered agreements," as a final means of horizontal enforcement of GATT rules.[43]

Alternatively, a non-violation complaint is brought to the DSB by a state which considers that benefits accruing to it under the GATT are being nullified or impaired as the result of "the application by another contracting party of any measure, whether or not it conflicts with the provisions of [the GATT]."[44] Thus, a non-violation complaint can be brought to the DSB with regard to a measure which is not itself in breach of any GATT rule, but which yet allegedly causes a nullification or impairment of benefits under the GATT, or which forms an

---

[39] See generally G. Sacerdoti, A. Yanovich, and J. Bohanes (eds), The WTO at Ten: The Contribution of the Dispute Settlement System (2006); R. Yerxa and B. Wilson (eds), Key Issues in WTO Dispute Settlement: The First Ten Years (2005); D. Palmeter and P. Mavroidis, Dispute Settlement in the World Trade Organization: Practice and Procedure (2004).

[40] DSU Article 19.1.   [41] Ibid.   [42] DSU Article 22.   [43] Ibid.

[44] GATT Article XXIII(1)(b).

impediment to "the attainment of any objective of the [GATT]."[45] As the GATT Panel reported in the 1990 *EEC-Oilseeds* case:

The idea underlying [the provisions of Article XXIII:1(b)] is that the improved competitive opportunities that can legitimately be expected from a tariff concession can be frustrated not only by measures proscribed by the General Agreement but also by measures consistent with that Agreement. In order to encourage contracting parties to make tariff concessions they must therefore be given a right of redress when a reciprocal concession is impaired by another contracting party as a result of the application of any measure, whether or not it conflicts with the General Agreement.[46]

Professors Matsushita, Schoenbaum, and Mavroidis have concluded that GATT jurisprudence establishes three conditions which must be met for a non-violation complaint to be successful:

1. A prior consolidated tariff commitment;
2. a subsequent governmental action that results in
3. negatively affecting the reasonable expectations created by the consolidated tariff commitment.[47]

A successful non-violation complaint does not result in a demand for the withdrawal of the measure in question, as the legality of measure itself is not in question. Rather, as Article 26.1(b) of the DSU provides:

where a measure has been found to nullify or impair benefits under, or impede the attainment of objectives, of the relevant covered agreement without violation thereof, there is no obligation to withdraw the measure. However, in such cases, the panel or the Appellate Body shall recommend that the Member concerned make a mutually satisfactory adjustment.

The panel and Appellate Body may suggest "ways and means of reaching a mutually satisfactory adjustment," although those suggestions as to means are not binding on the parties.[48] Still, Article 22 of the DSU, which makes no distinction between recommendations made in the context of violation complaints and recommendations made in the context of non-violation complaints, establishes that the "recommendations" of the panel and Appellate Body under

---

[45] GATT Article XXIII(1).

[46] Panel Report, *EEC—Payments and Subsidies Paid to Processors and Producers of Oilseeds and Related Animal-Feed Proteins*, adopted on January 25, 1990, BISD 37S/86, para. 144. See also See Panel Report, *Japan—Measures Affecting Consumer Photographic Film and Paper*, WT/DS44/R, adopted April 22, 1998.

[47] M. Matsushita, T. Schoenbaum, and P. Mavroidis, THE WORLD TRADE ORGANIZATION: LAW, PRACTICE AND POLICY (2003) 85. See also E.-U. Petersmann, *Violation Complaints and Non-violation Complaints in Public International Trade Law*, 34 GERMAN YEARBOOK OF INTERNATIONAL LAW 175, 227 (1991); *EEC—Payments and Subsidies Paid to Processors and Producers of Oilseeds and Related Animal-Feed Proteins*, 25 January 1990, GATT B.I.S.D. (37th Supp.) at 86, para. 147 *et seq.* (1990).

[48] DSU Article 26.1(c).

DSU Article 26.1(b) that there be a mutually satisfactory adjustment of some description are binding, just as in the context of violation complaints, and must be carried out through some means to be agreed between the parties. If these recommendations are not carried out, then just as in the context of violation complaints, the remedies of compensation and countermeasures may be sought by the aggrieved member state.[49]

With regard to questions concerning WMD dual-use export controls, it would seem most advisable for a WTO member state wishing to challenge another member's export control licensing regime under GATT rules, to bring both a violation complaint and a non-violation complaint against the state maintaining these measures. This strategy was pursued by the United States in the 1998 *Japan-Film* case, in which it claimed that certain measures enacted by the Japanese Government were both in violation of substantive provisions of the GATT, and at the same time additionally the cause of nullification or impairment of GATT benefits accruing to the United States pursuant to Article XXIII(1)(b).[50] This strategy was tacitly accepted by the WTO Panel, as it proceeded to consider both the violation complaints and the non-violation complaint in turn.

In the violation complaint, the state bringing the action will attempt to make a prima facie case that the export control licensing regulations of another state constitute a breach of GATT Articles I and XI. Per DSU Article 3.8, if this case can be made prima facie, the existence of a nullification or impairment of benefits under GATT Article XXIII to the complaining party will per se be established. If the complaining state is successful in making this prima facie case, the responding state must then justify its regulation as falling under the Article XXI(b)(ii) exception.

---

[49] Panel Report, *Japan—Measures Affecting Consumer Photographic Film and Paper*, WT/DS44/R, adopted April 22, 1998, paras 6.30 and 6.40; Panel Report, *EEC—Payments and Subsidies Paid to Processors and Producers of Oilseeds and Related Animal-Feed Proteins*, adopted on January 25 1990, BISD 37S/86, para. 148 ("The CONTRACTING PARTIES have decided that a finding of impairment does not authorize them to request the impairing contracting party to remove a measure not inconsistent with the General Agreement; such a finding merely allows the contracting party frustrated in its expectation to request, in accordance with Article XXIII:2, an authorization to suspend the application of concessions or other obligations under the General Agreement. The recognition of the legitimacy of an expectation thus essentially means the recognition of the legitimacy of such a request. The recognition of the legitimacy of an expectation relating to the use of production subsidies therefore in no way prevents a contracting party from using production subsidies consistently with the General Agreement; it merely delineates the scope of the protection of a negotiated balance of concessions.")

[50] Panel Report, *Japan—Measures Affecting Consumer Photographic Film and Paper*, WT/DS44/R, adopted April 22 1998, paras 1.20 and 3.20. See this strategy employed also in the *EC–Asbestos* case (Appellate Body Report *European Communities—Measures Affecting Asbestos and Asbestos-Containing Products*, WT/DS135/AB/R, adopted April 5, 2001).

A. Burden of Proof

This section's first observation occurs at this point in the proceedings. WTO case law has clearly established the principle that a state which seeks to justify its actions under an exception to a substantive obligation, which it has been shown prima facie to have breached, must bear the burden of proof in establishing that the subject state measure is properly to be contemplated within the scope of the exception claimed to justify it. As the Appellate Body held in the 1997 *Shirts and Blouses* case:

India has argued that it is "customary GATT practice" that the party invoking a provision which is identified as an exception must offer proof that the conditions set out in that provision are met. We acknowledge that several GATT 1947 and WTO panels have required such proof of a party invoking a defence, such as those found in Article XX or Article XI:2(c)(i), to a claim of violation of a GATT obligation, such as those found in Articles I:1, II:1, III or XI:1. Articles XX and XI:(2)(c)(i) are limited exceptions from obligations under certain other provisions of the GATT 1994, not positive rules establishing obligations in themselves. They are in the nature of affirmative defences. It is only reasonable that the burden of establishing such a defence should rest on the party asserting it.[51]

This principle requires states seeking to invoke an exception to a general obligation, such as the exceptions contained in GATT Article XX, to carry a positive burden of proof, to some quotient to be determined by reference to the particularities of the issue, through which the state must objectively establish that the subject regulation falls within the justifying terms of the exception. In the context of WMD dual-use export control regulations and the Article XXI(b)(ii) exception, this burden would thus require a state seeking to justify a regulation imposing export controls under this exception from general GATT rules, to produce not only evidence of the good faith character of its subjective determination that the measure is "necessary for the protection of its essential security interests," but also evidence that the regulation does in fact objectively relate to "traffic in other goods and materials as is carried on directly or indirectly for the purpose of supplying a military establishment."[52]

---

[51] Appellate Body Report, *United States—Measure Affecting Imports of Woven Wool Shirts and Blouses from India*, WT/DS33/AB/R, para. IV. See also U.S. arguments relying on this conclusion in the 1998 *Beef Hormones* case, Appellate Body Report, *EC Measures Concerning Meat and Meat Products*, WT/DS26/AB/R, WT/DS48/AB/R, adopted February 13, 1998, DSR 1998:I, 135, para. II(B)(1).

[52] Panel Report, *Japan—Measures Affecting Consumer Photographic Film and Paper*, WT/DS44/R, adopted April 22, 1998, para. 10.430 ("The ordinary meaning of *measure* as it is used in Article XXIII:1(b) certainly encompasses a law or regulation enacted by a government. But in our view, it is broader than that and includes other governmental actions short of legally enforceable enactments.")

Thus, states wishing to avail themselves of the Article XXI(b)(ii) exception to justify the maintenance of export control regulation of WMD dual-use goods, and official decisions based thereon, would be required to produce evidence of the reasoning supporting the subjective determination of the security necessity of the regulation. They would also be required to produce evidence of the limited objective effect of those regulations relating *only* to traffic carried on directly or indirectly for the purpose of supplying a military establishment. This evidence would be weighed by the panel or Appellate Body as any other evidence, and a determination made as to whether the evidence presented was sufficient to satisfy the established quotient.

In cases concerning the application of the GATT Article XX exception in both the environmental area (e.g. the *Tuna-Dolphin* case) and the public health area (e.g. the *Beef Hormones* case), this principle has been applied quite notoriously rigorously, and the burdens of production and persuasion have been stringently set upon the party claiming the exception to prove its actions are consistent with what has at times been, and still arguably is post *Shrimp-Turtle* and *EC-Asbestos*, quite a narrow and restrictive reading of the terms of the exceptional provisions in the article.[53] One of the primary theories for such a restrictive reading has been the prioritization of the functioning of the general rule, with its advantageous effects upon the predictability of the normative order, as well as upon the general unrestricted flow of international trade which is a fundamental objective of the WTO.[54]

It would no doubt be argued by some that while this principle of burden of proof requirement for states claiming exception, and the corollary practice of interpreting exceptions narrowly, while applicable to Article XX exceptions, would not be found to be applicable in the Article XXI context because of the particularity of state interests in the area of national security.[55] However, a similar burden of proof has recently been applied analogously by the ICJ in the *Oil Platforms* case to a similar context of treaty interpretation.[56] In that case, the United States sought

---

[53] Panel Report, *United States—Restrictions on Imports of Tuna*, WT/DS21/R (September 3, 1991); *United States—Restrictions on Imports of Tuna*, DS29/R, 1994; Appellate Body Report, *EC Measures Concerning Meat and Meat Products*, WT/DS26/AB/R, WT/DS48/AB/R, adopted February 13,1998, DSR 1998:I, 135; *United States—Import Prohibition of Certain Shrimp and Shrimp Products*, WT/DS58/R, adopted November 6, 1998; Appellate Body Report, *European Communities—Measures Affecting Asbestos and Asbestos-Containing Products*, WT/DS135/AB/R, adopted April 5, 2001. See, e.g., the very demanding interpretation of the terms "necessary" in Article XX(d) adopted in *United States—Section 337 of the Tariff Act of 1930*, GATT Panel Report, adopted November 7, 1989, 36th Supp. BISD 345 (1990).

[54] See J. Bhagwati, "Trade and Environment: The False Conflict?" in D. Zaelke et al. (eds), TRADE AND THE ENVIRONMENT: LAW, ECONOMICS AND POLICY (1993).

[55] See, however, the statement of the Czechoslovakian representative in the 1949 *U.S.–Czechoslovakia* case reviewed above, recalling that many delegations at the Havana conference negotiating the GATT "wished to have these security exceptions interpreted as narrowly as possible in order to avoid misuses." GATT/CP.3/39 (June 8, 1949) (Reply of the Head of the Czechoslovak Delegation).

[56] *Islamic Republic of Iran v. United States of America* ICJ Reports 2003, 161.

to except its forceful action of attacking Iranian oil platforms, from the general obligations of the 1955 Treaty of Amity, Economic Relations and Consular Rights between itself and Iran, by reference to Article XX(1)(d) of the treaty, which provided that nothing in the treaty was to be understood to preclude the application by either state of measures "... necessary to protect its essential security interests." The U.S. was required by the Court to produce evidence regarding the precursor missile attack upon the U.S. flagged vessel the *Sea Isle City*, and the precursor mining attack upon the *USS Samuel B. Roberts*, which it alleged gave rise to its right to engage in acts of self-defense which, while prima facie in breach of the basic obligations of Article X(1) of the treaty, were nevertheless justified under the Article XX(1)(d) exception to those obligations. To this end, the U.S. produced, inter alia, satellite photographs of purported missile sites in the area, as well as fragments of the missile which struck the *Sea Isle City*.[57]

The Court in its judgment proceeded to interpret the Article XX(1)(d) exception by reference to other principles of international law, and in particular the U.N. Charter rules on the use of force. In so interpreting this security exception, and in limiting its scope by reference to other rules of international law, the ICJ removed any doubt that the exception was self-judging in its scope on the part of claiming states, or in any way beyond judicial review. After considering the evidence put forward by the United States, in the end the Court found this evidence to be insufficient to meet the burden of proof which the U.S. bore to justify its claim to exception under Article XX(1)(d) from the basic obligations of the treaty.[58]

The judgment of the ICJ in the *Oil Platforms* case illustrates the procedural appropriateness of the imposition by international tribunals of a burden of proof upon a state claiming exception from the general obligations of a treaty, even in areas of national security sensitivity and the international use of force. It can therefore be concluded that arguments seeking to exempt the provisions of GATT Article XXI from the general principles of burden of proof and restrictive application of exceptions to general obligations, established in GATT/WTO jurisprudence, should be found to be unpersuasive.

Furthermore, on the issue of WMD dual-use export controls particularly, because of the significant overlap of WMD dual-use goods with normal commerce, the conferral of a burden of proof upon a state attempting to claim exception under Article XXI(b)(ii), as well as the restrictive interpretation of this provision of the Article XXI security exception, would appear to be supported by the same concerns which have led to such treatment in the Article XX area of jurisprudence. Such concerns include the prioritization of the functioning of the general obligations of the GATT, with their advantageous effects upon

---

[57] See J.A. Green, *The Oil Platforms Case: An Error in Judgment?*, 9 JOURNAL OF CONFLICT AND SECURITY LAW 357, 362–363 (2004).

[58] *Islamic Republic of Iran v. United States of America*, ICJ Reports 2003, 161, para. 72.

the predictability of the international trade normative order, as well as upon the general unrestricted flow of international trade, both of which are fundamental objectives of the WTO system.[59]

The imposition of a rigorous burden of proof upon states justifying WMD dual-use export control programs by reference to Article XXI(b)(ii) within the context of violation complaints before WTO Panels will in a measure implement the normative objectivity which has been clearly found to exist in the character of the provisions of the Article XXI exception. It will force states seeking to exempt their actions by reference to this provision to present to an independent arbiter, in a transparent process, the evidence on which it has based both its subjective determinations and objective assessments. Such a requirement will help to remove from this provision of the Article XXI exception the concerns, particularly held in the developing world, that it comprises a latent escape clause from GATT obligations, exercisable unilaterally by developed states without accountability or independent review for soundness. This will particularly be the case if some representations of developed states justifying elements of their export control programs are found by the WTO Panels or Appellate Body, to be insufficient to meet the requirements of the exception, and thus that the subject export control regulations are in violation of fundamental obligations of the GATT.

The question could be raised as to whether the imposition of a burden of proof requirement upon states claiming exception under Article XXI(b)(ii) will run into difficulty because of the provisions of Article XXI(a), which states:

Nothing in this Agreement shall be construed...to require any contracting party to furnish any information the disclosure of which it considers contrary to its essential security interests.

In most cases of WMD dual-use export control regulations, the reasoning behind the regulations and the evidence of the operation and effect of the regulations will not be particularly sensitive. However, it is conceivable that sensitive intelligence information could form a basis for the maintenance and functioning of particular regulations. Nevertheless, in the end, Article XXI(a) will not form a bar to the imposition of a burden of proof upon states claiming exception for their export control programs under Article XXI(b)(ii). Article XXI(a) stands, as do each of the provisions of Article XXI, as an exception to the general rules of the GATT, and provides that no general rule shall be construed to require member states to divulge information the disclosure of which they deem to be contrary to their essential security interest. In the context under consideration herein, which is the context of a state seeking to meet a procedural burden of proof in order to establish that its actions are within an exception to the general GATT rules, Article XXI(a)

---

[59] See J. Bhagwati, "Trade and Environment: The False Conflict?" in D. Zaelke et al. (eds), TRADE AND THE ENVIRONMENT: LAW, ECONOMICS AND POLICY (1993).

has no bearing. A state respondent in a violation complaint regarding its export control regulations may choose not to divulge certain information it considers sensitive, and it will be perfectly within its rights under all GATT obligations in doing so. In such a situation, nothing in the GATT is being construed to require the respondent state to furnish information the disclosure of which it considers contrary to its essential security interests. However, that unwillingness to disclose may preclude the respondent state from meeting the procedural burden of proof necessary to qualify for the Article XXI(b)(ii) exception to fundamental GATT obligations, and Article XXI(a) comprises no impediment to this requirement.

B. Countermeasures

If the violation complaint is successful, and the respondent state cannot meet the burden of proof to justify its export control regulation pursuant to Article XXI(b)(ii), then the normal DSU procedures will be followed with regard to remedies arising from that successful complaint. Whether or not the violation complaint is successful, however, the panel or Appellate Body can proceed to consider the non-violation complaint regarding the same regulations of the respondent state.[60]

In the non-violation complaint context, the complaining state is not attempting to show a prima facie breach of a GATT obligation. Thus, it cannot take advantage of the DSU Article 3.8 establishment of per se nullification or impairment of benefit. Rather, pursuant to DSU Article 26, the complaining state will be required to "present a detailed justification in support" of its complaint, including evidence establishing nullification or impairment of benefits and objectives of the GATT, and evidence establishing that this nullification or impairment is being caused by the subject state action.[61] This requirement sets a relatively high, but not impossible, threshold for complaining parties.[62]

As noted above, three conditions necessary for a successful non-violation complaint can be distilled from GATT/WTO jurisprudence:

1. A prior consolidated tariff commitment;
2. a subsequent governmental action that results in
3. negatively affecting the reasonable expectations created by the consolidated tariff commitment.[63]

---

[60] See Appellate Body Report, *European Communities—Measures Affecting Asbestos and Asbestos-Containing Products*, WT/DS135/AB/R, adopted April 5, 2001.

[61] See Panel Report, *Japan—Measures Affecting Consumer Photographic Film and Paper*, WT/DS44/R, adopted April 22,1998.

[62] Panel Report, *EEC—Payments and Subsidies Paid to Processors and Producers of Oilseeds and Related Animal-Feed Proteins*, adopted January 25, 1990, BISD 37S/86, paras 151–152.

[63] Quoted from M. Matsushita, T. Schoenbaum, and P. Mavroidis, THE WORLD TRADE ORGANIZATION: LAW, PRACTICE AND POLICY (2003) 85.

In the context of WMD dual-use export control regulations, therefore, a complaining state must establish that the tariff commitments which the respondent state has made with regard to particular goods, have given rise to reasonable expectations of a certain volume of unrestricted flows of trade in those particular goods between the complaining state and the respondent state. It must then establish that subsequent government action instituting a particular export control regulation or decision, has negatively affected, and is continuing to negatively affect, those reasonable expectations.

Thus, non-violation complaints in the WMD dual-use export control context will be most likely to succeed in circumstances in which tariff commitments on the part of the respondent state are in place, and a subsequently passed regulation or official decision (including a particular license denial) imposes export controls on goods which were the subject of those tariff commitments. In such a case, the reasonable expectations of the complaining state, i.e. the state against which the export control regulation or decision was targeted, may be shown to have been frustrated by the regulation or decision which has had the effect of decreasing the reasonably expected volume of trade in those goods as between the parties.

Such a non-violation complaint would be in harmony with the underlying principles of the WTO, and particularly with the general principle of non-discrimination, which is itself a reasonable expectation of WTO members, and which as noted above is an inescapable victim of national export control regulations.

As observed above, a successful non-violation complaint will result in a recommendation "that the Member concerned make a mutually satisfactory adjustment."[64] The panel and Appellate Body may "suggest ways and means of reaching a mutually satisfactory adjustment," although those suggestions as to means are not binding on the parties, nor is there any obligation on the part of the responding state to withdraw the subject regulation.[65] However, the recommendations of the panel and Appellate Body under DSU Article 26.1(b) that there be a mutually satisfactory adjustment of some description are binding and must be carried out through some means to be agreed between the parties. If these recommendations are not carried out, the remedies of compensation and countermeasures may be sought by the aggrieved member state.

Thus, the ultimate remedy granted to a state which brings a successful non-violation complaint, is the same remedy which may be granted to a state which brings a violation complaint. Countermeasures to be applied by the aggrieved state may be authorized by the DSB to offset the value of the denied import of the export controlled goods. Ultimately, therefore, the non-violation complaint process does bear teeth, and is a meaningful remedy for a state which feels that its reasonable expectations of benefit flowing from its own and other states'

---

[64] DSU Article 26(1)(b).   [65] DSU Article 26(1)(c).

obligations under the GATT have been frustrated, even if the state action which is the cause of that frustration is not technically a violation of GATT rules.

In the specific context of the Article XXI security exception, there is nothing particular to Article XXI as a legal provision which would appear to exempt it from susceptibility to the non-violation complaints procedure. Nor are there particular considerations which would seem to make the granting of counter-measures, as the ultimate remedy to a successful non-violation complaining state, in any way inappropriate or inadvisable simply because a state action justified by reference to Article XXI is involved.

Article XXI(b) provides that WTO member states shall not be prevented by GATT obligations from taking specified actions which a state deems to be in its essential security interest. The use of the non-violation complaint process by a state which feels that its reasonable expectations of trade pursuant to GATT rules have been frustrated by an action taken by another state which falls within the exceptional terms of Article XXI(b), does not in any way legally prevent the state taking action pursuant to Article XXI(b) from doing so. Nor does a successful non-violation complaint against such an acting state make the action in question illegal. The non-violation complaint process, and remedies attached thereto, is simply a recognition that the concept of nullification and impair-ment of benefits under the GATT is not confined to the results of a breach of GATT rules, but rather additionally encompasses the reality that even lawful actions under the basic obligations of the GATT may do violence to the reason-able expectations of WTO members based upon the operation of those basic obligations. A non-violation complaint does not seek to apportion fault. It does, however, seek to fairly apportion the negative effects upon trade that flow from state actions which frustrate other states' reasonable expectations based upon their WTO membership.

The non-violation complaint process in the context of WMD dual-use export controls thus recognizes that states do have the right to restrict exports under Article XXI, and thus exempt themselves from the application of Articles I and XI to those restrictions. However, it also recognizes that these lawful export license denials of high-tech goods will negatively affect trade with other WTO members, in frustration of those members' reasonable expectations of non-discriminatory treatment under existing tariff commitments. It seeks, therefore, to fairly apportion this negative economic effect for the duration of the maintenance of the action by shifting some or all of that negative economic effect back to the state taking the expectation-frustrating action. Again, this apportionment can take place through the legal vehicle of compensation as defined in DSU Article XXII(2), or ultimately through the vehicle of counter-measures under DSU Article XXII(2) if the regulating state declines to voluntarily compensate.

Overall the non-violation complaint process in the area of WMD dual-use export controls strikes a fair balance between the interests of states in national security, and the interests of other states in non-discriminatory treatment and fairness under GATT rules. The application of remedial measures under DSU Article XXII, resulting from a successful non-violation complaint in this area, would be an important concession in allaying developing world concerns regarding the potential use of GATT Article XXI(b)(ii) as a general escape clause. Not only would it more fairly apportion the negative economic effects on trade of national export control regulations, but in doing so it would have the further effect of raising the cost of maintenance of export controls, making this cost justifiable to export controlling states only in cases of sincere national security concern. This latter effect, too, would increase confidence in the WTO system as a forum providing objectively determinable and enforceable rules of law ordering international trade, the rules of which are not subject to abuse at the whim of powerful states.

C. Summary

The effect of these observed procedural principles of GATT/WTO jurisprudence, if applied by WTO Panels and the Appellate Body as outlined herein to the area of WMD dual-use export controls, should serve to mediate or temper the effects of the unilateral and discriminatory exercise of the GATT Article XXI(b)(ii) exception by export controlling states.

PART II

NON-PROLIFERATION LAW AND THE UNITED NATIONS SYSTEM

4

Non-proliferation Law and the United Nations System: The U.N. Political Bodies

This chapter will discuss the role of the United Nations political bodies in creating, facilitating, maintaining, and enforcing international law on the subject of the proliferation of weapons of mass destruction.[1] As the cornerstone international organization in the area of international peace and security, the United Nations has had a long history of engagement with the issue of WMD proliferation, beginning with the very first General Assembly Resolution on January 24, 1946.[2] Indeed, the U.N. Charter itself gives to the political bodies of the organization specific powers to participate in the creation of new international law on issues of WMD proliferation, as well as special powers of enforcement of non-proliferation law to the U.N. Security Council.[3]

During the Cold War, the United Nations political bodies struggled to find a meaningful role to play in the area of WMD proliferation, as the two superpowers engaged in seemingly unbridled expansion of their nuclear arsenals. Despite some influence, particularly by the General Assembly, upon the negotiation of multi-lateral treaties such as the 1968 NPT, carried on outside of the U.N. framework, efforts by the political bodies during this period to use their non-proliferation lawmaking powers under the Charter met with little success.[4]

After the ending of the Cold War in 1991, the Security Council, which had been most affected in its ability to function effectively due to the long standing

---

[1] This chapter is an amended version of an article entitled *Nonproliferation Law and the United Nations System: Resolution 1540 and the Limits of the Power of the Security Council*, published at 20 LEIDEN JOURNAL OF INTERNATIONAL LAW No. 2 (2007). Used here by permission.

[2] See J. Goldblat, ARMS CONTROL (2nd edn, 2002) 34–37; G. Den Dekker, THE LAW OF ARMS CONTROL (2001) ch. 7; H. Kelsen, COLLECTIVE SECURITY UNDER INTERNATIONAL LAW (originally published in 1957, reprinted by the Naval War College in 2001); D. Sarooshi, THE UNITED NATIONS AND THE DEVELOPMENT OF COLLECTIVE SECURITY (1999); V. Gowland-Debbas, COLLECTIVE RESPONSES TO ILLEGAL ACTS IN INTERNATIONAL LAW (1990); V. Gowland-Debbas, UNITED NATIONS SANCTIONS AND INTERNATIONAL LAW (2001); C. Joyner (ed.), THE UNITED NATIONS AND INTERNATIONAL LAW (1997).

[3] See Articles 11(1), 26, 39, 41, 42.

[4] See J. Goldblat, ARMS CONTROL (2nd edn, 2002) 34–37.

tensions between two of its permanent members, enjoyed a renewal of its ability to find common cause among its member states in an array of international security issue areas, and a new found effectiveness in Council decision-making.[5] This renewed consensus produced resolutions under the Council's Chapter VII authority to maintain and restore international peace and security with regard to situations, in among other places, the Balkans, Haiti, Somalia, Rwanda, the Congo, Afghanistan, and Libya.[6] In the WMD non-proliferation issue area, this renewed ability of the Security Council to use its Chapter VII powers was illustrated in 1991, in the passage of Resolution 687, which imposed specific weapons-related prohibitions on Iraq, and established an inspection and verification regime in order to compulsorily disarm Iraq of its WMD and related technologies possessions.[7]

However, the passage by the Council of Resolution 1540 in 2004 marked the beginning of a new chapter of Security Council action in the area of WMD proliferation, and manifested a distinct change in the Council's understanding of its role and powers under Chapter VII.[8] Through Resolution 1540, the Security Council used its binding authority under Article 25 of the Charter to impose upon all U.N. member states obligations to enact and enforce a range of non-proliferation-related regulations of universal scope and unlimited duration in their national legal systems, and to cooperate in international non-proliferation efforts.[9]

To many, the passage of Resolution 1540 was a long-awaited direct engagement by the Security Council in the area of WMD proliferation, and a welcome addition to the corpus of non-proliferation law. However this chapter will argue that, whatever its practical utilities, from an international jurisprudential standpoint Resolution 1540 is a legal travesty, and a dangerous departure from understandings of the authority of the Security Council pursuant to which the Council itself operated during the first 56 years of its existence.

The chapter will first review the powers of law creation and law enforcement granted to the political bodies of the United Nations under the Charter in the area of non-proliferation law, and will discuss their use (or more commonly disuse) since the Charter's founding. Consideration will then turn to the Security Council's passage of Resolution 1540 and to its meaning and import to the existing non-proliferation treaties and regimes system, as well as to a review of the harmony of the passage of this resolution with the limited powers of the Security

---

[5] See D. Malone (ed.), THE U.N. SECURITY COUNCIL: FROM THE COLD WAR TO THE 21ˢᵗ CENTURY (2004).

[6] For an account of these various cases in which the Council invoked its Chapter VII authority, see M. Hilaire, UNITED NATIONS LAW AND THE SECURITY COUNCIL (2005).

[7] SC Res. 678 (29 Nov. 1990). See Chapter 7 herein.

[8] SC Res. 1540 (24 April 2004).

[9] M. Asada, WMD Terrorism and Security Council Resolution 1540: Conditions for Legitimacy in International Legislation, IILJ Working Paper 2007/9, available at <http://www.iilj.org/publications/2007-9Asada.asp>.

Council under the Charter. It will conclude that in passing Resolution 1540, the Security Council acted *ultra vires* its authority under the Charter, and will argue that this action marks an alarming continuation of a trend in Security Council legislation first apparent in the passage of Resolution 1373 in 2001.[10]

I. The U.N. Charter and WMD Non-proliferation Law

The United Nations Charter makes no mention of the term "proliferation" and makes no distinction in the language of its provisions as between conventional and non-conventional weapons. Making such a distinction based upon particular weapons technologies only evolved as a customary practice after the advent of the nuclear weapons age in August 1945, only two months after the signing of the U.N. Charter in June of that year, although chemical and biological weapons had existed in various forms and been used in warfare for centuries, and had been addressed specifically in the 1925 Geneva Protocol.[11]

The Charter rather uses the terms "disarmament" and the "regulation of armaments" in three of its articles; Article 11(1), Article 26, and Article 47. These provisions address the subject of the regulation of military armaments generally through international law, as such technologies existed and were maintained in national arsenals at the time of the drafting of the Charter.[12] The U.N. Charter system which these provisions comprise was constructed to address issues of international arms control and to facilitate the generation of international law to regulate this issue area. As noted in the introduction to this volume, in terms of coverage, arms control law is a broader jurisprudential framework than is non-proliferation law, importantly conceptually including the legal regulation of development, possession, and proliferation of WMD, which comprises non-proliferation law as this volume utilizes that term, but also including the legal regulation of conventional weapons technologies.[13]

Thus, as the history of General Assembly and Security Council resolutions which will be reviewed below makes clear, the U.N. Charter system, comprised particularly of Articles 11(1) and 26, should be understood to have application to the creation, facilitation, and maintenance of WMD non-proliferation law, as these comprise a subset of issues within its general competence with regard to arms control law.

---

[10] SC Res. 1373 (September 28, 2001); See M. Happold, *Security Council Resolution 1373 and the Constitution of the United Nations*, 16 Leiden Journal of International Law 593 (2003).

[11] See Chapter 2 herein.

[12] See D. Cheever, *The U.N. and Disarmament*, 19 International Organization 453 (1965).

[13] See H. Schutz, "Arms Control", Encyclopaedia of Public International Law I, 259–267; H. Bull, The Control of the Arms Race: Disarmament and Arms Control in the Missile Age (2nd edn, 1965); J. Goldblat, Arms Control (2nd edn, 2002).

II. Review of Charter Provisions

Overall the subject of the regulation of military armaments receives significantly less attention, and less clarity, in the U.N. Charter than it did in the League of Nations Covenant, which in Article 8 declares as a principle of international law that "the maintenance of peace requires the reduction of national armaments to the lowest point consistent with national safety and the enforcement by common action of international obligations."[14] Article 8 proceeds to spell out the role of the League Council in helping states to establish minimum thresholds for maintenance of military armaments, and forbids the possession of armaments in excess of those limits without the consent of the Council. It further requires member states to engage in a "full and frank" exchange of information regarding the scale of their armaments.[15]

The difference in the context of the signing of the two documents largely explains the lesser emphasis in the Charter placed upon the idea of disarmament as an absolute principle. In the year leading up from the Dumbarton Oaks Conference in August 1944 to the final signing of the U.N. Charter in San Francisco in June 1945, the Charter framers were still at war, and thus had little interest in prescribing a new international legal system for universal disarmament.[16] Even in their thoughts regarding post-war plans, they abandoned the idea so central to the League of Nations Covenant that universal disarmament was necessary for the maintenance of peace. On the contrary, it was recognized that maintenance of military armaments would be necessary to effect the collective security system envisioned under the new Charter framework, which relied on the provision of forces by national governments to maintain international peace and security, under the direction of the Security Council.[17]

There was an acknowledgement that a general limitation of armaments could be a useful strategy to avoid excessive stockpiling of weapons, and reciprocal arms races that such production could engender, with negative effects upon national resource utilization and international security generally. However the

---

[14] See B. Simma et al. (eds), THE CHARTER OF THE UNITED NATIONS: A COMMENTARY (2nd edn, 2002) 465.

[15] See D. Hunter Miller, THE DRAFTING OF THE COVENANT (originally published 1928, reprinted 1998).

[16] See D. Cheever, *The U.N. and Disarmament*, 19 INTERNATIONAL ORGANIZATION 453 (1965); L. Sohn, CASES AND OTHER MATERIALS ON WORLD LAW; THE INTERPRETATION AND APPLICATION OF THE CHARTER OF THE UNITED NATIONS AND OF THE CONSTITUTIONS OF OTHER AGENCIES OF THE WORLD COMMUNITY (1950); B. Simma et al. (eds), THE CHARTER OF THE UNITED NATIONS: A COMMENTARY (2nd edn, 2002) 465–466; W. Benedicks, THE SAN FRANCISCO CONFERENCE ON INTERNATIONAL ORGANIZATION: APRIL-JUNE 1945 (1994); R. Hilderbrand, DUMBARTON OAKS: THE ORIGINS OF THE UNITED NATIONS AND THE SEARCH FOR POSTWAR SECURITY (1990); E.A. Luard, A HISTORY OF THE UNITED NATIONS (1982); S.C. Tiwari, GENESIS OF THE UNITED NATIONS (1968).

[17] B. Simma et al. (eds), THE CHARTER OF THE UNITED NATIONS: A COMMENTARY (2nd edn, 2002) 465–466.

U.N. Charter moved away from a reliance upon disarmament as a means to ensure international peace, and toward a broader concept of arms control within a collective security system, of which the maintenance of national armaments, particularly by major powers, was a necessary part.[18]

Thus, the Charter sought to strike a much more neutral position regarding the powers and responsibilities of its organs with regard to national armaments than the League of Nations Covenant had by substituting, or at least supplementing, references to disarmament with the more generalized term "regulation of armaments."[19] In Article 11(1), therefore, the Charter states that:

The General Assembly may consider the general principles of cooperation in the maintenance of international peace and security, including the principles governing disarmament and the regulation of armaments, and may make recommendations with regard to such principles to the Members or to the Security Council or to both.

Article 11(1) is a further specification, and not a limitation, of the general powers of consideration and recommendation granted to the General Assembly in Article 10.[20] The General Assembly under Article 11(1) is to consider "general principles of cooperation in the maintenance of international peace and security," a power which should be read to include consideration of abstract, general ideas about how member states should work together, and fundamental principles which should underpin the legal relationships which bind states in this area.[21] This power is apposite the General Assembly due to its character as the essential deliberative organ of the United Nations, and the only U.N. body comprised of all members of the organization, thus allowing the broadest possible spectrum of interests and perspectives to have input into the formulation of these basic principles governing state cooperation in international arms control efforts.[22]

Notwithstanding the relatively low emphasis placed upon arms control in the Charter generally, the General Assembly's first ever Resolution, passed at its 17th plenary meeting on January 24, 1946, was in exercise of its powers under Article 11(1). In Resolution 1, entitled "Establishment of a Commission to Deal with the Problems Raised by the Discovery of Atomic Energy," the General Assembly created the Atomic Energy Commission (AEC), which was

---

[18] Ibid.

[19] See J. Barton, "Disarmament", ENCYCLOPAEDIA OF PUBLIC INTERNATIONAL LAW I, 1072–1076.

[20] See B. Simma et al. (eds), THE CHARTER OF THE UNITED NATIONS: A COMMENTARY (2nd edn, 2002) 277–278.

[21] Ibid. at 277–280.

[22] L. Sohn, "Enhancing the Role of the General Assembly of the United Nations in Crystallizing International Law", in J. Makarczyk (ed.), THEORY OF INTERNATIONAL LAW AT THE THRESHOLD OF THE 21ˢᵗ CENTURY (1975) 549–561; O. Asamoah, THE LEGAL SIGNIFICANCE OF THE DECLARATIONS OF THE GENERAL ASSEMBLY OF THE UNITED NATIONS (1966); J. Castaneda, LEGAL EFFECTS OF UNITED NATIONS RESOLUTIONS (1969); J. Andrassy, *Uniting for Peace*, 50 AMERICAN JOURNAL OF INTERNATIONAL LAW 563 (1956); H. Kelsen, THE LAW OF THE UNITED NATIONS (1951); F. Morley, THE CHARTER OF THE UNITED NATIONS (1946).

to be composed of a representative of each state on the Security Council and Canada. The AEC was given a mandate to "proceed with utmost despatch and inquire into all phases of the problem" of the discovery of atomic energy, and to make specific proposals

a) for extending between all nations the exchange of basic scientific information for peaceful ends;
b) for control of atomic energy to the extent necessary to ensure its use only for peaceful purposes;
c) for the elimination from national armaments of atomic weapons and of all other major weapons adaptable to mass destruction; and
d) for effective safeguards by way of inspection and other means to protect complying States against the hazards of violation and evasions.[23]

The reason for the inclusion of this action in the very first General Assembly resolution was of course the fact that the world had only months earlier found out about the development by the United States of nuclear fission weapons, and their use on the cities of Hiroshima and Nagasaki, Japan in August 1945. In this resolution, the General Assembly extended as a matter of course its authority to consider issues of arms control, to include consideration of issues regarding nuclear weapons and "all other weapons adaptable to mass destruction," thereby clarifying the application of the Charter's terms to both conventional and WMD technologies, as that distinction began to be made from this time.

The early history of the AEC, perhaps not surprisingly, was to be a controversial one.[24] The U.S. Representative to the AEC, Bernard Baruch, presented a plan to the Security Council in June 1946 which included a proposal to establish a treaty–based organization to be called the International Atomic Development Authority (IADA), the task of which was to own, operate, manage, and license all atomic energy research and production facilities on behalf of the nations of the world. It was in essence a proposal to disarm all states of atomic weapons and create an international organization to control nuclear materials and distribute them equitably for peaceful uses, including the authority to maintain an inspection regime in all countries making use of such materials. The United States, as the sole possessor of the secrets of the full nuclear fuel cycle, was not to be subject to the authority of the IADA until the organization's control regime had been fully established, holding the atomic knowledge in "sacred trust" for all humankind, and of course maintaining a strategic advantage over the Soviet Union.[25]

The Soviet Union, for its part, forwarded a counter proposal which would entail the creation of two new treaty regimes; one to immediately and universally

[23] Para. 5.
[24] See H. Athanasopulos, Nuclear Disarmament in International law (2000) ch. 2; B. Bechhoefer, Postwar Negotiations for Arms Control (1961).
[25] See D. Cheever, *The U.N. and Disarmament*, 19 International Organization 453, 468– 470 (1965).

outlaw nuclear weapons, and the other to organize the controls of the AEC and guarantee procedures for sharing of nuclear information and technologies between states for peaceful purposes. These proposals, of course, would have neutralized the U.S. nuclear advantage, but would also have left disarmament efforts largely in the hands of national governments, with an international organization having only limited rights to conduct periodic inspections of nuclear facilities.[26]

The result of these conflicting proposals was a compromise reached in the General Assembly by the passage of Resolution 41 on December 14, 1946, which used the recommendation power of the General Assembly under Article 11(1) for the first time. Resolution 41 is divided into 9 paragraphs, in which the General Assembly makes two statements of recognition of "general principles of cooperation in the maintenance of international peace and security" and six "recommendations with regard to such principles" to the Security Council. The two statements of recognition are

1. the necessity of an early general regulation and reduction of armaments and armed forces;[27] and
2. that essential to the general regulation and reduction of armaments and armed forces, is the provision of practical and effective safeguards by way of inspection and other means to protect complying states against the hazards of violations and evasions.[28]

Based upon these statements of general principle, the General Assembly recommends in Resolution 41, inter alia, that

the Security Council expedite consideration of the reports which the Atomic Energy Commission will make to the Security Council and that it facilitate the work of the Commission, and also that the Security Council expedite consideration of a draft convention or conventions for the creation of an international system of control and inspection, these conventions to include the prohibition of atomic and all other major weapons adaptable now and in the future to mass destruction and the control of atomic energy to the extent necessary to ensure its use only for peaceful purposes.[29]

And further that

the Security Council give prompt consideration to formulating the practical measures, according to their priority, which are essential to provide for the general regulation and reduction of armaments and armed forces and to assure that such regulation and reduction of armaments and armed forces will be generally observed by all participants and not unilaterally by only some of the participants. The plans formulated by the Security Council shall be submitted by the Secretary-General to the Members of the United Nations for consideration at a special session of the General Assembly. The treaties or

---

[26] Ibid.   [27] Para. 1.   [28] Para. 5.   [29] Para. 4.

conventions approved by the General Assembly shall be submitted to the signatory States for ratification in accordance with Article 26 of the Charter.[30]

The Security Council responded to General Assembly Resolution 41 on February 14, 1947 with Security Council Resolution 18, in which it resolved:

1. to work out the practical measures for giving effect to General Assembly resolution [] 41...;[31]
2. to consider as soon as possible the report submitted by the Atomic Energy Commission and to take suitable actions to facilitate its work;[32] and
3. to set up a commission consisting of representatives of the members of the Security Council with instructions to prepare and submit to the Security Council...the proposals (a) for the general regulation and reduction of armaments and armed forces, and (b) for practical and effective safeguards in connection with the general regulation and reduction of armaments, which the commission may be in a position to formulate in order to ensure the implementation of the above-mentioned resolution [] of the General Assembly...[33]

The Security Council's relative quickness to accept the General Assembly's recommendations in Resolution 41, and willingness to implement them, is explainable by reference to the Security Council's duty in this area as specified in Article 26 of the U.N. Charter, cited by the General Assembly in Resolution 41. Article 26 provides:

In order to promote the establishment and maintenance of international peace and security with the least diversion for armaments of the world's human and economic resources, the Security Council shall be responsible for formulating, with the assistance of the Military Staff Committee referred to in Article 47, plans to be submitted to the Members of the United Nations for the establishment of a system for the regulation of armaments.

A number of points regarding the Security Council's role under Article 26 bear mention. First is to observe that Article 26, in addition to conferring powers and function upon the Security Council, also establishes responsibilities for the Council in carrying out its complementary role with the General Assembly in the exercise of its Article 11(1) powers. The Council is given the responsibility, on the basis of the recommendations of "general principles of cooperation" it receives from the General Assembly, and with the assistance of the Military Staff Committee, to formulate concrete plans in order to implement the general principles recommended by the Assembly. These plans are to compose a coherent "system" for the regulation of armaments, which would imply that the plans to be authored by the Council using this power are not to be situation specific, as in the case of an ad hoc response to a discrete event in international affairs. Rather,

---

[30] Para. 2.   [31] Para. 1.   [32] Para. 2.   [33] Para. 3.

these plans are to form the basis for a universally applicable, enduring system of "practical and effective" international arms control.[34]

The Security Council's responsibility to make concrete plans based on General Assembly recommendations of general principle is apposite that body, particularly as the membership of the Council was designed to consist of the great military powers. The conferral by the Charter of this power and responsibility upon the Council is a recognition of the likelihood that these states will have the largest military arsenals, and thus that their support will be required for any international plan for the regulation of armaments to be implementable.[35] It is also apposite because of the size of the Security Council, and the recognition that consensus on specific plans is more likely to be obtainable among a group the size of the Security Council than a group the size of the General Assembly. Thus, while Article 11(1) is in keeping with a principled notion of universal participation by the international community of states in the construction of fundamental principles which should order relations among states in the area of international arms control, Article 26 is a recognition of the practical exigencies of international politics which demand that the Security Council, despite its unrepresentative character, has a vital role in the construction of plans for an international arms control system.

However, Article 26 is not in fact as violative of principles of sovereign equality as it first appears. It must be noted that the Security Council under Article 26 only has the power to formulate plans. It must then submit those plans to the member states of the United Nations for their approval and for establishment through multilateral treaty as actual legal principles governing their relationships with each other. The Security Council's plans in and of themselves have no binding force upon members, and are merely hortatory offerings, although endowed with the gravitas of having been generated through the Charter system for creation of arms control law.[36] Members may however choose either to accept or reject these plans, in analogous fashion to the ratification of U.N.-approved treaties by member states. As Hans Kelsen has observed:

[W]ith respect to Article 26 of the Charter…the "plans" formulated by the Security Council "for the establishment of a system for the regulation of armaments" may provide for reduction of armaments; they must be "submitted to the members of the United Nations." That means that they are binding upon the members only if accepted by them.

[34] See B. Bechhoefer, Postwar Negotiations for Arms Control (1961); O. Bogdanov, *Outlawry of War and Disarmament*, Recueil des Cours 133 (1971-II) 15–42; B. Simma et al. (eds), The Charter of the United Nations: A Commentary (2nd edn, 2002) 466–468; J. Goldblat, *The Role of the United Nations in Arms Control: An Assessment*, 7 Arms Control 115–132 (1986); L. Goodrich, *The UN Security Council*, 12 International Organization 273–287 (1958).

[35] See D. Cheever, *The U.N. and Disarmament*, 19 International Organization 453, 464–466 (1965).

[36] See B. Simma et al. (eds), The Charter of the United Nations: A Commentary (2nd edn, 2002) 466–468.

The obligation is established by a treaty concluded by the members with the organization. Unlike Article 8, paragraph 4 of the [League of Nations] Covenant, Article 26 does not provide expressly for the "adoption" of the plan by the members, but if the plan of the Security Council is to be submitted to the members, it can be only for the purpose of being adopted by them.[37]

Thus under the Charter system, member states retain their full sovereignty over decisions to enter into legal relationships in the area of international arms control. This right is not presumptively subsumed under the Council's binding decision-making powers under Article 25, nor under its broad powers to maintain international peace and security under the articles of Chapter VII.[38]

Notwithstanding this inability to finally bring about new law in the area of international arms control under their own authority, the political organs of the United Nations are given an important role to play under the Charter system in facilitating cooperation and coordination between member states in reaching concrete agreements on the regulation of armaments.[39] This system is illustrated in the passage of General Assembly Resolution 41 and Security Council Resolution 18.

However, the subsequent history of the efforts commissioned by Resolution 18 was to comprise a cautionary tale for the practical implementation of this system. The studies and recommendations called for by the Security Council in Resolution 18 did not in the end result in plans being submitted to member states, as the commission created by the resolution was divided on fundamental issues.[40] This inability of the political organs of the U.N., and particularly the Security Council, to act due to political deadlock between the superpowers on issues of arms control was to become an often repeated outcome, and formed the primary cause of the failure of the United Nations to make any meaningful progress in developing multilateral arms control law through the succeeding decades of Cold War tensions.

This chapter will proceed to consider in further detail the role and record of each of the political organs in fulfilling their Charter mandates in the area of arms control law, and more particularly WMD non-proliferation law.[41] It will

---

[37] H. Kelsen, Collective Security Under International Law (originally published in 1957, here as reprinted by the Naval War College in 2001) 214.

[38] H. Kelsen, The Law of the United Nations (1951).

[39] See J. Goldblat, *The Role of the United Nations in Arms Control: An Assessment*, 7 Arms Control 115–132 (1986).

[40] See D. Cheever, *The U.N. and Disarmament*, 19 International Organization 453, 470 (1965).

[41] In Article 26 and Article 47 the Military Staff Committee is given an advisory role to the Security Council on an array of issues, including the regulation of armaments. The Military Staff Committee was mentioned in Resolution 18, and asked to submit a report to the Security Council on "the basic principles which should govern the organization of the United Nations armed force." The Committee did submit this report, and this remains its only significant accomplishment. It never exercised its advisory role under Article 26 in the area of armaments regulation. See B. Simma et al. (eds), The Charter of the United Nations: A Commentary (2nd edn, 2002) 770–775.

conclude that both the General Assembly and the Security Council have largely failed to fulfill the roles and mandates given them under the Charter in the area of non-proliferation law creation. It will then give particular consideration to the Security Council's recent use of its Chapter VII enforcement powers, instead of its Article 26 powers, to make non-proliferation law in the form of Security Council Resolution 1540.

III. The General Assembly

Consideration will first turn to a review of the efforts of the General Assembly and its subsidiary bodies in the area of non-proliferation law creation and maintenance, as well as that of the closely associated Conference on Disarmament.

A. The United Nations Disarmament Commission

In 1952 the Atomic Energy Commission and its sister agency the U.N. Commission for Conventional Armaments, were in effect consolidated into a new single entity which was to take the lead role as the forum for consideration of arms control issues. This first incarnation of the U.N. Disarmament Commission (UNDC), like the AEC, included in its membership all the members of the Security Council plus Canada, and was instructed to prepare a draft treaty on the regulation and reduction of all armed forces and armaments and the elimination of all weapons of mass destruction. However, the new consolidated Commission suffered from disunity among its members on fundamental issues, and was unable to make significant progress on a treaty text. Eventually the work of the Commission ground to a halt and it met only infrequently after 1959.[42]

The UNDC was revived in 1978, during the General Assembly's First Special Session on Disarmament, and was reorganized as an intersessional, subsidiary organ of the General Assembly, composed of all member states of the United Nations. Its mandate was given in General Assembly Resolution S-10/2 as follows:

The Disarmament Commission shall be a deliberative body, a subsidiary organ of the General Assembly, the function of which shall be to consider and make recommendations on various problems in the field of disarmament and to follow up the relevant decisions and recommendations of the special session devoted to disarmament. The Disarmament Commission should, *inter alia*, consider the elements of a comprehensive programme for disarmament to be submitted as recommendations to the General Assembly and, through it, to the negotiating body, the Committee on Disarmament.[43]

---

[42] See B. Simma et al. (eds), THE CHARTER OF THE UNITED NATIONS: A COMMENTARY (2nd edn, 2002) 473–475.

[43] GA Res. S-10/2 (June 30, 1978).

The UNDC currently meets for three weeks every Spring, and operates in working groups and in plenary sessions, the number of working groups being determined by the number of substantive issues on its agenda. It submits a report annually to the General Assembly. Since 1989, its agenda has been limited to no more than four substantive items, with only two being considered as a matter of practice in recent years, each usually considered for three consecutive years.[44] For the past several years, discussion at UNDC annual meetings has focused on two agenda items:

1. recommendations for achieving the objective of nuclear disarmament and non-proliferation of nuclear weapons; and
2. practical confidence-building measures in the field of conventional weapons.

However, it has produced few recommendations, and has in fact experienced considerable difficulty even agreeing upon its annual agenda.

B. Regular General Assembly Sessions

Debate in the UNDC tends to mirror that held in the First Committee of the General Assembly, which is one of the main committees of regular General Assembly sessions, and which since 1978 has dealt exclusively with arms control and other international security issues. Regular sessions of the General Assembly have produced numerous resolutions over the years on issues of arms control. A number of these have invoked or facilitated negotiations of important multi-lateral treaties addressing specific subjects of arms control.[45] One of the first, and perhaps the most important of these was the NPT, which was called for by the General Assembly as early as 1961.[46] In 1968, after the two superpowers had agreed upon the terms in principle, the Assembly passed the final text of the treaty in Resolution 2373.[47] Other important non-proliferation treaties endorsed or adopted by General Assembly resolution prior to coming into force include the 1967 Treaty on Principles Governing the Activities of States in the Exploration and Use of Outer Space; the 1971 Treaty on the Prohibition of the Emplacement of Nuclear Weapons and Other Weapons of Mass Destruction on the Sea-Bed and the Ocean Floor and in the Subsoil Thereof; the 1972 Biological Weapons Convention; the 1997 Chemical Weapons Convention; the 1996 Comprehensive Nuclear Test Ban Treaty; and most recently the 2005 International Convention for the Suppression of Acts of Nuclear Terrorism.

However, the vast majority of the resolutions of the Assembly on arms control topics have had little effect either on multilateral negotiations on legally binding instruments, or on the development of customary international law.

---

[44] See J. Goldblat, Arms Control (2nd edn, 2002) 34–37.
[45] Ibid.   [46] General Assembly Res. 1665 (December 4, 1961).
[47] General Assembly Res. 2373 (June 12, 1968).

General Assembly resolutions on arms control and non-proliferation issues, and particularly on nuclear issues, are prolific in number. There are often several resolutions passed annually, sometimes with divergent recommendations to resolutions passed in previous years. This track record of resolutions, many of which are passed with significant opposing minorities of states, has diluted the significance and influence of General Assembly resolutions on the development of international law in this area. They have come to be seen by many not as a reflection of the broad-based consensus of states on "general principles of cooperation in the maintenance of international peace and security," but as instruments of partisan diplomacy through which groups of states take turns making political points against each other to forward their own political agendas.[48]

C. Special Sessions

In addition to its work at regular sessions, the General Assembly has held three special sessions devoted to disarmament and arms control. The first special session was held in 1978, and was instrumental in improving the transparency of arms control negotiations and in making the U.N. agencies involved in arms control more representative particularly of non-nuclear states. The rejuvenation by the first special session of the UNDC, and its restructuring from a closed group comprised of Security Council members plus Canada, to a body on which all United Nations members are represented, is exemplary of this effort. The first special session further broadened participation in arms control debate by allowing non-governmental organizations and research institutions to address the General Assembly directly for the first time. The session set out a number of disarmament principles and established the broad frameworks of a work programme for negotiators.[49]

The second special session in 1982, however, largely failed to meet expectations. It was unable to agree on further aspects of a work programme, and spent considerable time and effort re-visiting the issues it had agreed upon four years earlier. The only positive result of the session was consensus on a World Disarmament Campaign, which was to be a partnership between states, non-governmental organizations, and the United Nations, with the purpose of educating the public and fostering greater public understanding of and support for disarmament. In 1992, the World Disarmament Campaign was renamed the U.N. Disarmament Information Programme.[50]

---

[48] See B. Simma et al. (eds), THE CHARTER OF THE UNITED NATIONS: A COMMENTARY (2nd edn, 2002) 280; J. Goldblat, ARMS CONTROL (2nd edn, 2002), 34–37; L. Sohn, "Enhancing the Role of the General Assembly of the United Nations in Crystallizing International Law," in J. Makararczyk (ed.), THEORY OF INTERNATIONAL LAW AT THE THRESHOLD OF THE 21st CENTURY (1975).

[49] See J. Goldblat, ARMS CONTROL (2nd edn, 2002) 34–37.   [50] Ibid.

The third special session held in 1988 was an even greater disappointment, with virtually no progress being made on multilateral arms control negotiations. Regional disputes formed one of the most substantial hindrances to negotiations, and blocked agreement on a final document.[51]

D. The Conference on Disarmament

In addition to re-establishing the UNDC, the final document of the first special session on disarmament in 1978 also sanctioned the work of another body comprising an important part of the organizational machinery of international arms control debate and negotiations.[52] The Conference on Disarmament (CD), based in Geneva, is the successor organization to the Ten-Nations Committee on Disarmament (1959–60); the Eighteen-Nations Committee on Disarmament (1962–69); the Conference of the Committee on Disarmament (1969–78); and the Committee on Disarmament (1979–83).[53]

In the 1978 Final Act the CD was given a broad and ambitious mandate by the General Assembly to

undertake the elaboration of a comprehensive programme of disarmament encompassing all measures thought to be advisable in order to ensure that the goal of general and complete disarmament under effective international control becomes a reality in a world in which international peace and security prevail and in which the new international economic order is strengthened and consolidated.[54]

It was designed to be the primary multilateral negotiating forum for the international community on issues of disarmament and arms control. The annual meetings of the CD last approximately six months, during which it is to deal with the 'decalogue' of issues agreed upon in its initial agenda mandate in 1978. These are:

1. Nuclear weapons in all aspects;
2. chemical weapons;
3. other weapons of mass destruction;
4. conventional weapons;
5. reduction of military budgets;
6. reduction of armed forces;
7. disarmament and development;
8. disarmament and international security;

[51] Ibid.
[52] <http://disarmament.un.org/gaspecialsession/10thsesprog.htm>.
[53] See J. Goldblat, Arms Control (2nd edn, 2002) 14–17; B. Simma et al. (eds), The Charter of the United Nations: A Commentary (2nd edn, 2002) 279–280.
[54] Para. 109.

9. collateral measures, confidence-building measures, and effective verification methods in relation to appropriate disarmament measures, acceptable to all States concerned; and

10. a comprehensive program of disarmament leading to general and complete disarmament under effective international control.[55]

In 1978 the CD was composed of 40 member states, including all 5 acknowledged nuclear weapon states and 35 other states representing geographical regions. In 1996 the CD decided to admit 23 more states to membership, and in 1999 5 more states were added (from 20 states requesting membership).[56]

The CD has a special relationship with the United Nations, in that it is not formally a U.N. organ, but does have a close working relationship with the organization. The CD adopts its own rules of procedure and its own agenda, usually influenced by recommendations from the U.N. General Assembly. The CD reports to the General Assembly at least annually. The budget of the CD is included in the budget of the United Nations. Meetings of the CD are held in United Nations facilities and are serviced by U.N. staff. The Secretary General of the CD is appointed by the U.N. Secretary General and acts as her/his personal representative to the Conference.[57]

Over its four decades of operation, the CD and its predecessor organizations have served as the negotiating and drafting *fora* for a number of multilateral arms control treaties. The most important of these are the 1968 NPT, the 1972 BWC, the 1993 CWC, and the 1996 CTBT. However, in recent years the CD has been significantly hampered in its work by difficult relations between its members, an outdated membership structure, and issue-linkaging between arms control issues that has stymied progress on all fronts.[58]

Despite its broad and inclusive "decalogue" agenda, the CD in practice only debates one issue in depth at each annual meeting, and must agree on a work programme on that issue for negotiations to proceed. In recent years a number of annual sessions have ended without agreement on a programme of work, or have failed to re-authorize programmes of work agreed in previous years, with the result that since the conclusion of the CTBT in 1996, negotiations at the CD have remained deadlocked. It has been argued by Jozef Goldblat, a pre-eminent commentator on arms control issues, that the CD must be significantly restructured in its membership and given more flexible operating procedures (the most pressing required change being a reworking of the CD's consensus approval rule) or risk complete abandonment as a negotiating forum.[59]

---

[55] See J. Goldblat, ARMS CONTROL (2nd edn, 2002) 14–17; B. Simma et al. (eds), THE CHARTER OF THE UNITED NATIONS: A COMMENTARY (2nd edn, 2002) 279–280.
[56] Ibid. [57] Ibid. [58] Ibid.
[59] *The Conference on Disarmament at the Crossroads: To Revitalize or Dissolve?* THE NONPROLIFERATION REVIEW, Vol. 7, 104 (2000).

E. Analysis of The General Assembly's Record in Exercise of its Article 11(1) Powers

The General Assembly, both in its plenary sessions and through its subsidiary bodies, has been the central forum within the United Nations for consideration of arms control and disarmament issues, including issues of WMD proliferation. It has been instrumental, particularly through its support of the Conference on Disarmament and its predecessors, in facilitating the negotiation and establishment of a number of the cornerstone multilateral treaties in this area including the NPT, BWC, and CWC.[60] However, when viewed in light of the fact that it has been working on these issues since the passage of its very first resolution in 1946, it is nevertheless fair to say that the results actually produced through the General Assembly's 60 years of efforts to fulfill its Article 11(1) mandate have been relatively modest.[61]

The challenges it has faced in its efforts to fulfill this mandate have of course included the difficulty in achieving consensus, or even majority agreement, among so large a group of states, on issues of such sensitivity and varied political meaning as those involved in military armaments regulation. This failure to achieve broad agreement was most pronounced during the decades of the Cold War when alliances of client states were drawn between the two superpowers. However, even the "new world order" of international cooperation achieved in some other areas since the early 1990s has not enabled the states of the General Assembly to find common ground on many issues of weapons regulation, and particularly on issues of nuclear technologies. Deep schisms have emerged between the developed and developing world over access to nuclear technologies and over nuclear disarmament.[62] These fundamental disagreements over nuclear technologies have foiled countless attempts to find "general principles of cooperation" acceptable to a broad spectrum of General Assembly members.

However, the General Assembly has in many ways also compromised its own ability to influence international debate on these issues by its sometimes unconsidered use of its Article 11(1) powers of recommendation. As mentioned previously, the passage of resolutions by bare majority on issues of high political sensitivity, simply to add leverage to one position or another on already controversial

---

[60] See F. Kalshoven, "Arms, Armaments and International Law," (1985-II) Recueil des Cours 191, at 310; O. Kimminich, "Disarmament," in R. Wolfrum (ed.), United Nations: Law, Policies and Practice (1995) 407.

[61] See B. Simma et al. (eds), The Charter of the United Nations: A Commentary (2nd edn, 2002) 280.

[62] See D.H. Joyner, *The Nuclear Suppliers Group: History and Functioning*, 11(2) International Trade Law & Regulation, at 33, 38–39 (2005); J. Simpson and T. Ogilvie-White (eds), NPT Briefing Book, Vol. 1: The Evolution of the Nuclear Nonproliferation Regime (2003); T. Ogilvie-White, *International Responses to Iranian Nuclear Defiance: The Non-Aligned Movement and the Issue of Non-Compliance*, 18 European Journal of International Law 453 (2007).

matters, has not contributed to the building of such broad-based consensus.[63] The General Assembly has in some instances of the passage of resolutions on issues of arms regulation, exercised questionable judgment, which at times has argued for reserve and for the abandonment of proposals which were of a divisive and unproductive nature.[64] This lack of judgment has resulted in a situation in which one does not find a clear, consistent pattern of principled recommendations to the member states or to the Security Council. Rather, the principles contained in General Assembly resolutions particularly on issues of nuclear weapons and related technologies, are highly varied, sometimes inconsistent, and not representative of broad agreement among General Assembly members.[65] This murky record of resolutions emanating from the General Assembly has contributed to the overall failure of the United Nations to play a meaningful role in efforts to build a comprehensive multilateral normative system on arms control and non-proliferation, leaving the non-proliferation law system which has evolved since the signing of the United Nations Charter to grow up through essentially *sui generis* movements outside of the formal United Nations framework.

IV. The Security Council

A. Analysis of the Security Council's Role in Fulfillment of its Article 26 Responsibilities

However, if the General Assembly has failed to fulfill its role under Article 11(1) of the Charter, despite its significant efforts and expenditures of time and resources on issues of arms control and non-proliferation, the Security Council's record of efforts to fulfill its role under Article 26 of the Charter has been virtually non-existent, at least since 1949.

The Security Council has had a supervisory role over a number of subsidiary bodies working in the area of arms control, most importantly including the Commission on Conventional Armaments (CCA) and the previously discussed Atomic Energy Commission.[66] However, since both subsidiary bodies were themselves composed primarily of the members of the Security Council, the political differences between the permanent members of the Council, which were most acute during the Cold War, trickled down into the operation of these bodies as well, such that there was frequent deadlock within the groups, resulting in failure even to agree upon reports to be submitted to the Security Council.[67]

---

[63] See, e.g. Resolution 5073 (1995).
[64] See, e.g. Resolution 5070[P] (1995).
[65] See J. Goldblat, ARMS CONTROL (2nd edn, 2002) 34–35.
[66] See B. Simma et al. (eds), THE CHARTER OF THE UNITED NATIONS: A COMMENTARY (2nd edn, 2002) 473–475.
[67] Ibid.

Despite frequent discussion within the Security Council of issues of arms control and proliferation, and their importance and relevance to international peace and security, the lack of agreed reports by these working groups, as well as the divisions in the Council itself, has resulted in almost six decades in which there has not been one clear instance of the Security Council exercising its Article 26 authority to formulate concrete "plans for the establishment of a system for the regulation of armaments," to be passed along to member states. Article 26 has thus remained essentially a dead letter within the Charter, even since the ending of the Cold War and the beginning of the renewed era of international cooperation ushered in thereby, which has witnessed a reinvigoration of the Security Council and its activities in other areas of international security concern.[68] In short, the Security Council has utterly failed to fulfill its responsibilities under Article 26. Article 26 is rarely even mentioned in Security Council resolutions, and the emphasis of the international community in the creation of non-proliferation law, at least until April 28, 2004, had very much switched to a focus on such non-U.N. fora as the Conference on Disarmament and other regional security groups such as the OSCE and COPREDAL.[69]

B. Analysis of the Security Council's Chapter VII Role and Powers

However, while not included in those Charter articles in which specific mention is made of arms control and weapons proliferation, the Security Council's powers under Chapter VII of the Charter certainly give it another role to play in non-proliferation law under the Charter system. This is an enforcement role, in which the Council may determine under Article 39 of the Charter "the existence of any threat to the peace, breach of the peace, or act of aggression" and, having made that determination, can move on to authorize action under Articles 40, 41, and 42 to restore international peace and security.[70]

Under Article 40, before taking enforcement measures, the Council can first call upon the parties to a dispute to take "provisional measures" calculated to resolve the dispute. An example of such provisional measures in the non-proliferation

---

[68] Ibid.

[69] Organisation for Security and Cooperation in Europe; Comision Preparatoria para la Desnuclearizacion de la America Latina.

[70] See E. de Wet, THE CHAPTER VII POWERS OF THE UNITED NATIONS SECURITY COUNCIL (2004), 133–145, 178–187; I. Brownlie, INTERNATIONAL LAW AND THE USE OF FORCE BY STATES (1963) 334–336; B. Conforti, THE LAW AND PRACTICE OF THE UNITED NATIONS (2nd edn, 2000) 151–209; See C. Gray, INTERNATIONAL LAW AND THE USE OF FORCE (2nd edn, 2004) 281; D. Schweigman, THE AUTHORITY OF THE SECURITY COUNCIL UNDER CHAPTER VII OF THE U.N. CHARTER (2001); H. Kelsen, *Collective Security and Collective Self Defense under the Charter of the United Nations*, 42 AMERICAN JOURNAL OF INTERNATIONAL LAW 783 (1948); I. Osterdahl, THREAT TO THE PEACE (1998); N. White, KEEPING THE PEACE: THE UNITED NATIONS AND THE MAINTENANCE OF INTERNATIONAL PEACE AND SECURITY (2nd edn, 1997).

law area can be found in Security Council Resolution 1696, passed on July 31, 2006, which demanded that Iran cease uranium enrichment activities on its soil, giving it a deadline of August 31, 2006 to comply with the demand.

If such provisional measures are ineffective in bringing a peaceful resolution to the conflict, the Council may authorize enforcement action under Articles 41 and 42. Under Article 41, the Council can authorize "measures not involving the use of armed force… to give effect to its decisions." These measures typically include the requirement of an imposition of diplomatic and economic sanctions by U.N. members as against the deemed authors of the threat, and are illustrated in the passage of Resolution 1718, passed on October 14, 2006, which imposed targeted economic sanctions on North Korea in response to its testing of a nuclear device five days earlier.[71]

If, however, the Council determines that these measures short of military force either are likely to be, or have proven to be ineffective, it may under Article 42 authorize the use of military force by U.N. members, as an exception to the general non-intervention obligation established in Article 2(4) of the Charter.[72]

The most notable case of the enforcement role of the Security Council in the non-proliferation law area is Resolution 687, passed on April 3, 1991. In Resolution 687, the Council addressed the threat posed by Iraq specifically with regard to its possession and threatened use of chemical and biological weapons, in violation particularly of the Geneva Protocol of 1925 and the BWC of 1972. It also acted on intelligence from member states regarding the presence in Iraq of nuclear weapons-related technologies, and activities geared toward the development of nuclear weapons, in violation of Iraq's obligations under the 1968 NPT. These violations and the threats posed by them had, of course, become all the more pressing by Iraq's unlawful invasion of Kuwait in 1990.[73]

In Resolution 687, the Security Council imposed specific weapons-related prohibitions on Iraq, in order to effectively disarm it of its WMD and related technologies possessions, including ballistic missiles of a range greater than 150 kilometers. Along with these prohibitions on possession, Resolution 687 re-authorized a mandate, first authorized in Resolution 661, for a broad range of international sanctions, including prohibitions on importation of goods of Iraqi origin, prohibitions on export to Iraq of a broad range of goods and services related to the production of WMD, as well as a range of other financial and economic sanctions.[74]

---

[71] On the effectiveness of economic sanctions generally, and so called "smart sanctions" particularly, see E. Shagabutdinova and J. Berejikian, *Deploying Sanctions while Protecting Human Rights: Are Humanitarian "Smart" Sanctions Effective?* 6 JOURNAL OF HUMAN RIGHTS (2007) 59–74.

[72] For a discussion of the role which Article 43 of the U.N. Charter was originally intended to play in the Chapter VII system, see D.H. Joyner, *The Kosovo Intervention: Legal Analysis and a More Persuasive Paradigm*, 13 EUROPEAN JOURNAL OF INTERNATIONAL LAW 597 (2002); C. Gray, INTERNATIONAL LAW AND THE USE OF FORCE (2nd edn, 2004) 195–217.

[73] See Chapter 7 below.   [74] SC Res. 661 (August 6, 1990).

The resolution further imposed upon Iraq the obligation to cooperate with an ad hoc United Nations weapons inspection regime, the United Nations Special Commission on Iraq (UNSCOM), later re-named the United Nations Monitoring, Verification and Inspection Commission (UNMOVIC). UNSCOM was tasked, along with the IAEA, with verifying Iraq's compliance with the disarmament provisions of the resolution.[75]

V. The Security Council as Legislator

A. Security Council Resolutions from 1945–2001

For purposes of the present analysis, it is important to note that Resolution 687 shared a number of important characteristics in common with almost every other Security Council resolution passed since 1945. Notwithstanding its broad endowments of power under the Charter, for the first 45 years of the existence of the United Nations, and due primarily to political tensions between the United States and the Soviet Union, the Security Council was able to exercise its binding Chapter VII authority only rarely.[76] The most famous such use occurred in June 1950 when, during a period of Soviet boycott of Security Council sessions, the Council passed Resolutions 82 and 83 authorizing U.N. member states to act forcefully to remove North Korean (DPRK) military forces back to the 38th parallel following the DPRK's June 25 attack on the Republic of Korea and crossing of the agreed administrative boundary.[77]

However, with the dissolution of the Soviet Union, the Security Council in the 1990s entered a phase of dramatically increased activity and both willingness and ability to exercise its Chapter VII authority. This trend began in earnest with Resolution 678 in 1990, which authorized U.N. member states to use military force to expel Iraqi forces from Kuwait. Thereafter, the Security Council used its Chapter VII authority to pass resolutions with regard to situations, in among other places, the Balkans, Haiti, Somalia, Rwanda, the Congo, Afghanistan, Libya, and Iraq.[78] The decisions and measures enacted through these resolutions were of a varied character. In addition to the authorization of force contained in Resolution 678, these measures included arms embargos as in the cases of Yugoslavia and Somalia; various economic sanctions regimes including those with regard to Afghanistan and Libya; a disarmament regime in Iraq; an interim force in Haiti to maintain order after the resignation of President Jean-Bertrand

---

[75] On UNSCOM and its efforts in Iraq, see J. Cirincione et al., DEADLY ARSENALS: NUCLEAR, BIOLOGICAL AND CHEMICAL THREATS (2nd edn, 2005) 329.

[76] See C. Gray, INTERNATIONAL LAW AND THE USE OF FORCE (2nd edn, 2004) 195–211.

[77] SC Res. 82 (June 25, 1950); SC Res. 83 (June 27, 1950).

[78] See C. Gray, INTERNATIONAL LAW AND THE USE OF FORCE (2nd edn, 2004) 195–211; M. Hilaire, UNITED NATIONS LAW AND THE SECURITY COUNCIL (2005).

Aristide; and, notably, the creation of two ad hoc international criminal tribunals in the cases of the former Yugoslavia and Rwanda.[79] However, as indicated previously, almost all of these resolutions shared common characteristics.[80]

First, in all cases the Council acted in response to a specific political or humanitarian situation that had arisen in international relations, i.e. it adopted a responsive as opposed to a proactive posture.[81] On this point there is little debate. On occasion the Council has been rightly criticized for its inaction in the face of argued threats to peace, or for its slowness to respond to such threats, but throughout the first 56 years of its existence, the Security Council was seldom if ever criticized for taking action in an excessively proactive or timely manner. The purposive essence of the Security Council's Chapter VII authority is to "maintain or restore international peace and security", wording which assumes a status quo of peace and security, and contemplates action authorized by the Council only in cases where there is change to that status quo. The Council's reactive, or responsive record of action throughout its history bears out this understanding.

Second, the decisions of the Council in most cases can be characterized as actions enforcing existing international law, whether specifically U.N. Charter law as in the case of the 1990 Iraqi invasion of Kuwait, or law contained in other international instruments such as the 1948 Genocide Convention in the case of Rwanda.[82] This is a more controversial accounting. Many scholars have commented on the subject of the proper characterization of the role of the Security Council within the U.N. Charter system of collective security.[83] Some, as Martti Koskenniemi, see a fairly clear separation between the roles of the political bodies of the United Nations, drawn between the concepts of justice (the responsibility

---

[79] See D. Malone (ed.), THE U.N. SECURITY COUNCIL: FROM THE COLD WAR TO THE 21st CENTURY (2004); M. HILAIRE, UNITED NATIONS LAW AND THE SECURITY COUNCIL (2005).

[80] See generally E. de Wet, THE CHAPTER VII POWERS OF THE UNITED NATIONS SECURITY COUNCIL (2004) 133–215; D. Schweigman, THE AUTHORITY OF THE SECURITY COUNCIL UNDER CHAPTER VII OF THE U.N. CHARTER (2001) 163–202.

[81] See M. Happold, *Security Council Resolution 1373 and the Constitution of the United Nations*, 16 LEIDEN JOURNAL OF INTERNATIONAL LAW 598–600 (2003).

[82] D.W. Bowett, "Judicial and Political Functions of the Security Council and the International Court of Justice," in H. Fox (ed.), THE CHANGING CONSTITUTION OF THE UNITED NATIONS (1997); M. Perrin de Brichambaut, "The Role of the United Nations Security Council in the International Legal System," in M. Byers (ed.), THE ROLE OF LAW IN INTERNATIONAL POLITICS (2000); V. Gowland-Debbas, "The Functions of the United Nations Security Council in the International Legal System," in M. Byers (ed.), THE ROLE OF LAW IN INTERNATIONAL POLITICS (2000).

[83] Ibid.; H. Kelsen, COLLECTIVE SECURITY UNDER INTERNATIONAL LAW (originally published in 1957, reprinted by the Naval War College in 2001); D. Sarooshi, THE UNITED NATIONS AND THE DEVELOPMENT OF COLLECTIVE SECURITY (1999); V. Gowland-Debbas, COLLECTIVE RESPONSES TO ILLEGAL ACTS IN INTERNATIONAL LAW (1990); V. Gowland-Debbas, UNITED NATIONS SANCTIONS AND INTERNATIONAL LAW (2001); C. Joyner (ed.), THE UNITED NATIONS AND INTERNATIONAL LAW (1997); M. Koskenniemi, *The Place of Law in Collective Security*, 17 MICHIGAN JOURNAL OF INTERNATIONAL LAW 455 (1996); M. Koskenniemi, *International Legislation Today: Limits and Possibilities*, 23 WISCONSIN LAW JOURNAL 61 (2005); M. Reisman, *The Constitutional Crisis in the United Nations*, 87 AMERICAN JOURNAL OF INTERNATIONAL LAW 83 (1993).

for pursuing which Koskenniemi places with the General Assembly) and order (which Koskenniemi sees as the primary role of the Security Council).[84]

It is of course correct that, as previously noted, the Council's Chapter VII authority is specified by the terms of the Charter to lie in the maintenance and restoration of international peace and security. This concept is not fully synonymous with the remediation of breaches of international law as a theoretical matter. However, in viewing the ever increasing breadth of the scope of international law's coverage *ratione materiae*, the very significant overlap between these two concepts becomes clear. And indeed, in many cases the Security Council has explicitly referenced breaches of international law as among the motivating reasons for authorizations under Chapter VII.[85] In numerous other cases, breaches of international law, while not explicitly referenced, are implicit in the motivating forces behind Chapter VII actions.[86] Indeed, in illustration of this overlap between concepts, it is difficult (though not impossible) to imagine a situation today which could escalate to a perceived threat to international peace and security, so as to trigger Security Council action under Article 39, without entailing one or more breaches of international law by target states or non-state actors.

Thus, while breaches of international law do not have a directly constitutive relationship with threats to international peace and security, in practice they can be concluded to have a definitional relationship with the determination of such a threat by the Security Council. Meaning that the identification of breaches of international law is a method used whenever possible by the Security Council in order to objectively demonstrate, even though there is no formal requirement for them to do so, that the subject behavior of a state or non-state actor has also created a threat to international peace and security. This observation further illustrates one of the important roles which law plays in international politics, i.e. serving as a commonly agreed set of standards for objectively legitimizing and delegitimizing state and non-state actor behavior.[87]

Thus, the overlapping and definitional relationship between the concepts of maintenance and restoration of international peace and security on the one hand, and remediation of breaches of international law on the other, is borne out in practice more than it is in theory. As Oscar Schachter has observed:

Under its terms, Article 41 may be used by the Security Council "to give effect to its decisions." It was not meant to provide sanctions for enforcing international legal obligations as such. The Security Council may presumably apply it against a state that has not violated any legal requirement if the Council decides that it is in the interest of maintaining peace and security. In practice, however, the Council has generally applied Article 41

---

[84] *The Police in the Temple: Order, Justice and the U.N.: A Dialectical View*, 6 EUROPEAN JOURNAL OF INTERNATIONAL LAW 1 (1995).

[85] See, e.g., Resolutions 664, 667, and 670 (1990); 713, 752, 757, 770, 787, 794, 837 (1992); 819, 810, 836 (1993); 925, 935 (1994).

[86] See, e.g., Resolutions 748 (1992); 1160, 1199 (1998).

[87] See Chapter 9 below.

sanctions against a state that has not complied with a Charter requirement or a significant legal obligation.[88]

Third, in each case, resolutions passed were targeted at specific, named countries, usually not more than one in a single resolution. On the basis of Article 25 of the Charter, these resolutions imposed obligations upon states, both upon the target state(s), and in many cases upon the general membership of the U.N. However those universal obligations, when they were present, had solely to do with maintaining or restoring international peace and security in discrete cases where that peace and security had been threatened by the actions of one or in a few cases a handful of states. Thus, the purpose of the resolutions was never to impose, in an abstract manner, obligations upon the general U.N. membership without reference to such a discrete situation of threat to international peace and security.[89] Particularly compelling on this point for the purpose of analysis herein is the observation of Georg Nolte, writing in 2000:

Security Council law must remain preliminary and situation specific. Even Kelsen only went so far as to assert that a Council decision might create new law for a concrete case. For example, the Council could one day be confronted with demands to enact, under Chapter VII, general rules concerning weapons of mass destruction or the protection of the environment... If this argument were accepted, however, the Security Council could then establish itself as a world legislator, a role for which it was not designed.[90]

Fourth, the binding applicability of each resolution was either explicitly or implicitly of a temporary duration, and resolutions almost without exception made this fact clear.[91] In many cases there was a particular event or situation spelled out in the resolution, the transpiring of which, as verified by the Council, was to terminate the obligations upon both the target state(s) and general U.N. membership. In all cases it was understood that once the situation which triggered the Council's determination of a threat to the peace under Article 39 had ceased to exist, through whatever means, the force of the resolution and the obligations it imposed were to end.[92]

Finally, in each case the Council acted in an ad hoc manner, meaning that it acted in each case as it arose and it did not try to project or predict the character

[88] "The U.N. Legal Order: An Overview," in C. Joyner, THE UNITED NATIONS AND INTERNATIONAL LAW (1997) 15.

[89] See M. Happold, *Security Council Resolution 1373 and the Constitution of the United Nations*, 16 LEIDEN JOURNAL OF INTERNATIONAL LAW 598–600 (2003); H. Kelsen, THE LAW OF THE UNITED NATIONS: A CRITICAL ANALYSIS OF ITS FUNDAMENTAL PROBLEMS (1951) 282–283.

[90] "The Limits of the Security Council's Powers and its Functions in the International Legal System: Some Reflections," in M. Byers (ed.), THE ROLE OF LAW IN INTERNATIONAL POLITICS (2000) 321.

[91] See P. Szasz, *The Security Council Starts Legislating*, 96 AMERICAN JOURNAL OF INTERNATIONAL LAW 901–902 (2002).

[92] Ibid.; E. de Wet, THE CHAPTER VII POWERS OF THE UNITED NATIONS SECURITY COUNCIL (2004) 308–310; M. Koskenniemi, *The Police in the Temple: Order, Justice and the UN—A Dialectical View*, 6 EUROPEAN JOURNAL OF INTERNATIONAL LAW 325, 339 (1995).

or particularities of similar situations which would arise in the future. Nor did it attempt to address such potentially arising future cases through a present normative statement.

What arises from an analysis of these common characteristics shared by almost all Security Council resolutions passed under its Chapter VII authority during the first 56 years of its existence, is the conclusion that the Security Council's own understanding of its Chapter VII role and authority was most analogous to that of an executive body, entrusted by all U.N. members with the responsibility and authority to maintain and restore international peace and security, primarily in cases where the generalized obligations of the U.N. Charter or other rules of international law had been breached. It understood that it was to use its powers under Chapter VII to authorize effective collective measures on a case-by-case basis, responding to the dynamics of international relations as they occurred, and through the passage of resolutions which authorized forceful or non-forceful measures, to be applied for a temporary duration as against the specific authors of threats to international peace.[93] As D.W. Bowett has concluded:

The obligations of member states stem from the U.N. charter, and the role of the Security Council is not to create or impose new obligations having no basis in the Charter, but rather to identify the conduct required of a Member State because of its pre-existing Charter obligations. Thus, the Council does not "legislate": it enforces Charter obligations.[94]

In so characterizing the Security Council's record of use of its Chapter VII authority during this period as analogous to that of an executive body, it must of course be borne in mind that comparisons of the sources and institutions of the international legal system to those of domestic legal systems are generally unhelpful.[95] The Security Council is not an "executive branch of government," meaningfully comparable to domestic governments. It is not a vertical orderer for the international legal system. To the extent the Security Council has an enforcement role in the international legal system as herein described, that role is incomplete and the Council has developed a highly dubious record in many respects

---

[93] See M. Happold, *Security Council Resolution 1373 and the Constitution of the United Nations*, 16 LEIDEN JOURNAL OF INTERNATIONAL LAW 593 (2003); M. Asada, WMD Terrorism and Security Council Resolution 1540: Conditions for Legitimacy in International Legislation, IILJ Working Paper 2007/9, available at <http://www.iilj.org/publications/2007–9Asada.asp>; J. Abr. Frowein and N. Krisch, "Introduction to Chapter VII," in B. Simma et al. (eds), THE CHARTER OF THE UNITED NATIONS: A COMMENTARY (2nd edn, 2002) 709; K. Zemanek, "Is the Security Council the Sole Judge of Its Own Legality?," in E. Yakpo and T. Boumedra (eds), LIBER AMICORUM JUDGE MOHAMMED BEDJAOUI (1999) 636–637; R. Lavalle, *A Novel, If Awkward, Exercise in International Law-Making: Security Council Resolution 1540*, NETHERLANDS INTERNATIONAL LAW REVIEW, Vol. 51, Issue 3, 428–435 (2004).

[94] D.W. Bowett, "Judicial and Political Functions of the Security Council and the International Court of Justice," in H. Fox (ed.), THE CHANGING CONSTITUTION OF THE UNITED NATIONS (1997).

[95] M. Reisman, *The Constitutional Crisis in the United Nations*, 87 AMERICAN JOURNAL OF INTERNATIONAL LAW 83 (1993).

in fulfilling that enforcement role. It is inconsistent and selective in its choice of situations to address. It has no police power in itself, but is rather depend-ant upon member states of the U.N. to implement its mandates. The list goes on. Notwithstanding these analytical incongruities, the characterization of the Security Council's self-understanding as an executive body is maintained herein primarily in order to distinguish its role and authority from other potential char-acterizations, in particular that of a legislative body, which characterization fails to accurately capture the Council's role and authorities much more profoundly than does that of an executive body, as will be demonstrated herein.

This understanding of the powers of the Security Council and its role as an executive organ within the U.N. framework, continued until the passage of Resolution 1373 in 2001, and, most relevant to the current analysis, Resolution 1540 in 2004.

B. Resolutions 1373 and 1540

Security Council Resolution 1373 was passed on September 28, 2001, only 17 days after the terrorist attacks on New York and Washington DC. The resolution begins by recalling the September 11 attacks and by "[r]econfirming that such acts, like any act of international terrorism, constitute a threat to international peace and security." It thus clearly grounds the jurisdiction of the Security Council over international terrorism pursuant to its powers of determination under Article 39 of the Charter.

In its operative paragraphs, Resolution 1373 "Decides that all states shall..." prevent and suppress the financing of terrorist acts, including by criminalizing terrorist fundraising and donation activities, and by freezing assets of known terrorist individuals or entities. It goes on to decide that all states shall refrain from providing any form of support, active or passive, to entities or persons involved in terrorist acts; take necessary steps to prevent the commission of terrorist acts; deny safe haven to those who finance, plan, or support terrorist acts; and ensure that any person who participates in terrorist acts is brought to justice.

It further calls on all states to cooperate in the fulfillment of these obligations through coordination of law enforcement activity and through increased infor-mation sharing between law enforcement agencies at the national level. It estab-lishes in Paragraph 6 a Committee of the Security Council (the Anti-Terrorism Committee) to monitor the implementation of the resolution. All UN member states are to report to the Committee within 90 days of adoption, and thereafter according to a timetable to be proposed by the Committee, on the steps they have taken to implement the resolution.

It is worth noting that in many respects Resolution 1373 mirrors the provi-sions of the 1999 Convention for the Suppression of the Financing of Terrorism. However unlike the Convention, it importantly does not include definitions of several key terms used in the text of the resolution, including "terrorism", "international terrorism", "terrorist acts", or "terrorists."[96]

On April 28, 2004 the Security Council passed Resolution 1540. This resolution was passed not coincidentally shortly after the revelation in February 2004 of the existence of a long standing clandestine nuclear materials smuggling ring headed by the father of Pakistan's gas centrifuge program, Dr. Abdul Qadeer Khan.[97]

In Resolution 1540, the Security Council undertook to address a number of fundamental limitations of the existing non-proliferation treaties and regimes system. In the Security Council meetings leading up to the passage of Resolution 1540, some of which were opened to comment from non-Council members, many states noted the need for such a resolution to close "gaps" in the coverage of existing non-proliferation treaty instruments. One such gap identified by states during these meetings has been previously identified as the problem of the non-universality of the system, a result of the fact that non-proliferation treaties, as all treaties, are adopted only voluntarily by states, and that for a variety of reasons many states, including some of significant proliferation concern, have remained outside the non-proliferation normative system.[98] As the representative of New Zealand noted:

[W]e place importance on the fact that the draft resolution would also impose restraints on those States that have deliberately chosen to stand outside the major disarmament and nonproliferation treaties to which most States, including my own, have committed themselves. This is a major gap that the draft resolution can begin to fill.[99]

A second major challenge to the non-proliferation treaties and regimes system is the fact that all existing restrictions within the regimes upon manufacture, possession, and trafficking in weapons-related technologies are addressed to states themselves.[100] Thus at the international level there is no substantive restriction on private parties, including business entities as well as other non-state actors, engaging in any of these activities. The utility of Resolution 1540 in addressing

---

[96] See M. Happold, *Security Council Resolution 1373 and the Constitution of the United Nations*, 16 Leiden Journal of International Law 593 (2003).

[97] See D.H. Joyner, "International Legal Responses to WMD Proliferation" in C. Hughes and R. Devetak (eds), The Globalization of Political Violence (2007).

[98] See S. Gahlaut and V. Zaborsky, *Do Regimes Have the Members They Need?*, Center for International Trade and Security Working Paper (Athens; Center for International Trade and Security, February 2003); R.T. Cupitt and I. Khripunov, *New Strategies for the Nuclear Suppliers Group (NSG)*, 16 Comparative Strategy 305 (1997); G.K. Bertsch and S. Grillot (eds), Arms on the Market: Reducing the Threat of Proliferation in the Former Soviet Union (1998).

[99] S/PV.4950 p. 21 (April 22, 2004).

[100] M. Asada, *WMD Terrorism and Security Council Resolution 1540: Conditions for Legitimacy in International Legislation*, IILJ Working Paper 2007/9, available at <http://www.iilj.org/publications/2007-9Asada.asp>; J. du Preez, *The 2005 NPT Review Conference: Can it Meet the Nuclear Challenge?*, Arms Control Today (April 2005).

this non-state actor gap in the non-proliferation treaties and regimes system was noted by numerous states, particularly in the context of international efforts to combat the phenomenon of terrorism. As the representative of Benin stated:

I would like to thank the States that have requested the holding of this open meeting, which makes it possible for us to open to all Member States the debate on the danger of the acquisition and use of weapons of mass destruction (WMD) by non-State actors. This danger relates above all to the emergence of non-State actors that vie with States for dominance in the area of violent force, a new phenomenon, a phenomenon that also highlights the existence of a legal void in the arsenal of contemporary international law and that calls for the community of nations to cooperate without delay to provide the means to prevent the danger.[101]

The resolution addresses the non-state actor problem described above in operative paragraph 1 in which it provides that "all States shall refrain from providing any form of support to non-state actors that attempt to develop, acquire, manufacture, possess, transport, transfer or use nuclear, chemical or biological weapons and their means of delivery." Furthermore, operative paragraph 2 provides that

all States, in accordance with their national procedures, shall adopt and enforce appropriate effective laws which prohibit any non-State actor to manufacture, acquire, possess, develop, transport, transfer or use nuclear, chemical or biological weapons and their means of delivery, in particular for terrorist purposes, as well as attempts to engage in any of the foregoing activities, participate in them as an accomplice, assist or finance them.

It then addresses in operative paragraph 3 the problem of non-universality of non-proliferation law by directly imposing an obligation upon states to establish and maintain effective export control laws and regulations at the national level,

including appropriate laws and regulations to control export, transit, trans-shipment and re-export and controls on providing funds and services related to such export and trans-shipment such as financing…as well as establishing end-user controls; and establishing and enforcing appropriate criminal or civil penalties for violations of such export control laws and regulations.

As in Resolution 1373, Resolution 1540 in operative paragraph 4 establishes a Committee of the Security Council to monitor the implementation by states of the obligations imposed by the resolution.

Although these two resolutions were adopted in very different contexts and are meant to cover quite different, although of course related, areas of law, they share important similarities in structure as well as in legal import. These two resolutions have been claimed by some commentators to have ushered in a new age of

---

[101] S/PV.4950 p. 12 (April 22, 2004). See additional statements to this effect from the representatives of, e.g., the Philippines, Brazil, Algeria, China, and Angola.

Security Council jurisprudence and to have signalled an intent by the Council to act as a legislative body, in supplementation of its executive functions.[102]

There had, before the passage of Resolution 1373, been other controversial acts of the Security Council which had caused debate on the topic of the proper role and powers of the Council.[103] Notable in this regard were the actions before the International Court of Justice stemming from the explosion of Pan Am flight 103 over Lockerbie, Scotland in 1988. During the resulting diplomatic tensions between the United States and the United Kingdom on the one part and Libya on the other, the Security Council in 1992 passed Resolution 748 in which the Council demanded that Libya hand over two men suspected of involvement in the Lockerbie bombing, and determined "that the failure by the Libyan Government to demonstrate by concrete actions its renunciation of terrorism and in particular its continued failure to respond fully and effectively to the requests in Resolution 731 constitute a threat to international peace and security."[104]

The suggestion was raised at the time by a number of commentators, and later formally put to the Court by Libya itself, that this determination was arguably prejudicial to Libya's rights under Article 14 of the 1971 Montreal Convention for the Suppression of Unlawful Acts against the Safety of Civil Aviation. There was also discomfort, expressed by several of the judges, regarding the Council's characterization of this situation as a threat to international peace and security, by which the Council invoked its powers under Chapter VII through the gateway criteria of Article 39. As Judge Shahubuddeen stated in his opinion:

The question now raised . . . is whether a decision of the Security Council may override the legal rights of states, and, if so, whether there are any limitations on the power of the Council to characterize a situation as one justifying the making of a decision entailing such consequences. Are there any limits to the Council's powers of appreciation? In the equilibrium of forces underpinning the United Nations within the evolving international order, is there a conceivable point beyond which a legal issue may properly arise as to the competence of the Security Council to produce such overriding results? If there are any limits, what are those limits, and what body, if other than the Security Council, is competent to say what those limits are?[105]

---

[102] See M. Happold, *Security Council Resolution 1373 and the Constitution of the United Nations*, 16 Leiden Journal of International Law 593 (2003); P. Szasz, *The Security Council Starts Legislating*, 96 American Journal of International Law 901–902 (2002).

[103] See M. Koskenniemi, *The Police in the Temple: Order, Justice and the U.N.—A Dialectical View*, 6 European Journal of International Law 325 (1995); K. Harper, *Does the United Nations Security Council Have the Competence to Act as a Court and Legislature?* 27 New York University Journal of International Law and Policy 103 (1994); B. Martenczuk, *The Security Council, the International Court and Judicial Review: What Lessons from Lockerbie?* 10 European Journal of International Law 517 (1999).

[104] SC Res. 748 (March 31, 1992).

[105] *Questions of Interpretation and Application of the 1971 Montreal Convention Arising from the Aerial Incident at Lockerbie (Libyan Arab Jamahiriya v. United Kingdom).* Request for the Indication of Provisional Measures, Order of April 14, 1992, ICJ Reports 1992, 3 at 142.

However, although in the *Lockerbie* cases there was an allegation that the Council had overstepped its prerogatives under the Charter, there was no hint of legislative aspirations in the Council's actions. The resolutions involved were clearly targeted against the acts and omissions of one state, Libya, and they set clear demands which, if met, would bring about the end of the mandate for exercise of Council authority. Thus they were in keeping with the Council's understood role, if perhaps excessively bold in construction.

Other examples of Security Council decisions more specifically alleged to constitute legislation include the previously discussed imposition of disarmament obligations on Iraq through Resolution 687, as well as the establishment by the Council of the ad hoc international criminal tribunals.

With regard to Resolution 687, while the obligations imposed upon Iraq did go beyond those it was bound to under the 1925 Geneva Protocol and 1972 BWC, and thus could be seen as new law created by the Council and operating upon Iraq, there were in this case decidedly un-legislative characteristics as well. The obligations imposed by Resolution 687 were clearly conceived to be temporary, ending as they would once Iraq's compliance with the terms of the resolution had been verified by UNSCOM and the IAEA. The resolution targeted only one country, and the sanctions regime which imposed obligations upon all UN members was only incidental to this primary normative object. And finally, this resolution was adopted in a reactive posture, the Council having been shown definitively through intelligence gained after the conclusion of the Gulf War that the Hussein regime had engaged in a clandestine and illegal weapons development and stockpiling program.

In the case of the ad hoc war crimes tribunals as well, in both cases of their establishment by the Council, the creation of these courts should properly be seen as special responses to specific situations of fundamental breach of international law. Each court was given a jurisdictional mandate tightly limited in both geography and chronology, as well as in subject matter. Further, the subject matter over which jurisdiction was to spread was essentially composed of breaches of already existing law, simply codified in the respective court statutes.

Because of the predominantly non-legislative characteristics of these and virtually all other Security Council decisions, it can be concluded that at the end of the decade of the 1990s, the Security Council had not yet passed a true piece of international legislation.[106] However, in the swelling of outrage and concern following the attacks of September 11, 2001, and, as has been alleged, with little foresight of the legal import of what they were doing, the Council

---

[106] See P. Szasz, *The Security Council Starts Legislating*, 96 AMERICAN JOURNAL OF INTERNATIONAL LAW 901–902 (2002); M. Happold, *Security Council Resolution 1373 and the Constitution of the United Nations*, 16 LEIDEN JOURNAL OF INTERNATIONAL LAW 593 (2003); M. Koskenniemi, *International Legislation Today: Limits and Possibilities*, 23 WISCONSIN INTERNATIONAL LAW JOURNAL 61 (2005).

passed Resolution 1373.[107] The Council passed this resolution not to respond specifically to the September 11 acts of terror themselves, nor to mete out any measure of punishment upon its perpetrators, nor to specifically target them or those states that aided and abetted them. The Council rather used the attacks as a backdrop and a catalyst for the establishment of a much broader and temporally indefinite normative regime addressing the subject of international terrorism.

The context of the passage of Resolution 1540 offers even less evidence of a specific situation of threat to international peace and security against which it is to be understood that the resolution operates, and to which it is to be understood to respond. Again, the revelation of the Khan network provided a circumstantial pretext which seemed to explain the prioritization of the subject of WMD proliferation and its address by the Council in Resolution 1540, but the resolution itself went far beyond simply responding to the existence of this network. It newly imposed a broad set of obligations upon all U.N. member states, which were purposed in changing permanently the structure and content of national legal systems.

These resolutions, simply put, cannot be described as ad hoc responses to events urgently arising in international politics. They are rather calculated, proactive, forward-looking normative creations. In both cases the Security Council simply determines that an entire class of actions which have been and which may be in the future committed potentially by any state, constitute a threat to international peace and security. The Council then decides in each case that all U.N. member states shall take extensive measures, broadly prescribed in the resolutions, including changes to their national legal systems, in order to combat these ill-defined present and future threats. The obligations imposed under both Resolutions 1373 and 1540 are not temporally limited, either explicitly or implicitly. Their duration is clearly meant to be indefinite. Moreover, there are no specifically targeted states. The obligations imposed in the resolutions are stated in an abstract manner, so as to make their application clearly universal.

C. The Limits of Chapter VII

The U.N. Charter in Article 24 confers upon the Security Council "primary responsibility for the maintenance of international peace and security." In the same paragraph the members of the United Nations "agree that in carrying out its duties under this responsibility, the Security Council acts on their behalf." This statement is the closest the Charter comes to attempting to remedy the non-democratic reality, made requisite by geopolitical circumstances in 1945, that the most powerful organ of the United Nations and the only organ capable

---

[107] See M. Happold, *Security Council Resolution 1373 and the Constitution of the United Nations*, 16 LEIDEN JOURNAL OF INTERNATIONAL LAW 593 (2003).

of issuing decisions binding upon all U.N. members, is composed of only 15 of those members (who now total 191), five of whom are given permanent status and have an effective veto power over every decision of the Council.

In this language seeming to imply a representative relationship between the Council and the rest of the U.N. membership, the Charter attempts to legitimize the declaration in Article 25 by the membership, that all U.N. members "agree to accept and carry out the decisions of the Security Council in accordance with the present Charter." Thus, Article 25 establishes the binding character of Security Council decisions upon the entirety of the U.N. membership.[108]

Although the specific powers granted to the Security Council under the Charter, and particularly in the articles of Chapter VII, are both broadly and vaguely worded, the Charter does however provide limits upon the discretion of the Council in its exercise of these powers. As the Council derives its powers from the Charter's terms, it is by the same process bound by the constraints and limitations of those terms. As the Appeals Chamber of the ICTY has observed:

The Security Council is an organ of an international organization, established by a treaty which serves as a constitutional framework for that organization. The Security Council is thus subjected to certain constitutional limitations, however broad its powers under the constitution may be. Those powers cannot, in any case, go beyond the limits of the jurisdiction of the organization at large, not to mention other specific limitations or those which may derive from the internal division of power within the organization. In any case, neither the text nor the spirit of the Charter conceives of the Security Council as *legibus solutus* (unbound by law).[109]

One such limiting provision upon the Council's power is Article 24(2), which provides that "In discharging these duties the Security Council shall act in accordance with the purposes and principles of the United Nations."[110] The purposes and principles of the United Nations to which this article refers are to be found in Articles 1 and 2 of the Charter, and include the right of states to self-determination, respect for human rights, the principle of sovereign equality, an obligation to act in good faith, and an obligation not to intervene in matters "essentially within the domestic jurisdiction" of member states. As the

---

[108] See the discussion of Article 24 as an independent source of authority for binding decisions of the Security Council in M. Happold, *Security Council Resolution 1373 and the Constitution of the United Nations*, 16 LEIDEN JOURNAL OF INTERNATIONAL LAW 593, 604–605 (2003).

[109] Appeals Chamber Decision on the Tadic Jurisdictional Motion, *Prosecutor v. Dusko Tadic a/k/a "Dule,"* Case No. IT-94-1-AR72, October 2, 1995, para. 28.

[110] D. Schweigman, THE AUTHORITY OF THE SECURITY COUNCIL UNDER CHAPTER VII OF THE U.N. CHARTER (2001) 29–33; H. Kelsen, THE LAW OF THE UNITED NATIONS (1964) 291–295; D. Akande, *The International Court of Justice and the Security Council: Is There Room for Judicial Control of Decisions of the Political Organs of the United Nations?*, 46 INTERNATIONAL AND COMPARATIVE LAW QUARTERLY (1997) 317–321; L.M. Goodrich, E. Hambro, and A.P. Simons, CHARTER OF THE UNITED NATIONS (1969) 27–28; J. Delbruck, "Article 24," in B. Simma, et al. (eds), THE CHARTER OF THE UNITED NATIONS: A COMMENTARY (1994) 397–407.

International Court of Justice stated in the *Certain Expenses Advisory Opinion* in 1962:

When the organization takes action which warrants the assertion that it was appropriate for the fulfilment of one of the stated purposes of the United Nations, the presumption is that such action is not *ultra vires* the organization.[111]

Another limiting provision is Article 25. As previously stated, the greatest import of the text of this article is the establishment of the universally binding character of Security Council decisions.[112] However, the fact that, under this provision, members agree to accept and carry out the decisions of the Security Council "in accordance with the present charter" suggests that the measure of this obedience should be contingent upon the validity of the Council's decisions and actions as held up to the standard of the provisions of the Charter, and further that it is conceivable that other provisions of the Charter might in some cases take precedence over conflicting Security Council decisions.[113] To paraphrase the article's meaning in this regard, U.N. members are not obligated to comply with the decisions of the Council one wit further than those decisions themselves comply with the provisions of the Charter.[114]

Some have suggested that the language "in accordance with the present charter" refers to the decisions of the Council rather than to the obligations of U.N. members, serving merely to emphasize the obedience due to the Council according to the provisions of the Charter. This interpretation however would render this last clause of the article almost completely redundant and therefore superfluous, thereby defying principles of clear and efficient textual construction. This interpretation is therefore less persuasive.[115]

Although the general purposes and principles of the United Nations are difficult to apply in a meaningful way so as to provide justiciable limitations on the powers of the Security Council under Article 24(2), in the non-proliferation issue area the process for creation of new non-proliferation law contained in Articles 11(1) and 26 described above does provide a clear, authoritative lawmaking procedure which can properly be called the U.N. Charter system for creation of non-proliferation law. As this explicitly provided system involves a clearly delineated division of roles and authorities between the organs of the

---

[111] 16 *Certain Expenses of the United Nations,* ICJ Reports 1962, 151, at 168.

[112] See R. Higgins, *The Advisory Opinion on Namibia: Which UN Resolutions are Binding Under Article 25 of the Charter?* 32 INTERNATIONAL AND COMPARATIVE LAW QUARTERLY 269–286 (1972).

[113] J. Delbruck, "Article 25," in B. Simma, et al. (eds), THE CHARTER OF THE UNITED NATIONS: A COMMENTARY (1994) 455; E. de Wet, THE CHAPTER VII POWERS OF THE UNITED NATIONS SECURITY COUNCIL (2004) 375–378; P. Rosgen, RECHTSSETZUNGAKTE DER VEREINTEN NATIONEN UND IHRER SONDERORGANISATIONEN. BESTANDSAUFNAHME UND VOLZUG IN DER BUNDESREPUBLIK DEUTSCHLAND (1985) 157.

[114] E.de Wet, THE CHAPTER VII POWERS OF THE UNITED NATIONS SECURITY COUNCIL (2004) 377.

[115] Ibid. at 375–378.

U.N., it thus comprises a limitation upon the authority of the Security Council deriving from "the internal division of power within the organization."[116] This limitation is therefore a part of the substantive law of the Charter in accordance with which, under Article 25, the Security Council is bound to act.[117]

Thus, while the provisions of the Charter in many instances provide limitations upon the powers of the Council which, though valid, are difficult to apply unambiguously, due to the presence of the lawmaking system contained in Articles 11(1) and 26, the non-proliferation law creation issue area fortunately does not labor under the same difficulty. It is argued herein that the Article 25 limitations on the Council's powers can be applied in the non-proliferation law issue area because of the presence of the criteria for legitimate lawmaking by U.N. bodies contained in Articles 11(1) and 26. Accordingly, any act by the Security Council which attempts to create "a system for the regulation of armaments" outside of the Article 11(1) and Article 26 institutional process is in breach of Article 25, and is thus an act *ultra vires* the Council's authority.[118]

It is argued that Security Council Resolution 1540 meets this test precisely. This resolution clearly attempts to establish a system for the regulation of WMD, which includes a universalized export control law requirement and a universalized requirement to enact laws on the subject of non-state actors. Therefore, to be valid as a source of binding obligation upon U.N. member states, it is argued that this system of obligations cannot be established through the Council's use of its Chapter VII powers, but must rather be constructed through the procedures provided for in Articles 11(1) and 26.

D. Analysis and Argument

The essential argument herein is that in passing what can only be viewed as an ostensible piece of international legislation in Resolution 1540, the Security Council has confused the proper scope of its enforcement powers under Chapter VII, with the proper scope of its long unused, limited lawmaking powers under Article 26, and has taken to itself by unilateral exercise of its Chapter VII powers a role which, under the Charter system, it is to share both with the General Assembly in the exercise of its Article 11(1) powers, as well as with the general membership of the United Nations, to whom it is directed under Article 26 to submit proposals for the creation of new international laws in the area of weapons proliferation.

This conclusion proceeds from the analysis that the post-September 11 war on terrorism has, for the first time in the history of the United Nations, led to an

---

[116] Appeals Chamber Decision on the Tadic Jurisdictional Motion, *Prosecutor v. Dusko Tadic a/k/a "Dule,"* Case No. IT-94-1-AR72, October 2, 1995, para. 28.

[117] Ibid.

[118] See M. Happold, *Security Council Resolution 1373 and the Constitution of the United Nations,* 16 Leiden Journal of International Law 593 (2003).

international security situation in which unified support can be achieved among the permanent members of the Security Council for such broadly conceived resolutions as Resolution 1540, which addresses a problem seen to be of global scope and threat to international peace and security. However, with this new found unity of purpose, it is argued that the proper Charter system for such lawmaking actions, with the express limitations on the role and powers of U.N. organs in this area laid out in the Charter, has been forgotten, or more likely ignored for the sake of political expediency.

After all, why go through a lengthy process entailing consideration in the General Assembly, recommendation to the Security Council, further consideration in the Council, then recommendation to member states for enactment through a treaty that will in the end likely only be adopted by states not of serious proliferation concern; when alternatively the Council may consider the issue in the first instance and instantiate the obligations through its own authority, in the process making the obligations universal?

The added political, legal, and chronological efficiency of the path chosen by the Security Council is not denied. For the members of the Security Council, and particularly for the permanent members who enjoy the most power from their positions on the Council, when considering the establishment of the obligations contained in Resolution 1540, the long unused Charter system for creation of non-proliferation law would certainly have looked less attractive, particularly as the amount of control they would have been able to exercise over the outcome of the approval process under the Charter system would have been severely diluted from that they would wield through the Chapter VII process.

However, none of these reasons of expedition and control give sufficient justification for going around the Charter system and assuming a lawmaking authority which was never intended to be exercised by the Council under the Charter. The Charter system in Articles 11(1) and 26 is the authoritative system for the creation of new non-proliferation law for good reasons. The system in Articles 11(1) and 26 divides roles among the political organs of the U.N., leaving the final and most important role of actual establishment as law of the principles generated through this institutional process, to the member states of the U.N. themselves. This system was created by the Charter framers in maintenance of the classical principles of state sovereignty and sovereign equality in international lawmaking, and was consistent with the resulting idea that the consent of states to be bound underlies the validity of all of the sources of international law, in the positivist tradition. This system was informed by the understanding that the consent given to Council authority in the first instance by states in Article 25 of the Charter does not equate to direct consent of states at the second instance to every substantive decision of the Council. And while this distinction is less troublesome in the domestic context under most theories of the positivist social compact, it is troubling to states in the international legal system which more jealously guard their sovereign autonomy under the sometimes maligned, but still quite virile Westphalian sovereignty paradigm.

Recent attempts by scholars to justify the role of the Security Council as lawmaker based upon its powers under the U.N. Charter take advantage of the breadth and vagueness of the textual recitations of those powers in making their arguments, but lose sight entirely of the spirit of the provisions and the proper place of the Council under a correct understanding of fundamental principles of international lawmaking.[119] This misunderstanding was not shared by members of the Council itself for the first 56 years of its operation, and these broadly phrased powers were exercised with due caution and reservation until the passage of Resolution 1373.

According to the Charter system for creation of non-proliferation law, then, what should have happened with the ideas behind Resolution 1540? Clearly these ideas fall under the category of "general principles of cooperation in the maintenance of international peace and security, including principles governing disarmament and the regulation of armaments." Thus, the process of law creation should have begun in the General Assembly with deliberations on the contours of such general principles, then proceeded to a recommendation by the General Assembly to the Security Council. The Security Council should then, in its Article 26 role, have been responsible for formulating a specific plan for implementing these general principles, taking full consideration of the recommendations made on the issue by the General Assembly. That discrete plan then, again according to Article 26, should have been submitted to the members of the United Nations. The members themselves, in their own sovereign capacities, would then have been responsible for the actual "establishment of a system for the regulation of armaments," i.e. the actual setting up of a legal framework in this area.

In fact, this process could have easily been followed in the case of the ideas behind Resolution 1540. The principles in the resolution itself could have been justified by reference to a number of General Assembly resolutions. The text of Resolution 1540, modified to comprise a treaty text but maintaining all of its significant principles, could then have been submitted to member states for their establishment as new international law. The reasons this was not done have little to do with procedural imperfections in the Charter system, and much more to do with motivations held by Council members of political expediency and control as well as universalized effectiveness, discussed above.

---

[119] See I. Johnstone, *Legislation and Adjudication in the U.N. Security Council: Bringing Down the Deliberative Deficit*, 102 AMERICAN JOURNAL OF INTERNATIONAL LAW 275 (2008); S. Talmon, *The Security Council as World Legislature*, 99 AMERICAN JOURNAL OF INTERNATIONAL LAW 175 (2005); F. Kirgis, *The Security Council's First Fifty Years*, 89 AMERICAN JOURNAL OF INTERNATIONAL LAW 506, 520–528 (1995); K. Harper, *Does the United Nations Security Council Have the Competence to Act as a Court and Legislature?*, 27 NEW YORK UNIVERSITY JOURNAL OF INTERNATIONAL LAW & POLICY 103, 126–129, 149 (1994); B. Kellman, *Criminalization and Control of WMD Proliferation: The Security Council Acts*, NONPROLIFERATION REVIEW, Vol. 11, No. 2, 159 (Summer 2004).

The Security Council, whose role in the Charter system for non-proliferation law creation is really a facilitative and definitional one, effectively bypassed the steps assigned to the General Assembly and to the member states by taking the issue to itself and acting both in the deliberative role assigned to the General Assembly, as well as the law creation role assigned to the members collectively. The argument in this chapter, therefore, is that the Security Council needs a clarification of its role in the area of non-proliferation law creation. It needs to have clarified to it that the system the Charter spells out in Articles 11(1) and 26 with regard to the role of U.N. bodies in the making of non-proliferation law is the *lex specialis* authoritative legal framework for such action, and not the legal framework of Chapter VII. The procedures set out in Articles 11(1) and 26 thus comprise a substantive limitation on the Council's powers under Chapter VII on the subject of the creation of new non-proliferation law.

E. The Security Council as Legislator?

The United Nations Security Council is simply not an international legislator, nor can it be. Even if the Council had a legitimate legal mandate arising from the Charter's provisions to act as a legislative body, it is ill-equipped institutionally, in terms of its membership structure and tenuous claim to any principle of representation of U.N. members, to assume such a role of law-giver to the international community.

The Council is composed of 15 states, with 5 states holding what can only be described as anachronistic proprietary rights, resulting from 60-year-old power politics. The Security Council was designed to be an authorizer of discrete uses of force, and at the time of its creation it was rationally designed for this purpose. It is not designed for any other purposes, and certainly not as a representative legislative body for creation of international law.[120]

---

[120] D.W. Bowett has argued that: "the [Security] Council does not 'legislate': it enforces Charter obligations." D.W. Bowett, "Judicial and Political Functions of the Security Council and the International Court of Justice," in H. Fox (ed.), THE CHANGING CONSTITUTION OF THE UNITED NATIONS (1997) 80. Oscar Schachter has noted "Neither the United Nations nor any of its specialized agencies was conceived as a legislative body." "The U.N. Legal Order: An Overview," in C. Joyner, THE UNITED NATIONS AND INTERNATIONAL LAW (1997) 15; Martti Koskenniemi states that: "No doubt, it is not possible to conceive the Security Council as a legitimate global lawmaker." M. Koskenniemi, *International Legislation Today: Limits and Possibilities*, WISCONSIN INTERNATIONAL LAW JOURNAL, Vol. 23, No. 1, 74 (2005). Georg Nolte describes the Security Council acting as a world legislature as "a role for which it was not designed." G. Nolte, "The Limits of the Security Council's Powers and its Functions in the International Legal System: Some Reflections," in M. Byers (ed.), THE ROLE OF LAW IN INTERNATIONAL POLITICS: ESSAYS IN INTERNATIONAL RELATIONS AND INTERNATIONAL LAW (2000) 322. See also M. Perrin de Brichambaut, "The Role of the United Nations Security Council in the International Legal System," in ibid. 275–276; A. Marschik, *The Security Council as World Legislator?: Theory, Practice and Consequences of an Expansion of Powers*, IILJ Working Paper 2005/18 (Institute for International Law and Justice, New York University, 2005), 7; G. Arangio-Ruiz, *On the Security Council's 'Law-Making'*, RIVISTA DI DIRITTO INTERNAZIONALE, Vol. 83, Fasc. 3, 628–629 (2000); Dissenting

In fact even discussing representation issues poses a bit of a straw man. The reason is that international organizations and international lawmaking generally do not function according to principles of collective representation of states along republican principles. As noted above, international lawmaking is fundamentally based upon the consent of states to be bound, even though this consensual basis of the sources of international law has not yet been perfectly realized.[121] However, the principles of state sovereignty and the sovereign equality of states as subjects of international law which the principle of consent safeguards, are fundamental tenets of the international legal system, and are in contrast with the orientations of rights of legal subjects recognized under developed national legal systems.

The ideas of democratic governance, through which the original sovereign authority of the state and the power to establish law binding upon all members of the legal system are deemed to be exercised by a subset of the population of the state, based upon principles of representation, finds no analogy in the international legal system. There has never been in classical understandings of international law and international lawmaking the idea that a subset of states, even a representative subset of states, could make decisions imposing substantive obligations upon other states without those states' direct consent.[122] This understanding applies a fortiori to the case of a non-representative group of states whose only claim to a representative character is its limited treaty mandate. As the ICTY Appeals Chamber stated in the *Tadic* case:

> It is clear that the legislative, executive, and judicial division of powers which is largely followed in most municipal systems does not apply to the international setting nor, more specifically, to the setting up of an international organization such as the United Nations … There is, however, no legislature, in the technical sense of the term, in the United Nations system and, more generally, no parliament in the world community. That is to say, there exists no corporate organ formally empowered to enact laws directly binding on international legal subjects.[123]

Thus, the idea that the Security Council could legitimately assume the role of a legislative body for the international community, notwithstanding the broad

---

Opinion of Judge Sir Gerald Fitzmaurice to the *Advisory Opinion on Namibia*, ICJ Reports 1971, 294, para. 115.

[121] See S. Hall, *The Persistent Spectre: Natural Law, International Order and the Limits of Legal Positivism*, 12 European Journal of International Law 269 (2001).

[122] See, e.g., M.O. Hudson, International Legislation, Vol. I (1931) xiii–xviii; A.D. McNair, *International Legislation*, 19 Iowa Law Review, 178 (1933–34); P.C. Jessup, "Parliamentary Diplomacy: An Examination of the Legal Quality of the Rules of Procedure of Organs of the United Nations," Recueil des Cours, tome 89, 203 (1956-I); K. Skubiszewski, *Enactment of Law by International Organizations*, British Yearbook of International Law, Vol. 41, 198–201 (1965–1966); idem., "New Source of the Law of Nations: Resolutions of International Organizations," in Recueil d'Études de Droit International en Hommage à Paul Guggenheim (Faculté de droit de l'Université de Genève, 1968) 509.

[123] *Prosecutor v. Tadic (Jurisdiction)* (Appeals Chamber, ICTY), (1995) 105 ILR 453, at 473.

reading of its treaty mandate given to it by some scholars, is opposed by basic principles underlying the international legal order.

It is significant to note that this clear role re-definition by the Security Council did not go unnoticed or uncriticized by other U.N. member states not members of the Council during meetings leading up to the passage of Resolution 1540.[124] The normally reserved Japanese delegate stated with concern that "[i]n adopting a binding Security Council resolution under Chapter VII of the United Nations Charter, the Security Council assumes a lawmaking function. The Security Council should, therefore, be cautious not to undermine the stability of the international legal framework."[125]

Egypt similarly observed:

We note a growing trend towards granting the Security Council additional legislative powers. Here, we wish to make it very clear that membership of the United Nations and the common desire to strengthen its role places a number of responsibilities on our shoulders in conformity with the provisions of the Charter as drafted by the founding Members. Thus, in defining the role of the Security Council in terms of the maintenance of international peace and security and of guaranteeing compliance by Member States with international law, the Charter does not give the Council legislative authority; it gives it the authority to safeguard the Charter and to monitor compliance with its provisions.[126]

Mexico also voiced its procedural concerns:

However, my delegation is concerned about the precedent that this draft resolution could set for the handling of other new issues on the world agenda. We are not only concerned about the proliferation of parallel regimes to those already established, using channels outside the norms of existing treaties, but also about the growing trend that the Security Council seeks to legislate, particularly with regard to issues that have their own regime of rights and obligations, even if incomplete when it comes to non-State actors. We require resolute commitments from States and, in order to achieve that, we need the wide participation and discussion of all actors.

Namibia further stated that it

recognizes that there are gaps in the existing multilateral legal instruments which need to be filled. However, such gaps can be filled by multilateral negotiated instruments and should not be filled by the Council measures, which are unbalanced and selective, as they represent only the views of those who drafted them.[127]

Nepal rather pointedly declared

the Security Council lacks competence in making treaties. We are afraid that the Council, through this draft resolution, is seeking to establish something tantamount to a treaty

---

[124] See R. Lavalle, *A Novel, If Awkward, Exercise in International Law-Making: Security Council Resolution 1540*, Netherlands International Law Review, Vol. 51, Issue 3, 428–435 (2004).
[125] S/PV.4950, 28.   [126] S/PV.4950 (Resumption 1), 3.
[127] S/PV.4950 (Resumption 1), 17.

by its fiat. This is likely to undermine the intergovernmental treaty-making process and implementation mechanisms.[128]

Cuba further maintained that "international legal obligations...must not be imposed upon [UN] Member States without their participation and their sovereign acceptance, through the signing and ratification of the corresponding treaties and agreements that have been negotiated multilaterally."[129]

India joined the voices of dissent by noting its "basic concerns over the increasing tendency of the Council in recent years to assume new and wider powers of legislation on behalf of the international community, with its resolutions binding on all States," noting that "[a]ny far-reaching assumption of authority by the Security Council to enact global legislation is not consistent with the provisions of the United Nations Charter," and declaring that it would "not accept any interpretation of the draft resolution that imposes obligations arising from treaties that India has not signed or ratified, consistent with the fundamental principles of international law and the law of treaties."[130]

In summing up concerns based in legislative overreaching, Iran stated:

The United Nations Charter entrusts the Security Council with the huge responsibility to maintain international peace and security, but it does not confer authority on the Council to act as a global legislature imposing obligations on States without their participation in the process. The draft resolution, in its present form, is a clear manifestation of the Council's departure from its Charter-based mandate.[131]

These problems with the assumption of a legislative role by the Security Council, both jurisprudential and institutional, taken together, comprise the legitimacy deficit of Resolution 1540 as a statement of binding international law.

F. Practical Effects

What, then, are the practical effects of this conclusion that Resolution 1540 was passed *ultra vires* the Security Council's authority? The Council not having possessed the authority to issue such a resolution, the decision thus rests upon no legal foundation, and thus has no binding effect upon members of the United Nations. In short, the procedural invalidity of Resolution 1540 results in its being null and void of legal effect.

There is a fine legal point to be made on the subject of laws deemed to be invalid procedurally, as to whether such a law is void *ab initio* (from its inception), or alternatively whether such a law is simply voidable, meaning that the valid legal effect of the law remains in place until the invalidity of the law is authoritatively

---

128 S/PV.4950 (Resumption 1), 14.   129 S/PV.4950, 30.
130 S/PV.4950, 23–24.   131 S/PV.4950, 32.

declared by a competent body.[132] The distinction between these two effects is to be found in whether there is an effective procedural remedy available through which such a determination can be made.[133] As Karl Zemanek has explained:

According to the general theory of law, the absence of a procedural remedy against an alleged illegal act, i.e. a procedure in which the act could be declared void (relative nullity), makes the act ipso facto null and void (absolute nullity).[134]

Eli Lauterpacht has noted further, "[T]he whole question of the effect of illegal acts is closely linked with that of the existence of suitable machinery for determining whether the act is in fact illegal."[135]

In the case of Security Council resolutions, there is only one body which could act as an independent procedural check, and which could potentially authoritatively declare a Council Resolution void of legal effect. This of course is the principal judicial organ of the United Nations, the International Court of Justice.

The question of the capacity of the International Court of Justice to review Security Council decisions for validity will be given fuller consideration in Chapter 5 below. As that discussion will conclude, it is clear from the Court's own jurisprudence as well as from the preponderance of academic literature on the subject, that the ICJ does possess the requisite jurisdiction *ratione materiae* to review decisions of the Security Council for validity under Charter law. The practical ability of the Court to exercise this role is significantly limited, however, due to aspects of its jurisdiction *ratione personae* under its statute, and particularly including both the fact that only states have the legal personality to be parties in a dispute before the Court, as well as the somewhat oxymoronic fact of the voluntary nature of state accession to the compulsory jurisdiction of the Court under the optional clause of the ICJ Statute, Article 36(2). Because of these limitations upon the Court's jurisdiction *ratione personae*, and the resulting inconsistency of

---

[132] See E. de Wet, *Judicial Review of the United Nations Security Council and General Assembly through Advisory Opinions of the International Court of Justice*, 10 SZIER 237, 268 (2000). ("A Voidable act is an act that produces all its effect in spite of the defects by which it is vitiated, as long as it is not annulled by the competent organ. It is only as a result of being annulled that the act loses, retroactively, its effectiveness.") On nullity see J.A. Frowein, "Nullity in International Law," III ENCYCLOPEDIA OF PUBLIC INTERNATIONAL LAW (1997) 743–747; R.Y. Jennings, "Nullity and Effectiveness in International Law," in D.W. Bowett et al., CAMBRIDGE ESSAYS IN INTERNATIONAL LAW: ESSAYS IN HONOR OF LORD MCNAIR (1965) 64–87.

[133] See D. Schweigman, THE AUTHORITY OF THE SECURITY COUNCIL UNDER CHAPTER VII OF THE U.N. CHARTER (2001) 282–285.

[134] "Is the Security Council the Sole Judge of Its Own Legality?" in E. Yakpo and T. Boumedra (eds), LIBER AMICORUM MOHAMMED BEDJAOUI (1992) 642. See also A. Verdross, 44 ANNUAIRE DE L'INSTITUT DE DROIT INTERNATIONAL, at 293, quoted by Lauterpacht in "The Legal Effect of Illegal Actions of International Organisations," in D. Bowett et al., CAMBRIDGE ESSAYS IN INTERNATIONAL LAW: ESSAYS IN HONOUR OF LORD MCNAIR (1965) 93. ("In principle, legally defective decisions are absolutely null, if no means of redress exist.")

[135] "The Legal Effect of Illegal Actions of International Organisations," in D. Bowett et al., CAMBRIDGE ESSAYS IN INTERNATIONAL LAW: ESSAYS IN HONOUR OF LORD MCNAIR (1965) 115.

the Court's ability to exercise jurisdiction over decisions of the Security Council, the ICJ does not presently constitute an effective procedural recourse for seeking authoritative pronouncements of the validity of Security Council decisions.[136]

Without an effective independent body which can authoritatively determine that an act of the Security Council is void, the conclusion must be reached that invalid acts of the Security Council are not simply voidable, but are in fact void *ab initio*, and are devoid of legal effect from the time of their pronouncement.[137] This indeed was the conclusion of Judge Morelli in his Separate Opinion in the *Certain Expenses* case:

> In the case of international organizations, and in particular acts of the United Nations, there is nothing comparable to the remedies existing in domestic law in connection with administrative acts. The consequence of this is that there is no possibility of applying the concept of voidability to the acts of the United Nations. If an act of an organ of the United Nations had to be considered as an invalid act, such invalidity could constitute only the absolute nullity of the act. In other words, there are only two alternatives for the acts of the Organization: either the act is fully valid, or it is an absolute nullity, because nullity is the only form in which invalidity of an act of the Organization can occur. An act of the Organization considered as invalid would be an act which had no legal effects, precisely because it would be an absolute nullity. The lack of effect of such an act could be alleged and a finding in that sense obtained at any time.[138]

Thus, because of the procedural invalidity of the Security Council's passage of Resolution 1540, the resolution itself is void of legal effect *ab initio*.

---

[136] See D. Schweigman, THE AUTHORITY OF THE SECURITY COUNCIL UNDER CHAPTER VII OF THE U.N. CHARTER (2001) 284. ("Although illegal decisions by the Council are voidable, in practice they will be considered null and void *ab initio*. This relates to the fact that the instances in which the Court can function as a procedural remedy against such decisions are limited, certainly more limited that the instances in which protests can be lodged against decisions.") Scholars taking a contrary view on the question of the effectiveness of ICJ review of Security Council decisions, and thus on the question of voidability, include E. de Wet, *Judicial Review of the United Nations Security Council and General Assembly through Advisory Opinions of the International Court of Justice*, 10 SZIER 237 (2000); G. Watson, *Constitutionalism, Judicial Review, and the World Court*, 34 HARVARD INTERNATIONAL LAW JOURNAL 1 (1993); J. Alvarez, *Legal Remedies and the United Nations à la Carte Problem*, 12 MICHIGAN JOURNAL OF INTERNATIONAL LAW 299, 286 (1991). ("If one accepts the presumptions of the *Expenses Case* and the premise that the Advisory Jurisdiction of the ICJ can provide a remedy, under institutional international law allegedly *ultra vires* acts are neither void *ab initio* nor invariably valid but potentially voidable if the member state challenging the act (1) establishes a prima facie case for invalidity and (2) seeks judicial resolution of the question.") It should be noted, however, that to the extent these scholarly views rest upon the ability of the ICJ to exercise is advisory jurisdiction to provide a remedy, that remedy is significantly undermined in its procedural effectiveness by the non-binding character of the Court's advisory jurisdiction. An advisory opinion, for all of its persuasive weight and importance, cannot be said to provide a formally binding determination of the validity of a Security Council resolution. Thus, the characterization of the Court's advisory jurisdiction as comprising an effective procedural remedy against invalid Security Council decisions is belied by the formal impotence of such statements by the Court.

[137] See D. Schweigman, THE AUTHORITY OF THE SECURITY COUNCIL UNDER CHAPTER VII OF THE U.N. CHARTER (2001) 284.

[138] *Certain Expenses* case, ICJ Reports 1962, 222.

5

Non-proliferation Law and the
United Nations System:
The International Court of Justice

Consideration will now turn away from the political bodies of the United Nations, and to a review of the International Court of Justice, the principal judicial organ of the United Nations, in the area of non-proliferation law. In the course of this examination of the past, present, and future role of the ICJ in this area, consideration will return to Security Council Resolution 1540 and other potential *ultra vires* acts by the Council, and the role of the ICJ in providing a judicial check upon the Chapter VII powers of the Council in the area of non-proliferation law specifically. However, before undertaking that specific analysis, the first section of this chapter will review the Court's prior jurisprudence in the non-proliferation law area more generally.

I. Role in the Past

In the past, the ICJ has not played a prominent role in developing international law on the subject of weapons of mass destruction proliferation. The ICJ, of course, is the principal judicial organ of the United Nations.[1] Its statute declares in Article 38(1) that its function is "to decide in accordance with international law such disputes as are submitted to it." Its jurisdiction is recognized in Article 36(2) to extend to "all legal disputes concerning . . . any question of international law." Thus, its jurisdiction *ratione materiae* clearly extends to questions arising under the sources of international law listed in Article 38(1) of its statute, including treaties and customary law, on subjects of WMD proliferation and use.[2] However, such questions have only rarely been properly placed before the Court for its determination.

---

[1] See ICJ Statute, Article 92.

[2] On the ICJ's jurisdiction, see generally A. Zimmermann, et al. (eds), THE STATUTE OF THE INTERNATIONAL COURT OF JUSTICE (2006) ch. II; T. Gill, ROSENNE'S THE WORLD COURT: WHAT IT IS AND HOW IT WORKS (6th edn, 2003) ch. 4.

There are a number of reasons for this paucity of jurisprudence at the World Court on non-proliferation law issues. Perhaps among the most obvious is the fact that situations in which states have felt their interests directly negatively affected by the development, possession, or use of WMD by another state, in breach of international legal sources, have been exceptional. There are currently only 12 states, out of the 191 states in the world, which are commonly known to possess, or are suspected of possessing, WMD arsenals.[3] For five of these states, their nuclear-weapon-state status under the 1968 Nuclear Nonproliferation Treaty is a recognition of the legality of their nuclear weapons arsenals (subject to their obligations under Article VI of the NPT as discussed above). The possession by states of WMD technologies, in and of itself, has not given rise to legal controversies easily capable of judicial determination; although in theory a case of possession-related breach of a non-proliferation treaty instrument such as the NPT, BWC, or CWC, could likely be sustained, at least in terms of standing requirements, by any other party to the same treaty.[4]

Actual military uses of WMD by states since the establishment of the Court in 1945 have been extremely limited, and include the use by Egypt of phosgene and mustard gas against Yemeni royalist troops in support of a military coup in 1963.[5] The most notable use of WMD since 1945 was the use of chemical weapons by Iraq during its war with Iran, which resulted in the deaths of approximately 50,000 Iranian soldiers and civilians.[6] Iraq further used chemical weapons to subdue the Iraqi Kurdish population in the north of the country in the late 1980s.[7]

Testing of WMD has also given rise to few occasions in which states have felt their interests illegally injured by other states. Testing of nuclear weapons has been the most sensitive due to the destructive impact of a nuclear explosion itself, as well as the potential environmental damage and threat to human health caused by the radioactive fallout of a nuclear weapon test. Due to these concerns, nuclear testing was addressed in the 1963 Partial Test Ban Treaty, the 1974 Threshold Test Ban Treaty, the 1976 Peaceful Nuclear Explosions Treaty, and finally the 1996 Comprehensive Test Ban Treaty. In accordance with the restrictions on testing in these instruments, nuclear explosions for testing purposes have relatively steadily decreased in frequency since the 1960s.[8] However, the abovementioned concerns were among those primarily prompting the reference to the ICJ of a case involving an atmospheric nuclear weapon test by France in 1973,

---

[3] J. Cirincione et al., DEADLY ARSENALS, NUCLEAR, BIOLOGICAL AND CHEMICAL THREATS (Carnegie Endowment, 2nd edn, 2005) 3.

[4] A. Zimmermann et al. (eds), THE STATUTE OF THE INTERNATIONAL COURT OF JUSTICE (2006) 612–626.

[5] J. Cirincione et al., DEADLY ARSENALS, NUCLEAR, BIOLOGICAL AND CHEMICAL THREATS (Carnegie Endowment, 2nd edn, 2005) 13.

[6] Ibid. at 66.

[7] See Chapter 7 below at 256.

[8] See J. Goldblat, ARMS CONTROL (2nd edn, 2002) 59.

one of the two most notable instances of the successful exercise of ICJ jurisdiction over the merits of a case involving non-proliferation law, which will be discussed more fully below.

The second reason for the infrequency of non-proliferation law cases before the ICJ is that when controversies regarding WMD possession, proliferation, and use have arisen among states, they have been viewed as intensely political matters, of high security sensitivity and of pressing urgency. Because of these characteristics of such controversies, the political bodies of the U.N., and particularly the Security Council, have been the *fora* of choice for dealing with such matters, and not the relatively slow moving, *ex post facto* judicial processes of the ICJ.

Indeed, both the BWC and CWC specifically direct members to refer issues of compliance with treaty obligations to the U.N. political bodies. In the case of the BWC, Article VI of the Convention directs any member which "finds that any other State Party is acting in breach of obligations deriving from the provisions of the Convention" to "lodge a complaint with the Security Council of the United Nations," along with "all possible evidence confirming its validity," for the Council's investigation and determination.

In the case of the CWC, the procedure for compliance determination is a bit more complex, with treaty members being directed in the first instance to bring complaints concerning the compliance of another member state to the Organisation for the Prohibition of Chemical Weapons (OPCW) Executive Council, which is to conduct a primary investigation and determination of the facts of the alleged breach, including through reliance upon the results of challenge inspections of suspected facilities in the respondent state. However, in Articles VIII(36) and XII(4) of the CWC, the text provides that the OPCW Executive Council "shall, in cases of particular gravity and urgency, bring the issue or matter, including relevant information and conclusions, directly to the attention of the United Nations General Assembly and the United Nations Security Council."[9]

The ICJ, whose fundamental role is to provide a determination of controversies regarding compliance with international legal obligations, is later mentioned only briefly in Article XIV of the CWC, and designated as an arbiter of disputes "relating to the interpretation or application of this Convention." In the BWC, no mention is made of the ICJ.

This orientation of dispute resolution roles and procedures in these non-proliferation treaties is of course the result of consideration both of the Security Council's "primary responsibility for the maintenance of international peace and security," under Article 24 of the U.N. Charter, as well as of the practical

---

[9] While not formally a part of the NPT, the IAEA Statute provides in the same vein in Article XII(C) that the IAEA Board of Governors, in exercising their supervisory role regarding safeguards agreements, shall report state non-compliance with a safeguards agreement to the Security Council and to the General Assembly.

advantages of the use of the political bodies, as opposed to the ICJ, for the settlement of disputes of this character.

When an issue of compliance with a non-proliferation treaty instrument, or rule of customary international law, is raised in a dispute between states, the likelihood is that that dispute will be not simply of an academic, or *ex post facto* character, but will rather be only one facet of a complex political dispute between the parties. This political dispute may, in part due to the presence of this legal dispute, be moving the parties toward contentious relations possibly including military conflict. Thus, what parties to such a dispute of high political sensitivity and moment primarily require is a dispute resolution mechanism which prioritizes mediation and moderation, as opposed to formal determination of legal liability between the parties.

In the context of the CWC, these offices are fulfilled by the OPCW Director General and the Executive Council, the latter organ acting in a dispute over compliance as a go-between among the states concerned, attempting to overcome communications and transparency problems through clarification efforts.[10] After this shuttle diplomacy between the parties, if a dispute over compliance persists, the Executive Council's role is to make determinations of fact and to recommend to the states involved, or to the treaty membership generally, measures "it deems appropriate to resolve the situation."[11] If these measures do not resolve the dispute, then reference of the matter can be made to the U.N. Security Council, which can if necessary use its binding authority under Article 25 of the Charter to obligate state compliance with the recommended course of action.[12]

Again, the primary need of the parties in such a situation of dispute over non-proliferation law is third party aid in order to settle the dispute among the parties in as non-confrontational and low-key a manner as possible, in order to avoid escalation of the dispute. Dispute moderation of this kind is indeed better provided by specific treaty organs or by the political bodies of the United Nations, rather than through the adversarial, and necessarily fault-finding, judicial processes of the ICJ. However, if escalation does occur, the need for political, not legal, resolution of the matter has a greater, not lesser claim to priority. Such cases of high political dispute between states, involving circumstances which may threaten international peace and security, are precisely the sort of issues for which the Security Council was created, and precisely the reason for the existence of its powers under Chapters VI and VII of the Charter.

Thus, due to the character of disputes between states on issues of non-proliferation law, recourse to judicial determination by the ICJ has been an option generally considered of lesser usefulness to the parties than recourse to other dispute resolution *fora*, and thus few such cases have been formally brought before the Court.

---

[10] See generally CWC Article IX.   [11] CWC Article IX(7).
[12] CWC Articles VIII(36) and XII(4).

Thirdly, even when circumstances have arisen in which states have felt their rights or interests significantly prejudiced through illegal possession, development, or proliferation of WMD, and have desired to avail themselves of the judicial determination processes of the ICJ, jurisdictional limitations of the Court itself have often made successful application of the court's jurisdiction to such controversies difficult or impossible.

As with any judicial body, the jurisdiction of the ICJ can be analyzed as consisting of two separate divisions: subject matter jurisdiction (jurisdiction *ratione materiae*), or the substantive issues over which the Court may properly exercise its jurisdiction; and personal jurisdiction (jurisdiction *ratione personae*), or the question of which persons or legal entities can appear as a party before the Court.[13]

In the case of the ICJ, its personal jurisdiction in contentious cases is clearly limited in its statute to states.[14] Thus, only states may appear as parties before the Court in contentious cases; a limitation which significantly excludes both natural persons (individuals) as well as non-governmental or inter-governmental organizations, although in the case of the latter some organs of inter-governmental organizations may apply for an advisory opinion by the Court.[15] Furthermore, the Court may only exercise contentious jurisdiction over states with their consent. The Court may not exercise its jurisdiction over a state simply by virtue of the state's character as a party to the ICJ Statute. Exercise of the Court's personal jurisdiction over a state requires a specific statement of consent by the state.[16]

This specific statement of consent may take various forms.[17] Consent may be given ad hoc by a state, within the context of a specific dispute. This consent often

---

[13] See I. Brownlie, Principles of Public International Law (6th edn, 2003) 680–690; J. Charney, *Compromissory Clauses and the Jurisdiction of the International Court of Justice*, 81 American Journal of International law 855 (1987); J. Crawford, *The Legal Effect of Automatic Reservations to the Jurisdiction of the International Court*, 50 British Yearbook of International Law 63 (1979); L. Damrosch, "Multilateral Disputes," in L. Damrosch, The International Court of Justice at a Crossroads (1987) 376–400; C. Gray, *The Use and Abuse of the International Court of Justice: Cases Concerning the Use of Force After Nicaragua*, 14 European Journal of International Law 867 (2003); E. Hambro, "The Jurisdiction of the International Court of Justice," Recueil des Cours 76, 121–215 (1950-I); A. Koroma, "Asserting Jurisdiction by the International Court of Justice," in P. Capps et al. (eds), Asserting Jurisdiction (2003) 189–198; F.L. Morrison, "Treaties as a Source of Jurisdiction, Especially in U.S. Practice," in L. Damrosch, The International Court of Justice at a Crossroads (1987) 58–81; J. Quintana, *The Nicaragua case and the Denunciation of Declarations of Acceptance of the Compulsory Jurisdiction of the International Court of Justice*, 11 Leiden Journal of International Law 97 (1998); P. Tomka, "The Special Agreement," in Edward McWhinney et al. (eds), Liber Amicorum Judge Shigeru Oda (2002) 553–565.

[14] See ICJ Statute Article 34(1).

[15] United Nations Charter Article 96.

[16] A. Zimmermann et al. (eds), The Statute of the International Court of Justice (2006) ch. II; T. Gill, Rosenne's The World Court: What it is and How it works (6th edn, 2003) ch. 4.

[17] In addition to those heads of jurisdiction covered herein, see I. Brownlie, Principles of Public International Law (6th edn, 2003) 680–690 for a discussion of the two lesser-used jurisdictional heads of *forum prorogatum* and jurisdiction to decide *ex aequo et bono*.

takes the form of a negotiated *compromis*, or statement of questions to the Court, by the parties. Consent may also be given *ante hoc* through inclusion of the Court as the forum of choice of the parties for dispute settlement in the provisions of a specific treaty instrument.[18]

Specific consent by a state to the exercise of the Court's jurisdiction may also be given *ex ante* through a declaration pursuant to Article 36(2) of the Court's Statute, often referred to as the 'optional clause' of the Statute, which provides that

[t]he states parties to the present Statute may at any time declare that they recognize as compulsory ipso facto and without special agreement, in relation to any other state accepting the same obligation, the jurisdiction of the Court in all legal disputes concerning

a. the interpretation of a treaty;
b. any question of international law;
c. the existence of any fact which, if established, would constitute a breach of an international obligation;
d. the nature or extent of the reparation to be made for the breach of an international obligation.

Such declarations recognizing *ex ante* the jurisdiction of the Court in proceedings properly initiated by or against the declaring state, create as among other similarly declaring states a subset of parties to the ICJ statute that have, in effect, consented to a system of compulsory jurisdiction before the Court, at least to the extent that such declarations remain in force and are not withdrawn or limited by reservation.[19] However, relatively few states have made such declarations under the optional clause (66 States as of January 2006), making this subset of states to whom the system of compulsory jurisdiction applies a distinct minority of the 192 states parties to the ICJ Statute itself.

Thus, in order for the Court to exercise its contentious jurisdiction over the decided majority of states parties of the ICJ Statute, including a supermajority of states with significant WMD arsenals (e.g. the United States, France, China, Russia, Israel, North Korea, Iran, Syria), the state must manifest specific consent to the exercise of jurisdiction either on an *ante hoc* basis through treaty provision (which is inapplicable in the context of the significant non-proliferation treaty instruments) or more conventionally on an ad hoc basis in the context of a particular dispute.

---

[18] Ibid.
[19] A. Zimmermann et al. (eds), THE STATUTE OF THE INTERNATIONAL COURT OF JUSTICE (2006) 626; S. Alexandrov, RESERVATIONS IN UNILATERAL DECLARATIONS ACCEPTING THE COMPULSORY JURISDICTION OF THE INTERNATIONAL COURT OF JUSTICE (1995); H. Briggs, "Reservations to the Acceptance of Compulsory Jurisdiction of the International Court of Justice," RECUEIL DES COURS 93, 223–367 (1958-I); E. Brown Weiss, "Reciprocity and the Optional Clause," in L. Damrosch, THE INTERNATIONAL COURT OF JUSTICE AT A CROSSROADS (1987) 82–105; E. Gordon, "Legal Disputes under Article 36(2) of the Statute," in L. Damrosch, THE INTERNATIONAL COURT OF JUSTICE AT A CROSSROADS (1987) 183–222; J. Merrills, "The Optional Clause at Eighty," in E. McWhinney et al.,(eds), LIBER AMICORUM JUDGE SHIGERU ODA (2002) 435–450.

This requirement of specific consent to the personal jurisdiction of the ICJ, and the limited membership of the subset of ICJ parties which have acceded to the compulsory jurisdiction of the Court through declaration pursuant to Article 36(2), has produced a severe limitation on the ability of states to successfully petition for the exercise of ICJ jurisdiction over disputes regarding alleged breaches of non-proliferation law. With so many important WMD possessing states not subject to the Court's compulsory jurisdiction, the ability of other WMD possessing states, or of states not possessing WMD, to challenge the possession, development, or proliferation of such weapons by these states, has been limited by the requirement of the specific consent of the WMD possessing state to the Court's jurisdiction in the particular context of each case. The sensitivity and national security importance of these issues to WMD possessing states, taken together with the lack of positive incentive to accede to the Court's jurisdiction in any such case, has produced very few such accessions, and therefore very few instances of the Court's successful extension of contentious jurisdiction over non-proliferation law cases.

A. The *Nuclear Test Cases*

The most notable instance in which the Court has exercised contentious jurisdiction over a non-proliferation law case is the *Nuclear Test Cases* between New Zealand, Australia, and France in 1973–74.[20] The South Pacific region had been used for testing of nuclear weapons, both through atmospheric explosions and through underground explosions, by several nuclear powers since the United States first tested in the Marshall Islands in 1946, where it continued to test until 1962. The United Kingdom began testing in Australia in 1952 and continued to do so until 1957, before moving their testing to Malden and the Christmas Islands in 1957 and 1958. France began developing its nuclear arsenal in the early 1950s and conducted its first test of a nuclear weapon in the French Sahara in 1960. After Algeria's independence in 1963, France decided to change its nuclear testing location to Mururoa Atoll in French Polynesia, where it began atmospheric testing on July 2, 1966.[21]

Though New Zealand and Australia had not formally protested to the earlier tests by the United States and the United Kingdom, by the mid-1960s there was a growing public awareness of the dangers of radioactive fallout associated

---

[20] *Nuclear Tests (New Zealand v. France)* ICJ Reports 1974, 457; *(Australia v. France)* ICJ Reports 1974, 253. See generally T. Franck, *Word Made Law: The Decision of the ICJ in the Nuclear Test Cases,* 69 AMERICAN JOURNAL OF INTERNATIONAL LAW 612 (1975); B. Kwiatkowska, *New Zealand v. France Nuclear Tests: The Dismissed Case of Lasting Significance,* 37 VIRGINIA JOURNAL OF INTERNATIONAL LAW 107 (1996); S. Tokarz, *A Golden Opportunity Dismissed: the New Zealand v. France Nuclear Tests Case,* 26 DENVER JOURNAL OF INTERNATIONAL LAW AND POLICY 745 (1998).

[21] See D. MacKay, *Nuclear Testing: New Zealand and France in the International Court of Justice,* 19 FORDHAM INTERNATIONAL LAW JOURNAL 1857 (2006).

particularly with atmospheric testing of nuclear weapons, both in terms of possible threats to human health, as well as of possible threats to the environment. There was also disgruntlement among the naval forces of New Zealand and Australia, as well as among commercial fishing fleets, arising from the French Government's cordoning off of the sea lanes surrounding Mururoa and establishing of an exclusion zone around the island, which many saw as an infringement of their rights of freedom of navigation under the international law of the sea.

Both New Zealand and Australia petitioned the French Government, expressing their serious concerns regarding the conducting of the nuclear tests and requesting their cessation. After years of fruitless protests, in late 1972 New Zealand and Australia began preparations to lodge a complaint against France with the International Court of Justice. On May 14, 1973, New Zealand submitted a Request for Interim Measures of Protection to the Court. A similar request was subsequently submitted by Australia.

The Applications asked the Court to declare that the testing of nuclear weapons by France in the South Pacific, which produced radioactive fallout, was in violation of New Zealand's and Australia's rights under international law, and that further testing would continue this breach of rights. These rights were argued to be based in various treaties and in rules of customary international law *erga omnes*.[22] On June 22, 1973, the Court ordered measures of protection to be applied, including that France should refrain from nuclear tests which would result in the deposit of radioactive fallout over the territory specified in the complaints until a formal judgment had been given by the Court.

The Court finally gave its judgment on both cases in December of 1974. The Court decided that because of statements by French officials indicating that there would be no further atmospheric tests in the region, there was no longer any object to the cases, and that therefore there was no issue on which the Court was required to give a judgment on the merits. As the opinion of the Court in response to the New Zealand application stated:

> Thus the Court faces a situation in which the objective of the Applicant has in effect been accomplished, inasmuch as the Court finds that France has undertaken the obligation to hold no further nuclear tests in the atmosphere of the South Pacific.[23]

In so finding, the Court relieved itself of the necessity of formally grounding its jurisdiction to hear the merits of the case, as the applicants had requested them to do. Thus, the Court did not move on to consider the more substantive questions of the argued non-compliance of French nuclear testing with its obligations under international law, and the alleged violence to the legal rights of New Zealand and Australia caused thereby.

[22] See generally, M. Byers, *Conceptualising the Relationship between Jus Cogens and Erga Omnes Rules*, 66 Nordic Journal of International Law 211 (1997).

[23] *Nuclear Tests (New Zealand v. France)* ICJ Reports 1974, 457, 475.

After the 1974 judgments, all French nuclear tests in the South Pacific were conducted underground. From 1974 until its moratorium on testing in 1992, France conducted 134 nuclear explosive tests in the South Pacific, detonating devices both at Mururoa and nearby Fangataufa Atoll. These tests continued to be protested by New Zealand and Australia, as well as other South Pacific states.[24]

Interestingly, a second chapter was opened on the legal history of the *Nuclear Test Cases* when, in June of 1995, French President Jacques Chirac announced that France would hold a final series of eight underground nuclear weapons tests in the South Pacific, to begin in September of that year. After formal protestation by a number of South Pacific states, New Zealand decided to attempt to re-open the earlier proceedings, relying upon a paragraph of the Court's judgment in its 1974 response to New Zealand's petition. Paragraph 63 of the Court's 1974 judgment stated:

Once the Court has found that a State has entered into a commitment concerning its future conduct it is not the Court's function to contemplate that it will not comply with it. However, the Court observes that if the basis of this Judgment were to be affected, the Applicant could request an examination of the situation in accordance with the provisions of the Statute...

Thus, New Zealand sought to argue that France's decision to engage in further nuclear testing in the South Pacific so affected the basis of the earlier judgment as to make valid a request for further examination of the matter by the Court. New Zealand considered that its chances for success in such a renewed action would be better than Australia's, as the latter's application in the 1974 case was specifically limited to a request that France stop atmospheric nuclear tests in the region, whereas New Zealand's application had not been so limited.[25]

However, a number of significant jurisdictional obstacles presented themselves. In January of 1974, while the earlier cases before the ICJ were ongoing, France had withdrawn its consent to the 1928 General Act for the Pacific Settlement of International Disputes which, read together with Articles 36(1) and 37 of the ICJ Statute, had afforded one of the bases argued by New Zealand for the jurisdiction *ratione personae* of the ICJ in the 1974 case. France had also, in the same month, withdrawn its declaration of accession to the compulsory jurisdiction of the ICJ pursuant to Article 36(2) of the ICJ Statute. Therefore, there was no basis for grounding jurisdiction for a new action against France in 1995. The only hope for New Zealand's legal team was to argue that there was a sufficient link between the threatened 1995 tests and the tests which had given rise to the case before the ICJ twenty years earlier, in order to ground the Court's jurisdiction in its statement in paragraph 63 of the 1974 judgment.[26]

---

[24] See D. MacKay, *Nuclear Testing: New Zealand and France in the International Court of Justice*, 19 Fordham International Law Journal 1857 (2006).
[25] Ibid.   [26] Ibid.

In its August 21 Request for an Examination of the Situation, New Zealand asked the Court to determine substantively that French underground testing of nuclear devices would be in breach of international environmental law, and that procedurally France was obligated to conduct an Environmental Impact Assessment before resuming testing in the region, pursuant to the terms of the 1986 Noumea Convention and customary international law.

New Zealand's jurisdictional argument to the Court has been described by Don MacKay, International Legal Advisor to the New Zealand Ministry of Foreign Affairs:

The continuity argument advanced by New Zealand, in essence, was that the Court concluded in 1974 that New Zealand's concerns about radioactive contamination of the environment were "matched" by France's promise to cease atmospheric testing. The Court had at that time assumed that underground testing would not damage the environment or breach international law. By 1995, that assumption had become demonstrably wrong. In terms of paragraph 63, New Zealand had, therefore, shown the basis of the Judgment to be affected by new underground testing. New Zealand could thus resume its 1974 case against France accordingly.[27]

France maintained that the 1974 case could not be re-opened on the basis of the new tests particularly as the previous case was limited to consideration of atmospheric testing, and argued that the Court could not now exercise jurisdiction over France even prima facie, due to lack of state consent.

The Court handed down its order on September 22, 2005.[28] The Court agreed with New Zealand that Paragraph 63 of the 1974 judgment did provide a procedure *sui generis* to allow New Zealand to re-open the case. However, in reference to the facts of the 1974 case, and the particular language of paragraph 63, the Court held that it could not find that the new tests would significantly "affect" the basis of the 1974 judgment, because the 1974 judgment had been specifically in reference to France's atmospheric nuclear tests, and that therefore only a resumption of atmospheric tests by France could trigger the right of New Zealand under Paragraph 63 to have the case re-opened.

The *Nuclear Test Cases* are illustrative of just some of the jurisprudential hurdles faced by states wishing to have the ICJ exercise its contentious jurisdiction over an issue of non-proliferation law. Both the 1974 and 1995 cases were defeated at the jurisdictional phase, with the Court declaring itself unable to reach the merits of the substantive case. The 1995 case is particularly striking in this regard, as due to the requirement of positive state consent to its jurisdiction, withheld by France in this instance, the Court was forced to try and find its jurisdiction for an important case in the non-proliferation law field in the language of a 20–year-old judgment on different facts. It is perhaps no wonder that three of the judges in the 1995 case issued dissenting separate opinions to the majority opinion, in which

---

[27] Ibid. at 1874.   [28] *Nuclear Tests (New Zealand v. France)* ICJ Reports 1995.

they discussed the substantive merits of the case at length, and expressed frustration that the Court was unable to rule on the merits of a case with such important legal substance. As Judge ad hoc Sir Geoffrey Palmer stated:

The essence of the approach taken represents a triumph of formalism over substance. The law appears as some disembodied construct that is far removed from the concerns of the real world. The law is frozen in time, nothing beyond 1974 has any relevance or importance in interpreting Paragraph 63, except a resumption of atmospheric testing. It is an approach that depends upon reading down the plain language of Paragraph 63, and sapping it of vitality. I find such an approach to legal reasoning arid and intellectually unsatisfying. When dealing with substantive issues of such overwhelming importance, decisions not to address those issues need to be convincing and carry legal conviction. In this case, however, the reasoning is laconic.[29]

Later in his dissenting opinion, Judge ad hoc Palmer goes on to consider larger issues of international jurisprudence presented by the *Nuclear Test Cases*, including on questions of the jurisdiction of the ICJ:

One of the signal weaknesses of international law is the fact that the jurisdiction of this Court rests at bottom on the consent of the States. Only about one-third of nations accept the compulsory jurisdiction of this Court under Article 36(2)...In general, the most powerful nations are not among the strongest adherents of compulsory jurisdiction for the Court...Arguments about consent and the logic of the situation in which the Court finds itself have in my opinion caused the Court to be cautious in the past, sometimes unnecessarily.[30]

B. The *Nuclear Weapons* Advisory Opinions

As noted above, in addition to contentious jurisdiction the Court may also, under Article 65 of its Statute, exercise advisory jurisdiction.[31] In Article 96 of the U.N. Charter, the General Assembly and the Security Council are authorized to refer questions of international law to the Court for its determination under its advisory jurisdiction. Article 96 also states that advisory opinions of the Court can be requested by "other organs of the United Nations and specialized agencies" if authorized by the General Assembly. As Ian Brownlie has explained: "The uses of the advisory jurisdiction are to assist the political organs in settling disputes and

---

[29] Ibid. at the Dissenting Opinion of Judge ad hoc Palmer, para. 96.
[30] Ibid. at paras 104 and 105.
[31] See generally I. Brownlie, PRINCIPLES OF PUBLIC INTERNATIONAL LAW (6th edn, 2003) 690–692; M. Aljaghoub, THE ADVISORY FUNCTION OF THE INTERNATIONAL COURT OF JUSTICE 1946–2005 (2006); A. Zimmermann et al. (eds), THE STATUTE OF THE INTERNATIONAL COURT OF JUSTICE (2006) 183–191, 1401–1468; T. Gill, ROSENNE'S THE WORLD COURT: WHAT IT IS AND HOW IT WORKS (6th edn, 2003) 86–91; D. Akande, *The Competence of International Organizations and the Advisory Jurisdiction of the International Court of Justice*, 9 EUROPEAN JOURNAL OF INTERNATIONAL LAW 437 (1998); D. Greig, *The Advisory Jurisdiction of the International Court of Justice and the Settlement of Disputes between States*, 15 INTERNATIONAL AND COMPARATIVE LAW QUARTERLY 325 (1966).

to provide authoritative guidance on points of law arising from the function of organs and specialized agencies."[32]

The Court's advisory jurisdiction differs from its jurisdiction over contentious cases in terms of jurisdiction *ratione personae*, in that a request for the Court's advisory jurisdiction cannot be made by states themselves, but rather exclusively by competent international political organs. The Court's jurisdiction *ratione materiae* is formally unchanged as between contentious and advisory cases; however the Court's jurisprudence has developed to limit the application of its advisory jurisdiction to questions either specifically related to the functions of the organ making the request, or of an abstract and general nature, not directly related to a particular legal dispute between states.[33] The Court's determinations under its advisory jurisdiction are non-binding in character, though highly respected and recognized as authoritative.[34]

Applying its advisory jurisdiction, the Court in 1996 conducted its best known foray into issues of international non-proliferation law, resulting in the production of two advisory opinions on the "legality of the threat or use of nuclear weapons." The first request for an advisory opinion came from the World Health Assembly, an organ of the World Health Organization. The Court eventually held that the Assembly lacked the authority to request an advisory opinion, and therefore did not reach a consideration of the merits of the Assembly's request.[35] However, a similar request was made on December 19, 1994 by the U.N. General Assembly, which in its Resolution 49/75K asked the Court to urgently render an advisory opinion on the question "Is the threat or use of nuclear weapons in any circumstances permitted under international law?"

Resolution 49/75K was passed by the General Assembly with 78 states voting in favor, 43 against, 38 abstaining, and 25 not voting. 42 states participated in the written stage of the pleadings before the Court, including all the declared nuclear weapons possessing states except China. The participants represented a cross-section of states in the General Assembly, many from the developing world taking an intense interest in the case. Twenty-two states participated in the oral hearings for the case, which were held from October 30 to November 15, 1995. On July 8, 1996, after a period of nearly eight months' deliberation, the Court issued both advisory opinions.

The Court's advisory opinion in response to the General Assembly's request has come to be regarded as one of the most, if not the most controversial decisions

---

[32] I. Brownlie, Principles of Public International Law (6th edn, 2003) 691.

[33] See ICJ Statute Article 68: "In the exercise of its advisory functions the Court shall further be guided by the provisions of the present Statute which apply in contentious cases to the extent to which it recognizes them to be applicable." See also Article 102 of the ICJ's Rules of Court. See the thorough discussion of the Court's jurisdiction *ratione materiae* in advisory cases in the *Nuclear Weapons Advisory Opinion*, paras 10–19.

[34] See I. Brownlie, Principles of Public International Law (6th edn, 2003). 691.

[35] *Legality of the Use by a State of Nuclear Weapons in Armed Conflict*, Advisory Opinion, ICJ Reports 1996, 66.

of the International Court of Justice.[36] Among the judges themselves, this fact is witnessed in the number of additional declarations (5), separate opinions (3), and particularly dissenting opinions (6) appended to the advisory opinion. This is the only occasion in the history of ICJ jurisprudence in which every one of the 14 judges sitting on the case felt compelled to issue a statement explaining their discomfort, to greater or lesser degrees, with elements of the Court's opinion. The dissenting opinions are particularly striking because of the intensity of disagreement on issues of law and applications to fact, as well as the exhaustive nature of several of the dissenting opinions in providing alternative, contrasting determinations of law from those adopted by the majority.

As always, the Court begins its consideration in the opinion with the question of its jurisdiction. It notes inter alia that, notwithstanding the undeniable political aspects of the question being put to it, the question is nevertheless a legal question, properly suited for and capable of judicial determination. As the Court states:

> The question put to the Court by the General Assembly is indeed a legal one, since the Court is asked to rule on the compatibility of the threat or use of nuclear weapons with the relevant principles and rules of international law . . . The fact that this question also has political aspects, as, in the nature of things, is the case with so many questions which arise in international life, does not suffice to deprive it of its character as a "legal question" and to "deprive the Court of a competence expressly conferred on it by its Statute." (*Application for Review of Judgment No. 158 of the United Nations Administrative Tribunal, Advisory Opinion, I.C.J. Reports 1973*, p. 172, para. 14)[37]

Having found that its jurisdiction over the case is well-founded, the Court proceeds to identify principles of international law relevant to the question put to it, and to determine the relevance and impact of various legal principles embodied in a number of substantive areas of law.

In the area of international human rights law, and specifically with reference to the provisions of the International Covenant on Civil and Political Rights (ICCPR), the Court notes the applicability of Article 6 of the ICCPR, which prohibits the arbitrary deprivation of human life, to the case of the threat or use of nuclear weapons. However, the Court holds that in the circumstance of a state of hostilities, the meaning of ICCPR Article 6 must be determined by the *lex*

---

[36] *Legality of the Use by a State of Nuclear Weapons in Armed Conflict*, Advisory Opinion, ICJ Reports 1996, 26. See generally P.Sands and L. Boisson de Chazournes (eds), INTERNATIONAL LAW, THE INTERNATIONAL COURT OF JUSTICE AND NUCLEAR WEAPONS (1999); V. Nanda and D. Krieger, NUCLEAR WEAPONS AND THE WORLD COURT (1998); R. Falk, *The Nuclear Weapons Advisory Opinion and the New Jurisprudence of Global Civil Society*, 7 TRANSNATIONAL LAW & CONTEMPORARY PROBLEMS 333 (1997); B.H. Weston, *Nuclear Weapons and the World Court: Ambiguity's Consensus*, 7 TRANSNATIONAL LAW & CONTEMPORARY PROBLEMS. 371 (1997); D. Stephens, *Human Rights and Armed Conflict—The Advisory Opinion of the International Court of Justice in the Nuclear Weapons Case*, 4 YALE HUMAN RIGHTS & DEVELOPMENT LAW JOURNAL 1 (2001).

[37] Ibid. at para. 13.

specialis pertaining to that circumstance, which is international humanitarian law. Thus, as the Court states:

[W]hether a particular loss of life, through the use of a certain weapon in warfare, is to be considered an arbitrary deprivation of life contrary to Article 6 of the Covenant, can only be decided by reference to the law applicable in armed conflict and not deduced from the terms of the Covenant itself.[38]

In the area of international environmental law the Court finds legal circumscriptions applicable to the threat or use of nuclear weapons, but not a universal prohibition. Rather, in a similar vein to its holding regarding Article 6 of the ICCPR, the Court notes the relationship between international environmental law and the substance of both international humanitarian law and international use of force law, and states that "[r]espect for the environment is one of the elements that go to assessing whether an action is in conformity with the principles of necessity and proportionality."[39]

The Court proceeds to find a similar lack of general prohibition on the threat or use of nuclear weapons in the law of genocide, noting that for the law of genocide to prohibit a threat or use of nuclear weapons, a specific intent of the kind proscribed in Article II of the 1948 Genocide Convention would need to be found, and that this would necessitate a fact specific inquiry.[40]

The Court then proceeds to a review both of the principles of international use of force law embodied in the U.N. Charter, as well as of the principles of international humanitarian law. The Court includes in its consideration of the law of armed conflict both international law in treaty and custom specifically on the question of the threat or use of nuclear weapons, using as its sources of law a number of non-proliferation treaties; as well as the legal principles of international humanitarian law, embodied in such sources as the Hague Conventions of 1899 and 1907, and the Geneva Conventions of 1864, 1906, 1929, and 1949, including the Additional Protocols of 1977.

The result of the Court's inquiry is that no universal prohibition on the threat or use of nuclear weapons is found in either international use of force law or the law of armed conflict, although the Court takes pains to clearly establish that the principles of international humanitarian law are controlling on nuclear weapons, and that in most foreseeable instances of the use of nuclear weapons in war, that use would be in breach of fundamental principles of humanitarian law, including proportionality and indiscriminate targeting of non-combatants.[41]

The Court grounds its reserved approach to this review of substantive areas of international law, and in particular its refusal to find in them a universal prohibition of the threat or use of nuclear weapons, upon the classic *Lotus* principle, which states the presumptive position in international law, founded

---

[38] Ibid. at para. 25.   [39] Ibid. at para. 30.   [40] Ibid. at para. 26.
[41] Ibid. at paras 74, and 105(2)(D)&(E).

in state sovereignty and state consent, that acts of states are legal unless specifically made illegal by a clearly identified source of international law. As the Court relates:

The use of the word "permitted" in the question put by the General Assembly was criticized before the Court by certain States on the ground that this implied that the threat or the use of nuclear weapons would only be permissible if authorization could be found in a treaty provision or in customary international law. Such a starting point, those States submitted, was incompatible with the very basis of international law, which rests upon the principles of sovereignty and consent; accordingly, and contrary to what was implied by use of the word "permitted", States are free to threaten or use nuclear weapons unless it can be shown that they are bound not to do so by reference to a prohibition in either treaty law or customary international law. Support for this contention was found in dicta of the Permanent Court of International Justice in the *"Lotus"* case that "restrictions upon the independence of States cannot...be presumed" and that international law leaves to States "a wide measure of discretion which is only limited in certain cases by prohibitive rules." (*P.C.I.J., Series A, No. 10,* pp. 18 and 19)[42]

In thus circumscribing its determinations, the Court seems to have been wary of creating a perception that it had gone further than provisions of positive law clearly dictate, fearing that particularly in such a high profile and contentious issue area, the Court would be criticized for having engaged in judicial legislation by the nuclear weapon states arguing for legality. As Judge Schwebel notes in his dissenting opinion: "More than any case in the history of the Court, this proceeding presents a titanic tension between State practice and legal principle. It is accordingly the more important not to confuse the international law we have with the international law we need." This reserve was, however, a subject of significant disagreement in several of the dissenting opinions.

However, it is on the relationship between principles of international use of force law (in particular the law of self-defense) and the principles of international humanitarian law, that the Court makes its most controversial, and to many enigmatic, holding. The Court, evenly split and only by the President's casting vote, holds in paragraph 105(2)(e) that:

It follows from the above-mentioned requirements that the threat or use of nuclear weapons would generally be contrary to the rules of international law applicable in armed conflict, and in particular the principles and rules of humanitarian law;

However, in view of the current state of international law, and of the elements of fact at its disposal, the Court cannot conclude definitively whether the threat or use of nuclear weapons would be lawful or unlawful in an extreme circumstance of self-defence, in which the very survival of a State would be at stake...

As many commentators, in addition to a number of the dissenting justices, have observed, this declaration by the Court that it could not give a conclusive

---

[42] Ibid. at para. 21.

legal determination on the core subject of the question put to it by the General Assembly amounts to a *non liquet*. *Non liquet* refers to a judicial finding that the law as applicable to a case is insufficient to allow the determination of a legal question one way or the other.[43] As Dan Bodansky explains, a *non liquet* can result from two distinguishable situations:

This indeterminacy in the law could, in theory, be of two types, one ontological and the other epistemological. First, a *non liquet* could result from a substantive gap in the law, such that the law fails to answer a legal question (in the case of the advisory opinion, whether the use of nuclear weapons in an extreme circumstance of self-defense is lawful or unlawful) . . .

In contrast, an epistemological *non liquet* does not presuppose an actual gap in the law. Even if the law were complete, a *non liquet* could still result if the law lacked sufficiently rich rules of reasoning to permit a court to answer every question.[44]

It is in fact unclear from the majority opinion itself the type of *non liquet*, ontological or epistemological, which occurs in paragraph 105(2)(e). However several dissenting judges voice their consternation, bordering on disbelief, that a case the central issue of which has been determined by the Court to lie at the nexus of international use of force law and international humanitarian law, two of the most developed areas of international law, could possibly result in a *non liquet* of either variety as its primary holding. As Judge Higgins writes:

The fact that its principles are broadly stated and often raise further questions that require a response can be no ground for a *non liquet*. It is exactly the judicial function to take principles of general application, to elaborate their meaning and to apply them to specific situations. This is precisely the role of the International Court, whether in contentious proceedings or in its advisory function . . . The learned editors of the 9th Edition of *Oppenheim's International Law* remind us: 'there is [not] always a clear and specific legal rule readily applicable to every international situation, but that every international situation is capable of being determined *as a matter of law*' (Jennings and Watts, Vol. I, p. 13). Nor is the situation changed by any suggestion that the problem is as much one of "antimony" or clashes between various elements in the law as much as alleged "vagueness" in the law. Even were there such an "antimony" (which, as I have indicated above, I doubt), the judge's role is precisely to decide which of two or more competing norms is applicable in the particular circumstances.

This refusal to give a legal determination notwithstanding the existence of developed law on point was perceived by a number of dissenting judges as an

---

[43] See generally R. Posner, The Problems of Jurisprudence (1990) 197; G. Fitzmaurice, "The Problem of Non-liquet: Prolegomena to a Restatement," Mélanges Offerts à Charles Rousseau (1974) 92–102; H. Lauterpacht, "Some Observations on the Prohibition of 'Non-Liquet' and the Completeness of the Law," in Eli Lauterpacht (ed.), Hersch Lauterpacht, International Law: Collected Papers, Vol. 2, (1975) 216.

[44] D. Bodansky, "*Non Liquet* and the Incompleteness of International Law," in P. Sands and L. Boisson de Chazournes (eds), International Law, the International Court of Justice and Nuclear Weapons (1999) 153, 154.

abrogation by the Court of its fundamental role as the principal judicial organ of the U.N. As Judge Schwebel argues:

This is an astounding conclusion to be reached by the International Court of Justice. Despite the fact that its Statute "forms an integral part" of the United Nations Charter, and despite the comprehensive and categorical terms of Article 2, paragraph 4, and Article 51 of that Charter, the Court concludes on the supreme issue of the threat or use of force of our age that it has no opinion... When it comes to the supreme interests of State, the Court discards the legal progress of the Twentieth Century, puts aside the provisions of the Charter of the United Nations of which it is "the principal judicial organ", and proclaims, in terms redolent of *Realpolitik*, its ambivalence about the most important provisions of modern international law. If this was to be its ultimate holding, the Court would have done better to have drawn on its undoubted discretion not to render an Opinion at all.

Judge Koroma adds his incredulity to that of the other dissenting judges in writing:

In my view, it is wholly incoherent in the light of the material before the Court to say that it cannot rule definitively on the matter now before it in view of the current state of the law and because of the elements of facts at its disposal, for neither the law nor the facts are so imprecise or inadequate as to prevent the Court from reaching a definitive conclusion on the matter. On the other hand, the Court's findings could be construed as suggesting either that there is a gap, a lacuna, in the existing law or that the Court is unable to reach a definitive conclusion on the matter because the law is imprecise or its content insufficient or that it simply does not exist. It does not appear to me any new principles are needed for a determination of the matter to be made. All that was requested of the Court was to apply the existing law. A finding of *non liquet* is wholly unfounded in the present case.

Whether of the ontological or epistemological variety, in its declaration of a *non liquet* in paragraph 105(2)(e) the majority seems to have broken from the guiding principle of the "*Lotus*" case which it used in its examination of other substantive areas of law.[45] The indeterminacy and unclarity found in the sources of international use of force law and international humanitarian law, and the lack of a clear prohibition on the threat or use of nuclear weapons found in those legal sources, if viewed through the lens of the "*Lotus*" principle and in keeping with the general principle of ICJ jurisprudence that *non liquet* should be avoided by the Court, would have been most consistently determined to produce an absence of universal obligation for states to refrain from the threat or use of nuclear weapons. This is particularly the case in light of the Court's recognition in paragraph 96 of its opinion of the existence of the "fundamental right of every state to survival, and thus its right to resort to self-defense, in accordance

---

[45] PCIJ, Ser. A, no. 10, 18.

with Article 51 of the Charter, when its survival is at stake." As Hans Kelsen has explained:

That neither conventional nor customary international law is applicable to a concrete case is logically not possible. Existing international law can always be applied to a concrete case, that is to say, to the question as to whether a state (or another subject of international law) is or is not obliged to behave in a certain way. If there is no norm of conventional or customary international law imposing upon the state (or another subject of international law) the obligation to behave in a certain way, the subject is under international law legally free to behave as it pleases; and by a decision to this effect existing international law is applied to the case . . . He who assumes that in such a case the existing law cannot be applied ignores the fundamental principle that what is not legally forbidden to the subject of the law is legally permitted to them.[46]

It is difficult to understand why in these substantive areas of law, the decision was taken by the majority not to point out this lack of universal legal prohibition as it had done in other substantive areas, that would have resulted in a legal determination of the legality of threat or use of nuclear weapons in some cases, and thus a proper judicial determination of the question put to the Court; but rather instead to say that the Court could not determine the result of the application of existing law to this question, almost as if the majority simply felt incapable of the task of legal interpretation set before them. However, Dan Bodansky has given a possible explanation for this decision:

If findings of *non liquet* are prohibited, then in some cases the Court may be faced with two equally unattractive options: fashioning a new rule of international law, which represents a pointless—perhaps even counterproductive—pursuit of utopia, or providing a legal apology for the status quo. This may well have been how the Court perceived its options in the *Nuclear Weapons* proceeding. I would suggest that it is not an uncommon dilemma, given the substantial gap in such areas as human rights and environmental protection between the law as traditionally conceived and the law as it should be. In such cases, a finding of *non liquet* offers an attractive alternative. It permits the Court neither to give legal approval to the status quo (by saying that whatever is not prohibited is *ipso facto* permitted), nor to undermine its credibility through rampant and potentially ineffectual lawmaking.[47]

But why did it come to this? Why did the Court allow itself to be put in this position, in which it perhaps felt that the declaration of a *non liquet* was its least worst option? Most enigmatically, why refuse to answer the central question of the General Assembly's request, when, as several of the dissenting judges point out, the Court could have used its discretion under Article 65 of the ICJ Statute

---

[46] H. Kelsen, Principles of International Law (2nd edn, revised and edited by Robert W. Tucker, 1966) 438–440.

[47] D. Bodansky, "*Non Liquet* and the Incompleteness of International Law," in P. Sands and L. Boisson de Chazournes (eds), International Law, the International Court of Justice and Nuclear Weapons (1999) 169–170.

to simply decline jurisdiction over the case in the first instance?[48] President Bedjaoui's separate declaration argues that in stating its inability to determine a legal answer to the question put to it, the Court was simply pointing out a deficiency in the law giving rise to legal uncertainty, and that doing so invited further lawmaking by states to remedy this deficiency.

However, this seems a less than satisfactory reason for the majority's failure to reach a legal determination. Should not this result and the attending embarrassment for the Court have been foreseen by the majority? And as such, as Judge Schwebel argues above, would it not have been more prudent for the Court not to have exercised its jurisdiction over the matter originally? Why did the Court indicate through its voluntary acceptance of jurisdiction that it would provide an answer to the question presented by the General Assembly, and then in the end refuse to provide such an answer? As Judge Shahubudeen summarized:

Overruling preliminary arguments, the Court, with near unanimity, decided to comply with the General Assembly's request for an advisory opinion on the question whether "the threat or use of nuclear weapons [is] in any circumstance permitted under international law". By a bare majority, it then proceeded to reply to the General Assembly's question by taking the position, on its own showing, that it cannot answer the substance of the question. I fear that the contradiction between promise and performance cannot, really, be concealed.

It would seem that the only, even partially satisfactory explanation for this rather schizophrenic approach to the advisory opinion by the Court is that the members of the majority who voted in favor of the holding in paragraph 105(2)(E) somehow changed their perception, or appreciation of the case and its justiciability after initially accepting jurisdiction over it. Perhaps they did not, at the initiation of the proceedings, fully appreciate the complexity of the case and the relevant law as well as the political implications of their opinion until the arguments were made by the various states. At that point, having already accepted jurisdiction but not feeling capable, or willing, to make a clear determination of the applicable law, they chose a declaration of *non liquet* as their least worst escape.

Whatever the reasoning, the Court's refusal to give a legal determination of the General Assembly's question regarding the legality of threat or use of nuclear weapons is perceived widely, and particularly among international lawyers, as a jurisprudential disaster, undermining of the credibility of the Court, and more generally of the meaningfulness of the role of international law in international affairs. This advisory opinion, in which the Court for the first and possibly last time was jurisdictionally able to reach substantive issues of non-proliferation law, and the Court's final declaration of its inability to determine that the substance of international law was of any consequence for the decisions of states on a central issue of WMD proliferation, is the principal legacy of the ICJ thus far

---

[48] See *Legal Consequences of the Construction of a Wall in the Occupied Palestinian Territory*, ICJ Reports 2004.

in the non-proliferation law area. This failure of the Court stands as a testament to the complexity of the issue area, and the difficulty of finding a clear place for international law on issues of such high politics and national security sensitivity.

Even though divided and controversial in its main holdings, it should be noted that the *Nuclear Weapons Advisory Opinion* does make a significant contribution to non-proliferation law in one of its other holdings in paragraph 105(2), in clarifying the obligations of states parties to the 1968 Nuclear Nonproliferation Treaty under NPT Article VI. In subparagraph 105(2)(f) the Court holds unanimously that:

There exists an obligation to pursue in good faith and bring to a conclusion negotiations leading to nuclear disarmament in all its aspects under strict and effective international control.

This holding by the ICJ represents the first instance since the establishment of the NPT wherein the NPT's terms have been given further explication and meaning through interpretation by a judicial body. Though in his dissenting opinion Judge Schwebel is likely correct in noting that, since paragraph 105(2)(f) was not in direct response to the question put to the Court by the General Assembly, this portion of the Court's opinion is *dictum*. However, Judge Schwebel is quite incorrect in stating that this pronouncement on the meaning of NPT Article VI is simply redundant of the treaty text itself. The Court's holding elaborates very usefully upon the meaning of Article VI, as to its nature as a substantive legal obligation with determinable terms and boundaries. Particularly useful in this regard is the Court's clarification that this obligation extends not only to the pursuit of negotiations in good faith "on a Treaty on general and complete disarmament," but also to the conclusion of those negotiations, i.e. to the production of a concrete, legally binding agreement among states setting out the details of how nuclear disarmament will be accomplished, and to eventual nuclear disarmament itself. As the Court further explains:

In these circumstances the Court appreciates the full importance of the recognition in Article VI of the Treaty on the Nonproliferation of Nuclear Weapons of an obligation to negotiate in good faith a nuclear disarmament...The legal import of that obligation goes beyond that of a mere obligation of conduct; the obligation involved here is an obligation to achieve a precise result—nuclear disarmament in all its aspects—by adopting a particular course of conduct, namely, the pursuit of negotiations on the matter in good faith.[49]

The obligation to conclude such negotiations and eventually to disarm, or as worded elsewhere herein, the obligation to move toward disarmament in good faith, was not unambiguously stated in the text of NPT Article VI.[50]

[49] ICJ Reports, 1996, 26 para. 99.
[50] In his dissent, Judge Schwebel is rightly doubtful of the expression of the Court's determination in paragraph 105(2)(f), though the text of this paragraph was adopted unanimously.

II. Role in the Present

However, despite this rather uninspiring record of the ICJ's involvement in the area of non-proliferation law in the past, returning to the discussion in Chapter 4 above regarding Security Council Resolution 1540 and the legislative aspirations of the Security Council generally, there may be an important role both at present and in the future for the ICJ to fill in maintaining the coherence of the U.N. Charter system for non-proliferation law creation, and in serving as a judicial check upon the political bodies of the United Nations, and particularly the Security Council.

As reviewed above, there is a procedural system spelled out in the Charter that should be followed as the *lex specialis* controlling paradigm for the creation of law by U.N. organs in the area of WMD non-proliferation. However, notwithstanding the presence of this system in the provisions of the U.N. Charter, the trend in the actual practice of the Security Council, as manifest in the passage of Resolutions 1373 and 1540, seems to be for the Council to ignore these Charter limitations and engage in a counterfeit presentment of international legislating. Because of the practical efficiencies, both legal and political, of this illegitimate use of the Security Council's Chapter VII powers reviewed above, there is every reason to expect that the Council will continue to pass pieces of legislation by means of its resolutions in the future, in the non-proliferation issue area as well as in other areas of international security concern. This manifest intent of the Council to take upon itself the mantle of international legislator should provide the catalyst for a renaissance of attention to old debates concerning the role and competencies of the organs of the United Nations, and specifically concerning the question of the authority of the ICJ to act as a judicial check upon the power of the Security Council by reviewing Security Council decisions for validity under Charter law.

It should be noted from the outset that the potential effectiveness of ICJ judicial review of Security Council decisions in the area of non-proliferation law is significantly greater than its potential effectiveness in other international security issue areas, including terrorism (the subject of Resolution 1373). This is due to the

He usefully clarifies that the obligation which is identified in paragraph 105(2)(f) must be understood to refer to the obligation expressed in Article VI of the NPT which, as the Court states in paragraph 100 "formally concerns" only NPT member states. The rather imprecise wording of paragraph 105(2)(f) leaves room for argument that the obligation identified therein is an obligation of a more general character in international law. However, as Judge Schwebel points out, there is simply no basis of authority for any obligation of this character apart from its expression in NPT Article VI. As noted in ch.1 n. 170 above, Article VI has not passed into parallel customary law due to the mixed record of state practice regarding disarmament. Thus, any suggestion that there exists either in customary law or other source of international law an obligation of nuclear disarmament which is separate from, or more expansive than the obligation contained in NPT Article VI, is wholly lacking in legal foundation.

presence in the U.N. Charter of justiciable standards and a clear procedural system for making non-proliferation law, contained in Articles 11(1) and 26, which as argued above provide a substantive limitation upon the Security Council's powers under Article 25 of the Charter. In other areas of Council decision-making under its Chapter VII powers, these clear justiciable standards and procedural mechanisms for law creation are lacking in the Charter. In these areas in which the Council can simply point to its broad *compétence de la compétence* over threats to international peace and security in Article 39, and its equally broad powers of compulsory sanctioning under Articles 41 and 42, legal arguments for limiting the Council's lawmaking reach will be more difficult to maintain, even though founded upon solid principles of institutional competence and the spirit of Charter law.

The argument in this chapter is thus a more discrete discussion of the authority of the ICJ, as well as the practical ability of the Court, to review Council decisions for validity in the area of non-proliferation law, in order to give authoritative voice to the limitations on Council authority contained in Articles 11 and 26 of the Charter. This chapter will not attempt to make more general arguments for ICJ judicial review of Security Council decisions in other issue areas, as this would require a much fuller treatment not only of the ICJ Statute but also of the provisions relating to the Chapter VII authority of the Security Council in the U.N. Charter, which would exceed the scope of this volume. It should be noted, however, that this more general argument has been made by others.[51]

A. The ICJ and Judicial Review

The idea of the ICJ serving as an institutional check upon the Security Council through exercise of a power of judicial review over decisions of the Council is one which has been discussed particularly by academic international lawyers for many years. From time to time there is a resurgence of interest in the subject, often prompted by a controversial use of the Security Council's Chapter VII powers, as occurred in the *Lockerbie* cases in 1998.[52]

---

[51] For analysis of this larger question and literature review see J. Alvarez, *Judging the Security Council*, 90 AMERICAN JOURNAL OF INTERNATIONAL LAW 1 (1996).

[52] *Questions of Interpretation and Application of the 1971 Montreal Convention arising from the Aerial Incident at Lockerbie (Libya v. UK; Libya v. USA)*, Provisional Measures, Order of April 14, 1992, ICJ Reports 1992, 3. See, e.g., B. Martenczuk, *The Security Council, the International Court and Judicial Review: What Lessons from Lockerbie?*, 10 EUROPEAN JOURNAL OF INTERNATIONAL LAW 517 (1999); D. Akande, *The International Court of Justice and the Security Council: Is there Room for Judicial Control of the Decisions of the Political Organs of the United Nations?* 46 INTERNATIONAL AND COMPARATIVE LAW QUARTERLY 309 (1997); E. de Wet, *Judicial Review as an Emerging General Principle of Law and Its Implications for the International Court of Justice*, 47 NETHERLANDS INTERNATIONAL LAW REVIEW 181 (2000); T. Franck, *The "Powers of Appreciation": Who is the Ultimate Guardian of UN Legality?*, 96 AMERICAN JOURNAL OF INTERNATIONAL LAW 519 (1992); S.I. Bortz, *Avoiding a Collision of Competence: The Relationship between the SC and the ICJ in light of Libya v. United States*, 2 FLORIDA STATE UNIVERSITY JOURNAL OF TRANSNATIONAL LAW & POLICY 353 (1993); B. Graefrath, *Leave to the Court What Belongs to the Court: The Libyan Case*, 4

Authors have quarreled over the question of whether the ICJ in fact possesses the authority, under the U.N. Charter and under its Statute, to assume judicial review powers in the exercise of its contentious jurisdiction, over decisions of other U.N. organs and particularly those of the Security Council. In support of their arguments, both proponents and detractors of the idea of judicial review by the ICJ cite evidence in the negotiating history of the drafting of the Charter, as well as the indeterminacy of Charter provisions.[53]

Often cited by proponents of ICJ review powers is the report of a Subcommittee on Interpretation of the U.N. Charter, adopted at the San Francisco Conference in 1945, which indicates that referral to the ICJ was at least one means of authoritative Charter interpretation foreseen by its drafters:

If two member states are at variance concerning the correct interpretation of the Charter, they are of course free to submit the dispute to the International Court of Justice as in the case of any other treaty. Similarly, it would always be open to the General Assembly or the Security Council, in appropriate circumstances, to ask the International Court of Justice for an advisory opinion concerning the meaning of a provision of the Charter. Should the General Assembly or the Security Council prefer another course, an ad hoc committee of jurists might be set up to examine the question and report its views, or recourse might be had to a joint conference. In brief, the members or the organs of the organization might have recourse to various expedients in order to obtain an appropriate interpretation.[54]

This competence of the Court to interpret the Charter in the context of a dispute between states would appear to include a review of decisions of the political organs of the U.N., which function under the authority of the Charter.

However, perhaps the most compelling evidence for the Court's limited power of review of Security Council decisions for Charter validity, comes not from the *travaux préparatoires* of the Charter, the material of which as with all legislative histories is equally susceptible to a wide range of varying interpretations, but rather from the later jurisprudence of the ICJ itself, and its own understanding of its powers.

Judge Shahabuddeen rather famously questioned the idea of the exclusive power of the Security Council to determine the validity of its own decisions under Charter law in his separate opinion in the 1998 *Lockerbie* case:

The question now raised...is whether a decision of the Security Council may override the legal rights of states, and, if so, whether there are any limitations on the power of the

EUROPEAN JOURNAL OF INTERNATIONAL LAW 184 (1993), M. Reisman, *The Constitutional Crisis in the United Nations*, 87 AMERICAN JOURNAL OF INTERNATIONAL LAW 83 (1993); C. Tomuschat, *The Lockerbie Case Before the International Court of Justice*, 48 REVIEW OF THE INTERNATIONAL COMMISSION OF JURISTS 38 (1992); G. Watson, *Constitutionalism, Judicial Review, and the World Court*, 34 HARVARD INTERNATIONAL LAW JOURNAL 1 (1993).

[53] See J. Alvarez, *Judging the Security Council*, 90 AMERICAN JOURNAL OF INTERNATIONAL LAW 1 (1996).

[54] Doc. 873, IV/2/37, 13 U.N.C.I.O. Docs. 653, 654 (1945).

Council to characterize a situation as one justifying the making of a decision entailing such consequences. Are there any limits to the Council's powers of appreciation? In the equilibrium of forces underpinning the United Nations within the evolving international order, is there a conceivable point beyond which a legal issue may properly arise as to the competence of the Security Council to produce such overriding results? If there are any limits, what are those limits, and what body, if other than the Security Council, is competent to say what those limits are?[55]

In the same case Judge Oda concurs in this questioning of the unchallengeability of Security Council decisions in his declaration:

Under the positive law of the United Nations Charter a resolution of the Security Council may have binding effect, irrespective whether it is consonant with international law derived from other sources. There is certainly nothing to oblige the Security Council, acting within its terms of reference, to carry out a full evaluation of the possibly relevant rules and circumstances before proceeding to the decisions it deems necessary.

Judge Lauterpacht declares in his opinion in an ICJ Order of September 13, 1993, with regard to U.N. Security Council Resolution 713:

The Court, as the principal judicial organ of the United Nations, is entitled, indeed bound, to ensure the rule of law within the United Nations system and, in cases properly brought before it, to insist on adherence by all United Nations organs to the rules governing their operation.[56]

Judge Skubiszewski similarly notes in his dissenting opinion in the 1995 *East Timor* case:

The Court is competent, and this is shown by several judgments and advisory opinions, to interpret and apply the resolutions of the Organization. The Court is competent to make findings on their lawfulness, in particular whether they were *intra vires*. This competence follows from its function as the principal judicial organ of the United Nations. The decisions of the Organization (in the broad sense which this notion has under the Charter provisions on voting) are subject to scrutiny by the Court with regard to their legality, validity and effect.[57]

In its 1970 opinion in the *Namibia* case, the Court explains in a more nuanced fashion that:

Undoubtedly, the Court does not possess powers of judicial review or appeal in respect of the decisions taken by the UN organs concerned. However, in the exercise of its judicial function and since objections have been advanced, the Court, in the course of its

---

[55] *Questions of Interpretation and Application of the 1971 Montreal Convention arising from the Aerial Incident at Lockerbie (Libya v. UK; Libya v. USA)*, Provisional Measures, Order of April 14, 1992, ICJ Reports 1992, 3, 142.

[56] *Application of the Convention on the Prevention and Punishment of the Crime of Genocide (Bosnia and Herzegovina v. Serbia and Montenegro)*, Further Request for the Indication of Provisional Measures, ICJ Reports 2007.

[57] *Case Concerning East Timor (Portugal v. Australia)* ICJ Reports 1995, 251, para. 86.

reasoning, will consider these objections before determining any legal consequences arising from those resolutions.[58]

In his separate opinion in the same case, Judge Onyeama states:

The Court's powers are clearly defined by the Statute, and do not include powers to review decisions of other organs of the United Nations; but when, as in the present proceedings, such decisions bear upon a case properly before the Court, and a correct judgment or opinion could not be rendered without determining the validity of such decisions, the Court could not possibly avoid such determination without abdicating its role as a judicial organ...I do not conceive it as compatible with the judicial function that the Court will proceed to state the consequences of acts whose validity is assumed, without itself testing the lawfulness of the origin of those acts.

The statements above from the *Namibia* case are particularly useful in explaining the nature of the power of judicial review over the decisions of the U.N. political organs, and particularly the Security Council, held by the ICJ, as well as the limits of that power. Taken together, the jurisprudence of the Court quite consistently establishes the principle that the Court does not possess a general power of direct review of the decisions of other U.N. organs, as some domestic high courts analogously have over their co-equal legislative and executive bodies. The ICJ's power of review is rather an implied, reserved judicial power of incidental review of the decisions of other Charter bodies when such a review is necessary to the resolution of a case properly before the Court and subject to its jurisdiction.[59] As Bernd Martenczuk explains:

Neither the Charter nor the jurisprudence of the Court would therefore support the claim that the Court is generally prevented from examining the validity of decisions of the UN political organs, including the Security Council, where such decisions have a bearing on a case before the Court. To this extent, it can be said that the Court may subject the resolutions of the Security Council to "judicial review." However, this review is implicit in the exercise of the judicial function of the Court; it does not constitute an independent "power of judicial review."[60]

---

[58] *Legal Consequences for States of the Continued Presence of South Africa in Namibia Notwithstanding Security Council Resolution 276*, ICJ Reports 1970, 45, para. 89.

[59] See B. Martenczuk, *The Security Council, the International Court and Judicial Review: What Lessons from Lockerbie?*, 10 EUROPEAN JOURNAL OF INTERNATIONAL LAW 517, 527 (1999); D. Schweigman, THE AUTHORITY OF THE SECURITY COUNCIL UNDER CHAPTER VII OF THE UN CHARTER: LEGAL LIMITS AND THE ROLE OF THE INTERNATIONAL COURT OF JUSTICE (2001) 267–271; F. King, *Sensible Scrutiny: The Yugoslavia Tribunal's Development of Limits on the Security Council's Powers under Chapter VII of the Charter*, 10 EMORY INTERNATIONAL LAW REVIEW 509, 532 (1996); *Prosecutor v. Dusko Tadic a/k/a "Dule,"* Case No. IT-94-1-AR72, 2 October 1995, ICTY, para. 21.

[60] B. Martenczuk, *The Security Council, the International Court and Judicial Review: What Lessons from Lockerbie?* 10 EUROPEAN JOURNAL OF INTERNATIONAL LAW 517, 527 (1999). This understanding of the limited, incidental power of review of decisions of other U.N. organs possessed by the Court due to its judicial role is thus in keeping with statements by ICJ Judges and others that the Court does not have a general power of judicial review over decisions of other U.N. bodies.

The nature of this power not as an explicit power afforded the Court in its Statute, but rather as a reserved power inherent in the judicial role of the Court, has prompted many commentators, particularly from the United States, to view the issue of ICJ judicial review through the lens of the U.S. Supreme Court's landmark *Marbury v. Madison* case of 1803, in which the Court established its power to review acts of the executive branch of the U.S. Government for validity under the U.S. Constitution.[61]

However, as other commentators have correctly pointed out, the particularities of the international legal environment and the unique characteristics of the ICJ itself as defined in the Charter and in its Statute, make such analogies to domestic courts' establishment of their powers of judicial review over national political bodies of questionable usefulness in many respects.[62]

Despite this general disanalogy, however, the primary jurisprudential logic employed by Chief Justice Marshall in the *Marbury* case does have equal application to the question of the ICJ's powers of incidental review of Security Council decisions.

The core reasoning in the *Marbury* case was not about the relationship between the court and the political branches of government, which is at the heart of the disanalogy between domestic and international institutions, but rather about the fundamental role of the judiciary itself. As Chief Justice Marshall states in the opinion:

It is emphatically the province and duty of the judicial department to say what the law is. Those who apply the rule to particular cases, must of necessity expound and interpret that rule. If two laws conflict with each other, the courts must decide on the operation of each.[63]

The reasoning here that a court cannot properly do its job unless it can interrogate the sources of law placed before it as the bases for its decision, in order to determine their correct interpretation and possible conflict with other sources of law before it, is as applicable to the ICJ as it was to the U.S. Supreme Court. The ICJ, again, is the principal judicial organ of the United Nations. Its statute declares in Article 38(1) that its function is "to decide in accordance with international law such disputes as are submitted to it." Its jurisdiction is recognized in Article 36(2) to extend to "all legal disputes concerning... any question of international law."

Decisions of the Security Council undoubtedly create international legal obligations for United Nations members, as stipulated in Article 25 of the Charter, and to that extent are sources of international law. When a decision of

---

[61] 5 U.S. 137 (1803). See, e.g., G.R. Watson, *Constitutionalism, Judicial Review, and the World Court*, 34 HARVARD INTERNATIONAL LAW JOURNAL 1 (1993); T.M. Franck, *The "Powers of Appreciation": Who Is the Ultimate Guardian of UN Legality?* 86 AMERICAN JOURNAL OF INTERNATIONAL LAW 519 (1992).

[62] See J. Alvarez, *Judging the Security Council*, 90 AMERICAN JOURNAL OF INTERNATIONAL LAW 1, 4–5 (1996).

[63] 5 U.S. 137 (1803).

the Security Council is properly brought before the ICJ as a source of law relevant to the Court's determination of the merits of a contentious case, the Court must be able to evaluate the scope and application of the decision as well as its possible conflict with other sources of law properly put before the Court, including the provisions of the U.N. Charter itself. If a U.N. member challenges the validity of a Security Council decision, in a contentious case properly before the Court, and the question of the validity of the decision is necessary for the resolution of the issue referred to the Court by the parties, the ICJ must be able to make a determination as to whether the decision is *ultra vires* the Security Council's authority granted to it under the Charter—i.e. whether the decision is in fact a valid obligation of international law.[64]

In the context of non-proliferation law, using the example of Resolution 1540, the necessity of the ICJ's incidental review of a decision of the Security Council could arise either through one state bringing a suit against another for non-compliance with Resolution 1540, or, which is perhaps more likely, through one state justifying a use of force or other violation of the sovereignty of another state using as the justificatory basis for this act the non-proliferation provisions of Resolution 1540. As noted in Chapter 8 below, Resolution 1540 has been used rhetorically as a justification for the Proliferation Security Initiative (PSI), which mandates the interdiction of foreign flagged vessels suspected of transporting WMD-related materials and technology to and from states of concern to PSI members. If such an interdiction were to take place on the high seas, and the interdicting state sought to justify its actions in breach of Article 110 of the Law of the Sea Convention, which prohibits such interdictions, at least in part on the basis of the provisions of Resolution 1540, then the question of the validity of Resolution 1540 as a source of international law would be necessary as a preliminary matter incidental to the determination of the veracity of the interdicting state's claim of reliance upon that decision of the Security Council as a justification for its actions. In such a case, the ICJ would have the authority to make a determination as to the validity of Resolution 1540 under Charter law, and use that determination in its further consideration of the primary question of the legality of the interdicting state's action.

It is also conceivable, as discussed in Chapter 3 above, that the necessity of the exercise of the ICJ's power of incidental review could arise in a dispute concerning Article XXI(c) of the General Agreement on Tariffs and Trade, which is effective in exempting sanctions or export controls authorized by the U.N. Security Council under either Chapter VI or Chapter VII of the U.N. Charter from the basic obligations of the GATT. In addition to targeted, ad hoc requirements codified in U.N. Security Council resolutions, this article could be read to

---

[64] D. Schweigman, The Authority of the Security Council under Chapter VII of the UN Charter: Legal Limits and the Role of the International Court of Justice (2001) 270, B. Martenczuk, *The Security Council, the International Court and Judicial Review: What Lessons from Lockerbie?* 10 European Journal of International Law 517 (1999).

include the broad and continuing obligations upon states imposed by Resolution 1540, inclusive of obligations regarding the maintenance of effective national export control systems. If a WTO member state were to justify its maintenance of WMD dual-use export controls by reference to Resolution 1540, through the operation of GATT Article XXI(c), it is conceivable that the target state of those export controls could challenge their maintenance against it in a contentious case before the ICJ, pursuant to the Court's broad jurisdiction *ratione materiae* as defined in Article 36(2) of its Statute, and particularly because of the presence of an issue of U.N. Charter law as a material element of the dispute. If this dispute were to be properly put before the ICJ, then the ICJ would arguably be required to exercise its powers of incidental review in order to determine, as a preliminary matter necessary to the overall resolution of the dispute, the question of the validity of Resolution 1540 as a matter of U.N. Charter law.

B. Litispendence and the Political/Security Question

Some have noted that this competence of the ICJ to review might be circumscribed by the principle of litispendence, which is a principle of both domestic and international law, and which can be a preliminary objection to the admissibility of a claim before a court.[65] Litispendence is essentially concerned with the existence of situations in which concurrent jurisdiction is had over the same matter by two separate organs possessing similar jurisdiction. The concern in the present context would be that, due to the Security Council's authority to maintain international peace and security under U.N. Charter Chapter VII, and the ICJ's authority to decide legal disputes properly brought before it under Article 36(2) of the ICJ Statute, the Security Council and the ICJ could potentially be concurrently seized of a matter, which would potentially serve as a basis for contesting the admissibility of a claim brought before the ICJ in such a situation.

However, the ICJ has consistently rejected objections to its jurisdiction based on the principle of litispendence. As David Schweigman has observed:

[The Court's] position has been that the Council and the Court are independent organs exercising "separate but complementary" functions...According to the International Court of Justice, the independence of the Court and the Council does not mean that

---

[65] *Questions of Interpretation and Application of the 1971 Montreal Convention arising from the Aerial Incident at Lockerbie (Libya v. UK; Libya v. USA)*, Provisional Measures, Order of April 14, 1992, ICJ Reports 1992, 3, Declaration of Judge Ni. See generally T. Elsen, LITISPENDENCE BETWEEN THE INTERNATIONAL COURT OF JUSTICE AND THE SECURITY COUNCIL (1986); D. Reichert, *Problems with Parallel and Duplicate Proceedings: The Litispendence Principles and International Arbitration*, 8 ARBITRATION INTERNATIONAL 237, 239 (1992); D. Ciobanu, "Litispendence between the International Court of Justice and the Political Organs of the United Nations," in L. Gross, ed., THE FUTURE OF THE INTERNATIONAL COURT OF JUSTICE (1976) 209–275, 215.

both organs should not cooperate in respect of a matter of which they are simultaneously seized. It means that the Court will not decline to exercise jurisdiction for the sole reason that the dispute brought to its attention is pending before the Council. This approach has been adopted by the Court in the *Hostages, Nicaragua,* and *Bosnia* cases.[66]

The Court has further made it clear that it will not be deterred from exercising its jurisdiction over legal questions properly placed before it, which arise in the context of situations of high political sensitivity. Some have argued in the past that questions which have a bearing upon ongoing political controversies should not be addressed by the Court. This logic is similar to the "political question doctrine" of judicial reserve applied by some domestic courts. This categorization of issues of political sensitivity as non-justiciable is made particularly in cases involving questions of international security and uses of force.[67]

However, the ICJ has stressed repeatedly that the political implications of legal issues before it have no bearing upon the justiciability of those legal issues.

In its 1988 judgment in the *Border and Transborder Armed Actions* case, the Court held that:

Political aspects may be present in any legal dispute brought before it. The Court, as a judicial organ, is however only concerned to establish, first, that the dispute before it is a legal dispute in the sense of a dispute capable of being settled by the application of principles and rules of international law and secondly, that the court has jurisdiction to deal with it, and that jurisdiction is not fettered by any circumstances rendering the application inadmissible.[68]

---

[66] D. Schweigman, The Authority of the Security Council Under Chapter VII of the U.N. Charter (2001), 260–261. See also *Legal Consequences of the Construction of a Wall in the Occupied Palestinian Territory*, ICJ Reports 2004; *Armed Activities on the Territory of the Congo (Democratic Republic of the Congo v. Uganda)*, Provisional Measures Order of July 11, 2000, ICJ Reports 2000; V. Gowland-Debbas, *The Relationship between the International Court of Justice and the Security Council in Light of the Lockerbie Case*, 88 American Journal of International Law 643, 658 (1994).

[67] The ICTY Trial Chamber described this doctrine by quoting from a U.S. Supreme Court Case: "Prominent on the surface of any case held to involve a political question is found a textually demonstrable constitutional commitment of the issue to a co-ordinate political department; or a lack of judicially discoverable and manageable standards for resolving it; or the impossibility of deciding without an initial policy determination of a kind clearly for non-judicial discretion; or the impossibility of a court's undertaking independent resolution without expressing lack of the respect due to co-ordinate branches of government; or an unusual need for unquestioning adherence to a political decision already made; or the potentiality of embarrassment from multifarious pronouncements by various departments on one question." *Baker v. Carr*, 369 U.S. 186, 217 (1962). Quoted in the Trial Chamber Decision on the Defence Motion on Jurisdiction, *Prosecutor v. Dusko Tadic a/k/a/ "Dule,"* Case No. IT-94-1-T, para. 24, August 10, 1995. See also D. Akande, *The Role of the International Court of Justice in the Maintenance of International Peace*, 8 African Journal of International & Comparative Law 592, 593 (1996); C. Greenwood, "The International Court of Justice and the Use of Force," in A. V. Lowe and M. Fitzmaurice (eds), Fifty Years of the International Court of Justice (1996) 373–385.

[68] *Case Concerning Border and Transborder Armed Actions (Jurisdiction and Admissibility), Nicaragua v. Honduras*, Judgment of 20 December 1988, ICJ Reports 1988, para. 52.

Similarly, in the Preliminary Objection phase of the Advisory Opinion requested by the World Health Organization on the *Legality of the Threat or Use of Nuclear Weapons*, the Court noted that:

The political nature of the motives which may be said to have inspired the request and the political implications that the opinion given might have are of no relevance in the establishment of its jurisdiction to give such an opinion.[69]

The question the Court will be concerned with is thus not whether political issues surround the legal issues presented to it, as such is the nature of most issues referred to the Court, but rather whether the specific question referred to the Court by the parties, to which the jurisdiction of the Court attaches, is capable of being resolved by reference to legal rules and principles. In the words of Vera Gowland-Debbas:

The distinction between a legal and a political dispute lies not in its inherent nature but in the distinction between a political and legal method of solving the dispute.[70]

On both the issue of litispendence and the political/security question issue, José Alvarez has very usefully explained:

The Court has decided that it is not precluded from considering either questions relating to peace and security or issues pending in the Council. An alternative rule instructing ICJ judges to ignore these questions or requiring automatic deference to the Council's wishes seems impracticable and unworkable; it tells judges that they may no longer fully adjudicate a broad range of basic legal issues. What is the Court supposed to do, for instance, the next time a party raises the contentious issue of damages or permissible countermeasures for internationally caused environmental harm? Is the Court not to pass on the question merely because, in Resolution 687, the Council found Iraq financially liable for such harm? Is the Court instead supposed to affirm, contrary to the views of many, that the issue has been resolved in favour of liability in all such cases merely because the Council found Iraq liable? Is the Court free to find that liability is due only after instances of aggression? or only after a Chapter VII finding? or whenever damage was intentionally caused? or whenever particularly grave damage results? Is the Court supposed to consider whether the Council or its members expressed views on the subject when it approved Resolution 687? Is the Court bound by such views no matter how ill-considered or contrary to other evidence of the state of the law? Whatever it does, the Court will find it difficult to avoid conveying a message about the state of the law on this controversial subject and, incidentally if not directly, on the scope (if not the validity) of the precedent set by the Council.[71]

---

[69] *Legality of the Use by a State of Nuclear Weapons in Armed Conflict*, Advisory Opinion, ICJ Reports 1996, 66, para. 13.

[70] *The Relationship between the International Court of Justice and the Security Council in the Light of the Lockerbie Case*, 88 AMERICAN JOURNAL OF INTERNATIONAL LAW 643, 652 (1994).

[71] J. Alvarez, *Judging the Security Council*, 90 AMERICAN JOURNAL OF INTERNATIONAL LAW 1, 23 (1996).

C. The Effect of a Finding of Illegality by the ICJ

If in a contentious proceeding the ICJ were to reach incidentally the question of the validity of a Security Council resolution, and if the Court were to find that the resolution was enacted *ultra vires* the Council's authority, or was for any other reason invalid, what would be the effect of that determination by the Court? The immediate binding effect of the decision of the Court would of course only apply to the parties before the Court in the present action.[72] However, the influence of such a determination, and its message to other states would have a far wider effect. If the ICJ were to declare a Council decision invalid in a contentious case, member states of the United Nations would most likely no longer feel obliged to abide by the decision, as no state can be bound to comply with an invalid source of law, and states would rightly predict that the Court would be consistent should the issue be raised again in a future case.[73] Legally speaking, as reviewed in Chapter 4 above, a decision of the Security Council found to have been enacted *ultra vires* the authority of the Council, would be void *ab initio*, and thus of no effect from its inception. This is no less the case in the context of an ICJ determination of such invalidity.

It will be recalled that the distinction between the recognition of an invalid rule as being either voidable or void *ab initio* was noted above to hinge upon the availability of an effective procedural remedy through which such a determination could be made. As concluded above, due to the limits placed upon the jurisdiction of the ICJ by the Charter and by its Statute, the ICJ does not constitute such an effective procedural remedy, in that there is no guarantee of consistency in the ability of the Court to act as such a procedural remedy. In the rare event that the Court could reach the merits of a non-proliferation law case, and in that context incidentally reach the question of the validity of a decision of the Security Council, this uncommon occurrence would not serve to alter this character of the Court under its current jurisdictional framework. Thus, in that unlikely but possible event, the effect of the Court's determination of invalidity would be that the decision of the Council is void *ab initio* and not simply voidable. If the situation were otherwise, and the Court's determination of invalidity only resulted in a state of voidability of the decision, where would the subsequent finding by a competent organ that the resolution is in fact void come from? It could not come from the Court, as at that point the issue would be *res judicata*. As noted above, no other independent organ with clear authority to make such a determination exists. Thus, there continues to be a lack of a procedural remedy through which the voidability of the decision can be resolved upon its being in fact void.

---

[72] ICJ Statute Article 59.
[73] See D. Schweigman, The Authority of the Security Council Under Chapter VII of the U.N. Charter (2001) 281.

D. Limits of the Court's Jurisdiction

Of course, for the Court to reach such an incidental review of a Security Council decision in a contentious proceeding, it must first be able to exercise jurisdiction over the case and the parties, and the issue of the validity of the decision has to be necessary to resolving the dispute properly put before the Court by the parties. Thus, the issue must qualify for the court's review both under its jurisdiction *ratione personae* and its jurisdiction *ratione materiae*. As discussed above, both of these elements of the Court's jurisdiction in contentious cases are subject to quite stringent limitations imposed both by the Charter and the ICJ Statute.

The difficulty of the Court's exercising its competence to review the validity of Security Council decisions for validity under its jurisdiction *ratione materiae* was illustrated in the *Lockerbie* case between Libya and the United Kingdom.[74] Here, the source of law used by the Court as its jurisdictional link to the subject of controversy between the parties was Article 14 of the 1971 Montreal Convention for the Suppression of Unlawful Acts against the Safety of Civil Aviation, which covered only questions concerning the interpretation or application of the Montreal Convention itself.[75] Article 7 of the Montreal Convention, which Libya asserted as an additional jurisdictional link, could conceivably have been interpreted to grant to Libya an implied right not to surrender the alleged offenders to another state. If interpreted in this fashion, Article 7 could have been found to be in conflict with Security Council Resolutions 748 and 883, and it would thus have been necessary for the Court to determine the validity of the Council resolutions in order for it to know what law should apply to the actions of the parties in dispute. However, Article 7 was implicitly construed by the Court more narrowly, as only to impose obligations upon Libya to refer suspects to its domestic officials for prosecution, and not to provide a right of non-surrender.[76] Thus, even though Libya wished to challenge the validity of these Security Council resolutions, and although the Court had exercised its jurisdiction *ratione personae* over the appropriate parties, it could not find a jurisdictional nexus, in the instrument upon which the Court's jurisdiction was based, to afford the Court the opportunity to conduct such a review.

However, as reviewed above the most difficult aspect of the exercise by the ICJ of its powers of review of Security Council resolutions in contentious cases in the non-proliferation law area, as in any other issue area, has to do with the limitations found in the ICJ Statute upon the Court's jurisdiction *ratione personae*. Most debilitating for the Court in this vein is the requirement of express

---

[74] *Questions of Interpretation and Application of the 1971 Montreal Convention Arising from the Aerial Incident at Lockerbie (Libyan Arab Jamahiriya v. United Kingdom).* Request for the Indication of Provisional Measures, Order of April, 14 1992, ICJ Reports 1992, 3.

[75] 974 UNTS 177.

[76] See B. Martenczuk, *The Security Council, the International Court and Judicial Review: What Lessons from Lockerbie?* 10 EUROPEAN JOURNAL OF INTERNATIONAL LAW 517, 629–531 (1999).

consent of parties to the exercise of the Court's jurisdiction, and the abovementioned fact that two-thirds of U.N. members, including almost all states possessing WMD, have not acceded to the compulsory jurisdiction of the Court
through the optional clause.[77]

Thus, while it can be established that the ICJ does have the competence to
engage in incidental review of Security Council decisions, and to determine the
validity of those decisions under Charter law, the Court is severely constrained
in its practical ability to exercise this competence, particularly in an issue area of
such high political and security sensitivity as non-proliferation law, due to these
other limitations upon its jurisdiction. Because of jurisdiction *ratione personae*
limitations particularly, and the ability of most states to avoid the jurisdiction
of the Court in cases of such security sensitivity, the prospect of the Court being
able to exercise its contentious jurisdiction over a dispute between states, on an
issue of non-proliferation law, and specifically on an issue of the validity of a
Security Council decision, is unfortunately quite dim.[78]

Nonetheless, this power of incidental review is within the Court's competence,
and is a power that should be exercised by the Court when it can be, in order to
preserve the Charter system and fill a needed role of institutional check upon the
power of the Security Council. This will require the Court to maintain a robust
understanding of its powers and role under the U.N. Charter, but one that is
completely in keeping with its role as the principal judicial organ of the United
Nations.[79]

E. Advisory Jurisdiction

In addition to the exercise of its jurisdiction over contentious cases between
states, the ICJ can of course alternatively use its advisory jurisdiction to give
its opinion on the validity of a Security Council resolution, if such an issue is
properly put before it by the Security Council, the General Assembly, or another
properly empowered body.[80] It could through this function, particularly in the

---

[77] See below at 203.

[78] See E. de Wet, *Judicial Review as an Emerging General Principle of Law and its Implications for the International Court of Justice*, 47 NETHERLANDS INTERNATIONAL LAW REVIEW 181–210, 199–202 (2000).

[79] See P. Kooijmans, *The ICJ in the 21ˢᵗ Century: Judicial Restraint, Judicial Activism, or Proactive Judicial Policy*, 56 INTERNATIONAL AND COMPARATIVE LAW QUARTERLY 741 (2007).

[80] See generally I. Brownlie, PRINCIPLES OF PUBLIC INTERNATIONAL LAW (6th edn, 2003) 690–692; M. Aljaghoub, THE ADVISORY FUNCTION OF THE INTERNATIONAL COURT OF JUSTICE 1946–2005 (2006); A. Zimmermann et al. (eds), THE STATUTE OF THE INTERNATIONAL COURT OF JUSTICE (2006) 183–191, 1401–1468; T. Gill, ROSENNE'S THE WORLD COURT: WHAT IT IS AND HOW IT WORKS (6th edn, 2003) 86–91; D. Akande, *The Competence of International Organizations and the Advisory Jurisdiction of the International Court of Justice*, 9 EUROPEAN JOURNAL OF INTERNATIONAL LAW 437 (1998); D. Greig, *The Advisory Jurisdiction of the International Court of Justice and the Settlement of Disputes between States*, 15 INTERNATIONAL AND COMPARATIVE LAW QUARTERLY 325 (1966).

non-proliferation law area, address the proper institutional roles of the various organs of the U.N. in the process of non-proliferation law creation laid out in Articles 11 and 26. It could use this advisory authority to determine that the Charter system in Articles 11 and 26 does indeed establish an exclusive, *lex specialis* procedural route for producing new international law in this area, and is therefore a substantive limit on the Chapter VII power of the Security Council.

While specifically addressing Resolution 1540 and the non-proliferation law issue area, the Court could additionally provide in its opinion some useful direction on the proper interpretation of the Council's role under the Charter system, and the limitations placed by the Charter on that role preventing the Council from acting in a legislative capacity.[81]

Such an advisory opinion by the ICJ would of course carry no formally binding effect upon states or upon the Security Council. However such an opinion would nonetheless likely be quite powerful in its effects, coming as it would from the highest court in the world on questions of international law, and particularly on interpretation of the U.N. Charter. Such an opinion by the ICJ would be a serious blow to the perceived legitimacy of any Security Council resolution so invalidated by the Court, and would send a strong message to the Security Council that it must use its power within the determinable bounds of the authority expressly given to the Council in the Charter.[82]

Of course, to be precise and consistent with the earlier argument in this chapter of the character of an *ultra vires* act of the Security Council as void *ab initio* and not simply voidable, it should be noted that the ICJ in exercising its advisory jurisdiction, would only formally be advising, or communicating, the fact of this already existing legal status of the resolution. The nature of the Court's opinion, therefore, if properly understood as advice regarding the already existing invalid state of the resolution, would only add to its influence.

In the case of Resolution 1540 (as the likelihood of the Security Council itself bringing the question of the validity of the Resolution to the ICJ is remote) there would be no question of the General Assembly's competence to make such a referral to the ICJ for an advisory opinion. Article 96 of the U.N. Charter authorizes the General Assembly to refer to the ICJ any question of international law for the Court's advisory opinion. While there is a strand of reasoning to the effect that advisory opinions may be requested only in issues arising directly under the requesting organ's jurisdiction, this reasoning is quite suspect given the general terms of the grant of authority in Article 96.[83] However, even under

---

[81] See P. Kooijmans, *The ICJ in the 21ˢᵗ Century: Judicial Restraint, Judicial Activism, or Proactive Judicial Policy*, 56 INTERNATIONAL AND COMPARATIVE LAW QUARTERLY 741 (2007).

[82] J. Alvarez, *Judging the Security Council*, 90 AMERICAN JOURNAL OF INTERNATIONAL LAW 1, 5 (1996); E. de Wet, *Judicial Review of the United Nations Security Council and General Assembly Through Advisory Opinions of the International Court of Justice*, 10 SZIER 237, 261–262 (2000).

[83] See the thorough discussion of the Court's jurisdiction *ratione materiae* in advisory cases in the *Nuclear Weapons Advisory Opinion*, paras 10–19.

such a limited interpretation, the question of the validity of Resolution 1540 fundamentally involves the jurisdiction of the General Assembly. Article 10 of the Charter gives the General Assembly a broad grant of competence over "any questions or matters" within the scope of the Charter. And of course, the General Assembly under Article 11 is granted the competence to "consider the general principles. . . . in the maintenance of international peace and security, including the principles governing disarmament and the regulation of armaments."

This latter provision, in addition to providing a general link between the jurisdiction of the General Assembly and the issues regulated by Resolution 1540, would also be a material part of the case to be considered by the Court in its advisory opinion, i.e. whether the jurisdiction of the General Assembly given it in Article 11 has been effectively usurped by the Council in its unilateral passage of Resolution 1540 through its Chapter VII powers.

It should be noted that the same principles developed by the Court with regard to its ability to exercise jurisdiction notwithstanding the argued limitations of that jurisdiction through the principles of litispendence and the political/security question, apply with equal force to the advisory opinion context. Thus, there would be no difficulties posed by these principles to the exercise of the Court's advisory jurisdiction over a question of non-proliferation law.

Due to the legitimacy problems under which the passage of Resolution 1540 labors, as reviewed earlier in Chapter 4, the conclusion is reached herein that the question of the legal validity of Resolution 1540 under U.N. Charter law is a question ripe for referral to the ICJ for the exercise of its advisory jurisdiction. The competence of the General Assembly to properly refer this legal question to the Court for an advisory opinion is beyond question. In addition, the practical likelihood of this occurrence is considerable, as there are many states members of the General Assembly who feel that in passing Resolution 1540, the Security Council has overstepped its bounds, and has shown its nature as an organized hypocrisy, through which the will of powerful states is imposed upon the rest of the world in the sheep's clothing of international law.[84] A movement in the Assembly purposed in referring the question of Resolution 1540's validity to the ICJ, and thereby allowing the Court to reign in the presumption of the Council to assume the role of international legislator without mandate, should not be difficult to maintain.

In summary, the advisory jurisdiction of the ICJ should not be forgotten as a very useful supplement to its contentious jurisdiction in the non-proliferation law area, and should be employed to allow the Court to give authoritative voice to the limits placed upon the Security Council's power by the provisions of the Charter, until the limitations placed upon the Court's jurisdiction in contentious cases can be changed, through amendment to the ICJ Statute, to allow

---

[84] See Chapter 4 above at 194–195 for statements from dissenting states. S. Krasner, SOVEREIGNTY: ORGANIZED HYPOCRISY? (1999).

the Court the ability to exercise its contentious jurisdiction more effectively and consistently, and thus the ability to make such pronouncements in a legally binding fashion.

III. Role in the Future

In order to have a system whereby incidental judicial review of Security Council decisions in the area of non-proliferation law, as well as other issue areas, could happen more effectively, the most important change to the existing structure of the ICJ's jurisdiction that must be made is the universalization of compulsory jurisdiction *ratione personae*, i.e. making membership in the U.N. Charter and acceptance of the compulsory jurisdiction of the ICJ a package deal.

From the standpoint of the history of both the ICJ and its predecessor, the Permanent Court of International Justice (PCIJ), this is by no means a new or radical proposal.[85] The question of whether universal compulsory jurisdiction should be an element of the jurisdictional framework of the PCIJ was argued over quite acrimoniously in 1920, by the Committee of Jurists tasked with the drafting of the Court's Statute.[86] A majority of the members of the Committee was in favor of a scheme under which the Court would be granted compulsory jurisdiction over all states members of its Statute, through the provisions of Articles 33 and 34 of the Committee's draft:

Art. 33: When a dispute has arisen between states, and it has been found impossible to settle it by diplomatic means...the party complaining may bring the case before the Court...

Art. 34: Between states which are Members of the League of Nations, the Court shall have jurisdiction (and this without any special convention giving it jurisdiction) to hear and determine cases of a legal nature concerning

a) the interpretation of a treaty;
b) any question of international law;
c) the existence of any fact, which if established, would constitute a breach of an international obligation;
d) the nature or extent of reparation to be made for the breach of an international obligation;
e) the interpretation of a sentence passed by the Court.[87]

---

[85] See generally I. Brownlie, PRINCIPLES OF PUBLIC INTERNATIONAL LAW (6th edn, 2003) 687; R. Prakesh Anand, COMPULSORY JURISDICTION OF THE INTERNATIONAL COURT OF JUSTICE (1961); M. Sameh Amr, THE ROLE OF THE INTERNATIONAL COURT OF JUSTICE AS THE PRINCIPAL JUDICIAL ORGAN OF THE UNITED NATIONS (2003); S. Rosenne, THE LAW AND PRACTICE OF THE INTERNATIONAL COURT, 1920–1996, Vol. II (1997).

[86] R. Prakesh Anand, COMPULSORY JURISDICTION OF THE INTERNATIONAL COURT OF JUSTICE (1961) 32.

[87] *Procès Verbaux*, 725–729.

Of this draft scheme, Lord Phillimore said:

We wanted a real Court to which a complaining state could come with its complaint, and request that the state complained of should be cited as a defendant. We felt that if the parties had got so far as agreeing to come and submit their disputes, they had already got a long way towards agreement, and that what we wanted to deal with were cases where the parties had not got so far.[88]

This draft was submitted to the Council of the League of Nations which, after lengthy debate, found that the draft entailed a modification of Articles 12 and 13 of the League of Nations Covenant on the subject of dispute settlement, and thus rejected the Committee's draft. However, the Rapporteur, Leon Bourgeois, made clear that the Council was not opposed to the compulsory jurisdiction of the Court per se:

The Council does not in any way wish to declare itself opposed to the actual idea of the compulsory jurisdiction of the Court in questions of a judicial nature. This is a development of the authority of the Court of Justice which may be extremely useful in effecting the general settlement of disputes between nations and the Council would certainly have no objection to the consideration of the problem at some future date.[89]

There was continued debate on the subject of the compulsory jurisdiction of the Court during the First Assembly of the League of Nations. Here too, it became clear that a majority of the members of the League supported the principle of universalized compulsory jurisdiction. However, among the powerful states there was a reluctance to embrace this power of the Court. They were reticent to bind themselves to the jurisdiction of the newly created Court, and urged that consideration of the issue be postponed until the Court had established itself and had won the trust of states through its jurisprudence. As Arthur Balfour, the British representative, stated:

It is quite true that we are ardent supporters of an International Court of Justice. It is quite true that we desire to see the applications to that Court made voluntarily and not compulsorily. That is not because we desire to check its extension to the furthest practicable fields, but because we are convinced that if these things are to be successful they must be allowed to grow. If they are to achieve all that their framers desire for them, they must be allowed to pursue that natural development which is the secret of all permanent success in human affairs and not least in that part of human affairs which deals with politics.[90]

Ultimately, the Statute of the PCIJ adopted in 1920 contained a compromise between the positions espoused in the Council; a compromise which was the

---

[88] "Scheme for the Permanent Court of International Justice," 7 Transactions of Grotius Society (1921) 93.

[89] Documents Concerning the Action Taken by the Council of the League of Nations under Article 14 of the Covenant, 47.

[90] League of Nations, *Records of the First Assembly*, Plenary Meetings, 488.

proposal of the Brazilian delegate Raoul Fernandes. This first incarnation of the "optional clause" was inserted as Article 36 of the PCIJ Statute and read as follows:

The jurisdiction of the Court comprises all cases which the parties refer to it and all matters specially provided for in treaties and conventions in force. The Members of the League of Nations and the States mentioned in the Annex to the Convention may, either when signing or ratifying the Protocol to which the present Statute is adjoined, or at a later moment, declare that they recognize as compulsory ipso facto and without special agreement, in relation to any other Member or State accepting the same obligation, the jurisdiction of the Court in all or any of the classes of legal disputes concerning

a) the interpretation of a treaty;
b) any question of international law;
c) the existence of any fact which, if established, would constitute a breach of an international obligation;
d) the nature or extent of the reparation to be made for the breach of an international obligation...

The declaration referred to above may be made unconditionally or on condition of reciprocity on the part of several or certain Members or States, or for a certain time.

In the event of a dispute as to whether the Court has jurisdiction, the matter shall be settled by the decision of the Court.

There was a great deal of dissatisfaction, particularly among the smaller states, with the decision of the Council and the Assembly of the League to not confer upon the Court the breadth of jurisdiction recommended by the Committee of Jurists. They felt that a Court without universal compulsory jurisdiction would represent little progress over the existing system for settlement of international disputes, principally including the Hague Court of Arbitration.[91] Bernard Loder of the Netherlands explained this frustration in a memorandum, stating:

Otherwise, why create this Court? In order to duplicate the Court of Arbitration? To continue a deplorable state of affairs and to administer justice between two contesting parties only after having obtained their mutual consent, and their agreement on the wording of the complaint and on the choice of judges? That is not worth the trouble. It is only too well known that those who feel themselves offenders in the eyes of the law and of justice know how to profit by their position; never agree to anything, and make exceptions and subterfuges serve their end.[92]

This state of voluntary acceptance of the compulsory jurisdiction of the Court, subject to (sometimes expansive) reservations made to the instrument of consent, continued as the jurisdictional framework of the PCIJ, until the dissolution of the organization in 1946. From 1921 to 1940, 45 states in all acceded to the compulsory jurisdiction of the Court under the optional clause of Article 36.

[91] See R. Prakesh Anand, COMPULSORY JURISDICTION OF THE INTERNATIONAL COURT OF JUSTICE (1961) 36.
[92] M. Hudson, INTERNATIONAL TRIBUNALS (1944) 77.

These accessions, in addition to the selection of the Court as the forum of choice for dispute settlement in a large number of bilateral and multilateral treaties, including the 1928 General Act on Pacific Settlement, gave the PCIJ a considerable jurisdictional reach.

In light of the international community's experience with the PCIJ's jurisdiction, and the high standing of the Court in the eyes of most states, when negotiations began on the successor organization of the United Nations, and its International Court of Justice following the Second World War, there was a concerted effort on the part of a significant majority of delegations at the Washington and San Francisco Conferences to place back on the agenda the proposals of the 1920 Committee of Jurists, as the jurisdictional framework for the ICJ.

The 1920 Committee's recommendations were once again made the subject of contentious debate among the special meeting of legal experts from 44 countries, held in Washington on April 9, 1945. Of these deliberations, which lasted until April 20, 1945, Ram Prakash Anand has written:

The compulsory jurisdiction of the Court was the subject of intense discussion. It was apparent in the debates before the Committee that a majority of the delegates considered that the time had arrived for a further advance towards compulsory jurisdiction that the compromise represented in the Optional Clause. No less than twenty delegates expressed themselves in favour of the adoption of compulsory jurisdiction, and four presented motions to amend Article 36 to this effect. Several, who opposed such action, objected not to the principle of compulsory jurisdiction, but on the ground that the question involved political issues which fell outside the province of a Committee of Jurists and should, therefore, be reserved for the United Nations Conference.[93]

The result of this 1945 Committee of Jurists was the production of two separate drafts, both submitted to the San Francisco Conference; one prepared on the basis of the optional clause compromise embodied in Article 36 of the Statute of the PCIJ, and another in which membership in the ICJ Statute would automatically include acceptance of the compulsory jurisdiction of the Court. Of this result of the Committee's debates, the report of Professor Jules Basdevant, Rapporteur of the Committee of Jurists, stated:

It does not seem doubtful that the majority of the Committee was in favour of compulsory jurisdiction, but it has been noted that, in spite of this predominant sentiment, it did not seem certain, nor even probable, that all the nations whose participation in the proposed International organization appears to be necessary, were now in a position to accept the rule of compulsory jurisdiction, and that the Dumbarton Oaks proposals did not seem to affirm it; some, while retaining their preference in this respect, thought that the counsel of prudence was not to go beyond the procedure of the Optional Clause inserted in Article 36, which has opened the way to the progressive adoption in less that

---

[93] R. Prakesh Anand, Compulsory Jurisdiction of the International Court of Justice (1961) 40.

10 years of compulsory jurisdiction by many States which in 1920 refused to subscribe to it. Placed on this basis, the problem was found to assume a political character, and the Committee thought that it should defer it to the San Francisco Conference.[94]

At the San Francisco Conference, the task of deciding between the two drafts presented by the Committee of Jurists fell to Committee IV/I, where the delegates from the United States and the Soviet Union argued strongly against the adoption of the proposal under which the Court would be granted automatic compulsory jurisdiction over all members of the Charter. The Soviet delegate went so far as to state that his government's ability to accept the Charter itself might be endangered if the compulsory jurisdiction of the Court was made an intrinsic part of membership in the organization.[95]

Expressing the view held by many of the less powerful states represented at the conference, the delegate from Mexico argued that the smaller states had, in accepting the sweeping powers of the Security Council over political disputes and agreeing to the permanent membership upon the Council of powerful states, manifested their trust and confidence in the great powers, and that in refusing to support the universal compulsory jurisdiction of the Court to settle legal disputes among states upon principles of international law, the great powers had failed to reciprocate that trust.[96]

Of these arguments by smaller states in support of the Court's compulsory jurisdiction, one of the U.S. delegates, Charles Fahy, noted:

I was deeply impressed by the strong feeling of the majority of the United Nations that the larger powers should not withhold judicial or legal questions from judicial decision by the International Court which all were agreed should be established. There was the strong feeling that impartial judicial settlement pointed the road to a rule of law in the international world, the ideal of our domestic order. They felt that for great powers to withhold from the Court assent to jurisdiction over legal questions was a means to the exercise of power without justice; and that justice under the law was not only an instrument of peace but a substitution of law for force.[97]

Despite this feeling of the majority of states, the Committee eventually accepted the view advanced by the U.K. delegate, that the participation in the International Court of Justice of the United States and the Soviet Union, both of which were opposed to the compulsory jurisdiction of the Court, made it a practical necessity to adopt again the compromise language of the optional clause, under which states could if they chose submit to the compulsory jurisdiction of the Court, but could also withhold that submission if their interests were seen to

---

[94] U.N.C.I.O. Doc., Volume XIV, 840.
[95] Summary Reports of the 14th and 17th Meetings of Committee IV/1, U.N.C.I.O. Doc., VOl. XIII, 223 ff and 246 ff.
[96] U.N.C.I.O. Doc., Vol. XIII, 227.
[97] C. Fahy, Hearings on Senate Resolution 196, 137.

dictate otherwise.[98] Thus, with a few relatively minor adjustments to its terms, Article 36 of the Statute of the PCIJ was adopted as Article 36 of the Statute of the ICJ. In his report to the plenary conference, the Rapporteur of Committee IV/I noted:

The desire to establish compulsory jurisdiction for the Court prevailed among the majority of the sub-committee. However, some of the delegates feared that insistence upon the realization of that idea would only impair the possibility of obtaining general accord to the Statute of the Court, as well as the Charter itself. It is in that spirit that the majority of the sub-committee recommends the adoption of the solution described above.[99]

Thus, due to the reluctance on the part of the United States and the Soviet Union to submit themselves to the compulsory jurisdiction of the ICJ, and the impracticability of sustaining the ICJ as a world court with general competence over international legal disputes without the participation of the two emerging superpowers, the compromise of the optional clause originally reached in 1920, was perpetuated in Article 36 of the ICJ Statute.

The argument herein is that in light of the trend toward assumption of legislative power by the Security Council apparent in the adoption of Resolution 1373 and Resolution 1540, and the aggrandizement of the power of the permanent members of the Council which this trend represents, there should now be a revisitation of the debate over the universalized compulsory jurisdiction of the ICJ, and an insistence by the majority of U.N. members, which have been in favor of such a jurisdictional framework for the Court since 1920, that the great powers now accept this amendment to the Court's Statute as an institutional aggrandizement of the Court to enable it to serve as a judicial check upon the Council's actions, necessarily concomitant with the assumption by the Security Council of legislative power.

Picking up on the comments made in 1945 by the Mexican delegate to the San Francisco Conference, while less powerful states did, upon signing the Charter, knowingly grant to powerful states disproportionate powers, by nature of their permanent status on the Security Council, to maintain and restore international peace and security, the assumption by the Security Council of a legislative power is clearly not a part of the compact into which states, and particularly less-powerful states, knowingly entered upon membership in the U.N. Charter system. In the non-proliferation law area particularly, this fact is made clear by the provisions for law creation contained in Articles 11 and 26 of the Charter reviewed above. If the Council wishes now to assume the power to impose the will of the great powers upon the entire U.N. membership through

---

[98] See U.N.C.I.O. Doc., Vol. XIII, 227; R. Prakesh Anand, Compulsory Jurisdiction of the International Court of Justice (1961) 43.

[99] Report of the Rapporteur of Committee IV/I, Doc. 913, IV/I/74, U.N.C.I.O. Doc., Vol. XIII, 391, 557–559.

legislative acts, and expects acceptance of this added power from the rest of the world, it must as a matter of fairness and good faith, make this reciprocal concession to less powerful states to allow the ICJ as the principal judicial body of the U.N. and independent arbiter of international law to have an effective power of review to determine the validity of those pronouncements by the Council under Charter law.

Granting this increased jurisdictional reach to the ICJ through formal amendment of Article 36 of the ICJ Statute, would facilitate the effective exercise by the Court of judicial review over decisions of the Security Council both in terms of the Court's jurisdiction *ratione materiae* and jurisdiction *ratione personae*.

In terms of the Court's jurisdiction *ratione personae*, it would obviously enable the Court to exercise jurisdiction over disputes arising between any states members of the United Nations. If the membership of the organization were to hold constant, this would increase the number of states subject to the compulsory jurisdiction of the Court threefold. This increase in personal jurisdiction, and therefore in the frequency of cases successfully brought before the Court, would make far more likely the convergence of facts and jurisdiction necessary to enable the Court to exercise its incidental powers of judicial review over Security Council decisions the validity of which is disputed by the parties.

In the non-proliferation law area, again if the membership of the organization were to hold constant, this change to the Court's jurisdictional framework would grant the Court compulsory jurisdiction over disputes involving actual known possessors of WMD, all but one of which as previously noted have not acceded to the Court's compulsory jurisdiction.[100]

In terms of the Court's jurisdiction *ratione materiae*, the universalization of compulsory jurisdiction would also greatly facilitate the Court's extension of jurisdiction to issues of non-proliferation law, and the discrete issue of the validity of Security Council decisions, as it would simplify the Court's extension of jurisdiction over the entirety of the dispute between the parties, and relieve the Court in many cases of the necessity of finding a nexus between the instrument(s) providing the Court's personal jurisdiction and the substantive issues in dispute, as it was forced to do inter alia in the *Lockerbie* case.[101] Under a system of universal compulsory jurisdiction of the ICJ, states would still be at liberty to agree in advance upon a statement of the particular issues to be presented to the Court, in the form of a *compromis*. However, the Court's compulsory personal jurisdiction over all U.N. members would allow for the greater use by states of unilateral petitions to the Court, naming a respondent state and unilaterally making representations as to the issues in dispute

---

[100] See below n. 203.
[101] *Questions of Interpretation and Application of the 1971 Montreal Convention arising from the Aerial Incident at Lockerbie (Libya v. UK; Libya v. USA)*, Provisional Measures, Order of April 14, 1992, ICJ Reports 1992, 3.

between the parties. It is this unilateral petition form which the Court has had the most difficulty entertaining due to its heretofore limited personal jurisdiction framework.[102]

Of course, universalizing compulsory jurisdiction would, in addition to further opening the gates of the Court's jurisdiction to decide upon the validity of Security Council decisions, have the parallel effect of facilitating the lodging of suits before the Court by powerful states based upon a claim that a respondent state has breached, or is otherwise not in full compliance with, a Council resolution such as Resolution 1540. Such suits might in fact be attractive to members of the Security Council as a means of enforcing valid resolutions of the Council, or at least of obtaining an independent determination of the non-compliance of the respondent with the Council decision. Such a determination by the Court would add legitimacy and credibility to any further enforcement action subsequently decided upon by the Council as against the breaching state.

Pursuant to Article 70 of the Court's Statute, the Court itself could begin the procedural process for amendment of Article 36 of the Statute, to make the Court's jurisdiction compulsory over all U.N. members. Such revised language would be consonant with the provisions in the Charter itself on the ICJ, and there would be no need to amend these Charter provisions.[103] After the communication of this proposal by the Court to the General Assembly, the proposed amendment would, under Article 108 of the Charter, then need to be approved by two-thirds of the members of the General Assembly, including all permanent members of the Security Council. It is at this point in the amendment process that the insistence of less powerful countries in the Assembly, including countries from the developing world, interested in the upholding of an international rule of law and the safeguarding of the U.N. Charter system, would be crucial to the success of the Court's proposal, along with pressure from within permanent members of the Security Council organized by non-governmental organizations and other international civil society movements.

Again, this chapter has considered one avenue of amendment to the fundamental documents of the United Nations for the purpose of increasing the effectiveness of the ICJ's exercise of incidental judicial review over decisions of the Security Council. For the Court to be an effective judicial review body in issue areas other than non-proliferation law creation, including Council legislation on the subject of international terrorism and in other areas of international security concern, a number of other alterations to the Charter, particularly, would likely need to be made. These include changes to the Charter text to clarify the Council's role and the limits of its powers, particularly through

---

[102] T. Gill, Rosenne's The World Court: What it is and How it works (6th edn, 2003) 81.
[103] See U.N. Charter Articles 2, 7, 33, 36, 92–96.

amendment of the vague provisions of Chapter VII. However, since such limitations are already set in the Charter text in Articles 11 and 26 in the area of non-proliferation law creation, as reviewed above, this treatment need not consider these other possible amendments.

IV. Conclusion to Chapters 4 and 5

From the passage of the very first General Assembly resolution, the United Nations has been concerned with the proliferation and threat of use of weapons of mass destruction. The General Assembly in particular has devoted a great deal of time and resources to issues of non-proliferation and disarmament, and has indirectly, through its facilitation of negotiating efforts in the Conference on Disarmament, contributed to the establishment of the cornerstone multilateral treaties regulating WMD proliferation. The Assembly continues to be the main international forum for multilateral participation, cutting across wealth and power strata among nations, in debates on issues of WMD proliferation, and in particular nuclear proliferation.

However the very size and composition of the United Nations, and particularly the General Assembly, while one of the institution's great strengths, has also made the realization of progress on these issues within the organization itself rare. Limitations upon the power of the organization, placed upon it by its foundational document the U.N. Charter, further limit the ability of its political organs, including the Security Council, to directly bring binding measures to bear upon the fundamental problems which have long plagued the international non-proliferation treaties and regimes system.

Notwithstanding these limitations of size and mandate, the United Nations will no doubt continue to be a central diplomatic forum for debate of issues of non-proliferation law, and of the utmost importance to international non-proliferation efforts in providing a forum and an institutional and procedural framework for communication and negotiation between states on these issues of highest national security sensitivity. The Security Council can, within its proper authorities, play an important role in enforcement of non-proliferation law through the exercise of its Chapter VII powers. Some of the Council's more recent activities in the non-proliferation area, including particularly its premature escalation of institutional pressure upon Iran, have not been well advised, and have not contributed to the maintenance of international peace and security, but have rather had the opposite effect of entrenching the WMD-related national aims it had hoped thereby to deter.

Though the ICJ has to date played only a minor role in developing non-proliferation law, a correct understanding of its full competence to act as an institutional check upon the authority of the Security Council underlies the hope that it will play a more significant and assertive role in maintaining U.N. Charter law in the future. This role could be strengthened considerably through a revisitation of arguments of long provenance regarding the Court's jurisdiction *ratione personae*, and amendment of Article 36 of its Statute to make its compulsory jurisdiction truly universal.

PART III

COUNTERPROLIFERATION POLICY

6

Counterproliferation Policy

As has been considered in the foregoing chapters of this volume, in the decades following World War II and the advent of the nuclear age, there arose through efforts of international diplomacy a web of treaties and other international normative regimes purposed in regulating the proliferation of WMD-related technologies. In addition to these technology specific, substantive treaties on possession, development, and proliferation (i.e. the NPT, BWC, and CWC) and related international normative regimes, this volume has considered rules of the World Trade Organization relative to international trade and the relevance of these rules to national law and policy regarding WMD proliferation. Consideration has been had also of the role of the various organs of United Nations, and of United Nations Charter law, in the area of WMD proliferation.

In this Part, consideration will shift away from these sources of international law and related administrative structures, all of which can in their own way be classed under the umbrella heading of non-proliferation law as this volume has utilized that term, and toward consideration of the relevance of international law to the policies of states relative to WMD proliferation, and to a particular consideration of the arguable shifting of some states' policies away from an emphasis on combating WMD proliferation through the facilitating rules and diplomatic networks embodied in these various sources of non-proliferation law, and toward a greater emphasis on combating WMD proliferation through more forceful, proactive, and often unilateral or small-coalition-based counterproliferation policies.[1]

A word on semantics. The terms non-proliferation and counterproliferation as used herein and elsewhere in literature on WMD proliferation are attempts to give some categorization to a variety of often interlinked concepts and policies.[2]

---

[1] See G.K. Bertsch and W.C. Potter (eds), Dangerous Weapons, Desperate States (1999); G.K. Bertsch et al. (eds), International Cooperation on Nonproliferation Export Controls (1994); F.V. Kratochwil, Rules, Norms and Decisions: On the Conditions of Practical and Legal Reasoning in International Relations and Domestic Affairs (1989); J. Goldstein and R.O. Keohane (eds), Ideas and Foreign Policy: Beliefs, Institutions and Political Change (1993); J. Dhanapala, *Multilateralism and the Future of the Global Nuclear Nonproliferation Regime*, The Nonproliferation Review (Fall 2001).

[2] See generally on all subjects of this chapter N.E. Busch and D.H. Joyner (eds), Combating Weapons of Mass Destruction: The Future of Nonproliferation Policy (2009).

In this sense the distinction may be rightly challenged as somewhat arbitrary. However, the purpose of this exercise in categorization is essentially to recognize sometimes subtle, and sometimes not so subtle, differences in both methodology and purpose which are to be found in policies and philosophies relative to WMD proliferation. Thus, non-proliferation activities may be broadly described as efforts calculated, if not perfectly effectively implemented, to keep the proliferation of WMD-related technologies to at least a status quo, and preferably to effect a reversal of proliferation trends through requirements of disarmament of existing materials stockpiles.

Activities under this category include the web of international legal instruments and supporting international normative regimes which have been constructed through multilateral diplomatic negotiation, primarily over the past 60 odd years since the founding of the United Nations system in 1945. As we have seen, these instruments and regimes primarily include possession, development, and proliferation treaties such as the NPT, BWC, and CWC and supporting parallel customary law;[3] international safeguards and inspection regimes such as the IAEA and OPCW; and multilateral export control regimes such as the Nuclear Suppliers Group, Australia Group, and Missile Technology Control Regime.[4] These various legal and diplomatic constructs have come to be collectively referred to as the "non-proliferation treaties and regimes" system, or as this volume has simply termed them, non-proliferation law.[5]

---

[3] Treaty on the Nonproliferation of Nuclear Weapons, opened for signature July 1, 1968, 21 U.S.T. 483, T.I.A.S. No. 6839, 729 U.N.T.S. 161; Convention on the Prohibition of the Development, Production and Stockpiling of Bacteriological (Biological) and Toxin Weapons and on Their Destruction, opened for signature April 10, 1972, 26 U.S.T. 583, T.I.A.S. No. 8062, 1015 U.N.T.S. 163; Convention on the Prohibition of the Development, Production and Stockpiling and Use of Chemical Weapons and on Their Destruction, opened for signature, January 13, 1993, Paris, entered into force April 29, 1997, 32 INTERNATIONAL LEGAL MATERIALS 800.

[4] See D.H. Joyner, *Restructuring the Multilateral Export Control Regime System*, 9 JOURNAL OF CONFLICT & SECURITY LAW 181 (2004).

[5] See D.S. Gualtieri, *The System of Nonproliferation Export Controls*, in COMMITMENT AND COMPLIANCE: THE ROLE OF NON-BINDING NORMS IN THE INTERNATIONAL LEGAL SYSTEM (D. Shelton (ed.) 2000); R. Forsberg et al., NONPROLIFERATION PRIMER: PREVENTING THE SPREAD OF NUCLEAR, CHEMICAL AND BIOLOGICAL WEAPONS (1995); B. Kellman, *Bridling the International Trade of Catastrophic Weaponry*, 43 AMERICAN UNIVERSITY LAW REVIEW 755 (1994); P. Van Ham, MANAGING NONPROLIFERATION REGIMES IN THE 1990's: POWER, POLITICS AND POLICIES (1993); T. Bernauer, THE CHEMISTRY OF REGIME FORMATION: EXPLAINING INTERNATIONAL COOPERATION FOR A COMPREHENSIVE BAN ON CHEMICAL WEAPONS (1993); M. Lipson, *The Reincarnation of COCOM: Explaining Post-Cold War Export Controls*, THE NONPROLIFERATION REVIEW (Winter 1999); G.K. Bertsch and S. Grillot, ARMS ON THE MARKET: REDUCING THE RISK OF PROLIFERATION IN THE FORMER SOVIET UNION (1998); R. Cupitt and S. Grillot, *COCOM is Dead, Long Live COCOM: Persistence and Change in Multilateral Security Institutions*, 27 BRITISH JOURNAL OF POLITICAL SCIENCE 361 (1997); E.H. Noehrenberg, MULTILATERAL EXPORT CONTROLS AND INTERNATIONAL REGIME THEORY: THE EFFECTIVENESS OF COCOM (1995). Regimes are defined by Stephen Krasner as the "principles, norms, rules and decision-making structures" that influence the behavior of states in various issue areas. See S.D. Krasner, *Structural Causes and Regime Consequences: Regimes as Intervening Variables*, in S.D. Krasner (ed.), INTERNATIONAL REGIMES 2 (1983).

However, notwithstanding all of the effort and resources expended by the international community in concluding and maintaining these treaty and other normative regimes, and their significant utility in accomplishing aims of non-proliferation of WMD and related materials and technologies, serious students of WMD proliferation have long understood that the non-proliferation system which they comprise is not a perfect system and was never designed or expected to bring about a zero proliferation reality. Borders are too porous, corruption at both high and low levels is too rampant in places where WMD materials and technologies are already insufficiently physically secure, and both legitimate commercial and illicit trafficking in WMD-related and dual-use items and technologies is too big a business for states to hope to control completely and effectively through inter-state treaties and monitoring mechanisms and supply-side export control regimes.[6]

As has been noted previously, the treaties and regimes approach to non-proliferation has, due to fundamental aspects of its normative character, a number of very real and important limitations with regard to its comprehensive character and ability to effectively combat WMD proliferation.[7] The first of these is the fact that all of the instruments and organizations comprising this system are entirely dependent upon the voluntary participation of states. One of the foremost problems challenging the effectiveness of such treaties and regimes, particularly due to the emergence of new supplier states after the Cold War as described above, is the phenomenon of many of these states, often including those states of most proliferation concern to other members of the international community, remaining outside of the non-proliferation treaties and regimes frameworks. This is what is known in proliferation studies circles as the non-universality or secondary proliferation problem.[8]

This problem has a number of causes. For some states, resistance to international non-proliferation regime membership has been a decision based upon

---

[6] See id.

[7] See J. Cirincione (ed.), Repairing the Regime: Preventing the Spread of Weapons of Mass Destruction (2000); M. Barletta and A. Sands (eds), *Nonproliferation Regimes at Risk*, Occasional Paper No. 3, Center for Nonproliferation Studies (Monterey: Monterey Institute for International Studies, 1999). On patterns of technology dissemination and the challenges presented thereby, see M. Moodie, "The Challenges of Chemical, Biological and Nuclear Weapons Enabling Technology," in P. Gasprani Alves and K. Hoffman (eds), The Transfer of Sensitive Technology and the Future of the Control Regimes (1997). See also W.W. Keller and J.E. Nolan, *Proliferation of Advanced Weaponry: Threat to Stability*, Foreign Policy (Winter 1997–1998); M. Hirsch, *The Great Technology Giveaway*, Foreign Affairs, September/October 1998.

[8] See C. Braun and C. Chyba, *Proliferation Rings: New Challenges to the Nuclear Nonproliferation Regime*, 29 International Security, No. 2, 5–49 (Fall 2004); S. Gahlaut and V. Zaborsky, *Do Regimes Have the Members They Need?*, Center for International Trade and Security Working Paper (Athens; Center for International Trade and Security, February 2003); R.T. Cupitt and I. Khripunov, *New Strategies for the Nuclear Suppliers Group (NSG)*, 16 Comparative Strategy 305 (1997); G.K. Bertsch and S. Grillot (eds), *Arms on the Market: Reducing the Threat of Proliferation in the Former Soviet Union* (1998).

political or philosophical dissent from the perceived aims of such regimes.[9] Trade in nuclear dual-use items, for example, is of particular interest to developing states at the early stages of energy production capacities. Many such states have voiced concern that the Nuclear Suppliers Group's regulation in this area is overly restrictive, and on a more fundamental level that the NSG itself is outside of the legal regime for multilateral regulation of nuclear materials, with the NPT as its cornerstone.[10] They have protested the characterization of NSG standards and policies as being authoritatively or normatively incumbent upon non-NSG members, whether NPT parties or not.[11] They have argued that the NSG is essentially a supplier-state cartel whose policies unduly target states legitimately attempting to develop civilian power generation facilities, and whose primary objective is to keep nuclear technologies within the fairly tight-knit community of existing nuclear states. This is only one example of the debates, often split along developed/developing and North/South lines, regarding the character and overall aims of the non-proliferation regime system. In large measure due to these disagreements, a number of states, importantly including India and Pakistan, have remained outside of the nuclear non-proliferation treaties and regimes system.

For some other states, resistance to inclusion in non-proliferation regimes has been grounded rather upon economic interest, and the opportunity to remain free to trade in weapons-related goods freely and profit through the ability to undercut non-proliferation regime member states by trading with states and non-state entities, and also in items and technologies, that are proscribed by the various regime instruments. One perennial state of concern in this vein is North Korea.

Many states, however, have not joined the regime system because they are not supplier states of sensitive items and technologies themselves, and have either insufficient resources or simply no intentions to acquire or produce WMD, and therefore have a fairly low foreign policy priority in joining multilateral non-proliferation treaties and regimes. This position, however, overlooks the dangerous reality that such states—and particularly those with insufficient resources to effectively police their territory and borders against illicit traffic in WMD-related technologies—are often prime transshipment targets for smuggling rings of varying levels of sophistication. This is particularly the case in troubled

---

[9] See A. Latham and B. Bow, *Multilateral Export Control Regimes: Bridging the North-South Divide*, Canadian Institute of International Affairs International Journal, 53, 3 (Summer 1998); J. Littlewood, The Biological Weapons Convention: A Failed Revolution (2005) ch. 6.

[10] J. Simpson and T. Ogilvie-White (eds), NPT Briefing Book, Vol. 1: The Evolution of the Nuclear Nonproliferation Regime (2003); T. Ogilvie-White, *International Responses to Iranian Nuclear Defiance: The Non-Aligned Movement and the Issue of Non-Compliance*, 18 European Journal of International Law 453 (2007).

[11] One basis for such characterizations is provided in the NSG Part 2 Guidelines, para. 9, which states: "In the interest of international peace and security, the adherence of all states to the Guidelines would be welcome."

regions of the world such as Eastern Europe, the Middle East, and Central and Southeast Asia.

A second major challenge to the non-proliferation treaties and regimes system, referred to as the non-state actor problem, is the fact that all existing restrictions within the treaties and regimes upon manufacture, development, possession, and trafficking in WMD-related technologies are addressed to states themselves.[12] Thus at the international level there is no substantive restriction on private parties, including business entities as well as other non-state actors, engaging in any of these activities. Of course, states that are members of the various treaties and regimes undertake to remedy this problem through national level legislation and regulation.[13] It will be recalled that the universalization of an obligation upon states to enact and enforce such regulations was one of the chief reasons for the passage of Security Council Resolution 1540. However, notwithstanding the passage of that resolution, national export control systems for WMD-related goods and technologies are underdeveloped and under-resourced in many system member states, and are virtually non-existent in many others.[14] Again, for many states, creating and maintaining effective export control and border protection systems within their territories is not high on their resource-allocation priority list for a variety of reasons, some of which are outlined above. Thus, the ability of non-state actors in many countries of the world to engage in WMD development programs and activities, essentially legally, can be seen as a major shortcoming of the classical non-proliferation treaties and regimes system.

Concerns flowing from these realities of WMD proliferation and the limits of the treaties and regimes system have been aggravated in recent years due to the emergence of state actors and sophisticated and maturing groups of non-state actors with both the resource base and either the ideological or strategic incentive to acquire and contemplate the use of WMD for the accomplishment of objectives perceived by many of the most powerful members of the international

---

[12] M. Asada, *WMD Terrorism and Security Council Resolution 1540: Conditions for Legitimacy in International Legislation*, IILJ Working Paper 2007/9, available at <http://www.iilj.org/publications/2007-9Asada.asp>; J. du Preez, *The 2005 NPT Review Conference: Can it Meet the Nuclear Challenge?*, ARMS CONTROL TODAY (April 2005).

[13] M. Asada, *National Implementation of the Chemical Weapons Convention in Japan: Its Relevance and Irrelevance to the Tokyo Subway Incident*, JAPANESE ANNUAL OF INTERNATIONAL LAW, No. 39 (1996); N. A. Sims, "National Implementation of International Obligations: Experience under the Multilateral Treaty Regime of the 1972 Convention on Biological and Toxin Weapons," in T. Stock and R. Sutherland (eds), *National Implementation of the Future Chemical Weapons Convention*, SIPRI Chemical & Biological Warfare Studies No. 11 (OUP, 1990) 59.

[14] P. Crail, *Implementing UN Security Council Resolution 1540: A Risk-Based Approach*, NONPROLIFERATION REVIEW, Vol. 13, No. 2 (July 2006); M. Asada, *WMD Terrorism and Security Council Resolution 1540: Conditions for Legitimacy in International Legislation*, IILJ Working Paper 2007/9, available at <http://www.iilj.org/publications/2007-9Asada.asp>; J. Carson Mark et al., "Can Terrorists Build Nuclear Weapons?" in P. Leventhal and Y. Alexander (eds), *Preventing Nuclear Terrorism: The Report and Papers of the International Task Force on Prevention of Nuclear Terrorism* (Lexington Books, 1987) 60; D. Fischer, STOPPING THE SPREAD OF NUCLEAR WEAPONS: THE PAST AND THE PROSPECTS (Routledge, 1992) 154.

community as being inimical to international peace and security. The rise to prominence and capability of complex and well-funded cross-border organizations, whose practices include the use of terroristic and/or violent actions calculated to bring about desired objectives grounded in what are alleged by their intended victims to be non-rational ideologies, suspected of having access to or being in the process of developing WMD, has in recent years formed a nexus of threat continually on the lips of international officials.[15]

Since the attacks of September 11, 2001 there have been a number of voices in the international community, and particularly from states which feel especially threatened by and vulnerable to WMD attacks staged by the aforementioned variety of ideology driven non-state actors, who have called for a refocusing of attention and a lesser reliance on the traditional treaties and regimes approach to stemming the proliferation of WMD. These commentators point to the previously described limitations of classical non-proliferation efforts and argue that, either as a supplement to or a replacement of this system of diplomatic relations and normative multilateral frameworks, states should increase their emphasis on and employment of proactive and forceful efforts of counterproliferation, including the use of both pre-emptive and preventive strategies for dealing with potential threats of WMD proliferation and use.[16]

Counterproliferation activities may be generally defined as efforts either to preclude specific actors from obtaining WMD-related materials and technologies or to degrade and destroy an actor's existing WMD capability. The blurry distinction between the two concepts is made clearer through a listing of activities usually classified as falling under the counterproliferation category, in juxtaposition to the treaties and regime frameworks previously described. Under the heading of counterproliferation activities can be grouped traditional efforts of deterrence and containment, efforts of defense and mitigation of attack, use of early detection technologies, interdiction of suspected transfers of sensitive items, and pre-emptive and preventive acts of force against either actual or potential possessors of WMD.

---

[15] See United Nations Security Council Resolutions 1373; M. Asada, *WMD Terrorism and Security Council Resolution 1540: Conditions for Legitimacy in International Legislation*, IILJ Working Paper 2007/9, available at <http://www.iilj.org/publications/2007-9Asada.asp>.

[16] M.E. Bunn, "Force, Preemption and WMD Proliferation," in N. Busch and D.H. Joyner (eds), COMBATING WEAPONS OF MASS DESTRUCTION: THE FUTURE OF INTERNATIONAL NON-PROLIFERATION POLICY (2009); J.D. Ellis, *The Best Defense: Counterproliferation and U.S. National Security*, THE WASHINGTON QUARTERLY 26:2 (Spring 2003); R.S. Litwak, *The New Calculus of Pre-emption*, SURVIVAL 44, no. 4 (Winter 2002–2003); J.D. Ellis and G.D. Kiefer, COMBATTING PROLIFERATION: STRATEGIC INTELLIGENCE AND NATIONAL POLICY (2003); H. Muller and M. Reiss, *Counterproliferation : Putting New Wine in Old Bottles*, THE WASHINGTON QUARTERLY 18:2 (Spring 1996); T.G. Mahnken, *A Critical Appraisal of the Defense Counterproliferation Initiative*, NATIONAL SECURITY STUDIES QUARTERLY 5:3 (Summer 1999); G. Andreani, *The Disarray of U.S. Nonproliferation Policy*, SURVIVAL 41:4 (Winter 1999); B. Roberts, *Proliferation and Nonproliferation in the 1990s: Looking for the Right Lessons*, NONPROLIFERATION REVIEW 6:4 (Fall 1999).

As is evident from the listing of activities subsumed under the two headings, neither is a newcomer to policy circles, and both varieties of activities have been carried out to a greater or lesser extent for many years through both national and international level efforts. However there is substantial evidence to support the assertion that the call of the aforementioned pro-counterproliferation commentators has been heard, and that, particularly in the policy positions of the United States and a relatively small number of other powerful states, the momentum of policy has begun to swing toward an increased emphasis on proactive and often unilateral or small-coalition-based counterproliferation activities and away from more multilateral and diplomacy/international law-based efforts of non-proliferation.[17]

While a shift toward counterproliferation policies can be seen in the statements of officials of a number of states, notably including Russia, Israel, Japan, India, Australia, and the United Kingdom, it has been most formally adopted by the United States in its stated foreign and security policy.[18] In both the September 2002 National Security Strategy document and the December 2002 National Strategy to Combat Weapons of Mass Destruction document, U.S. policymakers signalled a significant shift in WMD-related policies toward counterproliferation principles. As stated in the latter document:

We know from experience that we cannot always be successful in preventing and containing the proliferation of WMD to hostile states and terrorists... Because deterrence may not succeed, and because of the potentially devastating consequences of WMD use against our forces and civilian population, U.S. military forces and appropriate civilian agencies must have the capability to defend against WMD-armed adversaries, including in appropriate cases through preemptive measures.[19]

The National Security Strategy document discussed the concept of pre-emption further thus:

The United States has long maintained the option of preemptive actions to counter a sufficient threat to our national security. The greater the threat, the greater is the risk of inaction—and the more compelling the case for taking anticipatory action to defend ourselves, even if uncertainty remains as to the time and place of the enemy's attack.

[17] J.D. Ellis, *The Best Defense: Counterproliferation and U.S. National Security*, THE WASHINGTON QUARTERLY 26:2 (Spring 2003).

[18] M. Gordon and E. Schmitt, "U.S. Says Israeli Exercise Seemed Directed at Iran," *New York Times*, June 20, 2008; "India Mulls 'Pre-Emptive' Pakistan Strike, Cites U.S. Iraq War Precedent," *Agent France Press*, April 11, 2003. Available at <http://www.fromthewilderness.com/free/ww3/041403_india.html>; "Japan Mulling Action over N.Korea Missiles" by M. Yamaguchi, AP <http://news.yahoo.com/s/ap/20060710/ap_on_re_as/nkorea_missiles>; "Russia Won't Rule Out Pre-emptive Use of Force," *Los Angeles Times*, October 13, 2003. <http://straitstimes.asia1.com.sg/storyprintfriendly/0,1887,214354,00.html>; "Prime Minister Warns of Continuing Global Terror Threat," March 5, 2004 speech by Tony Blair. <http://www.number-10.gov.uk/output/page5461.asp>; "Terror-Preemption talk Roils Asia," by Dan Murphy, December 5, 2002, Christian Science Monitor. <http://www.globalpolicy.org/wtc/analysis/2002/1205preemption.htm>.

[19] Available at <http://www.whitehouse.gov/news/releases/2002/12/WMDStrategy.pdf>.

To forestall or prevent such hostile attacks by our adversaries, the United States will, if necessary, act preemptively... [I]n an age where the enemies of civilization openly and actively seek the world's most destructive technologies, the United States cannot remain idle while dangers gather.[20]

The place of the doctrine of pre-emption in U.S. counterproliferation policy was confirmed in the 2006 National Security Strategy document, which specifically sought to justify the doctrine on the basis of a right to pre-emptive self-defense in international law:

Meeting WMD proliferation challenges also requires effective international action... Taking action need not involve military force... If necessary, however, under long-standing principles of self-defense, we do not rule out the use of force before attacks occur, even if uncertainty remains as to the time and place of the enemy's attack.[21]

As Jason Ellis has succinctly written:

[T]he rise of counterproliferation to national stature really begins with the current administration... The Bush version gives continued importance to "strengthened" non-proliferation efforts but downgrades the prior treaties-and-regimes approach, elevating the status of proactive counterproliferation efforts to deter and defend against WMD and missile threats as well as effective consequence management should such weapons be used.[22]

Concerns regarding state use of pre-emptive force against other states and non-state actors, however, are not limited to the actions of the West or of developed states. There are real concerns that recent rhetoric by major powers legitimizing counterproliferation-oriented pre-emption will strengthen the resolve of a number of other states to apply the doctrine to their own regional conflicts. Indian Foreign Minister Yashwant Sinha was quoted in 2003 as stating that India had "a much better case to go for pre-emptive action against Pakistan than the United States has in Iraq," referencing of course the threat posed to India by Pakistan's nuclear arsenal.[23] Israel has also expressed alarm over recent statements by Iranian President Mahmoud Ahmadinejad that Israel should be "wiped off the map," leading to concern that Israel will act pre-emptively against Iran to degrade its capacity to produce nuclear weapons, following a pattern of pre-emptive uses of force which Israel followed in 1967 against Egypt, in 1981 against Iraq, and in 2007 against Syria.[24] Indeed, the degree to which the idea

---

[20] Available at <http://www.whitehouse.gov/nsc/nss.html>.

[21] Available at <http://www.whitehouse.gov/nsc/nss/2006/>; See also R.S. Litwak, *The New Calculus of Pre-emption*, Survival 44, no. 4 (Winter 2002–2003).

[22] J.D. Ellis, *The Best Defense: Counterproliferation and U.S. National Security*, The Washington Quarterly 26:2 (Spring 2003).

[23] "India Mulls 'Pre-Emptive' Pakistan Strike, Cites U.S. Iraq War Precedent," *Agent France Press*, April 11, 2003. Available at <http://www.fromthewilderness.com/free/ww3/041403_india.html>.

[24] "Israel's plans for Iran strikes," *Jane's*, July 16, 2004; M. Gordon and E. Schmitt, "U.S. Says Israeli Exercise Seemed Directed at Iran," *New York Times*, June 20, 2008. On September 6, 2007,

of dealing with WMD proliferation concerns by recourse to pre-emptive attacks has become a familiar and decreasingly broad conceptual leap generally in international society, was recently amply illustrated by the speed at which media outlets from around the world turned from questioning whether Iran's nuclear file would be referred by the International Atomic Energy Agency to the U.N. Security Council, to a race to confirm which states had not yet taken the idea of military force to deal with Iran "off the table."[25]

The two chapters which immediately follow will present case studies of counterproliferation-oriented pre-emptive uses of force. The first case study will be the 2003 military invasion of the state of Iraq by a coalition of states, led by the United States and the United Kingdom. The second case study is the Proliferation Security Initiative, an ongoing informal diplomatic program involving some 50 states at various levels of cooperation in logistic, law enforcement, and military efforts aimed at interdicting WMD-related items and technologies in transit, most often over the sea lanes.

These chapters will examine these concrete policy manifestations of the principles of counterproliferation, and will consider the harmony of these state actions with rules of international law. Both case studies present state actions to which the rules of international use of force law, or the *jus ad bellum*, are relevant, though as will be argued due to the legal canon *lex specialis derogat generali*, the Proliferation Security Initiative is more correctly analyzed primarily by reference to the rules of the law of the sea governing interdiction of vessels.

Chapter 9 will then present a number of observations and considerations leading on from the identification of this shift in states' policies from an emphasis on non-proliferation policies and activities to counterproliferation policies and activities, as illustrated in the two case studies. Consideration will be given particularly to the relational dynamics between this shift in states' policies, and international law; i.e. how international law affects or should affect counterproliferation policies, and vice versa.

Israeli warplanes attacked and destroyed a site in Syria which was later claimed to be a nuclear reactor site, constructed with the help of North Korea. See R. Wright, "N. Koreans Taped At Syrian Reactor: Video Played a Role in Israeli Raid," *Washington Post*, Thursday, April 24, 2008; D.E. Sanger, "U.S. Sees N. Korean Links to Reactor," *New York Times*, April 24, 2008.

[25] See also regarding North Korea, A. Carter and W. Perry, "The Case for a Preemptive Strike on North Korea's Missiles" *TIME.com*, July 8, 2006 (<http://www.time.com/time/world/article/0,8599,1211527,00.html?cnn=yes>).

7

The Challenges of Counterproliferation: Law and Policy of the Iraq Intervention

Allow the President to invade a neighboring nation whenever he shall deem it necessary to repel an invasion ... and you allow him to make war at pleasure ... If today he should choose to say he thinks it necessary to invade Canada to prevent the British from invading us, how could you stop him? You may say to him, "I see no probability of the British invading us," but he will say to you,
"Be silent; I see it, if you don't."

Abraham Lincoln, 1848

This chapter will present the U.S.-led coalition's 2003 intervention in Iraq as a case study of the implementation of counterproliferation strategy as opposed to non-proliferation strategy.[1] It will review those principles of international non-proliferation law which applied to the actions both of Iraq and of the coalition forces respectively in the context of this intervention, and will reach conclusions regarding the compliance of the actions of the two sides with those legal obligations. It will then discuss the implications of the intervention for considerations of the likely effectiveness and general advisability of the shift in emphasis in national policies away from the classic non-proliferation treaties and regimes system and toward more forceful and proactive strategies of counterproliferation, of which the intervention is an example.

The argument of this chapter is that the Iraq intervention of 2003 should properly be seen as a manifestation of this resetting of emphasis in the United States and in a limited number of other countries to favor counterproliferation efforts which, while sharing the classic non-proliferation aim of preventing the development, possession, and use of WMD, yet differ from traditional non-proliferation approaches in that they prescribe action in situations in which that use is not an imminent reality, but rather perceived to be a serious developing threat.[2] As a case

---

[1] This chapter is an amended version of a book chapter by the same title, published in A. Williams and P. Shiner (eds), THE IRAQ WAR AND INTERNATIONAL LAW (Hart, 2008). Used here by permission.

[2] The United States 2002 National Security Strategy document argues for a changed conception of the principle of imminence in light of the "capabilities and objectives of today's adversaries," 15.

study of the application of counterproliferation policy, moreover, it is argued that lessons should be learned from the 2003 Iraq intervention regarding both the legal and policy-oriented implications of this shift away from the non-proliferation treaties and regimes system.

I. Non-proliferation Law Relevant to the Actions of Iraq

In order to make this case, it will first be necessary to review the principles of non-proliferation law which are relevant to the actions of Iraq leading up to the 2003 intervention, and to establish Iraq's non-compliance with those obligations, as well as the legal implications of that non-compliance under the relevant legal sources.

A. Brief History of Iraq's WMD Programs

Saddam Hussein rose to power in Iraq at the head of the secular Baathist party in 1979. After the Iranian revolution of the same year, Iraq was seen by the West as a useful counterforce against Islamic fundamentalism in the Middle East, and Western states and private industries therefore supported the Hussein Government and provided it military support through the decade of the 1980s.[3]

Once in office, Hussein aggressively pursued his goal of making Iraq a regional power, and came to see the development of a WMD arsenal as key to fulfilling that ambition. During the 1980s he embarked upon major nuclear, chemical, and biological weapons programs as well as ballistic missile programs, convinced that these weapons technologies would allow Iraq to become pre-eminent over its regional rivals: Iran, Israel, and Turkey. This determination was made the more compelling following the destruction of the Iraqi nuclear reactor at Osirak by Israel in 1981.[4]

The Iran–Iraq war of 1980–88 was the primary catalyst for the development by Iraq of these non-conventional weapons programs. Iraqi forces invaded Iran on September 22, 1980, believing the campaign would be relatively quick; however the resistance by Iranian forces was stronger than anticipated, and the invasion became a protracted war of attrition lasting most of the next decade. In order to break this stalemate, Hussein turned to his fledgling WMD

---

³ J. Cirincione et al., Deadly Arsenals, Nuclear, Biological and Chemical Threats (Carnegie Endowment, 2nd edn, 2005) 331. See generally H. Blix, Disarming Iraq (2004); G. Pearson, The Search for Iraq's Weapons of Mass Destruction: Inspection, Verification and Nonproliferation (2005); A. Mauroni, Where are the WMD's? (2006), P.W. Galbraith, The End of Iraq (2007); T. Dodge, Inventing Iraq: The Failure of Nation Building and a History Denied (2005).

⁴ J. Cirincione et al., Deadly Arsenals, Nuclear, Biological and Chemical Threats (Carnegie Endowment, 2nd edn, 2005) 331.

development programs, accelerating research into nuclear and biological technologies, and using weapons resulting from his chemical weapons and ballistic missile programs on the battlefield. Iraq's chemical weapons program went from an initial production of mustard gas at one facility in the 1970s to full industrial scale production by 1983. Its biological weapons program from 1985–90 grew from a pathogen research program to full-scale production of weaponized agents and dissemination mechanisms. However, despite pressure from Hussein upon his nuclear scientists to expedite their development of the ultimate battlefield weapon, the Iraqi nuclear program, based on uranium enrichment through gas centrifuge cascade, progressed more slowly through the 1980s.[5]

For all of these programs, Iraq relied heavily on exports of materials and technologies from Western companies, some of which were undertaken in intentional circumvention of national export control laws. However, many of these export sales were executed in compliance with relevant licensing procedures, often with the exporting companies having no idea of the intended end-use of the items being exported. Through these legitimate imports, as well as through the dual-use materials black market, Iraq was able to develop an impressive array of WMD and ballistic missile research and development programs by the late 1980s.[6] The help received during this period from Western companies is illustrated in the 2004 conviction in the Netherlands of Dutch businessman Franz van Anraat on charges of complicity to genocide and war crimes.[7] Van Anraat had sold thousands of tons of chemical precursors for mustard gas and nerve gas to Iraq in the late 1980s. Both gases were used in the Iran–Iraq war, and in a 1988 attack on the Kurdish Iraqi town of Halabja in which more then 5,000 people were killed.

Iraqi forces invaded Kuwait on August 2, 1990, following allegations that Kuwaiti oil firms were slant-drilling oil from beneath Iraq's border. On November 29, 1990 the United Nations Security Council passed Resolution 678 which authorized U.N. members to use "all necessary means" to "uphold and implement Resolution 660," which had demanded that Iraq withdraw its forces from Kuwait, and "restore international peace and security." The resulting U.N. enforcement action lasted from January 17 to February 27, 1991 and resulted in the removal of Iraqi forces from Kuwait and their eventual defeat on Iraqi soil.

The Security Council passed Resolution 687 on April 3, 1991, in which it declared a formal ceasefire and demanded that Iraq

unconditionally accept the destruction, removal or rendering harmless under international supervision of all chemical and biological weapons and all stocks of agents and all related subsystems and components and all research, development, support and

---

[5] Ibid.
[6] J. Holmes and G. Bertsch, *Tighten Export Controls*, Defense News, May 5, 2003.
[7] "Dutchman Jailed over gassing of Kurds," The Times Online, December 23, 2005. Available at <http://www.timesonline.co.uk/tol/news/world/iraq/article782298.ece>.

manufacturing facilities; all ballistic missiles with a range greater than 150 kilometers and related major parts and repair and production facilities . . .

The Council further decided that Iraq "shall unconditionally agree not to acquire or develop nuclear weapons or nuclear-weapons-usable material or any subsystems or components or any research, development, support or manufacturing facilities related to the above."

Along with these prohibitions on possession, Resolution 687 re-authorized a mandate, first authorized in Resolution 661, for a broad range of international sanctions, including prohibitions on importation of goods of Iraqi origin, prohibitions on export to Iraq of a broad range of goods and services related to the production of WMD, as well as a range of other financial and economic sanctions. The resolution further imposed upon Iraq the obligation to cooperate with IAEA inspectors with regard to its nuclear technologies obligations, and with an ad hoc United Nations weapons inspection regime, the United Nations Special Commission on Iraq (UNSCOM), with regard to its chemical and biological weapons obligations. UNSCOM and the IAEA were tasked with verifying Iraq's compliance with the disarmament provisions of the resolution.

After several years of grudging cooperation with this monitoring and inspections regime, the Iraqi policy appeared to change to one of frustration of and non-cooperation with the international inspectors, even though this meant the forgoing of over $120 billion in oil revenues which the United Nations refused to release to Iraq as a consequence. The effects upon Iraqi civilians of the long-term economic sanctions regime imposed by U.N. resolutions was producing support for Hussein's Government in Arab countries. Bolstered by this support, in the fall of 1998 Hussein refused to allow full access by weapons inspectors to sites within Iraq unless the sanctions were lifted. The resulting stand-off between the inspectors and the Iraqi Government led to the decision on December 16, 1998 to withdraw the inspectors from the country. Two days of military strikes by the United States and the United Kingdom followed.[8]

On December 17, 1999, the Security Council passed Resolution 1284 which proposed a re-introduction of weapons inspectors into Iraq, led by the IAEA and the renamed United Nations Monitoring, Verification and Inspection Commission (UNMOVIC). However, Hussein once again refused to allow the inspectors access while the sanctions regime remained in force. The absence of inspectors on the ground in Iraq not only meant the end of on-site inspections of Iraqi weapons facilities, it also meant that the video monitoring of those facilities, and the other methods for safeguarding facilities against use in WMD development programs were not being maintained. Thus, there was no way to verify that the WMD programs, which had been significantly dismantled through the

---

[8] J. Cirincione et al., Deadly Arsenals, Nuclear, Biological and Chemical Threats (Carnegie Endowment, 2nd edn, 2005) 331–332.

inspections program, and as a result of the years of crippling economic sanctions, were not being restarted.[9]

From 1998–2002, the strategy of the West toward Iraq focused on containment and maintenance of the sanctions regime, though concerns regarding the effectiveness of this regime increased, as did fears that Hussein was rebuilding his WMD programs in defiance of U.N. Security Council Resolution 687 in the absence of the weapons inspectors. As time passed, the continued refusal by Iraq to cooperate with the U.N. inspection regime led many analysts to the presumption that Hussein now had something to hide, i.e. restarted WMD programs and resulting stockpiles particularly of chemical and biological weapons.[10]

Intelligence estimates compiled by Western intelligence agencies, and particularly in the United States, began to be based less upon direct evidence of what was going on in Iraq (as they had no access to such information) and more on projections of likely behaviour of Hussein and his regime based upon their past behavior.[11] The CIA's summary of intelligence on Iraq report to Congress in 1999 stated:

We do not have any direct evidence that Iraq has used the period since Desert Fox to reconstitute its WMD programs, although given its past behaviour, this type of acticity must be regarded as likely. The United Nations assesses that Baghdad has the capability to reinitiate both its CW and BW programs within a few weeks to months, but without an inspection monitoring program, it is difficult to determine if Iraq has done so.[12]

Beginning in late 2002, these intelligence estimates, and their interpretation by government officials and outside experts, began to contain a message of heightened concern and alarm regarding the perceived state of Iraq's WMD programs and resulting weapons stockpiles. U.S. administration officials repeatedly stated that Iraq had restarted its nuclear weapons program, that it had restarted industrial scale production of chemical and biological weapons and had stockpiled hundreds of tons of chemical and biological weapons, and that it had produced dozens of Scud missiles and aerial drones to deliver these weapons.[13] Secretary of State Colin Powell said in January 2003 that "Iraq continues to conceal quantities, vast quantities, of highly lethal material and weapons to deliver it."[14] Secretary of Defense Donald Rumsfeld went further in assuring that the United States knew the location of these chemical and

---

[9] Ibid.   [10] Ibid. at 332–333.   [11] Ibid. at 333.

[12] Central Intelligence Agency, Unclassified Report to Congress.

[13] J. Cirincione et al., DEADLY ARSENALS, NUCLEAR, BIOLOGICAL AND CHEMICAL THREATS (Carnegie Endowment, 2nd edn, 2005) 334–336.

[14] "Iraq Weapons Inspectors' 60-Day Report: Iraqi Non-Cooperation and Defiance of the UN," briefing in Washington DC, January 27, 2003. Available at <http://www.state.gov/secretary/rm/2003/16921.htm>.

biological weapons stockpiles: "We know where they are."[15] Secretary of State Condoleeza Rice said in June 2003 that the assessment of Iraq's possession and development of WMD was "not about a data point here or a data point there, but about what Saddam Hussein was doing. That he had weapons of mass destruction. That was the judgment."[16]

Official statements regarding Iraq's WMD programs reached their most definitive with the statement of President George W. Bush on March 17, 2003, which also included a reference to the assertion made for months by the U.S. administration that Iraq had "ties" with the al Qaeda terrorist organization:

> Intelligence gathered by this and other governments leaves no doubt that the Iraq regime continues to possess and conceal some of the most lethal weapons ever devised... the danger is clear: using chemical, biological, or one day nuclear weapons, obtained with the help of Iraq, the terrorists could fulfill their stated ambition and kill thousands or hundreds of thousands of innocent people in our country or any other.[17]

The United States led efforts at the United Nations to achieve the passage of a Security Council resolution clearly authorizing the use of force to disarm Iraq. These efforts, however, were countered by significant opposition from other permanent members of the Security Council, particularly including France and Russia. The result of this diplomatic discord was the passage on November 8, 2002 of Resolution 1441, in which the Security Council determined that Iraq "has been and remains in material breach of its obligations under relevant resolutions, including resolution 687 (1991)..." The Council further decided "to afford Iraq, by this resolution, a final opportunity to comply with its disarmament obligations under relevant resolutions of the Council..." and accordingly to establish "an enhanced inspection regime with the aim of bringing to full and verified completion the disarmament process established by resolution 687 (1991) and subsequent resolutions of the Council."[18]

The Council demanded that Iraq cooperate with the UNMOVIC and IAEA inspectors, and make a full and accurate accounting of all of its WMD-related

---

[15] Donald Rumsfeld, interview on *This Week with George Stephanopoulos*, ABC Television, March 30, 2003.

[16] Condoleeza Rice, interview on *This Week with George Stephanopoulos*, ABC Television, June 8, 2003.

[17] "Address to the Nation on War with Iraq," remarks in Cross Hall, Washington, March 17, 2003. Available at <http://www.whitehouse.gov/news/releases/2003/03/20030317-7.html>. On the suspected connection between Iraq and al Qaeda, in March 2008 the U.S. Joint Forces Command produced a definitive report, based upon a review of interviews and some 600,000 captured Iraqi documents, which concluded that there had in fact been no connection between the Hussein regime and al Qaeda. This report contradicted the statements of former Secretary of Defense, Donald Rumsfeld, who in September 2002 stated that the CIA had provided "bulletproof" evidence "that there are, in fact, al Qaeda in Iraq." See "Hussein's Iraq and al Qaeda Not Linked, Pentagon Says," CNN.com, March 14, 2008.

[18] See generally M. Byers, *Agreeing to Disagree: Security Council Resolution 1441 and Intentional Ambiguity*, 10 GLOBAL GOVERNANCE 165–186 (2004).

programs and stockpiles. It stressed that any failure to comply with the demands made in the resolution would constitute a "further material breach" of Iraq's obligations under Security Council resolutions. The Council decided to convene immediately upon the receipt of a report by the weapons inspectors "in order to consider the situation and the need for full compliance with all of the relevant Council resolutions in order to secure international peace and security." Finally, the Council recalled its warning to Iraq of "serious consequences" which would result from Iraq's failure to uphold its obligations.

The UNMOVIC and IAEA inspections began soon afterward and made significant progress, but the inspections ended in March without producing a report on their findings, when it became clear that hostilities were imminent. On March 19, 2003, the main invasion of Iraq by a U.S.-led coalition of military forces began. By May 1, President Bush announced that major combat operations in Iraq had ended, though the occupation and battle against insurgent forces was to continue.

The search for evidence of Iraq's WMD programs and weapons stockpiles had begun even before the invasion occurred, and continued afterward for months. In June, 2003 the Iraq Survey Group (ISG) assumed the lead in this effort.[19] Over the next year, the approximately 1,300 members of the ISG inspection team scoured Iraq looking for WMD development sites and weapons storage sites, and combing through thousands of documents trying to come up with evidence to support the pre-war allegations of active weapons programs. Neither U.N. inspectors nor the members of the ISG found any of the active programs, or any of the weapons stockpiles which had been cited as the primary reason for the invasion. UNMOVIC found 18 chemical artillery shells which had apparently been produced before 1990. Sixteen of these shells were empty, and two were filled with water.[20]

None of the allegations contained in U.S. and U.K. intelligence estimates concerning the activity of WMD programs in Iraq or the possession by Iraq of nuclear, chemical, or biological weapons proved to have been correct. In July 2004, both the U.S. Senate Intelligence Committee and the U.K. parliamentary inquiry (Butler Commission) tasked with presenting the findings of the post-war inspections, presented their reports. Both reports confirmed the inaccuracy of pre-war intelligence, and were highly critical of the intelligence failures which had led to the war.[21] According to the U.S. Senate report, most of the key pre-war intelligence judgments had "either overstated, or were not supported by, the

---

[19] See generally G.S. Pearson, THE SEARCH FOR IRAQ'S WEAPONS OF MASS DESTRUCTION (2005) ch. 7; H. Blix, DISARMING IRAQ (2004).

[20] J. Cirincione et al., DEADLY ARSENALS, NUCLEAR, BIOLOGICAL AND CHEMICAL THREATS (Carnegie Endowment, 2nd edn, 2005) 336–337.

[21] See S. Pullinger, "Lord Butler's Report on U.K. Intelligence," *Disarmament Diplomacy*, Issue 78 (July/August 2004); J. Cirincione, "Two Terrifying Reports: The U.S. Senate and the 9/11 Commission on Intelligence Failures before September 11 and the Iraq War," *Disarmament Diplomacy*, Issue 78 (July/August 2004).

underlying intelligence reporting. A series of failures... led to the mischaracterization of the intelligence."[22]

On the question of why Saddam Hussein had not cooperated with U.N. and IAEA inspectors when in fact, as now became apparent, he did not have WMD programs and stockpiles to hide, Kenneth Pollack has explained:

He may have feared that if his internal adversaries realized that he no longer had the capability to use these weapons, they would try to move against him... Saddam's standing among the Sunni elites who constituted his power base was linked to a great extent to his having made Iraq a regional power—which the elites saw as a product of Iraq's unconventional arsenal. Thus openly giving up his WMD could also have jeopardized his position with crucial supporters.[23]

B. Non-proliferation Law Violations

Notwithstanding the fact that no evidence of active Iraqi WMD programs, or WMD stockpiles, dating to the period after the 1991 Gulf War have been found, it is clear that prior to 1991 Iraq was in violation of its obligations under nonproliferation treaties, and that after 1991 it was in violation of its obligations under U.N. Security Council resolutions, including Resolution 687. This chapter will now proceed to a review of those breaches of non-proliferation law, and their implications, if any, for considerations of the legality of the 2003 Iraq intervention, as well as larger considerations of the likely effectiveness and advisability of counterproliferation policies generally.

1. Nuclear Weapons

Iraq ratified the Nuclear Nonproliferation Treaty (NPT) on October 29, 1969 and subsequently concluded an independent safeguards agreement with the IAEA. As a Non-Nuclear Weapon State it was obligated in NPT Article II not to acquire from any other state, or produce on its own, nuclear weapons or nuclear explosive devices, and not to receive foreign assistance in weapons development programs. Iraq first breached its NPT obligations through its efforts at its Osirak research reactor, which had been purchased from France in 1976, to generate plutonium for use in nuclear weapons. After the reactor at Osirak was destroyed by Israel in 1981, Iraq's efforts to produce fissile materials switched to uranium enrichment, using several different enrichment processes including chemical enrichment, gaseous diffusion, gas centrifuges, and electromagnetic isotope separation (EMIS). In its work on the nuclear fuel cycle and nuclear weapons production, it obtained the assistance of Western companies which transferred

[22] U.S. Senate, "Senate Report on the U.S. Intelligence Community's Pre-War Intelligence Assessments on Iraq," July 7, 2004. Available at <http://intelligence.senate.gov/iraqreport2.pdf>.
[23] "Spies, Lies and Weapons: What Went Wrong," *Atlantic Monthly*, January/February 2004, 22.

to Iraq classified design details of centrifuges, and high-tensile maraging steel for centrifuge manufacture.[24]

According to the IAEA, Hussein's original plan for the Iraqi nuclear weapons program was to produce its first implosion-type weapons by 1991. However, the uranium enrichment process lagged behind projected targets, and this goal became impossible. Despite a stepped-up program which was initiated after Iraq's invasion of Kuwait in 1990, by the time of the 1991 war with coalition forces, Iraqi scientists had as yet been unable to master the complexities of the high-explosive charges which must follow ignition, bombarding the fissile core of an implosion-type nuclear warhead with uniform shock waves to produce a critical mass of fissile material.[25]

The 1991 war and subsequent inspections and disarmament activities of the IAEA succeeded in fully dismantling the Iraqi nuclear weapons program. The IAEA secured all of the fissile materials and destroyed or removed all equipment and facilities relating to the program.[26] Although Iraq had never successfully produced a nuclear weapon, all of the activities it had engaged in during its decade-long concealed nuclear weapons program were both in breach of its safeguards agreement with the IAEA, and in fundamental breach of its substantive obligations under Article II of the NPT.

2. Biological Weapons

Iraq's international legal obligations in the biological weapons area present a slightly more complicated picture. Iraq did sign the BWC in 1972; however it did not deposit its instrument of ratification with the Depositary Governments until 1991. Since the BWC specifies in Article XIV that the Convention is subject to ratification, the substantive provisions of the BWC did not become binding on Iraq until 1991. Thus, Iraq's activities related to development and possession of biological weapons from 1991 were in breach of its obligations under the BWC.

However, the 1969 Vienna Convention on the Law of Treaties, which is recognized to codify customary law, provides in Article 18 that after signature of a treaty and before its ratification, a state is bound "to refrain from acts which would defeat the object and purpose of the treaty."[27] The object and purpose of the BWC being to forbid the development, possession, and proliferation of biological weapons, Iraq's activities in these areas from 1975 (when the BWC entered into force) to 1991 would fall under this provision, and therefore be a

---

[24] See G.S. Pearson, THE SEARCH FOR IRAQ'S WEAPONS OF MASS DESTRUCTION (2005) chs 8–9; J. Cirincione et al., DEADLY ARSENALS, NUCLEAR, BIOLOGICAL AND CHEMICAL THREATS (Carnegie Endowment, 2nd edn, 2005) 337–342.

[25] Ibid.   [26] Ibid.

[27] The ICJ has firmly established that Articles 31 and 32 of the VCLT reflect customary law. See, e.g., the *India/Malaysia* case, ICJ Reports 2002, para. 37; the *Libya/Chad* case, ICJ Reports 1994, paras 6, 21–22. See also I. Brownlie, PRINCIPLES OF PUBLIC INTERNATIONAL LAW (6th edn, 2003) 602–607; M. Shaw, INTERNATIONAL LAW (5th edn, 2003) 839.

violation not of the BWC, but of the Vienna Convention on the Law of Treaties and parallel customary international law.

Iraq's biological weapons program began in the 1970s, but increased dramatically in both scale and pace during the Iran–Iraq war of 1980–88. During this time Iraq produced both lethal pathogens (e.g. anthrax, botulinum toxin, and ricin) and incapacitating pathogens (e.g. aflatoxin, mycotoxins, hemorrhagic conjunctivitis virus, and rotavirus). Iraq also developed dissemination devices, testing the first such device in 1988. It tested and developed aerial bombs, rockets, missiles, and spray tanks as vehicles for dissemination of pathogens.[28]

Iraq's weaponization efforts increased in 1990, in anticipation of coming conflict. Al Hussein missiles were filled with aflatoxin, anthrax, and botulinum toxin and deployed in January 1991 to four sites in Iraq, where they remained throughout the Gulf War. After the war, Iraq's biological weapons and development program remained secret, through constant denial of their existence and active efforts to keep the program hidden from weapons inspectors. However, the location of the largest biological weapons research and development and production site at Al Hakam was revealed by Lieutenant-General Hussein Al-Kamal, Saddam Hussein's brother-in-law, after his defection in 1995. In 1996, UNSCOM destroyed the facility and materials at Al Hakam and transferred equipment from other R&D sites to Al Hakam to be dismantled.[29]

Iraq's long-maintained biological weapons program was in clear breach of its obligations under Articles I, II, and IV of the 1972 BWC, as well as its obligations under Article 18 of the 1969 Vienna Convention on the Law of Treaties. Its possession of biological weapons, and their concealment from UNSCOM inspectors subsequent to the passage of Resolution 687 in 1991, until their destruction in 1996, further constituted a breach of Iraq's obligations under Article 25 of the U.N. Charter.

3. *Chemical Weapons*

In the area of development, possession, and proliferation of chemical weapons, an international legal vacuum of sorts existed for most states until the signing of the 1993 CWC. Iraq has yet to sign the CWC, but as will be discussed below, this is a moot point because of the date of the destruction of the Iraqi chemical weapons program and its chemical weapons stockpiles.

Before the CWC, the only multilateral international legal instrument addressing chemical weapons, including chemical gas weapons, was the 1925 Geneva Protocol, which banned the "use in war" of "asphyxiating, poisonous or other gases, and of all analogous liquids, materials or devices," as well as the use

---

[28] G.S. Pearson, THE SEARCH FOR IRAQ'S WEAPONS OF MASS DESTRUCTION (2005) chs 8–9; J. Cirincione et al., DEADLY ARSENALS, NUCLEAR, BIOLOGICAL AND CHEMICAL THREATS (Carnegie Endowment, 2nd edn, 2005) 346–349.

[29] Ibid.

of bacteriological methods of warfare. Iraq acceded to the 1925 Geneva Protocol on September 8, 1931.[30]

Iraq's chemical weapons program was by far the most extensive, and productive, of its non-conventional weapons programs. Chemical weapons were also the only WMD Iraq actually used on the battlefield. Iraq's chemical weapons program began in the 1970s and expanded significantly during the Iran–Iraq war. Iraq produced mustard gas as well as the more complex compounds of tabun, cyclosarin, and sarin. These chemicals were weaponized by placement in artillery shells, grenades, mortars, aerial bombs, and rockets. It further deployed 50 Al Hussein missiles with warheads filled with chemical weapons as part of its battlefield forces during the 1991 Gulf War.[31]

Iraq used chemical weapons during its war with Iran on multiple occasions, resulting in the deaths of approximately 50,000 Iranian soldiers and civilians. Iraq further used chemical weapons to subdue the Iraqi Kurdish population in the north of the country in the late 1980s. The use of chemical weapons on the northern Iraqi town of Halabja on March 16, 1988, in which mustard gas, tabun, sarin, and the nerve agent VX were delivered by aerial bombs to kill approximately 5,000 people and injure 10,000 people, has been described as "the largest-scale chemical weapon attack against a civilian population in modern times."[32]

After the Gulf War, UNSCOM inspectors dismantled Iraq's chemical weapons program and destroyed 760 tons of chemical weapons and more than 3,275 tons of chemical precursors. Because of the scale of the program and the amount of chemicals produced through its industrial scale processes, as well as gaps in the accounting records delivered by Iraq to inspectors, concerns lingered as to whether all chemical weapons stockpiles and facilities had been detected and destroyed. These suspected residual stockpiles of chemical weapons, which some believed existed in secret, underground storage facilities, were at the heart of the concerns which eventually led to the 2003 intervention.[33] After the 2003 intervention, the head of the ISG, David Kay, stated that

multiple sources with varied access and reliability have told ISG that Iraq did not have a large, ongoing, centrally controlled CW program after 1991. Information found to date suggests that Iraq's large-scale capability to develop, produce, and fill new CW munitions was reduced—if not entirely destroyed—during operations Desert Storm and Desert Fox, 13 years of U.N. sanctions and U.N. inspections... Our efforts to collect and exploit

[30] See Chapter 2 below at 88.

[31] G.S. Pearson, THE SEARCH FOR IRAQ'S WEAPONS OF MASS DESTRUCTION (2005) chs 8–9; J. Cirincione et al., DEADLY ARSENALS, NUCLEAR, BIOLOGICAL AND CHEMICAL THREATS (Carnegie Endowment, 2nd edn, 2005) 342–345.

[32] Ibid.; quote from C.M. Gosden, "Chemical and Biological Weapons Threats to America: Are We Prepared?" Testimony before the Senate Select Committee on Intelligence, April 22, 1998.

[33] G.S. Pearson, THE SEARCH FOR IRAQ'S WEAPONS OF MASS DESTRUCTION (2005) chs 8–9; J. Cirincione et al., DEADLY ARSENALS, NUCLEAR, BIOLOGICAL AND CHEMICAL THREATS (Carnegie Endowment, 2nd edn, 2005) 342–346.

intelligence on Iraq's chemical weapons program have thus far yielded little reliable information on post-1001 CW stocks and CW agents production.[34]

Charles Duelfer, who succeeded Kay at the head of the ISG, stated more definitively in October 2004 that "ISG judges that Iraq unilaterally destroyed its undeclared chemical weapons stockpile in 1991."[35]

Thus, Iraq's non-signature of the 1993 CWC is not material to consideration of its breaches of international legal obligations during the Presidency of Saddam Hussein, as Iraq's chemical weapons program was no longer functioning, and its chemical weapons stocks had been destroyed, by 1991. However, the use of chemical weapons by Iraq against Iran during the Iran–Iraq war was in violation of Iraq's obligations under the 1925 Geneva Protocol. With regard to Iraq's use of chemical weapons against minority groups within Iraq, the prevailing legal opinion is that the limitation of the Geneva Protocol to the use of chemical weapons "in war" does not allow the application of its provisions to intra-state conflicts.[36] Thus, the horrific use of chemical weapons against the Iraqi Kurds in the late 1980s cannot be held to be a breach by Iraq of the Geneva Protocol obligations, although it almost certainly was a violation by Iraqi officials, including Saddam Hussein himself, of international humanitarian law and international criminal law.[37]

4. Ballistic Missiles

As reviewed in Chapter 1 herein, there are no multilateral international legal instruments or rules of customary international law addressing the development, possession, and proliferation of missiles. Therefore, the only international law which applies to Iraq's ballistic missile program and stockpiles is the provision in Security Council Resolution 687, passed in 1991, that Iraq's missile arsenal be limited to missiles with a range of no greater than 150 kilometers.

Before the 1991 Gulf War, Iraq had a large arsenal of short-range ballistic missiles, including single-stage, liquid-fueled Scud-Bs (with a 300-kilometer range and a 1,000-kilogram payload) which it had acquired from the Soviet Union. It also had developed three variants of the Scud-B itself, all of which had a range of around 600 kilometers. Iraq had weaponized both biological agents and chemical compounds by loading them into missiles, and was actively pursuing

---

[34] Testimony of David Kay to Congress in October 2, 2003.

[35] "Comprehensive Report of the Special Advisor to the DCI on Iraq's WMD," September 30, 2004. Available at <http://www.cia.gov/cia/reports/iraq_wmd_2004/index.html>.

[36] D. Turns, *Weapons in the ICRC Study on Customary International Humanitarian Law*, 11 JOURNAL OF CONFLICT AND SECURITY LAW 201, 220 (2006); idem, *At the "Vanishing Point" of International Humanitarian Law: Methods and Means of Warfare in Non-international Armed Conflicts*, 45 GERMAN YEARBOOK OF INTERNATIONAL LAW 115 (2002).

[37] M.J. Kelley, *The Tricky Nature of Proving Genocide against Saddam Hussein before the Iraqi Special Tribunal*, 38 CORNELL INTERNATIONAL LAW JOURNAL 983 (2005).

a program to develop the ability to mount a nuclear warhead on its Al Hussein modified Scud platform.[38]

In 1991 UNSCOM destroyed the 48 ballistic missiles which were declared to it with a range of over 150 kilometers. In March 1992, however, Iraq informed UNSCOM that it had not declared the existence of a further 85 missiles with ranges longer than the prescribed limit. Iraqi officials said, though, that they had destroyed those additional 85 missiles in October 1991 in a secret operation. By early 1995, UNSCOM was confident that it had located and destroyed Iraq's non-compliant missile arsenal. However, due to repeated instances of concealment of missiles and related facilities, and incompleteness of missile accounting produced by Iraqi officials, UNSCOM still had concerns regarding the comprehensiveness of their purge of missile stocks.[39]

Inspections carried out between November 2002 and March 2003 revealed the continued presence in Iraq's arsenal of Al Samoud 2 missiles which had a range exceeding 150 kilometers. Iraq began the destruction of these missiles on March 1, 2003 and had destroyed two-thirds of its Al Samoud 2 stocks by the time UNSCOM inspectors left, prior to the start of the war.[40]

While the vast majority of the Iraqi missile arsenal prohibited by Resolution 687 had been decommissioned during the early 1990s, the possession of these missiles after 1991, as well as the "substantial illegal procurement for all aspects of the missile programs" revealed by the ISG, did constitute a violation by Iraq of the terms of Security Council Resolution 687, and thus was a breach by Iraq of its obligations under Article 25 of the United Nations Charter.[41]

II. Non-proliferation Law Relevant to the Actions of the Coalition

Because of Iraq's breaches of its international non-proliferation law obligations, both real and imagined, and the threat that was deemed to exist therefrom both to the region and, through an alleged nexus to international terrorism, to the West as well, agreement was reached between the United States and the United Kingdom that action had to be taken to disarm Iraq once and for all and to remove the Saddam Hussein regime.[42] The question became, on what legal basis could such action be justified?

---

[38] See G.S. Pearson, THE SEARCH FOR IRAQ'S WEAPONS OF MASS DESTRUCTION (2005) chs 8–9; J. Cirincione et al., DEADLY ARSENALS, NUCLEAR, BIOLOGICAL AND CHEMICAL THREATS (Carnegie Endowment, 2nd edn, 2005) 350–355.

[39] Ibid.   [40] Ibid.

[41] Testimony of David Kay to Congress on October 2, 2003.

[42] See P. Sands, LAWLESS WORLD: AMERICA AND THE MAKING AND BREAKING OF GLOBAL RULES (2005), 182–184.

Looking first to the provisions of the substantive non-proliferation law instruments which Iraq had breached, there was seen to be little justification therein for forceful action against Iraq. The NPT makes no mention of disputes arising regarding the provisions of the treaty. Safeguards agreements with the IAEA are mandated under Article III; however, the IAEA is only empowered under its statute to determine breaches to its bilateral safeguards agreements, and has no authority to determine breaches of underlying NPT obligations. The IAEA statute provides for referral of cases from the IAEA to the Security Council if a breach of safeguards commitments has been determined.[43]

The BWC does contain provisions in Article VI regarding a situation in which any party to the treaty "finds that any other state party is acting in breach of obligations deriving from the provisions of the Convention." However, the prescribed procedure for registering such concerns is to lodge a complaint with the Security Council, which is to investigate the basis of the complaint.

Although the CWC, as discussed above, is not relevant to the case of Iraq, it too has provisions under which states are to pursue their complaints regarding another member state's compliance with the obligations of the treaty. In the case of the CWC, these procedures are more complex and involve the use of the OPCW as an intermediary between states parties to clarify information on chemical programs and, if necessary, to administer challenge inspections demanded by one state party as regarding another. However, the treaty provides in Article VIII(36) that "in cases of particular gravity and urgency" the OPCW Executive Council is to refer the issue directly to the United Nations Security Council.

Thus, under all three substantive non-proliferation law instruments, there are no provisions for unilateral enforcement of treaty obligations as between member states. Rather, all enforcement roads lead to the U.N. Security Council and to its authority under Chapter VII of the U.N. Charter.[44] And of course, there were Security Council resolutions specifically on the subject of Iraq and its WMD programs, stretching back to Resolution 687, demanding disarmament. These resolutions, all obligations of international non-proliferation law emanating from the Security Council's enforcement authority under the Charter, had been demonstrably flouted by Iraq, as detailed above, particularly in the areas of biological weapons and ballistic missiles.

But did violation of the substantive terms of these prior Security Council resolutions in itself give rise to a right of unilateral or coalition-based state enforcement action against Iraq, or was an explicit authorization by the Security Council necessary to provide a justification for such enforcement action? It was clear after the contentious passage of the ambiguously worded Resolution 1441

---

[43] See IAEA Statute Article XII(C).
[44] See C. Gray, INTERNATIONAL LAW AND THE USE OF FORCE (2nd edn, 2004) chs 7–8.

in November 2002 that no more specific authorization to use force against Iraq would be forthcoming from the Security Council.[45] Thus, if Security Council authorization to use force against Iraq were to serve as the legal basis for an enforcement action, that authorization would need to be found in resolutions already on the books.

This line of reasoning gave rise to the legal justificatory rubric adopted by the U.K. Attorney General in response to legal challenges to the war, and echoed by the U.S. State Department Legal Advisor in an article in the *American Journal of International Law*.[46] As summarized by the U.K. Attorney General, this justification proceeds thus:

1. In resolution 678 [of 1990] the Security Council authorized force against Iraq, to eject it from Kuwait and to restore peace and security in the area.
2. In resolution 687 [of 1991], which set out the ceasefire conditions after Operation Desert Storm, the Security Council imposed continuing obligations on Iraq to eliminate its weapons of mass destruction in order to restore international peace and security in the area. Resolution 687 suspended but did not terminate the authority to use force under resolution 678.
3. A material breach of resolution 687 revives the authority to use force under resolution 678.
4. In resolution 1441 the Security Council determined that Iraq has been and remains in material breach of resolution 687, because it has not fully complied with its obligations to disarm under that resolution.
5. The Security Council in resolution 1441 gave Iraq "a final opportunity to comply with its disarmament obligations" and warned Iraq of the "serious consequences" if it did not.
6. The Security Council also decided in resolution 1441 that, if Iraq failed at any time to comply with and cooperate fully in the implementation of resolution 1441, that would constitute a further material breach.
7. It is plain that Iraq has failed to comply and therefore Iraq was at the time of resolution 1441 and continues to be in material breach.
8. Thus, the authority to use force under resolution 678 has revived and so continues today.
9. Resolution 1441 would in terms have provided that a further decision of the Security Council to sanction force was required if that had been intended. Thus, all that resolution 1441 requires is reporting to and discussion by the Security Council of Iraq's failures, but not an express further decision to authorize force.[47]

---

[45] See M. Byers, *Agreeing to Disagree: Security Council Resolution 1441 and Intentional Ambiguity*, 10 GLOBAL GOVERNANCE 165–186 (2004).

[46] W.H. Taft and T. Buchwald, *Pre-emption, Iraq and International Law*, 97 AMERICAN JOURNAL OF INTERNATIONAL LAW 557 (2003).

[47] "Statement by the Attorney General, Lord Goldsmith, in Answer to a Parliamentary Question, Tuesday, 18 March 2003," *The Times* (London), 18 March 2003, p. 2.

Alternatively, were there other international legal bases for such an anti-proliferation oriented use of force against another state? When discussing the justifications for an intervention into Iraq prior to March 2003, U.S. officials particularly focused on the threat that Iraq posed to the United States, through its possession of WMD and connections to international terrorist organizations like al Qaeda.[48] They argued that this threat would only increase in time, as Iraq continued its WMD development programs. They stressed the need for the U.S. to act pre-emptively in order to defend itself by neutralizing this present and future threat. As President Bush stated during his March 17, 2003 televised demand that Saddam Hussein leave Iraq within 48 hours or risk war:

In this century, when evil men plot chemical, biological and nuclear terror, a policy of appeasement could bring destruction of a kind never before seen on this earth. Terrorists and terror states do not reveal these threats with fair notice, in formal declarations— and responding to such enemies only after they have struck first is not self-defense, it is suicide.[49]

President Bush went on to reference the U.N. Security Council resolutions which had been passed on Iraq, and the fruitless efforts of the United States to achieve passage of a further resolution clearly authorizing a renewed intervention campaign against Iraq. Distinguishing the coming action from action carried out under the U.N. paradigm, he went on to state: "The United Nations Security Council has not lived up to its responsibilities, so we will rise to ours."[50]

This policy of pre-emptive military strikes carried out either unilaterally or by an ad hoc coalition of willing states without authorization from the U.N. Security Council, against states and non-state actors who possess WMD and threaten the security of the United States, has come to be known as the "Bush Doctrine" of pre-emptive self-defense. This policy had its first official iteration in an address by President Bush to the graduating class at West Point Military Academy on June 1, 2002:

The gravest danger to freedom lies at the perilous crossroads of radicalism and technology. When the spread of chemical and biological and nuclear weapons, along with ballistic missile technology—when that occurs, even weak states and small groups could attain a catastrophic power to strike great nations. Our enemies have declared this very intention, and have been caught seeking these terrible weapons. They want the capability to

---

[48] J.B. Judis and S. Ackerman, "The Selling of the Iraq War: The First Casualty," *The New Republic Online*, Issue date June 30, 2003. Available at <http://www.tnr.com/doc.mhtml?i= 20030630&s=ackermanjudis063003>; S.R. Weisman, "Pre-emption: Idea with a Lineage Whose Time Has Come," *New York Times*, March 23, 2003; J. Garamone, "Rumsfeld Says Link Between Iraq, al Qaeda 'Not Debatable,'" American Forces Press Service, September 27, 2002. Available at <http://www.defenselink.mil/news/sep2002/n09272002_200209272.html>.

[49] Remarks by the President in Address to the Nation, The Cross Hall. Available at <http://www.whitehouse.gov/news/releases/2003/03/print/20030317-7.html>.

[50] Ibid.

blackmail us, or to harm us, or to harm our friends—and we will oppose them with all our power.

For much of the last century, America's defense relied on the Cold War doctrines of deterrence and containment. In some cases, those strategies still apply. But new threats also require new thinking... We cannot defend America and our friends by hoping for the best. We cannot put our faith in the word of tyrants, who solemnly sign nonproliferation treaties, and then systemically break them. If we wait for threats to fully materialize, we will have waited too long... We must take the battle to the enemy, disrupt his plans, and confront the worst threats before they emerge. In the world we have entered, the only path to safety is the path of action. And this nation will act... [O]ur security will require all Americans to be forward-looking and resolute, to be ready for preemptive action when necessary to defend our liberty and to defend our lives.[51]

The justification of this doctrine of pre-emption by reference to principles of self-defense in international law was included in the 2002 U.S. National Security Strategy Document, which stated:

For centuries, international law recognized that nations need not suffer an attack before they can lawfully take action to defend themselves against forces that present an imminent danger of attack. Legal scholars and international jurists often conditioned the legitimacy of preemption on the existence of an imminent threat—most often a visible mobilization of armies, navies, and air forces preparing to attack. We must adapt the concept of imminent threat to the capabilities and objectives of today's adversaries.[52]

The Bush Doctrine thus represents a legal justification for the 2003 Iraq intervention which is independent of and alternative to that offered in the U.K. Attorney General's opinion.[53]

The presence of both of these legal justificatory arguments in official rhetoric and national policy of the states participating in the intervention raises saliently the question of the proper interpretation of the 2003 Iraq intervention. Was it in fact a relatively straightforward non-proliferation action, i.e. simply an enforcement of non-proliferation law, undertaken legitimately by the established enforcement apparatus and procedures of the associated international organizational structure, as the U.K. Attorney General's arguments would attempt to persuade? Or should the intervention rather be viewed as something different; a counterproliferation action not essentially grounded in the legal structure of the non-proliferation treaties and regimes system, but rather on a theory of unilateral or small ad hoc coalition-based entitlement to engage in international uses of force, even including full-scale military conflict, against specific state(s) or non-state actor(s) considered to pose a WMD

---

[51] Available at <http://www.whitehouse.gov/news/releases/2002/06/20020601-3.html>.
[52] Available at <http://www.whitehouse.gov/nsc/nss.html>.
[53] See G. Simpson, *The War in Iraq and International Law*, 6 MELBOURNE JOURNAL OF INTERNATIONAL LAW 167, 171 (2005).

threat to international peace and security, based upon a non-conventional understanding of the inherent right of states to self-defense? And do either of these theories of anti-proliferation oriented action have any merit under international law?

A. U.N. Security Council Resolutions

There are a number of serious problems with the U.K. Attorney General's arguments, referenced above, which sought to legally ground the 2003 Iraq intervention by reference to Resolution 1441 and other previously passed Security Council resolutions.

First, while much is made by proponents of the Security Council resolution legal basis that Resolution 687 declared in operative paragraph 33 only that a "formal cease fire" was in effect, and not that the conflict was definitively finished, what is not as often referenced is operative paragraph 6 of Resolution 687, in which the Council

[n]otes that as soon as the Secretary-General notifies the Security Council of the completion of the deployment of the United Nations observer unit, the conditions will be established for the Member States cooperating with Kuwait in accordance with resolution 678 (1990) to bring their military presence in Iraq to an end consistent with resolution 686 (1991)...

By this provision, it appears clear that what was to follow the temporary ceasefire between Iraqi forces and military forces acting under Resolution 678's authorization of "all necessary means," was the deployment of another U.N. force with a much more limited mandate; i.e. to safeguard the IAEA and UNSCOM inspectors while they proceeded with their mandate. Once that deployment was complete, the Member States who had acted pursuant to Resolution 678 were to "bring their military presence in Iraq to an end," and this end was to be "consistent with resolution 686." Importantly, in operative paragraph 8 of Resolution 686 this is more clearly termed as a "definitive end to the hostilities." Thus, proponents of the Security Council resolution legal basis for the 2003 intervention make more out of the temporary nature of the "cease fire" declared in operative paragraph 33 of Resolution 687 than is warranted, in light of the fact that this legal status of temporary ceasefire was subsequently replaced by the legal status of the terms of operative paragraph 6 of Resolution 687, which provided for a definitive end to military action in Iraq under the authorization of Resolution 678.

Secondly, and as an additional argument rebutting the conclusion that Resolution 678, which authorized military action against Iraq in 1991, retained legal force on which to base a separate military action against Iraq 12 years later, is the textual construction of Resolution 678 itself. Operative paragraph 2 of Resolution 678 authorizes U.N. member states to use force against Iraq "to

uphold and implement Resolution 660 (1990) and all subsequent relevant resolutions and to restore international peace and security." Resolution 660 and the
other referenced resolutions relevant to Iraq were clearly focused on the invasion
by Iraq of Kuwait, and Resolution 660 is comprised solely of a demand by the
Security Council that Iraq pull its forces out of Kuwait and return its sovereign
status. Once this pullout and restoration was accomplished by April 2003, the
first clause of this paragraph ceased to confer authority upon U.N member states
to use force against Iraq.

The second clause of operative paragraph 2, the authority to "restore international peace and security," has become the basis for the claim by proponents
of the resolutions argument that the authorization to use force against Iraq in
Resolution 678 was still in force, and therefore could be "revived" in 2003 to justify a subsequent military campaign against Iraq. While the breadth of the terms
in the paragraph does permit this argument to be made, in a more circumspect
view of the implications, and future potential applications of this argument, it can
be seen to be a basis for dangerous precedent, and therefore not a persuasive legal
interpretation. The term "restore international peace and security" is commonly
used in Chapter VII resolutions authorizing military force for a simple reason;
this is the term used in Article 42 of the U.N. Charter which gives the Security
Council its authority to mandate such actions. The legal parameters of this term
have never been definitively clarified, however in practice it had never, prior to
the debates over a legal basis for the 2003 Iraq intervention, been referenced as a
basis for separate military actions spread out over a period of more than a decade,
as in this case. This term as used in Chapter VII resolutions, both before and
after the revival of Security Council activity in the 1990s, had been understood
to comport with the Security Council's role as an executive body, responding in
an ad hoc manner to specific, temporary threats to international peace and security as they occurred. In all cases it was understood that once the situation which
triggered the Council's determination of a threat to the peace under Article 39
had ceased to exist, through whatever means, the force of the resolution and the
obligations it imposed were to end.[54]

If this argument were conceded, and because of the common usage of this
term in Security Council resolutions under Chapter VII, all such resolutions
would essentially become a blank check authorizing force against the target state
on an indefinite basis. This is particularly the case if one accepts the complementary argument in the U.K. Attorney General's advice regarding the automati-
city of revival of Chapter VII authorizations of force by objective determination
of member states, and the lack of necessity for a revival of such authority of a

---

[54] See P. Szasz, *The Security Council Starts Legislating*, 96 AMERICAN JOURNAL OF
INTERNATIONAL LAW 901–902 (2002); E. de Wet, THE CHAPTER VII POWERS OF THE UNITED
NATIONS SECURITY COUNCIL (2004) 308–310; M. Koskenniemi, *The Police in the Temple: Order,
Justice and the UN—A Dialectical View*, 6 EUROPEAN JOURNAL OF INTERNATIONAL LAW 325, 339
(1995).

subsequent Security Council resolution. Under this reading, there are an ever increasing number of states which, having once been the subject of a Chapter VII resolution, are now and forever legally sitting ducks who have had their Article 2(4) rights under the Charter revoked indefinitely by a single Security Council resolution. The dangerous implications of such an interpretation of the legal nature of this term, commonly used in Chapter VII resolutions, argues strongly against its adoption.

Thirdly, the argument that a breach of the terms of Resolution 687 per se worked a revival of the authorization to use force against Iraq under Resolution 678 is a completely constructed idea in the U.K. Attorney General's opinion. No textual support for this assertion can be found in either Resolution 678 or Resolution 687.

On the subject of implementation, what Resolution 687 does say in operative paragraph 34 is that the Council itself "Decides to remain seized of the matter and to take such further steps as may be required for the implementation of the present resolution and to secure peace and security in the area." Far from implying an automatic revival of the authorization of member states to use force in Resolution 678 upon a breach of Resolution 687, this Paragraph specifies that it is for the Council, not member states, to take any further enforcement steps which may be required to implement Resolution 687. Thus, though the Council in Resolution 1441 did declare Iraq to be in material breach of its obligations under previous Security Council resolutions, the Council did not stipulate in Resolution 1441 that there would be specific consequences of this breach. On the contrary, the Council, using its declared discretion to determine what "further steps" were required for the implementation of Resolution 687, specifically gave Iraq another opportunity to bring itself into compliance with those obligations. Iraq's behavior with regard to this final opportunity was to be judged by UNMOVIC inspectors, who were to be re-introduced into the country, but whose work was cut short by the invasion on March 19, 2003. This argument of an automatic revival, without further action by the Security Council, of the mandate for member states to use force under Resolution 678 upon breach of Resolution 687 in the U.K. Attorney General's opinion, is therefore without foundation.

Fourthly, the Attorney General's opinion states that the fact of Iraq's non-compliance with the terms of Resolution 1441 was one which was objectively determinable by states themselves, and that no further Security Council resolution was required to confirm this fact before the authority to resume military action against Iraq was revived. This argument fails on a number of grounds. As previously discussed, the mandate to use force under Resolution 678 was given by the Security Council, acting under its Chapter VII powers. Subsequently, the ceasefire and thereafter the definitive end to hostilities declared in Resolution 687 were declared by the Security Council under its Chapter VII authority. It is only logical that if a decision was to be made, the result of which would be to once again revive, or more properly re-authorize the mandate given under

Resolution 678, the Security Council was the only entity empowered to make this decision.

Resolution 1441, indeed, provides the procedural method which was to be applied to enable the Council as a body to potentially make such a determination in the future. In operative paragraph 12, the Council "Decides to convene immediately upon receipt of a report in accordance with paragraphs 4 or 11 above, in order to consider the situation and the need for full compliance with all of the relevant Council resolutions in order to secure international peace and security." Thus, procedurally, a report was to be produced by the re-authorized and empowered UNMOVIC inspectors detailing the current state of Iraq's compliance with Resolution 678. That report was to be considered by the Security Council as a body prior to the Council potentially taking a further decision to re-authorize force by member states against Iraq. The dual notion that this process could be bypassed through the unilateral findings of Iraqi non-compliance by member states, and that an automatic right to use military force would result from this finding, is not supported by the text of Resolution 1441, and more importantly it is not supported by an understanding of the origin and right of exercise of Chapter VII authority, which rests with the Security Council as a body and not with its members individually.

Finally, and perhaps the most disturbing argument advanced by the U.K. Attorney General, is the notion that because Resolution 1441 did not expressly state the need for another Security Council resolution before the authority under Resolution 678 could be revived, the need for a further resolution did not exist, i.e. that in its silence, the Council was acknowledging the validity of the objective discernment of non-compliance and automatic revival of authority arguments. As the Attorney General explained to Parliament regarding the need for another resolution:

Had that been the intention, it would have provided that the Council would decide what needed to be done to restore international peace and security, not that it would consider the matter. The choice of words was deliberate; a proposal that there should be a requirement for a decision by the Council, a position maintained by several Council members, was not adopted.[55]

This argument reveals a deep misapprehension of the fundamental tenets of U.N. Charter law, a correct understanding of which provides the most powerful argument against the Attorney General's position regarding the justification of the 2003 intervention on the basis of Resolution 678. Security Council resolutions do not exist in an authority vacuum. They are exercises of the Security Council's power under Chapter VII of the Charter. However, the Charter has other provisions in addition to the Articles of Chapter VII, and the Council's powers

---

[55] "Iraq: Legal Basis for the Use of Force," annex to "Statement by the Attorney General, Lord Goldsmith," para. 11.

under those Articles must be read in conjunction with those other statements of rights and obligations in order to correctly understand the extent and limitations of the Security Council's powers.[56]

The Articles of Chapter VII, under which U.N. members can be authorized by the Council to use military force against another state, comprise a limited exception to the broad non-intervention obligation contained in Article 2(4) of the Charter, which states, "All Members shall refrain in their international relations from the threat or use of force against the territorial integrity or political independence of any state, or in any other manner inconsistent with the Purposes of the United Nations." This provision has consistently been interpreted by both the General Assembly and the International Court of Justice to comprise a broad and encompassing prohibition against the use of international force.[57] As the General Assembly declared in 1970:

No State or group of States has the right to intervene, directly or indirectly, for any reason whatever, in the internal or external affairs of any other State. Consequently, armed intervention and all other forms of interference or attempted threats against the personality of the State or against its political, economic, or cultural elements, are in violation of international law.[58]

This broad non-intervention norm provides an obligatory backdrop for all U.N. members, and its breach is the inescapable result of any international use of force committed by a U.N. member state which is neither based in the inherent right or self-defense recognized by Article 51, nor the subject of a specific exception to this rule contained in a Chapter VII resolution of the Security Council. Simply put, the rule in Article 2(4) of the Charter establishes a presumption of member state sovereignty which specifically includes non-intervention into the territory, or assault against the independent internal autonomy of any state. This presumption must be specifically overcome either by reference to the self-defense principles of Article 51, or through the clear, explicit, and definitive mandate of the Security Council in a resolution under Chapter VII.[59]

Thus, the silence of the Security Council in Resolution 1441 as to whether such a clear, explicit, and definitive mandate was necessary, has no legal implications. A clear, explicit, and definitive mandate is necessary in order to overcome

---

[56] See Vienna Convention on the Law of Treaties, Article 31 (1969); D. Schweigman, THE AUTHORITY OF THE SECURITY COUNCIL UNDER CHAPTER VII OF THE UN CHARTER (2001) ch. 4. See generally the discussion in Chapter 4 above at 187–189.

[57] *United Kingdom v. Albania*, ICJ Reports 1949, 4; *Nicaragua v. United States*, ICJ Reports 1986, 14, paras 190–191.

[58] Declaration on Principles of International Law concerning Friendly Relations and Co-Operation among States in Accordance with the Charter of the United Nations, GA Res 2625 (XXV) (October 24, 1970) (italics added); Supporting the authoritative status of this Declaration, see Article 31(2) and (3) of the Vienna Convention on the Law of Treaties regarding subsequent agreements by the parties to a treaty and the effect thereof upon treaty interpretation.

[59] See C. Gray, INTERNATIONAL LAW AND THE USE OF FORCE (2nd edn, 2004) ch. 2; M. Byers, WAR LAW (2005) 48.

the presumption of sovereignty established as a fundamental tenet of the U.N. Charter by Article 2(4).

This presumption of sovereignty established by Article 2(4) has been explained further by Jochen Frowein:

An old rule of interpretation of international treaties, frequently invoked before the Vienna Convention on the Law of Treaties, was the rule according to which treaties must be interpreted as respecting the sovereignty of States as far as possible. The idea behind that rule was that States may not be presumed to have given up their sovereign rights in a treaty. The Vienna Convention did not include such a rule. In fact, the International Law Commission was of the opinion that the starting point must always be the intention of the parties as expressed by the specific language of the treaty. This is in line with the nature of a treaty as an instrument in which the consensus among the parties has been expressed.

It is quite different with Security Council resolutions, particularly from the point of view of the state against whom enforcement measures are being taken. Such a resolution is the legal basis for the most severe encroachment upon the sovereignty of a member of the United Nations. It is submitted, therefore, that for the interpretation of such a resolution the old rule according to which limitations of sovereignty may not be lightly assumed is fully justified. Only where the use of force against a sovereign state is clearly authorized by a resolution this is [sic] in fact lawful under United Nations law.[60]

The absence of this clear, explicit, and definitive mandate by the Security Council in the case of the 2003 Iraq intervention places the actions of the U.S. and U.K.-led coalition squarely at odds with this presumption in Article 2(4). These actions thus constitute breaches of international law.[61]

III. Non-proliferation or Counterproliferation?

In summary, the U.K. Attorney General's argument, seeking to provide legal justification for the 2003 Iraq intervention in resolutions passed by the U.N. Security Council, depends upon extreme and unpersuasive interpretations of those resolutions, and upon fundamental misunderstandings of U.N. Charter law. As reviewed herein, more persuasive legal arguments conclude that these resolutions did not provide such a justification, and that the best legal judgment

---

[60] J. Abr. Frowein, "Unilateral Interpretation of Security Council Resolutions—a Threat to Collective Security?" in V. Götz, P. Selmer, and R. Wolfrum (eds), *Liber amicorum Günther Jaenicke—Zum 85. Geburtstag* (1998) 99 (as reprinted in M. Byers, *Agreeing to Disagree: Security Council Resolution 1441 and Intentional Ambiguity*, 10 GLOBAL GOVERNANCE 165–186 (2004).

[61] On arguments regarding the implicit authorization of force by the Security Council and their current status of acceptance by the international community, see C. Gray, INTERNATIONAL LAW AND THE USE OF FORCE (2nd edn, 2004) 264–281.

regarding the actions of the coalition of states which invaded Iraq in 2003 is that those actions were in violation of Article 2(4) of the United Nations Charter.

In fact, this line of legal argumentation is so tenuous and unpersuasive, that the dependence upon it by government lawyers in the U.K. and in other states gives credence to a number of conclusions regarding the circumstances surrounding its adoption. It was long suspected, and has now been persuasively shown by Philippe Sands among others, that this tortured legal analysis of U.N. Security Council resolutions was a line of non-proliferation law justification for the 2003 intervention which, far from being the starting point for considerations regarding that action, was invented by foreign ministry lawyers to provide a veneer of non-proliferation law cover, well after the substantive counterproliferation policy to invade Iraq was decided upon at higher political levels.

In his recent book entitled *Lawless World: America and the Making and Breaking of Global Rules*, Sands summarizes the proceedings of a high-level meeting between U.K. Prime Minister Tony Blair and a number of his cabinet ministers, including the Attorney General and the Foreign Minister, which took place in July 2002:

> They were reminded that the Prime Minister had told President Bush that the U.K. would support military action to bring about regime change, so long as a coalition had been created, the Israel–Palestine crisis was quiescent, and U.N. weapons inspectors had been given a further opportunity to eliminate Iraq's WMD. Those present were told that in Washington military action was now seen as inevitable... The Foreign Minister Jack Straw complained that the case was thin, not least because Saddam Hussein was not threatening neighbors and had a lesser WMD capability than Libya, North Korea or Iran. The meeting also considered the legal issues, including a March 2002 paper prepared by the Foreign Office legal advisers... The Attorney General confirmed that self-defense and humanitarian intervention were not justified, and that as matters then stood, claiming the authorization of the Security Council would be difficult. The Attorney General was instructed to consider legal advice with the Foreign Office and Ministry of Defence. The chosen route was to build up the intelligence to support the claim that Saddam had weapons of mass destruction, which could provide a potential legal justification. This meant persuading Bush to take the United Nations route, which Blair achieved by working with Colin Powell.[62]

This sequence of consideration makes it clear that the enforcement of Security Council resolutions and other breaches of substantive non-proliferation law by Iraq were a mere afterthought to policymakers considering the invasion of Iraq.[63] These justifications, based in the non-proliferation treaties and regimes system, were considered only after the decision to go to war had already been made on other grounds. The precise reasons for the decision by policymakers

---

[62] At 182–184 (Penguin, 2005).
[63] See also T. Friedman, "Because We Could," *New York Times*, June 4, 2003, at A31; S. McClellan, WHAT HAPPENED: INSIDE THE BUSH WHITE HOUSE AND WASHINGTON'S CULTURE OF DECEPTION (2008).

in the various coalition-state capitols to invade Iraq were undoubtedly complex and varied as among the states concerned, and will not be thoroughly analyzed herein. However, it is clear that at the highest levels of power, both in the United States and the United Kingdom, the enforcement of non-proliferation law was not among the primary motivating forces behind the decision to invade Iraq in 2003. With this understanding, the tenuousness of the legal arguments constructed to support this decision in non-proliferation law terms, become less surprising.

These considerations, both of political process and legal dubiousness, taken together, make the interpretive application to the 2003 Iraq intervention of the non-proliferation law and policy framework flatly unpersuasive. The Bush doctrine of counterproliferation-oriented pre-emptive military strikes, and its legal justification in self-defense law, comport much more closely with the pre-war statements of both U.S. President Bush and U.K. Prime Minister Blair regarding Iraq, which focused on the potential threat that Iraq posed to regional peace through possession of WMD, as well as to their own states through connections between the Iraqi administration and international terrorist groups, and the need to act pre-emptively in order to counter those threats before they were realized.

As Prime Minister Blair stated in the introductory section to the September 2002 dossier containing U.K. intelligence assessments of Iraq's WMD program:

I am in no doubt that the threat is serious and current, that [Saddam] has made progress on WMD, and that he has to be stopped. Saddam has used chemical weapons, not only against an enemy state, but against his own people. Intelligence reports make clear that he sees the building up of his WMD capability, and the belief overseas that he would use these weapons, as vital to his strategic interests, and in particular his goal of regional domination. And the document discloses that his military planning allows for some of the WMD to be ready within 45 minutes of an order to use them...In today's inter-dependent world, a major regional conflict does not stay confined to the region in question...The threat posed to international peace and security, when WMD are in the hands of a brutal and aggressive regime like Saddam's, is real. Unless we face up to the threat, not only do we risk undermining the authority of the UN, whose resolutions he defies, but more importantly and in the longer term, we place at risk the lives and prosperity of our own people.[64]

This rhetoric expresses a fairly classic counterproliferation strategy; to act proactively and forcefully, through unilateral or ad hoc coalition-based military action, in order to degrade or pre-empt a specific WMD threat posed against one's allies or against oneself. This, again, differs from non-proliferation strategy, which emphasizes diplomatic efforts through established international legal institutions and other international negotiating fora, and measures taken under the authority of international legal institutions, including the United Nations, to enforce established obligations under non-proliferation law.

---

[64] As reprinted in *The Guardian*, September 24, 2002. Available at <http://www.guardian.co.uk/Iraq/Story/0,,797883,00.html>.

The Security Council resolutions argument advanced by the U.K. Attorney General does succeed in muddying the conceptual water a bit in attempting this justification. As intended, it cleverly uses the sources of law and institutions associated with the non-proliferation treaties and regimes system in an attempt to cast the intervention simply as an enforcement action, duly authorized by the institutions of the international legal system. In the final analysis, however, because of the focus in official rhetoric not primarily upon Iraq's breaches of non-proliferation law per se as the primary reason for the intervention, but rather on the threat posed by Iraq's suspected WMD program to regional peace and stability, and to the intervening states themselves, and the need to act pre-emptively to counter that specific threat, the 2003 Iraq intervention fits much better under the counterproliferation paradigm than it does under the non-proliferation paradigm.

While at first blush this distinction between non-proliferation strategy and counterproliferation strategy may seem solely academic, the point of this analysis is to accurately categorize the actions of the coalition so that the proper lessons can be learned from it, and particularly from its failures, and applied to consideration of the future place of counterproliferation policies in national and international anti-proliferation strategy.

IV. Legal Issues

The first failing of the 2003 Iraq intervention as a manifestation of counterproliferation strategy based in international use of force law, was the failure of its proponents under this theory to provide a satisfactory legal basis for it, either by reference to existing treaty and customary law, or as a proposal to change existing customary law. The failure of the self-defense law argument in the context of the Iraq intervention has been explicated in detail in a myriad academic treatments since the war began, and this consensus judgment of the vast majority of objective, independent international lawyers has become clear.[65]

The basic legal point of reference, of course, is the U.N. Charter, which is the fundamental international legal source governing international uses of force. As

---

[65] See, e.g., G. Simpson, *The War in Iraq and International Law*, 6 MELBOURNE JOURNAL OF INTERNATIONAL LAW 167, 171 (2005); M. Byers, *Letting the Exception Prove the Rule*, 17 ETHICS AND INTERNATIONAL AFFAIRS 9 (2003); S. Chesterman, *Just War or Just Peace After September 11: Axes of Evil and Wars Against Terror in Iraq and Beyond*, 37 NEW YORK UNIVERSITY JOURNAL OF INTERNATIONAL LAW & POLICY 281 (2005); M. Shapiro, *Iraq: The Shifting Sands of Preemptive Self-Defense*, 97 AMERICAN JOURNAL OF INTERNATIONAL LAW 599 (2003), T. Franck, *What Happens Now? The United Nations after Iraq*, 97 AMERICAN JOURNAL OF INTERNATIONAL LAW 607 (2003); J. Habermas, *Interpreting the Fall of a Monument*, 4 GERMAN LAW JOURNAL 701 (2003); M.E. O'Connell, *Preserving the Peace: The Continuing Ban on War Between States*, 38 CALIFORNIA WESTERN INTERNATIONAL LAW JOURNAL 41 (2007); S. Murphy, *Assessing the Legality of Invading Iraq*, 92 GEORGETOWN LAW REVIEW 173, 177 (2005).

discussed above, in addition to the exception to the Article 2(4) non-intervention norm provided in the articles of Chapter VII, the only other exception to this obligation is found in Article 51, which recognizes the inherent right of states to self-defense.[66] In its entirety, Article 51 provides:

Nothing in the present Charter shall impair the inherent right of individual or collective self-defence if an armed attack occurs against a Member of the United Nations, until the Security Council has taken measures necessary to maintain international peace and security. Measures taken by Members in the exercise of this right of self-defence shall be immediately reported to the Security Council and shall not in any way affect the authority and responsibility of the Security Council under the present Charter to take at any time such action as it deems necessary in order to maintain or restore international peace and security.

Article 51 thus recognizes a temporary right of U.N. member states to take unilateral actions in self-defense "if an armed attack occurs" against them. With regard to the U.N. Charter's association with non-proliferation law, just as the articles of Chapter VII of the Charter may be understood to provide the Security Council a delineated role in enforcement of non-proliferation law obligations, similarly Article 51 may be understood to recognize a more limited enforcement role for U.N. member states themselves to engage in unilateral uses of international force against possessors of WMD, in delineated circumstances and subject to conditions imposed by both treaty and customary law.

Voluminous commentary has been produced on the meaning of the terms of Article 51, including upon the correct interpretation of the term "if an armed attack occurs."[67] If one employs the standard rules of treaty interpretation contained in Articles 31 and 32 of the 1969 Vienna Convention on the Law of Treaties, which mandates that the "ordinary meaning" of the terms is given primacy in interpretation, a solid argument can be made that the Article 51 right of self-defense can only be triggered subsequent to an armed attack having been made upon the state wishing to invoke that right, or at the earliest, as the attack is occurring. Ian Brownlie has argued this position thus:

[W]here the Charter has a specific provision relating to a particular legal category, to assert that this does not restrict the wider ambit of the customary law relating to that category or problem is to go beyond the bounds of logic. Why have treaty provisions at all?...It is submitted that a restrictive interpretation of the provisions of the Charter relating to the use of force would be more justifiable and that even as a matter of "plain" interpretation the permission in Article 51 is exceptional in the context of the Charter and exclusive of any customary right of self-defence.[68]

---

[66] See C. Gray, INTERNATIONAL LAW AND THE USE OF FORCE (2nd edn, 2004) ch. 4.

[67] See, e.g., *Nicaragua v United States of America* ICJ Reports 1986, 14; *Islamic Republic of Iran v United States of America,* ICJ Reports 2003, 16.

[68] I. Brownlie, INTERNATIONAL LAW AND THE USE OF FORCE BY STATES (1963) 156; See also B. Simma et al. (eds.), THE CHARTER OF THE UNITED NATIONS (2nd edn, 2002) 792; A. Rifaat, INTERNATIONAL AGGRESSION: A STUDY OF THE LEGAL CONCEPT (1979).

Brownlie's critique in this context was made to counter arguments which have been made to the effect that, notwithstanding the arguably plain meaning of the term "if an armed attack occurs," the description of the right in Article 51 as an "inherent right" implies that this treaty article was merely a codification of an already existing customary law right, and that it therefore must be read as being informed by the pre-existing scope and substance of that customary right. As Derek Bowett has argued:

> It is . . . fallacious to assume that members have only those rights which the Charter accords to them; on the contrary they have those rights which general international law accords to them except in so far as they have surrendered them under the Charter . . . [T]he view of Committee I at San Francisco was that this prohibition [Article 2(4)] left the right of self-defense unimpaired.[69]

Although addressing a different substantive question at the time, the ICJ in its 1986 *Nicaragua* decision lent support to this argument by holding that:

> Article 51 of the Charter is only meaningful on the basis that there is a 'natural' or 'inherent' right of self-defence, and it is hard to see how this can be other than of a customary nature . . . Moreover the Charter, having itself recognized the existence of this right, does not go on to regulate directly all aspects of its content. For example, it does not contain any specific rule whereby self-defence would warrant only measures which are proportional to the armed attack and necessary to respond to it, a rule well-established in customary international law. Moreover, a definition of the 'armed attack' which, if found to exist, authorizes the exercise of the 'inherent right' of self-defence, is not provided in the Charter, and is not part of treaty law. It cannot therefore be held that Article 51 is a provision which "subsumes and supervenes" customary international law. It rather demonstrates that in the field in question . . . customary international law continues to exist alongside treaty law.[70]

The principle in pre-Charter customary law which has caused the most controversy in the context of the interpretation of Article 51 is the right of anticipatory self-defense, which was recognized by both U.S. and U.K. diplomats in their correspondence during the 1841 *Caroline* incident. The following statement by Daniel Webster, U.S. Secretary of State at the time, has been generally accepted as a correct statement of this principle of customary international law pertaining at the time, inclusive of its substantive limiting principles of imminence, necessity, and proportionality:[71]

Mr. Webster to Mr. Fox (April 24, 1841)

It will be for . . . [Her Majesty's] Government to show a necessity of self-defense, instant, overwhelming, leaving no choice of means, and no moment for deliberation. It will be for

---

[69] D. Bowett, SELF-DEFENCE IN INTERNATIONAL LAW (1958) 185; See also M. McDougal and F. Feliciano, LAW AND MINIMUM WORLD PUBLIC ORDER (1961).
[70] Para. 176.
[71] See M. Shaw, INTERNATIONAL LAW (5th edn, 2003) 1024–1025. See also the Dissenting Opinion of Judge Schwebel in the *Nicaragua* Case, para. 200, in which he argues that the *Caroline* criteria are exclusively applicable to cases of anticipatory self-defense.

it to show, also, that the local authorities of Canada, even supposing the necessity of the moment authorised them to enter the territories of the United States at all, did nothing unreasonable or excessive; since the act, justified by the necessity of self-defense, must be limited by that necessity, and kept clearly within it.[72]

Ian Brownlie has suggested that state practice in between 1841 and 1945 served to even further limit the flexibility of the principle of anticipatory self-defense, leaving it in a tenuous state of existence at the time of drafting of the U.N. Charter.[73] This position would seem to be supported through even more recent events, such as the 1981 pre-emptive attack by Israel against the Iraqi nuclear reactor at Osirak. Resolution 487 of the U.N. Security Council, which was adopted unanimously, denounced the incident as a "clear violation of the Charter of the United Nations" notwithstanding Israel's reasonable (and later validated) claim regarding Iraq's nuclear weapons program and its connection to the site.[74] As Christine Gray has observed:

[T]he actual invocation of the right to anticipatory self-defense in practice is rare. States clearly prefer to rely on self-defense in response to an armed attack if they possibly can. In practice they prefer to take a wide view of armed attack rather than openly claim anticipatory self-defense. It is only when no conceivable case can be made that there has been an armed attack that they resort to anticipatory self-defense. This reluctance expressly to invoke anticipatory self-defense is in itself a clear indication of the doubtful status of this justification for the use of force. States take care to try to secure the widest possible support; they do not invoke a doctrine that they know will be unacceptable to the vast

---

[72] See THE PAPERS OF DANIEL WEBSTER, DIPLOMATIC PAPERS, 1841–1843, at 43 (K.E. Shewmaker et al. (eds), 1983). The *Caroline* was a U.S. registered steamer hired to ferry provisions across the Niagara river to supply Canadian rebels taking part in the insurrection against British colonial rule of Canada in 1837. On December 29, several boatloads of British soldiers came across the river onto the U.S. side and set fire to the *Caroline*, dragged her into the river current, and sent her blazing over Niagara Falls, killing one man in the process. The ensuing diplomatic correspondence between U.S. and U.K. officials has come to be regarded as a reliable statement of contemporary customary international law on anticipatory self-defense. On the principles of necessity and proportionality in customary international law, see I. Brownlie, INTERNATIONAL LAW AND THE USE OF FORCE BY STATES (1963) 257–264.

[73] I. Brownlie, PRINCIPLES OF PUBLIC INTERNATIONAL LAW (6th edn, 2003) 702.

[74] See L.Rene Beres and Y. Tsiddon-Chatto, " 'Sorry' Seems to be the Hardest Word" *The Jerusalem Post*, June 9, 2003; A. D'Amato, *Israel's Air Strike upon the Iraqi Nuclear Reactor*, 77 AMERICAN JOURNAL OF INTERNATIONAL LAW 584 (1983). On September 6, 2007, Israeli warplanes attacked and destroyed a site in Syria which was later claimed to be a nuclear reactor site, constructed with the help of North Korea. Information about the attack and the site have been difficult for the general public to discern, as both Israel and Syria have been less than forthcoming about the incident. Some details came to public light in April of 2008 when U.S. intelligence services gave a briefing to the U.S. Congress on the event. Due to the paucity of confirmed facts regarding the site and the attack, international opinion has at the time of this writing been difficult to gauge. Some have argued that the absence of formal censure by states has amounted to a tacit acquiescence to the strike. However the lack of certainty regarding the details of the site and the attack likely make such assessments premature. See R. Wright, "N. Koreans Taped At Syrian Reactor: Video Played a Role in Israeli Raid," *Washington Post*, Thursday, April 24, 2008; D.E. Sanger, "U.S. Sees N. Korean Links to Reactor," *New York Times*, April 24, 2008; M. Gordon and E. Schmitt, "U.S. Says Israeli Exercise Seemed Directed at Iran," *New York Times*, June 20, 2008.

majority of states. Certain writers, however, ignore this choice by states and argue that if states in fact act in anticipation of an armed attack this should count as anticipatory self-defense in state practice. This is another example of certain writers going beyond what states themselves say in justification of their action in order to argue for a wide right of self defense... A few of these commentators seem prepared to treat any US action as a precedent creating new legal justification for the use of force. Thus they use US actions as shifting the Charter paradigm and extending the right of self-defense. The lack of effective action against the USA as a sanction confirms them in this view. But the vast majority of other states remained firmly attached to a narrow conception of self-defense... The clear trend in state practice before 9/11 was to try to bring the action within Article 51 and to claim the existence of an armed attack rather than to argue expressly for a wider right under customary international law.[75]

However, even if one accepts the existence of the right of anticipatory self-defense, as iterated in the *Caroline* correspondence, and its legal validity as part of the contours of the Article 51 right of self-defense, this right of anticipatory self-defense clearly does not provide a sufficient legal basis for the 2003 Iraq intervention. The threat posed by Iraq's suspected WMD stockpiles, and its alleged connections to international terrorist networks, even if either had in fact existed, did not present a threat to either the U.S. or the U.K. that could, with a straight face, be characterized as presenting "a necessity of self-defense, instant, overwhelming, leaving no choice of means, and no moment for deliberation." This fact was recognized prior to the intervention by U.K. ministers, which recognition led them to seek for a legal grounding for the intervention in Security Council resolutions.[76] In the 2002 U.S. National Security Strategy document as well, this inability to legally ground counterproliferation-oriented pre-emptive military actions on existing self-defense law was also conceded. After essentially correctly describing the requirement of imminence in the customary right of anticipatory self-defense, the document states "We must adapt the concept of imminent threat to the capabilities and objectives of today's adversaries," thus recognizing that the sort of pre-emptive actions against possessors of WMD supported by the document would require a change to existing international law.[77]

Even if the imminence criterion were to be met in this case, it is important to remember that this is not the only requirement, nor as some would argue the

---

[75] C. Gray, INTERNATIONAL LAW AND THE USE OF FORCE, (2nd edn, 2004) 130, 133, 134. See also C. Gray, "The Principle of Non-Use of Force," in V. Lowe and C. Warbrick (eds.), THE UNITED NATIONS AND THE PRINCIPLES OF INTERNATIONAL LAW (1994); C. Gray, *The Use and Abuse of the International Court of Justice: Cases concerning the Use of Force after Nicaragua*, 14 EUROPEAN JOURNAL OF INTERNATIONAL LAW 867 (2003). For contrasting opinions on the subject of state practice in the area of anticipatory self-defense, see A. Arend and R. Beck, INTERNATIONAL LAW AND THE USE OF FORCE: BEYOND THE UN CHARTER PARADIGM (1993); M. Weisburd, USE OF FORCE (1997).

[76] See P. Sands, LAWLESS WORLD: AMERICA AND THE MAKING AND BREAKING OF GLOBAL RULES (2005) 182–184.

[77] Available at <http://www.whitehouse.gov/nsc/nss.html>.

most important requirement, imposed by customary international law upon international uses of force in self-defense. Whether of a reactive or anticipatory nature, all international uses of force in self-defense must meet the customary law requirements of necessity and proportionality.[78] The determination of necessity and proportionality is essentially a fact-based inquiry, and there is a relative paucity of cases which have been decided by international tribunals, in which clarification of the scope of these principles can be found. In the current author's opinion it is likely that neither of these criteria were met in the case of the 2003 Iraq intervention and succeeding occupation.

While debateable, the necessity of the intervention as a use of force in self-defense seems dubious, inter alia in consideration of the number and character of the states carrying out the intervention. None of these states, and certainly not the states taking leading roles in the operation, could have easily established that Iraq posed a direct threat to their own national security to any threshold of evidence beyond the speculative. Furthermore, the number of states in the intervening coalition and its diverse geographic make-up argue persuasively for the characterization of the intervention as one purposed in the promotion of collective security, and not the particularized self-defense of any one of the intervening states more than others. The spirit of the Charter system for use of force regulation would appear to impose upon an action possessed of these characteristics the requirement of prior, explicit authorization by the Security Council pursuant to its Chapter VII powers, and would be pained in the extreme to accord to it the legitimizing characterization of a necessary unilateral use of force in self-defense pursuant to Article 51.

As to proportionality, there is particular evidence of state practice supporting the notion that international uses of force which are followed by occupation, and particularly lengthy occupation, are extremely difficult to justify as proportionate uses of force in self-defense. For example, the Security Council repeatedly condemned both Israel's occupation of South Lebanon from 1978 to 2000 as well as South Africa's occupation of an area of Angola from 1981 to 1988 as being neither necessary nor proportionate, though both were argued to be legitimate uses of force in self-defense.[79] Given the limited nature of the direct security threat understood to be posed by Iraq toward coalition states themselves at the initiation of the intervention in March of 2003, the succeeding scope of the invasion inclusive of the toppling of the Government of Iraq, and the occupation of the state of Iraq by coalition forces which continues effectively, if not formally, to the

---

[78] See *Military and Paramilitary Activities in and Against Nicaragua*, ICJ Reports 1986, 14, para. 237; *Legality of the Threat or Use of Nuclear Weapons*, ICJ Reports 1996, 226, para. 141; *Islamic Republic of Iran v United States of America*, ICJ Reports 2003, 161, para. 43; C. Gray, INTERNATIONAL LAW AND THE USE OF FORCE (2nd edn, 2004) 120–126.

[79] On Israel, see 1978 UNYB 295, 306 and Security Council Resolution 425; On South Africa, see 1982 UNYB 312 and Security Council Resolution 545; C. Gray, INTERNATIONAL LAW AND THE USE OF FORCE (2nd edn, 2004) 126. ("Necessity and proportionality are also crucial in the rejection by states of the legality of prolonged occupation of territory in the name of self-defense.")

time of this writing in early 2008, are facts which argue persuasively against the proportionality of this use of force against Iraq.

In order to provide a legal basis for the Bush Doctrine of counterproliferation-oriented pre-emptive strikes, which mandates military strikes against states and non-state actors which are alleged to be developing, or in possession of WMD, and which are adjudged to present a threat either of direct use or of proliferation of those WMD to other dangerous actors, the right of self-defense recognized under Article 51 would need to be revised. The scope of this chapter will not allow a thorough treatment of the possible alternatives for revising this legal entitlement, nor of the likely effectiveness and juridical soundness of a right of pre-emptive self-defense so revised, though consideration will turn to these subjects in Chapter 9 hereafter. One point in this context, however—the argument that the 2003 Iraq intervention can be seen as an instance of state practice and related *opinio juris* in furtherance of a change to existing customary law, and that as such the intervention itself was legal in addition to contributing to the development of a revised custom-based right on which future forceful counterproliferation actions can be based—will be briefly reviewed.

Customary international law can indeed be modified by state practice which is inconsistent with a settled customary rule, if that practice is accompanied by *opinio juris* to the effect that the modified rule is consistent with elements of the already established rule.[80] This process has been described by the International Court of Justice in its 1986 *Nicaragua* judgment as occurring "if a state acts in a way *prima facie* inconsistent with a recognized rule, but defends its conduct by appealing to exceptions or justifications contained within the rule itself…"[81] In the same decision the Court further observed that "reliance by a state on a novel right, or an unprecedented exception to the principle might, if shared in principle by other states, tend toward a modification of customary international law."[82] If a state acts with this *opinio juris*, and if that novel justification is accepted by a large enough number of other states so as to provide a basis for concluding that a new rule of customary international law should be adopted in modification of an existing rule, the acting state's conduct is legal and additionally contributes as one instance of state practice toward the development of the new modified rule.[83]

---

[80] H. Thirlway, *The Sources of International Law*, in M. Evans (ed.), INTERNATIONAL LAW (2nd edn, 2006) 27.

[81] Para. 186.   [82] Para. 207.

[83] This process of the development of customary law at variance to existing custom is essentially similar in spirit to the observation in the 1969 Vienna Convention on the Law of Treaties, Article 31(3)(b), that in interpreting a treaty provision one should "take[] into account together with the context:…any subsequent practice in the application of the treaty which establishes the agreement of the parties regarding its interpretation." An analysis of this interpretive rule in the context of Article 51 of the U.N. Charter would proceed along the same lines as that related to amendment of custom, and would similarly fail to show sufficient practice to evidence an agreement of U.N. members that Article 51 should be interpreted to include an altered right of anticipatory or pre-emptive self-defense to that iterated in the *Caroline* case.

In the specific case of the 2003 Iraq intervention, while the statements of U.S. officials in the period leading up to the use of military force did seek to ground that act upon a principle of self-defense, there was never expressed an *opinio juris* which could be construed as proposing that the intervention, while not in compliance with existing international law, was justifiable as a modification of settled customary law principles. Indeed, to expect such a nuanced statement from political officials, conceding that the action was not in accordance with existing law, but was justifiable on the basis of this rather arcane rule of customary international law formation is likely unrealistic. However, U.S. government lawyers, from whom such a statement might be more reasonably expected, were silent as to even the possibility of legally justifying the intervention on self-defense law, let alone upon a customary modification of existing self-defense law. Interestingly, the legal justification adopted by U.S. State Department lawyers, as contained in an article in the *American Journal of International Law* co-written by the department's Legal Advisor William Taft, was centered upon the Security Council resolutions argument reviewed earlier.[84] Thus, as between U.S. political and legal officials, there appears to have been a marked lack of coordination, if not disagreement, regarding the legal principles on which the intervention was to be justified. Because of this lack of clear *opinio juris*, U.S. participation in the 2003 Iraq intervention cannot be justified as a proposed modification of existing customary law on self-defense.[85]

It is instructive for consideration of the future prospects for modification of international use of force law to include a counterproliferation right of pre-emption along the lines of that contained in the Bush doctrine, to note that the reason both political and legal officials did not make greater reference in their public statements to a pre-emptive self-defense right to justify the Iraq intervention was likely a reluctance to establish such a right in international law. Though such a right would have served their immediate purposes, officials surely realized that the formal establishment of such a doctrine in international use of force law could lead to the opening of a Pandora's box of dangers, as the right of counterproliferation-oriented pre-emptive strikes would then be referenceable by any state to justify actions which might be a source of great concern to the states considering action against Iraq. This long-term danger likely was perceived to outweigh the usefulness of a clearer legal justification based in self-defense law for the Iraq intervention in the minds of U.S. policymakers as well as legal advisors.

---

[84] W.H. Taft and T. Buchwald, *Pre-emption, Iraq and International Law*, 97 AMERICAN JOURNAL OF INTERNATIONAL LAW 557 (2003).

[85] On conflict of laws principles which would obtain if such a customary rule were to develop in conflict with U.N. Charter Article 51, see the analogous analysis of customary law in the humanitarian intervention context in D.H. Joyner, *The Kosovo Intervention: Legal Analysis and a More Persuasive Paradigm*, 13 EUROPEAN JOURNAL OF INTERNATIONAL LAW 597 (2002).

This was not a new calculus of the utility of legal vagueness in the sources of international use of force law. The same considerations of short-term usefulness of a customary law modification versus the long-term benefits of a clear, though contradictory treaty rule had resulted in the decision by intervening states in the context of the 1999 Kosovo intervention not to rely on a customary right of humanitarian intervention in order to mediate the obligations of Article 2(4), though such an argument would have given increased legal credibility to the immediate action.[86] Again in that context, it was feared that the actual establishment of such a legal right could provide legal cover for too many actions of dubious object by less well-meaning states, simply clothed in the garb of humanitarian intervention. Thus, in both cases the decision was made to more blatantly breach existing law when an argument for modification could at least to a degree have smoothed the legal road in the short term, out of a concern for the effects in international politics of the universal establishment of a modified customary right to use force.

In summary, then, the 2003 Iraq intervention by a coalition of states led by the U.S. and U.K. cannot be legally justified by reference either to existing international use of force law or to a legitimate effort to modify customary international law in this area. As such, without alternative legal justification, the action must be seen as a breach of U.N. Charter Article 2(4). This legal failing of the intervention as a manifestation of counterproliferation strategy is important because, while the intervention itself is unique, the principle of counterproliferation-oriented pre-emptive military strikes, which the intervention embodies, is an ongoing element of the stated foreign policy of the United States as well as a number of other states including Russia, Japan, Australia, Israel, and the United Kingdom.[87] There is every reason to expect that the legal challenges which will attend future actions in manifestation of this counterproliferation principle will be similar to those present in the 2003 Iraq case. Solutions to these problems which were not devised by officials and lawyers of the intervening states in this case will need to be devised if such future actions are to be deemed consistent with international use of force law.[88]

Before leaving the subject of international use of force law and the potentiality (unrealized in the Iraq intervention) of amendment to the meaning of Article 51 of the U.N. Charter to include a broader right of pre-emptive use of force than is

---

[86] Ibid.

[87] See below Chapter 6, n. 18.

[88] A legal justification of the 2003 Iraq intervention by reference to humanitarian intervention legal principles is not considered in this paper. This theory has been mentioned by some writers but in the present author's view this is both procedurally irrelevant and substantively meritless. Not only is there no *opinio juris* on the part of coalition state officials to base a claim in such a principle of customary international law, such that the issue is not effectively raised in this case, but the author has also elsewhere argued against the existence of the principle itself. See D.H. Joyner, *The Kosovo Intervention: Legal Analysis and a More Persuasive Paradigm*, 13 EUROPEAN JOURNAL OF INTERNATIONAL LAW 597 (2002).

currently allowed, even through incorporation of pre-Charter custom regarding anticipatory self-defense, and leaving aside larger questions of whether a satisfactory rule of counterproliferation-oriented pre-emptive use of force could ever be constructed as will be addressed in Chapter 9, the more discrete question of what specific acts of force might be justified by reference to a hypothetical broader right of pre-emptive use of force once established merits some brief consideration.

Pre-emptive international uses of force against developing WMD threats would of course, as any international use of force, have to be prosecuted in a manner which meets the requirements of proportionality, as that principle has developed both in international use of force law as well as in international humanitarian law.[89] For example, in the case of a use of force against a state alleged to be engaged in an illegal or otherwise threatening WMD development program, which has not yet produced weapons which pose a threat of *Caroline* imminence, the question arises, what would be the proper moment of threat to which the consideration of proportionality should be keyed? The moment of threat of the development program as it currently exists, or alternatively the moment of threat of the WMD development program as it may become, inclusive of its potential production of completed WMD? This determination of where along the line of present and potential maturity consideration of proportionality should be keyed to would be fundamental to a determination of what actions could be justified as proportionate in response to the threat.

If the consideration of proportionality is keyed to the development program itself, the threat of which per se to other countries would be low, uses of force which produce even minimal casualties on the part of the target state might well be seen to be disproportionate to the threat posed under U.N. Charter Article 51 proportionality analysis as well as under Article 51(5)(b) of the 1977 Additional Protocol I to the 1949 Geneva Conventions. This fact might preclude outright the use of aerial bombardment as a mode of attack upon facilities in some instances, due to the potential for collateral civilian casualties resulting even from "targeted" aerial strikes (e.g. of the type reportedly currently being considered by Israel in order to degrade Iran's suspected nuclear weapons program).[90]

However, since the potential threat which may be caused by the continuance of a WMD development program and its eventual culmination in the production of weapons is extremely difficult to predict at any point *ex ante* to its full maturity, a lesson amply demonstrated by the Iraq intervention of 2003, the only objectively measurable moment to which to key proportionality analysis would arguably be the threat of the development program as it currently exists at the time of attack. As above concluded, this determination will render minimal the collateral damage which would be deemed to be proportional resulting from a range

---

[89] See, e.g., *Advisory Opinion on the Threat or Use of Nuclear Weapons*, ICJ Reports 1996, para. 41; Article 51(5)(b) of the 1977 Additional Protocol I to the 1949 Geneva Conventions.
[90] See "U.S. Says Israeli Exercise Seemed Directed at Iran," *New York Times*, June 20, 2008.

of counterproliferation-oriented pre-emptive uses of force, based upon a broader hypothetical right of anticipatory self-defense than that currently enshrined in Article 51.

This consideration of the principle of proportionality, and the limits which it would place upon uses of force justified under a broader right of pre-emption serves to illustrate the low marginal additional utility which the establishment of such a rule would produce.

V. Policy/Practical Issues

However, the failings of the 2003 Iraq intervention are instructive in considering not only if counterproliferation actions can be legally justified, but also whether counterproliferation-oriented use of pre-emptive force is likely to be a practically feasible and effective doctrine for accomplishing the broader aims of international anti-proliferation efforts. These failings illustrate a number of formidable difficulties that will attend counterproliferation strategies as they are increasingly integrated into national foreign and defense policies.

A. Intelligence Accuracy

The most significant of these difficulties relate to intelligence, in terms of its collection, analysis, and sharing. In the final analysis, counterproliferation-oriented pre-emptive/preventive military strikes are all about intelligence, and intelligence, as the 2003 Iraq intervention proved beyond any doubt, is an art and not a science. The case of the Iraq intervention casts into serious doubt the suitability of the use of this art to provide a reliable factual basis on which to ground counterproliferation actions.

First there is the question of the accuracy of intelligence collection and analysis in preparation for, and used as the basis for legitimizing, counterproliferation-oriented pre-emptive strikes. In the case of the 2003 Iraq intervention, as discussed above, it has now become clear that the intelligence assessments made *ex ante* by coalition governments were significantly in error. Post-war inspections on the ground in Iraq have confirmed that assessments of Iraq's capabilities in all three WMD technology areas, in addition to missiles and other delivery devices, were either significantly exaggerated or completely groundless.[91] Similarly, pre-war assessments of Iraq's links to international terrorist organizations, and to the al Qaeda organization specifically, have now been found to have been entirely

---

[91] See, e.g., U.S. Senate, "Senate Report on the U.S. Intelligence Community's Pre-War Intelligence Assessments on Iraq," July 7, 2004. Available at <http://intelligence.senate.gov/iraqreport2.pdf>.

specious.[92] These intelligence gathering and analysis failures are a severe blow to the credibility of claims that a high degree of certainty can be achieved regarding an adversarial state or non-state actor's WMD capabilities and intentions, and that such intelligence assessments can reliably serve as a basis for a pre-emptive counterproliferation action. In this case, the most sophisticated and well-resourced intelligence agencies in the world were apparently essentially in agreement on seriously flawed intelligence assessments regarding the status of Iraq's WMD programs as well as the nature of the threat that Iraq potentially posed with them.

The Iraq case presents a particularly useful example of the problems faced by intelligence agencies in producing an accurate assessment of a state or non-state actor's WMD capabilities, when the target state is not only engaging in serious efforts to keep information on such programs secret, but is also intentionally presenting false information about those programs; either through positive statements of exaggerated ability, or simply by denying outside verification of information, which gives rise (as intended) to a suspicion of illicit activity. However, such counter-intelligence efforts should be expected in future cases where a state or on-state actor perceives itself being vetted as a candidate for pre-emptive counterproliferation action.

While a number of high-level government reports have been generated on the failings of intelligence assessment at the level of intelligence agencies within coalition governments, as of this writing in early 2008 none has yet been produced on the way those raw intelligence assessments were used by political officials in order to make the case to their respective publics for the necessity and justifiability of the intervention.[93] Thus, it is difficult to make conclusions regarding failures in the intelligence assessment and presentation process at this level. However the use or misuse of intelligence assessments by political officials is undoubtedly another point at which the imperfect nature of the use of intelligence as a basis for pre-emptive war can be perceived.

Such a significant failure to produce accurate intelligence assessments on which to base an action of this magnitude and potential destabilizing effect upon an area as sensitive as the Middle-East, will cast a long shadow into the future upon arguments that counterproliferation-oriented pre-emptive military strikes are a prudent part of a state's anti-proliferation policy framework. This new public mistrust of official statements regarding the WMD capability of states suspected of having clandestine WMD programs can be seen in popular responses to more recent claims regarding the status and direction of Iran's nuclear programs. These negative repercussions for the willingness of the public to trust such statements, as well as the chilling effect upon national officials to act on such assessments,

---

[92] See "Hussein's Iraq and al Qaeda Not Linked, Pentagon Says," CNN.com, March 14, 2008.
[93] Such a report by the U.S. Senate Intelligence Committee is expected later this year.

lest the outcome be as politically disastrous as has been the Iraq intervention, will doubtless continue for many years to come.

Overall, the failings of the 2003 Iraq intervention with regard to the accuracy of the intelligence assessments upon which it was based, serve to call into serious question the appropriateness and prudence of dependence upon modern intelligence gathering and assessment techniques as a basis for judgments regarding counterproliferation-oriented pre-emptive military strikes. And since such judgments cannot be made without the use of intelligence assessments, the prudence and likely effectiveness of pre-emptive counterproliferation as an increasingly emphasized part of national anti-proliferation policy is thereby cast into serious doubt.

B. Intelligence Sharing

Second, and in addition to the intelligence accuracy failure, the intervening coalition of states in the 2003 Iraq case failed to overcome problems of intelligence sharing among states engaged in pre-emptive counterproliferation actions, in their quest to gain multilateral approval for their intervention into Iraq. This failure illustrates the effects of these intelligence sharing problems upon the potential for maintaining an effective and viable system for *ex ante* authorizations of pre-emptive counterproliferation actions through the use of an international legal body such as the U.N. Security Council.

The difficulties of reliance upon a unilateral right of self-defense to justify pre-emptive counterproliferation actions, within the context of the system for *ex post* judgments regarding the legality of such an action (i.e. through judicial review by a competent international legal tribunal applying principles of international use of force law), have been reviewed above. In addition to these more legalistic problems with this route, this *ex post* judgment scenario is also problematic because it allows such actions, the results of which are likely to be severe and irreversible for the target state, to go forward before a judgment on legality is made. In such a context, a judgment of illegality by an international tribunal is likely to be seen as cold comfort to the target state, regardless of any compensatory judgment it may be awarded. Thus, some have argued that a better system would include the use of the U.N. Security Council as an *ex ante* authorizer of such action through its Chapter VII powers.[94]

However, for the Security Council to fill such a role of authorizer of counterproliferation-oriented pre-emptive uses of force, it would have to be a forum in which member states were comfortable in sharing highly sensitive

---

[94] See the United Nations Secretary General's High-Level Panel on Threats, Challenges and Change in its 2004 report entitled "A More Secure World: Our Shared Responsibility," para. 190 (<http://www.un.org/secureworld/report.pdf>)("[t]he short answer is that if there are good arguments for preventive military action, with good evidence to support them, they should be put to the Security Council, which can authorize such action if it chooses to").

intelligence information, in order to convince fellow Council members to support their application for authorization. It would further have to be a body among whose members there is likely to be substantial agreement regarding the sources and characteristics of threats warranting pre-emptive uses of force, so as to make states confident that efforts to work through the Council would be likely to be successful and worth the transactions costs as well as the inevitable risks of intelligence leaking to the target entity involved. However, as will be discussed in greater detail in Chapter 9 below, the Security Council does not meet either of these criteria as it is currently structured.

The intelligence which states collect on WMD threats of a nature which causes them such serious concern as to warrant a decision to use pre-emptive military force, is intelligence of the highest sensitivity, and will have been collected through means the secrecy of which the collecting state will protect at all costs. Information of this sensitivity will simply not be shared by states with a group as diverse as the Security Council, no matter who the collecting state is.

Sharing of intelligence of this degree of sensitivity sometimes occurs on an ad hoc basis between the closest of allies, for functional purposes, but would never be shared either openly or confidentially to the general membership of the Council or to U.N. staff. The risk of leakage to the target state, and general risks of divulgence of sources and methods, is simply too great, with insufficiently likely, and insufficiently substantial, gain from the effort. Although there have been proposals for the establishment of safeguards and confidence-building processes for sharing of intelligence within the U.N., none of these are likely to satisfy states when dealing with information of this level of sensitivity.[95] Thus while on February 6, 2003 U.S. Secretary of State Colin Powell gave a briefing to the U.N. Security Council in which he presented some intelligence information obtained by U.S. and other sources on Iraq's WMD programs, in a final bid to obtain a clear authorization of force from the Council, he was careful to say to the other members of the Council "I cannot tell you everything that we know."[96]

The second institutional limitation the Security Council faces in this area lies in the diversity of states comprising the Council's membership, and is the fact that members of the Security Council differ fundamentally at times in their perception and appreciation of WMD threats. The 2003 Iraq intervention is a salient example of such a divergence of views regarding both the existence and degree of imminence of WMD threats. In this case it became clear to those permanent members of the Council that wished to pursue forceful action under the authority of Chapter VII of the Charter, that that view was not shared by other permanent members of the Council. Thus, those states wishing to pursue such forceful action elected to pursue that action outside the Charter framework. Although

---

[95] See S. Chesterman, "Shared Secrets: Intelligence and Collective Security," Lowy Institute Paper, 10 (2006). Available at <http://iilj.org/research/documents/chesterman_shared_secrets_2006.pdf>.

[96] Transcript available at <http://edition.cnn.com/2003/US/02/05/sprj.irq.powell.transcript/>.

the Security Council acts as a body empowered with special legal rights, such disagreements and resultant inability to act as a body and to use those rights, are reminders that the Council is primarily an international political body, made up of States with divergent and often conflicting interests and world views. The expectation that such a group of states would in a consistent manner substantially agree in their perception of threats, so as to give states confidence that applications to the Council for pre-emptive force against WMD threats will likely find approval by nine members of the Council including all five permanent members, has little foundation. This fact argues against the prudential soundness of reliance upon the Security Council as a body with the capacity to act as an authorizer of pre-emptive uses of force.

Thus, the problems of sensitive intelligence sharing among states largely foreclose the option of having an *ex ante* authorization framework such as that offered by the U.N. Security Council, Chapter VII route. With resort to an *ex post* system of authorization, such as that offered by the unilateral self-defense paradigm and review by international tribunals, also presenting significant problems both of law and practicality, options for having a system of multilateral mandate, under international legal principles, for pre-emptive counterproliferation actions appear to be extremely limited. Without such multilateral mechanisms for mandate of counterproliferation actions, the principled basis of counterproliferation strategies as an element in national foreign policy becomes quite dubious. For without a mechanism for multilateral sanction or de-legitimization of such uses of force, the spectre of abuse of such counterproliferation principles, and their use as a pretext upon which to justify actions with other primary objects and motivating forces, looms large. Many, indeed, will argue that this is one of the real legacies of the 2003 Iraq intervention, i.e. that the genuine aims of economic and political power aggrandizement of coalition states were pursued, dressed in the sheep's clothing of pre-emptive self-defense.[97] The potential for such abuse of a principle exercisable only through unilateral action, or through secretive coalitions of willing states, further undermines the case for greater reliance upon counterproliferation strategies in national anti-proliferation policy.

C. Problems of Scope

In addition to failings relating to intelligence, many see in the Iraq intervention a failure by coalition governments to grasp the implications which were to flow from the excessive scope and ambition of the action, particularly in its inclusion of a full-scale invasion accompanied by political regime change and long-term occupation by foreign ground forces.[98] Counterproliferation actions purposed

---

[97] See D. Morgan and D.B. Ottaway, "In Iraq War Scenario, Oil is Key Issue," *Washington Post*, September 15, 2002; Page A01.

[98] See, e.g., P.W. Galbraith, The End of Iraq (2006).

in degrading a specific actor's WMD capabilities can take many forms of varying forcefulness and scope; from targeted inspection systems, to the imposition of economic sanctions, to police interdictions of suspect transfers, to outright military force. However, before the 2003 Iraq war, counterproliferation-oriented military action had been limited at the most extreme to targeted air strikes, such as the 1981 Israeli bombing of the Osirak reactor. Never before had counterproliferation been the primary policy basis for a full invasion of a state and for forced political regime change. As Joseph Cirincione et al. have aptly noted "The 2003 [Iraq] conflict was the world's first nonproliferation war."[99]

Incorporating full-scale invasion and regime change into a counterproliferation military action naturally makes the endeavor much more complicated, both from a principled/theoretical perspective as well as from a practical, logistical perspective. It also dramatically increases the costs both to the state(s) taking the action as well as to the target state, in terms of financial resource commitment as well as potentially in terms of human casualties incurred through the action.

The question thus becomes, does the addition of full-scale invasion and regime change to a counterproliferation action marginally increase the likelihood of success of the action in its aims of degrading the target state's WMD capabilities to a degree great enough to justify these additional complexities and costs? The purpose of joining an invasion and regime change to a counterproliferation military action is surely to increase the amount of control enjoyed by the intervening states over the process of disarmament, as well as the installation of a government or government system, which will be amenable to the policies of the intervening states, and thus make more likely the permanency of the disarmament.

However, as the unfolding saga of the post-war occupation of Iraq and its political and social strivings are making clear, the control by intervening states over a target state's political as well as security future post-counterproliferation action is by no means an assured result of even the most successful initial military campaigns. Indeed, while the future of Iraq post-Saddam Hussein remains to be seen, the fact that Iraq has at the time of this writing come to within a razor's edge of open civil war despite the installation of a democratic governmental process and the continuing presence of many thousands of both foreign and Iraqi security forces on the ground, shows the dangers of upsetting through insufficiently planned outside action what can be a very sensitive balance among peoples, cultures, and religions inside a state of proliferation concern. The very real future prospect of the collapse of the Iraqi state and its embroilment in factional political and religious civil war, which would produce a highly fluid security situation for whatever WMD-related items and technologies still exist in the country, demonstrates the very real possibility that counterproliferation actions of the scope of the 2003 Iraq intervention can, by inadvertently contributing to the breakdown

---

[99] J. Cirincione et al., DEADLY ARSENALS, NUCLEAR, BIOLOGICAL AND CHEMICAL THREATS (Carnegie Endowment, 2nd edn, 2005) 333.

of law and public order, lead to a greater proliferation threat than that which existed *ex ante*. This observation is simply in keeping with the unpredictable reality of the consequences of major wars.

In the case of Iraq, however, even if the governmental system installed by the intervening states does take root and produce a stable democratic reality for the future of Iraq, it should be noted that the proliferation-oriented advantages which will have been achieved by the addition of a full-scale invasion and political regime change in Iraq will have been minimal. This of course is in recognition of the discoveries made after the war to the effect that the years of economic sanctions and efforts of international inspectors in the years preceding the war had been largely effective in destroying Iraq's WMD programs, leaving only a few non-compliant missiles in Iraq's military arsenal by the time of the 2003 intervention.[100] Thus, whether the results of the invasion and regime change in Iraq are positive or negative for the future of the country generally, these additional aspects of the counterproliferation action against Iraq in 2003 will not have proven to significantly contribute to the proliferation-related accomplishments of the intervention. Thus, in the Iraq case, these additional highly costly increases to the scope of the counterproliferation action, cannot be justified as having increased the effectiveness of the action.

The fact that Iraq was such a unique example of a counterproliferation action the scope of which included a full-scale ground invasion and forced political regime change, does in some respects narrow its applicability as a model from which to glean lessons regarding the future place of counterproliferation strategies in national anti-proliferation policy. However, it is entirely possible, and perhaps likely, that counterproliferation actions of this scope will be seen repeatedly in the future, as powerful states attempt to deal with states and non-state actors they deem to pose a WMD threat to international peace and security, and which seem unresponsive not only to the non-proliferation treaties and regimes system, but also to classical counterproliferation doctrines of deterrence and containment. Particularly when the existing political regimes within such WMD threatening states display radical ideological tendencies, such that the rational basis underpinning such classical forms of dissuasion is determined to be absent from their foreign policymaking calculus, and they are at the same time determined to be active proliferators to other states and non-state actors of concern, powerful states may see no other way to ensure their future security than to take this extreme preventative action. Thus the lessons of the Iraq intervention, even as a case of a full-scale counterproliferation war, are likely to be valid and important notwithstanding the more limited likely reoccurrence of this particular type of counterproliferation action.

---

[100] J. Cirincione et al., Deadly Arsenals, Nuclear, Biological and Chemical Threats (Carnegie Endowment, 2nd edn, 2005) 336–337.

VI. Unintended Consequences

Finally, the 2003 Iraq intervention, even if it had been successful in stopping a WMD proliferation threat from Iraq, could be argued to have failed in a larger sense in having effected an overall disadvantage to international anti-proliferation efforts generally. The Iraq intervention appears, in addition to exacerbating already tense relations between Western states and states and other groups in the Islamic world, to have produced a subtle yet powerful reactive phenomenon in the minds and policies of officials in states which feel that they might be next on the U.S. list of states ripe for counterproliferation-oriented pre-emptive action and regime change.

Far from the intended indirect consequence of convincing such states to abandon their WMD programs or suffer a similar fate, the 2003 intervention into a state which had been forced to give up its WMD programs, thus leaving itself too weak to oppose invasion, appears rather to have produced the deleterious blowback effect of giving a highly rational motivation to officials of such states to expedite their WMD programs in order to deter such action. This line of reasoning is made the more rational by the difference in treatment accorded to North Korea, another member of President Bush's denominated "axis of evil," which has confirmed that it does possess nuclear weapons, and which has been spared any meaningful counterproliferation action.

Thus, for officials of a state like Iran which sees international attention beginning to focus upon it and its alleged WMD programs, this difference in treatment, as well as the general deterrent effect which they know would be achieved by the possession particularly of nuclear weapons technologies, the lesson of the 2003 Iraq intervention is one of an imperative not to allow one's own state to be placed in the same position of indefensibility as was Iraq, but rather to strengthen one's arsenals of both conventional and non-conventional weapons in order to gain the same powerful negotiating leverage which North Korea has apparently achieved through its open and notorious possession, and thus be enabled to approach negotiations from a position of strength.[101]

This blowback effect of the 2003 Iraq intervention is only one of the unintended negative results of this pre-emptive international use of force. Others may include an unforeseen alliance between the now Shiite Government of Iraq, and long-time Hussein rival, Iran, which would alter significantly the balance of power in an already tense and volatile region. Still another is the effect of the intervention and occupation upon international terrorist movements, and in particular the al Qaeda network. As the April 2006 U.S. National Intelligence Estimate (NIE) confirmed, the Iraq War has become, in a tragic irony, a catalyst

---

[101] See S. Boloorian, "Updated NIE Implies Constructive Pragmatism in Tehran," *BASIC Notes*, December 7, 2007. Available at <http://www.basicint.org/pubs/Notes/BN071207.htm>.

for the development and strengthening of international terrorist networks, both in providing a training ground for perfection of their skills and techniques, as well as a further incident of cause to stoke their antipathetic feelings toward the United States and the West generally. As the NIE states:

We assess that the Iraq jihad is shaping a new generation of terrorist leaders and operatives; perceived jihadist success there would inspire more fighters to continue the struggle elsewhere...The Iraq conflict has become the "cause celebre" for jihadists, breeding a deep resentment of US involvement in the Muslim world and cultivating supporters for the global jihadist movement.[102]

Fundamentally, uses of international force produce unpredictable results, and the Iraq intervention of 2003 was a particularly impactful use of international force because of its scope, as discussed above. However even relatively minor uses of international force can produce unintended, negative results if not for the immediate situation, then in the larger context of international political and security relationships. The nature of counterproliferation actions typically as forceful actions thus associates this unpredictability into the nature of results likely to be achieved through such action. This unpredictability and the potential for overall significantly negative net effects of counterproliferation actions, further undermines arguments for the prudence and likely effectiveness of counterproliferation as an increasingly emphasized element of national anti-proliferation policy.

VII. Conclusion

What, then, should be the lessons of the 2003 Iraq intervention regarding the challenges, both legal and policy-oriented, that accompany counterproliferation actions? It is certainly true that the Iraq case is only one data point, and so cannot be used as the definitive basis for judging the utility of counterproliferation policy across the board. However, it is an important data point, in an area where data points are always scarce, and a concrete illustration of counterproliferation strategies which have been an increasingly emphasized part of states' anti-proliferation policies.

Legally, the Iraq intervention is an example of the inherent difficulty of conforming counterproliferation strategies, which emphasize pre-emptive, forceful actions, to existing international law, which favors reservation of action until threats become demonstrably imminent. It further raises the troubling question of whether such actions could be legally squared with any principle of international law which could be devised to regulate international uses of force,

---

[102] <http://www.dni.gov/press_releases/Declassified_NIE_Key_Judgments.pdf>.

and which possesses important rule of law characteristics such as predictability and objective verifiability.

In terms of its other policy-oriented implications for consideration of counterproliferation as a useful and prudent strategy, the 2003 intervention certainly cannot be said to be a resounding affirmation of the effectiveness and likely marginal utility of counterproliferation strategies over traditional non-proliferation strategies. This is the case not only because of the intelligence assessment and sharing problems it exemplifies, and the non-multilateral nature of the intervention itself, but its desirability as a poster case for pre-emption is also significantly compromised by the fact that in this case the strategy of pre-emptive military force was accompanied by a full-scale invasion, political regime change, and extended occupation, which has in WMD proliferation terms accomplished nothing, and which has opened a Pandora's box of complexities in rebuilding the country *ex post*, and caused other significant unintended negative collateral effects.

Thus, while the 2003 Iraq intervention is a manifestation of counterproliferation policy, it is one that proponents of counterproliferation will not be keen to cite in the future when arguing for the wider use and effectiveness of counterproliferation strategies in combating WMD threats. In fact, it is a case the failures of which they will continuously be forced to explain, and the weaknesses of which they will need to distinguish from future cases in which counterproliferation actions are proposed.

8

The Challenges of Counterproliferation:
The Proliferation Security Initiative

In a speech given at Wawel Royal Castle in Krakow, Poland on May 31, 2003, U.S. President George Bush declared:[1]

The greatest threat to peace is the spread of nuclear, chemical and biological weapons. And we must work together to stop proliferation...When weapons of mass destruction or their components are in transit, we must have the means and authority to seize them. So today I announce a new effort to fight proliferation called the Proliferation Security Initiative. The United States and a number of our close allies, including Poland, have begun working on new agreements to search planes and ships carrying suspect cargo and to seize illegal weapons or missile technologies. Over time, we will extend this partnership as broadly as possible to keep the world's most destructive weapons away from our shores and out of the hands of our common enemies.[2]

The speech was given approximately five months after the United States Navy had participated in an incident involving a North Korean merchant ship which was to serve as the catalyst for this significant change in U.S. policy related to weapons of mass destruction proliferation.

I. The *So San*

At dawn on Monday, December 9, 2002 two Spanish Navy ships, the *Navarra* and the *Patino*, signalled the freighter *So San* which was at the time approximately 600 miles off the Yemeni coast in international waters.[3] The ship was registered in Cambodia but sailing without a flag, and was believed to be transporting goods

---

[1] This chapter is an amended version of an article entitled *The Proliferation Security Initiative: Nonproliferation, Counterproliferation and International Law*, published at 30 YALE JOURNAL OF INTERNATIONAL LAW 507 (2005). Used here by permission.

[2] 'Remarks by the President to the People of Poland, Wawel Royal Castle, Krakow, Poland, May 31, 2003'; The White House, Office of the Press Secretary. Avaliable at <http://www.whitehouse.gov/news/releases/2003/05/20030531-3.html>.

[3] See generally T. Ricks and P. Slevin, "Spain and U.S. Seize N. Korean Missiles," *Washington Post*, December 11, 2002; "Scud Missiles are Ours, Says Yemen," CNN.com, December 11, 2002. Available at <http://archives.cnn.com/2002/WORLD/asiapcf/east/12/11/scud.ship/>.

from North Korea—U.S. intelligence satellites and Navy ships had been tracking the ship since it left the North Korean Port of Nampo in mid-November. When the freighter attempted to evade capture, the Spanish ships fired warning shots first into the water in front of the ship and then across its bow. When it failed to respond, a helicopter was dispatched from the *Patino* carrying seven Spanish Special Forces troops, who boarded the ships using fast ropes.[4]

The crew of about 20 were put under guard and the ship was searched. It was clearly evident that the ship's original name and identification number had been painted over, and as clear that the ship was crewed by Koreans. The captain claimed that the last port of call had been China, and that the ship was transporting 2,000 pounds of concrete to Yemen, which was verified by the ship's manifest. When Spanish troops began to inspect the ship's cargo, however, they found, partially hidden by the 40,000 bags of cement also in the hold, large containers of missile parts and additional containers of an unknown chemical. The Captain of the *Patino* then called in U.S. military explosives experts aboard the *USS Nassau*, who were able to verify the items as composite parts of 15 mid-range Scud missiles, with 15 conventional warheads and 85 drums of a chemical called inhibited red fuming nitric acid—used as an oxidizer in Scud missile fuel.[5]

Then commenced a flurry of communiqués and phone calls through which it was discovered that the ship was indeed headed for Yemen, and that the Yemeni Government openly confirmed the order of the missile components. It had apparently agreed to purchase them in 1999 to help upgrade the small number of Scud missiles it already possessed. Yemeni officials denied any intent to conceal the shipment, blaming the deceptive storage underneath bags of cement on North Korea. Yemeni Foreign Minister Abubakr al-Qirbi stated: "The shipment is part of contracts signed some time ago. It belongs to the Yemeni Government and its army and is meant for defensive purposes."[6] Al-Qirbi summoned the U.S. Ambassador to the capital of Sanaa to lodge a formal protest over the seizure of the shipment.[7]

For the next two days Washington officials debated a course of action in light of the discovery and of the Yemeni Government's claim of right. After consulting with key foreign policymakers as well as lawyers at the State Department and elsewhere, President Bush signed off on the decision to release the ship and its cargo. Speaking at a luncheon in Washington on December 11, Secretary of State Colin Powell stated:

[A]fter getting assurances directly from the President of Yemen, President Salih, that this was the last of a group of shipments that go back some years and had been contracted for some years ago, this would be the end of it and we had assurances that these missiles

---

[4] Ibid.   [5] Ibid.
[6] "North Korea: U.S., Spanish Forces Seize Scud Shipment," *NTI Global Security Newswire* (December 11, 2002). Available at <http://www.nti.org/d_newswire/issues/thisweek/2002_12_13_misp.html>.
[7] Ibid.

were for Yemeni defensive purposes and under no circumstances would they be going anywhere else.

And on that basis, and also in acknowledgement of the fact that it was on international water and it was a sale that was out in the open and consistent with international law, a little while ago we directed the ship to continue to its destination. And I conveyed that to the president of Yemen just a little while ago.[8]

II. The Proliferation Security Initiative

In the aftermath of these events, head-scratching ensued in Washington, as the full import of what had just happened became disturbingly clear. Here had been a North Korean ship—commonly known to be the worst proliferator of missile technology—found conclusively to be carrying a cargo of concealed missiles capable of being armed with warheads carrying any one of a number of dangerous chemicals, biological agents, or even nuclear weapons, on its way to a region of the world at the top of Washington's worry list; and when action had been taken to seize the weapons and prevent their delivery, it was discovered that in fact there was no justification under international law for seizing the missiles. There was in fact nothing illegal going on—no treaties were being violated. In the eyes of existing law it was simply a sale of goods from one state to another, and if anything the Spanish and American ships involved in the forced inspection had arguably crossed over a legal line in abridging the *So San*'s right to free passage through international waters. There was a common consensus among senior U.S. officials, particularly at the Defense Department, that this was simply an unacceptable status quo and that something had to be done.[9]

Thus was born the Proliferation Security Initiative (PSI), through which, according to former U.S. Under-Secretary of State John Bolton, the United States expresses its hope to

work with other concerned states to develop new means to disrupt the proliferation trade at sea, in the air, and on land. The initiative reflects the need for a more dynamic, proactive approach to the global proliferation problem. It envisions partnerships of states working in concert, employing their national capabilities to develop a broad range of legal, diplomatic, economic, military and other tools to interdict threatening shipments of WMD- and missile-related equipment and technologies.[10]

---

[8] Secretary of State Colin L. Powell at the American Academy of Diplomacy Annual Awards Presentation Luncheon, December 11, 2002 (U.S. Department of State, Office of the Spokesman). Available at <http://www.usconsulate.org.hk/uscn/state/2002/121101.htm>.

[9] M. Byers, *Policing the High Seas: The Proliferation Security Initiative*, 98 AMERICAN JOURNAL OF INTERNATIONAL LAW No. 3 (July 2004).

[10] Statement by John R. Bolton, US Under-Secretary for Arms Control and International Security, before the House of Representatives' Committee on International Relations (June 4, 2003). Available at <http://www.nti.org/e_research/official_docs/dos/dos060403.pdf>.

After President Bush's announcement of the initiative in May 2003, meetings were held in the Summer of 2003 in Madrid, Spain and Brisbane, Australia among the 11 states initially signing on as participants in the "small group of like-minded countries" taking up this U.S.-led initiative—Australia, France, Germany, Italy, Japan, Netherlands, Poland, Portugal, Spain, United Kingdom, and the United States. By September, the group had moved on to conducting collaborative exercises, in which mock interdictions of ships were staged by ships and troops from various member nations working in concert. On September 4, the White House issued a Statement of Interdiction Principles which outlined the joint commitment of PSI members, and invited other similarly minded states to likewise commit "to undertake effective measures, either alone or in concert with other states, for interdicting the transfer or transport of WMD, their delivery systems, and related materials to and from states and non-state actors of proliferation concern."[11] The Statement of Interdiction Principles lays out in some detail the "actions in support of interdiction efforts regarding cargoes of WMD, their delivery systems, or related materials" which PSI members and participants contemplated to undertake.[12]

The complexity and scope of these exercises has been increased over the past several years, with mock interdictions taking place in areas of the world most highly trafficked by WMD-related materials traders and smugglers—notably in the Mediterranean and Arabian Seas, and the Pacific Ocean. The number of states endorsing the PSI has also increased to over 70, notably including Russia. By December 2003, Under-Secretary of State Bolton had confirmed that interdictions under the PSI framework had already taken place with more to follow, explaining that most such interdictions would not be made known to the public out of concern for the ongoing effectiveness of the program.[13] This pattern of secrecy regarding the progress of the PSI has been continued, with statements from participating governments typically cryptic and minimalist regarding operational details. As U.S. Under-Secretary of State Robert G. Joseph reported in June 2006: "Between April 2005 and April 2006, the United States worked successfully with multiple PSI partners in Europe, Asia and the Middle East

---

[11] Fact Sheet, Proliferation Security Initiative, Statement of Interdiction Principles, White House Office of the Press Secretary. Available at <http://www.whitehouse.gov/news/releases/2003/09/20030904-11.html>.

[12] Ibid. On the PSI generally see A. Winner and J. Holmes, "The Proliferation Security Initiative: A Global Prohibition Regime in the Making?" in N. Busch and D.H. Joyner (eds), COMBATING WEAPONS OF MASS DESTRUCTION: THE FUTURE OF NONPROLIFERATION POLICY (2009); C. Allen, MARITIME COUNTERPROLIFERATION OPERATIONS AND THE RULE OF LAW (2007); T.D. Lehrman, *Enhancing the Proliferation Security Initiative: The Case for a Decentralized Nonproliferation Architecture*, 45 VIRGINIA JOURNAL OF INTERNATIONAL LAW 223 (2004); A. Winner, *The Proliferation Security Initiative: The New Face of Interdiction*, 28 WASHINGTON QUARTERLY 129 (2005); Congressional Research Service, *Weapons of Mass Destruction Counterproliferation: Legal Issues for Ships and Aircraft*, Oct. 1, 2003, CRS Report RL32097.

[13] Interview with John Bolton conducted by Wade Boese. Published by ARMS CONTROL TODAY, December 11, 2003. Available at <http://www.armscontrol.org/act/2003_12/PSI.asp>.

on roughly two dozen separate occasions to prevent transfers of equipment and materials to WMD and missile programs in countries of concern."[14]

However, the solidarity of this coalition of the willing has been shaken as the commonly agreed general principles at the heart of the PSI have become operationalized.[15] Officials in a number of national capitals, as well as non-governmental members of the international community, have become more aware and concerned about the questionable existence of an international legal basis on which to legitimize interdictions of merchant ships and aircraft operating in sea zones in which their national authority is not absolute.[16]

This chapter will present the PSI as a second case study of the implementation of counterproliferation policy, and as a further example of the shift in some states' policies away from an emphasis on non-proliferation efforts and toward an emphasis on counterproliferation efforts, as that distinction has been defined herein. The chapter will provide an analysis of the PSI set against the backdrop of relevant international legal frameworks; specifically international use of force law and the international law of the sea. It will also provide analysis on the subject of the relative utility of the PSI as a part of international efforts to combat the proliferation of WMD-related technologies and materials.

III. International Law

A. Self-defense

Since self-defense has been offered as one justificatory rubric for implementation of the PSI, this section will proceed to briefly consider the PSI by reference to principles of international use of force law, and particularly principles of anticipatory self-defense.[17]

The contours of the modern right of self-defense in international use of force law have been discussed in Chapter 7 above. From this consideration, it will be remembered that, for parties to the U.N. Charter, resort to a right of anticipatory self-defense must be seen to be questionable in light of the plain meaning of the text of Article 51 of that document.[18] Nevertheless some have contended that the "inherent right" language in Article 51 has worked a retention of the rights of

---

[14] "Broadening and Deepening Our Proliferation Security Initiative Cooperation," Available at <http://www.state.gov/t/us/rm/68269.htm>.

[15] See M. Heupel, *The Proliferation Security Initiative: Advancing Commitment and Capacity for WMD Interdictions*, Disarmament Forum, Vol. 4, 57, 59 (2007); A. Kaliadine, *Russia in the PSI: The Modalities of Russian Participation in the Proliferation Security Initiative*, WMD Commission Paper no. 29 (2005); A. Newman and B. Williams, *The Proliferation Security Initiative: The Asia-Pacific Context*, The Nonproliferation Review, Vol. 12, no. 2, 303 (2005).

[16] "US Plans to Seize Suspects at Will," *Times Online*, July 11, 2003.

[17] G. Sheridan, "US 'free' to tackle N Korea," *The Australian*, July 9, 2003.

[18] See Chapter 7 below at n. 283.

self-defense operable under pre-Charter customary law for U.N. Charter members.[19] As discussed above, this is a plausible position, but in the final analysis does little to help those wishing to justify a broad right of pre-emptive use of force, and particularly one which seeks to justify uses of force against threats, including WMD-related threats, which are in relatively early stages of development, and which have not yet progressed to being imminent in time and practicality. For even if a right of anticipatory self-defense is recognized, it must still be held to be limited at least by the *Caroline* factors of imminence, necessity, and proportionality, if not in an even more restrained fashion as Ian Brownlie has urged.[20]

Under these limiting factors particularly, anticipatory self-defense would seem an inapposite and unworkable principle in the context of the PSI. The entire thrust of the principles underlying the PSI is a preventive one, i.e. to prevent the acquisition of potentially dangerous technologies by states and non-state actors of concern. This locates the PSI as being one relatively definitive step removed from addressing as its primary aim threats of WMD use which rise to the level of *Caroline* imminence. There has never been expressed by proponents of the PSI an understanding of an imminence of threat from particular foreign target vessels which under the *Caroline* formula would trigger even the customary right of anticipatory self-defense on the part of interdicting states.

The idea of preventive self-defense, which may be described as an attack against another state (or in the PSI context a vessel under the jurisdiction and flag of another state) farther back down the *ex ante* chronological line when a threat is feared or suspected but there is no evidence that materialization of the threat is imminent, finds no foundation as a principle of customary international law in modern times and any attempt to justify this extreme interpretation of a right includable in the legal concept of the right of self-defense by reference to the U.N. Charter is a clear exercise in futility.

In summary, therefore, the modern right of states to self-defense as contained in any respected interpretation of Article 51 of the U.N. Charter and related customary law is not sufficient to act as a broad justifying principle for the PSI.[21] Not only is the sort of preventive right which would be necessary for the task not to be found in modern international use of force law, but additionally and importantly there is in existence law on the particular subjects at issue that is both *lex specialis* and *lex posterior* to those sources of use of force law which have been referenced, and therefore to be taken in priority as a governing legal framework.[22] Here

---

[19] See Chapter 7 below at 281.

[20] See Chapter 7 below at 282. On the principles of necessity and proportionality in customary international law, see I. Brownlie, INTERNATIONAL LAW AND THE USE OF FORCE BY STATES (1963) 257–264.

[21] C. Allen, MARITIME COUNTERPROLIFERATION OPERATIONS AND THE RULE OF LAW (2007) 171.

[22] See D.J. Harris, CASES & MATERIALS ON INTERNATIONAL LAW (5th edn, 1998) 901. ("The 1982 Law of the Sea Convention, Article 110(1), makes no provision for jurisdiction over vessels on the high seas on the basis of self-defence.") On the canons of interpretation *Lex specialis derogat*

reference is made to the international law of the sea, and specifically to both the 1958 Geneva Conventions and the 1982 Law of the Sea Convention and related customary law, which address in a much more focused manner the rights and duties of both coastal states and seagoing vessels including aircraft, and which as will be seen have concrete and developed provisions regarding interdiction of foreign vessels. It is within the parameters of this body of law, and not the law of self-defense generally, that the PSI must be legitimized if at all.

B. The Law of the Sea

Since the signing of the Treaty of Westphalia in 1648 and the establishment of the principle of state sovereignty as a geopolitical paradigm shift in evolution from the principles of feudalism, states have jealously guarded and defended the right to be the sole source of legal prescription over their subject territory and to legitimately rule within their borders without interference of outside authorities.[23] Within this sphere of entitlement, international law has come to classify state authority as being near absolute and exclusionary. This classification applies not only to the land territory of a state, but also to its internal waters (e.g. rivers, bays, harbors) with extremely limited exceptions.[24] In recognition of this authority, international law does not accord foreign ships a general right of access to a state's ports. States have a wide authority to prescribe conditions regulating entry to ports, and may close ports to all international trade if they so desire. Once a foreign vessel has entered a state's port, it surrenders itself to the territorial jurisdiction of the state and the state may enforce its national laws upon the ship and those on board, subject to the normal considerations of diplomatic and sovereign immunities which most often come into play in the case of warships.[25]

As consideration turns from the land territory of a state to the waters immediately adjacent to its coastline (i.e. the sea area past the baseline),[26] however, the absolute character of state authority to regulate and to enforce national law becomes compromised by other principles of international law which have developed as part of the law of the sea.

Along with a state's rights to control its land and internal waters' territory, it quickly became generally accepted that states had rights also to control the sea

---

legi generali (the more specific law trumps the more general law) and *Lex posterior derogat legi priori* (the law which is later in time trumps the earlier law), see M. Villiger, Customary International Law and Treaties (1985) 36.

[23] See S. Krasner, Sovereignty (1999) ch. 1.

[24] See M.S. McDougal and W.T. Burke, The Public Order of the Oceans (1962) 327–373; L. Bouchez, The Regime of Bays in International Law (1964).

[25] See R.R. Churchill and A.V. Lowe, The Law of the Sea (3rd edn, 1999) 61–62.

[26] See M. Reisman and G. Westerman, Straight Baselines in International Boundary Delimitation (1992).

area directly adjacent to them. However for centuries both the breadth of the sea area to which this right of control attached, as well as the precise nature of the juridical competence of states over it, were evolving as principles of international law. In time it became settled that there was a legal distinction between the sea area directly adjacent to a state's coastline, or territorial sea as it came to be termed, and the sea area farther away from its coast. The breadth of the territorial sea was eventually determined to extend up to 12 miles from the baseline, and all sea area farther than 12 miles out came to be considered part of the high seas or "international waters," subject to an entirely different legal regime of prescriptions with much greater limitation on the authority of states to unilaterally regulate.[27]

1. Sources

First a note on the sources of international law in this area. The law of the sea is one of the oldest substantive areas of international law. The history of normative regulation of the sea lanes stretches back to medieval pronouncements of rules governing maritime commerce found in collections such as the *Consolato del mare* and the English *Black Book of the Admiralty*.[28] The evolution of international legal principles in this area has continued through to modern times, and in the twentieth century found codified expression in a number of significant multilateral treaties as well as through customary international law.[29]

In terms of treaty law, the 1958 Geneva Conventions—consisting of the Convention on the Territorial Sea and the Contiguous Zone (TSC), the Convention on the High Seas (HSC), the Convention on Fishing and Conservation of the Living Resources of the High Seas (FC), and the Convention on the Continental Shelf (CCS)—were a landmark achievement of international regulation of the world's seas in terms of comprehensiveness both of subject

---

[27] See 1982 United Nations Law of the Sea Convention, Article 3; I. Brownlie, Principles of Public International law (6th edn, 2003) 180–181.

[28] See R.P. Anand, The Origin and Development of the Law of the Sea (1983). On the history of international law see generally W. Grewe, The Epochs of International Law (translated and revised by M. Byers, 2000); D.J. Bederman, International Law in Antiquity (2001); M. Koskenniemi, The Gentle Civilizer of Nations: The Rise and Fall of International Law, 1870–1960 (2002); A. Nussbaum, A Concise History of the Law of Nations (1954); W. Preiser, *History of the Law of Nations: Ancient Times to 1648*, in Encyclopedia of Public International Law II 716–749 (1995).

[29] D. Bowett, Law of the Sea (1967); E.D. Brown, The International Law of the Sea (1994); C.J. Colombos, The International Law of the Sea (6th edn, 1967); R.J. Dupuy and D. Vignes (eds), A Handbook on the New Law of the Sea (1991); M.S. McDougal and W.T. Burke, The Public Order of the Oceans (1962); H. Smith, The Law and Custom of the Sea (1959); J. Wang, Ocean Politics and Law (1992); S. Oda, International Law and the Resources of the Sea (1979); D.P. O'Connell, The International Law of the Sea (1984); R.P. Anand, The Origin and Development of the Law of the Sea (1983); V. Prescott, The Maritime Political Boundaries of the World (1985); T. Fulton, The Sovereignty of the Sea (1911).

matter covered and number of states parties.[30] However, the increasing presence in the United Nations of newly independent states which had had no say in the drafting of the 1958 Geneva Conventions, particularly and importantly in the area of national authority to regulate the seabed led to initiatives in subsequent decades to amend the law contained in the 1958 conventions. Thus in 1970 the U.N. General Assembly in Resolution 2570 called for the convening of a United Nations conference purposed in producing a new comprehensive law of the sea convention.

The result of the Third United Nations Conference on the Law of the Sea was the signing in 1982 of the United Nations Convention on the Law of the Sea (LOSC).[31] The number of LOSC states parties currently stands at 157, including almost all of the major seagoing nations of the world.[32] For parties to both the 1958 Geneva Conventions and the LOSC, the LOSC takes pre-eminence by its terms.[33]

However, important to discussions regarding the United States and its obligations under the international law of the sea is the somewhat anomalous fact that, while a party to the 1958 Geneva Conventions, the U.S. has never acceded to the 1982 LOSC. The main differences as previously noted between the 1958 Geneva Conventions and the 1982 LOSC are in regard of regulation of the deep seabed, and indeed it is this sensitive issue area which has prevented the U.S from. signing the 1982 treaty.[34] However the two legal regimes are virtually identical on matters of right of innocent passage and interdiction which will be the focus of this study, rendering this anomaly insignificant in this context. In areas in which the treaty regimes do differ, it is important to note that the 1982 LOSC has with little doubt passed in its entirety into parallel customary international law, thereby binding the United States to its provisions as well.[35]

2. Territorial Sea

Over the area of the territorial sea, as it became defined as a principle of international law, states have asserted, and international law has come to

---

[30] 516 U.N.T.S. 205; 450 U.N.T.S. 11; 559 U.N.T.S. 285; 499 U.N.T.S. 311.

[31] 21 INTERNATIONAL LEGAL MATERIALS 1245.

[32] See <http://www.un.org/Depts/los/convention_agreements/convention_overview_convention.htm>.

[33] Article 311.

[34] See R.R. Churchill and A.V. Lowe, THE LAW OF THE SEA (3rd edn, 1999) 237. On July 29, 1994, the United States signed the 1994 Agreement Relating to the Implementation of Part XI of the U.N. Convention on the Law of the Sea. On October 7, 1994, President Clinton transmitted to the Senate the 1982 LOSC and 1994 Agreement Relating to the Implementation of Part XI of the LOSC. The package was referred to the Senate Committee on Foreign Relations. On November 16, 1994, the LOSC entered into force but without accession by the United States. On July 28, 1996, the Agreement Relating to Part XI of the LOSC entered into force, but without U.S. ratification. See M.A. Browne, "The Law of the Sea Convention and U.S. Policy," CRS Report for Congress, February 14, 2001.

[35] See R.R. Churchill and A.V. Lowe, THE LAW OF THE SEA (3rd edn, 1999) at 24.

recognize, the essential extension of state sovereignty from its land territory.[36] The 1958 Territorial Sea Convention expresses this understanding thus:

(1) The sovereignty of a state extends, beyond its land territory and its internal waters, to a belt of sea adjacent to its coast, described as the territorial sea.
(2) This sovereignty is exercised subject to the provisions of these articles and to other rules of international law.

The most significant principle comprising the sovereignty of states over their territorial sea is the right of innocent passage, as that concept has evolved in the 1958 Territorial Sea Convention and in other sources of international law. As a preliminary point it should be noted that the right of innocent passage through the territorial sea area is limited to sea vessels and does not extend to aircraft in the air space above the territorial sea. Due to the danger to states inherent in the abilities of aircraft to travel and maneuver at high speed and avoid detection, no right of innocent passage either over a state's land territory or the territorial sea has ever been conceded. Over aircraft in these areas, therefore, state sovereignty is at its apex.[37]

However, for sea vessels a right of innocent passage through territorial waters has long been maintained and has achieved a status of legal entitlement in international law. Essentially the right of foreign ships to innocent passage through the territorial sea extends to ships "passing" through the territorial sea area. This passage principle has evolved to include both direct passage through the territorial sea as well as passage with the intent of anchoring at port, inasmuch as that anchoring is incident to normal navigation or trade or to *force majeure*.[38]

The concept of "innocence" as an element of this right has been more complicated in its evolution. During the nineteenth and early twentieth-centuries, the concept of innocence in passage through the territorial sea was thought to refer primarily to the disposition of the passage relative to the national law of the state having sovereignty over the territorial sea—i.e. innocence was lost when the laws

---

[36] Ibid. at ch. 4; P. Allott, *Language, Method and the Nature of International Law*, 45 BRITISH YEARBOOK OF INTERNATIONAL LAW 79 (1971); W.E. Butler, *Innocent Passage and the 1982 Convention: The Influence of Soviet Law and Policy*, 81 AMERICAN JOURNAL OF INTERNATIONAL LAW 331 (1987); P.T. Fenn, *Origins of the Theory of Territorial Waters*, 20 AMERICAN JOURNAL OF INTERNATIONAL LAW 465 (1926); E. Franck, *The USSR Position on the Issue of Innocent Passage of Warships Through Foreign Territorial Waters*, 18 JOURNAL OF MARITIME LAW AND COMMERCE 33 (1987); T.W. Fulton, *Sovereignty of the Seas. An Historical Account of the Claims of England to the Dominion of the British Seas* (1911); P.C. Jessup, THE LAW OF TERRITORIAL WATERS AND MARITIME JURISDICTION (1927); L.T. Lee, *Jurisdiction over Foreign Merchant Ships in the Territorial Sea. An Analysis of the Geneva Convention on the Law of the Sea*, 55 AMERICAN JOURNAL OF INTERNATIONAL LAW 77 (1961); D.P. O'Connell, *The Juridical Status of the Territorial Sea*, 45 BRITISH YEARBOOK OF INTERNATIONAL LAW 303 (1971); J.K. Oudendijk, STATUS AND EXTENT OF ADJACENT WATERS (1970); D.R. Rothwell, *Coastal State Sovereignty and Innocent Passage: The Voyage of the Lusitania Expresso*, 16 MARINE POLICY 427 (1992); A. Roach and R. Smith, UNITED STATES RESPONSES TO EXCESSIVE MARITIME CLAIMS (2nd edn, 1996).
[37] See R.R. Churchill and A.V. Lowe, THE LAW OF THE SEA (3rd edn, 1999) ch. 4.
[38] Ibid.

of the coastal state were violated.[39] The 1930 Hague Conference adopted a text which loosened this strict tie to national law: "Passage is not innocent when a vessel makes use of the territorial sea of a coastal state for the purpose of doing any act prejudicial to the security, to the public policy or to the fiscal interests of that state."[40] While not requiring a breach of national law for innocence to be lost, this provision did require some act on the part of the vessel other than the mere act of passage for a loss of innocence to occur.[41] The International Law Commission's draft articles in 1956 essentially adopted this view.[42]

The Commission's draft article was not accepted at the 1958 conference, however, and Article 14(4) of the Territorial Sea Convention was constructed to read: "Passage is innocent so long as it is not prejudicial to the peace, good order or security of the coastal state. Such passage shall take place in conformity with these articles and with other rules of international law." Churchill and Lowe in their standard work on the law of the sea have commented on this provision thus:

This final text, which seems to be consistent with the actual practice of states, and so with customary law, clearly does not require the commission of any particular act, or violation of any law, before innocence is lost. Nor does violation of a coastal law necessarily remove innocence, unless the violation actually prejudices coastal interests.[43]

This relatively vague provision in the 1958 TSC was substantially added to in the 1982 LOSC. Article 19 of the LOSC retains the text of the 1958 Article 14(4) as paragraph 1. However, in paragraph 2 the article goes on to provide that "passage of a foreign ship shall be considered to be prejudicial to the peace, good order or security of the coastal state, if in the territorial sea it engages in any of the following activities..." The article proceeds to list those activities, which include weapons practice; spying; propaganda; launching or taking on board aircraft or military devices; embarking or disembarking persons or goods contrary to customs, fiscal, immigration, or sanitary regulations; and interference with coastal communication or other facilities. The article then lists two broader additions to this list:

(a) any threat or use of force against the sovereignty, territorial integrity or political independence of the coastal state, or in any other manner in violation of the principles of international law embodied in the Charter of the United Nations;...

(l) any other activity not having a direct bearing on passage.

---

[39] Ibid.

[40] League of Nations Doc. C. 351(b). M. 145(b). 1930. v, p. 213, reproduced in S. Rosenne, LEAGUE OF NATIONS CONFERENCE FOR THE CODIFICATION OF INTERNATIONAL LAW (1930), pg. 1415 (1975).

[41] See R.R. Churchill and A.V. Lowe, THE LAW OF THE SEA (3rd edn, 1999) 83.

[42] ILC Yearbook 1956, Vol. II, 272. See also the full discussion of the concept of innocence in the ICJ's *Corfu Channel* case in ICJ Reports 1949.

[43] R.R. Churchill and A.V. Lowe, THE LAW OF THE SEA (3rd edn, 1999) 85.

The addition of a delineated list of activities which, if engaged in by a ship in passage through the territorial sea, would work a loss of innocence of that ship under the right of innocent passage was intended to add objectivity to determinations regarding this right and to make such judgments less subject to interpretation by the coastal state.[44] As drafted, it appears to emphasize activities, or actions, and the necessity of engaging in some action other than mere passage for the loss of innocence to occur. However, in the absence of language explicitly rebutting the presumption, the list must be interpreted as non-exhaustive, and with the retention of the 1958 language in the first paragraph, this emphasis on activity cannot be taken as dispositive in requiring action in addition to other factors attaching to the passage.[45] Noteworthy in the context of this chapter's examination is the fact that the reference in paragraph (2)(a) of Article 19 is arguably wide enough to include threats of force against states other than the coastal state.[46]

Interestingly, the question of the import of the listed activities in Article 19 of the LOSC was addressed in a bilateral treaty between the United States and the USSR in 1989. Paragraph 3 of the Uniform Interpretation of Norms of International Law Governing Innocent Passage states: "Article 19 of the Convention of 1982 sets out in paragraph 2 an exhaustive list of activities that would render passage not innocent. A ship passing through the territorial sea that does not engage in any of those activities is in innocent passage."[47] While the binding weight of this interpretive declaration is certainly confined to the two parties to the treaty, its influence in customary international law is likely to be significant.[48]

As the 1958 TSC states in Article 16(1), in a provision echoed by 1982 LOSC Article 25(1), once innocence is lost, so too is the right of innocent passage, and the foreign vessel is at that point subject to the full sovereignty of the coastal state, which may arrest the vessel for a breach of its national laws.[49]

3. The Exclusive Economic Zone

The Exclusive Economic Zone (EEZ) is a fairly recent concept in the law of the sea, and is a compromise of sorts reached among those states that desired a full 200-mile territorial sea and those states which were wary of the extension of state sovereignty over so vast an area.[50] The EEZ is something of a

---

[44] Ibid. at 85. [45] Ibid. [46] Ibid.
[47] 14 LOSB 12–13 (1989).
[48] R.R. Churchill and A.V. Lowe, THE LAW OF THE SEA (3rd edn, 1999) 86.
[49] Ibid. at 87.
[50] See D. Attard, THE EXCLUSIVE ECONOMIC ZONE IN INTERNATIONAL LAW (1987); E.D. Brown, *The Exclusive Economic Zone. Criteria and Machinery for the Resolution of International Conflicts Between Different Users of the EEZ*, 4 MARITIME POLICY AND MANAGEMENT 325 (1977); W.T. Burke, *National Legislation on Ocean Authority Zones and the Contemporary Law of the Sea*, 9 OCEAN DEVELOPMENT AND INTERNATIONAL LAW 289 (1981); J. Charney, *The Exclusive Economic Zone and Public International Law*, 15 OCEAN DEVELOPMENT AND INTERNATIONAL LAW 233

hybrid between the territorial sea and the high seas as those concepts classically evolved, and can be claimed by states in an area not to exceed 200 miles beginning at the 12-mile territorial sea mark. As regards the freedom of navigation which is most pertinent to discussion and analysis here, Article 58 of the LOSC which describes this freedom in the EEZ context brings this law into almost complete harmony with the corresponding provisions regarding freedom of navigation, including aircraft overflight, on the high seas and indeed references those high seas provisions. Thus, for the purposes of this treatment the two areas of the EEZ (with the EEZ including also the contiguous zone if any) and the high seas will be considered to be subject to the same legal regime as described below.

4. *The High Seas*

As previously mentioned, since the recognition of a legal delineation between the territorial sea (and later the EEZ), and the sea area beyond, two quite different legal regimes have evolved to govern the two separated areas.[51] Firstly noteworthy is the fact that the legal concept of the high seas includes not only the water column but also the super-adjacent airspace as well as the seabed and subsoil subject.[52] The legal regime governing the high seas has classically been defined by its primary emphasis on the principles of freedom of universal usage and the exclusivity of jurisdiction over vessels of the flag state.[53] The dominance of these principles in the high seas regime is in marked contrast to the character of legal regulation of the territorial sea discussed earlier and is indicative of a significant decrease in the authority of states over foreign vessels. This decrease is of course a historical recognition of the importance to all seagoing states of an ordered

---

(1985); T.A. Clingan (ed.), LAW OF THE SEA: STATE PRACTICE IN ZONES OF SPECIAL JURISDICTION (1982); L. Juda, *The Exclusive Economic Zone and Ocean Management*, 18 OCEAN DEVELOPMENT AND INTERNATIONAL LAW 305 (1987); B. Kwiatkowska, THE 200 MILE EXCLUSIVE ECONOMIC ZONE IN THE NEW LAW OF THE SEA (1989); R.R. Churchill and A.V. Lowe, THE LAW OF THE SEA (3rd edn, 1999) 161.

[51] On the high seas regime and related issues see C.H. Alexandrowicz, *Freitas versus Grotius*, 35 BRITISH YEARBOOK OF INTERNATIONAL LAW 162 (1959); N. Grief, PUBLIC INTERNATIONAL LAW IN THE AIRSPACE OF THE HIGH SEAS (1994); Sir Arthur Jennings and Sir Arthur Watts (eds), OPPENHEIM'S INTERNATIONAL LAW Vol. I (9th edn, 1992); B. Kwiatkowska, *Creeping Jurisdiction Beyond 200 Miles in the light of the 1982 Law of the Sea Convention and State Practice*, 22 OCEAN DEVELOPMENT AND INTERNATIONAL LAW 153 (1991); E. Margolis, *The Hydrogen Bomb Experiments and International Law*, 64 YALE LAW JOURNAL 629 (1955); T.L. McDorman, *Stateless Fishing Vessels, International Law and the UN High Seas Fisheries Conference*, 25 JOURNAL OF MARITIME LAW AND COMMERCE 531 (1994); D.P. O'Connell, THE INTERNATIONAL LAW OF THE SEA (1984); N.M. Poulantzas, THE RIGHT OF HOT PURSUIT IN INTERNATIONAL LAW (1969); N. Ronzitti (ed.), MARITIME TERRORISM AND INTERNATIONAL LAW (1990); I.A. Shearer, *Problems of Jurisdiction and Law Enforcement against Delinquent Vessels*, 35 INTERNATIONAL AND COMPARATIVE LAW QUARTERLY 320 (1986); R.R. Churchill and A.V. Lowe, THE LAW OF THE SEA (3rd edn, 1999) ch. 11.

[52] See R.R. Churchill and A.V. Lowe, THE LAW OF THE SEA (3rd edn, 1999) 204.

[53] Ibid. at 203.

system of regulation of the high seas, and through that system the assurance of unmolested commerce and transit over the vast expanses of water that cover two-thirds of the globe. It is a subject to which special accord has traditionally been granted by states, in recognition of the inability of any state to unilaterally police so large an area and the consequent reliance of states upon mutual good faith in upholding principles of law laid down in treaties and the customary practice of states.[54]

The 1958 HSC and the 1982 LOSC share largely identical provisions outlining the high seas legal regime. Some of the most notable provisions are excerpted below using the text of the 1982 LOSC:

Article 87

1. The high seas are open to all States, whether coastal or landlocked. Freedom of the high seas is exercised under the conditions laid down by this convention and by other rules of international law. It comprises, *inter alia*, for both coastal and landlocked states:

   a) freedom of navigation;
   b) freedom of overflight:...

These freedoms shall be exercised by all States with due regard for the interests of other States in their exercise of the freedom of the high seas...

Article 89

No State may validly purport to subject any part of the high seas to its sovereignty.

Article 92

Ships shall sail under the flag of one state only and, save in exceptional cases expressly provided for in international treaties or in this Convention, shall be subject to its exclusive jurisdiction on the high seas...

For the purposes of the present discussion of the PSI, Article 92 of the LOSC is perhaps the most noteworthy of these provisions. Generally the rule of exclusive jurisdiction in the flag state of a vessel is binding and applicable in the context of both legislative and enforcement jurisdiction.[55] However, this exclusivity of jurisdiction is not absolute. Exceptions to this broad norm, in which other states may share jurisdiction over a vessel with its flag state and may under that jurisdiction exercise authority to "visit" the vessel, i.e. to interdict its passage by arresting and boarding it, are listed in detailed fashion in Article 110 of the LOSC.[56] It is of critical importance in terms of legal analysis to note that not only are these exceptions specifically listed, they are listed, unlike the freedoms alluded to in Article 87, in an explicitly exhaustive manner. These provisions are again substantially identically rendered in the 1958 HSC but will be excerpted here from the LOSC.

---

[54] Ibid. at 203–208.   [55] Ibid. at 208.   [56] Ibid. at 209–210.

Article 110

Except where acts of interference derive from powers conferred by treaty, a warship which encounters on the high seas a foreign ship ... is not justified in boarding it unless there is reasonable ground for suspecting that: ...

The article proceeds to list five grounds of suspicion which can trigger the further procedures laid out in the article for verification of the vessel's right to fly its flag and, potentially, for a search of the ship. Interestingly, Article 110 does not, however, explicitly grant to an interdicting state the right of subsequent arrest or detention of a vessel, nor seizure of its cargo, even if its suspicions of activity listed under paragraphs a) through e) of the article are confirmed. This omission is consistent with the title of Article 110, which is conspicuously termed "Right of Visit."[57] Particular note is also to be taken of Article 110(4) which states that "these provisions apply *mutatis mutandis* to military aircraft."

The five listed grounds for suspicion are the vessel's engagement in piracy; engagement in the slave trade; engagement in unauthorized broadcasting; being without nationality; or a case in which "through flying a foreign flag or refusing to show its flag, the ship is, in reality, of the same nationality as the warship." Of these, only two are even colorable candidates for providing a basis for interdiction in a situation in which PSI-related objectives are being pursued.

There has been some mention of attempts to expand the notion of piracy to cover activities related to WMD trafficking at which the PSI was conceived to be aimed.[58] While it would certainly be helpful for the prosecution of PSI principles to have such activities covered by established law on piracy, the issue is in fact deserving of little attention due to the total implausibility of this effort. Piracy is a long standing offense under international law and has received a vast amount of treatment both in legal sources and in academic literature.[59] It is defined explicitly in Article 15 of the HSC and Article 101 of the LOSC. The definition of piracy in these sources, with LOSC Article 101 being of course the operative source for the LOSC Article 110 right of interdiction, is in no way permissive of the sort of interpretive latitude necessarily wielded in attempts to include within the offense of piracy the simple shipment of WMD-related materials and technology without some additional act to bring the case under this established rubric.

---

[57] R.R. Churchill and A.V. Lowe, THE LAW OF THE SEA (3rd edn, 1999) 210.

[58] Interview with John Bolton conducted by Wade Boese. Published by ARMS CONTROL TODAY, December 11, 2003. Available at <http://www.armscontrol.org/act/2003_12/PSI.asp>.

[59] See A.P. Rubin, ETHICS AND AUTHORITY IN INTERNATIONAL LAW (1997); T.A. Walker, A HISTORY OF THE LAW OF NATIONS, VOL. I (1899); B.H. Dubner, THE LAW OF INTERNATIONAL SEA PIRACY (1979); H. Halberstam, *Terrorism on the High Seas: the Achile Lauro, Piracy and the IMO Convention on Maritime Safety*, 82 AMERICAN JOURNAL OF INTERNATIONAL LAW 269 (1988); N. Ronzitti, MARITIME TERRORISM AND INTERNATIONAL LAW (1990); A.P. Rubin, THE LAW OF PIRACY (1988). For current treaty law see also the 1988 International Convention for the Suppression of Unlawful Acts against the Safety of Maritime Navigation.

Secondly, and more significantly, much attention has been given to the possibility of use of the "stateless ship" exception in Article 110 as a basis for interdictions under the PSI framework.[60] Into this "stateless" category are assimilated unflagged vessels, vessels which have either had their right to sail under a particular flag revoked or had their desired flag unrecognized, and vessels that sail under two or more flags, changing them according to convenience.[61] Of such stateless ships Churchill and Lowe have written:

> Ships without nationality are in a curious position. Their "statelessness" will not, of itself, entitle each and every State to assert jurisdiction over them, for there is not in every case any recognised basis upon which jurisdiction could be asserted over stateless ships on the high seas... [I]t has been held, for example, that such ships enjoy the protection of no State, the implication being that if jurisdiction were asserted no State would be competent to complain of a violation of international law. Widely accepted as this view is, it ignores the possibility of diplomatic protection being exercised by the national States of the individuals on such stateless ships. The better view appears to be that there is a need for some jurisdictional nexus in order that a State may extend its laws to those on board a stateless ship and enforce the laws against them.[62]

In the context of the PSI it is conceivable that an arguable assertion of such a jurisdictional link might be made, as it has been made in the context of drug trafficking, of the severity of the threat produced by the activity, and that in a case in which a state meets the criteria for statelessness, interdictions and inspections could be conducted under the authority of LOSC Article 110. Again, however, the issues of further detention and arrest and confiscation of goods are not clarified by Article 110 and are only clarified with regard to verified pirate vessels in other Articles of the LOSC and HSE, which allow for their seizure and for the prosecution of individuals on board suspected of piracy.[63]

Other than through this described process of establishing a jurisdictional link in the context of assertion of a right of interdiction of stateless ships, however, nothing in LOSC Article 110 justifies interdictions of vessels on the high seas for the purposes contemplated by the PSI. In fact, as previously stated, Article 110 is explicitly exhaustive of bases of interdiction on the high seas, and thus serves to occupy the field on this issue, which in fact has the effect of posing a significant

---

[60] Transcript: *"Legitimacy" in International Affairs: The American Perspective in Theory and Operation*, John R. Bolton, Under-Secretary for Arms Control and International Security, Remarks to the Federalist Society, Washington D.C., November 13, 2003.

[61] See H. Myers, The Nationality of Ships (1967); S. Talmon, Recognition of Governments in International Law (1998); T.L. McDorman, *Stateless Fishing Vessels, International Law and the UN High Seas Fisheries Conference*, 25 Journal of Maritime Law and Commerce 531 (1994); R.R. Churchill and A.V. Lowe, The Law of the Sea (3rd edn, 1999) 213.

[62] R.R. Churchill and A.V. Lowe, The Law of the Sea (3rd edn, 1999) 214.

[63] HSC 19, 21, 22; LOSC 105, 106, 107.

legal stumbling block to any assertion of authority to interdict foreign ships and aircraft on the high seas à *la* PSI.[64]

IV. Legality of Actions Pursuant to the PSI

Having reviewed relevant principles of international law in both the areas of international use of force law and the law of the sea, consideration will now turn to a more targeted examination of the principles of the PSI as laid out in the Statement of Interdiction Principles released by the United States and in other statements by officials involved in the PSI, and the legality of actions to be taken in pursuance thereof.[65] To begin with it must be noted that the precise scope and character of the actions contemplated to be included under the PSI framework is a matter of some unclarity. For example some statements particularly by former Under-Secretary Bolton have seemed to indicate that the PSI could include interdictions of vessels believed to be carrying WMD-related materials upon the high seas.[66] Other iterations of the policy parameters of the PSI, such as the above referenced unclassified version of the Statement of Interdiction Principles, have conspicuously avoided reference to the high seas (although not ruling out the possibility), focusing instead on interdiction efforts within states' land territory, internal waters, and territorial seas. In light of these contradictory statements, and the further fact, as noted previously, that it has been made clear that most interdictions will not be reported for public response and critique, this chapter will proceed to consider possibilities for interdiction of vessels in transit through the entire range of possible legal regimes, from areas of clear state territorial jurisdiction out to and including the high seas.

A. State Territory

As previously noted, within the territory of a state—including land territory, internal waters, and super-adjacent airspace—the state has virtually complete jurisdiction both to legislate and enforce. Thus national laws could be constructed at the discretion of national lawmaking bodies and in accordance with constitutional or other governing national legal sources, in order to provide for

---

[64] See generally A. de Smet, *Policing on the High Seas; with Special Reference to the North Sea,* NEW DIRECTION IN THE LAW OF THE SEA, Vol. III, 193–205 (1973–1981); I.A. Shearer, *Problems of Jurisdiction and Law Enforcement against Delinquent Vessels,* 35 INTERNATIONAL AND COMPARATIVE LAW QUARTERLY 320 (1986); T. Treves, *Intervention en haute mer et navires étrangers,* 41 ANNUAIRE FRANCAIS DE DROIT INTERNATIONAL 651 (1995); A. van Swanenberg, *Interference with Ships on the High Seas,* 10 INTERNATIONAL AND COMPARATIVE LAW QUARTERLY 785 (1961).

[65] See generally C. Allen, MARITIME COUNTERPROLIFERATION OPERATIONS AND THE RULE OF LAW (2007) 155.

[66] Interview with John Bolton conducted by Wade Boese. Published by ARMS CONTROL TODAY, December 11, 2003. Available at <http://www.armscontrol.org/act/2003_12/PSI.asp>.

interdictions of PSI-related suspect shipments in either land, sea, or air transit through these areas. This competence to legislate and enforce would of course extend to any vessel, foreign or domestic, and to any state or foreign national involved in these transactions subject only to sovereign and diplomatic immunity protections under international law. Up to this point there is very little contention, and what legal questions there are are generally related to the harmonization of such provisions with national foundational legal authorities, and specifically to the precise standards for reasonableness of suspicion which would have to be met under those authorities for interdictions to legitimately take place, including whether information provided by other states would be sufficient for such purposes.

Also as previously noted states may prescribe conditions on entry to their ports and airfields including customs-related requirements for boarding and searching of vessels prior to entry and for seizure of items the possession and/or importation of which is proscribed by national law. Properly constructed, therefore, national laws could legitimize many PSI-related interdictions of both domestic and foreign vessels and aircraft in transit through areas of state territory.

B. Territorial Sea

As the scope of possible interdiction activities moves out beyond the area of states' territorial jurisdiction to include interdictions within the territorial sea area, analysis of the legality of those activities becomes more complicated. Based upon the principles of law previously reviewed, it should be possible to construct national law principles legitimizing coastal state interdiction of both foreign and domestic aircraft in transit through airspace over its own territorial sea under the PSI framework without running foul of international law. It should also be possible through these national legal sources to legitimize seizure of goods made illegal by those sources, which could include WMD-related items of PSI concern. Furthermore it should be possible for a coastal state to interdict seagoing vessels under its flag in its own territorial sea as long as principles creating such a right to interdict are established in national legal sources. Seagoing vessels as well as aircraft are of course subject to the jurisdiction of their flag state wherever they are found.

The interdiction of foreign seagoing vessels in the territorial sea by a coastal state, however, will necessitate either obtaining the consent of the flag state to the interdiction, or in the absence of this consent, overcoming those vessels' right of innocent passage described above. Notwithstanding the significant presumption of retention of the right of innocent passage, in the final analysis, in the particular case of suspected WMD-proliferation activities, this would likely not present too great a hurdle for coastal states to clear. As explained above, the current law applicable to this question, contained in Article 19 of the LOSC, is subject to interpretation which should allow a coastal state to deem the right of innocent passage lost simply through aspects of the character of passage of a vessel through the territorial sea, and not to require some additional act to be taken by the vessel for this purpose. In the modern climate of concern regarding proliferation of WMD and the fairly straightforward nature of characterizing such proliferation inclusive of activities of transit of WMD-related materials, as threats to the security of both the coastal state and, drawing upon the particular language of Article 19, to other states as well, it should be relatively unproblematic for coastal states to legitimize the overcoming of the right of innocent passage through their territorial waters of seagoing vessels regarding which there is a reasonable basis of suspicion of involvement in these activities, and particularly if such transfers are in violation of the national law of the coastal state. Short of an egregious abuse of this discretion, such a determination would not likely be found to be in excess of a coastal state's rights to safeguard its security.

In a case in which the right of innocent passage has been deemed lost, seagoing vessels in the territorial sea as noted above are subject to the full jurisdiction, legislative and enforcement, of the coastal state. Thus as long as these principles are established in national law, the arrest, boarding, searching, and seizure of illegal items found on board, as well as the prosecution of crew members, should be possible for the coastal state to legitimize under international law.

C. High Seas

The analysis thus far of the legality of actions contemplated under the PSI should be relatively welcome to proponents of the program, as within the full sovereignty zone and in the territorial sea area there should be a fairly wide latitude granted by international law for national laws properly constructed to allow for activities falling under the PSI's mandate. However, this latitude essentially ceases when consideration turns to the area of the high seas and its relevant legal regime described above. As the foregoing analysis shows, states may exercise their legislative and enforcement jurisdiction over both seagoing vessels and aircraft under their flag in the high seas area and thus practice the principles of the PSI upon them, including boarding, searching, and seizure of goods. States may also be able to use the principle of stateless vessels to legitimize "visitations" (i.e. arrest and boarding) of aircraft and seagoing vessels not under their flag on the high seas. However, the right of a state to effect a continuing arrest of the vessel or aircraft and to confiscate items found under this entitlement is quite tenuous.[67]

Other than in this latter class of cases, interdictions of foreign flagged vessels or aircraft on the high seas unless sanctioned *ex ante* by the flag state are illegal under international law not only for members of the 1982 LOSC, but due to the customary law status likely achieved by those principles, for any state. The only

---

[67] See R.R. Churchill and A.V. Lowe, THE LAW OF THE SEA (3rd edn, 1999) 205–218.

available means of legally exempting interdiction activities on the high seas from the relevant confines of Article 110 of the LOSC for parties to the same would be to take advantage of the first clause of the text of the article, which reads: "Except where acts of interference derive from powers conferred by treaty..." Here the drafters of Article 110 wished to leave open the possibility of subsequent or already extant treaties among groups of LOSC parties to amend as among themselves the right of interdiction covered in the article, for example through the conclusion of boarding agreements. And indeed, in pursuance of the principles of the PSI, the United States for example has concluded bilateral boarding agreements with significant flag states including Belize, Croatia, Cyprus, Liberia, the Marshall Islands, and Panama, which together provide a legal basis for interdictions of more than half of world shipping.[68] Thus states upon which the principles of the LOSC are legally binding can essentially rewrite the interdiction principles of Article 110 pursuant to this provision through the establishment of conflicting principles in other treaty instruments.

This recognition has been the impetus behind recent efforts, particularly on the part of the United States, to achieve consensus on amendments to the 1988 International Convention for the Suppression of Unlawful Acts Against the Safety of Maritime Navigation (SUA) to include in that instrument provisions allowing for interdiction of vessels engaged in weapons and WMD-related goods trafficking.[69] These efforts resulted in the adoption by the International Maritime Organization in 2005 of a Protocol to the 1988 SUA, which in its Article 3*bis* states that a person commits an offence within the meaning of the Convention if that person unlawfully and intentionally transports on board a seagoing vessel radioactive material, biological, chemical, or nuclear weapons, or related precursor or dual-use goods and technologies. The 2005 SUA Protocol has yet to come into force. Even if it does come into force, however, this addition to non-proliferation law will arguably do little to remedy the problem of legalizing PSI-related interdictions on the high seas. For a Protocol to the SUA to be meritorious in excepting a state from the strictures of Article 110 of the LOSC, not only the interdicting state but also the target state (i.e. flag state of the vessel to be interdicted) would have to be members of the SUA Protocol.[70] This again runs into the non-universality problem of non-proliferation law, and the fact that many states of proliferation concern to the international community are not parties to non-proliferation treaties. The only other means, although both practically and legally more questionable, would be for the SUA Protocol, if it does come into force, to achieve the status of customary law in derogation of both the treaty and parallel customary law of LOSC Article 110. In the end, this potentiality,

---

[68] "Key Facts: Overview of the International Shipping Industry," available at <http://www. marisec.org/shippingfacts/home/>.

[69] John Bolton interview with ARMS CONTROL TODAY, December 11, 2003. Available at <http:// www.armscontrol.org/act/2003_12/PSI.asp>.

[70] See <http://www.imo.org/home.asp>.

however remote, may have been the primary motivating factor influencing the conclusion of the 2005 SUA Protocol.

Also under this clause, however, could arguably be included the authorization and direction of interdictions by the United Nations Security Council acting under Chapter VII of the United Nations Charter, as the Charter specifies in Article 25 that all decisions of the Security Council including Chapter VII resolutions are binding upon all Charter members and are thus arguably includable under the category of member state obligations/entitlements under a separate treaty framework. Although the members of the PSI have up to the present declined to seek the support of the UN Security Council for the PSI, former Under-Secretary Bolton has indicated that Security Council action under Chapter VII could provide supplementary authority for PSI-related actions in the future in cases in which sufficient authority cannot be found elsewhere.[71]

D. Chapter VII

In this context it bears brief mention that arguments which have been made for the passing of a Security Council resolution under Chapter VII essentially establishing a legal framework for the PSI to be applied chronologically *ad infinitum* and in whatever cases appear to match whatever standards might be laid out in such a resolution, misunderstand the conception that body has always had of its rightful exercise of authority, as discussed extensively in Chapter 4 above.[72]

However, temporary and ad hoc authorizations of force by the Security Council under Chapter VII could through this clause establish a legal basis for interdiction

---

[71] It has additionally been argued that, since Article 51 of the U.N. Charter recognizes the right of self-defense, that right in all of its breadth may be relied upon by interdicting states through operation of the chapeaux of Article 110. This argument, however, misunderstands the distinction between inherent rights of states, inuring due to their fundamental attributes of statehood on the one hand, and rights collectively agreed through the operation of positive law, including treaties. The right of states to self-defense is not simply a power conferred by treaty. It is a right recognized as existing "inherently" in Article 51 of the UN Charter, in order to clarify the limitations of the proscription in Article 2(4). However, no state would accept that the right of self-defense is only operable because of its recognition in Article 51. The right of self-defense is a right of states, existing in custom and in general international law *ab initio*. The recognition that self-defense is a general right of states under international law, and not simply a right conferred by treaty means that interdictions of commercial vessels on the high seas during peacetime done on the grounds of self-defense are therefore not, in the words of Article 110 of the Law of the Sea Convention "acts of interference deriv[ing] from powers conferred by treaty." This in turn means that Article 110's specification that interdictions on the high seas may not be undertaken except under the categories specified in the article, is not subject to the further exception of self-defense, but rather is *lex specialis* to that general right and therefore is to be taken in priority in determining governing law. This is notwithstanding the appearance of Article 51 in the United Nations Charter, as again Article 51 only recognizes this already existing right of states. Article 51 does not therefore comprise an obligation of United Nations Members, as established by the Charter, such as to be taken in priority over obligations in other international agreements pursuant to UN Charter Article 103.

[72] See Chapter 4 below at 180.

of particular vessels suspected of involvement in transit of WMD-related materials. The process of obtaining such a resolution, along with attendant transactions costs of persuading a sufficient number of Security Council members, including all permanent members, to allow the measure to pass, is clearly not an attractive one for PSI participants, particularly as time is of the essence after the detection of a suspect vessel. This is not to mention the groaning among national intelligence agencies which will accompany any proposal to share intelligence with a group as disparate as the Security Council, as would be necessary to establish a reasonable basis for belief of a target vessel's suspect activity and obtain the support of that body for an interdiction. Thus the Security Council route, while an option for legitimizing PSI interdictions on the high seas in the absence of authority elsewhere, carries with it the same difficulties as reviewed in Chapter 7 above in consideration of *ex ante* authorizations of counterproliferation-oriented pre-emptive uses of force generally, and for those reasons is not likely to be a mode of choice among PSI participants.[73] Although as described above, there are few other authorities on which to rely for such interdictions.

E. Security Council Resolution 1540

Before moving on, it is important to note again the possible impact of Security Council Resolution 1540 on the issue of the PSI and the legality particularly of high seas interdictions. For the moment, therefore, the validity of Resolution 1540 will be assumed, notwithstanding this volume's conclusions in Chapter 4 above.[74] One provision of Resolution 1540 has been argued by some to represent additional or independent international legal authority for the prosecution of the PSI.[75] In operative paragraph 10, the Security Council "calls upon all States, in accordance with their national legal authorities and legislation and consistent with international law, to take cooperative action to prevent illicit trafficking in nuclear, chemical or biological weapons, their means of delivery, and related materials."

While at first blush this paragraph may seem to provide an additional legal support to the PSI, which was no doubt the intent of some of the resolution's drafters,[76] the legal character of the text of this paragraph can be distinguished from that of the text in operative paragraphs 1 through 3 of the resolution. In operative paragraphs 1 through 3, the Council "*decides* that all states shall" take specific actions related to the regulation of WMD proliferation within their domestic legal systems. This language signifies that the Council is exercising its

---

[73] See Chapter 7 below at 291.

[74] See Chapter 4 below at 197.

[75] See C.A. Kalinoski, "U.N. Security Council Resolution 1540 Calls on Members to Control WMD's," *The Export Practitioner*, Vol. 19 No. 1 (January 2005).

[76] See M. Byers, *Agreeing to Disagree: Security Council Resolution 1441 and International Ambiguity*, 10 GLOBAL GOVERNANCE 165–186 (2004).

Chapter VII and Article 25 authority to impose obligations upon states in their capacity as parties to the U.N. Charter, and to issue binding new decisions on matters of both substance and procedure. In operative paragraphs 4 through 7 the Council then further *decides* to establish a committee to accept compliance reports from member states, and takes other steps aimed at implementation. However in operative paragraphs 8 through 10, the Council noticeably changes its phraseology. It importantly only *calls upon* states to take much more ill-defined and broadly termed action to counter the general threat of proliferation, in the manner of an exhortation to states made on behalf of the United Nations in its capacity as an international organization, signifying a change in the legal character of the text from obligation-imposing to invitation-making.

Thus, the text of operative paragraph 10 does not bestow any additional authority upon states to prosecute the PSI in aggrandizement of any existing entitlements they hold under international law, and importantly it further does not exempt states from any international legal obligations they otherwise have. It is simply an invitation from the U.N. Security Council to states to cooperate in efforts to combat WMD proliferation in a manner consistent with existing domestic and international laws. As Paul Szasz has observed with regard to other similar Security Council Resolutions:

In recent years, however, the Security Council has increasingly adopted decisions that deal not with any particular conflict or situation but, rather, with conflicts in general. Thus, it has addressed the protection of children and civilians, the role of women with respect to peace and security, humanitarian questions, and even international terrorism. Nevertheless, the operative paragraphs of these resolutions that are addressed to states are not formulated in compulsory terms but, for the most part, merely "call upon" states or parties to a conflict, or even more weakly just "urge" them—terminology that is understood as not implying compulsion. Other provisions "condemn" certain practices but, again, without requiring states to refrain from them. Consequently, these decisions of the Council also cannot be considered as establishing new rules of international law.[77]

Support for this interpretation of the provisions of Resolution 1540 particularly can further be found in the statements of state representatives, including particularly permanent members of the Security Council, in the discussions leading up to the passage of Resolution 1540. As the representative of France noted:

Lastly, there are widespread misgivings with respect to the reference in the draft resolution to Chapter VII of the Charter, which has sparked concerns about a potential use of force to ensure the draft resolution's implementation. I should like to allay that fear by addressing the problem in depth. We believe that we can mitigate this concern

---

[77] P. Szasz, *The Security Council Starts Legislating*, 96 AMERICAN JOURNAL OF INTERNATIONAL LAW 901, 902 (2002). See also M. Byers, *Policing the High Seas: The Proliferation Security Initiative*, 98 AMERICAN JOURNAL OF INTERNATIONAL LAW 526, 532 (2004); S.D. Bailey, THE PROCEDURE OF THE U.N. SECURITY COUNCIL (1975) 204–205; S. Talmon, *The Security Council as World Legislature*, 99 AMERICAN JOURNAL OF INTERNATIONAL LAW 175, 186 (2005).

by enhancing the follow-up mechanism, which must protect the legitimate interests of States and coordinate Security Council cooperation with them . . . we are resolved to promote implementation based on cooperation and respect for the sovereignty of States and to preclude any coercion that is not justified, considered or authorized by the Council.[78]

Similarly, the representative of the United States stated:

The draft resolution is placed under Chapter VII in order to send the important political message of the seriousness with which the Council views the threat to international peace and security. It also is placed under Chapter VII because the Council is acting under that Chapter and levying binding requirements. However, the draft resolution is not about enforcement.[79]

Most definitively of all, the representative of the United Kingdom stated:

What this draft resolution does not do is authorize enforcement action against States or against non-State actors in the territory of another country. The draft resolution makes clear that it will be the Council that will monitor its implementation. Any enforcement action would require a new Council decision.[80]

Finally, in addition to this textual analysis of Security Council Resolution 1540 and its relevance to the PSI, as informed by reference to the *travaux préparatoires* of the resolution itself, it should be noted that further applicable to this issue is the principle of interpretation of Security Council resolutions which establishes a presumption in favor of the inviolability of state sovereignty.[81] This principle was discussed in Chapter 7 above in the context of the Security Council resolutions which some have cited as having authorized the 2003 military intervention into Iraq.[82] This presumption of state sovereignty, as a cornerstone of the international legal system codified in U.N. Charter Article 2(4), serves to require clear, explicit, and definitive authorizations by the Security Council acting under its Chapter VII powers, in order to legitimize actions violating state sovereignty taken in pursuance thereof. The implication or tortured construction of such authorization is never sufficient to overcome this foundational presumption.[83]

V. Legal Issues

In light of the foregoing discussion of the legality of actions contemplated to be performed under the PSI framework, and particularly in consideration of the

---

[78] S/PV.4950 p. 8 (April 22, 2004).   [79] S/PV.4950 p. 17 (April 22, 2004).
[80] S/PV.4950 p. 12 (April 22, 2004).
[81] J. Abr. Frowein, "Unilateral Interpretation of Security Council Resolutions—a Threat to Collective Security?" in V. Götz, P. Selmer, and R. Wolfrum (eds), LIBER AMICORUM GÜNTHER JAENICKE—ZUM 85. GEBURTSTAG (1998) 99 (as reprinted in M. Byers, *Agreeing to Disagree: Security Council Resolution 1441 and Intentional Ambiguity*, 10 GLOBAL GOVERNANCE 165–186 (2004).
[82] See Chapter 7 below at 276.
[83] See C. Gray, INTERNATIONAL LAW AND THE USE OF FORCE (2nd edn, 2004) 281.

continuing possibility of PSI-based interdictions on the high seas, at least two sets of questions bearing on this analysis are raised. The first has to do with the jurisprudential soundness of proceeding against the threat of WMD proliferation along the path outlined by the PSI, according to which legal efforts are expended primarily on justifying interdictions of vessels thought to be carrying WMD-related items, in place of efforts to in fact make illegal the transfer of the items themselves. This focus represents a clear manifestation of the shift in emphasis away from non-proliferation law and toward counterproliferation policy which has been identified herein, and its consideration illustrates some of the legal problems which can attend this shift in emphasis generally.

In legal terms this focus on interdiction represents cart before the horse logic. Interdiction, under either domestic or international law, is essentially an enforcement mechanism, not a substantive judgment on the legality of the target activity. This is the reason that LOSC Article 110 limits the legitimate subjects for interdiction to those vessels engaged in only five possible activities—i.e. activities which in other sources of law are themselves made substantively illegal.

The clearest example of this notion is to be found in the area of drug trafficking—one of the activities listed for justifiable interdiction in Article 110. Drug trafficking on the high seas is made an illegal activity under a number of international conventions most notably including the 1988 Vienna Convention Against Illicit Traffic in Narcotic Drugs and Psychotropic Substances, which both defines the activities covered under its proscriptive terms and in detail lays out measures authorized for their suppression.[84] Similarly, as previously noted, in addition to its classical delineation in customary law, the crime of piracy is defined in detail both in Article 15 of the HSC (Article 101 of the LOSC) and in the 1988 SUA, which in Article 3 provides a clear explication of the parameters of that offense.[85] Analogous sources substantively addressing the illegality under international law of the other activities on the high seas made subject to interdiction actions in LOSC Article 110 can also be referenced.[86] The LOSC is therefore best read narrowly as simply providing non-flag states the legal justification under some circumstances for interdiction of these already illegal activities.

[84] See W.C. Gilmore, *Drug Trafficking by Sea: the 1988 United Nations Convention Against Illicit Traffic in Narcotic Drugs and Psychotropic Substances*, 15 MARINE POLICY 183 (1991); *Narcotic Interdiction at Sea: The 1995 Council of Europe Agreement*, 20 MARINE POLICY 3 (1996); *Narcotics Interdiction at Sea: UK-US Cooperation*, 13 MARINE POLICY 218 (1989); J. Siddle, *Anglo-American Cooperation in the Suppression of Drug Smuggling*, 31 INTERNATIONAL AND COMPARATIVE LAW QUARTERLY 726 (1982); J.D. Stieb, *Survey of United States Jurisdiction over High Seas Narcotic Trafficking*, 19 GEORGIA JOURNAL OF COMPARATIVE & INTERNATIONAL LAW 119 (1989).

[85] See below n. 58 on piracy.

[86] See, e.g., 1927 International Convention to Suppress the Slave Trade and Slavery; 1965 European Agreement for the Prevention of Broadcasts Transmitted from Stations outside National Territories, and below n. 60 on stateless vessels.

Trafficking in WMD-related items and technology, however, is an entirely different matter. As discussed herein, the formal rules of non-proliferation law are limited in their effective coverage of cross-border transfers of WMD-related materials and technology. While importantly including broad prohibitive norms regarding WMD-related materials transfer, the cornerstone treaties contain very limited guidance on implementation of these norms. In the case of the NPT and BWC, there is no authoritative treaty definition even of the single-use materials the transfer of which is proscribed in their non-proliferation provisions. And in all three cornerstone non-proliferation treaties, there is insufficient definition of dual-use materials subject to transfer prohibition. As has been discussed above, some member states of the NPT, BWC, and CWC have attempted to fill in the gaps left by the treaties in the area of implementation, through the establishment and maintenance of multilateral export control regimes (the NSG and the Australia Group in particular). However, the guidelines of these regimes are formally non-binding upon their participants, and thus do not expand the corpus of formal non-proliferation law on the subject of cross-border transfers.

With regard to Resolution 1540, again assuming its validity *arguendo*, the provisions of this decision only bind U.N. member states to establish laws in their domestic jurisdictions regulating sensitive exports and non-state actor behavior with regard to sensitive items and technologies, and deny them state support. This does possibly establish international legal obligations for states, although it is not clear exactly what those obligations are with regard to direct and official state transfers of WMD-related items and technologies. These transfers may in fact not be covered by domestic export controls, which are as a rule focused on regulating exports by private parties and can generally be overridden by state policy imperative. However, even more importantly, non-state actor behavior is still not made the subject of direct international legal coverage through Resolution 1540, such as to give rise to breaches of international law by private parties engaging in WMD-related materials transfer.

These facts of the limited coverage of formal non-proliferation law beg the implementation question of which shipments should be the focus of PSI efforts? Would shipments from all countries or only a select few be candidates for interdiction? Similarly, information on transfers of which items and technologies would trigger a reasonable suspicion of illegitimate sensitive items transfer? In the absence of objectively verifiable law on the subject, according to what standard would such determinations be made? And perhaps most saliently, who would make these determinations? In fact the very same considerations which have bedeviled efforts to treat the subject of WMD-related materials transfer through formal non-proliferation law with specificity and objectivity are the same considerations which make these questions in the PSI context unanswerable, except to reply that such determinations would be made either unilaterally or in consultation with a small number of other PSI participants and on no objective international legal basis whatsoever.

As a domestic law analogy, imagine a statute authorizing police forces to stop and search all automobiles traveling on public roads which are suspected of carrying children to soccer practice, and providing for the seizure of all athletic equipment found in the vehicle. The reverse logic in this hypo of sanctioning interdictions of substantively legal activities is readily apparent. The application to the PSI context is of course that while trafficking in WMD-related items and technologies is perhaps more sinister than the conduct described above, it is in fact in many cases no more illegal under existing law and therefore as illustrative of corrupted logic in the establishment of interdiction principles. In the domestic context, such enforcement action upon activity not substantively illegal would likely be in breach of constitutional or other foundational protections against arbitrary arrest and detention, and unreasonable searches and seizures, and would be found to constitute a failure to accord due process of law to the subject of the enforcement action. While due process rights do exist in international human rights law, among other places in Articles 9, 14, and 15 of the International Covenant on Civil and Political Rights, it is unlikely that those rights would be found to be either applicable to the particular context of interdiction of foreign-flagged vessels engaged in commercial transit of goods over the sea lanes (i.e. due to the *lex specialis* nature of the law of the sea), or operative in such a case even if found to be applicable.[87] Still, however, the presence of such protections under both international law and the domestic law of most liberal democratic states (i.e. as general principles of law) might bolster arguments of a state made the target of PSI interdiction activities before an international tribunal of the illegitimate character of such activities under LOSC Article 110.[88]

This observation of the logic and jurisprudential correctness within the law of the sea regime of having norms on substantive illegality precede norms on interdiction in the context of the PSI can perhaps be applied as a lesson more generally to counterproliferation policies which are sought to be implemented by the use of international force. LOSC Article 110 can perhaps best be understood as a *lex specialis* use of force law regime, contracted into by states in order to deal with the particular issue of troublesome non-flag vessels on the high seas. Pursuant to this reasoning, Article 110 can therefore be understood simply as a branch or manifestation of international use of force law specifically applicable in the law of the sea context. Furthermore, the observation herein regarding the presence of legal standards and their breach as a prerequisite to the legitimate use of international force also transfers fairly well to the broader system of international use of force law, with the U.N. Charter as its cornerstone.

---

[87] See generally T. Morrison, *United States v. Suerte: The Fifth Circuit Fails to Address International Law Principles in Examining Due Process Concerns Raised under the Extraterritorial Application of the Maritime Drug Law Enforcement Act*, 27 TULANE MARITIME LAW JOURNAL 631 (2003).

[88] See Article 38(1)(c), Statute of the International Court of Justice (1945).

Within the Charter system of use of force law, Article 2(4) establishes a broad non-intervention rule with only two exceptions: Article 51 on self-defense and the articles of Chapter VII. Article 51 is worded so as to allow unilateral self-defense temporarily, and only "if an armed attack occurs" against a member of the U.N. That precursor armed attack would by definition be a breach of Article 2(4), and would whether committed by a U.N. member or non-member, be in breach of the substance of Article 2(4) which is now a rule of *jus cogens*.[89] Thus, the U.N. Charter system can be persuasively understood as having been designed to legitimize a use of force in self-defense only if that use of force is taken in response to a violation of international law.

As for the other exception to the Charter's prohibition of international uses of force, Chapter VII empowers the U.N. Security Council to authorize international uses of force against states or non-state actors who have caused a "threat to the peace, breach of the peace, or act of aggression." The overlapping and definitional relationship between the concepts of remediation of breaches of international law on the one hand, and the maintenance or restoration of international peace and security on the other, was discussed in Chapter 4 above.[90] As concluded in that discussion, the Security Council's own understanding of its Chapter VII role and authority during the first 56 years of its existence was most analogous to that of an executive body, entrusted by all U.N. members with the responsibility and authority to maintain and restore international peace and security, primarily in cases where the generalized obligations of the U.N. Charter or other rules of international law had been breached. Thus, the exception from Article 2(4)'s prohibition contained in the articles of Chapter VII can be persuasively read to comprise a power vested in the Security Council to authorize international uses of force primarily, if not exclusively, in response to a previous violation of international law. Indeed, as noted previously, it is difficult to imagine actions by a state or non-state actor which would rise to the level of being perceived to cause a "threat to the peace, breach of the peace, or act of aggression" but which did not entail breaches of substantive rules of international law.

The question of anticipatory self-defense, or some expanded version thereof, as a matter of U.N. Charter law is, as discussed previously, quite controversial. As will be reviewed in Chapter 9 below, it was the wisdom of the drafters of the U.N. Charter to design the rules on international use of force to make them as clear, transparent, and objectively verifiable as possible, so as to leave as little debatable legal ground as possible on a subject of such importance to international stability. In short, it was their intention to create definitive legal standards which would need to be met before an international use of force could legally be taken. This included the prerequisite of definitive legal standards having been violated by the target of such an international use of force.

---

[89] I. Brownlie, PRINCIPLES OF PUBLIC INTERNATIONAL LAW (6th edn, 2003) 489.
[90] See Chapter 4 below at 178.

Thus, in all levels and manifestations of existing international use of force law can be divined a principle of system construction pursuant to which uses of force are only recognized as legal when they are taken in response to a substantively illegal act on the part of the target state.[91] Applying this principle of system construction to considerations of an expanded hypothetical right of counterproliferation-oriented pre-emptive self-defense, of a type which would be necessary to justify the most aggressive PSI-based interdictions, or the 2003 Iraq intervention, illuminates jurisprudential problems which would be inherent in its existence and application. In a nutshell, the further forward along the *ex ante* chronological line a pre-emptive use of force occurs, the less likely it is to be in response to an illegal action on the part of the target state or non-state actor, as the *sine qua non* of such a pre-emptive use of force is its occurrence before the material dangerous action of the target state or non-state actor. Thus the jurisprudential system requirement of such a precursor illegal act on the part of the target state all but prohibits, logically, such an expanded pre-emptive right.

While the subject of the present and future of the *jus ad bellum* will be taken up in greater detail in Chapter 9 below, the lessons which can be gleaned from the case of the PSI with regard to the importance of clear legal standards upon which to base lawful and legitimate counterproliferation-oriented international uses of force are proposed to be of significant meaning and prudential recommendation for considerations of the implementation of counterproliferation policy, and particularly as that policy is sought to be implemented through pre-emptive uses of international force.

VI. Policy/Practical Issues

The second set of questions goes more to the utility of the PSI as a policy matter, yet has bearing on the legal issues discussed herein. The fundamental question is whether there is sufficient utility in the potential operation of the PSI to justify such jurisprudential difficulties in prosecution as have been discussed to this point, as well as the potential destabilization particularly of the high seas regime which could result from over virulent, or even abusive, application of PSI interdiction principles.

As described above, established rules of international law all but prohibit PSI interdictions of vessels on the high seas by non-flag states. This then leaves open the possibility, partially realized by the United States, of negotiating *ex ante* boarding agreements with flag states, though this requires the expenditure of a great deal of political capital to achieve and, in the end, will likely only be achieved with states that are not of great proliferation concern. It also leaves some

---

[91] See D. Rodin, "The Problem with Prevention," in H. Shue and D. Rodin (eds), PREEMPTION: MILITARY ACTION AND MORAL JUSTIFICATION (2007).

rights in coastal states as discussed regarding both flag and non-flag vessels in the territorial sea and of course enforcement actions in state territory. The question must therefore be asked, with a scope of legal application so limited by international law, of what utility is the initiative if its aim is truly to significantly decrease international shipments of WMD-related items and technologies by or to states or non-state actors of proliferation concern?

In this context it is important to note that transfers of completed weapons systems of the type seen in the case of the *So San* described above are quite exceptional and do not fairly represent what are the most commonly used and at the same time most difficult modes of sensitive technology transfer to combat. Reference is made here specifically to international trade and trafficking in dual-use goods. Of the current hot spots of proliferation concern, a generalized statement can be made to the effect that the greatest facilitator of WMD development programs either in the nuclear, chemical, or biological weapons context is not single-use items—i.e. fissile materials, poisonous chemicals, or dangerous biological agents and toxins. Rather, the greatest concern is the transfer to states and non-state actors of concern of the means of indigenous production of these materials as well as the technology to turn them into weapons of mass destruction. Dual-use goods of a wide variety which are sought for this purpose are both requisite to obtain and increasingly difficult to regulate on both the national and multilateral level.

The international transfer of such items and the proliferation threat caused thereby are not most effectively targeted through principles of interdiction in transit. Trade in dual-use goods is far too great in volume and complex in flow for such an approach. As discussed previously, the international transfer of dual-use items is addressed through multilateral export control regimes, and these regimes can and do play an important role in standardizing and harmonizing the national export control policies of member states. It is true, however, that the problem of secondary proliferation is not well addressed through the existing structure of the multilateral export control regimes and associated proliferation treaty instruments. And proponents of the PSI will argue that even if interdictions cannot legally be staged against all ships, there is utility in the program in that it may force proliferators to use only ships under the flag of non-PSI participants for proliferation activities, thus potentially raising transactions costs. They point as well to the potential deterrent effect upon commercial shipping companies which even a limited number of interdictions would have, in motivating such actors to increase their diligence in acquiring information on cargo and creating disincentives to enter into questionable freight contracts.[92]

The limited marginal utility of these possible effects is not denied. However it should be noted that, due to the secrecy surrounding PSI-related operations, even

---

[92] February 12, 2004 author interview with a senior official of the U.S. Defense Department on condition of non-attribution.

careful observers of proliferation issues are divided on the question of the results of the program thus far. Indeed, one leading commentator has recently observed that to date the PSI is "not yet responsible for successfully interdicting a single vessel."[93] With such skepticism among leading analysts, it is difficult to see how a deterrent effect among target actors is to be expected.

Again, though, being able to claim some relatively minor marginal utility of a policy is not the same as showing that its utility is sufficient to outweigh its potential costs. These costs come in a variety of forms, but most important in the case of the PSI is the potential cost to the legal order of the sea lanes, and particularly the high seas, if there were to come to public knowledge cases resembling the *So San* in which PSI interdictions occur on the high seas. As noted previously, in light of statements by some PSI participant state officials, and unassisted by the secrecy surrounding the prosecution of the PSI, it is not known whether PSI-related high seas interdictions are being carried out. The destabilization of the high seas legal order, which would be accomplished either through blatant violation of the law of the sea, or through extreme and unrespected legal interpretations thereof, could have serious reciprocal implications for commercial shipping, including for the merchant fleets of PSI participants.

A corollary question is whether, in a reality of scarce resources both physical and political, are gaps in the non-proliferation treaties and regimes system better addressed through the PSI than through other means? Are the resources of the international community best devoted to the PSI; a counterproliferation-oriented interdiction program of limited legal scope of application, the principles and motivations of which are likely to give rise to actions of questionable legality in an area of law of great importance to international order, and which is to be prosecuted among a group of states whose territorial waters, state territory, and boarding agreement coalitions could be fairly easily avoided by savvy and determined smugglers? Or might these resources rather be better allocated to additional non-proliferation efforts such as export control assistance programs, aid and development programs, and to less invasive counterproliferation programs such as the U.S. Customs and Border Protection Agency's Container Security Initiative, pursuant to which U.S. Customs officials are posted at a growing number of foreign ports including important transshipment points with inspection powers granted by the host government?[94]

In point of fact, the PSI seems in its original incarnation, potentially inclusive of the aggressive use of interdictions on the high seas, to have been almost tailor made to deal with only one threat, the proliferation of missile technologies. And

---

[93] M. Reiss, *Foreword*, in N. Busch and D.H. Joyner (eds), Combating Weapons of Mass Destruction: The Future of Nonproliferation Policy (2009). See also A. Winner and J. Holmes, "The Proliferation Security Initiative: A Global Prohibition Regime in the Making?" in N. Busch and D.H. Joyner (eds), Combating Weapons of Mass Destruction: The Future of Nonproliferation Policy (2009).

[94] See <http://www.cbp.gov/xp/cgov/border_security/international_activities/csi/>.

there is to be frank only one state which has consistently sold missiles to other states and actors requiring delivery over long distances by sea. It is the same state of origin of the missiles on board the *SoSan*—i.e. the only "rogue" state that is not only of development but also of significant proliferation concern. This is not to say that the threat posed by North Korean proliferation of missile technologies is not a serious one. North Korea is in possession of both short and medium range missiles with further development of ballistic missile capabilities reportedly advancing.[95] The proliferation of such advanced delivery systems to states with WMD development programs is clearly a legitimate concern for foreign policy-makers of states potentially the targets of these technologies, particularly in light of the fact as discussed in Chapter 1 above that proliferation of missile technologies has been the issue area least effectively addressed by non-proliferation law.[96] However, the recognition of the limited utility of the PSI in its aggressive form to the missile proliferation threat from North Korea does decrease in measure the justifiability of actions under the PSI framework which violate settled principles of international law, and particularly principles as vital to the ordered character of international commerce as those under the umbrella of the law of the sea. This consideration in turn should cause concern regarding the question of the PSI's character as the highest possible use of the scarce resources of the international community.

To be fair, in the past few years, the application of the PSI's principles does seem to have been rather significantly toned down and made less aggressive both in the rhetoric surrounding it, as well as in the small bits of information regarding actual PSI-based interdictions which have trickled into the public domain.[97] The change in rhetoric seems largely attributable to the departure of John Bolton, the firebrand U.S. diplomat and conceptual creator and coordinator of the PSI, from his position at the U.S. State Department.[98] However, through anecdotal evidence it can be surmised that the character of the program itself seems also to have been more tightly circumscribed in its scope than in its early days. When speaking of the effectiveness of the PSI, rather than pointing to instances of high seas interdictions, the 2003 case of the *BBC China* is frequently held up as something of a poster-child of PSI success.[99] In that case, a German owned merchant ship was interdicted by Italian authorities while docked at the Italian port

---

[95] See <http://cns.miis.edu/research/korea/overview.htm>.

[96] See Chapter 1 below at 40.

[97] M. Heupel, *The Proliferation Security Initiative: Advancing Commitment and Capacity for WMD Interdictions*, Disarmament Forum, Vol. 4, 57, 60 (2007).

[98] See A. Winner and J. Holmes, "The Proliferation Security Initiative: A Global Prohibition Regime in the Making?" in N. Busch and D.H. Joyner (eds), Combating Weapons of Mass Destruction: The Future of Nonproliferation Policy (2009).

[99] Though some observers dispute whether the *BBC China* case was in fact an implementation of PSI principles. See G. Corera, "Taming a Tyrant," *The Sunday Times*, June 25, 2006. Available at <http://www.timesonline.co.uk/article/0,,2092–2241879_1,00.html>.

of Taranto and found to be carrying uranium centrifuge parts bound for Libya, after coordination between U.S. and U.K. intelligence agencies, the German Government, and the Italian Government.

The PSI does seem to have been re-molded, in a sense, into a somewhat more modest program focusing, as in the case of the *BBC China*, on the international coordination of efforts to produce interdictions within participating state territory including ports, or within a participating state's territorial sea. This more reserved *modus operandi* has the potential to cure most if not all of the international legal problems which have been perceived to be present, or at least potentially present, in the past prosecution of the PSI. However, the secrecy surrounding the operation of the PSI remains, and thus fears of aggressive use of PSI principles in violation of international law cannot be fully abated.

If, however, the PSI were to be implemented in its scaled back form in accordance with the rules of international law, and if it were at the same time to be made a more transparent program about which more information was shared with members of international civil society, it could represent a very useful foil with other examples of counterproliferation policy of much larger scope and impact upon international relations, and of much more serious legal and policy concern, such as the 2003 intervention in Iraq. Indeed, a modest program of interdiction of WMD-related materials in transit, in which interdictions were seen to take place by states within their own sovereign territory, including their ports and territorial sea, in accordance with their national laws regarding transit of such materials, and in a relatively transparent fashion in which a meaningful amount of information regarding such interdictions was shared openly, could conceivably find widespread support in the international community, and if understood within its inherent limitations, could be viewed as a useful and legitimate demand-side addition to the non-proliferation treaties and regimes system.

In the end, as a policy/practical matter, the relative utility of the PSI has a great deal to do with the scope and method of its application. An aggressive prosecution of the PSI, including interdictions of non-flag merchant vessels on the high seas, presents substantial costs including considerations of damage to the order of the law of the sea, with arguably only minor benefits to international efforts to combat WMD proliferation. Alternatively, in a more humble form focusing on interdictions by PSI participant states within their own sovereign territory, including their own ports and territorial sea, and in accordance with their own substantive national legal prohibitions upon transfer of subject materials, and particularly if combined with greater transparency, the PSI could be seen to present a much better cost/benefit ratio, and thus be largely supportable as a modest counterproliferation-oriented addition to the non-proliferation system.

VII. Conclusion

Though analyzed herein essentially under the rubric of the international law of the sea, the PSI is at its essence a counterproliferation-oriented pre-emptive use of force, analogous thereby at a base level with the 2003 Iraq intervention. As this chapter has discussed, the PSI presents potentially problematic issues of legal and jurisprudential concern, from which more general lessons can be learned regarding counterproliferation-oriented pre-emptive uses of force. When viewed from a policy standpoint as well, its utility as a function of costs versus benefits, particularly in its more aggressive modes of prosecution, is also questionable. However, both legal and policy-related concerns could be substantially allayed through the operationalization of the PSI's principles in a more reserved and transparent manner. The considerations upon which these judgments are made in the context of the PSI, it is submitted, could be usefully applied more generally to other implementations of counterproliferation policy in order to determine their overall merit and prudence.

9

Jus ad Bellum in the Age of WMD Proliferation

This chapter will discuss the normative question of what should be the character of the rules and institutions of international law covering international uses of force, in the age of proliferation of weapons of mass destruction technologies.[1] It will posit that international use of force law is currently in a state of crisis, precipitated by the proliferation of WMD technologies and the revised set of national security calculations, which determine when and why states choose to use force internationally, that have been thrust upon states as a result. It will review a number of options which have been proposed for changing the substance of international laws and institutions which currently regulate this area, in order to make them responsive to this change in international security realities, and more effective and useful to states. However it will conclude that none of these proposals truly grasps the nettle of the problems facing states in the post-proliferated age, and the challenge of designing and maintaining effective and supportable rules and institutions in this area. It will argue that more fundamental changes to the character of these rules and institutions are necessary if they are to fulfill a needed role in providing standards for international behavior in this most vital area of international relations. Using both international legal theory and international relations theory, it will argue specifically that international law regulating uses of force should be de-formalized, and maintained not as legally binding rules, but as politically persuasive norms. This change in the character of rules in this area, it will be argued, would help to preserve the integrity of the rest of the formal corpus of international law, while accomplishing virtually the same results in influencing state behavior and in normativizing international relations in this area, as do the current formal rules of the *jus ad bellum*.

A word on the intent of this chapter before proceeding. The analysis and proposals in this chapter are the result of long deliberation regarding the crisis moment which the *jus ad bellum* currently faces largely as a result of WMD proliferation. The resulting analysis and proposals will no doubt be considered by some to be somewhat revolutionary, and perhaps even radical. While they are

---

[1] This chapter is an amended version of an article by the same title published at 40 George Washington International Law Review, Issue 1 (2008).

indeed intended to be new and challenging, it will be argued that they are in fact based upon sound theoretical underpinnings, to be found in both international legal theory and international relations theory. It will further be argued that they are a rational product of a realistic assessment of the current crisis and its consequences for international legal regulation in this area.

It cannot be overemphasized that the proposals contained herein are not intended to undermine international law. Quite the contrary, they are specifically intended to bring the character of international law in the area of international uses of force into harmony with the reality of the modern security landscape which states face, and thus ultimately to strengthen the formal corpus of international law generally. With regard specifically to the *jus ad bellum*, the deformalization thesis advanced herein should be understood not simply as a normative regression, but rather as a tactical normative retreat made necessary by fundamental changes in circumstance. This normative direction could, and should, be reversed in future when the infrastructure of the international legal system is better able to provide effective regulation in this most sensitive and important area of international relations.

I. Proliferation, Pre-emption and Use of Force Law

A. Crisis? What Crisis?

The first issue for consideration in this analysis is whether in fact there is currently a crisis in international use of force law, brought about by WMD proliferation and changed security realities for states. Some would doubtless reject this as an alarmist position, and maintain that while the instruments and means of international violence have certainly changed since the United Nations Charter, the primary source of governing international law in this area, was founded in 1945, the considerations which states must undertake when deciding to use force internationally have not fundamentally changed since that time, and that therefore no urgent change to existing law is required. This conclusion indeed was apparently reached by the United Nations Secretary General's High-Level Panel on Threats, Challenges and Change in its 2004 report entitled "A More Secure World: Our Shared Responsibility."[2] In its report, the High-Level Panel found that there was no need either for re-writing or re-interpreting Article 51 of the U.N. Charter on self-defense, or for fundamentally changing the role of the Security Council as the sole authorizer of international uses of force other than those justified by reference to Article 51, including those purposed in addressing WMD threats. To quote from the report, "[t]he short answer is that if there are good arguments for

---

[2] <http://www.un.org/secureworld/report.pdf>. See also A.S. Weiner, *The Use of Force and Contemporary Security Threats: Old Medicine for New Ills?* 59 STANFORD LAW REVIEW 415, 419–420 (2007).

preventive military action, with good evidence to support them, they should be put to the Security Council, which can authorize such action if it chooses to."[3]

However, this static approach seems at odds with the stated opinion of the former Secretary General himself, who in September of 2003 expressed this crisis to the U.N. General Assembly as follows:

All of us know there are new threats that must be faced—or, perhaps, old threats in new and dangerous combinations: new forms of terrorism, and the proliferation of weapons of mass destruction...Where we disagree, it seems, is on how to respond to these threats. Article 51 of the Charter prescribes that all States, if attacked, retain the inherent right of self-defence. But until now it has been understood that when States go beyond that, and decide to use force to deal with broader threats to international peace and security, they need the unique legitimacy provided by the United Nations. Now, some say this understanding is no longer tenable, since an "armed attack" with weapons of mass destruction could be launched at any time, without warning, or by a clandestine group.

Rather than wait for that to happen, they argue, States have the right and obligation to use force pre-emptively, even on the territory of other States, and even while weapons systems that might be used to attack them are still being developed. According to this argument, States are not obliged to wait until there is agreement in the Security Council. Instead, they reserve the right to act unilaterally, or in ad hoc coalitions. This logic represents a fundamental challenge to the principles on which, however imperfectly, world peace and stability have rested for the last fifty-eight years.

Excellencies, we have come to a fork in the road. This may be a moment no less decisive than 1945 itself, when the United Nations was founded.[4]

As indicated in these remarks, the fundamental challenge to U.N. Charter law which the former Secretary General perceived has been most saliently presented in the context of debates regarding the legality of anticipatory, or pre-emptive self-defense is in situations where states feel that they are threatened by a target state or non-state actor's development, possession, or threat of use of WMD. Former Secretary General Annan's remarks above were of course made during the 2003 diplomatic stand-off over whether, and on what legal justification, to use force against Iraq in order to forcibly disarm it of its suspected WMD stockpiles. However, debates regarding the use of pre-emptive force to prevent states and non-state actors "of concern" from developing and using WMD have not been limited to the case of Iraq. Indeed, an even more recent example of such a pre-emptive use of force was presented by Israel's September 6, 2007 unilateral attack upon a site in Syria which was later claimed to be a nuclear reactor site, constructed with the help of North Korea.[5]

---

[3] Para. 190.

[4] Secretary General's Address to the General Assembly, September 23, 2003. Available at <http://www.un.org/webcast/ga/58/statements/sg2eng030923>.

[5] See R. Wright, "N. Koreans Taped At Syrian Reactor: Video Played a Role in Israeli Raid," *Washington Post*, Thursday, April 24, 2008; D.E. Sanger, "U.S. Sees N. Korean Links to Reactor," *New York Times*, April 24, 2008.

B. Counterproliferation Policy and International Use of Force Law

As discussed in Chapter 6 above, the post-September 11 international security climate has seen a general shifting in the policy positions of the United States and a number of other relatively powerful states, toward an increased emphasis on proactive and often unilateral or small-coalition-based strategies of counterproliferation, and away from more multilateral and diplomacy-based efforts of non-proliferation.[6] While non-proliferation efforts have classically depended upon diplomacy and upon individual state implementation of treaty law and of rules agreed in other normative regimes of both a formal and informal character, counterproliferation efforts are generally designed to forcefully preclude specific actors from obtaining WMD-related materials and technologies or to degrade and destroy an actor's existing WMD capability. Such counterproliferation efforts include interdiction of suspected transfers of sensitive items, and pre-emptive acts of force against either actual or potential possessors of WMD.[7]

Two examples of the implementation of counterproliferation policy—the 2003 intervention in Iraq and the Proliferation Security Initiative—have been considered from the perspectives of both international law and policy. While these case studies can be distinguished from each other along a number of lines, including scope, and although the primary legal analysis of the PSI has been conducted, necessarily, by reference to the specialized legal regime of the international law of the sea, as concluded in Chapter 8; both the 2003 Iraq intervention and the PSI are at their essence examples of counterproliferation-oriented pre-emptive use of international force.[8] As such, the legal/jurisprudential considerations which have been had in the context of both case studies have relevance to the question of the harmony of counterproliferation-oriented pre-emptive uses of force with principles of international use of force law.[9]

As former Secretary General Annan's comments above express, and as has been demonstrated herein through legal analysis of the two case studies, the witnessed trend in policy emphasis toward pre-emptive, forceful counterproliferation actions does not sit easily with existing principles of international use of force law, with the U.N. Charter as its cornerstone. The fundamental problem in the context of counterproliferation-oriented pre-emptive uses of force is that this

---

[6] See Chapter 6 below at 245.

[7] See J.D. Ellis, *The Best Defense: Counterproliferation and U.S. National Security*, THE WASHINGTON QUARTERLY 26:2 (Spring 2003); R.S. Litwak, *The New Calculus of Pre-emption*, SURVIVAL 44:4 (Winter 2002).

[8] See Chapter 8 below at 332.

[9] Note the explanation in Chapter 8 at 325 above that LOSC Article 110 can perhaps best be understood as a *lex specialis* use of force law regime, contracted into by states in order to deal with the particular issue of troublesome non-flag merchant vessels on the high seas. Article 110 can therefore be understood simply as a branch or manifestation of international use of force law specifically applicable in the law of the sea context.

policy, as expressed by the United States and other states, and as carried out in practice in some recent cases, calls for uses of force against states and non-state actors who are simply in possession of WMD or who are in even earlier stages of development or possession of WMD or WMD-related materials, without the existence of an immediate threat that such weapons will be used in an armed attack against the state pursuing the policy of pre-emption.[10] Imminence, again, is a key criterion which must be satisfied in order to justify a self-defensive action by reference to the customary law right of anticipatory self-defense. Therefore, an implementation of this policy, in which unilateral international force is used by a state prior to actual armed attack, against state or non-state actors that simply possess or are developing WMD, without the existence of a meaningful threat to use such weapons which satisfies the criteria set out in the *Caroline* case, does not satisfy the requirements for justification under either the text of Article 51 or the customary right of anticipatory self-defense which it arguably incorporates, and therefore constitutes a violation of U.N. Charter Article 2(4).[11]

Notwithstanding this legal incongruity, the policy of counterproliferation-oriented pre-emption continues to be seen by a number of states as a necessary, final option to be used against WMD threats when no other tools appear to be working.[12] The idea that states must, per the text of Article 51 or the restrictive interpretation of anticipatory self-defense prescribed by customary law, wait for a WMD attack to have already taken place against them, or at least for indisputable evidence of a threat of use of WMD against them which leaves them "no choice of means and no moment for deliberation" before they are allowed to act in self-defense, is to the minds of many policymakers a wholly unrealistic notion, and unworkable in practice.

This then exposes the heart of the problem facing modern states in their desires both to vigorously pursue policies seen as necessary to their national security, and

[10] See D. Luban, "Preventive War and Human Rights," in H. Shue and D. Rodin (eds), PREEMPTION: MILITARY ACTION AND MORAL JUSTIFICATION (2007), arguing inter alia for a conspiracy analogy in the context of counterproliferation-oriented pre-emption. This analogy would be helpful in reconciling the jurisprudential concerns expressed in Chapter 8 above with unilateral pre-emptive actions taken in circumstances meeting the *Caroline* criteria of imminence, and thus justifiable under (what is argued to comprise) the customary law of anticipatory self-defense. See also the several chapters responding to Luban's arguments in the same volume.

[11] See Chapter 7 below at 279.

[12] In addition to statements supporting pre-emptive use of force made by U.S. officials, see below similar statements of officials from Russia, Australia, the United Kingdom, Japan, India, and Israel. "India Mulls 'Pre-Emptive' Pakistan Strike, Cites U.S. Iraq War Precedent," *Agent France Press*, April 11, 2003. Available at <http://www.fromthewilderness.com/free/ww3/041403_india.html>; "Israel's plans for Iran strikes," *Jane's*, July 16, 2004; "Japan Mulling Action over N.Korea Missiles" by M. Yamaguchi, AP <http://news.yahoo.com/s/ap/20060710/ap_on_re_as/nkorea_missiles>; "Russia Won't Rule Out Pre-emptive Use of Force," Los Angeles Times, October 13, 2003 <http://straitstimes.asia1.com.sg/storyprintfriendly/0,1887,214354,00.html>; "Prime Minister Warns of Continuing Global Terror Threat," March 5, 2004 speech by Tony Blair <http://www.number-10.gov.uk/output/page5461.asp>; "Terror-Preemption talk Roils Asia," by Dan Murphy, December 5, 2002, Christian Science Monitor <http://www.globalpolicy.org/wtc/analysis/2002/1205preemption.htm>.

at the same time to support and comply with international law, and comprises the cause of the current crisis in international use of force law. The U.N. Charter, now nearly 60 years old, is in the minds of many policymakers in states that are shifting their emphasis toward counterproliferation, an anachronism; a set of norms which, if accurately reflective of the principled universe which states inhabited within the context of the evolution of military technology and geopolitics in 1945, is currently unfit for the task of providing a set of workable and supportable principles for governing this most sensitive area of international relations.

These policymakers point not only to the proliferation of WMD technologies themselves, which have worked an evolution in the instruments of violence and the amount of damage that can be done in a single "armed attack," but also to the emergence of sophisticated non-state actors who, it is feared, will be able to use these weapons, changing the rules on where states must look to predict and manage threats, as well as the effectiveness of classical doctrines such as deterrence and containment for managing these threats.[13] These doctrines, while employed with some success in inter-state security tensions, seem likely to be largely ineffective against the fluid assets and operative networks of international non-state actors, and particularly those driven by extreme ideological motives.[14] As Daniel Poneman has explained:

Obviously, deterrence depends on having a return address which one can target and send an opponent a response to that which has just been received. However, terrorists do not often leave return addresses. Moreover, deterrence depends on a particular view of human nature. If you read Hobbes's Leviathan, you understand that, at the least, you need a minimal sense of self-preservation to rely upon if you expect notions of deterrence to obtain. In a terrorist context—in which, if not the leaders, then certainly the cannon fodder they send in to do the suicide bombings, are not driven by the desire for self-preservation—you can no longer count on deterrence.[15]

While some observers might characterize these views regarding the threat posed by WMD and the anachronistic character of existing international use of force law as extreme and reactionary, or perhaps even paranoid, the fact remains that many policymakers in counterproliferation-focused states genuinely believe that it is necessary for the security of their states that they are able to use force preemptively against these new threats before they develop the qualities of demonstrable immediacy necessary to square such actions with existing use of force

[13] Remarks by U.S. President Bush in Address to the Nation, The Cross Hall. Available at <http://www.whitehouse.gov/news/releases/2003/03/print/20030317–7.html>; Also Speech at West Point Military Academy on June 1, 2002, available at <http://www.whitehouse.gov/news/releases/2002/06/20020601-3.html>; Also remarks by U.K. Prime Minister Tony Blair in preface to the U.K. Government's dossier on Iraq's WMD programs, as reprinted in *The Guardian*, September 24, 2002. Available at <http://www.guardian.co.uk/Iraq/Story/0,,797883,00.html>.

[14] See D. Smith, DETERRING AMERICA: ROGUE STATES AND THE PROLIFERATION OF WEAPONS OF MASS DESTRUCTION (2006).

[15] "A New Bargain," in J. Pilat (ed.), ATOMS FOR PEACE: A FUTURE AFTER FIFTY YEARS? (2007) 179–180.

law. Moreover, it is clear that a number of these states will continue to act in pursuance of these beliefs, and of counterproliferation policies of pre-emption, regardless of the formal, technical requirements of international law.

This, then is the heart of the crisis: a significant number of states now believe that their vital national security interests require them to act in a manner that is in breach of the laws governing international uses of force laid down in the U.N. Charter. This is not a temporary policy shift, nor are actions taken in pursuance of counterproliferation policies isolated or extraordinary events. Policies of counterproliferation-oriented pre-emptive use of force are a part of a systematic rethinking within a significant number of states about the security environment in which states find themselves, and the policy options those states feel they must maintain in order to defend themselves against modern threats, and to pursue their essential interests internationally.[16] This is a revision of thought that is likely to persist and mature within these states, and it is likely that, as WMD proliferation inevitably spreads and becomes more intimately a part of the security concerns of a growing number of states, those states too will arrive at the conclusion that traditional non-proliferation efforts based in multilateralism and diplomacy, and utilizing strategies such as deterrence and containment, are not wholly sufficient to deal with these realities. They will likely conclude, as others have done, that policies of pre-emptive use of force against states and non-state actors that threaten them with WMD, and who will not sufficiently respond to or be managed by these classic strategies, are a necessary addition to the policy options at their disposal.

Therefore, at the heart of the current crisis in international use of force law is a continuing, and likely increasing gap between the provisions of existing law and the perceptions of a significant number of important states of the realities of the international political issue area that law is meant to regulate—a classic gap between law and reality caused by the law simply lagging behind the dynamics of technological and geopolitical change.[17] Such a situation, in which the law is

---

[16] M.E. Bunn, "Force, Preemption and WMD Proliferation," in N. Busch and D.H. Joyner (eds), COMBATING WEAPONS OF MASS DESTRUCTION: THE FUTURE OF INTERNATIONAL NON-PROLIFERATION POLICY (2009); J.D. Ellis, *The Best Defense: Counterproliferation and U.S. National Security*, THE WASHINGTON QUARTERLY 26:2 (Spring 2003); R.S. Litwak, *The New Calculus of Pre-emption*, SURVIVAL 44, No. 4 (Winter 2002–2003); J.D. Ellis and G.D. Kiefer, COMBATTING PROLIFERATION: STRATEGIC INTELLIGENCE AND NATIONAL POLICY (2003).

[17] See H.J. Morgenthau, *Positivism, Functionalism and International Law*, 34 AMERICAN JOURNAL OF INTERNATIONAL LAW 260, 260 (1940); M. Glennon, *The Fog of Law: Self-Defense, Inherence, and Incoherence in Article 51 of the United Nations Charter*, 25 HARVARD JOURNAL OF LAW & PUBLIC POLICY 540, 549 (2002); A.-M. Slaughter and W. Burke-White, *An International Constitutional Moment*, 43 HARVARD INTERNATIONAL LAW JOURNAL 1, 2 (2002); R.F. Turner, *Operation Iraqi Freedom: Legal and Policy Considerations*, 27 HARVARD JOURNAL OF LAW AND PUBLIC POLICY 765, 793 (2004); R. Wedgwood, *The Fall of Saddam Hussein: Security Council Mandates and Preemptive Self-Defense*, 97 AMERICAN JOURNAL OF INTERNATIONAL LAW 576, 583 (2003); A. Clark Arend, *International Law and the Preemptive Use of Military Force*, WASHINGTON QUARTERLY 89 (Spring 2003); R.N. Gardner, *Neither Bush nor the "Jurisprudes,"* 97 AMERICAN JOURNAL OF INTERNATIONAL LAW, 585 (2003); J.E. Stromseth, *Law and Force After Iraq: A*

seen by its subjects to be out of touch with the "on the ground" realities of the decisions and actions it is intended to govern, in any area of the law, is simply unsustainable, and as in any other area of law the result of this gap is decreasing confidence in the law and its institutions of maintenance, a decreasing perception of the validity of the law, increasing antagonism toward the law, and resultant non-compliance with the reason-offending rules. This indeed was one of the fundamental reasons underlying the decision by Western powers to invade Iraq in 2003, and is the reason that fears abound regarding future acts of force outside the U.N. Charter use of force system by counterproliferation-focused states, in places like Iran and North Korea.

C. Disproportionate Significance?

Still, it is certainly true that only relatively powerful states would consider engaging in a counterproliferation-oriented pre-emptive use of force. This is of course because only a relatively few states in the world have the capacity to project power through military force internationally, with confidence that they will be able to successfully withstand responsive uses of force against them. Some will no doubt argue as a consequence of this fact, that there are simply too few states anxiously concerned with this issue, and willing to act in furtherance of pre-emptive strike policies, for it to be cited as the cause of a "crisis" in international use of force law.

It should be borne in mind, however, that while numerically in the minority, these powerful actors are a disproportionately important subset of states to consider with regard to the current status and future character and substance of international use of force law for a number of interconnected reasons. Firstly, among this subset are states which, correctly or not, feel particularly threatened by the possibility of WMD attacks against them. For some states this is due to long standing regional inter-state disputes, the parties to which have or are in the process of developing WMD arsenals.[18] For other states, this is because of aspects of their political or cultural identity, or their international influence and activity, which they perceive have increased the likelihood of asymmetric attacks against them by terrorists and others, particularly non-state actors using WMD.[19] This fact of perceived particular threat, together with the abovementioned capacity of such states to act internationally in pursuance of a broad understanding of

---

Transitional Moment, 97 American Journal of International Law 628, 629 (2003); J.C. Yoo and W. Trachman, *Less than Bargained for: The Use of Force and the Declining Relevance of the United Nations*, 5 Chicago Journal of International Law 379, 381 (2005).

[18] "India Mulls 'Pre-Emptive' Pakistan Strike, Cites U.S. Iraq War Precedent," *Agent France Press*, April 11, 2003. Available at <http://www.fromthewilderness.com/free/ww3/041403_india.html>; "Israel's plans for Iran strikes," *Jane's*, July 16, 2004.

[19] Remarks by U.K. Prime Minister Tony Blair in preface to the U.K. Government's dossier on Iraq's WMD programs, as reprinted in *The Guardian*, September 24, 2002. Available at <http://www.guardian.co.uk/Iraq/Story/0,,797883,00.html>.

their vital national interests, produces a peculiar and important subset of states that are both most likely to want to have the legal option to engage in counterproliferation-oriented pre-emptive acts of force, and at the same time most likely to have the power and influence in international relations to either alter or opt out of treaties, as well as to employ the means of creation of customary law, in order to bring about such desired legal changes.[20]

In addition to their disproportionate motivation for and influence in changing relevant sources of law, these powerful actors are of particular importance in considering the future of international use of force law because they are among the relatively few states in the world against whom the horizontal enforcement mechanisms of international law—i.e. issue linkaging, diplomatic or economic pressuring, or direct military force—are unlikely to be effective should they alternatively decide that acting in a way that is formally in breach of the law is in their vital national interests, even if the majority of states recognize the action as illegal.[21] The 2003 Iraq intervention is, again, a perfect example of this ability.

For all of these reasons, it is argued herein that it is possible for the perceptions and actions of a relatively small subset of powerful states to form the basis for a crisis in international use of force law. It is further submitted, in agreement with former Secretary General Annan's statements, that the current state of international use of force law is indeed a state of crisis, the resolution of which is of fundamental importance to the future of the United Nations and to the U.N. Charter system for use of force regulation.

In his September 2003 remarks to the General Assembly, the Secretary General went on to discuss the founding ideals of the U.N. Charter and to conclude, "[n]ow we must decide whether it is possible to continue on the basis agreed then, or whether radical changes are needed. And we must not shy away from questions about the adequacy, and effectiveness, of the rules and instruments at our disposal."[22] There are indeed a number of possibilities for reform or amendment of relevant provisions of use of force law, and the organs of the United Nations, many of which have been proposed and discussed at length by others as alternatives for bridging the gap and bringing the law into harmony with the realities of international security concerns, though none of the proposals has met with generalized approval among members of the United Nations.[23] This chapter will

---

[20] M. Byers, CUSTOM, POWER, AND THE POWER OF RULES (1999).

[21] See A. Chayes and A. Chayes, *On Compliance*, 47 INTERNATIONAL ORGANIZATION 175 (1993); A.T. Guzman, HOW INTERNATIONAL LAW WORKS (2008); idem., *A Compliance Based Theory of International Law*, 90 CALIFORNIA LAW REVIEW (2002); H.H. Koh, *Why Do Nations Obey International Law?*, 106 YALE LAW JOURNAL 2599 (1997).

[22] Secretary General's Address to the General Assembly, September 23, 2003. Available at <http://www.un.org/webcast/ga/58/statements/sg2eng030923>.

[23] See, e.g., Y.Z. Blum, *Proposals for UN Security Council Reform*, 99 AMERICAN JOURNAL OF INTERNATIONAL LAW 632 (2005); I. Arias, *Humanitarian Intervention: Could the Security Council Kill the United Nations?*, 23 FORDHAM INTERNATIONAL LAW JOURNAL 1005, 1026 (2000); T. Franck, RECOURSE TO FORCE (2002); D. Malone, ed., THE U.N. SECURITY COUNCIL: FROM THE COLD WAR TO THE 21st CENTURY (2004); B. Fassbender, U.N. SECURITY COUNCIL REFORM AND

proceed by reviewing the most noteworthy of these proposals, on the subjects of the composition and decision-making processes of the Security Council, and the construction and application of the law on self-defense contained in Article 51.

It will then go on, however, to propose a somewhat different and more revolutionary path which the international community could choose to take in reforming the provision of international norms in the area of international uses of force. This proposal would involve a change to the fundamental character of the norms governing uses of force, to make them more practically useful to states and more in keeping both with the demands of states for greater flexibility in respond-ing to threats, and with what will be argued to be a more correct understanding of the proper role of international norms in this specific issue area of international relations. This analysis will be based upon an understanding drawn from inter-national legal theory that international law, in its current evolutionary state, is better able to regulate some areas of international relations through formal law than others; and the corollary understanding that some areas of international relations are better given normative underpinning and standardization through the use of informal, non-binding norms.

The proposal will further seek to use understandings from international relations literature, particularly from the sub-field of liberal institutionalism, to show that such informal norms can still have a significant influence upon state action, and can be of significant aid to states in overcoming the hindering forces of anarchy in international politics through the facilitation of cooperation. In fact, it will argue that these norms can accomplish in the area of use of force law virtually everything that formal rules can accomplish, without causing the unnecessary negative collateral effects for the rest of the formal corpus of inter-national law which have been occasioned by its breach by powerful states in highly publicized and splashy instances of state interest non-alignment.

II. Possibilities for Change

A. The Security Council

Among proposals for amendment to the provisions and procedures of the U.N. Charter system for use of force regulation, none has been more discussed than the idea of amending the make-up and decision-making procedures of the Security Council in order to make it a more credible, supportable, and effective body in the exercise of its authority granted under the U.N. Charter.[24] These

THE RIGHT OF VETO (1998); J. Muller (ed.), REFORMING THE UNITED NATIONS: THE STRUGGLE FOR LEGITIMACY AND EFFECTIVENESS (2006).

[24] See, e.g., Y.Z. Blum, *Proposals for UN Security Council Reform*, 99 AMERICAN JOURNAL OF INTERNATIONAL LAW 632 (2005); B. Fassbender, U.N. SECURITY COUNCIL REFORM AND THE RIGHT OF VETO (1998).

proposals essentially recognize that the 1945 political accord which provided for a 10-member rotating membership of the Security Council, plus the allocation of permanent member status and special veto rights to five specific states on the Council, is both unsatisfactory of modern ideas of democratic representation in international organizations, and unreflective of modern realities of states' power and influence.

Proposals for amendment of the Security Council have been many and varied, but can be categorized in summary as proposals for changing a) the size of the Council; b) the membership of the Council; c) the identity of permanent members of the Council (if any); d) the powers of permanent members; and (e) the procedures for Security Council decision-making.

One set of proposals for changing the size and membership of the Security Council was made by the 2004 High-Level Panel Report.[25] The Panel concluded that a decision to enlarge the Security Council's membership was "a necessity," and that it should be guided primarily by principles of increased democratic representation of U.N. members, particularly from the developing world, and of accountability in decision-making. Realization of these principles, it argued, was necessary for the Council to be seen as a legitimate, credible body in taking decisions regarding international uses of force.[26]

The Panel produced two proposals for amendment to the size and composition of the Security Council, involving a distribution of seats among four regional areas: Africa, Asia and Pacific, Europe, and the Americas. Under Model A, 6 new permanent seats on the Council would be created along with 3 two-term non-permanent seats, resulting in a revised overall Council membership of 24 states, evenly divided among the four geographic regions (see Table A).[27]

Table A

Regional area	No. of States	Permanent seats (continuing)	Proposed new permanent seats	Proposed two-year seats (non-renewable)	Total
Africa	53	0	2	4	6
Asia and Pacific	56	1	2	3	6
Europe	47	3	1	2	6
Americas	35	1	1	4	6
Totals model A	191	5	6	13	24

[25] <http://www.un.org/secureworld/report.pdf>.　　[26] Para. 250.
[27] Tables A and B reprinted from the United Nations Secretary General's High-Level Panel on Threats, Challenges and Change, 2004 Report entitled "A More Secure World: Our Shared Responsibility." <http://www.un.org/secureworld/report.pdf>.

Table B

Regional area	No. of States	Permanent seats (continuing)	Proposed four-year renewable seats	Proposed two-year seats (non-renewable)	Total
Africa	53	0	2	4	6
Asia and Pacific	56	1	2	3	6
Europe	47	3	2	1	6
Americas	35	1	2	3	6
Totals model B	191	5	8	11	24

As an alternative construction, under Model B no new permanent seats would be created, but 8 four-year renewable-term seats and 1 two-year non-permanent seat would be created, and divided evenly among the four regions (see Table B).

Although the Panel's Model A proposed the creation of new permanent seats on the Council, it did not provide for veto powers for those new permanent members, to equal the powers coincident with permanent member status under the existing Charter structure. Indeed, neither model provided for either expansion of veto powers or circumscription of the existing veto powers of permanent members. However, proposals from other sources have included alternatives for revoking the veto rights of permanent members entirely, or for establishing new decision-making rules for the Council which would mediate the effect of permanent members' veto, such as by allowing a supermajority of the Security Council to override the veto of one of the permanent members, or requiring the Council to take up a measure for "second consideration" if it was first defeated by only one permanent member's veto. In such a case of second consideration, the measure would only be defeated by the votes of two permanent members.[28] These and other proposals for amending the distribution of power among Security Council members, and for changing the Council's voting procedures, have been primarily aimed at improving the efficiency of Security Council decision-making, and at decreasing instances of stalemate in the Council and resultant inaction in the face of threats.

A number of these proposals for amendment of the Security Council and its decision-making procedures have received substantial political support, particularly on the issue of enlargement of the Security Council. A number of alternative plans have been put forward, and variously endorsed by groups of states, including some existing permanent Council members.[29] There was some significant hope that the issue of Security Council

[28] See I. Arias, *Humanitarian Intervention: Could the Security Council Kill the United Nations?* 23 FORDHAM INTERNATIONAL LAW JOURNAL 1005, 1025, 1026 (2000).
[29] <http://news.bbc.co.uk/1/hi/world/americas/4673977.stm>.

enlargement would be made part of the formal agenda for the United Nations' 2005 World Summit. However, this hope, as most hopes for progress in United Nations reform efforts at the World Summit, was not realized.[30]

Even if politically possible, however, the problems with this entire line of thinking in the counterproliferation-oriented pre-emption context are several and fundamental. As discussed above in Chapter 7 in the context of the 2003 Iraq intervention, for the Security Council to fill the role of *ex ante* authorizer, through its Chapter VII powers, of counterproliferation-oriented pre-emptive uses of force, it would have to be a forum in which member states were comfortable in sharing highly sensitive intelligence information, in order to convince fellow Council members to support their application for authorization. It would further have to be a body among whose members there is likely to be substantial agreement regarding the sources and characteristics of threats warranting pre-emptive uses of force, so as to make states confident that efforts to work through the Council would be likely to be successful and worth the transactions costs and inevitable risks of intelligence leaking to the target entity involved.[31]

However, the Security Council does not meet either of these criteria as it is currently structured, and, more to the point, none of the proposals which have been offered for amending it would serve to substantially address these limitations of the institutional capacity of the Council to act in such cases. The intelligence which states collect on WMD threats of a nature which causes them such serious concern as to warrant a decision to use pre-emptive military force is intelligence of the highest sensitivity, and will have been collected through means the secrecy of which the collecting state will protect at all costs. Information of this sensitivity will simply not be shared by states with a group as diverse as the Security Council, no matter who the collecting state is. Sharing of intelligence of this degree of sensitivity sometimes occurs between the closest of allies, for functional purposes, but would never be shared either openly or confidentially to the general membership of the Council or to U.N. staff. The risk of leakage to the target state, and general risks of divulgence of sources and methods, is simply too great with insufficient likely gain from the effort. Although there have been proposals for the establishment of safeguards and confidence-building processes for sharing of intelligence within the U.N., none of these are likely to satisfy states when dealing with information of this level of sensitivity.[32] An expanded Security Council membership, made regionally even more diverse, would further decrease the likelihood of sensitive information being shared, and thus further diminish

---

[30] "U.N. Reform Agenda Watered Down" CNN.com, September 14, 2005 (<http://edition.cnn.com/2005/us/09/14/un.reform/index.html>). (Quoting Secretary General Annan: "The big item missing is non-proliferation and disarmament. This is a real disgrace... when we are all concerned with weapons of mass destruction and that they may get into the wrong hands.")

[31] See Chapter 7 below at 292. See also S. Chesterman, "Shared Secrets: Intelligence and Collective Security," Lowy Institute Paper, 10 (2006). Available at <http://iilj.org/research/documents/chesterman_shared_secrets_2006.pdf>.

[32] Ibid.

the feasibility of the Security Council's filling a meaningful role in authorizing counterproliferation-oriented pre-emptions.

The second institutional limitation the Security Council faces in this area again lies in the diversity of states comprising the Council's membership, and is the fact that members of the Security Council differ fundamentally at times in their perception and appreciation of WMD threats. Both the case of Iraq in 2003, as well as the ongoing case of Iran's nuclear program are salient examples of such a divergence of views regarding both the existence and degree of imminence of WMD threats. In both cases it became clear to those permanent members of the Council that wished to pursue forceful action under the authority of Chapter VII of the Charter, that that view was not shared by other permanent members of the Council. Thus, in both cases, those wishing to pursue such forceful action elected to pursue that action outside of the Charter framework.[33]

Although the Security Council acts as a body empowered with special legal rights, such disagreements and resultant inability to act as a body and to use those rights, are reminders that the Council is primarily an international political body, made up of States with divergent and often conflicting interests and world views. The expectation that such a group of states would in a consistent manner substantially agree in their perception of threats, so as to give states confidence that applications to the Council for pre-emptive force against WMD threats will likely find approval by nine members of the Council including all five permanent members, has little foundation. This fact argues against the prudential soundness of the reliance placed upon the Security Council, as a body with the capacity to act as an authorizer of pre-emptive uses of force, by the 2004 High-Level Report as reflected in their statement quoted above.[34] Again, proposals for increasing the size of the Council and the number and diversity of its membership, would only serve to exacerbate this problem further, and would make the possibility of such consistent agreement less, not more likely, and thus further compromise the Council's ability to fulfill such a role.

It is argued herein that proposals for reform of the Security Council and its procedures, with a purpose in making the Council better able to function as an *ex ante* authorizer of counterproliferation-oriented pre-emptive uses of force, fail entirely to grasp the nettle of the serious institutional limitations upon the Council's capacity to act in this role. As shown above, the proposals which enjoy the broadest political support, i.e. those for enlarging and diversifying the Council's membership, would in fact produce effects retrograde to these aims. The 2004 High-Level Panel Report's emphasis upon such amendment, and not

---

[33] See Dafna Linzer, "U.S. Urges Financial Sanctions on Iran," *Washington Post*, May 29, 2006. Available at <http://www.washingtonpost.com/wp-dyn/content/article/2006/05/28/AR 2006052800999_pf.html>.

[34] See below n. 3 "[t]he short answer is that if there are good arguments for preventive military action, with good evidence to support them, they should be put to the Security Council, which can authorize such action if it chooses to."

upon more fundamental change to the underlying rules of international use of force law, it is therefore submitted, is largely misplaced.[35]

Article 51

The other most frequently discussed area for possible amendment to the U.N. Charter system of use of force law, particularly in consideration of the concerns some states have regarding WMD proliferation and international terrorism, and the need for pre-emptive uses of force to address these threats, is the U.N. Charter law on self-defense, contained in Article 51.[36] This provision and its relevance to debates regarding counterproliferation-oriented pre-emptive uses of force, including the argued inclusion from customary law of a right of anticipatory self-defense within its broader interpretation, have been discussed in Chapters 7 and 8 above. As concluded through that discussion, Article 51, even with its broader interpretation to include the customary law right of anticipatory self-defense, is not sufficient to legally justify pre-emptive strikes of the sort prescribed by some powerful states' national counterproliferation policies.[37]

The question of amendment thus becomes, is there some other formulation of the right of self-defense which might be agreed by states through amendment to the U.N. Charter or authoritative process of interpretation of that document, or through the development of a more expansive right of anticipatory self-defense in customary law, which would at once allow states the normative and procedural flexibility they desire to legally justify unilateral acts of force against developing WMD threats, while at the same time preserving a predictable, objectively verifiable rule of law on the subject of self-defense in international law?

The strength of Article 51 as currently textually constructed is its clarity, in establishing a "bright line" rule for unilateral self-defense which requires there to be an *ex ante* "armed attack" against a state before it may invoke its temporary right of unilateral self-defense and use force against the state or non-state actor that has attacked it, in order to repel the current attack and prevent further attacks. This standard, although still controversial in the details of its interpretation and application, does establish a fairly workable standard in principle that is capable of objective, independent determination by other states *ex ante*, and by authoritative arbiters *ex post*. However, this clarity and definition also comprise the weakness of Article 51, as its provisions are applied to the modern realities some states feel are present in their security calculations, and particularly with regard to the threat of use of WMD as discussed above.

---

[35] Ibid.

[36] See, e.g., M. Doyle, STRIKING FIRST: PREEMPTION AND PREVENTION IN INTERNATIONAL CONFLICT (2008); J.C. Yoo and W. Trachman, *Less Than Bargained For: The Use of Force and the Declining Relevance of the United Nations*, 5 CHICAGO JOURNAL OF INTERNATIONAL LAW 379, 386 (2004).

[37] See Chapter 7 below at 279.

In considering possibilities for amendment to Article 51, states with counterproliferation-oriented pre-emptive strike policies likely would wish for either formal amendment or authoritative re-interpretation through subsequent state practice, to produce a right of anticipatory self-defense which allows for a pre-emptive attack when a state has evidence (perhaps even if only circumstantial, and likely not open to review by other states) of WMD development or possession by another state or non-state actor, and a reasonable basis in fact (perhaps comprised largely by historical antipathy, and prior examples of aggressive acts or "ties" to terrorist organizations) to suspect that those WMD might be used to threaten them at some point in the future. This standard sounds vague and indeterminate because it is vague and indeterminate, but in reality it is the sort of normative construction that would be necessary in order to justify the pre-emptive acts of force contemplated by some national counterproliferation policies and official statements.[38] This level of vagueness and subjectivity with regard to evidentiary standards, burden of evidentiary production, perception of threat, and imminence of threat, is precisely what would be required in order to give such states the legal flexibility they would need to pursue such policies.

However, flexibility and vagueness in law on the one hand, and objective predictability and verifiability in law on the other, are very difficult to engineer simultaneously into the same legal provision.[39] As the vagueness and subjectivity of the right of self-defense increases through such flexible construction, so the ability of other states to judge *ex ante*, and authoritative arbiters to judge *ex post* the compliance of the action with the normative standard, decreases in measure. In a similar variance, as this ability of third parties to adjudge the compliance of a self-defending state's action with the applicable international legal standard decreases, so in proportion does the character of that standard as a rule of law.[40] As conceded above, the existing law of self-defense contained in Article 51 is, despite being an overall workable standard in principle, controversial enough in its discrete application to facts. Increasing the level of normative vagueness and subjectivity of its provisions would serve only to exacerbate this problem.

Added to this problem of effective norm construction, is the institutional problem within the international legal system of the relative absence of practical means of authoritative adjudication of disputes, including those regarding use of force law generally and self-defense law in particular.[41] This problem is of course

---

[38] See, e.g., the December 2002 U.S. National Strategy to Combat Weapons of Mass Destruction. Available at <http://www.whitehouse.gov/nsc/nss.html>. ("We must adapt the concept of imminent threat to the capabilities and objectives of today's adversaries.")

[39] See generally T. Endicott, Vagueness in Law (2000); B. Leiter (ed.), Objectivity in Law and Morals (2000).

[40] See L.E. Ribstein, *Law v. Trust*, 81 Boston University Law Review 553 (2001).

[41] See C. Lipson, *Why are Some International Agreements Informal?*, 45 International Organization 495, 504–505 (1991). See generally C. Gray, *The Use and Abuse of the International*

essentially the product of the voluntary jurisdictional basis of international judicial bodies such as the International Court of Justice, and the election by many states not to accede to the compulsory jurisdiction of the Court.[42] This ability of states to avoid the jurisdiction of international judicial bodies on questions of self-defense law has significantly hampered the development of authoritative interpretations of the provisions of Article 51 and their consistent application, notwithstanding the fact that they are, as previously discussed, relatively straightforward. An expansive and more flexible rule of anticipatory self-defense will only increase controversies regarding the correct interpretation of the law, as an authoritative interpreter is effectively absent.

The difficulty of satisfactory rule construction in the area of self-defense, and the international legal system's incapacity to adjudicate self-defense rules effectively, taken together, make reliance on amendment of Article 51 to include a broader, more flexible right of anticipatory self-defense unlikely to be the answer to the crisis caused by powerful states' desires to pursue policies of counterproliferation-oriented pre-emption in disharmony with existing international use of force law.

III. Deformalization

A. Overstretching

Neither amendment of the Security Council's membership or its procedures, nor reconstitution or reinterpretation of self-defense law under Article 51 seem to hold much promise for meaningful resolution of the crisis caused by the gap between law and reality at the nexus of states' counterproliferation policies and international use of force law. Indeed there seem to be no real prospects for amendment to the Charter, or to related customary law on the use of force that could address effectively both the desires of states with counterproliferation policies for normative flexibility, and the requirements of those interested in international law as a legal system for such amended provisions governing use of force to possess the important rule-of-law characteristics of predictability and objective verifiability.

It is argued herein that this crisis, which appears to be unresolvable through amendment to the formal sources of international use of force law, exposes in salient fashion an underlying but long-ignored truth about the *jus ad bellum*. This is that, at the current state of evolution of its sources and institutions of adjudication and enforcement, international law as a legal system simply does not have

---

Court of Justice: Cases Concerning the Use of Force after Nicaragua, 14 European Journal of International Law 867 (2003).

[42] See Chapter 5 below at 203.

either the normative or structural tools necessary to govern this area of international interaction, i.e. international use of force by states, in a credible and supportable way.

This truth was obscured for 45 years by the coincident, cotemporaneous existence in international politics of bipolar power dynamics and the possession by the two Cold War powers of nuclear arsenals which produced an antagonistic but relatively stable international security situation because of the powerful escalating dynamic of mutually assured destruction.[43] This dynamic, which could be triggered by even the most minor initial transgression between a superpower and the client state of the other superpower (see the Cuban Missile Crisis of 1962), kept serious international conflicts in anyway involving powerful states to a minimum.[44]

This, of course, was also the founding ideal of the United Nations: the prevention of uses of force by powerful states against less powerful states. The prevention of war between powerful states themselves was of course the ultimate objective of the Charter framers, who had lived through the devastation of two world wars involving armed conflict between powerful states, but they recognized that wars initiated between powerful states are rare because of the high costs involved and resulting deterrent effect. They realized that, as in the case of the previous two world wars, conflict between powerful states is more often precipitated by powerful states' conflict with and use of force against less-powerful states and non-state actors which, because of alliances with other powerful states or the threat of further spread of influence and power which might eventually threaten them, draws other powerful states into the conflict and results in powerful states being pitted against each other.[45]

Because of this empirical record of superpower stability during the Cold War, many lauded the success of the U.N. Charter system for use of force regulation as having had a causal effect in producing this result.[46] The change to the empirical data produced after the fall of the Soviet Union in the 1990s however,

---

[43] See K. Waltz, *More May be Better*, in S.D. Sagan and K.N. Waltz, THE SPREAD OF NUCLEAR WEAPONS (2nd edn, 2003).

[44] See E. Weede, *Extended Deterrence, Superpower Control, and Militarized Interstate Disputes, 1962–1976*, 26 JOURNAL OF PEACE RESEARCH 7–17 (1989). See generally L. Goldstein, PREVENTIVE ATTACK AND WEAPONS OF MASS DESTRUCTION: A COMPARATIVE HISTORICAL ANALYSIS (2006).

[45] See B. Simma et al. (eds), THE CHARTER OF THE UNITED NATIONS: A COMMENTARY (2nd edn, 2002) 119–120; L. Goldstein, PREVENTIVE ATTACK AND WEAPONS OF MASS DESTRUCTION: A COMPARATIVE HISTORICAL ANALYSIS (2006); D. Malone (ed.), THE U.N. SECURITY COUNCIL: FROM THE COLD WAR TO THE 21st CENTURY (2004) 5. ("The Council initially viewed its role as preventing a third world war. As the Cold War came to define global politics, the Council moved to tackle prevention of regional conflicts (often between client states or proxies of the superpowers) from spilling into a global conflagration.")

[46] See C. Kegley and G. Raymond. *International Legal Norms and the Preservation of Peace, 1820–1964: Some Evidence and Bivariate Relationships*, 8 INTERNATIONAL INTERACTIONS 171–187 (1981); H.K. Tillema and J.R. Van Wingen, *Law and Power in Military Intervention*, 26 INTERNATIONAL STUDIES QUARTERLY 220–250 (1982).

during which uses of force by powerful states against less-powerful states became more frequent, casts significant doubt upon such attributions of success to the United Nations system.[47] This increase in the frequency of armed conflicts involving powerful states argues strongly that the attribution of causation to the United Nations use of force system as having been a primary independent variable effecting the relatively inactive period of powerful state use of force during the Cold War, was in fact a specious claim, and that the observed reluctance of powerful states to use force during this period was more validly explained by larger contextual geopolitical forces and not by the effect of international use of force law upon state behavior.[48]

The post-September 11 climate of concern regarding international terrorism and the proliferation of WMD, and the resulting change in emphasis in many powerful states' national security policies to counterproliferation strategies in disharmony with the Charter system, foreshadows a continuation of this increased incidence of powerful states' use of force against less powerful states. Large scale actions similar to the 2003 Iraq intervention, as well as smaller scale breaches of sovereignty as per the PSI, will likely continue to occur in coming decades in the name of counterproliferation, as powerful states try to slow the inevitable spread of WMD to states and non-state actors of concern to them.[49] As these high-profile breaches of international use of force law continue to occur over the protestation of the majority of states, they will do

---

[47] See M. Kaldor, New and Old Wars: Organized Violence in a Global Era (2001); L. Goldstein, Preventive Attack and Weapons of Mass Destruction: A Comparative Historical Analysis (2006). J.J. Mearsheimer, *Why We Will Soon Miss the Cold War*, The Atlantic, August 1990, 35–50. See generally M. Doyle, Striking First: Preemption and Prevention in International Conflict (2008).

[48] See J.J. Mearsheimer, The False Promise of International Institutions, International Security, Vol. 19, No. 3 (Winter 1994/1995); J. Grieco, *Anarchy and the Limits of Cooperation: A Realist Critique of the Newest Liberal Institutionalism*, International Organization, vol. 42 (Summer 1988). This is not to say that use of force law as codified in the UN Charter has no effect as an independent variable upon state action. See I. Hurd, After Anarchy: Legitimacy & Power in the United Nations Security Council (2008). Rather, it is to say that use of force law was not a significant independent variable producing Cold War stability. The argument will be made herein that international norms can matter, even in the area of international use of force, although norms of a hard law character are inappropriate for regulation of this area currently. In summary, the argument herein is that soft law will matter as an independent variable in this area as much as any norms can matter in this area currently.

[49] L. Goldstein, Preventive Attack and Weapons of Mass Destruction: A Comparative Historical Analysis (2006) 155. ("Reconsidering the possible constraints on a given superior power, note that in the post-Cold War world, the United States is not likely to be limited by an adversary's conventional strength, as was often the case in the Cold War... Nor is the proliferator likely to find effective alliance partner, since there is no longer any alternative superpower. These two conditions are the defining elements of the post-Cold War international system. We must consider that only norms and geography are left to constrain the United States from fighting a series of volatile counterproliferation wars. These conditions existed before 11 September 2001 and before the articulation of the Bush Doctrine. The September 11 terror attacks appear to have significantly weakened norms in U.S. political culture that discourage preventive attack. Therefore, the post-September 11 world has witnessed a further exaggeration of the instability resulting from radical asymmetry in WMD rivalries. The U.S. military has been working for well over a

more and more damage to the perceived credibility not only of international use of force law and the U.N. Charter system, but to the rest of the formal corpus of international law as well.

Thus, it is argued herein that international lawyers and governments must finally come to terms with the reality of the structural capacities and limitations of the international legal system in the area of use of force regulation, and rigorously and honestly reassess what international use of force law can and cannot be expected to accomplish, as well as the costs to the perceived credibility of the rest of the formal corpus of international law which will be sustained through continued unwarranted excess in these expectations. It is argued that this crisis moment reveals fundamental problems with the application of the formal sources of international law to this area of international interaction, and that a more elemental reconceptualization of the prudential character and attributes of international norms regulating uses of force is required.

It must be remembered that international use of force law is a relatively late development in the history of international law, only reaching its maturity in a broad, multilateral prohibition on the use of force as part of the post-World War II renaissance of reliance upon international norms and institutions, after the profound skepticism regarding the effectiveness of the Kellog-Briand Pact and the League of Nations during the late inter-war years.[50] As with a number of the other new projects which expanded exponentially the range of international interaction covered by international law during this time (e.g. international criminal law, international human rights law), international use of force law was an idealistic extension of the formal sources of international law, born from the hope of using international standards of behavior to dissuade states from engaging in the sorts of actions which, in the words of the U.N. Charter Preamble, had "twice in our lifetime… brought untold sorrow to mankind…"[51] It was hoped that, as with the other more traditional areas of international legal coverage, even unwilling states would self-interestedly comply with these rules because of the expectations of the broader international community and resulting issue linkages to their economic prosperity, and because of the power of the states which had established the U.N. Charter and which took the five permanent seats on the Security Council. However, this was by far the furthest extension of the idea of regulating international behavior through binding legal norms, and would be the greatest test of the horizontal pressuring forces which had been relatively effective in producing compliance with international rules governing navigation and

decade at digesting the lessons of the early 1990's, actively preparing for contests with regional adversaries.")

[50] See G. Simpson, *The Situation on the Legal Theory Front*, 11 European Journal of International Law 448 (2000); S. Neff, War and the Law of Nations: A General History (2005).

[51] See C. Joyner (ed.), The United Nations and International Law (1997) chs 1 and 4.

trade by sea, diplomatic relations, and territorial acquisition and boundaries for centuries.[52]

The post-Cold War history of powerful state uses of force, and particularly that history since September 11, 2001, culminating in the present crisis between law and reality on the subject of counterproliferation-oriented pre-emption, is evidence that this most sensitive area of international relations has exceeded the regulating capacity of the formal sources of international law, and the normative and structural limitations of international law as a legal system.[53] The absence both of effective and reliable means for adjudication of disputes by international judicial bodies and of effective vertical enforcement mechanisms upon powerful states, while not crippling to the effective regulation of these other areas of international interaction through the sources of international law and horizontal pressure and issue-linkage-based compliance forces, renders international use of force law both normatively and structurally incapable of effectively regulating its subject matter. In sum, international use of force law is simply an overstretching of the competencies of formal international law.

B. International Legal Theory

To explain this conclusion further, it will be necessary to briefly review a number of prominent jurisprudential theories on the validity of international law. The oldest of these, and one which still provides the underpinning for many fundamental rules of international law, is the idea that the validity of legal rules is based upon principles existing apart from human creation, and discoverable by human reason, whether emanating from the divine or simply inherent in the natural order of human society.[54] This natural law tradition was the sole conception of legal validity of both domestic and international law up until the nineteenth century, and is most prominently associated with scholars from antiquity including Cicero and St. Augustine, then with medieval scholastics including notably Thomas Aquinas, then with later medieval and enlightenment scholars including Hugo Grotius and Samuel von Pufendorf.

While subject to significant variations in theme through the centuries, the basic idea of this school of jurisprudential thought is that the validity of law or of a legal system in its entirety is based upon the harmony of the substantive rules

---

[52] See A. Guzman, How International Law Works (2008); See A. Chayes and A. Chayes, *On Compliance*, 47 International Organization 175 (1993); A.T. Guzman, *A Compliance Based Theory of International Law*, 90 California Law Review (2002); H.H. Koh, *Why Do Nations Obey International Law?* 106 Yale Law Journal 2599 (1997).

[53] L. Goldstein, Preventive Attack and Weapons of Mass Destruction: A Comparative Historical Analysis (2006) 155.

[54] See M.D.A. Freeman, Lloyd's Introduction to Jurisprudence (7th edn, 2001); S. Hall, *The Persistent Spectre: Natural Law, International Order and the Limits of Legal Positivism*, 12 European Journal of International Law 269 (2001); R.J. Beck et al. (eds), International Rules (1996); R. Tuck, The Rights of War and Peace (1999).

themselves with higher principles of the *jus naturale*. While not wholly representative of all variations of natural law theory, the Thomist maxim *lex injusta non est lex* (an unjust law is not a law) gives an indication of this connection between the substance of law and principles of justice or morality contained in the *philosophia perennis*, commonly associated with natural law theory. It is from this natural law foundation that international law incorporated fundamental rules such as *pacta sunt servanda*, or the obligation to comply with treaty commitments, as well as a host of other "general principles of law recognized by civilized nations."[55]

The empirical revolution in the scholarly sciences in the nineteenth century contributed to the maturation, and eventual dominance over natural law theory, of legal positivism. Legal positivism, as developed by Jeremy Bentham and John Austin, and as revised particularly with regard to international law by Georg Jellinek and Heinrich Triepel, holds that the primary validity of international law is based in the processes of its creation, and not upon the conformity of its substance with higher principles of morality.[56] Positivism severed the necessary connection of law with justice, and focused inquiries concerning validity upon the consent of sovereign states, expressed either explicitly or implicitly, to be bound to international obligations. Legal positivism accepts only such empirically verifiable processes, and objectively discernible rules created as a result thereof, as having the character of international law.

Earlier positivist writings, and particularly those of John Austin, further required consistent and reliable sanctions from a hierarchical sovereign as punishment for breach of rules, as a definitional requirement for validity of a legal system. It was on this subject that, according to Austin, international law failed as a legal system, and was classed by him simply as a form of "positive morality."[57] Later positivists, culminating in the work of H.L.A. Hart, rejected this narrow view of the role of coercion in the requisite characteristics of a valid legal system. According to Hart there is a meaningful difference to be had between the validity of rules which states are *obliged* (i.e. coerced) to obey, and the validity of those which they are *obligated* (i.e. normatively bound) to obey. Hart focused his inquiries into validity upon the obligations of states and not upon rules which force alone—which Hart equated to rules enforced by gangsters—motivates them to obey. Nevertheless, Hart concluded that because international law was composed only of primary, substantive rules, and lacked important secondary or structural/institutional rules regulating the administration of the primary

---

[55] Statute of the International Court of Justice, Article 38(1).

[56] See G. Jellinek, ALLGEMEINE STAATSLEHRE (3rd edn, 1914); H. Triepel, VOLKERRECHT UND LANDSRECHT (1899); M.D.A. Freeman, LLOYD'S INTRODUCTION TO JURISPRUDENCE (7th edn, 2001); S. Hall, *The Persistent Spectre: Natural Law, International Order and the Limits of Legal Positivism*, 12 EUROPEAN JOURNAL OF INTERNATIONAL LAW 269 (2001); R.J. Beck, et al. (eds), INTERNATIONAL RULES (1996); R. Tuck, THE RIGHTS OF WAR AND PEACE (1999).

[57] J. Austin, *The Province of Jurisprudence Determined*, in C. Morris (ed.), THE GREAT LEGAL PHILOSOPHERS (1971).

rules, it was not a valid legal system, but rather simply a collection of valid legal rules.[58]

Notwithstanding the doubts of some influential positivist writers regarding the validity of international law, either as a legal system or simply as legal rules, and despite the lingering presence of rules of international law which could only be explained by reference to natural law theory,[59] positivism from the late nineteenth century, and continuing to the present time, became the primary theory which international lawyers used to validate their legal science. Pursuant to positivism's focus on the process of law creation, international lawyers grounded the validity of the sources of international law upon state consent, and found this consent to be present (although at times through tortured logical processes) in rules created by treaties, customary law, and general principles.

In his earlier writings, before turning his back on international law and playing a founding role in developing realist political thought after World War II, Hans Morgenthau developed a theory which, although ostensibly rejecting positivism out of hand as the primary theory of validity of international law, incorporated both elements of natural law and Austinian legal positivism to form what Morgenthau referred to as a "functionalist theory" of international law.[60] In his functionalist theory, Morgenthau criticizes legal positivism as being at once both too narrow and too broad to fully explain the validity of international law. Too narrow because it does not include recognition of "ethico-legal" principles and other considerations (e.g. *pacta sunt servanda*) which are a part of the corpus of international law. Too broad because it mandates the inclusion in the corpus of international law of rules which have been enacted by states through positivist processes, but that are not in harmony with the actual practice of states.

He identifies this excessive breadth as a gap between law and reality, in which the law recognizes rules which states create through consent, but with which they do not in fact comply, and is critical of international lawyers for having allowed such a gap to come into existence. As he wrote in 1940:

If an event in the physical world contradicts all scientific forecasts, and thus challenges the assumptions on which the forecasts have been based, it is the natural reaction of scientific inquiry to re-examine the foundations of the specific science and attempt to reconcile scientific findings and empirical facts. The social sciences do not react in the

---

[58] H.L.A. Hart, THE CONCEPT OF LAW (2nd edn, 1994).

[59] Including the doctrine of *pacta sunt servanda*, which mandates observance of treaty commitments, and rules of customary international law and general principles of law, only the manifestations and not the substance of which can be explained by legal positivism. See S. Hall, *The Persistent Spectre: Natural Law, International Order and the Limits of Legal Positivism*, 12 EUROPEAN JOURNAL OF INTERNATIONAL LAW 269 (2001).

[60] H.J. Morgenthau, *Positivism, Functionalism and International Law*, 34 AMERICAN JOURNAL OF INTERNATIONAL LAW 260, 260 (1940).

same way. They have an inveterate tendency to stick to their assumptions and to suffer constant defeat from experience rather than to change their assumptions in the light of contradicting facts. This resistance to change is uppermost in the history of international law…Instead of asking whether the devices were adequate to the problems which they were supposed to solve, it was the general attitude of the internationalists to take the appropriateness of the devices for granted and to blame the facts for the failure.[61]

Morgenthau rather proposes a theory of validity which takes into account the relationship of law with wider social and political forces which form the context in which states exist. This theory, he argues, has the ability not only to make legally valid those ethico-legal principles which are accepted as law by states, but which positivism cannot countenance, but also to exclude from the formal corpus of valid international law those rules which positivism does sanction, but which are not observed by states.

Whereas natural law focused on the substance of rules and positivism focused on the processes of rule creation, Morgenthau's functionalism places primacy upon the application of rules of law to state practice, and particularly upon the capacity of the legal system to consistently and predictably enforce compliance with substantive legal rules.[62] As he states:

A rule of international law does not, as positivism was prone to believe, receive its validity from its enactment into a legal instrument, as, for instance, an international treaty. There are rules of international law which are valid, although not enacted in such legal instruments, and there are rules of international law which are not valid, although enacted in such instruments…A rule, be it legal, moral, or conventional, is valid when its violation is likely to be followed by an unfavorable reaction, that is, a sanction against its violator. An alleged ruled, the violation of which is not followed by a sanction, is a mere idea, a wish, a suggestion, but not a valid rule.[63]

---

[61] Ibid. at 260.

[62] See the more recent reiteration of this idea in A. Guzman, *A Compliance-Based Theory of International Law*, 90 CALIFORNIA LAW REVIEW 1823 (2002). Additional scholarship on the issue of the relationship between international law and state compliance includes idem., HOW INTERNATIONAL LAW WORKS (2008); A. Chayes and A. Chayes, *On Compliance*, 47 INTERNATIONAL ORGANIZATION 175 (1993); idem., THE NEW SOVEREIGNTY: COMPLIANCE WITH INTERNATIONAL REGULATORY AGREEMENTS (1995); M.E. Keck and K. Sikkink, ACTIVISTS BEYOND BORDERS: ADVOCACY NETWORKS IN INTERNATIONAL POLITICS (1998); T.M. Franck, *Legitimacy in the International System*, 82 AMERICAN JOURNAL OF INTERNATIONAL LAW 705, 705 (1988); H.H. Koh, *How Is International Human Rights Law Enforced?*, 74 INDIANA LAW JOURNAL 1397 (1999); O.A. Hathaway, *Between Power and Principle: An Integrated Theory of International Law*, 72 UNIVERSITY OF CHICAGO LAW REVIEW 469 (2005); M.A. Chinen, *Game Theory and Customary International Law: A Response to Professors Goldsmith and Posner*, 23 MICHIGAN JOURNAL OF INTERNATIONAL LAW 143, 155 (2001); R. Goodman and D. Jinks, *How to Influence States: Socialization and International Human Rights Law*, 54 DUKE LAW JOURNAL 621 (2004); H.H. Koh, *Why Do Nations Obey International Law?* 106 YALE LAW JOURNAL 2599 (1997).

[63] H.J. Morgenthau, *Positivism, Functionalism and International Law*, 34 AMERICAN JOURNAL OF INTERNATIONAL LAW 260, 276 (1940). This does at first glance look like a simple restatement of Austin, but it differs in important ways. First, Austin would not have recognized

Each of these jurisprudential theories, which can only be briefly summarized here, has persuasive power in partially explaining the validity of modern international law. Natural law still is the only theory that can account for the foundational rule of *pacta sunt servanda* as well as the binding nature of both customary law and general principles of law.[64] Legal positivism, however, importantly removes the primary explanation for the sources of international law from the subjectivity of natural law's metaphysical underpinnings and grounds validity in state consent, analogously in accord with mature domestic legal systems.

However, on the question of prudential areas of coverage for the formal corpus of international law and the potential problem of overstretching identified above, Morgenthau's functionalism is most useful. This is because, as is evident from the continuing necessity of appealing to natural law to account for validity of some fundamental aspects of its normative structure, international law, if a legal system at all, is in its embryonic developmental stages as compared to mature domestic legal systems.[65] At this stage of its evolution, care must be taken not to relegate to the coverage of formal international law those areas of international interaction which are beyond the capacity of the sources and structures of the international legal system to regulate effectively. Doing so, as argued above, will only damage the credibility and perceived legitimacy of the legal system as a whole, and thereby slow or potentially permanently derail its evolutionary progress.

In keeping with the functionalist approach advocated by Morgenthau, therefore, the overstretching argument above with regard to the *jus ad bellum* can be restated as follows. The non-compulsory jurisdiction of judicial bodies and horizontal enforcement processes which international law has always depended upon to produce compliance can be expected to work well in relatively low politics areas, where expectations of reciprocity are strong and the likely cost of compliance is fairly low. Within this category may be grouped most of the traditional areas of international legal coverage. However, these enforcement processes should not be expected to work well in high politics areas, where issues concern vital national survival and prosperity interests, and where the expectation of reciprocity is dubious and costs of compliance are potentially high. The paradigmatic

the legal validity of ethico-legal principles as Morgenthau does. Second, Austin would not have accepted the sanctions Morgenthau discusses as genuine sanctions, as they do not necessarily flow vertically downwards from a sovereign. Rather, Morgenthau accepts Triepel's identification of the sovereign in the international legal order as being the community of states. He thus accepts horizontal sanctions as providing for the definitional element of enforcement in functionalist theory.

[64] See S. Hall, *The Persistent Spectre: Natural Law, International Order and the Limits of Legal Positivism*, 12 European Journal of International Law 269 (2001).

[65] See H. Kelsen, Law and Peace in International Relations, Lecture 2, (1942).

example of such an issue area in the latter category is state use of international force, particularly in self-defense.[66]

It is important to clarify that most areas of international law, i.e. particularly those part of the formal corpus of international law before World War II, do qualify as valid law even under Morgenthau's functionalist criteria. In most of these areas it is realistic to expect some meaningful sanction (including loss of trust and reputation, issue linkaging, economic sanctions, and military force at the most extreme) albeit horizontally, which is likely to produce compliance.[67] But it is important to understand that these forces are likely to produce compliance in these areas *because states are not far away from compliance to begin with*; meaning the cost of compliance, even when states think their short-term interests are better served by breaching, is seen to be outweighed by the long-term benefits of compliance, and thus they are more easily pressured into line. Again, in these areas the political and economic stakes in each instance are relatively low and the cost of compliance with the relevant international rules is also relatively low. These factors, along with an expectation of reciprocal compliance by other states which, along with their own compliance results in the efficiencies designed to be produced by the normative regime, are likely to provide sufficient bases for choosing to comply.

Use of force as an issue area candidate for international legal coverage presents a very different set of decision-making calculi for states when considering compliance, however. The above listed horizontal pressuring forces should not be expected to produce compliance with incongruous international rules by a state considering using force, if that state considers that its vital national interests of security and prosperity are at stake and can only be safeguarded through the use of force. This is particularly true if the state is powerful, and can therefore expect to deter and at the extreme resist the application of such sanctions, up to and including military force, imposed by other states. In such a case, the state will reasonably consider that the cost of compliance with the rule (when its judgment is that doing so will threaten its vital national interests) will be too great to be offset by long-term benefits of compliance. This is particularly the case in such areas of high politics and national sovereignty sensitivity, because states will not expect other states to reciprocally comply in similar situations, but will expect those states also to breach in furtherance of their perceived vital self-interest. Thus, there is not the reasonable expectation in reciprocity producing the efficiencies

---

[66] See A. Guzman, *A Compliance-Based Theory of International Law*, 90 California Law Review 1823 (2002).

[67] See A. Guzman, How International Law Works (2008); A. Chayes and A. Chayes, *On Compliance*, 47 International Organization 175 (1993); A.T. Guzman, *A Compliance Based Theory of International Law*, 90 California Law Review (2002); H.H. Koh, *Why Do Nations Obey International Law?* 106 Yale Law Journal 2599 (1997).

the system was designed to produce—in this case international peace and security—that there is in lower politics areas.[68]

The unlikelihood of the normatively indeterminate, horizontal pressure forces of the international legal system producing compliance, particularly by powerful states in the area of state uses of force, therefore results in the invalidity of international use of force law, according to Morgenthau's critique.

C. Hard and Soft International Law

Eric Posner and Jack Goldsmith's recent book entitled *The Limits of International Law* approaches the question of the limitations of international law as a legal system from a very different direction; that of international relations theory and specifically rational choice analysis.[69] They argue that international law is essentially epiphenomenal; that it is the product of states' interests and power, and that it does not meaningfully influence state action except through the limited role of defining the relationship between states at any given moment which has been agreed as optimal for states' coordination or cooperation. They reject any "non-instrumental" considerations (e.g. belief that compliance is the most legitimate option or is required by concerns of moral principle, including the greater good) for state compliance with international law. According to their model, since states will only comply with international law when they perceive it to be in their interests to do so, expectations for the usefulness of international law in influencing state behavior and in producing positive results in international interactions beyond what states feel is justified by their short-term interests to achieve, should be modest.

Posner and Goldsmith's model is quite a strict version of rationalism, and shares with other rational choice literature the fundamental flaw of insufficiently clarifying the distinction between short-term and long-term, or micro and macro state interests, and of failing to consider the impact of this distinction upon their analysis, in this case of the usefulness of international law.[70] Their conclusion that international law should not be expected to cause states to act contrary to their interests is produced because of their very narrow definition of state interest, which essentially only includes short-term or micro state interests, and excludes longer term or macro state interests, such as interests in order, peace, and prosperity. It is these macro interests which states have traditionally sought to secure through the development of international law, and which states

---

[68] See R. Scott and P. Stephan, THE LIMITS OF LEVIATHAN (2006).

[69] (2005). But see A. Guzman, HOW INTERNATIONAL LAW WORKS (2008).

[70] See R. Cryer, *The Limits of Objective Rationalism* (Book Review), in 82 INTERNATIONAL AFFAIRS 183 (2006); M. Koskenniemi, *The Place of Law in Collective Security* 17 MICHIGAN JOURNAL OF INTERNATIONAL LAW 455 (1996); A. Wendt, SOCIAL THEORY OF INTERNATIONAL POLITICS (1999).

have traditionally been willing to sacrifice their short-term interests to achieve. International law can therefore better be explained as having a reflective, two-way relationship of causal effect, in that it is created out of states' long-term interests, but also serves to reflect these long-term or macro interests back upon international interactions in order to limit states' actions which seek to serve short-term or micro interests undermining of these original long-term or macro interests.

However, this generalized discussion of state interests with regard to inter-national law highlights precisely another significant circumscription of the explanatory power of Posner and Goldsmith's model. In furnishing their "com-prehensive analysis of international law" Posner and Goldsmith make no dis-tinction in the operation of international law, and the role of states' power and interest in that operation, as between substantive areas of its coverage. As dis-cussed previously, the interest calculations involved in state decision-making can be substantially different depending on which set of issues form the context for that decision. This is because the issue context will be largely determinate of both the nature and scope of the state interests involved, which in turn determines the cost–benefit calculus for states, as well as states' expectations of reciprocity. Posner and Goldsmith's generalized treatment of the role of states' power and interest in the operation of international law makes for a much less sophisticated explanatory theory than one which takes account of the differences between the highly varied international issue areas combined under international law's regu-latory remit, and their particular respective requirements for and susceptibilities to international normative regulation.

The only literature in international relations which has attempted to explain the operation of international norms in a manner capable of distinguishing between substantive areas of international interaction is the excellent legalization thesis developed by Robert Keohane et al. in a special issue of *International Organization* in 2000, and particularly as applied by Kenneth Abbot and Duncan Snidal in their article entitled "Hard and Soft Law in International Governance."[71] The legalization thesis posits that formalization, or legalization, in the structure of international institutions can be separated into at least three broad sub-categories— obligation, precision, and delegation—the sum of the relative presence of each being the functional determinant of the degree of legalization present in the regime. As described by Keohane et al.:

"Legalization" refers to a particular set of characteristics that institutions may (or may not) possess. These characteristics are defined along three dimensions: obligation, precision, and delegation. *Obligation* means that states or other actors are bound by a rule or commitment or by a set of rules or commitments. Specifically, it means that they are *legally* bound by a rule or commitment in the sense that their behavior thereunder is sub-ject to scrutiny under the general rules, procedures, and discourse of international law,

---

[71] "Legalization in World Politics," Vol. 54, No. 3.

and often of domestic law as well. *Precision* means that rules unambiguously define the conduct they require, authorize, or proscribe. *Delegation* means that third parties have been granted authority to implement, interpret, and apply the rules; to resolve disputes; and (possibly) to make further rules.[72]

The legalization thesis essentially advances the idea that formalization or legalization of international interactions happens along a spectrum, with the place of any particular issue-specific regime along that spectrum being determined by the relative presence in the international norms addressing that regime of these three determinants, and not according to the rigid law/non-law distinction imposed by classical international legal theory.[73]

Abbot and Snidal proceed to apply this thesis by reviewing the advantages and disadvantages of hard law (i.e. legally binding commitments), as compared to soft law (i.e. non-legally-binding commitments), and arguing that international actors deliberately choose the form of normative regulation they wish to employ to address an area of international interaction, on the basis of the particularities of that issue area and the appropriateness of the form of regulation, either hard or soft, to regulate those particular circumstances.

Thus they argue that hard law will be chosen in issue areas where priority has been placed upon maximizing the credibility of commitments and minimizing future transactions costs associated with renegotiation of commitments, and where problems of incomplete contracting can be addressed through hard law because of the existence of substantial consensus on general principles, notwithstanding the difficulty of predicting specific applications. They argue that soft law, by contrast, will be chosen to address areas of international interaction in which costs of initial contracting are high, where sovereignty costs are potentially severe (as in issue areas involving national security), where uncertainty of the issue area is high (as through dynamic technological change), and where necessity of compromise is great due to fundamental disagreements over principles.[74]

---

[72] R. Keohane et al., *The Concept of Legalization*, 54 INTERNATIONAL ORGANIZATION 401 (2000).

[73] See also C. Lipson, *Why are Some International Agreements Informal?* 45 INTERNATIONAL ORGANIZATION 495, 504–505 (1991).

[74] With regard to arms control agreements, inclusive of the non-proliferation law treaties reviewed herein, the Abbott and Snidal analysis appears to place such agreements somewhat further down the spectrum towards the appropriateness of hard law regulation, noting that "states should use hard legalization to increase the credibility of commitments when noncompliance is difficult to detect, as in most arms control situations." They note that, while arms control treaties are understandable uses of formality of commitment as a regulatory vehicle, they tend also to be "minimally institutionalized." To phrase the point in terms of their three factors, arms control agreements tend to be high in obligation and low in both precision and delegation. See K. Abbot and D. Snidal, *Hard and Soft Law in International Governance*, INTERNATIONAL ORGANIZATION, Vol. 54, No. 3, 429 & 440 (2000). See generally A. Stein, "Coordination and Collaboration: Regimes in an Anarchic World," in NEOREALISM AND NEOLIBERALISM: THE CONTEMPORARY DEBATE (D.A. Baldwin (ed.), 1993); J. Grieco, "Understanding the Problem of Institutional Cooperation," in NEOREALISM AND NEOLIBERALISM: THE CONTEMPORARY DEBATE (D.A. Baldwin (ed.), 1993);

Applying the "spectrum" model of the legalization thesis, and being guided by the Abbott and Snidal analysis, there would appear to be no more persuasive candidate for international normative regulation through deformalized soft law, or non-binding commitments, than the issue area of international uses of force, as particularly manifest in the lesser-included issue area of international uses of force against WMD threats. If the gap between law and reality in this area is accepted, as also therefore the need for some normative change, then the daunting prospect of some new multilateral binding agreement on use of force law presents a case of extremely high initial contracting costs for instituting this change in hard law. Sovereignty costs in this issue area are clearly at their zenith, due to modern threats to national security including the potential and very real threat of use of WMD against states by other states and non-state actors. The issue area is highly uncertain, in that the necessities of normative regulation have evolved and continue to evolve as influenced by the dynamic changes to both the means of violence and to the political and economic phenomena (e.g. the facilitation of WMD dual-use trade through the forces of globalization) which shape the threats facing states. And the fundamental disagreements among states concerning principles of legitimate self-defense, particularly on the subject of counterproliferation-oriented pre-emptive strikes as described above, heighten the need for normative compromise in this area. Thus, all of the criteria for prudential application of soft law, instead of hard law, to the issue area are satisfied.[75]

D. Argument

The foregoing arguments based in both international legal theory and international relations theory support the following conclusions

1. that the *jus ad bellum* constitutes an overstretching of the normative and structural capacities of the formal sources of international law in their current evolutionary status; and

2. that as a consequence of a) this overstretching, b) the resulting gap between law and reality in the area of counterproliferation-oriented pre-emption, and c) the harm caused by this gap not only to the perceived legitimacy of use of force law but to the perceived legitimacy of the rest of the formal corpus of

---

L.L. Martin, Coercive Cooperation: Explaining Multilateral Economic Sanctions (1993); R.T. Cupitt and W.J. Long, "Multilateral Cooperation and Nuclear Nonproliferation," in The Proliferation Puzzle: Why Nuclear Weapons Spread and What Results (Z.S. Davis and B. Frankel (eds.), 1993); G. Bunn and D. Holloway, *Arms Control Without Treaties?* Stanford University CISAC Working Paper (February 1998). For an examination of the multilateral export control regimes by reference to the Abbot and Snidal model, see D.H. Joyner, *Restructuring the Multilateral Export Control Regime System*, 9 Journal of Conflict & Security Law 181 (2004).

[75] See also D. Shelton (ed.), Commitment & Compliance: The Role of Non-Binding Norms in the International Legal System (2000).

international law, the body of formal international law now constituting international use of force law should be normatively re-characterized as comprising non-binding commitments, or soft law.

Before proceeding with a further explanation of these conclusions, it is important to distinguish this deformalization thesis from other more extreme arguments relating to the prudential character of international norms in this area, and particularly those of Michael Glennon, which might be termed the "legal nihilist" approach to use of force law.[76]

Glennon's exhaustive writing on the subject of the character and usefulness of international law particularly in the area of use of force law can be summarized as follows. Glennon argues that the rules of the U.N. Charter regulating international uses of force are hopelessly unrealistic and impractical, and that because of this impracticality a gap between the law and state practice has been maintained since the Charter was established. He argues that because of this gap, policymakers do not consider international use of force rules as constituting binding law, and therefore tend to ignore them in their policy decisions. As a result of this consistent disregard and breach, he argues, international use of force law has fallen into desuetude, or has become invalid as law. Therefore, he argues, it should continue to be disregarded by policymakers.

Glennon is satisfied (and indeed appears pleased) that there are effectively no international norms which should influence state behavior in their international uses of force. He offers no replacement norms for those he says have fallen into invalidity through non-compliance, simply leaving it to states to decide for themselves which standards if any should guide their behavior in this area of interaction, without any principled framework around which international pressure can be mounted to convince the forceful state that the conduct, while perhaps politically expedient, runs foul of long standing principles to which the state itself has assented. The only hope he offers for standards to guide states in this area in the future is the potential evolution of customary law through state practice.

While sharing some of the same observations regarding the gap between law and reality in international use of force law, the arguments for deformalization in this chapter are quite different than Glennon's normative nihilism. The argument herein is that use of force law should largely retain the substance or definition of its standards, but should simply be re-characterized by states, through positive acts of renunciation and redrafting of documents, primarily including the U.N. Charter, and revised processes of declaration of assent to those agreements as comprising non-binding commitments rather than binding law.

---

[76] M. Glennon, *The Fog of Law: Self-Defense, Inherence, and Incoherence in Article 51 of the United Nations Charter*, 25 HARVARD JOURNAL OF LAW & PUBLIC POLICY 39 (2002); *The Rise and Fall of the U.N. Charter's Use of Force Rules*, 27 HASTINGS INTERNATIONAL & COMPARATIVE LAW REVIEW 497 (2004); *How International Rules Die*, 93 GEORGETOWN LAW JOURNAL 939 (2005).

These actions, along with further state practice and *opinio juris* pursuant to the revised understanding of the character of use of force principles, would in time further work a modification of relevant customary law. Some would surely call this distinction specious, and would maintain that in the absence of Hart's secondary administrative rules and a vertical orderer, international law has never been anything but a collection of non-binding, hortatory recommendations.[77]

However, it is argued herein that this distinction is meaningful and that the revised non-binding form of these rules would retain to this important area of international interaction a normative core of mutually agreed standards among states, through explicit agreement in documentary form, which would provide a principled locus around which efforts of domestic and international compliance pressure could be focused, and that this retention of explicit standards is both normatively and practically superior to the devilishly indeterminate processes of custom for purposes of influencing state behavior.[78]

While maintaining this normative core of referenceable standards, however, such deformalized commitments would have the added advantage of avoiding the unnecessary complications, tortured legal and practical fictions, and increasing harm to the perceived legitimacy of international law which will necessarily accompany the continued application of formal, binding rules to this international issue area.

With regard to the substance of such deformalized rules, as argued above in the first instance, the definition of such standards need not depart from their construction in existing legal documents, including most importantly the U.N. Charter. However, as Abbot and Snidal point out, one of the many utilities of soft law regulation is the facility of such norms for amendment with far lower transactions costs than those incurred in efforts to amend formal, binding agreements.[79] The recognition of an agreement as non-binding allows states to renegotiate the language of standards in a much less pressured environment, both due to the fact that they know their actions may never be as strictly decried

---

[77] See A. Guzman, *A Compliance-Based Theory of International Law*, 90 CALIFORNIA LAW REVIEW 1823 (2002).

[78] See J. Checkel, *Why Comply?: Social Learning and European Identity Change*, 55 INTERNATIONAL ORGANIZATION 3 (2001). This conclusion has some theoretical kinship to the arguments of the managerial school of regime theory, in which compliance with regime norms is asserted to be more likely achieved through persuasive and "managerial" approaches rather than by the use of coercive sanctions built into the structure of regimes. See A. Chayes and A. Chayes, THE NEW SOVEREIGNTY: COMPLIANCE WITH INTERNATIONAL REGULATORY AGREEMENTS (1995). It is also in keeping with the definition of international regimes put forward by Stephen D. Krasner as "sets of implicit or explicit principles, norms, rules, and decision-making procedures around which actors' expectations converge in a given area of international relations." *Structural Causes and Regime Consequences: Regimes as Intervening Variables*, in INTERNATIONAL REGIMES (S. Krasner (ed.), 1983).

[79] K. Abbot and D. Snidal, *Hard and Soft Law in International Governance*, 54 INTERNATIONAL ORGANIZATION 421 (2000).

as illegitimate based upon such non-binding standards, as well as the fact that the domestic procedures and scrutiny which accompany the initial establishment as well as subsequent amendment to soft law agreements are often not nearly as onerous as those which accompany the establishment or amendment of hard law agreements.

Thus, it is likely that such soft law standards could be drafted, or subsequently amended, to incorporate an increased measure of specificity in the definition or explication of standards on issues which in their hard law incarnation have eluded further explication due to significant disagreement among states. Examples of normative regimes in which specificity has been achieved precisely due to the non-binding nature of commitments include the multilateral export control regimes as normative addenda to binding non-proliferation treaties, as well as the 1975 Helsinki Final Act of the Conference on Security and Cooperation in Europe.[80]

In the use of force context, issues which might receive such added specificity, or explication in a soft law instrument include both anticipatory self-defense and humanitarian intervention. It is worth briefly noting in this context that the controversies which have long subsisted regarding the current restrictive state of international law on the subject of humanitarian interventions, and the gap between law and reality which has appeared in this area (as particularly manifest in the 1999 Kosovo intervention) serve only to support the deformalization thesis for the *jus ad bellum*.[81]

It is likely that such increased specificity would not take the form of more clearly defined or determinate standards, since the disagreements which prevented such clarity in hard law form will persist. Rather, this specificity is more likely to take the form of agreed considerations which should guide state decision-making in such areas. These considerations could include both standards which have evolved in custom, such as necessity and proportionality, as well as other factors such as evidentiary standards and legitimating purposes which may be agreed in principle, though left in their specific application to state discretion.[82] This non-binding commitment form would thus provide a normative environment in which the sovereignty sensitive, technologically and politically dynamic issue area of international uses of force could be more dynamically responded to with more specific, explicitly, and objectively agreed normative content than is currently possible through hard law forms of regulation.

---

[80] See D.H. Joyner, *Restructuring the Multilateral Export Control Regime System*, 9 JOURNAL OF CONFLICT & SECURITY LAW 181 (2004).

[81] See D.H. Joyner, *The Kosovo Intervention: Legal Analysis and a More Persuasive Paradigm*, 13 EUROPEAN JOURNAL OF INTERNATIONAL LAW 597 (2002); B.S. Brown, *Humanitarian Intervention at a Crossroads*, 41 WILLIAM AND MARY LAW REVIEW 1683, 1691(2000).

[82] See M. Doyle, STRIKING FIRST: PREEMPTION AND PREVENTION IN INTERNATIONAL CONFLICT (2008); H. Shue, "What Would a Justified Preventive Military Attack Look Like?" in H. Shue and D. Rodin, PREEMPTION: MILITARY ACTION AND MORAL JUSTIFICATION (2007).

A further insight from the Abbot and Snidal analysis also bears mention. That is that soft law, in many instances, because of its relative malleability, can function as a very useful precursor to harder forms of regulation, by allowing states to experiment with the definition of standards in a less normatively and politically threatening environment than that of binding multilateral treaties.[83] If the standards embodied in such soft law agreements eventually successfully narrowed the gap between international rules and state practice, the reverse process of formalization of those norms would be relatively straightforward. As noted at the beginning of this chapter, the deformalization thesis, therefore, while at first blush appearing to work a retrogression in norms addressing uses of force, would be better characterized as a tactical normative retreat the direction of which could easily be reversed in future.

Thus, while Glennon argues for an absence of normative standards in the area of international uses of force, the argument herein is for a retention of the same or better international standards, simply with a different normative character.

The rejoinder to this deformalization thesis from many international lawyers however will be to argue that the formal, legally binding character of norms governing uses of force is important, and that this argued dilution of the character of norms addressing uses of force would work a significant decrease in the influence of those norms upon state behavior for a number of reasons, and thus to their value in preserving international peace and order. Concern would be no doubt expressed that this path would lead inexorably to a returning of the international normative environment to the *bellum omnium contra omnes* status of pre-*jus ad bellum* international relations, resulting from each state having a largely unregulated *compétence de guerre*. It is to these objections to the deformalization thesis that consideration will now turn.

IV. Is Soft Law Meaningful?

The idea that soft law, or non-binding international norms matter (i.e. influence state action) is in fact much easier to argue than the idea of hard law or formally binding norms having any greater marginal effect on state behavior than soft law norms have. The former argument is supported by extensive and well-developed literature in the field of international relations theory, and in

---

[83] K. Abbot and D. Snidal, *Hard and Soft Law in International Governance*, 54 INTERNATIONAL ORGANIZATION 421 (2000).

the sub-field of liberal institutionalism particularly.[84] As Robert Keohane et al. have written:

In certain respects the study of international institutions in political science has been directed to demonstrating that informal institutions—not legalized and lacking any centralized enforcement—could still be effective. On the basis of institutionalist theory one should expect frequent informal agreements, some formal rules, and loopholes that provide flexibility in response to political exigencies...Institutionalist theory has explained how cooperation endures without legalization, but it has not explained legalization.[85]

---

[84] See, e.g., R. Keohane and L. Martin, *The Promise of Institutionalist Theory*, INTERNATIONAL SECURITY 20(1), 39–51 (Summer 1995); R. Keohane, AFTER HEGEMONY: COOPERATION AND DISCORD IN THE WORLD POLITICAL ECONOMY (1984); K. Oye (ed.), COOPERATION UNDER ANARCHY (1986); O. Young, *Political Leadership and Regime Formation: On the Development of Institutions in International Society*, 45 INTERNATIONAL ORGANIZATION 281 (1991); A.-M. Slaughter Burley, *International Law and International Relations Theory: A Dual Agenda* 87 AMERICAN JOURNAL OF INTERNATIONAL LAW 205 (1993); R. Jervis, *Security Regimes*, in INTERNATIONAL REGIMES (S. Krasner (ed.) 1983). Among international lawyers, opinions regarding the recognition of the utility of non-binding norms, as well as the term "soft law" have been mixed. However, it is generally accepted that non-binding norms do have an impact on state behavior, and are thus important to consider from a legal perspective. As Oscar Schacter has noted "States entering into a non-legal commitment generally view it as a political (or moral) obligation and intend to carry it out in good faith. Other parties and other states concerned have reasons to expect such compliance and to rely on it...[P]olitical texts which express commitments and positions of one kind or another are governed by the general principle of good faith." INTERNATIONAL LAW IN THEORY AND PRACTICE 178 (1982). See also O. Schachter, *The Twilight Existence of Nonbinding International Agreements*, 71 AMERICAN JOURNAL OF INTERNATIONAL LAW 296 (1977). When questioned about soft law instruments by the U.S. Senate Foreign Relations Committee, then U.S. Secretary of State Henry Kissinger once remarked that the United States is not "morally or politically free to act as if they did not exist. On the contrary, they are important statements of diplomatic policy and engage the good faith of the United States as long as the circumstances that gave rise to them continue." *US Department of State Bulletin* 73 (1975) 613, quoted in the Congressional Research Service study *Treaties and other International Agreements: The Role of the United States Senate*, 103rd Congress, 1st Session (November 1993) 38. See generally D. Shelton (ed.), COMMITMENT & COMPLIANCE: THE ROLE OF NON-BINDING NORMS IN THE INTERNATIONAL LEGAL SYSTEM (2000); A. Boyle and C. Chinkin, THE MAKING OF INTERNATIONAL LAW (2007). For a contrary view, see J. Sztucki, "Reflections on International 'Soft Law,'" in J. Ramberg et al. (eds), FESTSKRIFT TILL LARS HJERNER—STUDIES IN INTERNATIONAL LAW (1990) ("*Primo*, the term is inadequate and misleading. There are no two levels or 'species' of law—something is law or is not law. *Secundo*, the concept is counterproductive or even dangerous. On the one hand, it creates illusory expectations of (perhaps even insistence on) compliance with what no one is obliged to comply; and on the other hand, it exposes binding legal norms for risks of neglect, and international law as a whole for risks of erosion, by blurring the threshold between what is legally binding and what is not.") 550–551. However, as D.J. Harris has responded, "While it may be paradoxical and confusing to call something "law" when it is *not* law, the concept is nonetheless useful to describe instruments that clearly have an impact on international relations and that may later harden into custom or become the basis of a treaty." CASES AND MATERIALS ON INTERNATIONAL LAW 65 (5th edn, 1998). In the non-proliferation context in particular, see G. Bunn, *The Legal Status of U.S. Negative Security Assurances to Non-Nuclear Weapon States*, THE NONPROLIFERATION REVIEW (Spring/Summer 1997).

[85] *Introduction: Legalization and World Politics*, 54 INTERNATIONAL ORGANIZATION 392 (2000).

To argue that a deformalization of international use of force law to produce a system of non-binding commitments would result in a loss of influence of those standards upon state behavior, and thereby devolve the world into Hobbesian anarchy from which the formal rules have saved it for the past 60 years, is simply an unsupportable causal statement. To make this argument in light of the model proposed herein, it would have to be shown that there is something specifically about the formality of the norms in this area that has had, or should be expected to have, a significant marginal effect on bringing about peace and order, i.e. the absence of war, over and above what soft law norms would have been able, or should be expected to be able to achieve. As with many areas of international relations, it is probably impossible empirically to do this because of the absence of a control case, but again, what empirical work there is in international relations literature simply does not bear out this argument. This literature does however bear out the argument that the existence of international norms does have a marginal effect on state behavior over and above the non-existence of norms. This evidence would seem to support the conclusion that it is the weight of a norm as a recognized and supported international community standard, with the corresponding moral, reputational, precedential, and reciprocity factors militating for its observance, that in fact effects compliance and not the precise status of the norm in the relative hierarchy of legality imposed by the international legal system.[86] As Charles Lipson has written:

High costs of self-enforcement and the dangers of opportunism are important obstacles to extralegal agreements. Indeed, the costs may be prohibitive if they leave unsolved such basic problems as moral hazard and time inconsistency. The same obstacles are inherent features of interstate bargaining and must be resolved if agreements are to be concluded and carried out. Resolving them depends on the parties' preference orderings, the transparency of their preferences and choices (asymmetrical information), and the private institutional mechanisms set up to secure their bargains. It has little to do, however, with whether an international agreement is considered "legally binding" or not.[87]

Similarly, Ian Hurd has recently explained:

"Legitimacy," as I use the term, refers to an actor's normative belief that a rule or institution ought to be obeyed. It is a subjective quality, relational between actor and institution, and is defined by the actor's *perception* of the institution... Such a perception affects behavior, because it is internalized by the actor and comes to help define how the actor sees its interests... In this sense, saying that a rule is accepted as legitimate by some

---

[86] This of course presupposes a degree of transparency in the workings of institutions such that there is adequate information disclosure regarding norms around which pressure can be brought to bear upon states in favor of its observance. See M. Finnemore, *Norms, Culture and World Politics: Insights from Sociology's Institutionalism*, 50 INTERNATIONAL ORGANIZATION 325 (1996); T. Franck, THE POWER OF LEGITIMACY AMONG NATIONS (1990). See generally D.H. Joyner, *Restructuring the Multilateral Export Control Regime System* 9 JOURNAL OF CONFLICT & SECURITY LAW 181 (2004).

[87] See C. Lipson, *Why are Some International Agreements Informal?* 45 INTERNATIONAL ORGANIZATION 495, 507 (1991).

actor says nothing about its justice in the eyes of an outside observer. Further, an actor's belief in the legitimacy of a norm, and thus its following of that norm, need not correlate to the actor being "law-abiding," or submissive to official regulations. Often, precisely the opposite is true: a normative conviction about legitimacy might lead to *non*compliance with laws when laws are seen as conflicting with the conviction.[88]

Thus, in issue areas where hard law forms carry more costs than benefits, it is quite reasonable to assume, as argued above, that it would be highly preferable to have specific, soft commitments rather than to have more vague, binding commitments, as the specificity of the norm is more likely to form a principled locus around which efforts of domestic and international compliance pressure may be focused.[89]

The latter position placing primacy on the binding character of norms regulating international uses of force is, however, argued consistently by traditional international lawyers.[90] They argue that the formality of the rule expresses its importance and centrality to the system of norms, thus conveying a message to states that breaching will incur more disapproval and more likely sanctions from the international community than would breach of a soft law norm. They argue that because of this flagging of importance, states will be less likely to breach the rule. They further argue that hard law provides a better normative locus for both international and domestic compliance pressuring forces, enabling such movements to use the gravitas-laden rhetoric of illegality to delegitimize breaches of international standards.

It is not denied that such assertions are at least in some cases correct and therefore can add to the marginal influence of hard law norms on state behavior over the influence of soft law norms. However, these positive factors accompanying formality must be taken together with negative factors accompanying it in order to arrive at a true picture of the marginal advantage of formality, particularly in the issue area under consideration herein. In the international use of force area specifically, as in other areas of high politics, the fact of bindingness in normative regulation can itself produce negative effects at least partially counteracting any benefits accruing from it.

---

[88] AFTER ANARCHY: LEGITIMACY & POWER IN THE UNITED NATIONS SECURITY COUNCIL (2008) 7–8.

[89] G.W. Downs et al., *Is the Good News About Compliance Good News About Cooperation?*, 50 INTERNATIONAL ORGANIZATION (1996); J. Goldstein and L.L. Martin, *Legalization, Trade Liberalization and Domestic Politics: A Cautionary Note*, 54 INTERNATIONAL ORGANIZATION 603 (2000); see also J. Trachtman, *Bananas, Direct Effect and Compliance*, 10 EUROPEAN JOURNAL OF INTERNATIONAL LAW 655 (1999) ("hard law is not necessarily good law, and [] strengthened implementation, including possible direct effect, is not necessarily desirable. This seems obvious once we recognize that, putting aside for a moment transaction costs and strategic costs, states generally have the level of compliance that they want. The correct role for scholars and for lawyers involved with these issues is to help political decision-makers to identify circumstances in which, due to such problems, states have not achieved the desired level of compliance.")

[90] See, e.g., N. Krisch, *International Law in Times of Hegemony: Unequal Power and the Shaping of the International Legal Order*, 16 EUROPEAN JOURNAL OF INTERNATIONAL LAW 369 (2005).

As Charles Lipson explains, binding law is often established in such issue areas in order to reflect long-term interests back upon state behavior and thereby give added incentive for not breaching the rules precisely because it is known that the issue area contains concerns of high politics and is thus highly sensitive for policymakers in the short term. Because of this high political sensitivity in the short term, these are of course the issue areas in which states are most likely to breach when their short-term interests appear to them to overshadow their longer term interests. Therefore, paradoxically, the original desire to give added incentive to comply ends up installing a formal legal framework in an area most likely to see those formal laws breached in times of extremity. These original high intentions thus in actuality produce an effect deleterious to the assumptions which underlay them, as the high-profile breaches of formal, binding agreements which they facilitate, harm the perceived credibility of the very norms being used, and by extension the legal system as a whole.[91]

Therefore, in some issue areas it will be conceded that bindingness may indeed give added weight of influence upon state practice, facilitating predictability and surety of commitments, and raising the political costs of non-compliance, and can thus be a very useful legal fiction to maintain. However, as with the horizontal structural forces producing compliance pressuring in the international legal system, it is argued that this marginal advantage in influence achieved from bindingness is likely to occur only meaningfully in low politics areas where—because of low costs of compliance, damage to short-term interests being deemed compensated by achievement of long-term interests, and reasonable expectations of reciprocity being maintained—the decision-making environment is one wherein states *are already close to compliance anyway*.

In high politics areas, any marginal effect on state behavior toward compliance derived from bindingness is likely to be minor in degree, and, most importantly, is highly likely to be outweighed in states' policymaking calculus, per the Lipson paradox, in the very situations in which it would be hoped that norms would matter, i.e. when situations arise in which states perceive compliance as being harmful to their vital national survival and prosperity interests.[92]

We must accept that, at the current state of evolution of international law as a legal system, in high politics areas like international uses of force, it is not the bindingness of the norm that makes for high levels of compliance. It is rather the strength of and consensus regarding wider social and political concerns and values which the norm expresses. Only these considerations, and active forces of compliance pressuring brought to bear in support thereof, can hope to truly influence state action, not considerations of the character of the norm itself. Thus in international use of force law, non-binding norms can be expected to have just

---

[91] See C. Lipson, *Why are Some International Agreements Informal?*, 45 INTERNATIONAL ORGANIZATION 495, 512 (1991).

[92] Ibid.; A. Guzman, *A Compliance-Based Theory of International Law*, 90 CALIFORNIA LAW REVIEW 1823 (2002).

as much of an influence on state behavior as binding ones have had, particularly if because of their non-binding character, they can be made more specific and thus serve more effectively as normative loci around which international compliance pressure can be focused.

V. Practical Effects/Benefits

The essential practical benefits of such a deformalization of international use of force law are that it would provide norms to which states would positivistic-ally and explicitly assent and that would be acknowledged to apply to this area of international relations on the one hand, but which would allow states with legitimate concerns, as particularly expressed in WMD counterproliferation strategies, the flexibility they need to deal with modern threats to their vital national security and prosperity interests on the other. With such standards in place, states seen by the international community to act in disharmony with such agreed standards could be made subject to precisely the same methods of compliance pressure which now serve as sanctions for breaches of binding, hard law rules. Unilateral or multilateral sanctions could be imposed on the basis of these standards, and if necessary, military force could be used, as coordinated by international regimes with duly delegated institutional discretion. The court of world opinion regarding compliance with these standards would still be in constant session. And again, using such soft law sources, it is as explained above reasonable to hope that standards of conduct would be given more spe-cificity and explication than is currently the case in hard law forms, making even more effective such efforts of compliance pressuring by the international community.

However, with such regulation through soft law instruments, we would be spared the continuous and inevitably fruitless rhetorical battles regarding formal legality of state actions regarding international uses of force, in an insti-tutional environment in which we are unlikely to ever get authoritative state-ments or adjudications of who is right and who is wrong. Those arguments could still be usefully maintained in other issue areas in which compliance pressures, combined with formal legality, combined with increased willingness to submit such disputes to international judicial resolution, are more likely to make such breaches fewer in number and of less serious effect when they do occur. The deformalization argument herein is essentially a proposal to preserve to those areas in which it is meaningful and likely to be useful, the added weight of formal bindingness of rules, and to relieve issue areas in which it is likely not to be meaningful and unlikely to be useful from its inefficiencies. To place it in Morgenthauian terms, to save for normative regimes in those issue areas in which meaningful sanctions are likely and are likely to compel compliance, the moniker and trappings of valid law.

VI. Relationship of the Deformalization
Thesis with Foregoing Chapters

The analysis and proposals in the preceding chapters, and particularly in Chapters 4 and 5, have assumed that the current structural paradigm of the United Nations, inclusive of the character of the U.N. Charter as formal law, will remain constant. However, should the international community choose to implement the deformalization proposals in the instant chapter, what would be the implications for the U.N. Charter organizational system? As noted previously, a deformalized U.N. Charter system would essentially retain its principled structure and content. Furthermore, the organs of administration created by the Charter and their respective roles could also remain largely unchanged. In fact, very little of the activity of the United Nations as an organization is at all dependent upon the status of the U.N. Charter as a formal treaty.

The United Nations as an organization could still serve all of its functions as a center for multilateral diplomacy on a wide array of issues of international concern, and could play essentially similar roles to those it has always played in facilitating communication among states, in coordinating negotiations on new treaties, in advancing issues of importance to the international community including human rights, and in issuing normative pronouncements. There could still be a General Assembly with its associated subsidiary committees and bodies.

The only changes to the functioning of the United Nations which would be occasioned by the adoption and implementation of the deformalization thesis by the international community would have to do with the role and authority of the Security Council, and these changes would still in fact arguably change little in practice. As the Charter would no longer be a treaty, the Security Council would have no authority to issue legally binding decisions—in effect Article 25 would be left out of the revised Charter document. There could indeed still be a Security Council under the deformalized U.N. structure, which would continue to be a specialized deliberative body, with primary responsibility for issues of international peace and security. The Council could issue decisions either approving or condemning particular state actions, and making recommendations for the resolution of international disputes as it ever has done. It could even continue to play a meaningful role in the legitimization or delegitimization of forceful measures up to and including international uses of force, in exercise of its Chapter VII role—though to be clear, since there would no longer be a formal legal prohibition on international force, pursuant to the *Lotus* principle there would be no need to have such uses of force formally authorized.[93] Rather,

---

[93] See below at 211–212.

the Council's role in this regard would be that of legitimacy determination for forceful measures up to and including uses of force. As Ian Hurd has recently demonstrated, fulfilling this role of legitimacy determination and promulgation has been the Council's primary contribution as a part of the U.N. Charter system.[94]

As has been argued above, the effectiveness of an international commitment or institution has more to do with the presence of generally supported norms than it does with the character of those norms as legal or non-legal. Thus, if states agreed to continue the Security Council's mandate as a legitimizer of forceful actions, and so long as the Council demonstrated by its record that it could act in a supportable and legitimate manner in this role, the lack of formal legal authority underpinning its decisions should have little bearing on the Council's ability to function in this role—as indeed it would be difficult to demonstrate that the effectiveness of the Council has in the past been enhanced by its possession of formal legal authority per se.[95]

It should be briefly noted that a deformalization of the U.N. Charter would have no necessary effect upon the role and functioning of the International Court of Justice. The ICJ Statute is essentially separate from the Charter, and the ICJ could continue to function as it ever has.

VII. Conclusion

This chapter has described one possible option for the future of the *jus ad bellum*. Because of its revolutionary nature it will no doubt be met with skepticism and quickly dismissed by many. However, it is argued that at the current crisis moment, we must be willing to take bold and creative steps in order to bring the character and organization of this important area of international normative regulation into line with what are reasonable expectations for the capacity and usefulness of international norms in an area of such high politics and state sovereignty sensitivity. As stressed herein, addressing this crisis moment need not simply be a question of the maintenance or not of international norms in this issue area, but rather a question of what kind of international norms would be best suited for the purpose of standardizing international behavior in this issue area to the extent realistically possible, given the current evolutionary state of the international legal system. It has been argued that the continuing negative implications of allowing formal international law to be overstretched to include within its regulation issue areas that it simply cannot reasonably be expected

---

[94] After Anarchy: Legitimacy & Power in the United Nations Security Council (2008).

[95] Ibid.; C. Lipson, *Why are Some International Agreements Informal?*, 45 International Organization 495, 507 (1991); See also J. Trachtman, *Bananas, Direct Effect and Compliance*, 10 European Journal of International Law 655 (1999).

to regulate effectively at the current stage of its evolutionary progression, will include decreasing respect for international law generally, and, albeit unfairly, a lessening of the perceived authority of international law in other areas in which it does in fact function relatively well. It is hoped that international lawyers will have the intellectual integrity not to be bound to the status quo simply for its own sake, and that we will be willing to think and act in the best interests of the future of international law generally, to enable it to better fulfill its important role in international relations.

Concluding Thoughts

It is hoped that the explanation and analysis in the foregoing chapters will contribute to an understanding of how international law regulates WMD proliferation, as well as how international law regulates state responses to WMD proliferation. This analysis also, however, raises important systemic questions for international law in this area. The most compelling and fundamental of these is the question of whether the formal sources of international law, at their current state of normative evolution, indeed have the tools and supporting normative and institutional structures, to enable the international legal system to regulate effectively this sovereignty sensitive area. This question is presented by the gap between law and reality which has been identified and which may be summarized as follows.

The non-proliferation treaties and regimes system, based necessarily upon state consent, voluntary participation, and international legal personality, is inherently limited in its ability to regulate effectively WMD proliferation. Among the limitations of this system are the non-universality or secondary proliferation problem, and the non-state actor problem, as described in Chapter 6 of this book.

However, attempts by states to supplement or replace this non-proliferation law paradigm, and address these limitations through more forceful and proactive efforts of counterproliferation, often fall foul of rules of international law governing, inter alia, the use of force and the law of the sea. Examples of this actual and potential inconsistency have been given in case studies of the Proliferation Security Initiative and the 2003 Iraq intervention. Notwithstanding these legal difficulties, some states will likely increasingly see the utility of counterproliferation action in combating WMD proliferation as outweighing the costs of such action, including costs arising from widely acknowledged breaches of the letter of international law.

Furthermore, as discussed in Chapter 4 of this book, the efforts of the United Nations to close loopholes in the non-proliferation system have thus far led only to the confused passing of a piece of ostensible international legislation by the Security Council; a decision which itself runs counter to U.N. Charter law and serves only to muddy the waters of international legal regulation in this area.

The composite result of these related normative dynamics is that the non-proliferation treaties and regimes system, while hugely important and meaningful in delegitimizing activities which contribute to the proliferation of WMD, is not fully sufficient in itself to address effectively the problem of WMD proliferation. However, other rules of international law serve in many instances to prohibit state actions which might supplement the effectiveness of this system. And the efforts of the United Nations to address the problems of legal regulation in this area have to this point been unfruitful.

What remains is a serious, ongoing challenge to international security posed by the proliferation of WMD, and a gap between current international law and the perceived reality of this threat which the best efforts of states through the international legal system have thus far been unable to address effectively. As noted in the Introduction to this book, while this gap is principally to be located within the context of the international law on the use of force, it is in fact a composite result of the limitations of non-proliferation law, the realities of WMD proliferation, and the limited possibilities for normative construction in international law on the use of force. This gap is therefore a systemic gap in the sources of international law meaningfully related to the regulation of WMD proliferation and the regulation of state responses to that proliferation.

This realization raises yet further questions, including whether in light of this gap between law and reality, counterproliferation-oriented uses of force in violation of international law are likely to become more commonplace. If so, what will be the effect of the accumulation of such actions upon the future of international law, particularly in regulating the use of force? How should international law respond to this challenge to one of its central areas of regulation? Is it indeed possible, given the sources of international law, for an amended system of international use of force law to be devised which provides for the flexibility which some states seek for the purpose of combating WMD proliferation, while still providing an objectively verifiable rule of law in this important issue area? The analysis in Chapter 9 of this book considers these questions and offers one possible way forward for addressing some of these concerns, specifically in the law governing the international use of force.

In the end, there are few clear answers to the questions which the gap between law and reality in the area of WMD proliferation pose to the international community. Finding the right answers is one of the greatest challenges facing those who care about the future of international law.

Index